THE SPIRIT OF THE TAROT

THE SPIRIT OF THE TAROT
Numbers as Initiators of the Major Arcana

*Claudine Aegerter
and Berenice Benjelloun*

AEON

First published in 2009 by
Aeon Books Ltd
118 Finchley Road
London NW3 5HT

British Library Cataloguing in Publication Data

A C.I.P. for this book is available from the British Library

ISBN-13: 978-1-90465-835-1

Typeset by Vikatan Publishing Solutions (P) Ltd., Chennai, India

Printed in Great Britain

www.aeonbooks.co.uk

CONTENTS

INTRODUCTION

Humanity is at the present time at a crossroads, or point of transition. The human kingdom represents the latest state of biological evolution on planet Earth, so further expansion of the mind beyond its intellectual boundaries must take place, if we are to realise the true potential of who we are as human beings and understand the purpose of our existence. It is our responsibility to lead the way in service to the whole process of life in this Solar System. Up to now, mankind has been the frightened brave species, expressing group survival through our behaviour and mentality. By extending ourselves beyond our safe place, we can see ourselves as vehicles for a greater energy and a greater plan. We then step into the realm of the next kingdom in the evolutionary process; that of the Soul. The Tarot, seen as an initiatic tool, offers a perception of the inner work that a human being has to achieve as he associates with his Soul. This leads to contact with the higher mind and its universal experience.

This is a new exploration of the Tarot, which reveals the esoteric numerological links underlying this ancient system. It also connects the journey of the Tarot to the initiatic teachings, which express the idea of the work of the expansion of consciousness. This expansion takes place through the realisation that there is more to life than the outer form. As we explore beyond those physical, emotional and mental aspects in us that we call the personality, we find another energy that is not so easy to define and which seems to move us at a deeper level; this is the Soul. It is by being receptive to its mystery that we can start to connect to the universal collective energy of the Spirit. The different stages in this pioneering expansion into the unknown, unseen world of Soul and Spirit are reflected in the twenty-two cards of the Major Arcana. They provide a structure or map on which that journey can be recognised. The symbols on the cards are translated into practical steps that can be applied to the everyday lives of those who seek greater consciousness.

When natural man first awakened by opening the doors of awareness and consciousness, the whole of the greater story was revealed, so that everything was seen for what it is. The wise seers of those times had the insight to understand the revelation as a mind looking at its creation, seeing the origin of everything in the greater mind. The story of manifested life had to be retraced and given out in codes and symbols to measure time and space; this was done with the help of geometrical shapes representing numbers and spiralling symbols for the understanding of the cycles of numbers.

These seers elaborated on the initial symbols of 1, 2 and 3 as a blueprint, out of which the final structure of 4, 5, 6 and 7 emerges. These are the seven rays of manifestation. Through the ages the descriptions of the movement of the creator as he built the worlds as we know them, took the many different forms of the stories or myths that are linked to every culture and religion. The original symbols themselves do not belong to any particular group or sect; it is always the same revelation of the unfolding of a higher consciousness, capable of being of service to the great mind of the universe. As the tribal consciousness took control of most of mankind on the planet, it became dangerous for this knowledge to be given out, so it was hidden, the mysteries being kept in the depth of the Ancient Wisdom. Then later, the idea of drawing pictures which related to that universal story was materialised and one of the end results was what we now know as the Tarot. The Tarot illustrates the mystery of the alchemical process of transmuting matter back into light, personality into Soul.

The cards carry pictorial symbols which, at the time they were made, were linked to what was known of the ancient traditions, such as the Ancient Egyptian, Hebraic, Christian and Islamic cultures. Like parables, they tell the hidden story in a universal language that can be translated according to the understanding of the reader. The Tarot is a book for disciples and aspirants, or those who are open and ready to hear the symbolic language of the Soul. The first language was number, then the language of pictures and myths kept the knowledge of initiatic enlightenment alive.

As we get to know the world and so become ourselves, the world becomes itself. The Gospel of St John tells us, "The wind blows where it wants; we hear its voice but we do not know whence it comes, or where it is going. It is the same for whomever is born of Spirit". Once we remove the idea that we're doing anything, but are still participating in action then we're not even really doing it; it is happening through us. For example, if we think we are writing a book, we are trying too hard. If we simply make ourselves available, the book will come through us and our skills will be used. By all means try to know who we are, where we are, what we're doing, or what's the next best thing. However, as John Lennon's song says, "How do I know where to go, when I don't even know where to turn, or where I stand, or where I face?" This one speaks as a Fool of God. Spirit comes through the wind and it is with the air and the fire that we spiritualise the earth and the water, for they are divine once we have seen the light. So if we're not doing something because we are waiting to face the right direction, we are not a Fool of God! Fly with the wind, burn with the fire, or flow with the water, it does not matter which; we are on Earth and it is of beauty.

'In these happy nights I was helped in the secret,
Nobody could see me and I could not perceive anything
To guide me, only the light burning in my heart'.

Numbers give us a never-ending appreciation of the cycles of manifestation of life as it progresses towards its apotheosis. Each card is a stage in our personal transformation. The Tarot is a pictorial crystallisation of the mysterious language of number to guide us through the cycles of spiritual transformation. Each chapter can only be understood in relation to the one before and the one after, just as with numbers. We can really only truly understand a Number 2 or a Number 3 if we've understood what the Number 1 was about; a Number 1 by itself without time and space has no chance of realising itself! If the blade is alive in the fire, in the air, in the rock and in the water, we have to pull it out and go where it takes us. Each card by itself is one aspect of whom we are, but all of them together make a book of esoteric life, of man becoming his future, the essence of love and wisdom, Heaven and Earth – a Soul.

The brotherhood of Soul is an initiatic brotherhood that does not bring us into conformity and even less into uniformity, but more into harmony by and through the wonderful diversity of the expressions of the one life. We know that we are all one and are making the glorious pattern of the one life together, so it is not for one cell to say; "Do as I do", but in the words of Albert Einstein, "I love you as I am".

This book – The Spirit of the Tarot – enables the receptive reader to return to the original understanding of number behind the pictorial symbols on the cards. This knowledge has been kept going through the intellect. The aim of this book is to go behind the intellectual understanding and bring in a natural intuitive flow, by linking with the numbers.

Each picture is a crystallised depiction of mindsets from ages past, reaching right back to that first explosion of understanding. This symbolism and knowledge has been held and kept going by the Ancient Wisdom schools, ready to emerge at the time and place of greatest need and receptivity. The merging of symbol and intuition then can take place and the resulting wisdom is used and applied in practical ways. We need to be open and allow in that which stirs us, so that the work of recognition can happen, helping the process of intuition to develop from within. The story depicted on the card (exoteric) then amalgamates with the holding of the hidden knowledge (esoteric) so that intuition can result. The aim is to allow a more universal flow of intelligence to bypass the symbolism. By recognising the message behind the symbol, the wisdom of the ages can be translated into practical everyday life.

This is not a book about using the Tarot as a method of prediction, but rather as a guide through which we can look at the state of our awareness of the world as it is today. It offers a new perspective on the traumas and crises that face us. This new perception comes from the point of view of Soul.

Each of the twenty-two chapters is based on a different card in the Major Arcana, presented and explored in the numerical sequence in which it occurs in the Oswald Wirth Tarot pack. A detailed and in-depth description of the symbolism and qualities of the particular card in question is given, as well as how what we learn from it can be applied to everyday life.

The book can be read as the ongoing journey of the Soul, or can be used as an oracle, by meditating for a few instants on a troubled perception of a problem and opening the book at random. It might then be helpful to read the complete chapter for a further insight.

The readers would be those who are looking for a new way forward into their understanding of how they can help to bring a positive collective vision to bear on the struggle that humanity is undergoing in the present age. The eradication of physical, emotional and intellectual poverty has to be the concern of every human being on the planet. The many groups working on relieving famine, war trauma, disease, lack of education and environmental genocide, demonstrate the hope of a more compassionate humanity. The ultimate necessity is a global rise in consciousness. The blindingly obvious realisation that we are one body, one Soul and one mind will generate more goodwill to nurture our planet with its wonderful web of life, than any pre-occupation with self-preservation could do. The one great Soul will naturally guide and heal its children into loving acts of goodwill.

Key Themes to unlock this book

Although some of the words in these chapters are commonly used in many other contexts, the meanings we ascribe to them in this book are specific to this field and we wanted to convey the meaning of some of these words to readers that may not be so familiar with these topics, so that the message of the book is clearer.

CO-CREATIVITY

Co-creativity takes place when the personality is fully attentive and at the service of the Soul; the Soul in turn then obeys faithfully the direction given by its spiritual higher mind. At this point the skills of the instrument can be used for the greater purpose of the unfolding of the plan of love, light and life on Earth. The higher mind itself would be driven by the karmic necessity of the great life we live in.

GOD

God is the sum total of all that exists, visible and invisible – one entity, omnipresent and omnipotent. Not personal to any religion or belief system, but accessible by any person willing to relate to that which is greater than the self. It is the unknown, unseen energy that works in mysterious ways, through any belief system or religion. In God we live and move and have our being.

INITIATION

'Initiation may be defined in two ways. It is first of all the entering into a new and wider dimensional world, by the expansion of man's consciousness, so that he can include and encompass that which he now excludes and from which he normally separates himself in his thinking and acts. It is secondly the entering into man of those energies which are distinctive of the Soul and of the Soul alone – the forces of intelligent love and of spiritual will. These are dynamic energies and they actuate all who are liberated Souls.

The Soul- in its own nature – is group consciousness, and has no individual ambitions or individual interests, and is not at all interested in the aims of its personality. It is the Soul which is the initiate. Initiation is a process whereby the spiritual man within the personality becomes aware of himself as the Soul, with Soul powers, Soul relationships and Soul purpose. The moment a man realises this, even in a small measure, it is the group of which he is conscious'. *From 'Ponder on this'- published by the Lucis Trust.*

JESUS

Jesus is a generic name for a specific aspect of mankind's Soul. A prophetic aspect of revelation. The essential message is that the higher mind uses and knows the kingdom of God, not as only material here on Earth, but as an inner spiritual transformation for the future, revealing the immortality of higher consciousness and so becoming the Soul.

A witness, 'a son' of the greater life (God). The only way to achieve transformation of the consciousness into Soul here on Earth is for the higher consciousness to follow the unique source back home. Home is the great sea of universal love that links every tiny life within the great life of the universe. This intelligent love is the only way we can truly relate to each other and to the other kingdoms in nature.

When the intelligent love of the Soul (Jesus) has completely taken over, the little will of the personality aligns to the spiritual will of the Soul and the realised Soul emerges; we call this the Christ. The following defines the Christ realised Soul:–

> 'Christ is the light of the world, the embodiment of love and the indicator of divine purpose. He is the source of all light and energy which flood throughout the world of human consciousness at this period in the annual cycle. The Christ of history and the Christ in the human heart are planetary events.
>
> At the centre of all life on this planet stands the Christ, the relation between life and form, Spirit and matter, the innermost consciousness of all creation awaiting revelation. Because of the position the Christ occupies in the evolution of our planetary life, he is the focal point of all endeavour, the "way" of spiritual enfoldment, for "no man cometh to the Father but by me". He belongs to all humanity irrespective of nation, race, religion, social or cultural background. He is "the same great identity" which those of different ideologies recognise under different names.

The Christ is God-man, human-divine, a fusion of the vertical way of at-one-ment and the horizontal way of service. He is total human experience fused with the inner life force which gives coherence, intelligence and purpose to life on Earth.

The Christ is a Person, a Presence, and a Principle. He brings together in one sweep of continuous energy flow, the cosmic fountainhead, the planetary manifestation and the human expression. He is power and livingness, love and wisdom, light and understanding.

He is the builder of the new world, the new age: the driving power within the human heart and mind which produces the new forms of the new and coming civilisation. He is the magnetic and attractive force which "lifts up" and redeems the density of materialism. He ignites the spark of divinity within each human being. He is the fiery love of God for man which inspires sacrifice and renunciation.

The Christ is the archetype of the true Aquarian: he is cooperative, inclusive, intelligent and active. His motive is love of humanity: his keynote is service.

He is the Way, the truth and the life for all mankind. He is the beacon in the darkness, the essence of divine truth and reality, the guarantor of ultimate spiritual achievement for "as he is so can we be in this world".'

Full definition of The Christ from the Lucis trust.

MASS CONSCIOUSNESS

Mass consciousness is the everyday consciousness of humanity which focuses entirely on all the expressions of survival, from the fear of life, to being the most powerful person. The mass consciousness is driven by the urge to gratify the subconscious needs.

MISERICORD

Dictionary (Petit Robert). Misericord is having a heart sensitive to others pain and unhappiness; pity through which forgiveness is given to a guilty person. Proverb – 'To each sin, misericord' – meaning every mistake is forgiven. Goodness, charity, commiseration, compassion, pity are the sisters of misericord. Divine misericord is absolution.

From 'misereri' – sadness with pity, and 'chord' – heart.

Dictionary (Websters). Mercy or compassion. From 'misereri' – to feel pity.

PERSONALITY

The personality consists of the outer manifestation of the human individual. To begin with it is a vehicle through which the individual can express him or herself in the world. It is made up of the physical (5 senses), the emotional and mental (intellect) aspects of the self. Once the individual begins to see beyond the illusionary material world, the personality starts to change its nature and as a result undergoes what can be seen from the outer reality as a crisis or break down. Through this process the higher mind or Soul is able to come into the consciousness and take the individual to a more collective understanding of the world. Eventually the Soul takes over, revealing the original true purpose of the personality, which is to be a vehicle for the Soul.

SORCERER'S APPRENTICE

The Sorcerer, through deep knowledge of the laws of nature, will aim to affect persons, things or events; this is seen as magic by the onlooker. The apprentice may try his spells before he is ready to control the whole of the experiment; this often results in disaster.

SOUL

Soul is the name given to the mediator between Spirit and matter. It is that invisible immortal aspect of the self which links man to the eternal in him. Within the Soul we carry the whole of our evolution or the sum total of the multitudinal experiences that we have gone through in all of our lives; it is only through linking to our Soul that we are able to take all the misunderstandings back to their source and so gain wisdom, clarity and compassion. Soul is a state of being beyond the personal little self and therefore takes us into the collective consciousness, which is united and connected to the wholeness of life on this planet. The voice of the Soul resonates through to us and is translated into noble qualities which we aspire to, such as intelligent goodness and enduring mindfulness. These give us inspiration for a world of truth, love, peace, joy, equality, and justice. All these terms are intended to be representative of the highest levels of consciousness, so we speak of clear truth, unconditional love, peace for all and so on. These qualities are transpersonal; to attain them in their purest forms requires a great deal of work on the little self, as we move from the personal to the collective. This is the enormous task which humanity is just starting to engage with. A great part of this work is to see our fellow human beings as Souls and reflect that back to them, in order to uplift the goal of personality to expand beyond its limitations. In this way we bring the perception of the Soul kingdom into play, each individual working in the group, for the group. As the Soul or essence is strengthened, it begins to reveal its true purpose, which is to be a vehicle for Spirit through its intuitive intelligence.

SPIRIT

Spirit is so expansive that it is difficult to say much about it, except to say that it is everywhere and in everything; it flows through life at every single level. It is the dance of the great creator, whose intent is in the movement; it is the breath of God. The great work is to bring Spirit and matter together into a state of fusion. At the present time the energy of Soul is needed to act as a mediator or vehicle within which these two principles can be synthesized. In the book we use 'Spirit' as meaning universal truth and divine light.

SUBCONSCIOUS

The subconscious represents a state of unconsciousness solely occupied by the active and reactive aspect of man. In the subconscious mind all mankind's distortions of the pure instinct of the unconscious are found. They are brought about through the misunderstandings of the newly-found emotional and mental body of man, as he rises into the human kingdom from the animal kingdom. Action which stems from the subconscious results in behaviour which is not reflective or self-conscious. The semi-conscious emotional/mental aspects cause pain in the driven human being, as he strives to make sense of what drives him. This begins the work of releasing the subconscious misunderstandings in the Soul, through the bringing in of awareness and greater consciousness.

TETRAKTYS

This simple form holds the memory or blueprint of the divine intent and therefore the understanding behind all the different systems or tools used by different spiritual traditions, such as Astrology, Tarot and the Kabala. As the energy of Spirit moves through time and space, the blueprint can transform the divine intent into manifestation, so that matter and form can mirror back to the God we live in, an appreciation of the unfolding of his intent.

So the Spirit comes down, still holding the beautiful and pure ideas of the blueprint and the concept, enabling us as humans to see ourselves in a mirror. At the final state of higher consciousness, the God we live in is seeing itself in his own creation. The mirror cannot

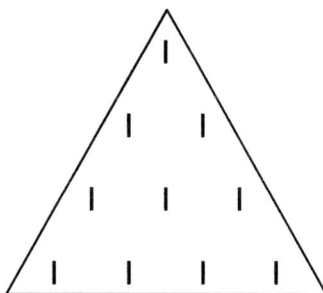

Figure 1. The Divine Tetraktys.
The Divine Tetraktys contains the whole of the Ancient Wisdom
and if we ponder on it, all can be revealed.

happen without the tool of self-consciousness that we take with us on the descent into our subconscious, which is what we call hell. If we are not aware of the subconscious we are just being driven by nature, which has innocent purity but also terrifying behaviour in the cause of survival! This means that we don't know what we are doing, for we have no self-consciousness. The Soul instigates our descent into hell so that we can retrace all the steps which lead back to the original Trinity (father God/mother Earth – with us as witnesses to the end product) or source of life, this is how we find the mirror that shows us 'as above, so below.' The knowledge of intuitive perception accumulated over thousands of years, is called the Ancient Wisdom; this is held in the divine Tetraktys. We don't need any books because the Tetraktys holds it all; we can ponder on it and let numbers teach the way to enlightenment, for the idea of the swamp, the descent into hell, the purgatory stage and the redemption through the light of consciousness are all there. Through this knowledge comes the simple understanding that we have to start internalising the 'How' of our knowledge of the world to find the 'Why' – that's when the journey really starts.

UNCONSCIOUS
The absolute and primary principle of the Universe is unconscious, or in a state unaccompanied by conscious or self-conscious experience. The unconscious describes the entire experience of nature from the beginning of time, as it adapted to prevailing circumstances in order to survive as viable life. Pure instinct has its being in the unconscious. It is from this original, unconscious Active Intelligence that the creation of all life is sourced.

ACKNOWLEDGEMENTS

This book was developed from a series of talks given by Claudine Aegerter to the Connaissance School of Numerology over a period of 2 years. The aim of the talks was to bring out the hidden light or Spirit behind the ancient system of symbols known as The Tarot – hence the name 'The Spirit of the Tarot'.

The idea of making the talks into a book was instigated by members of the Association Internationale de Numerologues (AIN), of which the School is part. As a group, the School and the Association formed a receptive and willing body, whose thirst for spiritual waters invoked the precipitation needed to bring in these teachings.

Thanks go to:-

Lesley Smith, who faithfully transcribed the work from tapes to written word. Nicholas Aegerter, who helped with the illustrations and format and final editing. Inspiration was drawn from the Ancient Wisdom teachings, given out by the Lucis Trust and the writings of Madame Blavatsky. To Edmond Delcamp who wrote 'Le Tarot Initiatique, Symbolique et Esoterique' from which the initial idea for the talks was developed. The owners of the Oswald Wirth Tarot cards who have given their permission to use the images of their cards in this book.

Others involved were; Colin M. Baker, Margarita Coleman, Paul Elkerton, Jenny Myers, Christine Tonks and all the people who attended the talks on the Tarot. Also the many other members of the Association Internationale de Numerologues and the Connaissance School of Numerology, who gave their support.

Finally thanks to Claudine Aegerter, who was of course the great inspirer, joint editor and re-writer. The project completed its full cycle by coming back into her hands, to make sure that the original clarity of purpose and expression were retained.

I myself have been privileged to have worked on the project from the very beginning, and have all the way through, derived enormous inspiration from being able to hold this work together and finally see the completed book; there to inspire and provide a practical way of working with the greater energies of Soul and Spirit.

Berenice Benjelloun.

The Connaissance School of Numerology

The School was founded in 1993 with the aim of advancing the knowledge and practice of Numerology. Our approach with numbers is to let them be our teacher and to open our intuitive intelligence for, as Pythagoras said, "Number is the ruler of form and ideas and is the cause of gods and demons". We offer Foundation and Diploma courses in esoteric Numerology.

Association Internationale de Numerologues (AIN)

The Association Internationale de Numerologues has the following aims and objectives:

a) To promote the practice of Numerology as a profession.
b) To stimulate and encourage the development of Numerology
c) To represent the interests of professional numerologists
d) To serve the public good through the promotion and practice of Numerology
e) To build a brotherhood amongst numerologists world wide

The School and the Association are both based in Royston, Hertfordshire in the UK. We are located over the historic Royston Cave which is at a significant junction of the Michael and Mary ley lines.

Find out more on our website www.numerology.org.uk, or email us at support@numerology.org.

The Magician, Le Bateleur
In the beginning

The Magician or holder of the baton, is bright and wilful, full of potential and enthusiasm, yet he comes into the world knowing about the illusions and glamour of the world, so he is not going to be taken in by them. He is here to look for the greater truth and can only find it by being completely part of this world. He has all the elements of the Earth to use and he sees the whole of humanity reflected in him; by this means he can recognise what is real or illusionary within him. This is the work and the journey has begun.

1

The Magician is the beginning of the pack, The Fool is the end and in between these two, the work has to be done and the journey made. The Magician represents the first stage or the Number 1, so he holds all the keys and is the potential initiate. He is the start of the process of the Number 1 travelling through his inner landscape for transformation. He's represented as a man because he is the active principle. The Major Arcana was originally meant only for initiates and not for the average person, so he is someone who knows he is on the path of expanding consciousness.

He knows that the material world or the world of form is an illusion and that humanity is doomed to self-destruct if it stays in that illusion. We have to stay in physical incarnation long enough to learn to survive, so that eventually we can say "There must be more than this" and start to look beyond the material world. The Magician comes back knowing that he is not going to be taken in by the illusion of form, so he will rise above whatever he has to do in the world in order to find the higher view of the Soul, which he can then apply and work with in the world. He's coming back to research and find the truth and light, in a world dominated by illusion and glamour, glamour being the illusion of the emotional.

He has come to change the world, but he knows that it is his perception of the world that has to change. 'Be the change you want in others'. This means he has to make the change in himself and so spark the understanding of the process in others. This process is shown in Fig. 1.

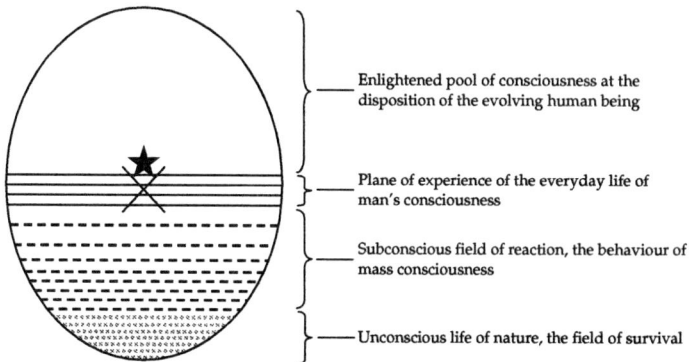

Figure 1. *The field of the work of the initiate.*

Inside the figure, labels read:

— Enlightened pool of consciousness at the disposition of the evolving human being

— Plane of experience of the everyday life of man's consciousness

— Subconscious field of reaction, the behaviour of mass consciousness

— Unconscious life of nature, the field of survival

Actually The Magician is the wrong name for him, because the sort of person we would normally call a magician would be someone who would perform and demonstrate magic tricks by showing a 'before' and 'after'. The Magician's more appropriate description is the French name for the card, which is 'Le Bateleur', meaning somebody who handles a baton to represent the power of his passion. The true Bateleur, or Magician, has to work with situations as they are; he simply cannot do anything else. He cannot escape the elements or the karmic laws and limits that bind humanity on the planet. We have people on the planet who do not respect the natural laws because they want to be seen as magicians, but the true Magician partakes in the situation and the laws down here on Earth, with the highest respect. In fact the way he's going to work is to stimulate and initiate, so that the work is done from within. Otherwise, he knows that it doesn't really happen – there might be an apparent change for five minutes and then things go back to where they were before.

The whole of life is movement and that movement has shaped the web of life in such a way that it can hold all the possibilities or potential. The psychic space of the planet is more polluted at the moment than the physical body of the planet. The mental and emotional levels are equally or more polluted, this is demonstrated in the way that we treat life and each other. This is what the Bateleur, or baton holder comes back into, so we may wonder why he's got a big smile on his face! He is happy because he's going for truth and love, for without those there is no way he would be able to escape the weight of the illusionary world. This world is not just heavy, it is very thick and sticky and also very appealing, like honey. So he's coming back into all the ties and karmic webbing that humanity has surrounded itself with. The average person is bound and tied in their own glamour and illusion. The cutting of these ties is the work that the initiate has to achieve within himself, using the very same tools of the everyday life experience in the world of matter. He has to inspire himself before he can inspire others to do the same.

The Magician sees himself as completely part of the world and therefore can use the world to recognise what is still true or untrue within him. He knows about 'as above, so below', therefore what is in front of him can have a strong reflection within him. He knows that for the unreal to be wiped out he needs to feel his human side intimately, so as not to go into the illusion that he is different. The elements are in him, humanity is in him and he has to recognise and accept that, if he wants the clarity and the purification of the mirror. He's smiling because he hasn't realised all of that yet!

Each card in the Major Arcana represents part of a whole, so in order to understand the place our Magician holds, looking at some of the other cards is helpful.

The first three cards, The Magician, The High Priestess and The Empress, represent the three major aspects of the unity of the God we live in, so in these three we see a depiction of the divine Trinity. It is through encountering The High Priestess in Number 2, that The Magician looks for pure mind or intuition through reflection, and then with The Empress in Number 3, he finds a way to apply these attributes to the world. Basically he's come back to search for and find, the truth of the divine light in a world that is dominated by illusion and glamour.

The Magician is the son in the Trinity. Son is a lovely word, because in the Anglo-Saxon language it is so close to the word 'sun', which also has a link with 'Soul'. In French the word for son is 'fils', which looks the same as the French word for thread, so this reminds us of the thread of Ariadne that Theseus carried with him into the underworld to enable him to find his way out again. This is the 'son' that is ready to go into the darkness of earthly life. That golden thread of inspiration from the Soul means he can come back and synthesise the receptive and active qualities of the God we live in, becoming the result of the union of the first two – the son.

So these first three cards depict the higher Trinity and then Number 4 is The Emperor; this is the concept of that Trinity that has to be crystallised. Through the vigilant guidance of the wise men and women of humanity, he is an active, masculine principle and this gives him authority. It is important to see the figures in the cards not as male and female, but rather as active and receptive. Sometimes some of the active figures are quite passive as well and vice versa, because a complete balance has been achieved.

It is interesting to see that Number 6 is called The Lovers, but in fact it is 'The Lover' and it could be masculine or feminine. This is an example of how words can influence and get in the way of true understanding. Eventually, as we work more with the symbols, the deeper level of interpretation will not come from the intellectual, but from somewhere more profound and subtle. So rather than trying to make sense of them via the intellect, we can allow them to speak to us from that deeper place. It is out of survival and despair that we've said that there must be more than what we find in ordinary life, so it is necessity that pushes the nature in us up to her lover. Then the intellect in man has to give up and look for another answer to the question, "Is this all there is?"

Number 12, The Hanged Man, represents the state that any initiate aspires to. He is depicted upside down, with his hands tied behind his back and he is in hell. All he can remember is how to be the wind and the fire and so he gives his life for the greater life. He is upside down because spiritually the world is actually the wrong way up, the true life being the inner not the outer. He can't actually do anything, because all he can do is serve and what he is doing doesn't even appear to be service to the world. In The Hanged Man we can see an upside down Number 4 made with the shape of his legs, which shows us that the Number 4 has reached the breaking point; here even the idea of pride has to be given up. Pride makes us think that we are special and that we can actually 'become God'. Then in Number 13 we remove the intellectual head to stop naming anything that may keep us tied to self appreciation. This is a Number 4 that has uplifted itself towards the Trinity; every notion of self has got to disappear so that the mind, free of the intellect, can see situations from a transpersonal point of view.

The Magician has a lovely happy face, but the face of the Fool is his other side. The Fool is the end result of the journey, where any self-protection has been removed. When we consider that, we can see why we have to be a Fool to come back again!

We're looking here at the exoteric way of grounding ideas in order to guide or frustrate the world, so that men can start asking questions and desire another way of life. When we are guiding others, we may say "Go for it!" even if everyone else says the opposite. A little bit of foolishness can get people a bit frustrated, but then they start to think for themselves. That is the way to be a Fool of God, which is our last card, The Fool. The fool in the court, the jester, or comedian, is the one that is doing all types of silly things, but in fact he is the one that is wise. In the past the jester would guide the king or the emperor, because he had one or two bits of wisdom in his little bag. This is the role of the initiate; it is not so much having a long face and telling the world the dread, or beauty of things to come, it is about saying 'go for it' and teaching people to laugh at themselves, because from the point of view of Soul we are only witnessing, so to want to be better than anyone else is a joke.

Basically, the problem is with all of us. We can perceive, sometimes we can even apply the higher pattern to the lower dimension and hopefully we are as honest, aware and awake as we can be with our reaction to the world. The world is us and it is within us. We know intellectually that we mustn't suffer disappointment, because that would mean that we are not there yet, or not 'it' yet. If we are honest with ourselves and if we recognise the world in us we cannot be disappointed, because if we stand from a point of where the world is at, where is the disappointment? We can't go lower than where we already are. That is where we all have to start and there's no way we are above anybody else. If we do get disappointed by the result of our actions, it only means that we think we are better than we are. We can tell others they did their best, but we do not apply the same rules for ourselves. So stop trying, keep going and keep doing!

There is a point of wisdom where we have to learn when something is not viable any more. We persevere and then there is a point where we have to ask, 'what is the pattern that I keep repeating? Has the karmic lesson been learnt? Is it a bad habit left behind, or should I persevere because I have not seen it yet? We all are very fragile and young and maybe we send our arrows in completely the wrong direction, but as long as we keep sending them, one day the goal becomes internalised. The characteristic of the action of the profane world is action for the sake of reaction and this will never exhaust its possibilities, or achieve a goal.

In the sacred world of the Magician, the actions are above all symbolic and so have the value of true ritual. From this point of view an action is not about learning to do a ritual, it is doing it with the knowledge and understanding of why we are doing it; that is what makes the magic. An action is performed with elegant poise. The vision of the mind is held with love, as in transpersonal harmony with the Soul, rather than for some self gratification or self-aggrandisement. It could be exactly the same action as the man next to us, but it is the understanding and the love that we put into it which makes all the difference. This is the purity of intent aligning us with the natural, abundant, creative force of Spirit, which makes nature come up every spring.

The Magician is confronted with all the problems to be solved. Once he comes into matter, he knows that straight away he's going to be faced with the sphinx; this is the work! If we look at Number 2, The High Priestess, her left arm is resting on a black sphinx which represents 'the dweller on the threshold', meaning all the dark shadows of the subconscious. His life will be full of enigma, questions and problems that he has to understand in order not to be eaten by the sphinx; in other words not to be taken in by the monsters of the subconscious. If he sees all the misunderstandings and pictures that the subconscious has presented to him as real, then he will be eaten by the meaning and go down again into the illusion and form of the small self, or personality. The work of this first card is extremely important, because this is where he is tested to see whether he can go through to the next level, for if he goes through when he is not ready, he faces annihilation, so it is an eternal life or cyclic death matter. If he doesn't pass that threshold he will stay in ordinary consciousness and become the magician who plays games and tricks people.

Once he has grasped the secret and been able to take the key and open the great door, he knows that there is no return. If he can't open it or chooses not to, he can retreat; that is the choice and this is what the average mass consciousness in humanity has done for thousands of years. Many who come to the door do not go through it, for they haven't enough of that incredible sacrificial fiery quality that the Number 1 has to have, so they go back to survival mode. It is like being faced with 'the fires of hell' and being prepared to go through them; actually those fires are the purifying fires of love. Number 1 can have some fool-hardiness and pride, which may make them go into the fire of sensual passion and so into degeneration and destruction, rather than the passion of the love of God of truth. But that is a choice and if we are foolhardy enough to take that choice, we should remember the message from eternity, that there is all the time in the world!

 The Magician's shoes are black, because that is the first colour of the great alchemical work, which takes place through the whole of the 22 cards of the Major Arcana. This first stage of the alchemical work is also called the work of the raven, for this black bird symbolises the work of exploring the subconscious, which is the very heart of the materia prima. In this first aspect of the work matter is represented esoterically by coal. Black coal represents the deepest, densest matter; it can be ignited to burn, giving flames and warmth. In the same way if we don't go into our subconscious to find the densest darkest places, we can't achieve the alchemical burning. The whole of the experience of matter is here represented by the coal, which is ready to be heated in the alchemical oven or athenor, so as to start the process of trans-substantiation. When we give ourselves in service, we give up all our experience of matter into the fire to be burned; in that process we can become 'no substance'. The black work is the beginning, so we start from the matter that is not yet aware of itself and not aware that it is informed by Spirit. This is the starting point of man, so we see it symbolised in Adam, the earthling, or the newborn child, in a time when life was based purely on animal instinct and survival. With the energy of The Magician this

Adam-man is asked to evolve, aspire and transcend, so becoming the spiritual human potential. If we look at The Magician's hat, it is shaped in the symbol of infinity and he's being asked to evolve to that infinite point, for as the initiate he has all the levels of consciousness within him.

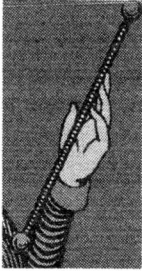

He has a wand, or baton, in his hand, to represent man with all the potential and illusions of power within mankind. We shouldn't be afraid to own our illusions, for if we are honest and able to understand their roots, we will transmute their energy into the force and ability to express our potential. The minute we see the illusions, we can transmute them and make a huge leap, then eventually by lifting and falling (only transmuting more coal into energy) again and again, we will have done that energetic rise in consciousness.

The Magician comes back realising that he holds all the possibilities in him and he is completely aware of how he has to handle matter. He has the baton in his hand, which is the symbol for the wands and on the table in front of him he has the cup, the sword and the pentacle. These are the four elements symbolising the tools that we have to help us proceed from the lower to the higher states. The wand is fire, the pentacle earth, the sword is air and the cup is water. He holds the wand in his left hand and he's pointing to the pentacle with the index finger of his right hand. He has contact with the wand of the active/masculine element, which is directed towards and received by, the pentacle of earth, the feminine/receptive element. The Magician himself is active, being a Number 1, because he acts on and in the world; he's the alchemist guiding the transmutation of those parts of the world he's going to expose. The sword, as air, is masculine/active, bringing Spirit into the receptive/feminine cup.

The wand is in his left hand. If we see a picture of someone in authority with a wand in the right hand, this is a false magician. This is because the right hand is the hand of rationalism and intellect, whereas the left hand is about feeling and receptivity. The red upper tip of the wand represents the fire of Spirit coming down; the lower blue tip symbolises receptivity to that greater energy, which has to be translated by the mind. The order or command is received from above through the left hand, so it is not him doing the ordering. This gives him the possibility of receiving intuitive power and knowledge and then implementing the vision into the material world, which is represented by the pentacle, or element Earth. He is really a 'way-through', for he doesn't do it himself. That is why he's a true Magician, for he understands and acts, but knows that the greater energy is working through him. This is what it means when it says in Genesis that the power and domination of the world is given to man, so that it can be used to work in the name of God. This is of course an incredibly high degree of achievement and we have to go through the purification of all our mistakes, which are only misunderstandings, to eventually become a true Magician or juggler. The word 'juggler' is another good name for this card, for it doesn't carry the pretensions of the ego that 'The Magician' does.

If we haven't elevated our minds into the knowledge that the world of matter and form is an illusion, then we become the type of magician that does magic in an illusionary way. We need to look at the distinction between the two magicians, for the difference is quite subtle. It is about applying the word of God to everyday life, rather than playing at moving or manifesting objects in the air. The real work could be something so simple as to be unnoticed.

The Magician has to be completely open, supple and receptive, for he never knows when the order is going to come and he always has to be ready to obey the higher impulse from within himself. He is getting himself ready to knock on that great inner door with the purpose of finding the universal truth.

The wand is a symbol of order or command; it has been found absolutely everywhere on the planet, right back to prehistoric times wands are found in tombs buried with tribal chiefs. The wand would be given to the wise one in the tribe, because they would be recognised as having ideas that were always beneficial to the group and therefore coming from a higher place. This is the spiritual will coming in to inform matter and the power conferred to mankind to dominate, use and transform the material world. It is a great challenge and can have an inverse action, for in the acceptance of power a man is dragged into the world, which then may hold and imprison him. When he dominates his world from that place, he can be confused if he focuses on that and starts to believe that he is 'God'. This means that he's not purified enough and his personality is being taken up by the idea of his own power.

Matter is not the prison for Spirit, rather it gives the freedom for Spirit to forever demonstrate and manifest new forms, new diversity, new beauty and new refinement. But if we haven't felt the heaviness and the incredible lure of form, we shouldn't even try to be a Magician. Matter becomes mere dust when we know it isn't real and can be transformed with ideas into new worlds. When we get taken in by matter, we feel the mass and the heaviness of it; we all recognise that feeling. From coal to diamond, we have to experience life on the earth as heavy, dark and oppressive, so as to associate with the suffering of humanity. Every time we go through an up-lift, we release the weight of what we're leaving behind. Remember the 8 of infinity, which tells us that every time we rise we have to go a bit lower, until eventually we touch the outer realm of our world.

The wand or baton is also used as a symbol of generation, with the idea of perpetrating a species, a race or an idea. Mass consciousness will use this energy as brute power. In this case it would be completely lost except for its other use – the instinct of reproduction, which is needed to perpetuate the race. In mankind the instinct of reproduction carries misunderstandings and distortions. The great illusion for mankind is that we think we choose, possess and dominate, when all the time we are only the instrument of propagation. So the initiate can easily revert to the state of the generative, biological man, rather than remembering where he comes from and what he's supposed to do. Because he is going deeper than he has ever gone before, he feels that the perseverance he has had to have to go through his many lives has all been in vain. All he needs is to become a witness, a Soul infused personality and maya will not fool him anymore.

The Magician, with his discriminating right hand of reason, shows us the pentacle, which is the sign that represents the Earth. It is the circle of Spirit, surrounding the cross of matter to show us that he is implementing Spirit into the world. The position of the hands is reflected in the feet. The right foot is stable and solid, so that the left one can step out from a good base. They are in the shape of a setsquare, which is another symbol used by the initiate, to do with measuring and sacred geometry; man as a corner stone for a temple. So the steps are taken from the solid ground of rationalism and common sense and the movement comes from feeling, receptivity and above all, passion.

This passion burns a path for the higher energies of love and light, to penetrate matter with the purpose of uplifting its consciousness. It is the passion that says "I'm going for it whether I'm going to be blamed or praised". The ultimate hallmark of any master has to be the passion of service and the fire of action. Passion receives the higher order when it is aligned to the higher will and then it is implemented into right action. The 'sad souls', or the souls without colour, who lived 'without attracting blame or praise' were the first people Dante saw in hell and these were people without passion. When we are 'going for it', that is when the doors of hell are open and the passion is there, ready to deliver action, devotion and sacrifice out of chaos. The passion of searching for the truth is the most dangerous passion there is, for it has to do with the slaying of an aspect of the personality, such as the glamour of being best loved of the emotional body, or the pride of the intellect. We can hold on to the idea that we are the gift, rather than understanding that the gift is working through us. When we know the latter we climb against the current many times, like the salmon, which is another symbol for the initiate. If we have not purified our personal intent or needs, it is not the fire of truth that is going to push us along, but the fire of disintegration, so the danger is real and involves survival of the Soul. There is nothing more dangerous than the pursuit of truth, but we have to be in love with it and then the danger doesn't seem real, because love holds and transmutes any misunderstanding we might have had. So we learn to master our passion and therefore learn to transmute it, but at the beginning if there is no passion, we might as well forget it, for esoterically we have to want to die for the truth. This means to let go of our self importance and our survival mechanism. This would make us a fool according to the everyday success story of the world!

If we have taken a 'wrong path' then we have more coal for burning. We can love and transmute that path into the right path; it is as simple as that. All mistakes are allowed and it is not even a question of allowing, for there's actually no mistake.

It is in the two or three cards after The Magician that discrimination and determination will be developed, because we can't ask a Number 1 to discriminate. If we receive an impulse from the higher self we have no time to discriminate! If our impulse is from the needs of mass consciousness then we have to start learning to discriminate, because by the time we come to The Empress we have to be able to tell the difference between the two, otherwise we will be using the power of the wand for the generation of more glamour, rather than the enlightenment of nature. If we want to keep on doing that, we can do it for eternity, but if we want to get onto the path of the Soul then we have to start to discriminate.

The pentacle is gold, for gold cannot decay or be corrupted and so it doesn't follow the rules of the material world. It is the gold in his purified solar plexus, the seat of emotional needs and impulse, which is preventing The Magician from being tainted, or brought down by mass consciousness and the lower passions.

The purity of his understanding of the material world cannot be soiled; he can live in the world without being spoilt or stained and can give orders without thinking that the power is his. We have to reach that stage of incorruptibility if we want to rise above the magnetic pull of needs and desires, for it is purified matter that allows spiritual action. The beautiful Celtic, or Antioch cross of the occident which is carved on the pentacle, symbolises the union of Spirit and matter. The Magician has his index finger on the centre of the cross, which is the goal, for only from the centre can we transform or transmute. Spirit has no other goal but the fusion with matter in order to release it from its unconscious state.

The cup on the table reminds us of the Grail cup, as well as all the other beautiful cups of initiation. It is full of red blood. It is a silver cup with a hexagonal stem, so its six sides tell us of the creation of all things, for it rises out of the Star of David as the perfect cup of nature. This speaks of the six amazing days of the creation of the material world in which man lives. Silver is the colour of the aspiration of nature to fuse with her maker. There is no other way that the mind can rise except by the taking of initiation and making the blood sacrifice, blood being a symbol for the living Soul. This means giving the love of one's life for a higher cause; this sacrifice can only stem out of the heart of matter, willing to give its experience up for the love of Spirit or truth. When somebody takes an initiation it is from within and however great the initiator in front of him is, it could not happen if the person were not ready for it. Even if Jesus (the Soul of mind) were the initiator it couldn't happen, for there is no possible sacrifice if it doesn't come from the heart or Soul of matter itself. That is why The Magician is not a magician in the ordinary sense, for he will not 'magic' things to happen. When the beautiful hexagonal Star of David (the perfected nature in mankind as king) has done its work of rising up and has offered its life's blood, or the experience of the Soul of nature to the process, it happens.

The cup is the greatest instrument of divination, because it will always reflect and always be receptive. It is the instrument of communion with the divine, for the cup receives the divine. Man must live in his becoming. Life is an unfolding evolution, rather than accountability, so we should not keep on measuring what we have done in the past. The cup of course is feminine and cannot give any other service but to receive.

It is the nature of the cup to receive and when she receives the light energy of the sword, she can only respond according to the level of her own understanding of the God we live in, so if the consciousness is purely focussed on nature, that energy will be transformed into babies, seasons or harvest. The cup can only form shapes that are a reflection of her own life, which is the perfection of nature imposing form on whatever she receives. This receptivity is not passive, it is receiving and creating, but it can only create a replica of itself. When suddenly the receptivity of the cup is uplifted into a higher dimension then that new vision can be replicated. For this reason it is important not to look down at the path of the life of nature, whose higher aspiration has to do with surviving in the physical. The more receptive we can be to the higher levels of thinking and ideals, the more of the new world we can manifest. The preparation for the future is held in the cup itself and this is truly what gives her the power of divination, because it is through the work of the pure, transparent, receptive feminine that the future can actually be seen in advance and materialised into ideas, words and actions. All we need to do is uplift our cups (inner sight) so that the new vision of humanity can be received; it is as simple as that. If the nature in us doesn't want to replace attachment to the survival of the form by the concept of a higher vision of love and harmony, it won't happen. The symbol of the cup is linked to the great mother, the Goddess, or Mary; she is that great field of life that holds the whole Solar System together. It is not just Earth, or the Goddess of nature materialising, but the great Goddess of receptivity, making certain that she faithfully reproduces her ideals. The transmutation of the world is in the cup, which is where the alchemy is happening.

You could call The Magician an alchemist who has to realise the great work. He acts on illusion so as to dissolve it and reveal reality. The sword and the cup are a necessary union of the two principles of mind and heart. Spirit has to go to the heart of matter for anything new and beautiful to happen, for new vision and new manifestation. If we use our heart or head alone we haven't got a complete vision. The head and heart have to be together. The process has to be loved with the passion of the heart and the light of Spirit has to be able to penetrate the darkness, to absorb its misunderstandings and this way clarifies the cup. This is mirroring the primordial union, when the Spirit came into the great womb of the Solar System; this is the evolution that we are re-enacting inwardly.

With the sword we are doing magic, for it is used to draw a circle of protection around The Magician. If we look at the handle it is in the shape of a gold cross. The blade is the penetrating Spirit used to vitalise matter, for we are not destroying with the sword of truth, but awakening and informing matter. That is why we need to understand that books or a person can't change our lives; they may be a catalyst, but the acceptance of a revelation comes when we are ready. While we are thinking that something from outside will do it for, or to us, we haven't contacted our own spark of responsibility to spiritualise truth. We need to kill the old for the new to be born.

It is not a bloody sword, but an incredible, wonderful sword, because it doesn't just free the teacher or the initiator, it frees the old patterns of the past. As the Spirit penetrates matter, there is a symbolic death and at the same time a real death, for it frees man from attachment to the pull of matter. Man evolves, elevates and transmutes the unconscious in his body by the acceleration of his vibration with the light of understanding. This light creates a circle of protection, for he must live in this world to increase the light. The cross of the hilt of the sword tells him to cut himself free, making certain that he has no auric or karmic ties around him, so that he doesn't still give out the idea that the world 'does' it to him, or that he does it to the world! It is about owning and taking complete responsibility for our ideas and actions and then we are our own true initiators.

The cup and the sword allow the movement of inspiration from the wand to the pentacle to take place and then the manifestation is complete. Without the sword we can see that the pentacle wouldn't be gold, for it could be corrupted by outer influences. The sword is the one that makes certain that we all have our own circle, that there are no ties to bind us, that nothing is pulling us down and that the gold of the solar plexus centre radiates, so enabling the whole of the body to become incorruptible.

These four elements, or the four aspects represented by wands, pentacles, cups and swords in the minor Arcana are the beginning of everyday life and the totality of the cosmic world at the same time. They tie up with the cosmic patterns of the stars and so link to the astrological signs.

The wand is fire, which is action and this is seen in Aries, which is the first sign to come in. This is the fiery direction that becomes domination in Leo. So Aries initiates a movement into a direction, or impulse. Leo is the dominating fire of life that has to find its own truth in dominating itself, then with Sagittarius the fire has to learn to point upwards and inwards. When the arrow keeps going downward, or towards the outer, we are looking at the Earth rather than looking at God, so then that fiery element goes into self-destruction. A fiery person that doesn't look within is definitely in danger of burning out. If we want to dominate the world with our good or bad ideas, we slide into power and the lust for more. We have to learn to dominate our passions.

The cup represents the element water, which in its highest meaning is the great water of Heaven. Rain is what links the creative creature and his God and water is psychic life. So we start with Cancer, the origin of life, the Mary or mother who is the awakener of the psychic life. Then in Scorpio we have the hidden life, the mystery, sexuality and death, which bring the questions that the anxious man is going to ask, about the transition towards the Spirit. Pisces, with the fishes, is completely submerged into the psychic life, revealing the difficulty with the two currents; one is going up and the other going down. It has to become the purified waters of the Soul, as Jesus (the Soul) demonstrated, by asking us to go beyond the physical and emotional worlds. Action has no value to man if it is not directed by the realm of the Soul, which is eventually the highest representation of the cup.

The sword, which is air, is Spirit informing the heart. In Gemini we have the mind that wakes up and its power touches everything. It has to find stability. In Libra, we find a balance between the desire to dominate in Leo and the acceptance of sacrifice in Virgo. This middle point can truly only be achieved in this world, for there is no other possible place where it can be found. Once we have the middle point we're home. Unless we can simultaneously experience life and witness it with detachment, we are not going to find the narrow door to the higher mind in the Soul. Air in Aquarius will allow the mind of humanity to go beyond the understanding of life as survival and will start to perceive the oneness of life in the cosmic waters. The mental/spiritual life of the air and the water will show us the way through. The mind of the average Aquarian has to work very hard at this point, to recognise other people's point of view and reality, as equally important as their own. It is one great mind made of trillions of points of view.

The pentacle represents matter and the biological life of our bodies; this is where all initiation must start. It doesn't matter which way we take, we have to go deeper and deeper into the Earth to reach the heart of the cells, which are the building blocks of life. This is the importance of the cave, for there is no birth without a cave and its potential of bursting into light. The test of probation on Earth gives man the trust or the backup of the world in which he lives. So we have the bull, Taurus, offering its endurance and developing the perseverance and the patience to find the light. Virgo has the resignation that forgets self through devotion, because we know that we hold the promise of the world in us. There is still a hint of accountability, judgement and criticism here, because Earth is the product of that fantastic Active Intelligence which will be able to see every single little detail that is not right, so it is only through devotion that we can completely resign ourselves to the idea that this is the way the world is; it is perfect as it is and not as we want it! Then in the great Capricorn we have the self-realised man, clothed in his own silence and secrets. He bears and holds the secret and he sometimes doesn't even realise that he's got a secret in him; all he knows is his silence. He has in front of him in his hand the entire created world; all the mental thoughts and all the possibilities. That is a heavy weight and we can see why Capricorn can either be so stern or the depressive comic.

To be an initiate is not to be a disincarnate 'master', meaning an entity that doesn't need to come back and experience matter; rather he is looking for the middle way. He has always known that wherever he is in matter, the middle way is so right that he doesn't need protection, because by being his own true nature he has become that middle way himself.

The Magician goes back into hell, meaning back into the dust of the past and although he's been there before, he's not done it on this particular round. He is very much in the world though he is engaged in taking possession of the means of domination of his personality; he must not see it as a way to get out. The Tarot is anthropocentric, meaning it is the journey of man through the medium in which we live, which is nature and it is only The Fool at the end of the journey who can take us back into this world, with more opportunity to love and understand. The mind has to soar and uplift, so as to truly understand that matter and form are the shadowy misunderstanding of a higher reality that is to come. Yet mankind has to be grounded enough to act in the world. Matter is the past and we're all past mistakes!

The table in front of The Magician has three visible legs and the fourth one is outside the picture. The three legs represent three of the four corners of Solomon's temple and are the pillars of strength, wisdom and beauty. The fourth pillar is there, but is not visible, for it is man himself, the initiate, who is there to give stability in space and time. It is his spiritual power that gives a strong, stable consistency to the material manifestation of the building of the edifice, so that we can go from the impermanence of manifestation to the clarity of Spirit. Number 3 is the beginning of manifestation and is the great Trinity that isn't yet viable, so the plan is drawn but is unstable. To make it viable we want the Number 1 to come back to make the fourth element; this is man with his spiritual courage and vision, rendering the great work of the Trinity viable. Without men recognising the Trinity in life, it cannot be perceived and named and therefore might not even exist. We bring it down into matter through our own recognition of love, strength, wisdom and beauty and through these the spiritual power is reborn.

In the manifested, material world the temple has four columns and a table has four legs, so another, more material way to see the fourth hidden leg would be as all the institutions. Everything that has to do with the secular world; groups, tribes, associations, nations and party politics: everything that gives stability to a society would be the fourth leg of that table. The initiate has replaced that by a spiritual foundation, rather than a material foundation and this is why we don't need to see it, for it is not of this world. This confirms the fact that our Magician is very much outside the secular world; even if he is working in it he's not at all taken in by it and so it has no authority over him. He has spiritual authority only, so that fourth leg really belongs to the higher plan of the Soul kingdom. This path that we are looking at is not for newcomers.

The red tulip is a recognised symbol for a superior initiation. When we see it depicted in ancient art that is its meaning. In the picture the little tulip is just opening, so it is the beginning of initiation that we're looking at. However, this does not mean that

The Magician is a beginner; if he were the little plant would just be sprouting green and not flowering, so it is not one of the first initiations we're looking at here. From within nature the stem of a plant reaches up towards the Sun. This stem is strong, with just a little bud opening, guided towards the light of the Sun. It reflects the colour red to show its passion.

His stockings are sky blue, with stripes of black to represent the heaviness of matter. The blue on his legs means that he is well balanced between Heaven and Earth. In the middle of his jacket is a blue panel with five buttons above the belt, to represent the five senses. The buttons are gold because his lower nature is completely purified and therefore obedient to the spiritual flow. Around his neck he has white, which represents purity of action and thought. Red is the colour of passion and of the blood, also it is sometimes seen as the colour of life at the material level. He has a good balance of red and green, which are complementary, to show the presence of both the life of matter and nature and the life of the Soul.

His sleeves are like wings, for once we become an initiate the hands become the wings of the Soul and they can manifest love. The arms and hands can hold and give love and healing and also do practical things such as making bread. If we put all our loving intent into whatever they are used for, we can see them as healers. They are the beginning of the exteriorised wings of the Soul. The yellow or gold which contours the hat and is coming out again on the shoulders, re-enforces the fact that he is entirely responsible for his own receptive capability, which is expressed by 'as I receive through the cup of my mind, I act'. This is a complete response of action to the vision. The service is from and for the Earth, so we have the colour green.

His belt is red, black and white, which are the colours of initiation. When these colours are seen on the belt that rests on the hips, it tells us that he has completely given his power to service and to the higher life. It says, "I have no intention for myself, so anything I do, is for the world". His belt is the belt of the initiation of the master. He has not yet realised that in the complete giving up of self-power, he is learning to dominate all his elements.

The gold background symbolises the golden thread of the Ancient Wisdom, which goes through all the cards.

His hat makes the Number 8 of infinity over his head and the shape of his head in his hat makes a circle of red, which shows us that he is a passionate Soul. It is the passion within nature and within the Soul itself, which will attract the Spirit through the mind.

This is the man standing on the world he lives in, with the power of his mind to attain the vision of infinite understanding. He has to have a passion for the truth and the vision of a completely free world. Here we're not talking about 'freedom' in the sense of feeling better because one is free of burdens, but freedom in the sense of more loving, giving, allowing and understanding. This vision of complete union with the divine through service to humanity is the opposite of freedom in the ordinary sense. But before that can be achieved, we have to be free of the ties of the world. Initiation goes through stages of nine levels of freedom, but the true purpose and the true becoming is complete fusion with the highest, through complete acceptance of what we aim to free from ourselves. He knows within himself that he is infinite in essence and the aim is to free the essence, not from matter, but rather to free him from the misunderstanding that he is a prisoner or victim in matter. By being in perfect union with a higher and inner being, which is pure essence and the source of all things, the notion of limitation becomes inconceivable. He finds his full realisation and lives his life as if it should never end. He is not an apprentice but a silent master; his mouth is shut, he is smiling and he is actively working in a normal place of work. It is said of the master, 'the world might think he belongs to it, but he stays in it so as to understand it better, in order to leave it behind'. He watches, he's a witness, he contemplates; he's in it but he doesn't truly belong to the world. 'The master doesn't work because he knows, he knows because he works'. That is exactly what our Number 1 is coming back to do; he's coming back for more understanding.

Thoughts are more important than words. Words can only express the value of thoughts, according to the measure and understanding of the world of form. In incarnation, man's thought must be exteriorised and so manifested in the world. He has to be independent, so he uses the energy not to adapt himself towards security, but to transform the world nearer to his vision. The other way of using the laws of nature is to make ourselves more comfortable and give ourselves more gratification; here we are looking at a completely different use.

The Magician wants to know the laws of nature, so that he can use them to make life easier for mankind, this way he allows others to become initiates themselves and reveal man's infinite possibilities. While we are using all the laws of nature in the struggle to survive, we will have not much of a chance to go beyond the everyday life and ask the vital questions. Transcendence and spiritualisation has to come from within us, so mankind has to have freedom from the dominance of the needs of survival; this is a practical truth for the times we live in.

The initiatic science seeks to understand the whole of nature, right back to its origins, so that the creator can find himself in nature. But before that, we have to make sure that needs, security and protection are not part of the intent. All the laws we have learnt and all the understanding of the power of mind to bring things to us, can be used psychically to control other people; this is black magic. The Magician on the other hand, uses honesty, clarity, strength and perseverance, to do the work and journey through the Major Arcana.

The name for this first card is 'I Am'. Man 'is' only if he has constant and full consciousness of the Soul and life within him for a full twenty four hours. This means that when we are lying down and falling asleep, we know why we are doing that and we know exactly what our subconscious is doing behind the scenes. That is what 'I Am' is about and The Magician is creating and bringing all the tools together in himself to achieve that. There have been several rounds, so it is not just a first-degree initiation and the round he's come back on might be the last one, for all we know. He symbolises all of us who have followed the inner path, learning to go through our cycles and our degrees.

He ceases to have a passive attitude and let life act on him. Nature and man suffer life; an initiate suffers, but he doesn't suffer life. He knows that life is in him and that he has to uplift the world and say, "Get away from me Satan", where Satan represents the subconscious. Jesus, representing the Soul, does this when he talks to Peter, who represents the material and physical body of the personality with its needs, fears and protective instinct. The Soul, or the initiate, has to truly oppose all his needs, fears and protective instinct and in so doing, he can actually absorb all the fears within matter. Then, with the quality of perseverance he carries on with all the cosmic forces behind him, helping him to uplift. The only way we are going to transmute all the patterns that are locked in the biological life, is by completely absorbing them into our own will and love. The opposition is actually done by absorption and that is a good way of opposing, isn't it!

When we are on the inner path of consciousness in life, it is a continuous effort to always go beyond ourselves, deeper and deeper where we do not want to go. We keep on going behind, behind and behind, it is incredibly simple. We look at our everyday life and keep on watching and knowing that we are doing it! Every time we say, "I don't want that any more", we are on the path and we can't go back, so we are going beyond ourselves. If we think we have reached our limits and we are still there tomorrow, then we haven't reached the centre. To keep going beyond your limits is called endurance and we are going in the right direction. We are not talking about not using our discriminating power, for there are things one mustn't endure and we are all intelligent enough to know what they might be. Every time we say, "No I can't any more" we discover there is more love, understanding, humility, giving and more 'Thy will be done'. This means we are on the right path.

Until we associate completely with the fact that we are the person in front of us, whatever they are doing, we are stopping our spiritualisation and inward motion. Freedom is within and out is in.

If we thought ourselves to be superior to humanity, we could not absorb and uplift it. If the Spirit in us was not able to reach the heart of matter and therefore the heart of all the molecules and cells, the wisdom of the planet could not be delivered. It is only in this world that real absorption, experiential knowledge and real freedom can happen; we are not running away here, we are going deeper. When we talk about the initiate being out of this world it is not as an angel on a cloud, it is deep in the very centre of matter that we become atomic and nowhere else. We become atomic inside and we go back to the real willpower of life, which will touch on the building blocks of Spirit and matter from millions of years ago. That is what erases all the misunderstandings within the genetic patterns and renders them completely bright, clear and spiritual; the way through is at the very heart of matter. We have to internalise with our minds, because it is the mind that does that journey and frees the mind-sets of the mental body. It is therefore that spiritual movement within that is going to cleanse all the misunderstandings, fears and the pains of the Soul of nature, nature being the emotional body of Earth. That spiritual energy sends a blast, like a little atomic bomb into the genetic pool, so that we can truly become the beings of light we are supposed to be, carrying the blueprint of creation.

The High Priestess, La Papesse
Meeting the Mystery

la Papesse

There is no higher manifestation of the divine intention than The High Priestess, the female Pope. Wearing a crown with two rings and a red cloak lined with green, she is seated on a throne in front of a veil. Here she protects the access to the great mystery. She is Isis, the metaphysical form of the Goddess and she represents love-wisdom. In one hand she holds the book of life, in the other the silver and gold keys, for she has all knowledge of both the natural and esoteric realms. Her left arm rests on a black sphinx. This Sphinx is the dweller on the threshold, the black Dog of Hell, representing our subconscious minds and this is what the initiate faces as he comes before her. Her face is partly obscured and her expression blank, for there is no easy access here. If the initiate is ready and few are, he will receive the higher revelation, will see beyond the veil and be changed forever.

23

The right use of the Tarot is as a spiritual teaching aid. All systems are only tools; the intention and the energy we invest when using the tools will define the result. Here we are aiming to put drops of gold back into the Tarot cards, for one tiny unit of truth and light changes an ocean of misleading darkness. The work is to go into the subconscious where something is festering in ignorance; to take us in there we need the ancient symbol of the dog, represented here by the black sphinx.

There are two qualities symbolised by the dog; there is the dog who is a server of God and there is the big black dog of Hell, who likes to be fed and the more he is fed the more he grows. The way we feed this black dog of Hell is by not knowing ourselves and being automatons, enacting out all our subconscious reactions without being aware of what is going on. We are all subject to this behaviour; the initiate's only work is to become completely aware of every single atom of shadow within him and so become aware of the input of his inner relationship with the outer world. This way he won't be caught by it, play its game and fall back into automatism. It is only when we can be aware of the origin of our reactions that we can start to be of use to the God we live in. This process doesn't happen in five minutes, which is why there are twenty-two cards in the Arcana. It is a very thorough process, turning around every stone and every little memory cell, because each one of them might still contain a little hologram of a situation where we are 'playing the game'. We are looking for little pools of hate, pain and regrets, so as to bring the light of love from our Soul into them. Every single corner of our sub-conscious that we feed unknowingly creates an entity within our aura, for all thoughts are creative. With every need, want and link we forge with somebody, we create a tie. This is what we have to face with The High Priestess. Are we as pure of intention, as free of needs as we think we are?

The High Priestess symbolises the highest manifestation of the authority of the divine wisdom on the planet. She is removed and silent. She scrutinises us and her presence warns that if we are going to come any nearer, it is not going to be a picnic.

Everything manifested is a symbol for an unseen cause. As we begin to understand life as symbolic, we access our inner wisdom and the material world of form has less effect on us. The High Priest-ess is therefore to be seen as a symbol, rather than a woman sitting on a throne. The aim of the journey is to understand that the world is within us and the fact that we see the world in a particular way is because it is already in our brain. This is an essential requirement for going through the veil of Isis, she is the metaphysical form of the Goddess.

The Magician in the first card now stands before her. He is already a potential initiate and he smiles, for he thinks that he has found a pot of honey. She says to him: "You want to come and show me what you have learned so far? You want to go further? Then look at me, look at me long and hard!" If we won't face her and go forward through her, then the journey is not for us. Going through the veil is the aim of the whole twenty two cards, so in a way at this point we are almost at the end. The High Priestess is the grace/wisdom aspect of the Goddess. She is metaphysical so she can only be perceived by the metaphysical mind in us. On the other side of the veil are the cause of life and the divine knowledge. She has to guard the door so that no imprudent intruder can step through. She holds the secret.

The Magician, the Number 1, is able to have a transforming effect on the manifested world; in fact we can all have an effect on the manifested world, but not in a conscious way. We can bring a culture down, we can bring another culture in and we can pollute the planet; we do all this within nature's unconscious cycle of transformation. The great catastrophes or wars are part of this, because they are 'weather' effects that needed to happen to the planet within a greater context and they help humanity to wake up to its responsibility. When we look at all the people and at the beneficent or destructive leaders, what we see is a superficial expression, which occurs when things either need to be manifested in a particular way, or destroyed. At those times some people are used as puppets or tools in major world events, when the time is right for something to happen to shake us. However, these people are different from the great ones, whom we would call the Masters. Those who have the ability to affect things can be stimulated through these events to realise the new vision and new hope. When The Magician comes in he is ready to receive a higher revelation.

In the experience of being truly alive, our senses are so instinctively pure, that we don't even know that we are sensing through them. In this state we can read the landscape for miles, like a wild beast. This is what our senses should be used for rather than to be used for the gratification of whether we like chocolate, or the colour red, or a particular piece of music. Whilst we are strongly centred on using the senses for pleasure, we are still quite a way from fully understanding the impact of what it is to be a true initiate. The true initiate can appreciate colours and chocolate and it doesn't mean that we mustn't like these things, but rather that we do not need any of them. We appreciate these things because our senses are there, but in that pure state of being truly alive we do not need any sensation and if suddenly we lost all our senses, we would not miss anything at all. Have you experienced being alive, without the senses being used for sensations? This state is always approached with a sense of dread, because it is the complete unknown: it is the divine or what is behind the veil and if we go through without being ready, madness is certain.

The initiate has come back to the world and from day one has a smile on his face. Is he naïve, over confident, or could it be dread, because what he is going to face is an unknown space? It is the space that holds all the wisdom so far and the secret of how God manifested it. This is Number 2, the great Isis or the great space. It has within it all the dust, beauty and brightness, all the life and death experiences for millions of years that have been and are to be, manifested, explored and brought back into the light.

When the initiate is truly alive, he always has that sense of dread and it is not because he doesn't dare. We have learned to survive physically by the senses telling us what is around so that we can act accordingly; for example, if I am a rabbit and five inches away there is a fox, I run away. The acceleration of picking up the message and having to go is what we call excitement. It is life and death, it is sex and survival. Anything that accelerates the senses to make us move is an over-the-top reaction, except when it is for survival and to save our skin. Most of us in the western world should not be 'in excitement' because we are not living at a time where we have a hunter behind us about to kill us. However, the rest of the world lives on the edge of survival, so we can hold compassion for them. If mass consciousness is still using excitement in creating its own hysterical shows as part of daily life, it is really only because it has not yet grown up, for modern man is very young on the planet in comparison to the millions of years of biological life. Man is like a two or three year old infant still sucking his thumb; this is not a judgment or condemnation, just a statement of fact.

Using the senses to feel alive comforts us. We can get addicted to the laboratory rather than the research, like an artist who gets addicted to the beauty of the colours, rather than refining his art until he understands that art isn't necessary. The fact that we need comfort is because we still have the survival aspect in us and so we find other modes besides the natural flight, fight, or rut instincts, to stimulate excitement. The rut in the animal kingdom is not really excitement, though we have described it as such, it is just the mind-less push of biologic or organic creativity. This is very relevant in The High Priestess, for we have the two pillars of life that are con-stantly mating and that is why they support the temple. When you have the rut in nature, you have the two pillars in action in order to procreate species. We describe it as excitement because mankind has experimented with all the deviations of the sexual act, but in real-ity sex is plain and simple and doesn't have all the bits and pieces, complicating and hiding its true nature. We had to make sensual excitement part of our luggage in order to plunge into the mud of the subconscious and see what is exciting down there, otherwise we would just never have gone for the experience, for who wants to go and get excited on dust? The gift of the senses thus enables us to do the work of purification.

So The High Priestess puts fear and dread into us. When we real-ise that all is mind moving into space, as witnesses we are being used as we have abused; this is what the veil is going to reveal. Biological life has been used from the beginning of time for the purpose of birth-ing awareness. We are learning to give our material life in service, as a way through for the higher consciousness. Form is only yesterday's intent and understanding that needed manifesting, so that through it the great life can recognise itself by us being aware of our reactions. We understand that service is the only thing that we are here to do, so this is our use. Service should not be a means to achieve sainthood or mastery, for in the real energetic life there is nothing else we can be used for. The reality is that we are being used, so we are servants and it is the complete non emotional acceptance of that fait accompli that is the truth. We have to fall in love with the great life beyond the emotional to reach this stage of acceptance. We play lots of games to find out what the experience of being alive feels like from every angle and now we have to put the games away. The High Priestess or Isis knows that she serves the servants of God, who are full of love and compassion and all manner of beautiful things. She serves them because she knows that they can't pass through that doorway with emotional luggage, so she is there to help them look into their sub-conscious emotional needs. The world of God is a world of energy, where love is magnetic and truth is light. In this world of energy, matter is only a way to recognise what the space is made of and to see how beautiful the dance of the energy is. The High Priestess causes dread, because we have to drop all the dreams of childhood; we even have to drop the dreams of the initiate who thinks he is going to help some great God in the sky to save the planet. We really have to die to all that, so that the mind can soar and realise that it is just a spark of light. The message is 'Just die to everything you aspired to achieve and become, so as to be truly alive'. This is what is meant by the veil tearing, when Jesus was dying on the cross. At this point, Jesus the Soul was pierced by the incoming divine mind, removing any hope of personal glory. The higher mind in the Soul has no other agenda than service to the great life.

If we have come in front of The High Priestess here, it is because we have surpassed and risen above the little mysteries of life such as science and psychology, which help make us into individuals who can manage life a little bit better. We would have to take several more leaps in consciousness to be in the presence of The High Priestess. These leaps will reveal the existence of the Soul principle, until eventually we learn to associate with the concept of Soul. Higher intelligence has to be reached though Soul, so aspiration has to be strong enough and high enough, for Soul to come down and manifest the star of Bethlehem. The star is that part in us where the Soul has reached the higher self and associates with that point of light.

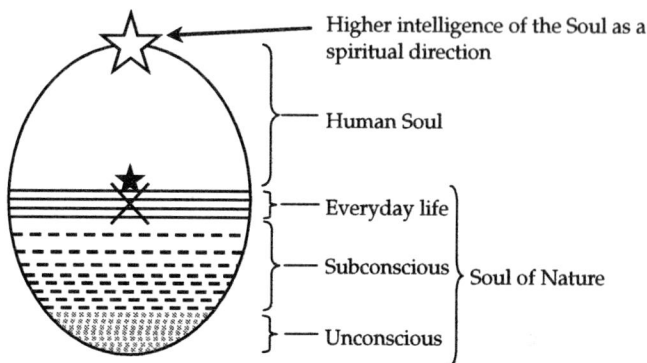

Figure 1. The Star of Bethlehem.
Aligning with the point of light within the Soul.

When we are in the depth of our despair, we think that no human being has ever suffered as much as us, or ever gone so low. We are very good at holding onto self-pity, but once we finish with self-pity we slowly come up. As we come up we don't stop at self, because having gone a bit higher, we feel as though we are as Jesus – then we realise we have to come and serve. We come down again quickly because we are happy and eager to serve; beware of the excitement of that!

The idea is to bring the light down into the subconscious and even if we do it out of pride or weakness, it doesn't matter, because we are bringing the light in. It is always our own experience and hopefully every time we plunge a little deeper we are gathering a bit more of the mystery.

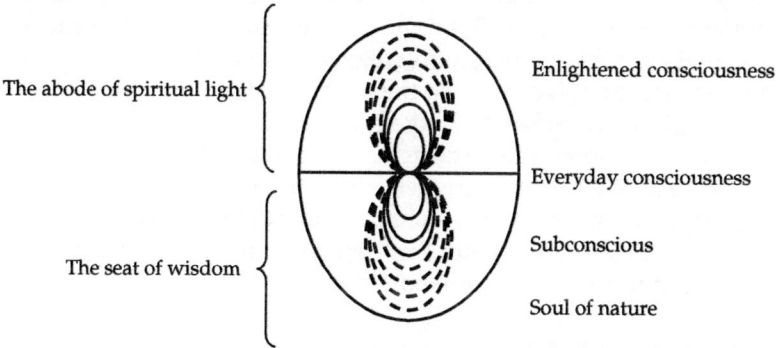

The abode of spiritual light

Enlightened consciousness

Everyday consciousness

Subconscious

The seat of wisdom

Soul of nature

Figure 2. 'As above so below'.

The movement of the light into the sphere of work. Bringing the wisdom back into the consciousness of humanity, so that it can rise proportionately to its descent, to meet the higher mind of the Soul.

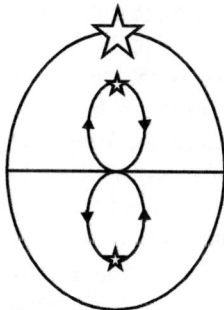

Figure 3. *The star comes down increasingly bringing light into the darkness.*

Then the light of the star directs and works with the pure instinct of nature.

The light has met, cleansed, understood and loved whatever it meets with, so it has sublimated the whole of the space. If we come back to a life of crises which sends us into despair and we identify with the despair, then we haven't stopped getting excited about the experience of the situation, so we are not going to be able to sublimate all the knowledge that we have. To increase our contribution to the realisation of the plan, we must stop focussing on self and stop imprinting through the emotional and intellectual senses. We are useful when we meet the situation and are able to look at it from above with the viewpoint of the star. The star is with us always.

An intense feeling of despair or joy, would give us the opportunity to travel with our star (higher mind) to its source in the cellular memory where it is held. Then the light of reality can transmute the personal guilt/victim perception that we have of this specific recurring emotional/mind-set, into the acceptance of having been used by the light for a rescue job on the subconscious Soul of nature. That is how we 'redeem', although actually nothing needs redeeming in the sense of sin. The world was created or 'deemed' and all we are doing is revisiting every single little pebble of that creation to name it. We don't have to own it or carry it on our shoulders, because we can revisit it and be in there completely with truth, to leave it in peace.

With awareness, we know when we have put ourselves in a dreadful situation, so we don't make any fuss because we know it will be gone tomorrow; we don't hold onto it unless we feel self-pity and guilt.

Any pain that we feel is added onto the original pain. We have to go beyond pain and see from the humble point of view of the fallen Star that there is nothing to it, it is not done to us, it is life happening and from there we can see that a big crisis is just a bruise. There can be a bruise on our body, or on the body of the planet which could manifest as a catastrophe, such as an earthquake or a famine. A bruise is just a lot of damaged cells and when we visit our own personal life crises, the crystallised scars can be seen for what they are, the past, experienced, named and depersonalised by the light of the Soul and the love of service.

 We have to face the guardian on the seat, The High Priestess. She is holding two keys in her left hand, which is resting on the head of the sphinx. In her right hand she holds the book of life, which symbolises truth, so she's putting us in front of the psychic trial of getting real. She tells us that we don't get real through intellectual knowledge or emotional visualisation workshops, for anything that has to do with the personality's experience is not real. We can only get real through using the psychic realm, or the realm of the Soul; this is the only way our work can be done. The realm of the Soul is one with the higher mind and the Soul of nature, the work is aligning the mind of man with the higher mind of the Soul and the love/wisdom

of the Soul of nature. This is truly going to happen on the psychic level through the Soul, so is the beginning of the true death of the illusion of the personality; this is why there is a feeling of dread. We are talking about the Soul wanting to be active and really having to fish out all these pains and problems, so that once and for all we don't take matter, intellect or the big emotional body, as the Queen of the heavens, which they are not. The personality is only a puppet, a vehicle for the mind to follow, to find more fuel to transmute into light.

The work of the Soul starts in a psychic trial. If we start it too soon, mental disorder comes in, which always happens to a few and is a necessity in every group. For the normal Soul group it is natural to have a few individuals going beyond reason, to allow the whole group to align to psychic understanding and the use of true, non-intellectual intelligence. The warning is, be careful, don't undergo the trial too soon out of personal aggrandisement, because that can destabilise the fragile instrument and so necessitate a lot of healing work. If we use too many physical ways to reach God, such as overuse of exoteric or mechanical rituals, or chemical substances, we can be derailed. The way through is a natural process that must be witnessed, so the true spiritual path is humble and has nothing to do with pride, or wanting to save the world. Looking back at our childhoods, we may have been already somewhere in front of the veil but didn't recognise it until somebody described the landscape; that is the natural way.

When we see that the testing ground is everyday life and that nobody is holding our hand, true initiation can happen. Then if we can have the courage to dive in where our emotional/mental reaction takes us, the Soul perception can disperse the shadows. Though we are all important in the scheme of things, as individuals we do not matter, so we must remove our personal selves from the vision. As we remove the personality from a happening, whether bad or good, we can be grateful that we can mine from it more coal to burn.

We are talking about alchemy, hidden knowledge, or transmutation. The Magician is master of the secrets and this has allowed him to come in front of The High Priestess with her keys, which hold the unlocking of the secrets. He is wary, for if the veil is lifted just in one corner, he will have the realisation that it is all energy and that we really are of no consequence. Then even if the veil is quickly put back he cannot draw back, for he's had a glimpse of the world as an energetic entity. If we have seen that and yet still live strongly in the sensory, intellectual way, we will be deeply troubled by our ways and will perceive them as weakness and failures, until we accept being used by a greater power. We tend to forget the whole picture as we get taken in by everyday life, maybe because the monkey in us is a bit too proud, or maybe because we haven't fully recognised its tricks yet.

The humble character of the Soul will love those people who help to cut the emotional ties. It is important to remember that it is those ties that hold us back, not the people. When we see behind the veil, we can look at our environment with a new appreciation of where we are and we are able to recognise all the personal emotional ties that are holding us back. The love aspect becomes purer and stronger if we dissolve the ties of need. We may go through several groups of friends or loved ones in a life-time; they help us to do that energetic work of severing our links to the lower emotional. We have to bring our immediate emotional response back to pure instinct, to recognise our natural survival needs rather than emotional attachment.

With groups and couples we have interaction rather than leaders, for there is no above or below and no one is more evolved than another. It is the power of the love of the work that is important, for it measures evolution and without that there is no group. The same applies in 'use and being used' and 'abuse and being abused'; the abuser is also the abused. If the victim can look at the fact that he is also the perpetrator, because he or she had to experience the abuse, then eventually we see that they both undertook the experience and both have to stop playing the game. There is nothing to abuse, there is only spiritual energy floating through a space bringing up shapes and forms, so that it can recognise its evolution at the time. Once that level of understanding is reached, we won't put ourselves into those situations as abused or abuser. The initiate won't engage in it mentally or emotionally, because matter is of no importance. The body is only a manifestation at the time, a tool being used by energies and the world is an energetic world. We cannot take seriously what happens to our personalities in that sense, but Soul can inform them so that the instrument can translate what needs to be understood through it. Being able to gather the emotion from that type of experience is more than important and worthy, though the experience itself is not important. The emotions have to be named and purified by the higher mind, so that we understand which feelings are personal. The feelings are there because the personality thinks it is important and doesn't understand its link to divinity. The way through to this understanding is through the Soul work, when we start activating the star of Bethlehem. The three-fold personality has to give up all its needs to be the instrument of the Soul, which in turn has to give all its love to be at the service of the karmic spiritual energy that moulds the Universe – so who is using who?

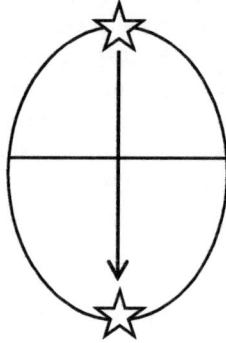

Figure 4. *The final alignment of the personality/Soul/Spirit connection.*

The unveiling has to be realised all the way down, so the star has to drop down into the great sea of the subconscious, restoring wisdom to everyday life.

The work is done only through taking the conscious mind into the unconscious, which is the Soul of nature and was there before us. Nature had to find a unit in herself that could be a little star, a torch, or a light and so she gave birth to awareness in the human kingdom. We go in and feel everything, eventually realising it is not ours! We should not personalise what we feel; we are only little light-bearers going into the experience to feel and name it. The initiate has understood that the content of his subconscious is part of the previous experience in the unconscious of nature, that is why he can walk up and down with his torch and nothing bothers him. The feelings of 'It is unfair' and 'I am being used' are not there; he is not afraid of anything he finds there, because he is cleansing and bringing in more and more light. Once the big star is at the bottom in the full light, we have redemption or re-creation and everything is seen for what it is. The Star comes down increasingly, for the Soul knows it has come back for service and is full of enthusiasm. The amnesia that the Soul had when it first comes back can only be dissipated through the one that experiences (Soul), when the experiment and experience make one. We go in and dig deep and look at everything from that very deeply felt, emotional hurt that the world carries. As we become more and more aware, we vaguely remember having been there before, so the work that needs doing becomes clearer and clearer. We have the star and the light, so we need not

be overwhelmed by emotions, because we realise they are not personal. We are in a big sea of emotion and have to ride it to see where
it takes us. The waves take us to a point of rest at the top, when we
think we are the saviour. Then when we are at the bottom, we drop
the self-pity and feel the black velvety rest of the overshadowing
of the wisdom of the world. Suddenly peace is there and the Soul
brings comfort in the subconscious amongst the monsters, except
there are no monsters! So we keep on doing the work, deeper and
quicker. What a privilege it is to look, understand and be aware, so
that we can translate the process. We can thank God we are doing
the work! It is all about knowing that the personality is of no consequence. We can liken it to screaming at a horror film; even though
we know it is not real, we can still be afraid, but we know the difference between the drama and the real thing. We scream because we
know we can go into drama and it is okay, it is not really happening,
the real alchemy is in silence.

The High Priestess is herself a veil in a way because all that she is
going to confer to us, with her keys and her book, is what we truly
have to absorb. We are talking about Soul work, for Soul absorbs
and retains. Soul is a sea of memory, or a memory bank and she is
showing us that. We don't see the other side of her throne, just as
with The Magician we only saw three of the four legs of his table,
the other one being hidden. Her right side is not seen, but we can
imagine the white sphinx there hidden by her cloak.

Whether or not we are facing The High Priestess, the humanity of our nature needs to be completely honoured, loved and cel-
ebrated. There used to be an official near the Pope whose job it was
to remind him 'you are only a man', just in case he was losing a
bit of humility in thinking he was God on the planet. It is a tradition that should be kept. Do we want to become a God and escape
being a man? Why would we want to escape? It is the same with
the work we are doing, if we don't completely own one hundred
percent what we are at the time with love, compassion and humility, whether we are the abused or the abuser, then we cannot fuse
with the higher understanding of the Soul that is infused with the
light of the Star.

Through the wisdom of The High Priestess and the secret of
knowing that we are not this, that, or the other, we can actually fuse
with the divine through the mind, the Soul and the higher intelligence. When this is happening we may not be able to describe or
sense what is going on. We must go through the intense purification
of sulphur, for that is what is expected. Ancient Wisdom says that

until the sixth initiation we are still in illusion, so there's still a lot of burning and dissolving to be done.

The Silver Key that The High Priestess holds gives knowledge of the natural things; being in her left hand it shows receptivity and intuition. Silver is the beautiful energy that wants to rise up with hope and 'esperance', travelling right up to the higher mind to meet the lover. We have to start where we stand and we stand in nature, so we must have all the knowledge of the natural world. The silver will take us to the flower of what the intellect can do, which is philosophy. Philosophy is a wonderful supreme science and a natural tool, which enables the intellect to uplift itself. The intellect works through philosophy in a beautiful and refined way, but it is still a human science. Religion is one of the flowers of human science.

The leaves on the silver key represent the three virtues of religion, which are the beginning of the work of faith, hope and charity. They are still of the personality and require that the personality thinks and aligns to goodwill. Then, once the intellect is dropped, they are not needed. Faith is unnecessary because we know; we don't need hope because we are in the now; we don't need charity because we have compassion. We don't matter and yet we are priceless! On the way there is always an exoteric lane and an esoteric path. A lane leads to a path and when we are going towards the esoteric path there will always have been an intellectual lane beforehand, such as a teaching, a guru, or something else exterior. The esoteric is hidden inside and the minute we go there we work with Soul.

The intellect is the intermediary principle and the way through, for it is only through the intellect that we are able to translate the knowledge and vision of the Soul. Whichever form of expression we use; words, arts or sciences, we still have to use mind. To have rendered the intellect into a very well ordered, obedient servant to some higher quest is something quite beautiful. To be seen as intellectually clever can bring difficulties, because even if we have been touched by the Soul, this does not obviate the fierce battle between the intellect and Soul. The seat of the Soul is in the heart and therefore in the emotional body, but the first contact with Soul is through the intellect. Active Intelligence is the divine side of intellect. A rise in consciousness has to come from a contact with the higher mind and the will. It manifests as a change of perception; it is the perception of everything from the point of view of the Soul that enables the rise to happen. We don't have to get rid of problems, but rather transmute them by seeing them as teaching aids.

So the silver key of science that The High Priestess holds in her hand symbolises all the qualities that have lifted us right up to a refined level of concrete knowledge. Though it is refined the knowledge is still dogma; for example, we have a fixed idea that a plant is a plant and it grows like this or that, according to its species and its chemistry with the soil and the light. While a thing is seen scientifically it is a dogma, whether it is religion or science. Because of this we know that the next initiation has to happen from within, for there is no deeper truth than the one that comes from our inner chemistry, just as there is no possible plant unless the seed is taken from the heart of the plant so it can unfold into the flower and the fruit. When we have used all these beautiful social, initiatic paths at the level of matter, we have to kill the perception of ourselves as we are at that time, so as to be reborn into a different awareness; this is what we mean by the initiate killing his initiator. The plant in our example is then seen or perceived as a specific symbol of sacrifice; a gift, rather than what it is seen as purely biologically.

On the top of the Gold Key is the symbol for sulphur, which in alchemy represents the burning and dissolving of matter and of anything that is impure. The Gold key holds wisdom and to be an effective channel for wisdom we need reason. Reason, which is another side of the intellect, has to be regarded as important, as long as it doesn't become an end in itself. If it does, then all we keep doing is reasoning and so stay in the closed circle of the intellect. Having the light coming in with reason to express it, is the only right use of reason and intellect. Gold is the esoteric knowledge, which gives life, reality and gnosis and will only deliver all that after purification with sulphur. Sulphur symbolises total purification and there is no realisation if we are not purified. If we are truly to be a tool, we must be completely clear so that what comes through us when the star comes up can be seen for what it is. Sulphur eliminates anything that is not eternal. It instigates a painful purification, because in the silence of our minds it destroys anything that has no value and is a lie. What it destroys are all the easy convictions of a lazy faith, which puts its trust into exteriorised affirmations and mantras that are recited from the lips but have no uplift, because they have not been experienced or understood. We think that if we keep on saying the same thing time and time again, we will go to Heaven! The natural way is in silence and it is only truly when man is in the silence of his own solitude that he can find his own God. Remember Moses, the prophet or the intellect at the service of the higher mind, when he told God "Oh Lord, you made me powerful and alone".

The initiate, having found his inner truth, has to take it beyond the God of religion, or the God that took him to where he is. He must rise above all dogma, wherever it comes from, in order to have a vision beyond his own preoccupation. This is initiation – to merge with a higher vibration of perception. Science is fantastic, because it is the job of the intellect to name everything, so that we know the body of the God we live in at the physical and chemical level. In the same way, religion is wonderful because there are tens of millions of people on the planet who need to be carried and protected by a structure. A religious service is wonderful, although if we rely on it to feel comforted and protected we have to recognise this as a need. We have to learn to participate humbly in its symbolism, rather than participating because it is beautiful and makes us feel better. It doesn't matter which faith it is, all religious services are touching, because it is about the Soul of mankind moving towards God through a structure, which is as old as the beginning of the rise of consciousness in nature and it is beautiful. However, the true transformation can only happen inside, in silence. 'The word is silver and the silence is golden' – the word is the translation through the intellect and then silence is golden, because the understanding is complete and undiluted by the poverty of the intellect.

'The Word' is a teaching, given by a teacher or master. Silence is a re-thinking of the word, so that it can be assimilated by the pupil for his own understanding. It is a harmonious value that he vibrates with and can in turn pass on. We have all read books that have moved us, because we recognised truth in them and realised that we are made of that truth and can appropriate it. It doesn't matter who has written or said these truths, we feel the duty to pass them on because they changed us.

If we repeat what is read in a book in our own words as we feel it and know it, it will have a hundred times more value than reading directly from the book, because it will be Soul given, rather than intellectually sent. That is the power of transmutation. An example is a great and beautiful sentence sounded by a poet or master; we take it in and resonate with it in the cave of the heart, so bringing another facet to it and making it more beautiful. Then when it comes through us it is able to touch somebody else. If we find something that resonates in us, it is our duty to bring a specific sound out of that inner resonance. Only when we are ready to see the great truths, will they come and vibrate in us. The will is there in the heart of every atom of life and for a while nobody resonates with its sound, then suddenly some of us do and start sounding, so that somebody else picks it up. This is how more and more sound is created; it is truly bringing the word of God right into every breath of everyday life. Some people might hear us and say; "Yes, that is it, I'm going to start a business at the corner of the street and feed the poor". They are interpreting that particular sounding in their own way and yet the original great sentence was, 'I am the bread and I am the life'. They have translated it into something practical and that translation has come from within them, which is why it is important to only follow the esoteric way from within. Silence is golden, but silence without the silver of the intellect doesn't communicate its peace to the ones who need the vibration of the teaching and the word.

When we have completely exhausted the experiences of life through seeking and nothing has worked, then we are at the beginning of the threshold and realise that 'life is going to do it for us'. If all the exoteric ways weren't there, we wouldn't get to the end of that lane, for once we have tried everything and it hasn't satisfied us, we can scratch our heads and realise there is something else. When that is done, we can become our own teacher. One of the great beauties of experiencing as much as we can is that eventually we realise that there is no satisfaction and nothing has come out of all the experience. We can go and learn from another book of knowledge and it will just be the same, so eventually we realise that all these things are superficial and that knowledge, pleasure, dogma and using the physical, the form and the intellect, ultimately gets us nowhere. People, who make the biggest mistakes in an experiential way, can often cut the link with the superficial form more quickly.

Once all this is seen and it is understood that the value of it is only superficial, we should ask ourselves; "Which law drives life that make us so subservient to what holds the material in place?" Whenever that question is asked, we are then starting on the occult path. The question might not be asked again for another 40 years, or 40 lives, but there is hope because it has been felt and sounded. From that first question the man will not stop searching, even if he takes a lot of holidays in between. He is very much in the dark to start with and just going with his feelings like a blind man, trying to convince himself that what he has done in the past isn't futile or worthless, so he will say that maybe the past is real life. He has to recognise all his weaknesses, temptations and hates, so he has to start to hate everything that his life has been, as he contrasts it with where he wants to go. He has been in the profane world, the world of the superficiality of matter, form and greed and then he begins to think that there has got to be something else, so he starts looking. He goes deeper and deeper; he starts to hate what is in his mind, seeing it as mediocre and manipulative. All his past and the way he has always lead his life, suddenly looks very gross and ugly and he starts hating what he had previously loved, to the point of losing his Spirit. If we don't do it like that, we don't do it properly and we are not good searchers. He will keep on until he gets to the inner door of the temple of Solomon, the Holy of Holies, where only the high priests go. The higher mind reaches the depth of all the experiences of the human heart, where the love/wisdom princess awaits her knights in shining light. This is the wisdom of the initiate who can gaze, look and understand the enigma that is put in front of him.

The keys cannot be separate, for they work together. The golden key symbolises the life giving esoteric energy and its handle is shaped like an Ankh. This tells us that it is only the inner knowledge of the Soul that gives life. We're alive if we are in nature and it is therefore the Soul of nature in the world, that sustains biological life, but we are only truly alive as a human being if we are fed by the light of the Soul, which is the inner life. When this is realised, we can knock on the door of the inner temple. We must exhaust the knowledge of the material world if we do not want to fall back under its influence.

The power of the initiate is not so much what he can do; it is an inner power and so doesn't have to manifest in any specific way. Like The High Priestess, the initiate is somebody very dangerous to come near to. This is not because he would harm anybody, but because there is something in his clarity that will bring people in front of themselves. The black sphinx of The High Priestess is doing exactly this, mirroring what the initiate has in him and if he has something to face, that is his enigma. This is 'Man know thyself' and if the man doesn't know himself, the black sphinx is there to show him exactly what it is that he doesn't know. Knowing ourselves is only being aware of our behaviour, which is driven by our subconscious. It is having a little light down there in the subconscious and always being honest and strong enough to say "I vibrate to that, I react to this and I react to that, so I understand why this happened and why someone might commit a crime, because I have already recognised that in myself". When we can do that we automatically defuse it and there is no blame, because there is only an act that occurred, which doesn't need to be repeated. An act is only a movement in time and isn't permanent. We have all been violators, because we are only repeating the step that nature took to survive, so we need to recognise that and be strong, as it is our work to go through the inner purifying flame. Self-development can cause distress; we can see the word differently, as 'de-stress' and stop stressing about it, let the tension go and relax.

The steel of the sword of truth has to be purified. When we really come in front of our own truth we must have the courage to take the sword, put it into the fire again to be purified and then dip it straight into the water. Things need to be destroyed quite quickly, so that all the impurities in the metal can be burnt out. The more we put the blade into the fire to be beaten into alignment, the stronger the steel becomes. The steel symbolises the spiritual will and the stronger and purer it is, the more the intuition and light can come through it. It is therefore dangerous in everyday life, because when we are going for self-purification, we can get obsessed by it and that can destabilise the instrument mentally, as we bring the shadows up to the surface. We may be too self-obsessed and so fall back into think- ing that the world is there for us.

The work will bring pain, but also elevation and uplift, or rebel- lion and fall. Rebellion is the important and necessary first step towards listening to the higher mind, as in its extremes it ignores anything from the outside. We can see an example of this in the rebel- lious adolescent who wants to be seen to be the best and the most obnoxious, yet at the same time wants to be loved; that is personal- ity. With the rebellious adolescent, we must wait until the silliness has stopped and then help them to comply if they want to be good in society. If the person sees the possibility of rising and yet refuses to work on the inner plane, as they carry on in their rebellion, then they are not at ease in the world. The opportunity for change is there but they do not want to hear the inner call, so they keep on being socially dysfunctional; it is a disorder, or un-ease. Rebellion is a state which makes us hate any outer authority that restricts us, because the Soul is after its own inner guidance and once we have got hold of that, we naturally comply with the laws of the land to show that the work has been done. These two states have the same aim and one comes after the other, so remember not to judge for we all have to fall.

When the initiate comes in front of The High Priestess her face is blank and unreadable. He will misread her if he thinks she is a brick wall, because that is not the case. She completely ignores him because if she had any expression on her face that said "Come on,

I know how you feel", or "Don't be an idiot", it could stop the man in front of her from accomplishing his mission. The mission is to unfold his destiny and to follow his own star, which is the true seed of divinity. As he faces her he is aware that he could get lost, for he doesn't know if it is life eternal on the other side of the veil or not and he's aware of the dread of not knowing. She completely ignores all that and so appears to be stern and impartial. He has to decide from within himself to stay and knock at the door. His persistence is a true sign of courage, which says that the steel of his inner truth has been sufficiently tempered.

Whenever we are very close to the truth, discrimination through the intellect must be used; otherwise the initiate at the door hasn't really rendered his intellect useful. The only job the intellect has, after he has gone through that door, is to serve. Right up to the door he has had to see whether he is taking his intellect seriously or not, but after going through it discrimination becomes a spiritual quality. We still have to weigh everything up carefully, because we remember that mistakes are always likely. Even Jesus (the Soul) on the cross was weighing up and asking; "Is this really happening?"

He could go on living the double life, for on the one hand the initiate or disciple is driven towards the goal of illumination or fusion with the highest; on the other hand he knows that he is weakened with temptation and can be charmed. In taking the next step and going through the door, he will have to let go of that double life and then it is really a single life, with the focus on the highest, but staying with the behaviour of the profane. There are no more excuses of "I am only human and I am not completely aware", which allowed him to go back and play the game. Jesus (the Soul) said; "When you are in a foreign land you eat and behave as a foreigner" so the initiate does not say, "I am special and I am different", but rather obeys the social laws of the country he is in and the laws of the Earth, even if he knows these laws are temporary. The laws are temporary in the sense that they will carry on until the Earth herself is divine and then we will be under divine laws, rather than the laws of life and death. If he pleads ignorance that is covering up the fact that he still wants to enjoy the sensual life.

The real word for The High Priestess is gnossos, or connaissance, which is what we are born with. The wisdom is not that we are in the world, but that the world is in us. At this stage we know that, because we have learned to understand what incredible instruments we are. We are a memory-bank for the God we live in and we each have the capability of entering every single room in that great vault of knowledge. Each cell in our bodies is a room that we can enter into and decipher the knowledge therein; this is the kind of instrument we are. The world is actually not out there, except when we need to check the little black dogs we have within us, which are our reactions as we play the game. Once we truly know the world is within us, then everything is accepted and loved and there is no problem. We can go and visit any room with as much courage, honesty and love as we can fathom within us, for we are custodians of our house; that is what makes us true co-creators. Creation isn't to do with planting trees; it is to do with truly understanding that the world is the way it is because of an idea or a mental process. Each word or thought creates a true entity. Self work is necessary, also witnessing and service are a by-product of the greater plan, which is to make planet Earth sacred. In this work we are essential but not most important, for we ourselves are just by-products by which the planet can move on.

The whole of the planet's psyche is polluted by a murky, lustful, wishful, wanting, needy atmosphere. Cleansing our thoughts, desires and needs is necessary, so that our instruments can exteriorise the good will and pure intent of the Soul into the highest attainment, by the work of service; this doesn't mean being a 'goody-goody'. If we can hold that intent, then even when we are living for biological survival, we can recreate the world with the power of our thoughts; for example the more people think peace, the more peace will happen. If we see the possibility of that, we can see how it is going to replace the lower needs. All of us are breathing an atmosphere that is full of this polluted mind stuff. If we put together all the wishes and lust that occur between men and women in just one day on the planet, it isn't surprising that there is rape and abuse. In a time of war it happens through the de-humanised men who are used for these wars. That violent energy has to manifest through an instrument, so let's not put the entire fault on the rapist or the killer, they just happen to be the weakest instrument at the time; it is the sum of all our thoughts that makes it happen. In knowing this, our initiate must always focus on the highest vision, for we are forever recreating the world with our thoughts. Originally the world was a manifestation in form of the highest possibilities of biological perfection, but now it has given birth to consciousness through mankind. We have recognised that we are in the world to observe it, so it has become the laboratory for the consciousness to unfold into its full potential. We go in and are driven by lust and greed, and then we have to become aware of our behaviour in order to stop playing the game. Once we liked it, but now we must hate it; eventually we go beyond love or hate by dropping it and focussing elsewhere. At that point we are not in the body or in the personality anymore, but are guided by the Masters of Wisdom.

We really do create everything with our thoughts all the time, so mass consciousness is constantly creating the world we see now. Changing this takes courage and honesty and it doesn't hurt us, but we don't do it at all if we are afraid of losing the game. We have to be in the market place, waiting for someone to wake up. This knowledge cannot be taught in books, because it has to be an inner process. It is the same type of thing in family relationships, for the whole human family is working towards the complete acceptance that our sole purpose is to be used in service. It can seem violent that we have to be killed and have to suffer earthquakes and war in the name of God, but it is the same as having millions of cells in our bodies dying every day; that death is an unfolding of new life.

There are more and more of us who have greater awareness now, so the mass consciousness can't dominate in such a malevolent way any more. It is a tiny opening, but it has more power than anything we can imagine, because we are plugged into the enormous power point of Spirit. Power, in the sense of force or light, is not without danger. When we hear "Let us not fall into temptation", this is a reality that we have vaguely understood as "Don't let me go for one more bar of chocolate". Temptations are only a measure of the power we have, so if all we are worried about is the temptation of the bar of chocolate, then our powers are quite gentle. There are no absolute sins to do with temptation. Absolute sin is only when we have lifted ourselves up to the higher level of consciousness and want to use the power gained to manipulate the energy for our own purposes; this is serious black art. Sin can only be against Spirit, so we cannot sin through lack of awareness or ignorance of nature, we can only sin in the light of Spirit, which is to use the force knowingly for our own benefit. This is why we have to be so vigilant in the cleansing of the instrument. All so-called sins are there to teach us to align and to be aware. If we think we are afraid to fall into temptation, we have had it, because it is the power of thought that does it. Temptation only comes through self-interest. Dread is okay because we are in front of something incredible, but we need to go bravely forward with no intention of falling back, for that would feed that power into the personality. So falling back is a sin which stems from fear of falling and is about wanting to be more powerful than the other one. We have to be consciously aware of all our thoughts. It is important to choose a focus that is completely detached from self and to dare to lose any interest or intent towards self. The dread is normal, but let's not turn it into excitement, fear, or whatever it was that we carried on our backs, otherwise we will fall back into our mindsets and carry on playing the game.

We are being asked not to live a double life, for in the process of lifting the veil we have to be honest and true all the time. If we can do that there is no sin, because we can see it as it happens. As an instrument we are covered with dust; as we see the dust we can transmute it into pure energy. This becomes easier in time and eventually, when we are focussed on the truth rather than on ourselves, it just happens without having to try. It is the truth that is important and we cannot plead ignorance any more once the veil is lifted. There can be a heavy disturbance about having to go further, because, when we are in front of the sphinx we are faced with how much we have fed the black dog of hell. For lives and lives we trod that beautiful path, we had visions, we even taught people. Then suddenly we are truly looking at ourselves and we see the pitiless reality of the system we live in. It is truly awe-ful when we are put in front of the formidable divine; it is a consuming process.

The Tiara of The High Priestess has two crowns, tiers, or circles. They represent the senses and the intellect and the crescent moon on top shows the psychic aspect. The Pope at Number 5 wears the purple pontifical tiara, which has three tiers, representing the physical, emotional and mental worlds, of which he is completely in charge. The High Priestess has a white veil coming down from the crown and over her shoulders, to show that she is about mystery, being half-hidden. The Veil represents purity, knowledge and wisdom. We cannot pass through the veil without meeting the big iron gates of death; they are iron because we are talking of alchemy in the sense of will and we need a strong will to get through them. As with the Devil, in Number 15, where we have chains of iron, these gates, symbolising the senses have to be broken, but it is easier to break chains of iron than break the chains of the senses. We have to go forward and not look back and as long as the veil is not lifted, it is still possible to stop.

The Moon represents the psychic sense, or the ability to go into Soul to get the esoteric or hidden knowledge. The Moon has many symbols and from the esoteric point of view of the Ancient Wisdom, it represents the subconscious aspect. The physical moon is dead and getting smaller, because as we go more and more into the subconscious and bring more and more light in, it is going to disappear. It represents the dark side of our past and it holds, just as our cells hold, all the memory of the things that are of the instinctual pure planet. It is actually in the process of decay and it consists of all the bits and pieces we are visiting when we visit our deviations, our misunderstandings and our self-pity. Planet Earth herself has no self-pity, for she is tough and survives. The Moon represents the subconscious, self-pitying Soul of nature and is the shadow of the Earth from deep in the past. Earth has had to put the past aside and carry on and do the work of God and use the light reflecting on its past for its unfolding. So when we go into our subconscious, we are revisiting the decaying body of the past, in order to clean the psychic atmosphere that we inhabit; we have to do that because if we didn't go there and see it, we wouldn't redeem it and stop the game of seeing ourselves as victims.

Seen from the highest point of view, this is the great hermaphrodite Moon, which enables us to do the work. She is both receptive and giving, for she receives the light and gives it out. It is not the grandmother moon, who says how much better it was in her time when everything was right, it is the eternal Goddess Moon, the one that can receive the light from the lover and give it to the children. She is the priestess, the wisdom of both male and female and is the purest aspect of the intellect transmuted into a receptive vessel for the light of Spirit. So this is another appreciation of the Moon, which has to do with transmutation. She will receive the light in the cup of the crescent moon, translate it and give it out, for it is the crescent moon that is detached from the world and says "I am one with my Lord".

Those who are influenced by the lower moon don't want to hear the call of their Soul, so the needs and pain of being a human being are given priority and the self-pitying whingeing moon takes over, decomposition takes place and the opportunity to rise is not taken. When we truly go into Soul, time and space disappear into the great egg of infinity.

 The black and white chequerboard floor is a link to the Ancient Wisdom and is often depicted in masonic rituals. It makes us aware that the world we live in is made of contrasts and opposites; in this awareness we start understanding that we are walking on the path of initiation. Black and white will always come in to show us that we are starting to evaluate, recognise, think and discriminate, so this can be the beginning of the path. This is the world of appearance

and we have to be clear that we are going to see it all uniquely, this is why we have to truly understand that we are an instrument and not an 'individual' in the personal sense. The totality of everyone's vision of objects or ideas is the complete vision that the God we live in will have of the world. We can look at one thing, but we will all see it differently; if one of us doesn't look, then the God we live in has to look again, because what is being looked at hasn't been seen in its entirety. God has to know himself from every single one of his cells.

We can't be important as individuals, but we are important as small units of awareness. Until we completely own our reactions to life for what they are, we are not really serving the God we live in. We really have to be at ease with where we are at, whatever that is, with no judgment. God needs all the little pairs of eyes for the vision to be complete, according to his life and truth. The vulgar is fine, so go and get it! By hiding it, all we are doing is feeding a little monster that will grow, until eventually we dislike the people in that vulgar house. In the end this leads to political war against those people in that vulgar house; this is how it works. This is where we know we only exist as a comparison, opposition, or an association with others, because personality gets its worth by comparing. Blessed and lucky are the animals when they are not tainted by our auras, because they do not compare, associate, or oppose with their mind. It is about comparing one world of appearance with another and, from where we stand, we think we are the only right one. The fact that we compare and associate re-enforces separateness, so when we find a group or religion to associate with, that will keep us in the world of appearance. This is a tricky one because people can have opposite views on the same subject and all come from the best possible intent. Nobody is wrong or right and it is a world of complete harmony and balance, so we have to see the world as it is with all its different facets, balancing within ourselves all the time and still hold true to ourselves. The yin and yang symbol is a sphere rather than just flat and is forever doing that dance, until it comes back completely clear. The only way to get there is by recognising that we are Soul and therefore the witness.

There cannot be any absolute positions, for if people take their thoughts for absolute we would be stuck in an impasse, with no more movement. The yin and yang is going round and coming back, like the spiralling expression of the 1 to 9 seen from the top and bottom. We know it is a world of impermanence, of movement and contrasts. It is a world that has to know itself, therefore every single thing has to be experienced and seen. We know as well that by itself it has no value; this is very important when we do the work of looking in. The initiate knows he has no value in himself, but it is his duty to try to wake things up, because they will only have a value when they are filled with spiritual truth.

The only value that the superficial world of contrast, appearances and association has is in how much we can take from it or make of it. This is quite a sad statement, but it is so. We give value to the things of the world which we can take; things such as eating, enjoying ourselves, being greedy, playing the martyr, so the value we give to the world is also what we want to take from it. From a positive point of view we know it is a learning process, but on another level it is abuse. The lenses of science, philosophy and religion are great, but they are limited as well. The value of the world is not in itself, but in us and it is up to us to make it sacred because in itself it has no value whatsoever. This is why we must remake, rebuild and remodel the world according to our understanding and our thoughts. There are as many worlds as there are thinking individuals; to every one his truth; that is how we build the world. We have to impress faith, hope and charity in people's hearts. So far it is mainly mass-consciousness that builds the world, but this is changing rapidly, for as individual consciousness rises we can manifest a higher order of peace and love, to infuse minds and hearts and bring in more tolerance and understanding to religion, science and philosophy. Goodwill is love in action.

The High Priestess rests her feet on a green cushion, green being the colour of life and nature, which allows Earth to breathe through the vegetable kingdom. The plant life can be seen as a beautiful symbol for mankind's work with the light. After germination the little flowers yield fruit and whether it is a big bush or a tree, it starts with a tiny shoot before it becomes a stem or a trunk. Through exposure to light chlorophyll gives the little plant its green colour, crystallises it and mixes it with minerals so that it can hold the light. This means that when we eat a plant, we eat light. Viridis, the colour green, has the same root as 'vir' which is the word for man, so we are the green shoots of God and the holders of light, here to materialise and express it. The plant kingdom is as evolved as it can be. We are trying to fuse with the light to make it part of our body, so we feed on the plants. Green is the principle of active life; it is the manifestation of light and its action in matter.

It is the colour of life in spring, which brings support and hope to everything. All of this is why her feet rest on a green cushion. She is the Goddess of knowledge (Gnossos) and has the power over everything alive and over the principle of life.

In the card the two columns are those of the Temple of Solomon. They are called Joachim and Boaz and they represent the strong masculine and feminine aspects, which are the forces that hold the world together in love and strength. They perpetuate manifestation and are just outside the temple so that the Holy of Holies will eventually become the world.

The emblem at the top of each column is the stylised flower, the fleur-de-lys, which represents purity, the Trinity and man as king. These are protective symbols and are there to keep away all the malevolent influences that could come and disturb the houses of Yahweh, the God of time. Standing stones were used in the past for this purpose, because man was very sensitive to energies and could hear and feel the life vibrating within big stones, especially if they happen to be on ley-lines. At that time they took these stones to be the dwelling places for the Gods. When the Tarot cards were originally made, the symbols which are depicted were the common language among the initiates and therefore they can be seen as vehicles for the ancient knowledge, rather than promoting particular religions or philosophies.

The High Priestess' red cloak is lined with green, for as has been said, green is the colour of life. The coat is red as a sign of spiritual domination. She wears it because she is the side of the manifestation of God that says that knowledge is the wisdom principle. She is the love-wisdom aspect; she holds the life of the second Solar System and is in communication with the divine. We must not see her as an entity, because she is a manifestation of a characteristic of divine wisdom.

In the story of Adam and Eve in Genesis, the snake tells Eve "You will be like the Gods", which meant that if the intellect were developed man would know all there is to know about the planet. This was true, because the Gods of that time were the elemental Gods of fire, earth, wind and water and the whole of life on the planet was at their mercy. The snake was just the intellect that was saying, "Come on, these are only elemental Gods, aren't you going to understand them and become master of them?" We have to rehabilitate the snake, because he has been seen as the villain who put Adam and Eve out of paradise. Man was not chased out of paradise, rather he perceived with clarity what paradise really was, which was animal man in complete ignorance and with no self-awareness whatsoever. The minute that mankind observed and started to think and understand the environment, he was on the side of the snake. So the intellect took over and was not baulked by the old Gods, because they are only elementals; however, we have to realise that our bodies are made up of the elementals. The snake was a wake-up call, saying, "Come on nature, we have to rise here". So we started looking at the opposites of black and white and started playing the game. With The Magician we become capable of rising above the idea that we are God on the planet, so rising above the elemental Gods. Eventually we can let go of the little snake of the intellect, which has served us well by taking us to philosophy, religion and healing; the next step is to learn to communicate with the divine. As the intellect translates the wisdom, the light of the higher mind will shape it as a diamond.

This whole process happens via the occult or the inner life and cannot be found in form. It is a metaphysical pursuit and therefore it escapes the senses; this is why it is secret, because it is in the dark. It can only be passed on to initiates who have had many trials and meditated on them very strongly and profoundly, in silence and solitude. Everybody on the planet would have had a hard life, with a few exceptions, but it is only the ones who have been able to go in, meditate, 'raise the bread' and 'make the wine' within themselves, who will understand the symbol. They will have gone through the alchemical process of having made something of their hardships through the solitude and silence; this has brought them into wisdom, love and compassion. However, there are those who will pass by all this and not see anything in it.

This is where the Star of Bethlehem translates as the light of the higher mind in the Soul, raising the house of bread, bread being the symbol for the biological life of human-kind. We each have our little Star of Bethlehem to take us to the Soul in the dark. The word Bethlehem means 'house of Bread'. We are told in the Bible that bread has to be earned by the sweat of the brow, meaning it is hard work to be born into the world. That is what the bread symbolises, complete sacrifice and complete willingness to give of self, by going right down into the collective sub-conscious to do some of the burning. Bread is a representation of food as well as representing the body of the God we live in, so it is sacred. Bread has gone through three processes of transmutation; the grain has been ground; the dough has been kneaded, then raised and baked. The disciple undertakes these three processes (symbolically representing the work of the first three initiations) in order at the end to become the complete initiate. Bread is a complete spiritual food that represents the body of Christ, meaning the biological life that we have to sustain, so that eventually it is there to be given as sacrifice. In the Bible bread symbolises the body, while the blood/wine represents the Soul.

The book, which The High Priestess holds in her right hand, is the sacred book of beginnings and endings, of yin and yang, feminine and masculine. It is not knowledge; it is inner connaissance, an inner eternal renewal or renaissance as the two divine energies perpetually fuse their love into life. The High Priestess is a mistress who will not suffer or accept us having any other teacher. We must not think that the world is going to do it for us; it is in us. Yin and yang is not an opposition, but a complete dance of the world, revealing its dangerous beauty to the slavish mind, or its secret to the initiate.

This is the Number 8, symbol of infinity, the spiral without end. Eventually it becomes a complete sphere and ends when all is light. Each time a star falls, it keeps the memory of the light and the sparkle of where it came from. In the world of yin & yang we know that we are coming back, just like the day knows that it is has been born out of darkness and the darkness knows that it holds the light in itself. That is truly the beginning of great wisdom if we understand it fully. It is the star falling as a sacrifice, knowing that it holds the memory of the light.

If we truly see life as energetic, any limitation is only an appearance or an illusion. Spirit is not a prisoner in matter and we are not limited by it; we are free to create whatever we want in matter because it is the manifestation of Spirit. As long as we have completely accepted the process of manifestation, the only thing that limits Spirit is the lack of the will of its instrument to want to be truly alive. There is actually no limitation by matter, in fact it is the opposite and the possibilities of creating a new world are absolutely limitless. Yes, we have to be patient, but even that concept is a limitation. We are of course essentially unstable, even when we come back with a bit of understanding in our mind, because we do live in the world of transmutation and instability. Looked at from the inner perspective, we can see that the superficiality of the world is only a cartoon caricature of the level of consciousness prevalent at the time. That idea should spur us never to fall back into the old ways, for who wants to be a Donald Duck!

The initiate keeps in himself the love of everything that is still held in the bitter dark prison of pain; by the time he can do that there cannot be any 'self' left. While we are preoccupied by any type of 'self', we are going to expect the world to feed us on self love, self respect, or self-worth. The minute we stop focussing on self we hold the whole world in love, because we are in love, but not with self. We are not after any self-worth because the worth we have is the worth and respect of God. We are not lacking anything, because we have put it all into God and therefore made it sacred.

At this point we will automatically hold the profane world in love, for we have understood that it is within us, so we're going to hold it until the end. This can only really happen when we have dropped self; that is when the profane world itself will see us as a real danger. If we look at the prophets, most of them were put to death; the same happened to Jesus the Soul. Purity and fearlessness can be taken as an insult by those who, at some stage of their inner work are rebelling against the acceptance of their imperfection. They have so many little points of darkness that they think we are judging and sneering. Even if we give compassion, they will take it as false charity because they cannot read us; we have become an aspect of The High Priestess. They know that there is danger for the personality here and they don't like it, because it might mean that they have to look at themselves. When they see us, what they are really looking at is themselves, so they are throwing a stone at us, because we come and disturb. The purity of the initiate will stir the profane world.

The profane is known by everybody; it is the social life, the professional life, the personality, the theatre, the position, the drama.

The sacred is not recognised by most people, but will be perceived by the ones who are more advanced on the path. This is because they don't see the social life; they see the face of the inner life, the true reality of the human being. You are looking for the name of that essence – the true you.

The profane and the sacred will be merged as life.

The intellect has given us everything it can by the time it has achieved the realisation of its powerlessness; this is the greatest gift from the mother to the son. The intellect is the best thing that nature could give to the son of mind and she says, "I can't do any more for you now, you are by yourself. I can't protect you, I can't explain life, I can't drive you; you must go and do it by yourself". How many good mothers would be completely silent and stop 'supporting' in the sense of feeding with the intellect? How many mothers would truly know not to give any advice to their children unless they are asked for it? This non-interference is the greatest gift we can give our children. When the intellect has understood that it has to give up and that it is completely powerless, then man can start to grow into the 'angel' of his own Soul. Then the Soul is a reflection between divinity and man, so is receptive to God. The light fecunds the Soul, so she attracts the light and it feeds her with knowledge and intuition. In perceiving the light she is feminine, but when she becomes the intellect and translates, she becomes masculine or active.

The Black Sphinx is not really frightening; he's just doing the job of making certain that anything hidden within us must come to the surface. When we meet him, all the thoughts that most of us cannot control and all the needs and wants that we have ever accumulated, are going to rise to be dissolved in the light of the Soul. This continues as we come up, until we come to the point of initiation, which is the point of death of the old patterns. Those undercurrents and chain reactions within us that we think we have no control over, will come in front of us and are actual entities. We are talking about 'abuse and the abuser' and the sub-personalities; all of these give us an excuse not to own them. We have to know that these are us, we created them and they are not separate from us. What right have we, when we have created these things in ourselves, to say that they belong to someone else! They are all ours and have to be owned. By meeting them and seeing all the things we have done in their names, we can blow them out like soap bubbles to be dissolved in the light. The problem is that we don't want to recognise them so we create many subtle cover-ups, but they all have to be visited. The re-visiting is happening in this lifetime, but the entities were created over many lifetimes, not because of particular situations, but because it is our job to put a name on nature's experience, so we have to create situations to exteriorise the feelings.

We dissolve the problems by completely associating with them; it doesn't take that long, even if it feels like it. We are not just helping our own individual case, but bursting a huge entity in the world that cries out that it is being used and abused, therefore we are working in the collective. There is a job to be done and it can only be done by the work of completely owning, releasing and transmuting. There can be so much disgust and hate; we must name and see these negatives, then soothe, love and understand them on behalf of the God we live in. We can't blame our grandmother for being self-pitying! We can go to her and tell her we love her! The minute we do that she is happy and for five minutes she is free of self-pity; that is a great relief for the world!

Life is clever; it will put us in front of a karmic pattern that needs looking at and which will be very close to one of our shadows. That is why we have to remember it is in us and is not the other person's fault. If we refuse the knowledge from within, we refuse ourselves and the God in us and start the work of self-destruction. As we self-destruct all aspects of true spirituality within us will stop. The inner life will die within us if we do not accept our work. If we want the world to do it for us, then we are as nature, destroyed and renewed until the light of awareness gives birth in the cave of the heart once more.

The big difference between our initiate and the ordinary man is that the ordinary man is taken in by life and is a puppet of life. The initiate knows that he is a channel for releasing spiritual energy on behalf of something greater than himself, so he is not being taken in by the shadows of life. It is like a great river; either we are buffeted like a puppet, or the river is in us and we can let the waters of life flow when it is needed. It carries us and if we think something needs to be done, we will do it automatically.

'Man know thyself', is what we are doing when we have recognised everything we have been. We must find ourselves in all the events of our existence and understand the situations, attitudes and reactions. We have made strangers of ourselves because we haven't wanted to see a lot of the things that have happened to us. Sometimes we didn't know whether we liked them or not, so we had to hide those experiences just in case we didn't like them; this game can go on for a long time. Because we were uncertain whether an experience was good or bad we covered it up and kept playing the game, hoping we would get the answer. We call it confrontation when we look, but the confrontation only comes from the intellect, which retains all the virtual experiences that we have lived. The dweller on the threshold fights, because the pain and the drama of the previous experiences feel so real; these are the ones that will be burned by the sulphur, because of the resistance. When we as personalities are resisting and causing problems, we cannot blame things on past lives, for our past experiences were opportunities to wake up and witness. The sphinx will keep staring but will not speak, for a dialogue would be too easy and helpful, so it is up to us to get the message.

If we know that life is a state of unfolding and no action is definitive, then we can meet the dweller or guardian on the threshold and start doing the work of cleansing. By revisiting past situations with the intense awareness of the perception of the Soul, we see them for what they are. Whether we find a manipulating abuser or a manipulated victim, it matters not, because it is only a part of the great dance and everything can be harmonised.

An initiation can only happen when the mind comes into the darkness of the flesh of the Soul of nature, to see whether it can receive the star, we don't get initiation up there in the stars. In the past, every initiation started with a descent underground or a retreat into the desert. It had to be night and it had to be done alone; this is symbolic of the process of the inner work. The mystical star shows the descent of spirit into matter and the ascent back; the deeper it goes down, the higher it will shoot up towards the source, like a firework into the skies.

The keynote to this card is that, through true will and vision the unfolding of the Soul can happen. The work of descending into the cave has been an act of will and the intelligence of man cannot content itself with the intellectual life.

The wisdom of The High Priestess is the wisdom of Isis, the high sacred science of the initiate and the sacred world. We are talking of the beginning and the end, the lost and found and above all, grace. We are not doing anything from a personal angle, because we are doing it on behalf of our brothers and sisters. It can only be grace because we are not coming back to judge, but to love. There is no judgment or punishment here, only awareness and that is what grace is, to know that whatever the other human being is doing, you are doing it as well and it is all okay, but 'Shall we stop doing it now? Let's go in!' The good news is that there is no punishing God; there is only the book of life and the key of life. We are unfolding into the true, the beautiful and the good and all this comes through the wisdom personified in The High Priestess. She is the true bride of Spirit and truth.

She is the teacher, who translates through her silver key what the golden key has understood in silence. So there is no action and no words. She is silent, she teaches by her presence. We are also reminded that we must not keep silent if a person needs help; we have to speak and use right actions, so the word or the intellect mustn't be excluded.

The High Priestess is the Queen of the elementals because the pure hermaphrodite cross is upon her chest and each corner is crossed with a black cross, so it is sanctified. This is the card of alchemy; The High Priestess has made sacred the world of matter by purification. The message is that our higher mind has to intimately meet and make one with the wisdom within us.

The Empress, L'Impératrice
The web of life

At *The Empress* the first part of the cycle is complete, for the first three *cards together form the Trinity. She is the third principle of Active Intelligence that enables the work of Spirit to be expressed in matter though the universal mind. She is winged; her halo of stars speaks of unconditional love and purified matter, for she is Mary the universal mother. Her blue coat tells us that she is focussed on infinity, which she brings down into the world of matter. Her left foot, resting on the inverted crescent moon, reminds us not to be taken in by the illusion and drama of everyday life. She is the star of love and light that we must find in ourselves, to enable us to transform the dark shadows within.*

The world we live in is not real, but virtual. It is entirely created by the interpretation that our minds give to it. The beauty of the greater plan is that each mind is unique and therefore the creation is being seen from as many perspectives as is possible. That is why we have to have a great respect for everybody's point of view, because all those combined views make up the level of perception that the God we live in is at, as it looks at itself. They are all God's point of view even if they are the opposite of ours.

We are all little points of light or stars. The star symbolises spirituality in the world of virtuality and the higher mind in the Soul. The Star we are is the original forgotten sound which can guide us to our original self. Sound is the medium between concept and creation and it has the same role as the Soul. It is forgotten because it is inaudible and invisible and the first manifestation of it was too bright, so it is hidden in the densest place. The sound is inaudible because we haven't reached the right level of consciousness to be able to hear it. We take a name (which is sound) to focus our mind, as we listen for that forgotten sound, which is the first manifestation of the creative energy coming into the time and space of the Solar System.

We have to sense the Soul of the Mary of nature to decipher the sound that we are seeking, because all manifestation ended up in a crystallised form, such as an animal or plant, which then can be named. Everything vibrates to a sound and then the matter that is subsequently created is the final destination of that sound at the time. As we re-incarnate with the guidance of our inner light, the crystallisation of our name becomes more and more invisible as we develop the understanding of the symbol that we perceive, then we can reflect it into our etheric mirror. We know that the impulse from the Great Architect comes from within the sound, so the sound is only the result of the movement of the impulse, re-organising the original chaotic sound into crystallised units. That first point of manifestation breaking through from the spiritual will into space, was the forgotten name of God and our name was part of it. This is the secret that all the traditions are helping us to bring back, because it is the origin or source of everything on Earth. Our original name is part of that first sound, which is made of light. The Star is a virtual mirror of the brighter self. The brighter we become the more cosmic we are. Finding the sound in the present automatically mirrors back the Star.

In Number 1 we saw that The Magician is truly a juggler or Baton-holder, who holds the baton to direct energy and learn to achieve another level of understanding. This means that eventually he will allow the divine energy that flows through him to be in charge. If he thinks he is in charge he's playing at being God, but by allowing that flow, understanding the world that is around him and knowing what his needs are, he won't fall into any illusion. He is learning non-action, but at the same time he has to be very active, for if he doesn't act he will never understand what non-action is. When people are using their instrument very intensively they eventually let things happen through them. For example if we sing a lot, eventually it isn't us singing but the Spirit of singing coming through us; we are just letting it happen.

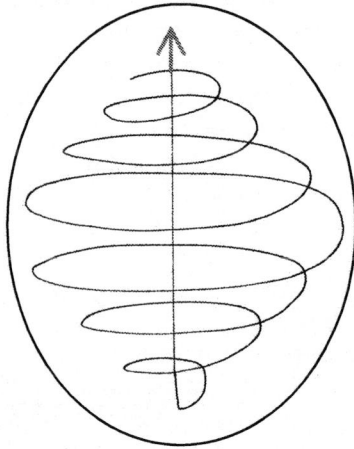

Figure 1. Spiral.

Movement of Spirit into the space of the universal egg.

The Magician comes in and is faced straight away with that moving spiral. He is going to have to go through many rounds of it before he will achieve higher initiation. The first thing that he has to do is to open the door to wisdom. This is not human or shamanic wisdom, but divine wisdom represented by The High Priestess. She is not funny and she is not going to say, "I will touch your cheek with a feather and make it better", rather she will stare at your cheek and it will hurt even more. This wisdom is not subject to the laws we know of and it doesn't come through recognition, for the divine wisdom is beyond that. It is the veil that we need to come through if we are going to have a chance to follow our cosmic star.

We are looking here at the great energetic work of alchemy, which is about being able to internalise the whole understanding, then transmute the water of the emotional body into love and wisdom. It is an energetic work and we only truly exteriorise and emanate the star we are by internalising and rendering ourselves alchemical.

The initiate comes back carrying an awful lot of knowledge; he knows he can be a magician but he is aware that there is a lot to do to avoid the pitfalls. At this point a lot of people will withdraw; a few others will jump in before they are ready and what they will find is awesome to them and might blow their minds away, because they haven't done much of that deep internal work. Those that are ready have to start doing the inner work before the veil is lifted. The second card, The High Priestess, is the great door to higher consciousness and is the alpha omega of all there is. The initiate has to have enough humility to be ready to come in front of The High Priestess, for she is the aim of the whole of the Tarot deck. This aim is to acquire divine wisdom and fuse with the divine mind. The rest of the major Arcana tell us about all the energetic trials we have to go through to achieve the initiation. It is a transforming journey. So every time this break through is not achieved we cannot go onto the next stage. It is not a drama or a test, it is just an energetic process that we have to endure and accept.

It is a question of choice. We all have heavy luggage and if we keep on with the drama we know by playing the same old games, it is because we want to. When we make the choice to serve ourselves, we are denying our Star and denying God, so making the load even heavier for ourselves and everyone else. The minute we make a true choice of affirmation to look up or away from whatever game we are playing, it is instant and we need not play that game again. It is not controlling, hiding, or covering up any more, because we can now see that the game is only a habit we can remove. The virtual reality we live in can be dispelled, but if our true self loves it better we can choose to go back into it. Any tenuous, tiny particle of an emotional link that we attach onto the game makes us stay in it. It is not about love/hate; it is not being a victim, or being weak; neither is it saying "It is to do with my childhood" or "It is past-life". It is none of those, it is a question of what we want to love; either an impersonal God, or a self-centred little god of personality. Both are still God, so nobody punishes or judges, we just have to recognise which one we love the best.

If we go into the practice of affirmation in order to drop some negative emotional mindset and later find we haven't dropped it, we need to see whether we are using the name of truth as a witness to feed and reinforce our malaise. If we love drama best and love the survival nature of God better than the uplifting part, we might be using the power of the light to further and feed our infant drama even more. If we realise that this is what we are doing, we need to stop it straight away for this is the path of self-destruction, which can drag others down with its magnetic powers. There is nothing cleverer than a twisted intellect that feeds the 'black dog of hell' or the 'the dweller the threshold'. This is Active Intelligence that hasn't recognised its divinity and thinks it is the only God, in fact it is just one aspect of the divinity wanting to remain in charge of everything. This is when the human being is encouraged by the emotional game that the personality is using, which involves being clever in order to resist the Soul's message. Most personalities resist the break-through to the Soul, through the belief that they are masters of their own lives. They think that if they don't persist in this affirmation, they will be martyrs or victims again and never be themselves. This is the cleverest trick in the book of affirmation! It re-enforces the walls of separation so that the inner light is never seen amongst the glitzy light of glamour.

It is so important that we drop the covering up and the games we play, so as to involve deep into the inner light. The little black dog of hell really only wants one thing, which is to obey a master, so let it be the light that it obeys! The love-hate of the drama is very strong and we are all in it. Any tiny critical little thought we have about ourselves, or about other people is of the drama nature; all these are manifestations of the little black dog of hell! If we think we are too fat or to thin for instance, we have the capability of either doing something about it, or just knowing why and liking the way we are at the time. We need to de-focus the mind from the emotional drama that wants the game of feeling bad or guilty; this drama takes the mind away from the light. If we bring the light in to look at the size of our bellies that is quite funny, but it is also a tragic misuse and a self-centred use of light. Whatever we think about ourselves, whether it is over inflated like; "I'm a great spiritual person" or coming down on ourselves as in "I'm a worm", both are virtual, self-centred and the wasteful use of the light. Looking inside can only relate to the outside and what we see out there we have within; the knowledge of that is what renders us transparent. Whatever reactions come into our instrument, we should allow them for we need them. It is only through owning our reactions and understanding them with compassion, that we can reach transparency. To sin by pride or by false meekness doesn't allow the work to carry on. The question is, do we react honestly and admit there's a reaction or a bit of shadow there? Do we have a look at it and clear it or do we react because we like the game? If it is the latter, this is addiction setting in.

Without The Empress we are in Maya or illusion in whatever we do. The Empress is Active Intelligence that has completely regained its divinity. We are in the process of beginning to recognise what we have to do with our minds; without the qualities of The Empress we cannot ever begin to do the work. In starting that work, we look for our own original sound by trying out many different songs. In that process we may find some vibrations that are in tune with parts of our sound or Soul, vibrating to its spiritual guidance. When we travel deep into our space we might find some aspects of ourselves that we don't like, this is when the work of transmutation has to take place. We need to remember the first sound behind our name; to do that we have to let ourselves drop as if we were falling from a mountain. Then, as we fall deeper and deeper, we will align with our sound and eventually it will become the chord, or silver thread.

Once we have connected to it we will be able to go anywhere with it, because we will always be completely aligned with the original sound within ourselves and always be at home.

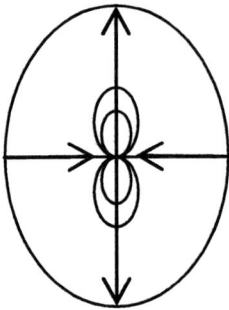

Figure 2. *The work of the evolving consciousness.*

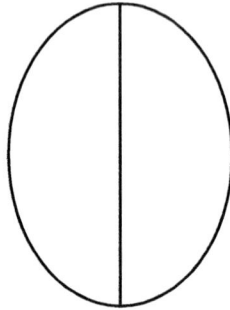

Figure 3. *The goal of the disciple.*

The alignment of the Soul-driven personality with its higher mind has the ultimate goal of building a direct link to the divine plan.

The naming of the animals that God asked Adam to do, is so important because it was saying "If, on my behalf, you can make sounds which represent all things, such as trees, cats or clouds, then you are actually vibrating with those things that you are naming and so bringing them back to me".

We can qualify this further by saying "Beautiful flower, sweet cat and great tree" and even if it is 'murky yuck', all that can be brought back to God, for they are all part of God and God knows how to love. If there is only love, simplicity, humility and the understanding of the process, then transmutation predominates and we may ask "Why should anyone want to be the best and what for?" We are all alchemical instruments and not one of us is better as an instrument than any other. Who cares which one goes first and which one is recognised or is the fairest? As we drop all the descriptions such as, 'fairest', 'prettiest' and 'cleverest' by owning them and admitting that we wanted to be this or that, we can transmute them. The question is always "What do I love best? Do I love God best, or my position in the system?" Once we know the answer to that, we stop feeding the drama and everything else that might look like a fall isn't one. Everything difficult that comes up is like a bubble coming to the surface and is released. So we should not pull it back by thinking that we are bad again or by hating it, because that is feeding the drama; we can just love the process of witnessing.

All the Tarot cards are archetypes. We are all archetypes, because it is a virtual world; we are as we thought, loved and feared yesterday. Archetypes are illusionary thought forms, but they are a necessary part of recognising the big drama we play. Archetypes are mostly elemental gods and thought-forms. We are required to fly with the archetype without getting lost; this is how we survive in the inner world of the psyche and the mind. Archetypes are not reality, but they are ways and mind-sets that help us to recognise each energy we are dealing with, so enabling us to touch the fire without burning.

The only archetype that is not virtual is the great life we live in; energetically this is just movement in space. It is important to depersonalise the greater entity we live in, otherwise we go back into the archetype of the father-mother God. This is a beautiful concept but is still an archetype. It is an energetic life, that is all and though that is a mind-set too, it is the clearest mind-set we can have so it stops us from going back into the emotional. If we can only see the world as archetypal we might have locked ourselves into a virtual system, whereas if we really see it as energy, see matter as crystallised Spirit and Spirit as refined matter, it is so much easier to have a transpersonal point of view.

The whole of life is symbolic and archetypal; it is only a film or tapestry. The Empress is the beginning of the esoteric life or mind. Being the goddess of clear reason she is serene and poised. We need to remember that if we recognise a good or bad archetype in someone else, we have been there ourselves.

The initiate comes right into the market place in order to learn, for the only viable place to wield energy is in matter, on the Earth. He knows that he can't give his life to God because it already belongs to God, but because he has understood the idea of fusion and aligning he is able to go through the door for the last purification. Divine wisdom, or the second aspect of the Trinity is in every single one of the atoms of our body; it is really here in matter, not somewhere up in the clouds. The alchemical process is one of recognising and dissolving the separative little self into the light and heat of the Soul, again and again. The initiate is dealing with the daily reaction of the heavy matter of his body and he knows that his brain/body apparatus is a wonderful sounding board. It enables him to align progressively to the light that is flowing through him, revealing the understanding of all the wisdom and knowledge that his karmic biological lives have gathered. He knows as well that there is no more intellectual knowledge to explore, for we can keep on reading books for a long time until eventually we realise that it doesn't actually change anything, since we are still reacting to life and have to experience these lessons to release the wisdom. We know that the reactions are not there to be taken personally, therefore there is a deeper burning that enables a true transmutation to happen. This is the giving up of self, but at the same time knowing that it is not up to us to give ourselves to the greater life, because we already belong to it; this enables us to avoid the martyr archetype.

The High Priestess is the guardian of the door; she is also an archetype and we need to absorb and translate the 'pass-me-not' of cosmic wisdom. So we should not take ourselves seriously, because whichever archetype we have projected for ourselves, we can forget ourselves in knowing that we are just an instrument or cell for the greater life we live in. Removing an archetype can be a tricky thing, because behind it there is nothing but reality and reality is quite shocking. This is because we recognise the games that we are playing. To do this we have to be completely dead to any self-intent and while we think either that we have nothing left to give up, or so much to let go, we put ourselves in the realm of the archetype of the self-obsessed! After The Empress, the rest of the Major Arcana describes the conditions and the right ingredients for the alchemical process to be realised within the initiate, so that he can pass through the opened door to divine wisdom.

The inner man is where the great Saturn of Capricorn operates, for this is the initiate. He has climbed the mountain and is very single minded and resilient to the point of stubbornness, so as to reach the top. It is important to transmute stubbornness into the spiritual quality of endurance and use it when it is needed. If we know stubborn people, we should help them to use their stubbornness for the work of the light. To climb the mountain we have to be as tough as the mountain, but remember we do not have to carry it on our shoulders, the mountain carries us on its back and the mountain invites us to its summit. Once we have understood that we can climb it, so we have to make light of the task. Endurance is a wonderful quality; this is the lesson, for if we mean to live as we affirm we mustn't move from our affirmation. The mountain will come and go, but that affirmation will remain.

The French word for Empress is 'Imperatrice' and is linked to the word 'imperative', which means absolutely necessary. It is imperative that the mind is clear, poised and impersonal. Because it is a virtual world, man is there to recreate it through his own thoughts; this means changing his perception, so The Empress works though impressing thoughts. If there are enough of us seeing the world in a particular way, it will happen. So we have to understand the importance of how we perceive the world and in which direction we align our mind.

The Empress is Active Intelligence, which knows itself as a mind with a mission. It is intelligence being conscious of itself and therefore can open to the higher spiritual truth. With The Empress we have started to understand that it is a virtual world created by our minds and because each mind is unique, the creation is seen from as many angles and points of view as is possible. If we understand this, we can respect everybody's point of view, knowing that we are all an expression of the great life.

The Empress is a mighty hermaphrodite – she is Mercury in all its beauty. She is a perfectly receptive intellect. The intellect is the masculine characteristic of the personality, but because she has rendered it receptive she is represented as feminine. This is why we get the double qualities of masculine and feminine in her. She is the quality of mind that becomes the silver thread, linking the divine to the higher intelligence of the initiate as he goes back into life. He can then make sense of the process, redeem it and render it sacred through a pure heart and an open and loving mind. She teaches the human family to recognise its spiritual heritage and to develop wisdom.

The book that The High Priestess was holding is now opened by The Empress. To open that book requires intelligence and wisdom; this is why Number 3, The Empress, represents intelligence. It is the wisdom of application which appears in humans as eternal wisdom, when a state of humility is present. It is that intelligence and wisdom that The Emperor will give to the initiate. The Empress represents Active Intelligence, which pervades the whole of the system and enables it to manifest in its manifold glory.

The High Priestess has to be veiled, for she's a mystery and therefore she will only address a minority. On the other hand The Empress is available for everybody to see and appeals to all men of goodwill, meaning those who can listen to the message of life. It is here that we start to point our will towards good and God and away from ourselves.

The Empress is mercurial; she is the equivalent of Athena (Greek), or Minerva (Roman). She's the intellect when it is self-conscious. The initiate has to have a complete understanding of life at the intellectual level to be able to use all the knowledge that is locked into Active Intelligence or life on this Earth. If the intellect is developed it can then fly and reach the higher mind, so The Empress has a completely open, playful mind, obsessed with the love of understanding the energy behind things and the knowledge that truth is universal. In this way the eternal student becomes the eternal teacher. People's level of perception reflects how much endurance they can bring to bear on coping with the suffering of reality. Most human beings are still cocooned in the mind-set that all they need to do is to be comfortable at home in front of the TV with two nice meals a day, thank you very much!

The intellect, curiosity and open mind of The Empress help to break down the mind-sets where we are stuck in prejudices and preconceptions. Ultimately she searches for the one universal truth and so she knows that all the little truths along the way are quite useful, even if they aren't complete.

She has a peaceful, placid face to symbolise the mature intellect. She's at peace with her environment, because she's in complete possession of the mind that has created it. The mind learns speedily and eventually, through knowledge and open mindedness, it knows how to discriminate, eliminate and choose – this is what The Empress does. If the result of her work is not practical and viable, the higher intelligence will soon abort it. Nothing is ever wasted, everything is used in the best possible way.

Her feet being in contact with the Earth brings a grounded quality to whatever The Empress has to do. It is only because of this quality that self re-creation can happen, and then it is through her own effort and her love of fusing with the truth that she knows how to re-create. She knows she is only the messenger and not God, so she sees her limitation. The breaking through of the intellectual life is absolutely necessary for the initiate to access the cosmic wisdom, so in her we see the willingness to break through and uplift her mind beyond the control she thought she had over creation; this is why she has wings.

When our intellect is flowing with life, love, discrimination and observation, it is marvelling at its own Active Intelligence and we have to bring it back to terra firma to apply its findings practically. Without the grounding and assimilation, the vision and the knowledge aren't used.

The planetary preoccupation of the survival of matter is needed as much as anything else; it is all the same divine process. We tend to open our hearts and feel pain for tiny unimportant things, when we should know that we are here for one job only; yet for that important job we have no time. This is where humanity is. We have to see how much beauty there is on the planet and cherish it all as we would our child; this is the incredible job we have to do. In the next few hundred years we have to de-personalise any hurt that has been done to us. The hurt had to happen in the first place for we had to feel and know it, but now we have to own our part of it so that when we tell people that there is no guilt in humanity, only responsibility, we sound real. Until we are grounded we can't do that, for without the grounding the vision can't be used by the Earth as it stays in the higher planes.

Our repeated incarnation is, to a large extent, motivated by the gathering of our experiences; it is through this that we acquire a good solid base of understanding and knowledge. This is what awareness is: we come in, we go through an experiment and then affirm that we already know about that particular one, so we need never go back in and do it again, unless we recognise an addiction to the feeling of unease through the experience. The light that comes in through the 'déjà-vu' feeling enables us not to be taken in by anything degenerative and wasteful.

One of the poignant aspects of transformation can be illustrated by what happens when the butterfly comes out of its chrysalis; for a few minutes it is wet and cannot fly because its wings have to dry. It has had to let go of its protective case and there's an incredible fragility in that instant, when for a few minutes it is completely at the mercy of any bird or anything that can eat it. This is like baby humanity, completely in danger because it is so new. We are co-creators and as such our perception and discrimination has to be right, for God uses us for witnesses. Suddenly we are out there and it is so new and so different, that we might lose our minds because we don't recognise anything. Sound is so important, for if we are so lost that we don't recognise the room we are sitting in, sounding our name can re-crystallise our skills and put us on auto-pilot. Our name is the sound that the family group has given us and it is what grounds and cocoons us. We can also sound a special, sacred name such as Mary, Allah, or a mantra. These will carry us through pain, but our name will remind us of our responsibility to the group.

Ultimately we have to let go of the concept of freedom. Like the intellect, freedom is separation because it makes us want to stand apart and be different. However, we do not acquire freedom of mind without knowing what freedom is about. A truly free mind, which is a pure mind, has a connection with the divine via the Soul, so it has learnt freedom in the real sense. If it hasn't understood that freedom creates separation, it will be a rebellious mind and against the idea of God. To reach God the mind has to fuse with an unknown mind vibration, which is the opposite of separation and is a giving up. Freedom is good in that it pushes us up and gives us our autonomy, but it is not inclusive, it is separative. We have to assimilate, love and transmute all the pride and needs so as to acquire a mind free of fear and separation. This is why we have to learn through endurance to be really tough, as we could get lost on the way to a more rarefied vibration of the higher mind.

Think of experience as intelligence. An animal doesn't do an experience; it just lives, whereas we 'do' an experience. Eventually we know that no experience or knowledge fulfils, for it is insufficient and lacking, but we really have to do it to find that out, even if someone advises us not to. If we do not do it then we do not understand. This is why we cannot ever blame the courageous souls who have made all the mistakes, for if we haven't made the mistakes then we don't know when to stop. We can only watch in compassion when the experience takes over, for if we know how to stop we must have got lost sometimes before.

If we look at the pattern of an average life, nobody tries to teach a tiny child something by reasoning; rather we do it by distracting and changing the mood of the child. The minute there are some faculties of reasoning then the initial teaching we give a child has to be dogmatic, so we give them hard knowledge and exams. The intellect is developed first for it is the flower of nature, then the true fruit will be the intelligence of the Soul. As a child develops the teaching is less imperative, allowing the child to think for itself more and more. In most cases the child will think as the society around it dictates, for example through TV or fashion, but that cannot be helped. So if you are a teacher you will look for children who aren't taken up by society, sleeping, or sweets; these are the bright ones who have the autonomy to think for themselves and so can free and separate themselves from the mass consciousness. Then the problem is that they get so used to being separate, that at a later stage that separateness can stop them working with group, whereas the real intelligence develops from fusing, co-operating and communicating. We might reach a very high level, but we need to watch out for the mind-set of 'I am lonely, nobody understands me'. Adaptation is so important; the group work will teach everyone in it how to best utilise the incoming light according to each unique capability of the instruments. Some are receptors, some are translators, some are best at distributing the crystallised outcome to the public and so on.

Active Intelligence is the instrument and when the fully obedient personality aligns to its Soul/spiritual direction, Active Intelligence rules the waves. People can be full of light but restricted in expressing that light, so their capabilities and faculties must be encouraged and fuelled in the best way, for everything is of use. The idea is to find the best possible way of shining, by letting the light use our skills. Sometimes a simple pane of glass can be more useful for our purposes at the time than a multifaceted crystal. We can only fly from a solid base, where we know how to use what we have in the most economical way for the task ahead. The Empress will naturally give us the best solution to any question and will hold it humbly for the Soul to smile.

There are many contradictions in us that scramble our minds. When we go deep into the knowledge, we look into ourselves and humanity and see both good and bad. The contradictions are so painful that we have difficulty finding the way to bring the good into the bad, so we look for the next method or teacher to sort it out for us. As long as we hope for a fix, a book, or a method that is going to do it for us, we live in contradiction and false hope. The mind is lost, so we have to turn towards the Soul, for this is the only compassionate place where our mind can get the cosmic joke when the higher mind winks at it.

In Dante the envoy of the Soul is Beatrice, whose name means blessed, therefore fusion with the mind of God. We have gone to hell, then we have to come back again; the Soul will guide us out of the darkness. The life of the Soul holds the sum total of all the experiences that the mind as Spirit, has gone through as it dances with matter. Purgatory is not a place but a state of mind in which we allow all the emotions we have to torture our conscience, as our new awareness of responsibility and reality is too hard to take.

We have to trace the whole of our lives backwards, to remove the drama of it, in order to love it all completely. All the minute little emotional ties we have with people or with situations will still link us to purgatory. It is only the vision of Soul, in touch with the higher mind, that can dissolve all that. Soul has a link with the higher quality of mind as well as the intellect, so these two have to talk to each other.

We have to love and forgive all the details of our lives, as we had to go bravely where angels will not dare to tread. This is our job; to live our lives fully and be well equipped in experiences for the Soul to do its work. The Soul will eventually guide us up from the contradictory experience of the world we live in, with all its thousand and one possibilities or contradictions, then the progressive alignment of light and wisdom will culminate at the Soul's crucifixion. The veil has to be torn for the Soul to die, as it fuses with its last karmic incarnation. It is a death but at the same time it is a fantastic rebirth, where the atomic substance of our being will have the quality of Soul and therefore the love-wisdom energy, working at one with Active Intelligence.

The Empress is the quality of mind which determines the nature of whatever is in manifestation. The Soul is in charge of bringing in the divine energy and its manifestation into the awareness of life. All the love-hate relationships we've had with the world of illusion are linked with the fact that these two have to recognise that they are one, so that we can have the wonderful understanding behind it. So don't be attached to what stirs you, it is not yours! See it for what it is; it is the two cosmic lovers wanting to fuse. Our Soul awareness is the third one, making it whole.

The Empress prepares us for the spiritual life and this is where endurance comes in. Endurance is being able to look into your Soul clearly to see all the things you haven't done in the Spirit of truth. Until we do that, the Soul is completely lost in the game and all that happens is addiction. We are addicted to life through the part of our Soul which is in biology and has survived by having fiercely addictive behaviour; addicted to survival as it is held in all the different species of nature, in all its kingdoms. We live on the edge of this universe in a very old, dark and dense past vibration. So we have the difficult task of exploring and restoring clear perception. Meanwhile we are subject to illusion, drama and maya, which are fed by the imagination of our species, thinking we can rule the world! Imagination is a wonderful tool, but we have to recognise those times when we use it to keep ourselves locked into the drama.

The Soul of nature loves drama, because it is made of feelings; feeling is its nature. Active Intelligence responds to nature's spiritual input through the urge of its Soul, so we retrieve our Active Intelligence through our Soul, which is in touch with Spirit. The Empress' foot on the inverted moon crescent demonstrates her dominion over the exalted Soul of nature. She has the solutions, she is in control. She can use her imagination, dreams and the whole realm of the astral, yet not be swamped or taken in by them. She is discriminating and can see which part of the puzzle is needed; she has them all and more! She directs rather than follows, using all her resources to manifest the next phase of the vision.

Without Active Intelligence nothing could work on the planet, for it has all the possibilities of imagination and dreams that can receive the message of the divine. It is in contact with the vision, but is not in a dreamy state so is in active control. Survival, protection, playing games and selling ourselves should all be seen for what they are, put in perspective and understood as the great attributes of nature's abundant gifts. If this level of comprehension of our work is not achieved, there can be no progress towards our source, or the end of our journey.

The mind of man has infinite possibilities; only a tiny little aspect of those will be realised and expressed in one life. None of the experiences we have had in virtuality really matter, because what we are actually doing is looking for ourselves, looking for our name, or our allocated job. We are reflective grains of dust that grow into bigger stars, so the shine starts to show. As each one grows bigger and bigger, the thread which guides us back home to the source becomes more and more apparent.

Active Intelligence is absolutely everywhere to be seen and it has to become self-aware. The Empress is Queen of the kingdom that doesn't know its divinity. It is only through mankind that Active Intelligence becomes Queen, for we are truly the mediators. Our role is to realise that we are Souls, for the Soul is the mediator and bridges the Spirit/matter gap. It is so important now to train the human family to understand that that is what we are. We are not animal man, we are Active Intelligence in motion and our true nature is Soul, which knows itself as sound. Eventually in contemplation, Active Intelligence will hear the harmonious silence of the wisdom within.

The Empress will freely dispense her knowledge and the treasure of her science. She doesn't need to keep any doors shut and it is out for all to see. She gives hope to those who want to reach the point of light, sounding "I'm the way"; this is the Soul of mind. There are no tricks and no severity, but many will not use, receive, or even see the fullness of what she offers, because they will still be using it for their own security and pleasure. She's a teacher walking alongside the initiate, but she never imposes anything on him, it is up to him to go and ask her for help. He has to use his Active Intelligent mind to go and fathom the puzzle.

Active Intelligence is an intelligent faculty bringing clarity into everything, dispersing darkness and giving strength where there is doubt and hesitation. It is the crystallisation of the esoteric mind and so brings uplifting. So far in man's evolution we have used Active Intelligence as though we owned it, for self-aggrandisement and power, calling it our own truth but now we need to serve the truth, which is quite an up-turn. Truth cannot be domesticated to make us comfortable. Though there is a desire to contemplate the truth with no protection, its simplicity can be devastating when our heart is free of all vanity and self-centredness.

Our tragedy lies in the fact that we do not love the greater life, but rather want the greater life to love us. However, this can change overnight if we make that decision. So we need to look at our affirmations to make sure that we are not using them to reinforce our little selves thereby our self-centredness and so reinforcing the drama, because that can be addictive and is a wasteful use of the light. Nature had to be self absorbed until she found the moment when she gave birth to consciousness in the human species; we have to rise above survival to give nature back her divinity.

In the story of Theseus and Ariadne, Theseus goes into the labyrinth to confront the Minotaur, a ferocious creature who is half man and half bull. The Minotaur requires a Cretan youth as a sacrifice every year, so the people of Crete need a hero to go and kill the Minotaur. This creature represents the past and the old God from a previous culture, so it is no good giving youth to him because it only goes to feed the black dog of illusion. In all the stories and legends a hero is needed to go into the past or the dark night, so as to kill the illusion and the attachment to the past; he can only go when he knows that he has eternity in him and therefore is no longer afraid of death. It is only the initiate who can do that type of work. If we know we are going to die for something much greater than what is going on at the time, there is not the problem of being afraid of death. All that is experienced is the virtual death of the personality as it goes down and re-lives the past, but this is not real. Princess Ariadne gives a golden thread to Theseus, as a guide to help him come out of the labyrinth safely, the thread being a symbol for the Soul, linking him to the eternal life.

Mass consciousness is driven by the subconscious experiences held in the Soul of nature and therefore is the basic human being. When we reincarnate we take our biological suit from the karmic pool of human DNA. Our lighted mind reflects on our reactions to life and our thoughts go back up the stream to the source of those reactions, revealing the films of locked in emotions. We have projected so many situations to be recognised, named and seen as nature's survival tricks. Nature is then redeemed by the greatness of her intelligence.

The idea of confession in Roman Catholicism, is to help people say "Yes, I've done that" as we make the confession to the priest who wears black. Black represents the black work, which is the first stage of the alchemic process and symbolises the deepest understanding of the ordinary life that is driven by the subconscious. We need to confess our sins, or our subconscious reactions, but in reality we just need to recognise what has been done in the past with the true light of the new perception, which brings no blame. In reality these past actions are not sins, because they are seen for what they are. This is the work we have to do to be at ease with our humanity and follow the guiding thread of The Empress, for she links the initiate to the divine. In this way he can make sense of the process and render it sacred, by using the perception that comes from a pure heart and a loving mind.

She has a blue cloak because she's focussed on the infinity that will only be reached with The Fool at the end of the journey. The Fool renounces all attachments to beauty, vanity and desires. All the things that we imagine are there for us and that we think we need, such as fame, pleasure and security, are given up. We take continuously, but the objects themselves that we receive don't offer what we want. Their virtuality is there to make us see what is in us; such is the incredible quality of mind. When we are centred on self-aggrandisement and power we plunder the world to have more and to protect what we have, when actually what we seek is the eternity of peace of mind, which does not reside in the world of dusty possessions. When we feed the world with the love that comes through our hearts and eyes, we give it back its beauty and sacredness and feed the connection we have with the divine. However, we are so used to taking from it, like the baby taking from its mother, that we've become very spoilt children.

The Empress has her cloak over her knees and arm; this signifies that she's available to everyone, unlike The High Priestess who has her cloak over her shoulders to tell us that she is only available to the initiate. The Empress' cloak is blue, lined with green; blue being the colour of clarity, the higher mind and higher intelligence, whereas green is the colour of the beauty and wisdom of manifested life. So we are here to bring the blue sky of infinity into the green world of life and that is the way we inspire and uplift it. But before man can fly he has to assimilate everything that is human in him, so that he can become the universal man. The blue also tells us that she is not a mystery like The High Priestess, for she is there to be seen by all men of goodwill. She asks us to listen to the goodwill message of the life which is in front of us.

She holds a sceptre with a cross on it, which means she has authority over the Earth, because she is the flower and procreator of it. This is a true spiritual authority, so she is flooded with light. She obeys the divine justice that stems out of love, which will help people align to her ways and cooperate with each other in her intelligence. All manifestation is held in the process of death and re-birth until the system, through mankind, realises that it is made of energy moving into space and organises its manifestation for precognitive awareness only. We will be locked in time and space on the wheel of life until this happens. This manifestation is reflected in the element water, which is able to hold the memory of biological life on the planet. We cannot possess someone else's form, or hold anyone else's water; divine justice naturally doesn't allow this, it would go against the beauty of the plan, for Active Intelligence obeys the great laws of the non interference of the divine mind. True beauty is an inner process of revelation, which harmonises the petals of beingness, as we let life unfold.

Superficial politeness has to be taught, but the more we recognise and perceive things from the point of view of energy, the more naturally polite we are, because we don't want to interfere either with another's individual space, or the collective environment.

The Empress holds a Coat of Arms in her right hand, on which there is a silver eagle on a red background, with its wings outstretched. The eagle is a bird that can stare at the sun without blinking, so it symbolises the highest possible aspiration of the human mind, which is to soar towards the mind of God and stare at God's light without blinking. This is the desire to contemplate truth in all its splendour, with no protection.

A coat of arms is a symbol that is there for us to recognise a particular family, school or group. It is a symbolic representation of the genealogy behind the person or group. It is a very potent symbol which fixes a goal and states an aim. The message is clear for mankind; "Become the truth, the love and the wisdom through your intelligent nature!"

The Circle of Stars round her head consists of nine visible stars and three that can't be seen, so there are twelve altogether. These symbolise the twelve signs of the Zodiac, the twelve apostles and the totality of all the experiences of creation. The three stars that are not visible are those that are working at the transfiguration of the alchemic year in the dark. The crown of stars is Mercurial. With The Empress we are looking at the universal mind, so she has to be very pure of intent. Universal intelligence wants to fuse with universal love, so she has to fly high to surpass and go beyond herself.

If we are looking at the zodiac then Saturn is the highest star right on top, for it has to reach the peak of all intellectual research, which is wisdom devoid of illusion and vanity; this is the mind which will dominate this world. The transfiguration of this world is the ideal, the free and the true. The whole of creation is moved towards spiritualization by transubstantiation, this is the great work of alchemy. So in terms of the zodiac archetype of Saturn, we have Capricorn at the top, being the symbol of the concrete world, for man is nothing if he hasn't got his head in the stars. This enables the great work to be exteriorised through the higher thoughts and mind of man. It is impossible to separate man from the cosmos and if he can understand the truth, he can co-create, meet and fuse with the divine through his work.

Once self-awareness is born and reasoning happens, light and understanding can come in. Eventually, when our mind has learned to reach the Active Intelligence within the Soul, we look at an object or being and we can see clearly what is behind the form; we perceive its Soul rather than its form. Thus the higher intelligence is developed and that thought process feeds itself. Imagination and dreams are important, so as long as there's a bit of the Saturn element there to keep it real and viable, for the mind fertilises itself from one simple understanding. The reality is that it is the perception we put on life's manifestation that is truly important, rather than the object we are looking at. The thing in front of us is only there to help our mind retrace its steps.

Eventually, when we have removed the consideration of the personality, we see things for what they are. If we want to get rid of an addiction and see it for what it is, we should stand in front of the object of our addiction and try to see that part inside us that is saying "I want it". The object of desire that we thought was real actually isn't; it is virtual. The trigger to the addiction is the wanting to experience a specific set of feelings, not the object. If we realise that the need to play a game is feeding us, we own it and are at the beginning of transforming our coal into hot fire of sublimation: this is alchemy. The aim is not to separate ourselves, but to absorb the addiction so that we can own our inner drama and dissipate our shadows.

In this world we are addicted to form. It keeps our mind in the virtual world and stops our internalising, so our intelligence is blinded and overshadowed by pictures, there to give ourselves what we want to think. Our lives become driven by phantom forms, which come out of our needs and we let the unscrupulous merchant of false gold dictate our every move and thought! We are poor little stars, lost in a false paradise; let's reclaim our minds, smile, rise and shine! We only react to the world through what is inside us. We are at the beginning of the great rise in consciousness of mankind. This is a great wakeup call from the Earth to its people. We need to cleanse all the layers of accumulated shadows from the densest matter, to the rarefied mental thoughts of the cleverest human being. The light is reaching deep into our history so far and bringing out all the monsters. So as long as we see it from the greater perspective of humanity and the Earth being one body, we can help the process by not interfering through blame, criticism or judgment.

Jesus, the Soul, said that we have to hate the world in order to reach the divine mind; this does work if we can see hate not as a feeling, but as a tool which enables us to cut away from the drama of the past and embrace the work with a more compassionate mind.

We all have to be self-centred and selfish on the way to finding our centre and losing ourselves. When we are very pre-occupied with self we detach ourselves and make ourselves into the deep spiral that precipitates us into the depth of our existence, our Soul. Adam and Eve represent the moment in time when mankind was part of nature and became self-centred, so allowing the fall or the individualisation of the mind in mankind to happen. We had to fall to enable us to look at all the things we had been playing with;

this is the work. There is no shame or judgment in this, for it was the work that was needed and required, so that freedom of choice could come in; we can make a conscious decision to do the work, or let our needs live our lives for us! We can't have self-awareness without being self-centred and we can't precipitate into hell without having a choice. The first idea was to precipitate self-awareness into the darkness without a choice, and then the great Luciferian angel took pity on us and precipitated itself to give us the gift of discrimination. So the first real sacrifice was that of Lucifer coming down; without that influence we wouldn't have had the choice. The word Lucifer means 'bringer of light', so this energy is truly a messenger of Spirit, coming down into matter. The consequent disturbance that is thus stimulated in the crystallised mindsets has caused Lucifer to be associated with evil; this is a great misunderstanding and distortion.

The energy of Lucifer makes us do the work faster than was expected, enables us to suffer with awareness of mind and puts pain in its context as being a by-product of the work. Consequently the pain is more intense but the process is quickened; it would have been a long, slow process without Luciferian awareness of mind and we might still not have succeeded in understanding that this is a virtual world. When a light comes in, it has to find another light in the darkness, so as to have a point of recognition. The first light is the one that came by choice; the whole story of Adam and Eve is always about choice. When we are given dominion we are going to use it for ourselves to begin with.

When the mind has understanding through love in the heart, it can transcend any mindset which presents itself, especially the one of freedom. This is what is meant by; "The more I love the more I understand, the more I understand, the more I love". The only thing love wants is to forget itself and fuse with the light. If we truly transcend the self, then we go back home to meet our star and freedom is useless, for what is the use of freedom when we are in love? Freedom is only a notion, a mental mind-set and virtuality. It is autonomy, dominion, possession and power; love is the opposite. Love holds, builds; freedom separates and destroys.

Light has got to have a mirror to excite itself. Through falling in love with God, who represents the loving self, we become love. If we don't love self, we can't love God. If we do not love God we deny the purest part of ourselves. Pride is the reason that the mind will not consider some entity more intelligent than self!

The white lily by the left arm of The Empress is a symbol of purity of mind. She is pure of personal intent and so holds the idea of virginity and innocence of action. She is Mary, the universal mother, carrying the intelligence that humans can achieve. She is Number 3, the true hermaphrodite, who re-births and fecunds itself. As the mind is purified, she becomes Mary the Cosmic mother, the flower of purified matter and Active Intelligence in all her beauty. The Trinity is one person and Mary is the creative side; she is not a woman, but a symbol of what the becoming of mankind could become. Mary is co-creating all the time, because she is the creative aspect of the one creation. The Empress teaches us that through Active Intelligence we are witnessing the universal re-birthing. All creation comes through her, for she renews everything endlessly. She has an incredible amount of power and is the creative logo in the true sense.

There are many levels of transformation that we can undergo. There are nine degrees of initiation, four of those necessitate reincarnation in form; the next three proceed with the complete removal of attraction to the planetary life in the mind of the initiate. The last two are to do with this mind fusing with the cosmic life. Even if we have left personality behind, we still have more levels of transmutation to go through and all these are only really levels of refinement of energy back to the source of all. The personality will still be there with all its qualities after the fourth initiation, but the qualities that would have been centred towards aggrandisement or protection will have been refined and turned towards the work, rather than towards the personality. They are all called death, because we give up aspects of ourselves. We have less resistance and more fusing with the light of the Soul, in order to let wisdom teach us the next step.

All we are here for is to name, meaning to render nature self-conscious. As we name we love, because as we recognise and understand, we love. We are talking about connaissance, which is the pure science of human beings, a science we are born with. This universal intelligence is the deep intimate knowledge that allows assimilation, absorption and the way back to the lost sound. It is only when we touch the heart of an atom of a living organism, that we can hear its sound and know the vibration of its Soul. As our Soul connects with that sound, we can communicate with it. Listen with your heart to your dog or cat and hear the sound that they make. This way we find the dog in us, so can ask a question and get an answer. When we become one with our dog, we become as humble as a dog, for we see the God in ourselves and hear the answer. Remember, it was thirty thousand years ago that the first jackal came to work with man and it came about through the pure, deep, intimate knowledge of Active Intelligence. If we are not pure we are going to anthropomorphise, or see everything in the image of man. If we haven't got the human being out of the way, all we are doing is reflecting ourselves in the poor little dog or cat.

The more we inspire, the more we die: the more inspired we are, the more alive in the eyes of God. We are breathing the breath of God in and out all the time, the great life breathes us into its heart when we are inspired!

The key to this card is the affirmation of truth and its consequences according to the divine plan. We tend to affirm, then deny and then wonder why it doesn't work. For example we can recognise "I'm addicted to chocolate!" and then say; "I mustn't eat it!" which is a denial. So we take the light of understanding in and immediately destroy it. The true work is to find out why the addiction is there (remember it is only a stuck record) and then love it. So we see the truth, we affirm and we feel privileged to do a fair bit of work on behalf of the group and the life we live in. In this way the judgment is done, we unite the Spirit with the wisdom, the locked light within matter is released and the two make one bright explosion; that is what makes the star.

We become co-creators when our minds have become totally absorbed in the mind of God, so that as we think, we think on behalf of the great life of the planet. We may only have done that for a total of three minutes in ten lives and we may not even know when it happened, but it doesn't matter, for that is what we are meant to do.

When we have recognised the divinity of Active Intelligence a blessing is bestowed from the light, rendering sacred the manifestation. As we see truth we create truth, so becoming a true co-creator. If only ten percent of the population suddenly saw the light, we would have a new dawn of peace within thirty years. What we see around us are yesterday's thoughts and we create the future with the thoughts of today.

Everything in nature is automatic. One thing that makes us different is that we have a choice and the gift of self-consciousness, whereas nature has no choice. So we can choose either the automatic life, or our own inner truth serving the creator. We can ask ourselves the question, "Are we choosing to serve and receive the blessings of the Holy Spirit?" Because what comes next is not a May day fair on the village green, but a mayday distress signal to the universe.

The Emperor, L'Empereur
Creating the structure

The Emperor sits on a yellow cube on which we see the emblem of a black eagle; black symbolises the first stage of the alchemic work. Both he and the eagle are looking to the west, the place of death. In his right hand he holds a baton, in his left hand a green orb with a cross on top. The thick plait around his neck represents the three paths of the initiate going back to the beginning of time, woven together to hold the higher vision for the future of the world. The apron from his helmet covers the nape of his neck, so protecting him from any external influences, for he must be an impartial judge. He orders and uplifts us, preparing us for the next stage when the mass consciousness of the world is raised into the sacred. The Emperor is in all of us, for 4 is the number of the human kingdom.

The first three cards gave us the three aspects of the divinity as they organise their qualities to project the idea of the creative Logos:

1. In The Magician (the mind of the initiate) we see the birth of concept. The Magician is the instrument that can direct the new energy through his baton, so that the next part of the journey unfolds.
2. The timeless fecund egg of all wisdom is the great cosmic Mother, The High Priestess. The lower mind cannot access these refined vibrations unless it has given up all the illusionary ideas about its own importance. At this stage transparency is required.
3. The Empress gives us the clearly received vision of the plan or blue-print. She is ready to give of her etheric fabric to inform the next level of precipitation. This happens from the light of the concept reflected in her pure intellect.

These first three cards embody the three great rays of aspect: will, Love/Wisdom and Active Intelligence, as named by the Ancient Wisdom. They are the symbols of the Trinity or the 3 in 1. At this point they are in place; it is out of the third aspect of Active Intelligence that the whole of creation can proceed.

The Emperor, the Number 4, is the 1 born out of the 3; this is the transitional leap in the journey enabling the original intent to be further crystallised. In the journey from Spirit to matter, everything is a differentiation in vibration of the eternally moving mind/Spirit of the universe, within the mother of all possibilities – space. This is the movement that is seen in everything, from the all-knowing, all-seeing, all-pervading essence of the universe to the dim awareness of our tiny lives on this dark little planet, then eventually to even deeper levels of the amnesia of basic organic life.

Spirit is the quality of life that carries universal truth; light is the truth we are able to see as 'the light of the end of the tunnel', or when we say "Let there be light". The initiate is learning to respond to these emanations of the great Source of life and he aspires to align with them, gaining intuitive knowledge in the process. As the life of the greater truth comes in, The Empress, or the purified intellect, is the instrument which provides the reflection for the incoming light.

The Emperor is the quality of mind which can focus intensively on the blueprint, as he has to faithfully precipitate a viable structure for the vision he has perceived. He knows that it is the mind that captures the light and the vision, he has to release it to set in motion the fiery whirling lives of Spirit, so that they can attract and gather the right quality of matter for the manifestation of the next phase of the plan.

We all create our tomorrow with our thoughts; today is only what we projected yesterday. If we can internalise today's experience and learn to depersonalise it, we are on our way back to our source, doing our true job of witnessing from the perspective of Soul. This is how the spiritual journey of the unit in nature, which we call the human being, starts finding its place in the scheme of things and this is relevant to Number 4. So here the Number 4 (the one that is born out of the 3 of Active Intelligence) will, through sheer endurance, bring the chaos of the aeons of experience that is in the creative experiment, into the cohesive, harmonious and symbiotic life of our Solar System; thus it corresponds to the idea of the fourth ray, harmony through conflict. In this way the 4 can reflect the perfect dance of the cosmos, so that in time a new phase of self-awareness in nature can prevail. The initiate has to become The Emperor in his world.

At this stage, mental focus has to be held. The mind has to work outside the emotions, needs and wants. If it does not it would easily be diverted by the monstrous shadow rising out of the depth of matter, as the lighted mind reveals the many survival tricks of nature's darkest past. The Emperor has to bring the light, will, force and power into matter so that matter can be organised out of chaos and acquire the possibility of seeing its own spirituality. The Emperor has to achieve all of that without using any kind of weapons.

If we understand that the law of 3 is the blue-print for divine creation, then we can look at the procession of the cards, 1 to 22 as they are organised by this law.

1	2	3
4	5	6
7	8	9
10/1	11/2	12/3
13/4	14/5	15/6
16/7	17/8	18/9
19/1	20/2	21/3
22/4		

(Note in this table that we are using the following convention; in numerology we reduce a double digit number into one, by adding its digits together.)

If we look at the first descending column, starting with the 1, 4, 7 and continuing with 10/1, 13/4, 16/7, 19/1 and 20/2, this shows the procession of 1, 4, 7, 1, 4, 7, 1, 4. Here we go from the vision that becomes viable, to its perfect manifestation which is a mirror back to the vision. The 4, born out of the 3 and the 7, is the result of the 1 fusing into the 6.

Equally the middle column 2, 5, 8, 11/2, 14/5, 17/8 and 22, shows the procession of 2, 5, 8, 2, 5, 8, 2, which speaks of the journey from the divine wisdom to the scientific inquisitive mind of man, then back to its karmic work of fusing higher intelligence and wisdom.

Finally the right hand column gives us 3, 6, 9, 12/3, 15/6, 18/9 and 21/3, which is 3, 6, 9, 3, 6, 9, and 3. This represents Active Intelligence perfecting the finished vehicle of the Holy Grail (which is represented by the 6), so that it can mirror itself back to its Source.

When we add up the lines horizontally, they all come to 6; the perfect number. It represents the perfect beauty of the ultimate message for creation, the six days of the scriptures.

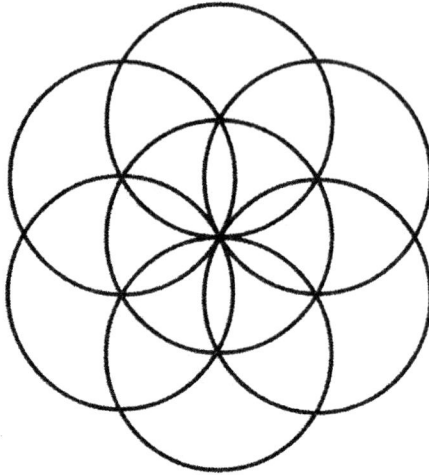

Figure 1. The 6 circles.

$1 + 2 + 3 = 6$ *The perfect solution.*
$4 + 5 + 6 = 15/6$ *Through nature, the witnessing mind is born.*
$7 + 8 + 9 = 24/6$ *In time and space, the wisdom of the Soul emerges.*
$10 + 11 + 12 = 33/6$ *The Soul/witness, sacrifices to the greater life.*
$13 + 14 + 15 = 42/6$ *Dutiful love is the way.*
$16 + 17 + 18 = 51/6$ *The spiritual warrior brings truth into the heart.*
$19 + 20 + 21 = 60/6$ *The cup of vision, with all its perfected possibilities.*
$22 \quad\quad = 4$ *The viability of nature to be the perfect mirror through the mind of the initiate, is established.*

The initiate's transition from the 3 to the 4 is encapsulated in the symbol of the energy of the 34/7, which can be described as systematic, organised, spiritual growth; this describes faithfully this movement in time. The steady mind of The Emperor knows this transformation will take time; he has the strong balance of care and tough love, necessary to meet the responsibility of the task.

The Emperor's main quality is misericord. He has known the deepest despair and found mankind's condition wretched until, with his mind, he has transmuted the despair into wisdom, through the acceptance and understanding of our place in the universe. With this quality he takes on the burden of our pain as he pushes us towards crucifixion, for he knows that we cannot be free of our miserable ignorance if we do not pass through to the next level of initiation. He can only do this work with love; otherwise he would be a dogmatic tyrant.

This quality of mind (misericord) is the result of being completely at one with the misery of mankind, for when we have done it all, seen it all and risen above it, then, on our descent, we understand every single atom in humanity's body that is going through misery. This work is beyond dogma, it is the karmic will implemented. We will not feel the love aspect until we find a harmonious blend of understanding and acceptance. The righteousness and severity of The Emperor are the obvious qualities of the 4, but when we perceive it as true service and love; we can apply misericord to the way we look at people and situations, rendering life so much more generous.

The Emperor's visionary mind has to crystallise into matter the quality of mind which is self-aware in the 5. He knows that he has to have the clarity of reflecting the Trinity into the future; this has to happen in matter. He is not matter, but represents that phase in our life when we have had an idea, we have seen some light, we have come home to our true self at some level and then we have to implement it. From the 4 to the 5, which can be seen as a 45, we have misericord or the deepest wisdom coming out of the deepest despair. The Emperor has to reflect and implement harmony out of conflict. Mankind has to have dominion over his own nature.

The Emperor's most important tool is intuition. He has to receive the concept from the 3 (Active Intelligence) and with as little compromise as possible, bring the vision into the building bricks of matter. He wears a helmet on his head to protect this quality of intuition, for he might fall into the heavy mindsets of the past and go back into self-interest.

We are in a thick soup of self-survival and self-interest; we have to be aware of that all the time. We can kid ourselves that we have let go of most of our own protective behaviour, but when we really *have* let it go we don't know that we have! It is when we are no longer concerned about what others think of us physically, emotionally or spiritually that we can follow the greater will and have no interest in what the world is thinking about us.

The Emperor has the world on his shoulders. The 4, 5 and 6 represent man or humanity. Looking at it esoterically mankind comes first in order, so the primal idea is mankind. Maintaining dominion is what is being looked for in the story of the evolution through the different kingdoms. Humanity was already conceived in the mind of God in the original space, but it was the way to bring it into being which wasn't truly fathomed. The physical shape that humanity would take was immaterial; the important thing was that it should be the best possible instrument to serve the great life. The world of nature is not a principle, it is the fleeting moment of sensation and a step towards the gem of mankind; this is the Number 5 in the middle that can use all the senses, including the higher ones, to perceive what is. Humanity is the one that has to keep on discriminating and going through fire by using the power of truth and honesty, so as to eventually become useful as a witness.

When you read the Ancient Wisdom, there is always the idea that man came first, which is the opposite of what biology tells us. This is because the idea or the initial concept was of a creature that could become completely aware, so that God could see himself. The animals are experimental steps on the way to man. We have the animal instincts, but because of the addiction to sensation we have misused these pure instincts, so until we have restored and mastered the right use of the instincts, we have to watch ourselves.

The difficulty for the 4 comes from the fact that all the tiniest details of manifestation have to be recorded, yet it must not be taken in by the picture, or outer appearance. When the 4 finds its uplift in the 13/4 it sees the complete vision, then in the steady opening of the channel of the 22/4, we have the perfect vibration for all the esoteric schools to be used as channels for intuition.

Many people often misuse their intellect and so we see that they have no idea of boundaries, politeness, or how to help and serve; these are the qualities of the right use of the intellect. They are not aware of their immediate environment, or their historic or scientific background. If we haven't got the boundaries of the intellect that provide a structure, we only think of our immediate self-gratification rather than the bigger picture of our destiny. Because of this we make mistakes and don't take responsibility for them. This leads to having no boundaries and not wanting to grow up, and then eventually we will learn through our own mistakes to square again and become our own Emperors. The people who have adhered to those boundaries are applying the laws of The Emperor.

The Emperor holds the karmic law. He comes after The Empress, who represents supreme intelligence, universal consciousness and is the Mother of all. She offers us all the possibilities of a virtual world. In the journey of the 1 to 3, everything is seen and is possible, so there is expansion. A 3 that doesn't expand is a 3 that uses a shallow intellectual energy and so eventually goes into self-destruction, for we cannot regenerate ourselves if we stay at the surface. The 4 has to be out on the surface to bring the idea into manifestation, yet at the same time has to hold the depths of the inner expansion of the 1 to 3. This can cause conflict if they only stay on the surface and concretise their position there, where everything looks like gold. Power doesn't last very long if it hasn't got its base in the purity of the inner world of the imagination and intuition. In any civilisation, if power is not fed from a very deep source, then it has no chance of changing or rearranging the world for the future, which is what the 4 has to do. The 4 is a true inner way, yet it uses everything in matter that is used by the world except magic, because magic is not the permanent true way of uplifting the elemental world.

Once the Soul is aligned with the personality, there are only three ways to manifest; this is why The Emperor has a plait with three strands around his neck. This plait represents the long chain of initiates who have come before us to give help in three different ways. It is a beautiful canvas; it is the veil of Mary, or the Holy Ghost.

The Emperor is not the creator; he is the one who brings in the force and the influence for the creative process to happen. He is not matter, but he is the actualisation of the idea and because the idea is very pure and white he has to be sensitive to the movement of the energy, so as to know what is needed according to the will of God. He has come into the world of facts and deeds so he must be concrete and impose the structure, which is the energetic life of the God in which we live and the karmic principle, pushing the 'will to be' of the 1 into manifestation.

The Emperor has to be completely pure and centred on the job of adapting the idea to the level of the possibilities of manifestation, according to where the world is at the time. His eyes are looking far away, for he has to keep his eyes on that web or plan, from which he is reading all the virtual possibilities for the world. The male element in the Tarot always represents the active principle within us, which is recognised as truly doing the will of God for tomorrow. We are told we have to live in the present or the now and that the past is the past, but he doesn't live in the 'now', for he has understood the transitory quality of it, seeing that it is nature and only a step. He has the vision of where we are going; so he has to feed drops of that vision into the reorganisation of matter and then eventually the whole of matter is ready to see the vision for itself. This is a job and a half! The plan is the original past, so we must retrace our spatial past journey to fuse with the blueprint of our future.

He hasn't come to make the idea practical, but has come to mould the world according to its flexibility and adaptability. Adaptability is not an obvious attribute of the 4, but if the form only thinks of itself as practical and righteous, the point of creative genius is missed. What allows him to do the job is the fact that he can first adapt the idea to what the world needs at the time, so as to adapt the world to the new idea. For example, when we look at a person and we see what the potential of that person might be, our task would be to adapt the thought-form and the feeling of that person into the next step, so that eventually they arrive there. We can call that practical common sense, but that is not really what we are talking about here, rather we are saying, "Have you got the strength of character?" "Have you got the will?" and, "Have you got the intelligence to survive?" All the time it is an inner thing.

The Emperor has to mirror and apply the learning of the realm that is above him, then translate it so that the world can make sense of it and use it; this is why he has to look far ahead. If we look far ahead we don't look for immediate results, but we know it is going to happen one day. So we keep looking ahead, applying whatever our adaptable mind can provide according to what we can perceive from the messages on the web. He has come back to help everybody follow their own destiny; for he is the one that has the eye on the higher destiny of the plan. There lies the difficulty, because we all have free will. Many times we think we have made a choice and we make ourselves believe that we are on the path, but in reality we have turned our backs on the path. That applies to all of us. Following the path is a natural state, like grace and humility. When we think we have to make a choice, we are automatically outside the path. If we know exactly where our beam of light resides and we want to merge with it there is no choice, so we don't have to make one.

This little world is under the illusion of making a choice every day, but in reality it is grounded in anarchy and dissolution. The world has a tendency towards destruction, because all the little units want as easy a time as they can get and they do not want to accept responsibility for the damage they do. So The Emperor has to act with the force of persuasion and not the heavy "You must do it!" He must act, for how long would it take society to wake up if we didn't have all those lovely emperors? How long would it take humanity to come out of chaos and the swamp?

Because he has dominion in a world where so many people are still so far from the light he has to use force, which looks as if it is against them but is actually *for* them. He is very misunderstood, like a parent who smacks a child to prevent him from burning himself, after telling him to be careful because it is dangerous. It feels like it is 'against' the child but it is actually for his benefit. There is a fine line in this, so be careful!

When everything has been said and done (which from the beginning of time it has), we know that the one who is resisting the most and taking the longest to come round, is going to be the best Emperor. The Emperor would certainly throw out the one who is always saying, "Yes sir, no sir, I will do it sir", because that one is afraid of getting hurt. The question is always; "Has he got the will and the strength to go and be an Emperor?"

The level of consciousness of humanity, the karma of the life of the planet and of the Solar System, determines the exact manifestation of the expression of the God we live in at the time. We live in a huge energetic bubble which is all energy and movement. The development of the perception of God has occurred as human beings have become aware of their own environment. At first there were the four elemental gods of fire, water, earth and air, who were feared because they could punish and kill us. If we were good they would feed us, give us a good harvest, keep us warm and cook our food. We are made of these great elemental gods, but once we cease to pay homage to them we can have some kind of dominion over our own elementals. If we are not driven by our fires, or completely drowned in our waters; if we are not weighed down by the heaviness of our earth; if we are not completely flying and day-dreaming with our air element; if all four follow the will which is within us so that they harmoniously form the next materialisation of the idea in our heads, then we have good dominion over our elementals. This then means that the gods of old are not the gods that we are going to pray to. The way that the elementals worked and were understood was mainly through fear, so when the Spirit of truth descended into biology and mankind, it was quite a dramatic realisation to see that everything we think, do and care about has to do with survival. There were high initiates now and then, but most of the priests would have understood it according to the teaching they were given, which was to do with the elemental gods. The scriptures tell us that the fear of God is the beginning of wisdom, but the other way to look at it is not to fear, but to respect; if we respect our elementals then they can work for us. If we fear them, they automatically play the game. The Emperor has complete respect for the planet, therefore for all the elementals in mankind; it is that respect which will bring in 'thy will be done'. It is that force in the will of God to implement the plan that a person will completely respond to, rather than fear.

When mankind realised there was something much stronger than him, which was nature, then nature was definitely his God. The first attribute of that God was fear, for it was the power of nature which man feared. Man had to bow his head and respect that great God, who could eat him alive. As we grew and started to internalise, we had to completely revise all our understanding, for fear has to get out of the way. It is not about losing fear; for fear is the name we gave to the apprehension of the energy that tells us that our spiritual guidance wants us to move a bit deeper into matter. The first step is to be aware of something much bigger and greater than us, which can take our life in an instant; that teaches us to respect the elementals. Eventually, as our experience takes us more and more into the world of energy and matter we realise that our own life is eternal, for we have been here before. Even if the coat or body we have been occupying dies, it doesn't mean that the experience will die with it, so we end up believing in a much more metaphysical God. Mankind has the need to join and fuse with that greater metaphysical God, through faith, love and a complete giving over of his own life. It is the same in religion; at first it used the fear of God, so we had to obey, suffer and offer sacrifices to the gods without understanding the whole picture. It is the same with our children, we don't explain to a two year old that it is dangerous to cross the road for they won't understand; we just have to forbid them to cross the road without us. The child won't understand and it is the same with a lot of people, who believe in God and who haven't understood the internalisation process. Internalisation gives us the knowledge that the God we love is the higher vision that we want to reach within ourselves.

The majority of people still love a God they are afraid of. They fear God's judgement of their 'naughtiness'. In time we seek comfort and peace, to soothe the burden, so we follow a religion which offers a more promising Heaven. Religion is an alignment to a school of thought: it is not a need, it is a necessity. A necessity is a law of nature, there to give structure for mass consciousness to face the unavoidable truth about its condition. The way religion is given out or preached will comfort the weak and help the strong to find themselves.

The Emperor meditates all the time, but is also active. He is not going to ask us to go to a workshop to try to sort out whether we are truthful or not, for if we are not truthful he is going to trip us up. We all have a little bit of that old fear of God in us.

Look at our life and how it is; would any of the women among us be OK going out without makeup? What we believe people think of the way we look is the first stage of fear. The next stage is what they think of us as friends, lovers, mothers, brothers and colleagues. All of us are watching out for these things, so it is normal for the God of fear to be still quite present among us. It keeps us behaving the way society wants us to behave and it is not a bad thing, as it helps us to learn to control our natural urges; this is the beginning of controlling our physical elementals. The fear of The Emperor is a good thing because it makes us toe the line. The Emperor is moulding society and our minds to the way we have to go, for we have to respect other people and society, until it becomes natural to do so. We are self-centred to begin with and then eventually our inner higher self emerges.

The Emperor is looking towards the west and that symbolises death, materiality and Spirit having to go into matter. It is the death of Spirit as it goes into the dark until it can perceive itself as matter. He has to help every single little unit go towards its death, with the aim of letting go of fear, guilt and anything else personal, so that it can go forward and recognise itself as Spirit.

In Number 3, The Empress is not a feminine principle of generation, though we still call her the mother of all, because from her we are going to see the little ones grow up. The Emperor has the authority of the father so he requires obedience. If the children are going to be loved, forgiven and blessed by The Pope of the Tarot, they first have to show obedience. We are all going to get lost on the way and do all kinds of wayward things; The Emperor will keep presenting us with problems, so that we learn to keep to the straight and narrow path.

He is the principle of the authority of the word of God incarnate and it is that authority that will lead us to spiritualisation in the 5. We do not have authority over anything or anyone, unless we do it for them and not for ourselves. The problem with authority is that we tend to think that we are the boss who is going to be listened to, but we should know that authority is not exercised for the one who holds it, but for those who are subjected to it. The true shepherd doesn't keep his sheep safe for himself; he does it for the sake of the sheep. We need to be completely true, connected and selfless, then when we find the quality of The Emperor in us we have to trust it completely.

Whatever relationship we might have, if we are exercising something for self, that relationship is bound to go to destruction, unless we are talking about a higher God. If we seek the love of God for ourselves, we will eventually have to go through trials and tribulations until we no longer believe in that God anymore; this is the tragedy for many religious people, or people 'on the path'. If we really understand that we are only a piece of the jig-saw and an instrument and that the God we live in doesn't care whether we are doing well or not, then we stop expecting something from God. The quicker everybody understands that, the more work can be done on behalf of that energetic being. It is cold and simple, not lovey-dovey. Human love is a most beautiful flower, but it is still an emotion; the love we are talking about when we are talking about the love of God, is truly not an emotion. We give our lives many times on behalf of the love we feel as a human being, until we recognise the reality that what we have called love is based on a need for recognition and protection, so we had better take ourselves out of the drama! The play can go on without us, we are needed somewhere else.

Human love is truly a sublimation of all the other needs, wants and emotions; it is the opposite of logic and reason. If we truly love a God or a person enough to go beyond ourselves, we are sublimating our emotional body, which is the most beautiful thing. The love of God is truly transpersonal, it has nothing to do with human life; it is about having even given up love for ourselves. The Emperor doesn't love us in a lovey-dovey way, he doesn't care about us personally, but what he does care about is that the plan should be re-enacted into humanity.

The Emperor is completely fixed on the intent and the becoming. He regulates the present, but the present has absolutely no value in itself. The majority of people live strongly in the present, which is the world of nature, survival and the senses. We're all completely taken in by the form and sensation of what we have been looking at.

We can never repeat a sensual experience even if absolutely everything is as it was when we had that experience, because it is transitory. It might be exactly the same time of day, the same colours, the same people, but we are different. What that teaches us is that sensation is illusory and if we hold onto it and go back for more, we find out where we are and how detached we are from sensation. Are we taken in by sensations? Do we want more of them? Do we keep on going for the same thing? Sensation does feed the mind, so it is very important as a learning process and we repeat the experience in order to learn the lesson. However, that can be a nice excuse to keep on doing that same experience forever and it can become addictive, especially when we have understood that the first one can never be repeated. If we have done the experience once and we go "Wow! I want more", we are going to be looking for it through the senses. Our senses are really only there to help us work on behalf of the God we live in and be a witness, but while we are taken in and play with them, we are not good witnesses. We are just players at best, at worst we are used by the self-destructive elemental forces of nature.

The minute we have done something and felt it, we can gain the wisdom from that one experience without having to do it again. We just need to take it in, remember all the things that brought us there and then we will certainly go to the very heart of why the God we live in wanted us to have that experience. When we are working at aligning our three bodies of expression with our personality, we have to go and climb that mountain of maya and glamour up to addiction and near self-destruction, so as to let them all go. With the initiate, or disciple on the path, the inner life has to eventually overtake the sensory life. He has to debunk the idea of keeping on doing the experience, so as to know. However, we mustn't stop the youngsters doing what we have done, for they have to climb up the mountain for themselves.

When we see a film or read a book several times, we understand different things from it each time, which shows that our perception has changed. It is therefore perception, rather than sensation, that we are associated with. When we are working on aligning we generate a lot of emotions because we are disappointed, then we get cross when we don't get the thing we want, the way we wanted it. We have to find all these feelings in ourselves and name them on behalf of the God we live in. As we explore the experiences we can be taken in by the stimulation of the drama, on the other hand if we internalise the sensation it really can bring back an inner memory, which sheds a lot of light on what is or isn't true. Often when we are nearly letting things go, we will have loads of these memories coming back and we will start to see them with pity and love, with the knowledge that they have to go. As a rule we should not seek those memories, as they come out of the blue when we are ready to process them.

The world of sensation is just a by-product of the movement of Spirit in space and is transitory. The whole of our life is a virtual experience, but most people do not recognise it as virtual and take it for real every day. The minute we have a sensation it dies, for it is like the seasons in nature; every sensation has its spring, summer, autumn and winter. By going for more and more sensation and therefore more and more deaths, we are degenerating nature, rather than aligning to it. Nature doesn't do that, the trees and the animals align to their own nature and don't go for sensation, there's just ongoing life. Man has to keep the body alive until we have become completely self-aware. Man is a virtual being, a huge accumulator of virtuality and only a very small amount will manifest in a lifetime, so when we look at ourselves or somebody else, there are enormous possibilities. Imagine that the whole of humanity could understand for just one minute that this is a world where we witness, have dominion and care; this would bring the best possible result that mankind can have, which is peace on Earth. If we all thought that for an instant, peace could happen overnight through the power of thought, vision, will and alignment.

Most of the time, the senses make us feel that we are completely alive, when in fact we are completely unconscious. That state of being alive, which we like and is beautiful, is walking in the warm breeze, smelling the flowers and looking at the birds; isn't that what we all want for everybody at the level of the senses? But we do not *need* to feel happy because of the warm breeze on our faces, we feel it and we might say "What a wonderful God we live in", but we do not actually need it. The senses are as important as the intellect, they are wondrous, but if we are an initiate they are a ritual to remind us of the greater order. Flowers are here to give their love and beauty, they are the 'healing ointment' of the emotions and are ritualistic, but a ritual doesn't have to come with senses. The fact that we see the flowers as beautiful is an emotional perception and a call for the mind to seek uplift in the beauty. Some days when we look at a flower the ritual aspect of our perception brings back the awe, but other days it doesn't and then the flower looks flat and virtual: this is when we are nearer to the coldness of being a witness on behalf of the God we live in. This is not a day when we are having a 'down', but a day when we have the emotions emptied from us. We have to move on and The Emperor is the force that moves us on, so when we suddenly recognise that energetically we are moved by things called flowers, we remember all the memories of what that kingdom is doing. Then suddenly from within us wells a love and awe that we translate as beauty. It can be the same when we look at our old mother or father, who might not be beautiful on the surface, but as we look at them from our memories we find them beautiful. It is not a sensual beauty, for we are looking at it from the point of view of ritual. If we are looking at a flower and use the ritual to follow it back to its source, it will remind us of the generosity and beauty of the plant kingdom, so we look at the beauty of the essence rather than the form. The form is the ritual that reminds us of the essence.

The Emperor's vision is focussed on the work to be done in the present, which then moves into the future. The present is a passage, the past is dead and the future holds all the possibilities. The present is only an ocean, or a point of reference for the mind to understand that reality contains the three stages. The only real way is the eternal, but before we get there we have to remember to keep looking at the highest or deepest within us. The three stages of past, present and future are one; the present is the result of the action of yesterday and is the dying stage for tomorrow. If we want to keep on repeating the sensations, we want to stay in that transitory place where we are the result of yesterday and a dying phase of tomorrow. If we don't move on from there degeneration will follow.

The Emperor has received the supreme intelligence and all the possibilities, so with those he is going to act on the manifested world to exteriorise all that he can, so achieving an alchemical transmutation. It is his force of vision that can implement something according to the possibilities in front of him that will definitely help him with the alchemical transmutation of the world. He has only one aim, which is to uplift the profane, everyday mass consciousness of the world, so transforming it into the sacred. He orders, uplifts and prepares the world for the next stage. Today has no value in itself; also mankind has no value in itself, except as an instrument and today is an instrument for tomorrow, which is our original past.

First there is the idea, then the materialisation of that idea, then making it sacred. The Emperor is the strength and the force in mankind that allows him to go from the intellectual to the mystical plane, by using and acting on the material world. The idea descends into this world and incarnates with The Emperor, so that this world can be sublimated and offered to The Pope: it is all one process.

Nature is only truly alive when it is guided by an idea that penetrates its state of being. If we recognise what is in front of us from the point of view of The Emperor, then we start an ongoing process of complete respect, where we don't want anything for ourselves and we bless nature on behalf of the God we live in; this is when nature is truly alive. Before this happens nature doesn't know it is alive. The karmic idea has got to be seen for what it is. Then, within that, we can say that we make an effort to come back and help our little brothers. Once we fully realise that, we don't come screaming and kicking, or asleep, or wanting something for ourselves, but we know that there's only one thing we have come to do; that is work. This is truly about love. If we look at that misericord side of The Emperor, then to push somebody out of the nest when they need to go is to love them, for if they don't go the world doesn't have a chance for eternal life.

The Trinity at the top needs an instrument or structure that is going to ground it and implement its activities; this is the role of The Emperor in humanity. We cannot aspire to be anything else but the best possible grounding instrument.

The material world of form is a world of force, which works by a process of action and reaction. It looks very constant, strong, square and structured, so it seems as though we are prisoners in structure. Actually it is the opposite, the world is unstable and it is always moving. We become aware of the instability when we become like The Emperor and sit on a golden cube. Gold represents that which is constant, because it cannot be corrupted, in contrast nature is always in a constant state of action and reaction; this is what keeps it going. It is a vast field of magnetic forces, within which the only equilibrium that the diverse and opposing forces can hold, comes from the harmony of the cosmos. The Emperor has completely mastered his elements and form, so he is not driven, taken in by them or lost in them. He has complete mastery, so he knows he is here to help the plan move forward. His structure is not a structure as such, it is a cornerstone and he is going to help other people become cornerstones for the new world. The Emperor is the best incarnation of the force of the will of God, which is there to implement change and the transmutation of nature into the divine essence of its origin.

His body represents a triangle with his arms and legs crossed, this can be the symbol of the triangle of generation or Venus, but also represents sulphur and is very much like the sign for Jupiter. It is a fire symbol and the sulphur or fire comes in to stimulate, blaze, or initiate, so that the light can take over. This goes with the idea of The Emperor.

Figure 2. The symbol for Sulphur.   *Figure 3. The symbol for Jupiter.*

A helmet signifies active authority, unlike the crown of a king, which would be a more passive authority; this tells us that he is higher than a king. A king has to lose his head for the wisdom to come through; he is only there to serve the people according to the wisdom. A king is not active, he stands in for the authority of the divine, but The Emperor is an active authority, so he has the right to co-work with God to have dominion. He is a conductor for the fire of God.

The helmet has four faces, or four points, to symbolise the four directions, four elements and four kingdoms in nature. The top part has four points and is open, as a focus to attract and receive the cosmic energy and influences of the divine. It is the receptor and also a protector. The back of the helmet rim that covers his neck is to protect him from any influences coming from the Earth or matter, which would pull him down.

When we rule over a kingdom we have many people coming to us who need help; this is what he is there for. However, he must not be influenced by anybody, for it may cloud his judgement and make him biased. He is the impartial judge and the helmet protects him from making a wrong decision, at the same time it allows him to capture the light and intuition. The only way to do that as a personality is to be aligned, so that all the elementals as well as the personality, can receive the light without being disturbed. Alignment of personality takes a long time because if it is done too quickly, the physical, mental and emotional bodies can't take it and the tower or structure can crumble. Our Emperor is organised and aligned, so he can take the light. Protection is not quite the right word here; it is more about allowing the best possible organisation of everything that is available, so that the job can be done well. This is what a true protection is; therefore the best and most true protection we can have is alignment.

His helmet covers the nape of his neck, which is a part of the body where we are most fragile and vulnerable psychically; also from here we release a lot of emotional trauma. It is a place of entry, therefore a weak point.

The Emperor must at all costs remain master of himself, not just of the four realms, but of the psychic realm within him as well. The first immediate goal of initiation is to create a human being who can retain control over his elemental and psychic life, with the power of the sword of truth and righteousness. He has dominion over the terrestrial powers.

The reality of his defence is that he is completely aligned and has let go of any selfish interests. Because of this he cannot be corrupted and as he acts he leaves his imprint on the world. He is indifferent, but not disinterested; he has to uplift and purify and is not seduced by the world. His strength is greater than the attraction of any self-interest, for he sees beyond. All the dances we move to as part of the life on this planet are danced to bring out the weaknesses. Even if we may intend to be true, like Peter (the personality) in the story of the capture of Jesus (the Soul), the survival instinct of the personality takes over and the Soul is betrayed by the denial of the truth. Peter is the cornerstone of new humanity, but he betrayed Jesus three times. The three bodies, physical, emotional and intellectual were not yet fully aligned to the will of the Soul and each one reacted in turn, to demonstrate that it was not time yet for the crucifixion. He denied the Soul out of weakness and out of wanting to save his own skin. The world we live in does its little theatrical dramas, so that all our weakness can be seen and brought to the surface.

There is no way anyone can act as The Emperor, until he has gone through both an alignment to personality and the alignment of Soul to the Spirit. This is a personification of the will of God incarnate, which is the will in the Soul. He doesn't carry any weapon because he doesn't need one. His helmet is open to the divine, protecting him from charm and seduction of the psychic level. He has dominion over the world, which is the temple of the God we live in. He is a guide and a true judge; not the kind of judge who speaks of good and bad and tells us that we are naughty, but more like a referee who simply shows us the yellow card. He is watching over the destiny of the world and of mankind. He has acquired immunity before he can use his powers on the world.

The only way we can truly give manifestation and structure to an idea is by bringing in the energy of the 4. We may have a lot of good ideas, but this doesn't work on its own for very long. For an idea to be able to mould the world, it has to faithfully and painstakingly move through the scrutiny of the 4 and be personally out of the way, so that we can see all the details and all the ways that the idea can be implemented. We need to ask the questions: "Will it benefit society and will it benefit the world?" It needs the matrix, so it does need the internalisation of the quality of mind of The Emperor before we start, just as a rebirth always needs a term of gestation.

The Emperor is not a man of pity and forgiveness because that is not his job; his task is uncompromising. He is not there to soothe, but to make sure that everything moves to its end. He might be called to strike, not in judgement but because it is needed. He is truly a conscious instrument for the karmic laws.

When the missionaries went to far-off countries to spread the good news, they made certain they had a beard, because men who have beards have always been recognised as men to be respected and listened to. Hair holds the whole of our yesterday and when it is on the face it demonstrates spiritual will. So in The Emperor we are looking at a man who is displaying the fact that he has lived a long time and understands the great laws of the lord of time and karma. The Egyptians depicted their pharaohs with a well-knotted beard to denote wisdom at the etheric level, which is when the physical life is rendered available for service and the authority of dominion has been given.

When we put together three strands, which represent the three paths (1, 2 and 3) going back to the metaphysical divinity, we have complete union and complete strength. So the plait is a sign of initiation, representing the energy that holds the world together. If we have a vision for good, however crazy it might look and even if the opposite comes to pass, we should still hold it, because it is that vision that holds the world together and stops it from going into complete disintegration. Without the vision of the initiate it would truly be a chaotic, anarchic world; it is the vision that holds order. The initiate is not alone in holding it; in fact none of us is alone. The lighted three fold plait of the stream of consciousness represents all the past lives offered to the great life, so the initiate is part of the fabric of the long chain of men of goodwill. When a change is needed in a social institution, any new idea will always need many groups to hold the vision and to impress the right authority at the right time for it to be implemented.

It is the union of all the initiates that gives The Emperor the power to guide the manifested world. This union is a chain that never breaks, for it has been there from the beginning of time and is made up of all the ones who have ever worked by themselves or in groups, throughout the world. They make up that magnetic network of thoughts and it is through the magnetic field that we can receive information. To receive and to translate the plan is the work we do, so however feeble we might be at doing it, keeping on will make perfect. This union of minds and Souls is a protective web of love; the love is truth and light. Without it our world of racism, class hate, envy, war and separation would have degenerated and disintegrated a long time ago; we have to accept this. The fact that we haven't killed ourselves to extinction is because there is a true web of life watching over this planet, which was created by the thought forms of all the initiates that have been before us. This chain of intelligence and love gently guides the world towards its goal, for it is made up of those that have dedicated their lives to the work of love and sacrifice; of dying without hate.

The sun and moon are depicted on The Emperor's chest, which tells us that he has to create complete harmony over his yin and yang. This means he has to be active but also receptive. If he is going to receive the word of God and act on it, he has to listen first. A man or a woman who is all action and not receptive, can end up as a tyrant who gives out dogma; that is the problem with a strong personality. On the other hand a person who is completely internalised and does too much daydreaming, has no will. The Emperor is a good blend and balance of the intuitive and active, so these two poles come together in him. He receives the bright idea from the sun and takes it into the moon, so that it can be born. This is a generative principle, which requires both receptivity and activity and brings cohesion and harmony between the two aspects, fusing in the cross of sanctified matter – the cross linking Heaven and Earth.

The golden cube on which The Emperor is seated can be interpreted as either a masonic stone, or a petrified beam of light from the sun. All matter, including ourselves, is in essence crystallised light. Masonic stones usually had an obelisk sitting on top of them, to represent the channelling of the light of Spirit into matter.

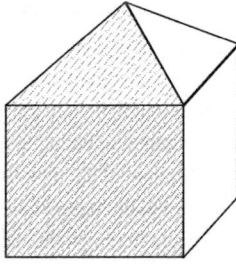

Figure 4. A Masonic stone.

The cube is Number 4, which is the number of humanity and the Earth. It is a symbol for matter and nature. The Emperor holds the structure which supports matter and stability is an attribute of the cube. The obedience, the service and the focused attitude of mind of The Emperor has transmuted the matter of his body into gold; gold tells us that it cannot be corrupted.

The world is forever moving, but it is the stability and the incorruptible nature of the will manifested in man that we are looking at here. The Emperor's focus on the vision does not influence the adaptability of his mind. Our problem is that we are always seeking balance, for most people want balance and harmony; in other words they want to be happy and well. The only stability we should seek to acquire is the stability of will and wisdom, for stability, balance and harmony in the physical is very transitory. The world we live in thinks that what we all need is a family, a partner, health and money, but the only true stability is a vision and the ability to apply it. If this applies to the former ideal, so be it, but the vision is the key.

The cube represents the power that knows that it is viable until the end of the world. It is not our power, but the force that comes through us. That golden cube goes through from revolution to revolution. It is durable and is not going to be overturned, because it has been given the ultimate power, which is to hold the vision. The Emperor is truly the first cornerstone of the New Jerusalem and so he is sitting on that golden cube; this tells us that he has dominion. He doesn't have to work at it, for he can trust it so completely that he doesn't have to do a thing. It is his throne, just as misericord is one of his aspects. He can judge and guide the world because he has achieved the constant stability of holding the vision. The cube is underneath him, but he doesn't have to stand on it, because that would mean he wants to leave it behind; sitting on something means we trust it. He's got his legs crossed for he's not going to run; he is at ease, for the vision will never fail him. He is not going to go into the excess of tyranny, for the cube is telling us he has gained his gold, so he is at peace with the world.

The Emperor is the foundation stone of the most important building, the sacred temple or church of humanity. From the beginning of time, the building of the temples or churches has always started with the ritual of laying the cornerstone. This job was traditionally done by kings or emperors, to honour God and ask for fertility and abundance for the community. The ritual was also about protection, being a warning to those who might come to destroy or damage it. No edifice was built without a cornerstone as a manifestation of the idea of God. The one who lays it holds the divine right to do so, that is why the kings or heads of state still do it. This has taken place since the beginning of time, because the sacred building always had the eye and the mind of the first initiate, king or priest, who officiated at the ritual.

We must not forget the part played by the great brotherhood of Initiates, who were the ones who crafted that plait before us. We do not thank them enough in our prayers, or recognise them in our daily lives, even though they have given their lives to create the ladder of light. We do not thank ourselves enough, for however weak we may be we still carry on holding a vision of peace for humanity. There are numerous beautiful Souls that gave their lives to do the work. This is not to do with thanking the gods of nature for giving us the harvest; it is foregoing today's harvest, so enabling the seeds of light to be anchored in the pure soil of the Soul for tomorrow's harvest.

Because The Emperor has done the alchemy, he is the result of the great work of the transmutation of all matter, as well as the purification of that which has been soiled, so matter is rendered pure and psychically precious. Because of this he can have dominion over the world he lives in.

The eagle in this card is black, whereas the eagle in Number 3 (The Empress) was white. Everything that she represented has to be put into action by The Emperor, who guides the people back up to the Trinity. The eagle is a bird of height, so it wants to rise, but this one is dark and heavy, for it has to work with the ignorance of mankind. Its darkness symbolises all the greed and the holding on to safety, as well as all the things we like and don't want to release. It is fierce, like a bird of prey is when it holds onto its prey and kills it with its beak. It has its wings well spread out and its talons are ready to grasp, but it is actually not holding onto anything. It is going to be flying, following our Emperor in rising and being transmuted into gold. Black is the first colour of the alchemic work, so we are seeing an eagle in the process of being transformed into gold. It wants to fly and is using the best in itself. It has hope, which is one of the great characteristics that The Emperor offers, so it is the hope of all the would-be flyers and transmuters. This is the equivalent of the Black Virgin. The black eagle knows it needs to change. This is like the initiate, who has the quality of the mind of The Emperor within him, so he knows that he will have to put his black eagle through the process of transmutation by going through a crucifixion. This is the energy coming through the 4. It is the balance between the spiritual aspiration and the separative downward pull of matter. The eagle is looking towards the West, which is the direction of death, for Spirit has to receive the heavy materiality of the technological mind of the west, in order to uplift it and make it its tool for good. The thirteen protrusions of its feathers (13/4), speak of that state of transformation that it is undergoing and it is uplifting with ease.

The sceptre in the right hand of The Emperor has a crescent Moon at its base, which represents receptivity. The Empress was in complete control of the whole of the psychic world, so her moon was turned down, but The Emperor has to receive so he uses it the other way up, to denote that he is not going to go into illusion. It is in his active hand, so that we know that man receives and has to act with intuition, rather than rationality. On the top of the sceptre is the fleur-de-lys, which tells us of the purity of all his actions. Between the moon and the fleur-de-lys, there are two little things that look like fishes, to represent the Spirit coming down into incarnation, then coming up again with matter after having transmuted it. This is the divine sacrifice. The fleur-de-lys is a symbolic flower rather than a real one, because we are all myth and symbolism; the only thing that is real is the power of pure intent. We are surrounded by transitory illusion, so nothing of what we see is truely viable unless it is manifested out of pure intent.

The globe or orb is green, with the cross of Spirit at the top, representing the alchemic transformation of humanity and of the Earth. It is held in The Emperor's left hand, for it has to have love and care from his feminine, nurturing side so that he can act with love. The balance is completed by the sceptre being in his other hand.

The flower under his right knee is an open tulip. In The Magician we saw a closed flower, a little bud, but here we see it open to symbolise the manifested initiate.

The golden egg shape on the sock on his left leg protects the vulnerable shin on the front of the leg. The socks are sky-blue to represent the truth, which touches the Earth as he walks, so like the Buddha he's pure. The intent is to bring the sky or cosmos down to the Earth. He has wisdom and his point of vulnerability is covered by gold, so he is rendered invulnerable. His red stockings tell us of action and fire, for he's an initiate who fires things up.

If we do not find in nature the way by which we can see ourselves, so enabling the God we live in to see itself, then there is no life. The only reality is perception, which is an attribute of Spirit. We are not the centre of the world for if we die life carries on, but if there are no more witnesses to allow awareness, there is no light in life because there is no perception.

A keyword of the 4 is 'severity', which tells us that it is only out of the experience of knowing every little bit of the suffering in the human chain that we can become an Emperor. He is severe because he is trying to take people out of their misery by saying to them "Go to your death quickly my son, you will feel better after". This idea is appropriate to mercy, or 'misericord', for it uplifts the one who exercises it as well as the one who needs it. It is energetic and magnetic, so the weak ones who want to become strong will be attracted to the strength of The Emperor. We keep on working at the process of rising up to God, without being able to know, feel, or understand that greater life and then God comes down to us. We work at being 'magnetic' enough and 'light' enough by transmuting and forgetting all the heavy, dense memories, so that we can magnetically be a good receptor for the plan and vision of the Solar System. A lot of us might want to go to another universe or into the heart of the Sun, but actually it happens the other way round; it is the heart of the Sun that comes into our hearts, because we are not of much use on the planet if we are actually on the Sun. If we become what we are channelling from another star we can be excellent teachers, but not for planet earth!

How can we ever get out of what is heavy, dense and useless, if we do not first put our nose in it? It is the same idea with the Sun; the minute we give room for that tiny bit of light in us, which is the awareness of Soul, by looking at our actions and reactions we can burn off all those weaknesses, so that the light of the Sun can keep on expanding in us. The problem is that most of us think that we are aware all the time when we are not; we think we have got the answer when we haven't. It is not about seeking answers, it is about being truthful.

We all have to remember stages we have been in so that we can heal them. The minute we have understood and healed something from the past, the door is closed underneath us; this is 'closing the door where evil dwells'. If, however, we are working through this life and suddenly we click and understand something for the first time, it is going to take a little bit more time, because we have to bring all the levels of reaction (mental, emotional and physical) into that little realisation or Sun, to be purified. Little by little we lighten the pot.

The Emperor puts everyone in front of themselves; it is that principle in us that we have to recognise. To be able to face ourselves is the beginning of being able to materialise a higher principle and a better world for tomorrow. The intent and hope may be true, but we have to face ourselves. Water will not boil until it has reached the right temperature, so keep watching yourself and that kettle will boil. This is watching in the sense of being a witness, so is different from self development. It does take time, but eventually the water boils.

The key to the 4 is discovering truth, working to ensure justice and then, when that is undertaken its power cannot be resisted. The first duty and the only justification of power, is to know and discover truth, without pretension, prejudice or self-interest; only then can we operate justice. This doesn't happen through brute force. If we are going to bring the kingdom of God onto the planet, then all the little units in humanity are going to be joyful and beautiful instruments. Justice then would mean that every single unit is going to be able to get back what it gives, which would be completely fair; this is nothing to do with good and bad. Everyone has to become truly realised so that they can be true witnesses. Everybody will have their share of light, but the way they are going to do it is by taking full responsibility for their actions and reactions. The personality has to respond to the Soul and accept truthful witnessing; the Soul has to respond to Spirit by loving the work it has undergone. This is a fantastic justice. The man who is true to himself is an Emperor, who is able to mould the world in the way it is going to be eventually. All he can do is guide, watch and help, but not impose himself on anybody else, although he has to persuade by saying "Well done, you are doing all right, carry on".

The Emperor gives us the understanding of three-fold golden plait of the co-creators, who are building the plan on Earth.

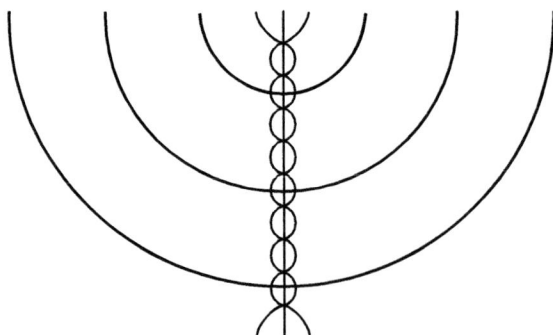

Figure 5. The golden plait.

The golden plait of the brothers of the wisdom.

When we understand it we realise it is the top of the triple Heaven, the 1 2 3 (as above so below) and once we see it we bring Heaven down to Earth so the Trinity can be manifested.

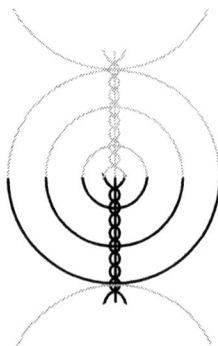

Figure 6. As above, so below.

Heaven coming down to Earth.

We are here to transmute through alchemy, for it is the power of pure thought and unconditional love that makes it happen.

The Magician was part of the active absolute, made of the first three or the Trinity, then to start the new line we have the active relative, in the form of The Emperor, who has to relate.

The active Absolute	1	2	3
The active relative	4	5	6

The Emperor is the vivifying principle. The 1, 2, 3 comes back as the Trinity into the web, then the 4 is the one that makes the form, not the one that creates; it is very important to understand the difference. The 4 has far too often been put as the one who puts the furniture together, but it is formative not creative. We are looking at the divine will in manifestation and the realisation of that in the world, which is brought into being by creation.

So we have three steps to take:

1. Realisation of the divine will by creation.
2. The realisation of an idea, by measuring all the possibilities of manifestation in order to bring in a solution.
3. Realisation of action conceived by the 2, through the direction of the 1.

The 4 has to give form to the realisation, so he will meet the resistance of matter as he brings more light (therefore possibilities of change) until a harmonious compromise is found and a new order has been realised.

We know that The Emperor is a transition point from one cycle to another; this transition enables mankind to move from nature to Spirit.

The 4 is definitely a first reflection of the 1. That first reflection, when it reflects the divine, is the will. The guidance of the will of the greater life is what our Soul is seeking.

At the human level, we are a reflection of Adam and the seed of the power of the greater life. At the natural level the reflection is the universal creative field, or the Soul of the universal nature. We mustn't forget the roots we came from in nature, because they are the ones that have to become gold through the perception of their divinity; they also give us the foundation for the golden future.

The Pope, Le Pape
The Blessing

The Pope holds the blessing of the primary religion, which is the knowledge that God is within us and not in rituals. He is not attached to any particular religion, therefore is not dressed in white as the traditional Pope would be. He is the fifth card and so concludes the first stage of the journey. His pure blessing is there for all, but it is only possible to receive it by making the choice to look up and so rise above the personal desires and dramas. The message is very simple and clear, reminding us to look beyond the outer form and see the energy of love and truth behind all things.

The Pope at Number 5, represents peace of mind, which is the state that is reached once the mind has explored all the experiences of the senses, all the sciences and all the philosophies. In this state it will perceive itself as wisdom, Active Intelligence and the obedient will. The higher mind it has become is falling in love with its reflection and it is that moment of deep peace that reveals the love aspect at its fullest. The understanding that we are all one great life is the 'coming home' feeling, where nothing else is needed; we are whole, we are blessed – so the giving out of the blessing can begin. Many numerologists will question this view of the 5, but this is the highest attainment that the mind of mankind can reach, just as the 12/3, The Hanged Man, is the highest expression of the Trinity in mankind.

Before the mind reaches this point, it will have to revisit every behaviour pattern that the experience of living has imprinted on an inquisitive human being, who seeks answers through knowledge in the never ending record of mindsets. When these mindsets are seen as his lot and his weakness, the initiate seeks the transforming inner path into wisdom. As he does this he is not even aware that this accumulated knowledge will play a big part in the personality's proud resistance to the inner light. He has to give back to God the little light of his mind, for he does not own it but he is it and so he belongs to God. He is not any of the archetypes that his pride would have projected to keep him subject to. We can see the danger of the knowledge in the mind of man, when he recognises that he is his creative mind and still believes in his own importance.

In Number 4, The Emperor, we experience the conflict that the mind might encounter as it learns to harmonise the many difficulties of the task of realising the concept 'as above, so below'. This is the role of mankind; what a responsibility! We have to watch out truthfully for these archetypes, from martyr to saviour, from servant to saint and so on. We need to find them in ourselves and dissolve their potent energies, thus releasing life from erroneous mindsets and structures. In the 4 we saw that the emotional, romantic aspect of love had to be transmuted into the cold light of reason, so that the action of mind on matter is for the greater good. What has to be done is for the best in the long term. We are all equal and brothers in the eyes of love/wisdom so we fight unfairness, but when we look at a situation we thought unfair and see the greater picture, we realise that it helped us to internalise and rise.

If you are a surgeon, there are times when it may be necessary to cut off a limb, so you would have to be completely insensitive to the pain that would be caused otherwise you couldn't do it. If you have a bad tooth you go to the dentist and he pulls it out; he knows it hurts but it is his job and he is helping you. He won't be thinking "Poor thing, I am going to hurt her, shall I do it?" he just does it. If we realise we have called somebody a name because we were cross, and understand that this came from our personality, not from Soul-Spirit, we have to have enough humility in us to forgive ourselves and know that the other person can do that as well, as can everybody else. If we are really hurt from the personality point of view, we bite back; then we can see and understand that reaction, so absolve and transmute it. That is fine and means that next time we might react from Soul with a similar effect, without even questioning it.

It is about being human in the best possible way and that means that boundaries and discipline are completely understood. The structure of a healthy, intelligent society is formulated to be good, for it stops complete degeneration and destruction. For an average human being to accept and follow the discipline of functioning within the boundaries of society is good, but at the same time Ancient Wisdom is teaching people to be able to see through the structure and recognise it. It is not brainwashing or persuading people; in fact it is the complete opposite. It is putting another picture next to the standard one, so as to allow people to think for themselves and bridge the gap between their Heaven and Earth.

When we put our hand up in blessing that gives a spiritual/Soul content to whatever we are in front of, whether it is plant, human or object. Then when we completely align the instrument, Soul and Spirit, we have only peace, love and truth in our hands so spiritual healing comes automatically. The harmonious vibration from the love/wisdom energy creates patterns that inspire a response within the receiver, so that a space for healing is created. For example, just by smiling we will help others to smile. The problem is that society has given us norms of harmony and beauty that are so limited and deformed. In the eyes of the disciple or would-be initiate the world is too small, mean, or just not good enough. He might ask "Am I dreaming? Is this really planet Earth? Is this really who I am?" This is the pain of the disciple. He has had his eyes full of starlight and gold dust, he has drunk the milk of Heaven and then comes back and denies himself every five minutes. He will have to relive the experiences with the full light of truth on to them, so that he doesn't leave some dark corners of festering emotions in the cup. The peace of mind that he has to achieve will serve him when he is uncoiling the memories that are locked in the organic cells of his body.

We need to depersonalise what we see as ourselves. The sensations of pleasure, guilt, or pain are so addictive that we keep going for more drama or disgust. The perception has to shift from "This is me" to "This is the job that I, the Soul, have to do". We need to see it in the context of the process of life and keep witnessing with compassion, for we are here to help people. Artistically, if we can bring something higher out of the dilemma of being human by using the senses at a higher level than self-gratification and then express what we feel, we are doing just right. This is what most people don't do enough. They would express the first thought of what they feel, but if the will to be completely honest is not there, they don't go to what is important behind the thought; for ninety-nine percent of the time that first thought is an intellectual cover-up.

We have to use the senses, so we are being fed excitement and it is important to go on expressing it outwardly so as to show other people the effect; then eventually it sublimates itself. We should give out everything that we are, until we feel there is nothing else to give; this applies to all the services and the sciences. While we feel we have more to express, then we should do it. We are the expression of the God we live in and we have to bring out truth from the depths of our feeling and be moved. It is a 'good citizen' syndrome to be afraid of being moved and afraid of saying "Look I'm weak". If we are moving in the waters, whether it is the deep subconscious waters or the higher waters, or the ones in between, that is what we have to express. When we are silent we are learning to discriminate inside and are checking our own honesty. After that it is a crime against humanity if we don't express our own humanity, for we have to demonstrate to others that it is possible to be at peace with it. How is an aspirant even going to be able to start taking a pen to draw a circle if we haven't expressed ours in many ways before?

The primary religion is about knowing that God is within us. Once we have understood that, all the other gods are elementals even if they are cosmic. The one having the experience is the God of the system in us and on behalf of that inner God we are expressing the Solar System. We cultivate endurance through pain, until one day we smile and say "What is next?" for the spiritual uplift is moving us on. If we do the experience of our addiction (and we are all addicted to life otherwise we would not be here), then it passes, it goes. If we do it humbly, with love in our hearts then we are doing well, but it is not a recipe for doing it forever, it must move on. We all carry our potential as a higher consciousness within us and also the action-reaction of our personal karmic biology.

The Pope is simple and beautiful. In Number 5, the five-pointed star is a symbol of the Christ. He is the true human, the biological being who is completely responding to and is at the service of the God within; that is what The Pope represents and in the card he's not meant to be the head of the Roman Catholic Church. The Tarot at its peak was drawn during the middle Ages, when the powerful in the land were the kings, Popes and emperors, so this is why those names are in the Tarot. The name that represents the highest possible authority on Earth of a spiritual order is The Pope, depicted in the fifth card.

The Pope of the Tarot, like Christ or Krishna, is the highest possible achievement of light and matter coming together in the service of God towards humanity. This quality of mind gives rise to wisdom, which is then made perfect in action. This is a description of a human being that has done everything and who comes back completely denuded of personal intent. The only thing that they come back for is to try and save the ones that are lost; this is the Christ or the Bodhisattva. It takes very little for us to be lost and in humanity today we are at a point of crisis, so a lot of people are lost. We need the courage to represent the life that is within. Some of us will have to go beyond recognised ideas and systems to remove some worn out veils of corruption, so that the new understanding can actually reveal a simpler truth.

The flow of energy through the Tarot has arrived at Number 5, which is half way through to the perfect 10. However, even to reach the perfection of the 5 we have to go all the way to 22 and back, many, many times. The Pope concludes the first five cards, coming just at that time when the true birth of the Christ within can take place; the higher mind of the soul and the love wisdom of the heart fuse. The Tarot describes the journey of the Soul on its initiatic path. From the beginning we are presented with the tools, the goal and the qualities of mind required to complete the journey. The Pope and the Hanged Man represent an achieved state, like grace or humility. We can't work at becoming a Pope; it is a state we arrive at, just as we can't work at becoming humble. To be as near as possible to that state is what is required, so that we can carry on through the next seventeen cards. So far in the first five cards all the qualities and attributes to aspire to, have been pointed out. We are not perfect, so there is a need to be vigilant all the time, because in the next seventeen cards there is always the possibility of losing ourselves. We need to check our equipment as we would do before climbing the Himalayas, by seeing that our back-pack is prepared for the job. In this way we are ready to go on to the next part of the journey, which is coming into life itself. Up to now we have been flying high with the concept. With The Magician, we had to be full of spiritual will to come into the world of illusion; this is the will to be able to see and push through, without being taken in. We need the will to acquire the deepest wisdom there is and to go into every single corner of the subconscious so that the veil can be lifted in Number 2, The High Priestess, who asks us to have pure thought, (which means not looking through our own personal glasses) and then reclaim the mind as Active Intelligence, to name and create the world in Number 3, The Empress. She can weave, she has understood the pattern and she can express it. When the idea, net or canvas is firmly there, The Emperor brings that blueprint into crystallisation, saying "Nothing will deter me from bringing the plan on Earth". Then after the pity and compassion of The Emperor, we have the blessing in Number 5, The Pope.

Nothing of what has been done or will be done is judged by the measure of manmade justice, only by love and truth. This kind of judgment is a blessing. If we have been a thief and what made us one is understood through love and compassion, then we do not need to be a thief any more. As long as what we have done has been lived, understood and completely seen, right to the root of what being a thief is, then we can stop being one. Everything has a root and a source and there is nothing more that nature wants than to make one with that source, which is God. To be moved by genuine compassion rather than self protection is glorious, to be in the drama of being human is also glorious, but wouldn't it be much simpler to stop being in the drama? Anything that is not moved by the spontaneity of the Spirit/Soul connection is self-gratification, including spiritual or philosophical pursuits.

The Pope is coming back with a clear heart and a pure mind and he is going to do his job. The Tarot is a book of man's esoteric life and makes a complete story. If we understand the first ten cards, we understand what our inner spiritual world is made of, but if we understand the whole twenty-two, we have understood what being an initiate is and we are at work; it is not just studying.

Life is energy organising itself and manifesting as systems. These systems can be seen as archetypes, but in reality all the systems are one and any system is a by-product, like the virtual life where the experiment of life takes place.

The first two cards indicate to the initiate all he will need to achieve to dissolve the black sphinx of misunderstandings. Once he has understood that he is responsible to Soul, he can't stop the process of transformation because the past mistakes keep presenting themselves for purification. If we stop asking questions because we feel we have come to a point or level where love and peace reigns in our lives, we have to watch it, because we might be kidding ourselves with some sensory experience that feels good, when in reality it is an illusionary state created by pride. On the other hand, we don't have to go and break a leg because we think we are too happy; we just need to be honest. The personality learns to align its desires, wants and hopes, to survive and succeed in the everyday world, but eventually when the alignment to Soul begins, these driving aspirations have to be directed towards others welfare.

Religions are right to bring hope to humanity; they are useful mindsets to help us be good citizens, because there is no work that Spirit can achieve if there isn't good citizenship. Even if at some time we have to confront our neighbours, good citizenship has got to be there. The essence within us pushes us towards more work, more truth and more love; not for self, but as service. Keep on being vigilant to see whether in us there is still some hope for salvation that remains from being afraid of Hell, or from pride and wanting to be first at the gate of Heaven.

The expression of the God we live in is inside us, but hope, salvation and pride have no place in us, when we are filled with the quality of love and wisdom. Certainty replaces hope, service is habitual and humility is our state. It is the ongoing, incessant journey of bringing Spirit down to Earth. Rather than hope it is certainty, for we know we are fulfilling our task; we can't stop doing it and there is nothing else we can do. To be truly able to do it, we have to get rid of all the hopes, because while we are hoping there is something in it for us or something in it for humanity. If there is something in it for humanity and we want to help our brother in that way, then think, "Why do I want to help my brother, what is the matter with me?" We've got a problem. We can feel our brother's pain, but we all know really that we can't do a thing for our brother, so we stop hoping. All we can do is carry on. People come for healing and we give 'hope', for humanity has got to hope and it gives us the opportunity to learn through what we are hoping for.

We will start to realise that there is something else in the world besides ourselves and that we have been taking ourselves too seriously. Look at what the world is going through; our suffering is peanuts! There is a lot of breaking down going on. The fact that we have the privilege of breaking our hearts over a peanut helps us to go to the very heart of our wants, so that we can de-crystallise them. We see that the journey is going to be coloured by what we want. The only requirement is to be completely true to what is happening in our lives at the time; this is the greatest pain of all. We may have done nothing more than squash a bee when we didn't want to and we are devastated. We can ask ourselves if we have ever experienced deep pain about something like that. See it, because these are the feelings that will eventually give us the white gloves of pure intent. We can ask "What is the fuss about and why is it so difficult to accept ourselves as we are?"

Society is the support of the body of humanity; it is a structure, so let's not kick the body of humanity by kicking society. Let's try to see whether we can put in more light, more soap, a better diet and all the other things it needs. Society is the expression of what humanity at the time can work out, just as our bodies are an expression of how we lived our lives yesterday. If we think of society like that, we can see how initiates will work within it by bringing more compassion and light into the structure of the house of humanity, so that eventually society can be completely bathed in the Sun. The change will not happen in our lifetimes, but that is no reason not to act.

Truth is not the firework display of suddenly seeing the Solar System in its full glory, it is homely and small. How can Spirit make atomic light happen in the heart of wisdom, if it doesn't go into the small atomic memory of our everyday life? That is the truth with love/wisdom. It is a road to Damascus experience when we let the understanding drop into the heart and the heart allows the fire to fuse with the light. The flashing light is suddenly saying, "My God, it is that simple!" There is no other truth, except when the light of Spirit in our little unit can reach yet another depth in the core of our wisdom. The Empress is the idea and the high spirituality and then The Pope is the divine flash in the mind of mankind's heart, because the truth of the human condition is perceived with love in the blessings given.

After 1 and 2 we have a goal, which is to aim for the wisdom on our journey and then 3 and 4 represent aspects of the skill of mind. Have we got the higher intelligence in place and the skill to implement the vision? Numerologically the 1 2 & 3 are the cosmic karmic mirror in which the initiate is asking the question, "What am I made of?" It is an energetic world and when consciousness comes in, then the space is going to allow the light to tear the veil so that it can say "Oh yes! I can see, I've got the map, I've got the plan". That is The Magician, The High Priestess and The Empress. Light comes in, needs to see and asks "What do I measure?" "What am I made of?"

"What do I feel?" The High Priestess gives the answer and corner by corner darkness is lifted gradually, as consciousness overtakes the blind cleverness of nature.

By the fourth level with The Emperor, we are going to find a way to humanise. We become our own ruler. Only when we have found the wisdom and have no personal intent can we guide, but in this case we are talking about more than guidance. The word is 'regulate', which has the same root as 'regal', or kingly. Rules and regulation all come from the same idea of the Spirit being in charge.

As we look at The Pope in the card, we see that he is an old man with a white beard and a red green-lined coat with a blue habit underneath it. He's holding a cross with his left hand, is giving a blessing with his right hand and he wears a Triple Crown. We can only see the top of his chair in the card and there are two clerics in front of him. He's gentle and it is a very simple card. We are not looking at this Pope as the religious, symbolic head of the church, but as the summit of achievement in spiritual religious authority. Religion comes from linking and binding things together just as we bind a book; this is symbolic of linking or re-linking with God.

The fifth card is a continuation of The Emperor, so we have the same levels of consciousness with two very different expressions. The Pope and The Emperor are two sides of the one coin. They are the manifestation of the religious power in life and the social-cultural everyday power; these two have always been fighting each other. Even in the days when the priests and the kings were one, there would have been an internal conflict. We know from the very first stories of the opposing brothers, whether it is Lucifer and Christ, or Cain and Abel, that there has always been a conflict within the psyche of mankind about how to apply the rule of God, as we try it this or that way.

The initiatic way, which is the inner way, has been vilified because the power of the social organising structure had to win over the inner way to begin with. What we regard as the truth in most religions is the exoteric or outer structure, like the ten commandments, which say: "Don't do it", rather than "I know I'm free, I've understood I lie every day, but I can see it and I know why I am doing it, so I will learn not to lie". The ancient Egyptian commandment was, "I haven't lied, I haven't killed, I haven't refused to help my brother". The difference between these two ways is that "I haven't", has been turned into the structured exoteric "Don't do it". For the initiate, however mean he has been, as long as he sees it and as long as he turns it into honesty and love one day, it is okay. However, the people had to be given a structure, so the religions had to tell them what not to do, otherwise they would never be aware of what they *were* doing. The battle of social versus religion, meaning outer versus inner has been going on from the beginning of awareness. How do we now apply the truth of God as we see it?

It is all to do with power and will. When will first comes in, it is force. Then when it reorganises and regulates itself, it becomes the power of the land or the power of the spiritual mind; power is the force that is able to find a way to regulate. When the social side or the structure of civilisation is stronger than the inner life, then it is Caesar the Emperor, for example, who wins over the religion of the land, which represents the inner life. All the highest aspirations are there in the idea of the perfect town, the perfect country and the unification of the world, so that we can be at peace. The greater life is there; it doesn't die, but it becomes extremely materialistic and superficial because we are only talking about the building or structure; religion then becomes a tool to reinforce the social order.

The ones who should apply divine justice and say, "I know my son, I love you, but don't do it again", are the judges and the policemen. They don't apply divine justice, instead they protect the state and the good citizens by giving out punishment. "We will call you a scum and make you into a scum"; this is the 'eye for an eye' type of morality, which is the old interpretation of the old fear of God mentality, rather than spirituality.

The role of religion is to surpass and rise above the social order, not to maintain the artificial hierarchy based on personal interest. Initiates are representatives of the true inner religion; every piece of love and truth in the initiate, however small it is, is there to create a reaction; this truly makes them act as a stirrer or devil's advocate. But we shouldn't *make* ourselves into stirrers, because the artificial stirrer is the worst possible aspect of the desire to be important. We can only be a devil's advocate if we are the brightest of the bright, having gone through all the love, compassion and blessings. These great sparks from Soul are the true devil's advocates and are the ones who come and push on the wheels of Job. They are the ones who are bright and faithful and so much into God, that they don't mind coming in to hurt one or two of us just to wake us up. If that isn't The Pope, what is? Can you see how much love there has to be for truth, for the God we live in and for humanity, to be able and come down and say, "Hold on mate, you are doing it for yourself'. With the temptation in the desert, Jesus' brightest, most honest side came up and asked "Do you think you are that pure? Well, I am going to put you in front of yourself". We should beware of the false devil's advocate. They either do it because they have understood some part of the mysteries and they are trying to play a role that isn't theirs, or they have seen the role from afar and their pride takes over, so that they sabotage themselves and everybody around them. Remember it is not so much about which lies we tell to others, it is always more about whether we are lying to ourselves.

With Caesar it is all about structure, therefore it has to be fixed and stable. There's nothing more difficult for a well-established society than to welcome change, because change represents instability and trouble. However, social change cannot happen without instability. In a culture it will take several generations to change, because the social structure will always resist change. The true nature of Spirit is to move, so the mystical life moves and its very nature is a continual evolution, so if we follow the warning of Buddha we don't go for pictures and crystallisation. When the mystical life or religion dominates, then it can become dogma, as we can see in religious fundamentalists through the ages where religion is applied with force.

There can be no social application or practical interest behind the spiritual base of faith in its truest sense of 'faith, hope and charity'. If faith is what rules the religious content of a country, it is still very much the spiritual trying to find a way to build a structure. It is not the job of religion to do that, it is The Emperor's job. That is why the Tarot has been wise and made two cards out of that power, for it is the same power but with different interpretations. The Emperor is the power that regulates the vision and what is to come. The Pope represents the natural peace of mind, that through its direct connection with the realised higher intelligence of the Soul offers blessings to those who are ready to receive them; then they can naturally obey the rule of The Emperor. There is no way The Emperor is going to bring Heaven on Earth in one day and it is not the job of those with a religious inner vision to become Emperors. The Pope will act in everyday life, but his light and authority will only be recognised by those who seek innocence. We understand that eventually the initiate functions with both aspects at once; the right side of the brain has a spatial intelligence, the left a data information function. When they work together we have a more universal intelligence.

All religions will have the fear of hell, karma and the idea of eternity in them. There isn't a system that does not have an appreciation of yesterday, today and tomorrow. The minute we put one single practical interest into our spiritual work, we are bartering, making conditions and exchanging; for example by saying "I won't do that because it will be bad karma and I will end up in hell for being a bad girl/boy". Are we at peace, or are we still bartering our life with the beliefs around us? We all have the bartering aspect in us, but we are talking here about going beyond ourselves. We cannot barter with God, because God doesn't want anything in exchange. God is the great energetic life. What we get is what comes back to us today from previous needs and thought forms that we have projected yesterday.

We are clinging so strongly to the material mother, but in truth there is only a flow of love, life and possibilities of manifestation. What we call love is the satisfaction of meeting and being with another person and life being unthinkable without them. That has the beginning of the understanding of true faithfulness and service to a God that doesn't require anything. True love is not preoccupied at all with whether it is going to get something back, or whether it is going to avoid something. Can you imagine the life we live in, which sustains absolutely everything, thinking "Is he going to love me back?" We are not allowing the flow of God through us and so we stop God 'becoming' by putting ourselves in the middle all the time and by being so obsessed by our own 'rabbit-hood'. What arrogant creatures we are! We are so self-obsessed with our long ears and our small fluffy tails and all the rest! Nothing is really of value that doesn't allow fusion of our lives with the greater life and we spend our lives protecting ourselves from more understanding, love and compassion (the true 'other'), because of our own blueprint of mindsets and desires.

Where there is true love for another, we become two minds or two lives who don't destroy each other by uniting. One doesn't absorb or annihilate the other, but on the contrary gives them the exaltation to have found the reality and supreme reason for life. This is what we are all after; fusion with the mind and love of God. The way we are learning to love is by loving another person without a battle; it is not "You haven't done this for me today!" It is nothing to do with bartering; it is entirely to do with allowing. The minute there is a reaction, we know that we are separating from the person and that is not love; in that we are also separating from God. The person in front of us whom we want to love to the hilt, doesn't have to be evolved or un-evolved, so long as they are the one we are with that we are going to love one hundred percent. This is fusion and true giving. To be alive is to truly love what is there in front of us, with no fear and no holding back. We should not question that, but we should discriminate, otherwise it could be a recipe for an awful lot of disintegration, which is of course the opposite of what is required. If the healer gives healing, hoping that the one that is being healed is not going to physically die, that is not using discrimination. Discriminate so as to see that the quality of the love we are offering matches the quality of the situation, but always stay open to receive grace through an accepted blessing from the Soul.

It is love that gives movement to Spirit and thereafter gives birth to life. Truth and light can only be revealed if the love aspect gives space for it. It is love of a cause that will drive the will to give up its life. When the Soul has achieved dominion over the personality it will die for its lover as it fuses with its etheric envelope, so that Spirit can directly guide the instrument. There is a fine quality of vibration that comes with spiritual truth, but actually for all of us it is love that makes the difference. The will to serve God is truly an act of love and here we are a blind server, so love doesn't even need to be talked about, because we love God so much that the only thing we are going to do is bring the will of God into action. Very often this doesn't look like an act of love; it is more like the surgeon cutting through to the clear reality, so there is a double edge to both blessing and surgery. The blessing is an act of God, so when it suddenly happens and the light comes in, we feel the pain where we are not in the truth; that is why the will of God is like the knife of a surgeon. Love has always got to come first, because if we bring the will of God down without loving and without thinking, we can do an awful lot of harm. This is the trouble with many high-flying spiritual or conceptual minds; if the intellect is still holding some type of spiritual pride, love finds it very hard to breathe in that type of atmosphere, because it is the opposite to that. Love is fusing, not conquering and does not say; "I am the best".

We live simultaneously in two planes of experience, for we have on one side the great understanding of love and wisdom and on the other we have to implement it through some rules and regulations. In the finding of intelligence, man can order his world so as to be free of the need for protection or conservation of material life. This means he can expand his spiritual powers and turn towards his mystic life.

It takes a lot of courage to bring the higher intelligence into matter, which means into our hearts, personality and subconscious. When spiritual will flows into the higher intelligence of the Soul, it brings the light in so we can look into our space; all the games and tricks of the personality/survival instinct are revealed! We have to let our mind drop over the edge of an imaginary cliff and then when we have fallen deep into the heart of the cellular memory, we release the light. Then we see the picture of the imprint on the cellular memory, because the light is shining through; that is true cinema. Seeing that picture, we know we have reached the root and truth of what we are looking at. If we have done the exercise correctly, we get the picture and so the negative has gone, never to return and haunt us again, though we may have to return several times, as fire falling into an unknown precipice is not an obvious, easy feast. When we really get back to the source and have traced the river to where it starts, we can then walk beyond the source. It is the same with cellular memory. While we are playing our own cinema, we are feeding that and creating so many layers that it becomes more and more difficult to get to the source. Once we finally decide to give ourselves up and really want to see ourselves as we are, we let ourselves drop into the heart of our source. We see where the illusion started and we get that flash of light; we are no longer haunted. If we have created sequels, we may have to go for more flashes to clear it. We are instruments for the light; we collect experiences so that we can understand them and take them back to their source. Eventually we become a true instrument with no personal cinema and the whole of the individual becomes one divine cell in the body of humanity. This is what the blessing is about; it puts a bit of light in a cell, so that the cell can open up its heart and fall into the fusion of love, then we can once and for all get rid of that negative picture. The blessing will only reach the person's heart if they allow the death of that negative memory.

We have accumulated a lot of things that we don't really want to admit to ourselves, but all that is required is to give those pictures back and transmute them into light. The thing that stops us doing that is holding onto our sense of self. The resistance we put up to becoming light is completely crazy! We know that there is no other place to find the source of life than the manifested world on this planet. This world is the only place where we can decode the karmic helix. It is a technical energetic and spiritual world and it is all those things at once. If there isn't a camera, a film, a projector and a dark room, it cannot happen. That is why the great ones come back to help us recognise those tools.

The higher the vibration, the higher the sensitivity (non emotional) of the instrument, the more discrimination has to be used.

At the higher levels, the consciousness is not taken in by the cinema and has even lost the appreciation of time, because it is not expecting a result. Consciousness knows that if someone doesn't open their heart now, in time they will, so it is within the time aspect that discrimination has to happen and this is truly where 'you don't give pearls to the swine' applies. We can give a blessing to the little pigs and they will be the first ones to glow pinker with it and that will be appropriate, but if there is no appreciation of the inner life anywhere in the land, don't go and battle for it. The Pope of the Tarot isn't an evangelist or somebody who goes into battle, he will only bless the ones who come to him. This is to do with time management; it is not worth wasting time and light on the ones who don't really want it, because it doesn't work and if he is trying to make it work he is not a Pope. It only works for those whose lives are already open to the work of God, or are at an impasse in their search.

The idea is to be able to come back into the world, see it for what it is from the standpoint of the light and be able either to bless or exorcise it; The Pope will use whichever means is appropriate. To work in this way we have to be separate from the world. We have to be 'in it, but not of it', for if we are partaking, in the sense of being taken in by what is happening, we cannot change it. We are partaking in it, but are not taken in by it. However, we are here to apply the law of God according to the law of the land and if the law of the land is hope, we have to speak of the idea of hope. At the same time we have to be completely detached, so that we compassionately bless the hope in the world. The being taken by it, would be to come from an emotional point within us and say "Yes, I hope", for that person. It is refined, but quite different; the idea is to partake in the game without waiting for the rewards. We are learning to be in the two worlds, so as to align to the world of 'here and now' and give a way of carrying on, so if hope is needed we should give it. There is a big difference between hope and expectations; hope is always giving it to God to deliver.

Love knows and ignores all laws and restrictions; we cannot change the world if we are ourselves overtaken by its restrictions. We are in a virtual world and as we think, we manifest, that is really all there is. That which The Pope can manifest is effective, meaning that it becomes reality rather than virtuality, for the higher truth is constant not temporal. Virtuality is not effective, for we only need to change in one second the mindset of the group of people and that reality crumbles, because it is virtual. This is one of the reasons why the golden thread of the Ancient Wisdom has never gone out of fashion, because it is the only effective representation of the plan we have so far; as we search and rise this is what we find. It is also a mindset, but it is effective because it is the highest possible picture we can have of the plan.

The initiate who created the Tarot made certain that Number 5, The Pope, wasn't seen as the Pope in Rome, otherwise he would be dressed in white. The colours we see in this card are gold for incorruptibility, green for life, blue for hope and red for sacrifice. These make the achievement complete and give life. The first work is the alignment of personality. As the mind is orientated towards the higher goal, through restriction, frustration and other obstacles many questions will be asked, resulting in more and more anxiety, choices and options. Then, breaking away and taking responsibility leads to more freedom and uplift, so there is readiness to do the work and the initiate is not taken in by anything. The Pope comes back to save those who are lost, he doesn't come back for those who are on their path and doing quite well.

The Pope's gloves are white; white represents purity and gloves indicate ritual. When there is a ritual that is meant to be an inner one, then gloves are worn. If we intend to render sacred an act of ritual, such as the Holy Communion, we are going to have to be completely free of personal intent so automatically our hands are white. At the moment of intent behind a healing, it is white light that comes out, then after that the colour changes according to what the body needs. It is possible that the ones who were performing rituals in the past might have emanated white light, so that is where the idea of wearing white gloves comes from. Wearing white gloves would also be to prevent contamination or soiling of the sacred act.

The Pope is the one who is able to go right into the muck and grunge to find that which is lost, for it is not to be found in the pure stream of water, with the singing birds under the apple tree! He does not need protection from the muck, because what is pure cannot be contaminated, but like the surgeon, he goes in with the scalpel. The gloves are both a protection for the body he is operating on and for the surgeon himself. The operation is being done with the best possible knowledge of what the body is; The Pope goes into the darkest parts of the body of humanity to work on bringing healing to those who are lost. There is a treble meaning to the gloves, for there is no personal intent, yet there is protection and the process is non- intrusive and harmless. People used to wear gloves when going to church on Sunday and originally white gloves could only be worn by those who had purified themselves, before going into the temple.

We're not kidding ourselves here for we know we are not Popes, but at the same time when we perform a sacred act we can have the intent to be three-fold pure by checking our three levels and asking "What am I doing it for?" so that we can be pure of intent. A true blessing can be given by anyone, if at the time they completely align with the light in their heart. Children are very good blessers, because that pure energy is in them. Without the inner purity man will not be able to go through the rest of the work without losing himself. All the work that needs to be done in the illusion of the virtual world is extremely pollutive; this is why purity of intent is extremely important. If we discover a flaw on the way, then we can bless it, bring the picture up and transmute it into light, rather than put another picture onto it straight away.

The Pope of the Tarot has a serene face because he is in possession of the light and so can go deep into the failure of others and understand it. He has to go into the heap of manure and light up a luminous flower, so this vibration makes him like Buddha walking on the Earth. He is holding hope for others and so he must have incorruptibility, because he has to go to any depths, anywhere and at any time. He is not here for those who uplift themselves, he has come back to heal those who are getting lost and cannot help themselves.

There are two ways, which are represented by the two brothers; one who is going to evolve in the natural slow way and the other one who takes the way of the light-bearer. The slow way is where man is God's beast of burden, who takes all the suffering on the yoke and toils and works on behalf of the God of nature. There is always the possibility that through suffering he will eventually wake up to the God of mind. The other way is the bright one who says, "No way will I work for this cruel God, I am going for the God of compassion who tells man to use his mind and wake up!" This one is Lucifer, the light bearer, who uses his mind to be as God. The other one is the brother, or carrier, who toils and works. Real life is somewhere in the middle, so it is both work and understanding. The God in us can talk to us and bless us, but we are going to have to work. An apple tree will never give us a peach because there is no peach kernel, or stone to represent the essence and Soul of peach. Even the God we live in, who is a completely ordered, perfect, harmonious, intelligent God, will not get a peach out of an apple tree. The luminous flower coming out of the manure has to be pushed by will and opened with love to become that flower.

One of the two clerics in the card is looking up with arms open and the other is looking down, saying "Save me". Which of them will become the luminous flower? It is the one who has fallen in love with the blessings and the light. The other one is saying "I can't do it, I'm down there". He wants, but he is full of self-pity and he is focused downwards onto his drama, pain and needs. The card shows us the attitudes that man can adopt in front of God. One is completely open and in love and the other is full of fear. The blond haired one represents the passive aspect, has his head in his hand and is making the symbol of the six with his sleeve. He is the self-pitying one, so he still wants help and is child-like. This is the infant with the self-pitying of the six, that still needs a cuddle. The dark haired one, who represents the active aspect, is ready to become a cup himself and his hair is a lovely dark blue, with violet, lavender and black; like metal.

Their coats are orange and repeat themselves as yin and yang, dark and light, with the little dot of the opposite into the other one, to symbolise the two aspects in us. These are the two ways to God. It is the will to meet God that counts, whatever the approach, so the slow way gets there as well, for the one who goes to God by the work of intelligent action, will one day feel the burning flame of love in his heart. When we rise with our mind, if we don't at some point fall into love and feel that burning flame, we don't rise any further. The other one, who starts working through love, will one day have the mental illumination that will make him understand the language. Through love we understand and through understanding we love, it is always the same, these are the two ways and eventually they become one.

Their bald patches are in the position of the crown chakra. This is about uncovering the crown of the hair of animal man, so that the other kingly crown can be put in place. Hair symbolises strength and power, so when we remove hair, it is removing the power of biological reproductive regeneration.

 The gesture The Pope is making with his right hand has two fingers pointing up to make certain that light from above goes into the life of that little seed. We are all seeds and flowers and the heart of the flower can be touched, so that we can be completely in love, giving ourselves up to fuse with the higher love. There is a choice right up to that point, of either looking down or up, but while we are thinking there is a

choice, we are in fact still choosing to look down. When we are not looking down any more then we know there is no choice. That is the illusion of the beauty of freedom; freedom is separation and if we are free of something we are separate from it. Real love is fusion not separation, but we first have to separate from all the things we might want or need, in order eventually to die to our needs and then we fuse with ourselves. That is the great dilemma with freedom: while we think we have it we have the illusion of being free.

Freedom as we understand it automatically entails the idea of having rights, like claiming our freedom from slavery, but rights will always have another side, which is responsibility; the two go hand in hand. If we have the right to something, we also have the responsibility to be able to exercise that right; consequently choice and freedom will always have the seed of failure in them. If we are really looking to see which way we are going, we are still going for freedom and choice, which means we still have to go through avenues that don't work. A true friend helps us go for defeat, so that we complete the route we have taken, that way we learn from it. The problem is that people often go for drama and self-pity. The real freedom from slavery will only be realised when we include human/animal life in the respect that we show towards our own loved ones; this is inclusion, not separation.

The Pope gives benediction to the crowd and it is not known who is ready to receive it. Because his hand is not completely open, it can be given to crowds without profanation of the sacrament of the blessing, so it is not 'casting pearls to swine', wasting energy, or rendering the sacred ineffective by not being received. To protect the sacred act he does not give benediction with open hands, this way only the ones who want to receive it do so. It is the same when benediction is given to a single person, it can only happen if they want to open their heart, so The Pope is treating the crowd as if it is one person. Acts of sacred ritual mustn't be done just for the crowds; they have to have the deeper meaning, for we are talking about a high level of spiritual evolution. The blessing allows the upward movement of the inner will of the person receiving the blessing, if they want to recognise the opportunity.

The Pope is gazing beyond, for all he sees is the love of God. He is a wise man who has achieved the sum of supreme knowledge, this is signified by his three layered crown; he comes back to be in the world of mankind. The first layer from the bottom has flowers and is the world of nature that man is in.

The second layer is the intermediary world of man, which is man fighting for his rights and freedom; the world of re-vindication. This is the crown of the king in man and the fleur-de-lys represents the potential purity of the human kingdom.

The third layer has triangles and circles on it, for here we are in pure thought and sacred geometry. It is a huge leap between the first human crown and the third one, which is the crown of the highest initiate. This last one is the world as energy or the angelic world. This crown would never be worn by earthly rulers or kings who are in service to mankind, for it is for the highest position and is an etheric crown, where man is of the etheric rather than of form and nature. Ancient Wisdom tells that matter is not a principle and that the etheric is our true nature. The Pope of the Tarot lives at this level, rather than in nature and form.

In that higher world, freedom doesn't really mean anything, because there is complete fusion of the intellect with the higher mind. It is a world of communion and fusion with divinity and it ignores anything else which is not that, such as laws and freedom. Here total love reigns. If we want to identify with something, then it only works through an act of love, for in the world of energy it is only that energetic principle of love that attracts that which it wants to fuse with. Even the love of knowledge is an egocentric affair, because knowledge will only really feed the ego or the self. With The Pope, consciousness has gone beyond self, so instead of being egocentric it is extracentric.

We can be so self-centred that we want to take from, identify and be loved by every single aspect of life. That is not being extra-centric, that is being so self-centred and superficial that we want to recognise self-love in everything around us. Most people relate to other people according to what they want from them. Am I sexy? Am I good? Am I pretty? Am I intelligent? This is what the message is all the time when people relate to other people.

Then there is the self-centredness of the person who is learning to find their centre and so everything in the world is only there to serve their spiritual advancement and understanding. We all go through this and it is the only way to eventually recognise that we are just an instrument. If we can drop the cinema and all the wants and every-thing else, then the love and understanding of God comes out from everything that one looks at and we have become extracentric. We are always learning; it is a continual process.

When we look at the cycles in nature that are represented by the zodiacal signs, we can see the energetic progression of the inner work. In the spring, when we have Aries moving to Gemini, the instinctual life will tend to go towards the intellect, which says "I want to be loved by everything I see", so it is a superficial way of wanting to grasp life. When we are looking at the basic will of life, the spring is very much to do with the adolescent obsession of wanting to be loved by everything and everyone and that obsession can manifest in different ways. This only applies to natural cycles, so if your star sign is between Aries to Gemini it doesn't mean you are like that.

From Cancer to Virgo, the individual goes within, worrying about the origins in order to achieve criticism, a systematic rational doubt and discrimination. We are going back into the centre, bringing everything back and really wanting to understand it, because we know we have to internalise.

In the third one, from Libra to Sagittarius, we have to balance the experience in matter with the spiritual experience, because in the fourth one, which is Capricorn to Pisces, we are going to come back and serve.

It is important not to classify ourselves according to our zodiacal sign, for there are so many different stages to each sign. In Aries, for example, you could be a spring lamb in the final phase of spiritual sacrifice, or you could come back as a very young Capricorn just to learn to take responsibility for your actions.

The first two crowns of the Pope (nature and mankind), rely on development in manifestation and the senses, which is often mistaken for sensitivity. In the third crown we see the true sensitivity that is extra sentient. This is the one of the higher mind in the Soul at the etheric level. With the first two, the transitory world of man relies on the senses, the third one relies on a sensitivity which is nothing to do with the senses; rather it is the sensitivity of Soul. The first two are quite similar because man is very much of nature, so the crowns look vaguely the same. The little crosses on the different layers of the crowns are changing their form as they rise up and the top one is not on the crown itself, but on the top of the dome. This shows that the first two will rise organically and then this third one is a spiritual, energetic rise.

By the time we get to be a king and are truly in charge of our counsel, we know where we are going; we have responsibility and a big court around us. The next stage is the one that will definitely test spiritual or intellectual pride for a lot of people, for by then we know we can only do it for ourselves and this is where The Pope would come in. We can be a king and have taken a path that leads us very quickly back down into the world of nature. This isn't a bad thing, for nature will eventually turn up with her goods as well, but the real test will be the test of pride. We know we can do it from within and we can only do it for ourselves, but now we have to recognise that we need help to jump to the next level. Because the will aspect is so important, it can make us not humble enough to ask for help, or to listen to help. "I will still do it my way, thank you very much". We have to be completely wilful at that stage, but can we accept that so far our kingship is not working any more? Can we accept that we are starting to feel quite desperate, because if that is all there is it is not enough? Many kings will carry on doing what they are doing by learning more tricks, like monkeys, to try to keep the castle going, instead of simplifying it. This is the stage where people start to make it more complicated. We are going from having a lot of knowledge, mastery and skills to "Let's get more simple"; it is not "Let's go and learn more" which would be going back into the intellectual supremacy and the power of notoriety. This is truly a time where we have to ask for help, not in the sense of "I'm drowning and I don't want to", but by opening up our arms, like the cleric on the left side of the card and giving our authority to the highest.

The blue crosses on the white gloves are purified hope. We are talking about people who are on the path but who are getting completely lost, so we cannot remove hope; we have to purify it in ourselves for the blessing to be effective. Crosses always represent spirituality guiding man, for a cross is one of the oldest symbols of Ancient Wisdom and esoteric knowledge. This wisdom carries and guides nature and the intermediate realm, the latter being the human kingdom.

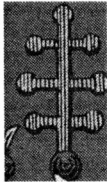

The Pope holds the triple cross, which represents the triple aspect of life. He holds the staff very softly, almost supporting his hand on it. This is the opposite of the manner in which The Emperor holds his staff, which is a dogmatic persuasion. With The Pope it is a comprehensive persuasion and it is out of understanding what is in front of him that he can persuade. He can rest on his staff, but he holds that wisdom firmly in his hand, not by grasping, but by being relaxed, because it is his nature and he is resting on it. He has understood.

The Sun is at the top of the staff, as the divine creator of life. The three branches have the signs of the six planets known to the ancients. His finger is on the green ball, which represents the Earth;

this tells us that he has rulership over Earth. Energetically it is the fire that dispenses its whole life to the system.

On the left side we have the higher Moon aspect, with Mercury on the other side, to represent imagination versus active or concrete intelligence.

Then on the next level down we have Venus, to show feeling and love as the way of the cold light of reason, with Mars as action. The two go together, because feeling cannot build without action and action is dangerous without feeling.

Jupiter and Saturn at the bottom tell us of faith and intelligence in spiritual philosophy and religion: intelligence looking for the help of a faith to understand and faith looking for some explanatory intelligence.

On the left is the path of the feminine (receptive) and the path of the masculine (active) is on the right side.

Receptive	Active
Higher Moon	Mercury
Venus	Mars
Jupiter	Saturn

When the Bodhisattva comes back and walks among men the only judgment he gives is love and understanding. We can see that though he himself is well beyond anything like judgment or hope, just the fact that he is here gives hope. That was the message of Jesus the Soul, who was a Bodhisattva in that sense and said "I can do it, so you can". This is the message of the Soul.

When we have achieved a higher level of an attainment, we truly need strength to come back into the heaviness of matter, so that our light can work here.

The Pope is the end of the first group of five and gives us the way of evolution. The rest of the cards are to do with the practical realisations in life that man will have to confront, so as to realise his evolution. We must be comforted and reassured that this first series ends with the benediction, because after this we are going into real life.

Let's not associate ourselves with pictures and symbols, because we have to be our own Buddha, our own Jesus, our own Soul, not the one that might be given to us as an example. If we want to be a healer or want to save the world, or if we have a saint or an idea in front of us that we want to emulate, we will never become our own saint or our own Buddha. The power of the senses and the inner cinema is so real, but these are bubbles that will have to be burst again and again.

There is no judgment, no pronouncement, just blessing. We are not here to be happy or unhappy, lucky or unlucky. We are here exactly where the will of God has put us, whether or not it aligns to our own little will at the time. If we are going on the road of the Bodhisattva, the task is to align to the greater will. All is energy and we will only find ourselves energetically in the place where we are going to be the most useful to the harmonious, balanced, greater life. Where we are is exactly where the greater life wants us to be at the time. Our personal life might not be balanced and that is exactly why we have to forget ourselves, for we are here to harmonise with the will of God, even if that means falling on our heads.

We don't see The Pope's seat because his status is that of a state of mind. The two pillars are reminiscent of the two pillars of Isis, The High Priestess, with the difference that he has brought them into life and matter; so instead of being on the metaphysical side of life, he has brought his living wisdom, living blessing and living love, into matter and life. This can be represented by the position of his two feet, which are creating luminous flowers every time he walks. Although he is sitting, he is not really sitting on a temporal throne; he is bringing the throne of the Holy of Holies (the spiritual abode of the Soul) into everyday life. The higher mind in love with wisdom is not preoccupied by ideas and systems to save the world; it is profound peace of mind at one with life, fecunding life with its holiness.

The Lover, L'Amoureux
Following the path of the heart

The Lover stands at a crossroad and has to choose which way to take next. The two women on either side of him represent the choices; on the one side he has the world of nature, with the simple, natural, easy life of the collective Soul; on the other side there is the crowned Queen, representing the Soul and initiation. The winged child is love, faith and the beginning of a new life: this child of the Sun holds a bow and arrow directed towards The Lover's heart, ready to instil in him an action born out of love. Will he give total commitment to the world of nature or to Soul? It is the will within him that will determine his direction and the love that will give the impetus for the movement. In this way he prepares for the next part of the journey, which will take him into everyday life.

The 1 has travelled deep into the unknown in the process of manifestation, associating itself with the measure of the space it moves in. This is the final landing where it has to include and accept everything it perceives as its own manifestation. A point of balance has to be achieved between the one mind and its space, where, through achieving the right attraction of forces, some fusion might occur, some light might brighten the space and the long process of naming can begin. This point of balance is a state of pre-fusion, where everything is being organised so that clarity of vision can really be achieved and we can see what we reject or accept. Spirit has reached the bottom of the cup and has come back aware. The realisation that the 1 who has the experience, the field of experience and the experience itself are one, is the epiphany moment of recognition of the self as the witness or the Soul, the 3 in 1.

In everyday life, if we recognise in others and in nature all the aspects that we have denied and refused in ourselves, then we can start the process of healing. This is to accept the pain, the burning of the dissolution and the transmutation of our ignorant past, by looking at the world with a more inclusive, loving open mind.

The initiate (the 1) knows that Isis (the 2) doesn't lift her veil at the beginning of the path. He needs the Active Intelligence of The Empress (the 3), the rigorous righteousness of The Emperor (the 4) and the compassion of The Pope (the 5), to achieve his passage through the two pillars of the Temple. He needs to find the mirror image of the sacred veil in himself. The polishing of his receptive cup with the power of his loving intelligence, will, with the light of his spiritual will, reveal the great wisdom he is seeking.

After many lifetimes of polishing and aligning its cup to the light of the Soul, the threefold personality will find the point of fusion that the initiate was seeking. Aeons will pass before humanity reaches this state of being, but for the individual cell of the body of humanity, which we call the aspirant, disciple or initiate, the time it will take will depend on the perfect balance between the forces of his spiritual will and the forces of the field of vibration that make up his physical environment.

When we look at the world, we look at ourselves. Because we have an idea of sainthood, beauty or harmony, we refuse at first to accept that it is ourselves we are looking at, for nothing is clean enough, beautiful enough, or good enough. We suddenly look at ourselves and at humanity and have the strong feeling that nothing has really been done; moreover what has been done is not good enough. Even nature, in her most uplifting beauty, hides thousands of murderers underneath her attractive tapestry. "I come from the vision of God and the stars and what do I see? War, abuse and decay everywhere!" The 6 has passion to drive it to seek love; it will find love anywhere and in everything, even in disdain or hate if it has to. We are looking at an accumulation of awareness where the animal instinct in nature has suddenly become distasteful. This is not the same as the perception of pure instinct, which will eventually be recognised as the will to be, which is divine. This is one of the jobs that mankind has to do on behalf of the God we live in, to go and fish out the misunderstanding, misuse and corruption of pure instinct.

I offer you a universe and you ask for freedom
I offer you a galaxy but you ask for peace
I offer you a planet and you ask for understanding
I offer you wealth; you shake your head in sadness
I offer you a wild flower, your laughter is a joy
I ask "What is your secret?" Thus came your reply –
I have two gifts been given, one is a gift of life, the other to be found
And used for the good of others and only this can be taken from me
By misunderstanding, greed and fear of me,
As I watch you turn to go, I wonder, are you the fool of fools,
    or the wisest of the wise,
Or a wise fool who knows. Each must find his own way to peace
    and inner self.

We have not been able to find out the author of this lovely poem; it is simple and very appropriate to Number 6. It truly tells us of that stage where we don't even want the wisdom, because nothing is good enough and then we go into our addictions, which make us feel oblivious, whether we hate or love.

The Lover will offer us the awareness of our addiction to the emotions, therefore teaching us to find our inner senses, which help us to detach from the pull of matter and to realise the wisdom. Even the meditation used by a wise man as the necessity of life will be used by most of us as a pleasure, to feel better or to feel superior. Everything is necessary, needed and holy, but it is the inner intent of the action or reaction which makes it either a prison or just a by-product.

When two personalities meet, it is like mixing two chemical substances. If there is any combination at all, both are transformed: this is the idea of the 6. When two people meet in a relationship it is an energetic process that happens, so we need to try to drop the romantic idea of love and attraction. We live in a planetary body that has a regulated life, this makes it more poignant and relevant because the love we feel is the only fuel we have which enables us to carry the will in the direction of the love.

Will moves according to nature when it is lost in the subconscious, while nature doesn't seek as her lover another guide apart from that of her own fabrication, which is the intellect. It suits her to keep the Spirit enthralled in her senses. Spirit will only be able to become the sole true guide and deliver the new vision, when the instrument within nature (humanity) can earth it safely, so nature will protect her progeny with fierce cunning. We see the example of so many sensitive people struggling to unfold their creativity under the intensity of a very brilliant spiritual urge, confusing the pain of transformation for depression and illness and holding on to addiction out of shame. Nothing is imposed on the system, the only imposition is the karmic will of the Solar System and this is an energetic happening.

It is only love that drives the will in the direction of the things that it loves. At first everything moves for gratification and survival, this is the love of nature where the need/love aspect directs the will. So it is extremely important to recognise what we want and love, because this is where our will keeps taking us until the higher love in the Soul and the will move as one.

The crossroads depicted in the card symbolise a time where a direction has to be chosen; the two women represent the two possible directions. The direction that The Lover is going to follow is that which leads to transformation; neither path is right or wrong. It would be an inappropriate judgment to think that the choice of the easy life of gratification is the downward path, for if the disciple hasn't engaged in all the needed experiences then he will need to do so.

This is the point at which he has to follow the direction that his love takes him, whatever that love is, so that transformation can happen. Even if the direction he takes leads to decay, he shouldn't be afraid to go for it. On the other hand, if he has actually done all the needed experiences and still chooses to go back on the path that follows the senses, this means he has an addiction; he has to recognise that, accept and tame it. The woman with flowers on her head represents that decaying process of nature, which is the manure of life. It is about dying and coming back again and again, in nature's recycling pattern. If the would-be initiate hasn't yet felt the fire that pushes him forward, he might need more experience; this is a tricky one, because we can all use this argument as an excuse to live for an addiction. Transformation can only happen with the love of the truth, the righteous and the good. We need to have love of life for itself, which removes the desire for self; in that love transformation will happen.

There is no birth of consciousness without pain; 'A man who has not passed through the inferno of his passions has never overcome them'. This is a relevant quote for the 6. The energetic way is the only way to bring about transmutation. If we do not make one with the things that are ours and that are part of the whole of humanity, we will never transmute them into unconditional love. This is the plight of the human being; he needs to understand that his passions are not so much his passions, but his job in this life: in this he works on behalf of the God we live in. This understanding lightens up the load, but at the same time makes it even more pressing, for the job has to be done: 'A man's got to do what a man's got to do'.

It would be a ridiculous and unwarranted assumption to imagine that we were more energetic or more intelligent than the men of the past, because what matters is not evolution but transformation. It is because of the beautiful, fiery sacrifice of the lives before ours that we can be in contact with higher realms. None of us would be bright enough to bring ideas, thoughts and love from far above the level of the mass-consciousness, if it weren't for the fact that others had done it before. It is that golden line of energetic thought and love that we benefit from when we connect to it. In the human kingdom there is enormous variation among individuals and their neuroses, so we need to approach each case with no assumption whatsoever. Looking at it from the higher point of view, human beings cannot be classified into neuroses or anything else, all we need to know is that there is energetic progress in the long march of fusion between light and matter. 'Knowledge rests not on truth alone, but on error also'.

With many of the great men and women who were true initiates, there was much personal suffering. A lot of them had to grapple with their private lives as well as their lives in the collective. Some found that very difficult, but as they brought in many new thoughts and ideas, the light of Spirit came into matter.

We are all in the same boat. Do you ever wonder why we still want the womb of self-gratification when we have understood so much? It has to do with responsibility and whom we love the best. If we love ourselves best, then we are only going to feed ourselves and take full responsibility for making ourselves as happy as we can, with the shadow of all the hurt that we will inflict on

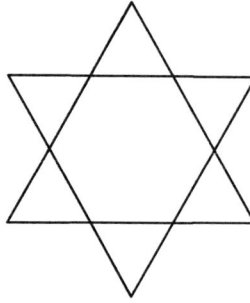

Figure 1. The symbol of the 6 – the Seal of Solomon.

This symbol holds within it triangles of fire and water, sacred geometry, the seal of Solomon and most importantly, the mystery of mysteries.

our environment. If we love our fellow human being best we have work to do, but we will have to be very careful not to take responsibility from them, for if we do we will serve their need rather than their development as a responsible unit. If we love the Spirit of truth best, then our Souls will respond to its call.

An egregore is an entity made up of the collective thought forms of human beings, such as we find in a religion, a professional body or a social establishment. Each human individual finds the family or egregore where its little thoughts will fit the best and then energy goes back from the egregore to feed each individual. It is like the womb of nature, but made by man's intellect. We have to ask ourselves, does what we love best belong to a particular intellectual class, race, or society? The most beautiful organisation, which to us is completely innocent, may be the thing we love the best, so we pray to it every day. This includes groups working at understanding Ancient Wisdom. All these groups are valid, but remember, they are egregores and if we establish our personality as belonging to a group we need to be very careful, for we could be limited by any rigidity in the entity of the egregore. It is always important to keep fluid and create a movement rather than an entity. The difference between an egregore and a group of people working towards a common vision is that with the vision they all move within it, not on behalf of the school or organisation, but on behalf of the movement of the vision. In that way the work is not sclerosed or crystallised and the responsibility is always to the love of truth, the love of the God we live in and the good of humanity. By striving to be as humble in our clarity as we can, it can keep on flowing and then we are in no danger of building an egregore. Egregores do need to be there to provide a structure and keep us on the road, as long as we don't limit ourselves by their structures.

Being alive on this planet we are faced with dealing with the practical everyday life and at the same time we have to be truly in love. We are in a situation where the level of evolution achieved in earlier lives gives us the opportunity for experience in this life, so we are exactly in the right place at the right time, according to our evolution, to experience the next level of life. We must recognise the experience as instructive rather than personal. This way we go through it and out of it, so as to see its place in the greater picture. The experience can only be individual, because we are like cells in a body. If we can come to a level where we are wise enough to feel the presence of the whole body and understand that it is a collective path, we do feel the hurt but feel it as natural and so we do not take it personally. As we recognise and look at the sufferings of mankind and all that mankind does to itself, we feel the depths of the pain twenty times more acutely, because we see it and feel it with clarity and the knowledge of where humankind is coming from. It is the tearing pain that nature has to go through when it is doing the experiencing in darkness, not the self-pitying drama of man. Someone can be completely distraught because of a distressing condition, finding it quite unbearable because they do not understand. They don't think they can survive it, but if they have seen it as part of the whole picture of humanity's work, even if they feel the pain more intensely, they are not so distraught because they know it will be sublimated through suffering in awareness.

In the animal world, an individual animal in pain has the great support of its group Soul in that experience. Unconsciously it knows it has to go into shock or flight, so it adopts the right position to deal with it; this is the 'unaware' wisdom of instinct. It is only in the human, where there is consciousness of individual pain that the real work starts.

The wise will eventually go back to the pure instinct of the group, so they will feel the pain and carry it, knowing that it will be alright because it will heal. But if we were wise already there wouldn't be much work done, so we have to individualise and go through being self-centred and egocentric, to the point where the whole universe seems as if it is against us, or for us, according to our point of view. We get to the point where we are swimming in pride, aloofness, detachment or disdain, according to which of these is our escape route. It could be downward into addiction, upwards into pride, or we could go into detachment and meditation; all of which are attractive. These activities are all necessary and useful, but need to be used with the right understanding. The only thing we are supposed to do is have experiences and then give them away. We must recognise our humanity; we have transmuted experience through the wisdom of our hearts, so we know it is all about the life of the God we live in.

The decision about which of the two directions to take, depends on our vision and communication with the environment. We can't decide which path others should take, but we can help them. We have to decide for ourselves which way to go, but we can't do it by ourselves. We can find the way only because of the previous generations of adepts, who have managed to go through the fire of their passions and give them up. They could do this because they accepted their humanity and accepted that they were part of every man, so letting go of being so proud, aloof, or degenerate. A lot of people go for self-destruction out of pride; this is a sort of spiritual rebellion that doesn't want to let go of the pride aspect. We all have some aspects of that, by wanting to be the most beautiful, or the bravest, or whatever.

There cannot be any transformation without the will to want it more than anything else; also we can't transform without input from a higher energy. This higher energy comes from the flames of love that burn eternally and the truth is that we are all one flame. We could keep on finding excuses to go on doing the human experience in ordinary life for infinity, by saying "We're only human", but once we reach the outer ashrams or the eternal, we can't use that as an excuse any more.

As the consciousness reincarnates, it always comes into a world that has gone through some sort of transmutation. If it is looking for a way out through the "We are only human" syndrome, it will follow its passion forever and will never end. This is natures' way of allowing the great magnetic body to do its transformation for us, by being in the mass consciousness of humanity. For example, if we understand that slavery isn't right, we come back in a world where mass consciousness has taken the great step of abolishing slavery, but then we see that one form of slavery has been replaced by another. Then we have to go and experience those more sophisticated forms of slavery because we have forgotten our understanding, which is that each man has got to think for himself. So if we say, "I am only human" and carry on and do as everyone else does, it is a false sense of freedom. It is no good waiting for humanity to come to that understanding, while being a slave in following the next thing that comes along. Isn't it better to be one of the pathfinders for the sake of the love of Humanity? But whatever we love best or whatever our passions are, even if it is self, we shouldn't feel bad, just recognise them without giving ourselves any excuses. However, we have to be careful, because we may go from passion to addiction, for addiction happens when we are still putting love into our burnt out passions.

When we are on the quick fiery path of the initiate, following what we love the best, understanding the truth of the Ancient Wisdom and the higher transcendental life, we can experience and understand the process of purifying the instrument or personality. What we are following is well beyond us, but we are serving it, so we do not need to go back into ourselves for more experience. By loving and feeling other people's plight at the Soul level perception, rather than at the emotional level, we will realise that we do not actually need to materialise and go through these experiences ourselves, because we are capable of feeling in depth and with awareness what they are feeling. Sometimes we can use the excuse of not having done an experience to go and do it, but instead all we need to do is completely identify with our fellow human beings. They are doing it, we are part of them and they are part of us. So by truly being able to put ourselves in others shoes we forget ourselves completely, then with compassionate love we can actually understand and feel what is going on. That is a shared, compassionate humanity and this is the way that we can help the other person understand themselves with peace in their heart. However, some of us can take responsibility when it is not ours, so selling ourselves either too short, or too high.

Mass consciousness says, "We are only human; let's have an easy enjoyable life and anything that requires effort is not natural". We know that all the group souls are specific expressions of the one Soul; each one has to have a characteristic, this is why we have the body of nations, with each being different. This way we can see how the one Soul is expressing itself through the different parts of that body, like the left arm or the right foot, with all the organs together taking responsibility for supporting that life. When we come back, we come as part of a wave of many lives, so we will reincarnate with familiar kindred souls. This is an energetic world, so the right vibration for a Soul's experience is obligatory and necessary for viability. If we reincarnate out of our previous group Soul, we will come in exactly at the right time to help or experience the group Soul that is incarnating at the time. We have a great big wave of life coming in, which is expressed in a race, culture, or country; these big waves have always got to be lifted up. There are two possibilities for a wave, it can either go into the ebb and flow, or, as the wave leaps up, we can go up with it and end up in a higher wave. It is an energetic process, where little drops of water are caught in a higher stream, for it is all one river. The aim of the initiate is to create such an energetic current of upward movement that it will take others with it by bringing a gust of lighted air into the mass of the body of water. This uplifts the individual droplets and there is the hope that they will catch the light by themselves and then go back into the stream to lighten up the darkness. It is all to do with love and thought; through these the material body can also be uplifted.

Before we individualised, we had human-animal group souls. The womb of the group Soul helps the little human entities to individualise; this is the only way that we are going to have millions of little eyes witnessing the life of nature for God. That great group Soul is the great biological and emotional mother of all those little sparks of light, which suddenly realise that they are individuals. Society is a biological result of that group Soul and is seen in all social structures, from the organisation of a village to the organisation of the largest country and we receive and take from society. There are all types of egregores coming from the individual people who work at pushing humanity forward, so what they give to an egregore is some kind of hope. It is a process of separation from the state of mass consciousness, in order to differentiate ourselves into more responsible, intelligent units. We have taken all this from the Soul of nature and we cannot give anything back until we recognise and understand the pure instinct within us. Pure instinct is noble and it gives back the Goddess her right to divinity.

Many parents expect something back from their children, but this is not nature's way, so while we are expecting something back we are out of God. When we are children we take, then we grow and become independent, taking the responsibility to give to our children. Then we let them go so that they can be independent and they in turn learn to give. The only way to teach them to give is to allow them their own pain and problems and not actually take those problems as ours, although we feel them greatly. That is how nature and pure instinct works. When we don't give back, we think we are due something back, like recognition, praise, or wealth: this is not the way the divine energy works. The divine doesn't want recognition and love, it *is* love and it knows itself. So we have to learn to recognise that while we are doing things for self, we are still in the womb, going for survival and self-gratification. When the road looks too hard, we go back for solace into the arms of 'mummy' (society) to get fed; this is alright when we are not strong, for the egregore of society is protective and is not to be broken down. But there is a time when society becomes inhibiting, then we have to have the courage to tear ourselves out of the womb. This is a rebirth and a real push out which we have to do, a breaking away. It is always done with an inward violence, because it is a cutting of the emotional umbilical cord that is attached to what gave us security and comfort; this is replaced by the support of one's own Soul. This is like a birth and however smooth a birth is, it is still a bloody affair.

The idea is for the mind to detach from the group Soul (not necessarily from an actual person) so that we are able to discriminate and see what is going on from the transpersonal point of view. While we are in the soup of mass consciousness, all we can do is stay in there and be a prisoner of it. The minute we start becoming a cook or a carer, we can put a higher perspective into the soup, so becoming more spiritual. Are we still in the soup? Then we haven't done our little birth yet. Not to worry, because we don't want a baby to come out of the womb before term; on the other hand, look and see if we are addicted to the soup. Even if we become a cook and a carer, we are still very much part of the group, working in it and no different from it. We might have 'closed a few doors where evil dwells', but this isn't effective if we cannot understand what we have closed the doors on. It is about complete openness, for even if we have closed the door on that experience, we mustn't think that we are above it. When we are in the Soul group, the brighter we become the deeper we have to go. In the initiation process we actually go underneath the people or the mass-consciousness, to hold the process of transformation and destruction. We take all the heat directly from the pan, then karma can do the work whether we like it or not. We can't do that holding if we don't want to associate with the dirty coat, for this is the densest manifestation of expression of the group. Do not forget that the one who carries this dirty coat might be the most courageous of us all! Eventually there are a lot of individuals thinking in similar ways, so it is not a group Soul but it is recognising the one Soul, which is made out of all these expressions.

Expression itself can become an addiction. We are here to express what the fusion of Spirit/matter/Soul in our particular combination is, but we can see that we can end up using that as an excuse to feed the egocentric love to infinity. Expression mostly still has to do with exhibitionism, but true expression is beingness. However, we do have to encourage people to express themselves.

We end up with strongly defined individual groups, which manifest solidarity and it is that solidarity which brings groups within groups to understand the oneness of life. To start with, the groups have to be as diverse as all the people in them and then eventually the one purpose will unite them, even though each one has their different tools and goals. The group Soul is neither good nor bad; it can only be in accordance with the measure of its participants.

The role of the initiate when he comes back is of considerable importance, because he has to take responsibility for the constitution and direction of the egregores. As we have said, an egregore is of human origin, coming from a thought form, so eventually we have to let them die, because the important thing is not the function of the institution but the flow of life through it. The egregore can only measure up to the level of the consciousness of its participants and we know that passion can create evil egregores. This passion has to be expressed and manifested because it is there in the subconscious; the job of the 6 is to burn out passion. While we are not taking complete responsibility for the situation we are supposed to be rising from, all we do is criticise everything around us. It is important to be very clear about our intent, for we live in a world that consecrates the ego.

The initiate has to come back into that obscure forest of humanity's group Soul, where he knows that most people are completely lost and so they have to find an egregore in order to find themselves. Some others just perceive the past in that dark forest, so they cannot find their way out without somebody helping them. At first they will come out of their group Soul into an egregore, from which they rise into some type of leadership role. Eventually they perceive the Soul; that is when somebody who is capable of initiating will appear. How are we going to ever come on the path if we do not start with a little bit of humility and ask; "Where is my teacher? Are you my teacher?" The true teacher will always tell us that we are our own teacher, for it is not enough to have understood a lot of theory – we have to go and do it. We shouldn't be shy in admitting our behaviour. We don't want to admit that we are silly or stupid, because we want to be like our 'higher' brothers in humanity; that is spiritual pride.

Once we have accumulated all that wisdom, we have to 'walk our talk', in everyday life, trials and temptations. Indifference to all that, may make us say; "I am wise like Buddha". Being condescending, having disdain, weakness and pride, all this is what we have to work on. We are still under illusion right up till the sixth initiation. Jesus Christ, the enlightened Soul, was going through the fourth initiation in consciousness at the crucifixion, so let's not kid ourselves! We have shadows and we must put the light on, so that we can see them. If we have any pain to do with the flesh and senses, for example how we look, or what we want, or love, see that these are illusion, they do not exist and they will die with us, for they are impermanent. Anything to do with the flesh and senses is relative, so there is no point in lying to ourselves and pretending by ignoring this. The rest is Spirit and absolute. We all use the weakness of the flesh to exercise our pride, but the weakness is not the worrying thing for it can be dropped overnight and is relative; it is everything else around it that is the problem. If we have spiritual pride or lack of self-worth, we try to be the best so as to hide the original problem.

The idea of feeling unloved or not loved for what one is, can lead to greed and love of food, which looks like something that needs to be cured. However, this is a sensory problem and what is real is the need to be loved. By treating the outward addiction we are giving the person an excuse not to recognise that we are love itself and that Soul contact through service and internalisation is the only cure. Pride can be expressed by great asceticism, by accumulating loads of possessions or rising to the top of one's art or profession. These all stem from the need to be the best loved. When we turn it around and let the skill of love flow through us, it overtakes everything we might have accumulated and transmutes it into even more gifts and love for the group.

When we are engaged in acquiring the things of this world we will automatically use the senses in a big way, because we love those things and they are a measure of our pride, whether it is status, cars, or property. The things themselves are illusionary and temporary; it is the pride itself that is the problem. The aesthete says; "Look at me, I don't need anything, I am so pure". They are in an ivory tower, which means they don't communicate with the world; this is also spiritual pride. We have to go through all these experiences to find out that we do not need to measure ourselves according to appearance or disappearance.

The fall of man is the only way to redemption, for it is only when we truly go down and recognise what we have done, that we can redeem ourselves. It is not so with the fall of Spirit, for here we are talking about a conscious fall, meaning an initiate who has awareness and yet is still being taken in by the sensory excuse of hiding some shadows; this is denying God. We all come back and are part of a web, in which we confront and transmute every single temptation. We are here to participate actively in the movement of the wave of life in which we find ourselves. If we feel that it is too much for us to do, we must put our hearts beyond ourselves and learn to love beyond where and who we are, this way we can start loving God. This is a big thing, because most of us would only love God by expecting protection back and this is not love of God. If we don't understand what it is we are supposed to love, the answer is that it is humanity with all its faults, the planet, the life we live in and the greater thing that is well beyond us. If that is too difficult, we should find a living creature such as a dog that opens our heart. Because we learn to put their needs first, we naturally do not blame them for their trespasses, so this takes our love beyond ourselves. If we learn to do that then we can start thinking the same way on others' behalf and that will bring us to the door of true love. While we think and feel from within the group Soul, or the mass consciousness, we only love ourselves. In thinking beyond ourselves, we drop that addiction to the self, so can learn to love beyond ourselves. The emotional pain we feel when a loved one falls into trouble through illness, accidents or behaviour is actually a pain for self, as we do not want the shame and disorder. When we see the karmic work that the group is invited to do out of this experience, we love beyond ourselves by accepting the situation. Then we feel the sharper pain of dissolving the shame, or the rejection, or any other self-centred emotion which might need to be seen.

Imagine what it would be like if we didn't have to come back and face all the temptations and all the shadows in ourselves. If we just looked at it on the mental/wisdom level then went into our cocoon and meditated we would probably feel great, but we would be like an engine that has never been tried or used. If we don't want to come back, this is denying life and the love of God. We all have had this desire not to come back, because we think that we can't endure more than we are already enduring. Actually the next time we can love more, because we have learned to love deeper and stronger through being back here. We may think that we are evolved enough not to come back, because when we are not feeling jealousy, hate, pride and lust we think we are alright, because we've understood, so we are in that warm bath of wisdom and love. But we cannot save ourselves if we have not encountered that which we must be saved from, so in falling we understand the weak and will know the words that can bring them back on the path. We need to experience all that in our flesh and minds. We must know the torture of doubt and of having made mistakes, so that we can direct ourselves with divine pity. We too have been lost and this is what pushes us towards someone else who is lost; it is not because it hurts us, it is because we know that something painful happened to us before, so it is going to happen to them.

Man has to understand man and offer him a helping hand, not through moral obligation or religious belief, or for reward, but helping the fallen one to be fully human in all his aspirations and weaknesses, with an intimate inner urge and warmth from the heart. This intimate inner urge is The Lover. We have been there before and been part of it, so we know there is nothing we can do except feel compassionate. When someone asks for pity, they ask for someone to understand their situation. The difference between compassion and pity is important to understand: compassion gives a sense of expansion, 'going beyond', which is an opening of the heart. We are in 'passion' with the person, without associating the pain with ourselves, so we are helping them to rise with the connection to the Soul. Pity is more to do with the understanding of the human condition, so is of wisdom rather than the love aspect. It has a sense of focus and holding.

The initiate has come back into everyday life with the whole metaphysical luggage; the apparatus is in place and he faces trials and temptation. He is quite protected, there is no fear in him and his eyes are closed. He has gone through the bloody forest of life before and he comes back with a full awareness of the dangers. He is now coming to experience and recap, after the initiation of having seen, felt and understood. He comes full of love, because he has to be clear enough about his love principle to be able to ask himself what he loves best. To be more loving and humble towards his brother is like a confirmation of his initiation; this is what the whole story of that cycle is about.

The crossroad represents the opposition between the divine and profane worlds. On the one side we have the path of wisdom and incorruptibility, taking man towards his destiny on the higher path. On the other side we have the easy and passive path, carried by the unconscious mass-conscious life of nature, with its tendency towards no responsibility. The path is coloured orange because orange is to do with moving in a specific direction, with intention. The woman on his right is in blue, which is the colour of psychic contact; she holds all the powers of duty and faith, given from initiation. The woman on his left represents the natural life. She is easy and passive, crowned with fragile flowers on her head. Both women pull on him. The one in blue is very gently saying no more than; "Can you pay attention?" The other one is a little bit more persuasive, because with the one hand she is holding his arm and with her other hand she is almost pushing him from the back, so the impetus is quite strong.

The woman dressed in blue is the Sun, or the Soul, so she will not put any constraints, or pressure on him. The blue of her dress shows spirituality and the red sleeve shows action. This shows us that there is no possible action worth doing if it isn't moved by the deepest, inner spirituality of the human being. Action is in vain if it is for self, or for immediate gratification. Eternal action is the only one worth doing; any other action is only the manifestation of thoughts, needs and wants. When it comes from above, from something beyond self then that action is truly divine. The effect of this on the world may not be seen for a long time and it takes more than one man or one group to do it, for it is action with no immediate effect. The deeper we become the truer we are, so when we have reached the depth at the centre it is very easy to get out of the way and just allow Soul to appear.

She represents duty to life, which is much more than simple duty; she is the life that has completely given over to the greater will. She has given her own will to the higher will of the one life; this is shown by the crown on her head. She will help the initiate regulate and align his instincts, so that they can be used purely, thus achieving the proper detachment from the group Soul. Then the whole of his being, right down to his instinctual life, can be completely realigned. All this is going to be spelled out by the responsibility that he is going to accept. She is definitely a mode of life and more than a picture, for she represents a whole way of living, which has to do with inspiration and always having one's sight on the metaphysical and the eternal. She is going to help the initiate not to follow the universal moral code of society if he thinks it is not right. She is truly the path of connaissance, or the knowledge in the sense of gnosis. Her qualities will give him effective action, because the influx doesn't come from the world but from that higher purpose, which instils a duty that obeys the higher will. Here we are not expecting a pragmatic, immediate goal, for we are well beyond the personal. We are not going to start thinking that if we are not succeeding we are no good, because the goal is beyond ourselves and we know we have to keep on. In the long term it is that type of everyday life that we live, with our action coming from above, with complete duty, respect and alignment to the fact that it is our life, but not our life; for it is a life of love and duty to a higher order. This is what will allow the eventual transubstantiation of the world.

The crown is gold and therefore represents incorruptibility, so she will not be stained. Her thoughts are governed by the will of God, so she doesn't put any pressure on the initiate, she only requires his attention and that has to come from him. There is no restriction, the only obligation that we have is to what comes from within; there is no obligation to a group or to anything external. Imposed obligation will only harbour resentment or martyrdom, the only obligation is to the God we live in. It is an inner search that moves a man towards what he wants, towards the light, or whatever is his goal. God doesn't redeem men against their will and helping people means saying; "I'm here" that is all, there is no threat and no promise. Nothing can modify the decision for there has to be complete freedom of choice; any little speck of forcing doesn't deliver, for a higher energy cannot be forced into a unit that is not ready and open enough to receive it.

The name of the card, The Lover, is relevant, because absolutely no movement is energetically possible from within man without the moving quality of love. We know that in the personality it is the emotions that move us; in the initiate it is love that moves him. However clear our wisdom may be and however well we might have understood the esoteric, occult side of life, without love we are very dangerous. Initiation will always start from the point of view of mental and spiritual understanding, but it cannot actually express itself and manifest if there isn't a movement of love. However, the apparatus has to be in place from the intellectual, higher mental point of view, otherwise we get lost in the illusion of everyday life. The Lover is ready to face his illusions and it is his faith in a deeper more inclusive love for the world that moves him into action. This, rather than work or deeds, will save through blessing. Knowledge per se will never reach perfection although it can reach near perfection, but to break through we have to want it, therefore real love has to give the energetic movement to push the knowledge through the barrier that it needs to surpass. We do it within ourselves, but we cannot do it without the mirror of what is around us, to reflect to us where it is we want to go, what it is we want to fuse with and what we want to love. It is that link or relationship between the knower and the thing that is known, which makes the movement, the assimilation and the oneness possible; not the hard, mercenary task of ploughing on with the job. The work will keep us going, but what will make us 'become' as we go, is love. It is always a process of assimilation, of losing ourselves by fusing with something bigger or smaller (if it is a small thing we love); it is always something beyond us.

That movement from the initiate (subject), to the thing that is wanted (object), gives a true respect and rapport between them and so does not subordinate one to the other. The meaning of the word respect is a difficult concept, as the word is used in so many situations where it is felt that there has been a lack of respect. In fact this is because we have not owned our reaction, so have put the responsibility of the hurt onto 'a lack of respect' from someone else. Eventually we understand everything that is alive and manifested is an expression of the God we live in, so has a rightful existence and should be respected. If there is no respect for something, there is no love for that part of God. It has to do with identification and affinity with the other and knowing it from within. It is not judgment, but sympathy; a shared feeling and total identification. It is about recognising God in the thing in front of us; this is only possible with the perception of the higher mind or Soul, which sees that everything is perfect and so has the highest understanding and respect for life. We can understand intellectually that there is another living being in front of us, but while we come from the intellect we come from judgment and explanation. We lose our wisdom when we look at life as something we can take from: this is an intellectual understanding and shows a lack of respect. A true understanding can suddenly make us drop into our hearts and experience the oneness of the human condition; it is love that enables that to happen.

The average man who is completely lost in his everyday survival and self-gratification will have a very hard time to understand another, unless he sees the other as exactly like him, in which case he will understand the man through his own glasses. In that position of love and understanding, we cannot judge, we can only describe.

Faith is a facet of love, because it is not conceivable without love. When we have love, faith is automatically a part of it. If we haven't got faith in what we are doing at the time, it is hardly worth pursuing. The scientist will never find anything; likewise the religious person can't help others on the path, without faith. The Lover in the card has his eyes shut, for he is being driven by faith; he knows inside that love will prevail to the end and he feeds on that in order to carry on. Faith can move mountains. Work and deeds have no value before faith and all the externalisations have temporal value, if there is no faith behind them, for it is the faith not the deed that ignites what is done. If we do good deeds and charity only because the 'good book' tells us to, we are going to be greatly disappointed, because God is not necessarily going to give us something back for it. Doing something for a reward is of man, not of God, for divinity is not a market, it is absolute. Meditation, good deeds, charity and all things that we do for reward are training grounds; as such they are not to be judged but encouraged, because within these acts the little penny can drop into the heart and the person may meet their Soul.

The woman dressed in blue represents love, faith and duty in its highest form. We don't do service because we are going to be rewarded, but we serve out of love because it is our nature. The mind is liberated because the will has become one with the universal will and so it is a complete manifestation of comprehension, through total love.

The Lover is one of the highest symbols of the Tarot, because he is truly in the position of coming back into life to make it sacred, through his focus on love, wisdom, duty and truth. He has achieved the death of the illusion of the self, so he is ready for action and is not worried about getting quick results.

The Child, with the Sun behind, represents love, faith and the beginning of a new life. When we bring love into action, we bring in awareness and love of the work on behalf of the higher cause, so then we can start a new life. That aspect of love has to be a child; unspoilt, clear and not afraid of life. It has only got a future and a glorious past, it comes from the Sun and therefore we have an aspect of divine love.

Eros is the love child with heavenly blue wings and a bow and arrow. The arrow is about action, so it has to strike, push and move. Neither Spirit nor Soul, nor love will decide which direction the man is going to take, for that is entirely up to him. It is definitely the kick-start. Love moves mountains, but it will not tell you which mountain to move; you have to choose. It is the will within him that is going to determine which way he is going to go; it is the love in him that is going to make him move. It is an internal state that dictates the direction, so where he is going to go is entirely up to his inner landscape. The arrow is the force of the love aspect, which will push him forward into that direction. Once this has happened, it is almost like a ball being catapulted out of a cannon; it is extremely difficult to get back. The more we move in one direction, the more difficult it is to change that direction; this is energetically true of any decision we have taken, regardless at what level. The love/want aspect of the thing we want to be with, or want to do and which moves us down any road we have chosen, takes us right to the very end. If the situation we find ourselves in is one where we realise we might have made a big mistake, then we need to understand that karmically we had to go and burn out that particular passion; this makes it into a healing and so it is alright. It was the manifestation of something that was within us that had to be exteriorised, so the love aspect of the Soul in us was wise enough to accompany us fully into the action of our mistake.

We have, in this card, the whole dilemma and the whole beauty of life. The desire for life and the will to be alive is very important, for refusing life is refusing God and is a rejection of his work. It is only on planet Earth that we can progress, because it is only here that we can 'walk our talk' for the sake of transformation. This requires a deep faith, which fills The Lover with love, so he can meet himself and the work. While we are seeing God as something that can make us feel better, we are still seeking comforts for our needs; this is entirely to do with the five senses. It is only on this little planet through biological awareness that we can see whether we are free of the addiction to the senses and of the love of drama that goes with them.

Having understood the relative value of what he is going to meet, the initiate understands that renouncing or giving up and wanting to die, are of no value by themselves. If he comes in with a bright spark, he realises that it is all an illusion, for the only absolute values are love and truth, which enable him to come back to face life without fear. Once we are here and have love and awareness, we are well placed, with heart and head aligned. Remember our origin, the Sun, for we are going back to it. Whenever we think "What is the point", this is only a reflection of the pitiful condition of mankind and is therefore relative and temporal; when we realise that, we ought to have no disillusion. The mind becomes aware of an egocentric movement towards the centre, which eventually makes us fall though that centre and realise, "I am dead, but I am still here. I'm hurting like I didn't think I could hurt and yet I am still here". In recognising that awareness, the 'I' becomes something much more permanent and so will survive the impermanent situation of the life on this planet. We feel it all strongly, so we can be in true despair and renounce love, yet even knowing that, all we are doing is rebelling against the human condition. We have been there before and so we know that we will survive it. Then the acceptance of our job description makes us more effective in our work and removes fear. When we are aware of the situation and environment around us, there is nothing that can be experienced in this Solar System that can 'kill' our Soul. Understanding this is awareness given back to the great life of the Sun.

We know that the more we give of our life, the more we serve and love. Venus, instead of renewing herself slowly with volcanic activity, does it all at once, turning herself inside out completely by burning herself. It is a complete act, there is no holding back. The evolved 6 works like this, taking everything into the inner furnace and transforming it all at once. This is symbolic of unconditionally surrendering to love and the karmic will as divine justice, for a complete transmutation.

When we have looked at the situation we are in as an opportunity for growth and for more love to be released, we are going deeper into our divine aspect. Then the pull of the images and illusions loses a lot of its strength. This means that we can come back with less and less fear, until eventually we are fearless. In the name of love we will be ready for anything; it is love that moves all our chakras to align and purify our personalities with the Soul, in the petals of sacrifice on our brows. Nothing gives more certainty than the deepest love and the certainty is what removes fear.

Our initiate is not judging – he is a good shepherd. He approaches the practical world with his arms crossed over his chest and his eyelids shut, to demonstrate that he does not need anything from this world, neither recognition nor appreciation. He goes in with his ideal vision that nothing can soil or destroy, so he cannot be eroded or corrupted. He is a shepherd who is affirming his choice by radiating love.

The Lover's hair is blonde, which represents a golden halo, or a yellow-golden aura around the head. This denotes that he has given his mind to love and purity. He has Soul connection, which is when things can be understood and seen, for he is completely receptive. He brings love to the world; a love that goes beyond freedom. Freedom is a way to rise up from one level of consciousness to the next, but by its own definition it is separative. Love is the opposite, for it fuses and unites. Here we are not concerned about our own freedom, because we have separated enough to reach the level where we see and understand the unity of all life. Freedom has been given to man so that he can find true love and be reunited with his source.

When we have understood, we stop fighting and rebelling. Anything which forces us, or puts pressure on us will only achieve an artificial sense of love and freedom. We have to start by rebelling against our parents and society, but eventually it is not the fight, it is the giving up of the opposition to life that brings in the love. The manifested world is a mirror because we perceive it as a reflection of our likes and dislikes. Whether in society, human beings, or the divine, we have in its reflection a comprehensive meeting of self held in the one life; that higher perception can only be achieved in the initiate beyond the need for freedom and at the end of rebellion.

It is the role of initiatic societies to reclaim all the notions belonging to the life in the absolute and to bring men towards divinity, through a path of love and identification with the entire creation. There is no other mission, no other job for initiatic groups. Ancient Wisdom has to regain its central role in everyday life to uplift humanity's consciousness. It has been misused only because people didn't know better and didn't go deep enough, or because they tried to be God on the planet. All we have to do is reaffirm what the original life was so that it doesn't get lost; more and more groups are working in that way. We are all an expression of the divine and our little planet expresses love and joy.

Love doesn't impose itself, neither will the Soul, but the Soul will be involved, because it is the result of experience. It is in Soul that we do all the mirroring; it is Soul that burns when the cellular memory has to be seen. It is the love from within the Soul that will render the template clear and bright, so that the pure instinct can reveal itself.

Some people who have plunged into the occult have understood a lot, so will criticise organised religion or the exoteric ways of doing things. Let the children play; it is the way we learn! Few churches tell us to understand or know, some may even tell us that personal research is dangerous, egocentric and even of the Devil; some tell us to accept, serve and bow our heads. If we go into that infantile servitude, how are we ever going to start thinking for ourselves and doing things in our own way, which is the only way we will find our inner path? It is by our own efforts that we will arise and realise ourselves. We will recognise by the same token that others are doing their own thing, so 'Live and let live'! Many people start the journey by hating, criticising and judging, but if we are already aware, we will know that once we have gone through the rebellious stage to gain the awareness, the rebellion eventually becomes determined courage and we accept and serve; quietly lowering our heads in humility.

The woman in green at The Lover's left side represents the easy life, which is about wanting to go back into the womb of nature, where we are fed, pleased and where things are 'done to' us. It has to be a woman because we are talking about the higher Soul of nature. She is dressed in the yellow and green of the passive and latent aspect of nature. Flowers are bright in the morning and dead by the evening, according to the cycles of nature; our desires, senses and needs are transient, like flowers in nature. If we follow their cycles we are in a vegetative state and we like it, so be aware of it. This state is being alive, but not really knowing we are alive; it is a life with no responsibility. It doesn't question life, or if it does the answer is "But we are only human". Anything that will come and disturb the peaceful rhythm, or even the stressful pattern that the person has made for themselves, is avoided. So it is living for one day at a time, seeing the bright flower without noticing the decay.

The one who chooses the way of nature lives entirely for himself, with no desire and no effort to detach himself from mass-consciousness. So he stays in his pleasures without the light of understanding, or without making any engagement with responsibility in the future. The consciousness is not awake yet, so there are no questions and no motion, for he is still in the womb and will let the wave carry him like a child. It is an extremely painful process to detach from the group of the mass consciousness; it is like the first man, Adam (representing humanity) being chased from paradise. How many children carry that same hurt in them, the first time they went to school, or the first time they were left with somebody else? We are looking at a pain that lingers on, as we hold on to the memory of being looked after by 'mummy'.

The breaking away of that state to overcome stagnation is painful and bloody. Many people will anaesthetise themselves with other thoughts, such as their social status, other people's opinions of them, reading their newspaper, or the fear of law and order. We busy our mind with all of this to avoid making this step. It is about safety in numbers and renouncing personal growth, so most will stay where they are.

What makes a person choose one path or the other, or decide to leave the easy-life path for the other one, is the vision of falling in love with a higher more demanding authority. The will aspect will always go for the thing it loves the most. Will is like the 8, it pushes us, helps us to succeed, even in failing while that is what we want. So the will pushes us in the direction that we choose; this is how free will operates. Also it is the vision from within the love aspect that will fuse with the will and take us down the road we choose; so it is what we love best that drives us. It is very much to do with what we've understood and how we feel within our own inner landscape.

Falling in love with a partner or a cause is definitely the love aspect from within wanting to exteriorise; it is only that which will render the self-love strong. When we speak of 'self-love' this is not the love of self, which is an egocentric thing, but loving the life within us or the higher self. Personal relationships help mirror our difficulties in loving the world as it is.

The man represents humanity in front of its past and future. The wave of life can either lift itself into the greater waves of universal life or fall back into the impasse of nature, where it can make itself felt through another flood or volcanic eruption, because that is the only way nature has found of breaking stagnation. When humanity en masse hasn't got enough initiates to bring up that big wave of higher life onto the planet, then nature takes care of it herself, creating another disaster; or we create a disaster such as war, so as to break the stagnation.

It is like the lower Sagittarian condition of being half animal, half man. His mind is flying up to the sky, he wants to understand and get answers; it is through that uplift that he can lift his animal mass-consciousness from the group. He throws loads of arrows in as many directions as he can, which are like all the wrong questions looking for the answers in the outside world. It is only the evolved Sagittarian who knows how to throw the arrow, because he has completely redeemed his animal side, so the arrow will come back and give the answer. The goal is to aim at the inner self so as to pierce something inside and get the clear water of love falling on us; to do that we have to receive the arrow into us and we have to dare to be hurt.

With Number 6 we have the seal of Solomon, which is beauty; it is made up of the two forces within that have to come together. Spirit comes into form to inspire matter to uplift, listen and sublimate; this is the role of the initiate. The Lover comes into society and the world to inform them. The ones who recognise the radiation of the Soul will want to sublimate themselves, so that they can start the work and carry it on.

There is a misunderstanding in the perception of Number 6, which is the idea that it is the contemplation of physical beauty that wakes up the desire for the eternal in man. Actually, it is the contemplation of the beauty of the mind behind Active Intelligence that does it. When we look at the diversity and the incredible intelligence of the manifestation in the physical, we cannot but be in awe; this creates the desire to know the eternal. The more we become a scientist with the eyes of a Lover, the more we are going to understand and love. The understanding that focussed on physical beauty as appearance and form was not at all what was meant; from that came our obsessions with the glamour of possession and therefore cultural perception of beauty. What was truly meant was the beauty of the intelligence behind the manifestation of life. We don't need to be scientists to appreciate and see the incredible diversity of the leaves when we walk through woodland. As well as the trees there are plants that grow in the shadows under the trees where the sun doesn't reach; their leaves are made so that they can take full advantage of what light is available. It is beautiful to look at that, for the intelligence required to make one leaf is quite amazing. We have to be careful about the illusion of beauty, because the beauty is really in the concept of the incredible multiplicity. There are only very few elements out of which life can be built, yet we look and see the endless diversity around us; this is the beauty. We will never be able to reinvent nature; all we can ever do is come away from our heavy technology and copy nature in her simplest form.

The key to Number 6 is the idea that iron chains are easier to break than chains made of flowers. The images that we put on the Tarot and on the numbers, all relate to everyday life, but at the same time are very symbolic, because they have to speak of the deeper aspects of life in the language of everyday life. If we gave these images to a classroom of children they will come out with a lot of truths, when they think about this idea. If we have iron chains everywhere we are really going to want to break them, in the same way as if we have no freedom we will want to break free. So it is very easy to see why we would want to rebel against the iron chains. If we put anything that is alive in a prison, it will try to break free, or else go mad; going mad is another way of breaking free and avoiding the situation we are in.

On the other hand the chains made of soft, sweet flowers, represent temptation, facility, happiness and an easy everyday life. This is much more difficult to let go of, because wanting to indulge will make us think; "We are only human and that is what we are here for anyway". It is actually difficult even to see that we are imprisoned by all these nice little flowers. We do not notice them and if we do, they look so innocent and fresh that we may feel there is no reason why we shouldn't enjoy life and feel good, for we are being told all the time to express and glorify ourselves. All of this is man-made and of the intellect not of nature, so nature is not guilty here and neither is Spirit. It is coming from little humanity that sees itself as God! We don't even see that the flowers are dying and the innocent are being sacrificed, or that it is all starting to decay. Decay attracts more decay into itself, so we go into self-abuse and we can't see the slavery of that. We say, "Let's get excited every day so as to feel alive", because that is what we think we are supposed to be doing. Man doesn't recognise his addiction; he thinks that everything is a good thing, as long as it brings us peace and happiness, or does not distress us. This doesn't mean that we must not help ourselves and that we must not render life happier, more beautiful, or healthier, but we have learned to let go of all the mindsets that this is all there is; this is the aim of life.

We are clad in both types of chains. The work is firstly to recognise that if we act with the action of our inner spiritual being, we still can enjoy the fruits of life, but are not doing anything in order to obtain them; secondly that we do not need them for our happiness, as inner peace and loving have replaced anxiety and wanting.

Be more yourself, more radiant, more into life and giving. This is the only way you can do your higher duty and let the love in you express itself. We're born out of a very beautiful instinctive Soul and we have used it and abused it for an easy life, so now it is time to bathe it in the light of its solar Lover – the Soul of mind.

The Chariot, Le Chariot
Making it easier

With the Chariot comes zeal. The Charioteer is a trailblazer, bringing back the light into the open cup of the Love; he is ready to 'walk his talk'. Holding the baton of authority he stands and looks ahead towards the goal. He brings in the fiery energy of Mars, which is tempered with the generosity and expansiveness of Jupiter. Before him sit two sphinxes, one black and one white; they are joined at the hip and represent the fusion of the conscious and subconscious minds. The four 'legs' of the Chariot reach up to the stars, two being coloured the green of the Earth and two the gold of Heaven. The Chariot is a war instrument, but it is a war on all that keeps us addicted to the sensory life, for the Charioteer has gone beyond himself and is becoming an instrument of co-creation, so as to bring the highest vision of mankind to the planet.

159

When man has understood and accepted his role in the creative process, he lends and aligns his mind to the mind of God. The further he rises the more he understands that he belongs to God, so his mind can fuse in ever more sacred spirals with the energy of past initiatic wisdom. The Tarot is the story of such an elevated mind coming back into matter, to work at the exteriorisation of the different qualities necessary to achieve further alignment. In this work many trials have to be faced to attain the goal of wisdom. Each card represents a turn of the Spiral in the journey towards wisdom.

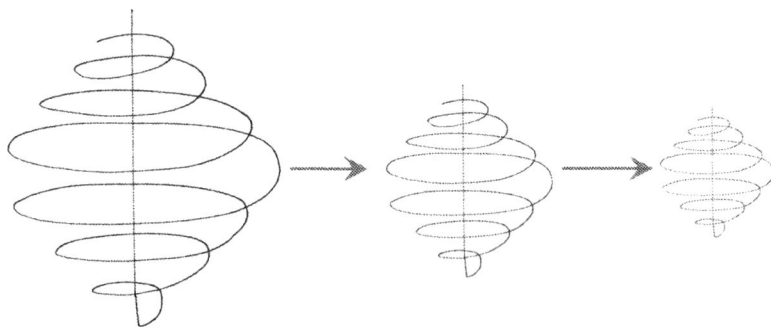

Figure 1. Spirals and spheres.

Each spiral itself represents a sphere which is created by the same movement, repeated time and time again and following a karmic path according to its own level of vibration and environment; it moves from the atomic to the universal- all is energy.

Each turn of the spiral is an energetic atmospheric sphere by itself, so we can see that when we rise from one level of vibration to the next, we carry quite a portion of the older vibration as shadows of untransmuted misunderstandings. When we move into another sphere of consciousness, we bring the wisdom and experience of the one we are just leaving into the new one, so everything positive and useful has been taken from the previous sphere. Because of this there is going to be a strong connection between specific cards, as the energy moves from one cycle to another.

We can now look at the 6 as the cup, where the concept has been harmonised in a final well defined process of creation. The cup receives the 1 (the Spirit of light), then flows with ever changing information and endeavours to manifest the message. So it is at the point of fusion of the light with the concept, that the 7 (magic) is seen as manifestation. The seventh stage is a bringer of the new spring and the ceremony of constant renewal. As we come into it we

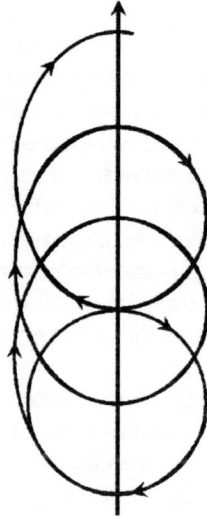

Figure 2. 'Before enlightenment chopping wood, after enlightenment chopping wood'.

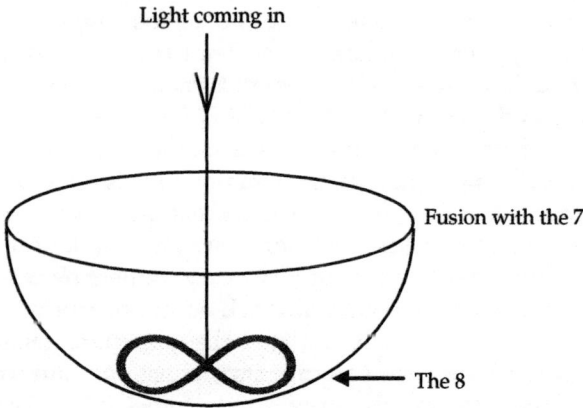

Light coming in

Fusion with the 7

The 8

Figure 3. The cup of the 6.

feel the death of the old and the rising of the new; this is what we call fear. Our Charioteer is exalted, so in him fear is transmuted into zeal. The next step in the 7 is to recognise what drives us. The 7 is the process of becoming the thing that our mind is contemplating.

The sixth card, The Lover, is the hinge by which the door can be opened. The 5 of the Pope moved the process on to the love aspect through his compassion and blessing, for without these qualities there is no possibility of a choice that will move the Soul. The rapport between The Pope and The Chariot is the same process, for without the blessing there is no ability to lift up and climb onto The Chariot. A lot of people will not use the energy of the blessing, so they don't use this opportunity to catch a glimpse of the light, because they are so focussed on pleasure, needs, wants and status. A blessing can be present even in small things, such as being touched by the beauty of what we are looking at. The observation of the beauty of nature gives us the possibility of uplifting ourselves, for it takes us into the pure Spirit of nature which is greater than us.

We have soiled and tainted the lens of our nature, because we have needed to go right into the subconscious and manifest all the past deeds in order to reveal the Holy Grail. We have to have the courage to bring our demons up into the light, so the Charioteer is going to make certain that the demons don't exist for him any more because he knows that they aren't real.

The Pope is the perfect 5, the measure of man and the becoming of the perfected Soul, so he blesses everything. Then there is the 10 (5 × 2), which is the perfect number in the sense of Spirit coming back with the greatest potential. We need all the attributes of the 5 to be able to turn sensuality and the scientist in us, into love/wisdom. When this happens, The Pope of the Tarot is like the Christ or the realised Soul of man. In this way man is rendered perfect, ready to shine out and do the work.

The Lover represents perfect balance and completion, so when the 6 is functioning at its highest then the stage is set and is perfect according to what is required for the situation. When the 1 comes back as a 7 into a new spiral of experience, the work of the initiate will start with the re-evaluation (8) of the judgment on its situation. This work will then have to be internalised in The Hermit (9).

If we look at the creativity of nature, the Active Intelligence aspect is awe-inspiring, for it is re-creating itself constantly, but we have to remember that the impulse for creativity comes from Spirit or universal truth, which is far beyond nature. The Soul of nature serves as a blueprint and a coded matrix for the most intelligent way to reproduce a concept, so that when Spirit comes in it will rush through unimpeded with its eternal zeal. This process has taken place over millions of years and it is extremely clever. Nature is so clever that we can bring back life from the past through DNA. However, we need to remember that it is not man doing it, but nature. The skill comes from the completed cup, which is represented by the 6 or the Soul of nature. This is the blueprint which has all the know-how to create the millions of possibilities of manifestation. The next step in the 7 is to be aware of the inspiration behind the creation. In nature everything is automatic and unconscious, so it suffers or accepts and just gives birth to itself. Nature creates pure instinct and that quality is attributed to Mary. When purity is there it is possible for pure self-awareness in truth to be born from it, in the same way as the light comes out of the dark; this is how Mary gave birth to Jesus, the human Soul. Through this conception the Spirit has touched Mary's heart and she has fallen in love with the creator. The result is the Soul of mind, which is Jesus, the light of the world.

To become a co-creator, any personal interest has to be transformed into forward moving energy, so that we can merge as far as we can with the omnipresent idea. As we follow that process we realise that any ideas that we have are not ours, for we are only channelling or mirroring whatever is around. The only thing we are supposed to do is to hold the thought that truth and love will prevail in the end, so touching on the deepest ideal within us as often as we can. This is what being a co-creator is and it is the only thing we are here to do. When we align to the highest possible idea or vision for mankind, we can actually bring our own vision into focus. Here we are not talking about our visualisation of what we or the planet will be tomorrow, we're talking about the certainty of something deeper, which makes us a beacon of light because there is no doubt in us.

The Chariot is the quality of mind meeting its goal in the heart of its being, giving it the depths of purpose and the utmost certainty that in the end truth and love will prevail. In our lives there is always a seed of what our becoming might be, or a vague shadow of what we were. The minute we see a manifestation of our seed or shadow it is like meeting ourselves, but if we haven't started to express what it is, we can recognise it as something almost impossible to get and we make a strong retreat into what we used to be and into what yesterday used to be like. It feels like falling back with a huge splash, because we thought we had mastered that shadow, or the 'becoming'. We can liken it to a rabbit in the full blazing headlights of a car, so transfixed and terrified by the light that it freezes and doesn't cross the road. The more accurate the vision of ourselves in the light, the more we resist and retreat into the stagnant past, for enlightenment is the death of what we think we are. Those under the influence of 7 have that tendency to want to die and not be here. They retreat so that they do not have to see reality for what it is, because they want to be better than what they are. This is a remnant of the 6 atmosphere that has to learn to love everything about life. They need to recognise that really what they want is to be at peace and accept life as it is, it is just that they have translated the experience as the fear of not being good enough. Now with The Chariot we transmute fear into zeal.

The 7 is the 1 fusing with the 6 giving fusion and movement, but without the great disciplines of restriction, choice and discrimination that we find in the 8, so with the 7 we are in for a very fast ride and a lot of fireworks. In the cycle of the 7 we have to check whether we are going off the rails with over-enthusiasm, or succumbing to doom and gloom. The mind is realising that it is experiencing the fusion of the creative light and the creative matrix; it experiences the act of creation within itself, as a witness. Its way ahead can only be on a tightrope between the act of creation and the witnessing, because it recognises that this is the job it has to do; it has to follow the process of the movement of creation through its own experience. The 7 gives the whole of its life to the movement of Spirit, which takes us back into the world to 'walk our talk'; this is why we are trail blazers for others.

A chariot is a traditional war instrument; this can be seen as the triumph of the strong over the weak, because it is an oppressive instrument used to run over adversaries. It goes for war, so has to win the battle over its enemies and oppressors. Our Chariot on the other hand, asks us to internalise that war, not as a contest of oppression, but as recognition that the life it is experiencing is a fusion of light and darkness. In this process the only thing that dies is misunderstanding, ignorance and fear. The only thing we have to fight is our resistance to that fusion. This resistance would be made up of all our survival and habitual instincts, which keeps us addicted to treading the mill rather than blazing the trail ahead. So we have to be ruthless with our laziness, our complacency and our excuses, for if we have come back to learn to be a co-creator, there is no time for self-indulgence. However, this is an internal process and the instrument itself deserves the rest it needs in order to be a good Chariot or carrier for the Spirit.

The intent and love is so strong that whatever he does to the self is understood to be part of that process. The zeal for truth is so strong that the mind will take its instrument through a much faster process of alignment, with the acceptance of whatever life is throwing its way. The process of the 7 is to gather a lot of speed towards its goal, so we are experiencing a lot more obstacles; these will be transmuted into spiritual energy. Eventually, the realisation comes that the addiction is to the drama itself, rather than to the problem that doesn't exist any more. We don't change every single atom of our body in five minutes, so when we are talking about the body of humanity as it is, changing it will take a very long time. We are not here in a prison or a dead-end although it may feel like that. At times the whole thing might feel a bit pointless, but it is not. Once Spirit recognises that the only way to exteriorise is through matter, then the inner movement can be used in a positive way; complete union with what we thought was our prison being the result. Once it is understood that what is happening is a materialisation of the concept that allows us to fly higher than yesterday, then we can see not only that it is not a prison, but it is a wonderful field in which we can grow hope for the next day. All of this realisation is done through acceptance, then if we suddenly have a big dip and ask "Do I have to be here?" we need to remember that we are here to change our concept of what life is, through the mind perceiving things differently.

With rationalisation the Soul will learn that restrictions are the necessary structure upon which dreams can be built, because they are there to help and give foundations. Any time we feel despair and are unable to move, we can rationalise and remember that it feels like that because we are at the edge of a new perception of reality. The restrictions we feel are only a measure of what is possible and viable, for the initiate obeys the karmic laws and adapts the vision to what is already there. When we are not aligned to the idea of exteriorising the divine, then we are not receptive to the light and we feel useless, because the way we are looking at life is of no value. The Magician (1), at the stage of The Chariot (7), has made the choice and is beginning to apply it. He has to 'walk his talk'.

We live now at a time when we can truly take part in the transmutation and transubstantiation of the world through applying the Spirit of truth to our lives; this is the aspiration that drives the Spirit into zeal. It doesn't matter which wave we might be riding, there are many different levels of consciousness. If we all want to be on the top step of the stairway to heaven it wouldn't be very helpful to the great life to create a big gap between us and the next person, for how on earth will anybody get up! It is better to be on the bottom step, inviting the willing Soul to tread the path. Anyway, it is not up to us to decide where we want to be, we are as we are, so we become humble. We can never be 'the top', because that is the sum total of everything. Even in the state of higher consciousness, when the mind is expanded, we fully understand that there is no way we can ever catch up with eternity, even if we have in us that last whisper of when everything is accomplished in the Universe. We are not the thing itself; we are just an expression of it. When we are open, receptive, aware and zealous we might not understand why people behave as they do, but when we recognise that the life force is in everyone else, we can regain our humble place in the human family and see that we are one and the same as our brothers.

There is no way that we can live life for someone else by taking up their karma, even through all the experience that we have brought back. But by giving ourselves up to Soul, we can perceive another person's past and see the whole potential of their future. Loving and understanding that person as they are is how the initiate becomes his work. This process requires the humble service to our fellow human beings and it has to be on behalf of the God we live in. So we are 'it' but at the same time we are not 'it', for we serve it. We are the by-product of the process of God recognising itself. As we fuse and align with the mind recognising itself, we give ourselves up to the cosmic wisdom.

The Charioteer has five gold studs on his chest, pointing from the throat to the heart, denoting the refining through the heart of the five senses, at the service of higher creativity. He has completed three degrees of Masonic work, so there are three larger gold studs in the apron. The apron is the symbol of the apprentice.

True zeal is what is needed to climb onto the Chariot, because we need enormous zeal to come out of the cocoon of easy living; we may even need to be stung by a mighty cosmic bee to do it! This is the stage where we really see our pain, so once we have made our decision, there is no way that we are going to avoid that sharp sting. The cosmic bee has only one function, which is to get the nectar and bring it back to the Queen bee following the direction according to the Sun. The Sun represents the spiritual impulse of the Soul. The function of the pain is to remind man of his pitiful condition on the planet if he stays in the animal world of nature. Pain is an integral part of the experience of the Charioteer, for he has to put himself through the fire of purification; this is the sharp sword of karmic alignment.

In the Lord's Prayer 'Lead us not into temptation' can be translated as: 'let's not go into pointless acts and free us from evil, as we become aware of our subconscious need for power; let our pride not blind us into action'. So we cease to play the game of veiling what our behaviour might tell us about ourselves.

The Sphinxes are black and white to represent the two aspects of the Soul, shadow and light. We know that man can only leave this world when he has resolved the question of the riddle; that happens when he has sublimated these two aspects. Consciousness, truth, and honesty have to be active all the time to transmute the shadow side. The personality wants to keep covering up, until the final fusing happens when there is nothing left to cover up. It is then, when we have given up that the great work is completed. On the one hand we have the urge for freedom, which moves us towards the light; on the other hand we carry the karmic luggage that keeps us firmly in the drama. These two have a tendency to separate, so the left hand doesn't know what the right hand is doing and vice versa. The idea is to make them work together; this is focussed awareness.

The white sphinx represents the receptive side of the brain, which will have a tendency for day-dreaming and metaphysical thoughts. It is the nature of this mind to always look for the new and the light. Because the mind is looking up it doesn't look for answers in its own subconscious, but has a tendency to look for the answers in books or other people's experiences. The mind will have to fuse intimately with the subconscious and see that this is the only 'book' it has to read.

The black sphinx represents the repeating of the same old hurts and behaviour patterns from the subconscious, so that they can be seen and explored. When they come together and fuse there is sublimation, wisdom and knowledge. The job of the 7 and the Charioteer is to keep bringing back the light into the cup of nature, so that eventually the two divergent aspects merge.

The two sphinxes are united by their rear ends, so they are actually one sphinx with two heads. They represent the Soul of nature and the Soul of mind in one unit, which is humanity or the aspirant/disciple/initiate. The black one is the subconscious and the white one is the conscious. They are fusing completely through the essential inner mastery of the Charioteer. This fusion of the two Souls is also strongly linked to the work of the 7. Once The Lover, (Number 6) has made the inner decision, he has to come back into life to 'walk his talk'. He has to go into the shadows with truth and life, because he knows that in the darkness there are the pearls of wisdom he seeks. These will enable him to transmute the obsessive protective survival instinct into the pure tools of action at the service of the Soul. Once we are in The Chariot, we want to win, so we have to know where we are going, but there are no reins for it is not an exterior violence that he applies to himself, but an inner work of fusion. This is the same process as the fusion

168 THE SPIRIT OF THE TAROT: NUMBERS AS INITIATORS

of the Spirit of Spring, which also has a 7 vibration and comes back so that nature can give her fruits; this one seeks to fuse the will of the higher mind with the will to be of nature. The harvest is the initiate. This is why the Charioteer has to have a very sharp karmic wind behind him, as he has to learn to travel the tightrope of fusion through the straight line of acceptance, so that he does not fall into drama or illusion.

What we see around us in our everyday lives mirrors our inner state of consciousness, so being completely aware of our reactions will show us the nature of our shadows. When they are seen, perceived, absorbed and understood, then we have fused the black and white sphinxes. This is about being completely and honestly aware of whom we are. For the average aspiring person this is a huge battle. As we behave and react we need to know instantly which shadow we are looking at, to understand the esoteric side of it and to bring in love for it so that we can transmute it. This is a mighty mastery, showing a high level of humility and a true giving up of the little self to the higher life. To do this needs all the zeal of the Charioteer for it is deadly painful. It is much easier to veil the shadow, to refuse to accept it and to project it onto somebody else. It is easier to go back to the drama we know, than to go down on our knees under the cutting truth of reality, for it is like a lost battle; anyway we are too puny and we want to be so mighty! The Charioteer has the potential in him to triumph; we need to be a prophet and a trailblazer, so one of the attributes of the Charioteer is triumph.

The Chariot is the beginning of a journey; what we are going to see on that journey are the inner and the outer realities. The mission is to become more and more honest with ourselves and more accepting of where and who we are. The practical externalisation of that process has to come from our skills, then the right use of those skills is what determines how much of the missionary will emerge. It is not what we are going to do, but the intent behind it that is the most important thing. If we use those skills for our own triumph we will soon be derailed. Here we are learning to wield energy on behalf of something greater, because that is the only task there is. There is a constant fusing and merging of receptivity and activity, which can be seen as passing on the message. The Charioteer, with the vision of love in front of him, has seen the virtuality of his own being, that is why he has given himself up to his zealous mission. He's depicted as calm and poised, for he is absolutely confident about his success.

The symbols on front of The Chariot represent sexuality, which on a higher level represents the fusion of two aspects of mind into the one divine energy. This happens through the movement of the cosmic Kundalini fire, which is that sexual energy that makes certain that nature carries on and that consciousness can be born out of it. It is a very scorpionic symbol, which includes within it the symbols for Jupiter and Mars. Mars is movement, action turned towards the future and life in expansion. Martian energy is not accurately understood; in the beginning it comes out through the will of Aries to sacrifice itself through the experiences of the Zodiac, then at a higher sphere it comes back blinded and washed out by the bright waters of love. Aries comes out like a fiery ball, full of love, which is expressed with all the will and zeal that can be mustered. Love prevails, so there could be the misunderstanding that he has got to inseminate everything in sight; that is the problem of Aries. In the young Aries this is not focussed, so the one thing they need is inspiration. If they don't have that the energy is used to destroy the mind. The sexual energy comes from the impulse that says "I love you"; we have to learn how to handle that properly. It is about mind coming into matter. Aries can follow the strong impulse to jump in and die and it doesn't matter if he takes the wrong or right road, because he has got to be sacrificed. Martian energy is mental and therefore ruthless. On the other hand, Jupiter brings generosity, the potential of life and expansion. This is represented in the symbol for Jupiter, which is a red circle with blue wings. This symbol as a whole represents the fiery energy of Mars coming back, to bring in the possibility of transmutation by Spirit.

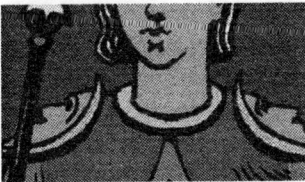

To make the whole process gentler the two shoulders of the Charioteer are crowned by the moon, representing the receptive, affectionate, loving, caring and regenerative aspect. Being on his shoulders, it shows the glory and the power of the Earth, making certain that the glory and the power are spiritual and not selfish or personal. The world is full of the power of the personality, which is shown by those men who only do things for themselves. Without all the attributes of the Moon, Mars and Jupiter, The Chariot can be like that. The face in each moon tells us of the work of making the whole of the subconscious conscious. This is the meeting of the 'Angel of the Face', which comes to light when the Soul sees its own life as a perception of the God we live in; the personality then sees the face of its Soul! To make that recognition we have to have our faces turned upwards to meet with Soul; it is a complete association at an intimate level with the idea that created us. The Charioteer has had a glimpse of the Angel of the Face, which carries him and allows that part of him which had the needs and the illusions, to die.

The Chariot itself is a Masonic altar: it is an inner journey, accommodating and transforming everyday life. It is white, so whatever mud or illusion the Charioteer has to go through his purity will protect him, for remember 'to the pure everything is pure'. This means that if we are pure we can go into the foulest place and it won't taint us, because we know that it is all part of creation. This is the cosmic mastery, which happens when the mind has aligned with the cosmic mind. It is the same altar that we saw in The Magician, but The Magician's altar had only three legs because he was working on the theory. The Chariot's altar has four legs, to denote action and the fact that he is walking his talk. He knows that he has come back to work with Earth, Fire, Air and Water, which can also be seen as Spades, Clubs, Diamonds and Hearts, or pentacles, wands, swords and cups. The Chariot is a table full of cosmic wisdom, for the legs reach up to Heaven. There are two green legs to represent Earth and two gold legs to represent Heaven; these are the inner and the outer coming together and fusing. It is that process which propels The Chariot into motion. In The Magician or the potential master, we had the tulip which signified initiation; now in The Chariot we have the master in the workshop of everyday life.

The multiplicity of situations and forms in everyday life is being perceived as the one life evolving into a state of constant expansion. This point of recognition in the 7 not only enables the Charioteer to be more aware, but gives him the work of being a trailblazer and an enlightener. The responsibility of becoming clearer and brighter is dangerous, as it could exteriorise in wanting to be the brightest and cleverest; we have to believe in our zeal for the work of the light and yet become more humble. We are giving the wrong message if we are putting ourselves forward as gurus. So many gurus are only human beings who have made a lot of mistakes, so have reached some lessons of wisdom and have forgotten that they are only on a step rather than being the altar itself; they think they are perfect when in fact they are only full of pride.

When we truly know that we are only witnesses, it is like being in each cell of our bodies and understanding why this cell is dying, why that one is not performing properly, or why another one is regenerating. That is really all it is, but with the difference that with our minds we can actually influence events by seeing the consequence of what is happening in front of us. This can be likened to knowing we are going to be ill if we eat too much chocolate or drink too much wine. It is the same at the level of humanity. When we have understood that it is one life, we can foresee the consequences and then automatically we can influence events with our thoughts and understanding, so seeing which way the event will go. We can even manifest an event not by actually doing anything, but by holding in our minds how it should happen. The reason why we still have war and strife is that most people are holding in their minds the idea that this is human nature. All that gloom and doom stuff is to do with fear and protection. However, the world is going forward very fast into a new vision for humanity and it will happen because there are enough of us holding the peace with the world vision. All the compassion in the world is useless if we don't apply discrimination and say "No, I don't play your game, it is not one I recognise as ethical".

As we develop a balance between our vision and everyday life, any viable action has to be on the human scale and align with the vision as much as possible. This is the inner fusion and it is enormously difficult. The first quality of The Chariot is to know how to dominate this world, meaning how to dominate the little self of personality. The Charioteer wants to release himself from the ties, which are all aspects of want and need; even wanting to be a healer is a tie. He has to cut all the ties that his personality might want to keep feeding on and get out of the prison, so that in the end he can realise that all we are is a 'way-by', a little instrument that shines in the dark.

The plight of all the people who have a strong influence of the 7 arises through others remarking on their quiet brightness; as a result they think they must be the best. This is the maya or illusion of the 7, that it cannot be a light bearer if it is not better than others, when really it is about doing the best that they can. Because of this, there is still the great fighting going on between light and dark, creating explosion and making the fusion happen. Where there is fusion there is pain, because when light and matter fuse, both die in creating life. By becoming more of the new we become less of what we thought we were. Confidence is a key, triumph ensues from the fact that the initiate comes back certain that he is going to do it; because of that, triumph is not the goal. The intent of merging with the light has been formulated in the 6. We have the potential; now we have to manifest its viability in the present. So at the point of fusion, which is the present, all the fears and uncertainty rise to the surface to be transmuted into positive action. A familiar aspect of our being has to die to become the conqueror. All the details that have to be seen and transformed may take over the consciousness and we can focus on irrelevant details, such as what other people think of us, or whether we will show our shortcomings. All of these irrelevant details can be used as excuses not to go further. In fact there is no failure in this life, so the Charioteer says "Let's go forward". It is his role to triumph over the fear, for he is the conqueror. Fear of failure is the main fear we are seeing here; this is about not being the best, or not being as good as the next one. They need all the zeal, love and generosity in the world to bring light into the swamp, so as to feel the wings of Spirit moving through the cells of the body. Fear of the enormous responsibility needs to be debunked, for we are only getting it wrong so that we *can* get it right. Fear of responsibility in that respect, is a fear of not getting it right and is false pride. Accepting the world's imperfections because it is in the process of 'becoming,' is to accept that we are not perfect! That is courage.

Be confident that we are going to come out into the light at the end of the road, for we have been blessed and confirmed by the Pope, who gives us the opportunity for the mind always to be turned toward the inner light of the Soul. From all of this, the perception is focussed on the truth, so we are not going to be caught by the illusion of this world. We know that we have the brightness of the stars of our inner landscape, for The Star is the vision itself. We are truly guided by the fusion with our inner light – 'the Star we are' – like the wise men travelling on their camels to find the Soul Jesus by following the cosmic Star. Any human Soul being born is a cosmic event!

We cannot fail if we understand that there is only one thing to give up: our own self-importance. How can we fail, for if we trip ourselves up, even that is not a failure, because the more we fall on our knees the more we can smile and say "Thank you". If we are able to recognise that we are acting out of pride, then that is a victory not a failure. So we cannot fail, all we have to let go of is an image of ourselves. That is not renouncing ourselves, for if we do we renounce God. We are here to shed as much of our preconceived intellectual appreciation of life as we can. This is the ongoing transformation of the world, from instinctive to cognitive, to the development of the intellect and eventually to the birth of the higher understanding.

We are here to learn to wield energy. If we look back at the sort of lives we have lived, we see a huge amount of energy wasted in the pursuit of nothing. The energy spent on making people believe that 'the more we have the more we need', could transform the world overnight, if it were used as a message of hope and goodwill. Human beings are the only hope for the world so far! So let's focus our energy away from our needs and see the reality in front of us, which asks us to take responsibility. We can become responsible in the flesh, in our organs and our biology. What is the flesh for, if not to move us to do the work of God? What are the eyes for, if not to perceive life with the optic as close as we can get to pure observation and witnessing and use that for the most objective truth? What is the mouth for, if not to bless the food we eat and the words we speak?

When we have the certainty in the depth of our being that the only use for life is to follow the inner path to truth, then we know that there is no other way than to climb into The Chariot of humanity. As we spin on the incoming energy and reach high to be clear, honest and understanding, we automatically attract wisdom and can have the confidence of the one who is going to work on behalf of something greater and bigger than himself.

Once we understand the plan, we redeem by co-creating. How can we not put our lives into the arms of the creator? We only go through a single moment once and we won't pass that way again, so we should not miss the opportunity to do some good in the sense of making the world a better place. That 'doing good' could even be telling someone off, it is not necessarily being a 'goodie-goodie'. We have to be non-judgmental and yet judge whether an action is right by observing its effect on the world. We may witness a war and react by declaring "This is not right" or we may see a rescue mission and decide that "This is the way". Both are showing us that their effect on the world is positive. The living world is greater than us and because it is the life that we are observing, we have to rely on the wisdom that we have brought forth into the observation.

The symbol of a sphinx reminds us that we are looking at a riddle, such as "Who are you?" or "Where do you come from?" we can't just refuse to look at it. The Charioteer is riding with the question so as to fuse with it and give himself an answer. He's understood the answer to the riddle "Who am I?" as "I am the one who is asking the question!" We all have to go through the nights of doubt and questioning because there is no possibility of certainty if we don't doubt. We have to affirm our existence with no other excuse or question, the answer is "I am"; everything is an affirmation of life.

The Charioteer has engaged with the riddle, to make sure he is going to sublimate and fuse intellect and intuition. He knows that in his worldly journey he is not going to be taken in, for if the world of form, expression and matter were an absolute it would give all the answers raised by man's existence, consciousness and awareness. Even science, in all its greatness, cannot give the answer to "Why?" – We need the metaphysical to answer that. The world of form is part of the absolute, but it is not *the* absolute, so the Charioteer knows he is not going to find the answer in his reactions, even though he has to look at them. The absolute is everything, including both the known observable world and the unseen unnamed life, which makes up its totality. If we die, it is irrelevant to wonder whether the world ceases to exist. What is relevant is the perception of the 'why' of what is, because that is what makes us potential co-creators. Everything is a mindset and maya (illusion) is the way we want to perceive it until we know better. It is always to do with understanding that there is no polarity of good or bad; everything is right and the end of the mindset is the end of manifestation. All the time we have to be a witness we have to accept we are in a virtual picture or a cinema, which is projecting its story constantly.

A proposed opinion from the scientific world states that everything in the Universe is a by-product from the production of black holes, so it is only through black holes that the Universe can renew itself. Our little world owes its existence to the fulfilling of that potential. In knowing that, we know that the greater potential is the most important thing, so we can apply the qualities of confidence, perseverance and endurance to our lives. Zeal is the best word to sum up all of that.

Our biological life on Earth is a flat veil or net on the surface of the planet, so when Spirit blows onto it creating movement, the idea of form is perceived; all the forms of life come from that movement. As the light projects onto the net, it moves and then reverberates into colour, sound, shape and form. When we go from the third dimension to the fourth, we realise that form is a film in time and space; it is all a question of projection and recognising that the reality of form only exists because it is held in the movement. The cup of nature is manifesting the theatre and what we see is a projection of the mind. The only thing we gain from this world of illusion is the awareness of our reaction to it. We have to reincarnate into the theatre to play the role of thinking that we are in form. We exist in one dimension, but the dimension of perception is the only real one; that is where we know that everything is a mental projection. If we really know that, then it is very odd to actually want something from this world of form. We are continuing to feed the illusion so as to survive a bit longer, because there is still much work to be done.

Many of us have had the experience of suddenly realising that the whole world is in a lens and we are looking through it. We actually exist in all dimensions, but we only manifest in the dimension that we think we exist in, just as what is after death is only what we think it will be. We manifest ourselves into a situation where we feel or think that the strongest experience is necessary; or we manifest what we want to have, or do. We can do it in any time, or simultaneously in more than one place at the same time. It is best not to play with that, because we can go on doing it forever; what we want to do is to stop wanting!

The less we focus on whether we are right or wrong and the less we think we have something to do with the outcome, the better. It is just bubbles upon bubbles of energy coming back into re-incarnation, manifesting many different outcomes from the mind; this goes on until we stop putting ourselves in the centre of the universe. Then we can see that we are a by-product for Spirit to move through us. The only projection that we need to make is the one that is the closest we can get to the optic of the God we live in and we have to accept that we will make many mistakes as we try to do this.

Zeal fuses the subconscious and the higher consciousness, in the service of bringing light and truth into this pitiful world. We are serving the highest and our brothers, so the clearer and the more sublimated our needs, shadows and reactions to the world, the faster our Chariots can go. At the same time it is okay if our Chariot is slow. Zeal is a product of emotional sublimation, mental perception and will; it evolves from 'my will' to 'Gods will'. Every single man, before he triumphs, has got to meet the conflict and see the unease of his own existence, without questioning or trying to appease the malaise. At the collective level that is where all the mystic cosmology comes and helps, because everything is explained so that we all know and understand that there is a pattern and a plan that is shown to us. So we can put a plaster on our painful questioning about the meaning of life, for if we vibrate to that plan we have something to get on with. The plan is given to the group Souls and it goes into making an egregore. In the end we have to break away from group thought, for there is no true triumph or certainty while we are attached to a collective myth or egregore.

It is the same idea as we read in St John of the Cross, when he tells us to go beyond our God. With our minds we have to go beyond the given cosmology and myth about life. Myths are only here to help us on our way, so we have to recreate our myths and our heroes; otherwise we go into superstition, stagnation and self-destruction. For mindsets to be valid and strong they have to catch the imagination to enable old ideas to be changed, but mindsets have to be checked all the time. Go along with the wind, for wind brings new seeds and new life; we have to be flexible enough to catch the new winds or new mindsets, so that we can go beyond the old myths. This doesn't mean that we can't use them, because there are good solid ones. For example, if we mix red with blue we will end up with purple, but we know very well that with slightly different quantities of colour we might end up with mauve, violet, or even magenta, which is a strong re-organiser of mindsets.

Most people are still in the womb of mass consciousness, because we are all held together by common thought and desire. This gives us a pattern of understanding to follow that obeys some kind of useful and safe rules and regulations, so that eventually the curious amongst us, who have more Spirit, can break that mould and go to the next expression. We might want to help others lift out of their moulds, but they have to do it from within themselves.

Most collective thoughts are like a dressing that we put on a wound. At the social level the dressing is what is right or wrong; at the psychic level it is what is true or false. When we break through into the reality of the 'why' there is no more need for a dressing. This is why we say the kingdom of heaven is for the violent, because we feel the pain that all these people are not daring to touch. Everything is there to be explored, worked out and digested; it takes a long time. At a higher level we recognise this process as transmutation, so we don't suffer from it in the same way but we still experience it very acutely. We know that it is a normal alchemical process of turning coal into diamonds; this is why we have to be so honest about the type of pain we are experiencing, because most of our pains are self-inflicted and degenerative rather than transformative. The mind at the Buddhic level has detached from its personal life and transpersonal perception is the way. Melancholy is an attitude of mind associated with the Buddhic level, as we accept that there is nothing we can do to lift our brothers to the higher vibration. Compassion reminds us of the pain in the process; we come back into the pain to show others that pain doesn't matter, because it is the by-product of transmutation.

We can all be trapped by our understanding of peace and self-contentment, like having everything we want or by being a good citizen, having all the experiences which go to make up a good life and giving thanks for that. The Chariot asks us to be careful not to take this kind of peace as the be all and end all, or as the ultimate goal. Jesus the Soul says, "I come to bring a sword, not peace". When Jesus (the Soul) has rendered himself completely at the service of the Father or spiritual truth he tells his disciples, who represent the many aspects of the personality, "I leave you with my peace", which is that place of deep acceptance and understanding where we witness the world and all its difficulties; only the love aspect is left as a reaction. We do not triumph if we do not fight the inner battle with ourselves, so we should not be gentle or sweet to ourselves; this is the jihad of Islam or the inner work of the disciple. We should not punish ourselves when we are weak, greedy and unkind, but we should apply the sword of truth and honesty, to see it, accept it and dissolve it. We have to conform to the outer world by being clean, wearing nice clothes and eating the food that we are given, but the inner process knows of the emptiness and attachment to the world of the senses. Asceticism is a necessary stage that helps us detach from the personal use of the senses and recognise that they are only tools to know the world. After that when we eat for example, we take in the colour, taste, texture and smell, not as a personal emotional reaction, but as a vibrational energetic experience – therefore a true 'witnessing'. If we put all our humanity into sharing with others by drinking and eating with them, we can actually sublimate the process by setting an example, so bringing the awe of nature into the group and uplifting it.

Before we get to The Chariot of our own autonomy, our mind is confined in a collective institution, so it wants to break out and find its own way of thinking. It has to rebel, to break away from the God of religions to enable it to come back to an intimately experienced authority and give itself up to this conscious perception, as the mind recognises that it is part of God. We should encourage people with their visions, for they are going for autonomy and individuality of Soul. We might gently turn over a pebble for someone, but we don't remove it; however, we may need to throw it in the air to wake them up! That is the way of the triumphal Chariot; it doesn't hesitate to use whatever is needed in the name of love and truth to clear the path. When we ask ourselves the question "Why is my life going that way?" and "Why are people calling me names?" it is because we are on The Chariot and The Chariot wants us to remove all the pebbles under the wheels. The people working at truth with zeal have very difficult lives of endurance and persistence. If we are going to understand and help others, then we are going to have to feel and experience the pain of the human condition.

There is no religious system, story or myth that doesn't depict the long painful march of mankind towards its goal. We often meet crossroads where we feel oppressed and want something new. This is shown in the story of the Jewish people when Moses led them to the Promised Land. To get there they had to endure so much that they didn't even want to listen to Moses any more. The Moses within us shows us the vision, telling us that there is a promised land somewhere, so we go forward on our Chariot; then suddenly we are hurting and want to give up! This is the story of The Chariot. At one point in the old story, the people wanted to go back to Egypt because they were starving; this is like our wanting to go back to our comforts. We might have been slaves to our senses, but we had all the comforts in our lives. Humanity has not yet found its Jerusalem, for we are still refusing to recognise brotherhood, but it won't be long before we do, even if it takes two thousand years, for that is a very short time in the history of the Solar System. The story of the Jewish people is the story of humanity. Once we reach the 'Promised Land', which is a different perception in consciousness and not a place, there is then the question of what we are going to do with it. The initiate teaches brotherhood and sharing the land, for we are one mind and that is what takes humanity forward.

As the Charioteer goes forward, he will have to fuse with the next experience because a 7 has to learn to accept and assimilate the human condition as his, without personalising the pain of the resistance. If we refuse to go through the pain, the conflict can carry on for a long time. Eventually the pain of fusing will be seen as the natural process of transmuting negative reaction energy into acceptance and endurance, which then fuels the zeal. We have to push ourselves beyond ourselves. Conflict is happening everywhere now, so align with it and learn to perceive it in a different way. Are we healing the past and releasing light into the world, or are we using that energy to make the same mistakes?

We are all addicted to the drama of the theatre. When we realise that the world is a projection, theatre or film, we reach a level of understanding where we know there is nothing in it for us. At that point we may say "Is it worth it?" Then we have to render ourselves selfless in order to carry on, because if we think that there is something in it for us we have not understood service. There is a level where the veil of illusion is so clear that we know we are only here as a conduit for things to happen through us. Happiness doesn't come into it, for if it does then there is something in it for us and we are acting to achieve some gratification. We can rejoice when we see some light of understanding coming into a conflict, but that is not happiness. Joy is beyond happiness, beyond ourselves and the senses; it is a collective state.

Zeal is the necessary tool to enable us to break away from the mass consciousness of the group. If the family group is quite evolved zeal will help it to leap into the next sphere of perception, as this would be the aim of the Soul; to uplift its love aspect into the realm of the higher intelligence. When the zeal has sublimated the resistance, it creates for a very short time a clear channel of intuition. There are aspects of the Ancient Wisdom that have been translated according to the level of consciousness of people from a distant past. There is therefore a need for a new interpretation, so that the simple truth that 'all is energy' cannot be used by clever minds in a dangerous way to manipulate others. Although we know that most of mass consciousness is completely driven by that type of manipulation, this is rapidly being checked by the large numbers of human souls rising in consciousness, as increasingly the average civilised, honest human being comes to the conclusion that only truth and love are important.

The brightness and quickness of mind of the 7 is always looking for the next challenge or the next direction. If they have a strong mindset about who they are, how they are going to do it and their goal, results will come for a while until suddenly life will start to be very difficult. Then they will meet a lot of obstacles, because they have to learn that they are not here to use their gift for their own purpose, or to make the world how they would like it to be, but rather to let the greater life use their gift for the bigger purpose. With the generous power of The Chariot we are internalising the domination of self, which leads to triumph and zeal as the Soul is turned towards the light and service.

The crown with three stars on the Charioteer's head shows that he has uplifted his mind to the third degree of the great work and is ready to blaze forward and fuse his mind with the cosmic level of consciousness. This cosmic level is represented by the twelve stars on the canopy of which four are out of view. The two sets of three stars on the canopy plus the three stars on his crown (making nine in total), tells us he is on his way to becoming a master of wisdom (9).

Being triumphant, the Charioteer has to have a baton or wand, to tell us that he has the authority to walk the talk of the Magician. On the top of the baton is the point of alignment to perfection, which keeps him on the track of his fiery inner potential. The red ball on

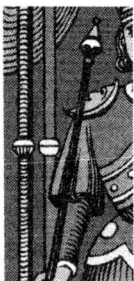

the top of the baton tells us that the aim is known. The white part represents pure intent, so the result will be a pure action enacted to reveal the potential. The pose is natural rather than authoritative and aggressive, because the impulse comes from the Soul, rather than the glamour of the personality, so he holds the wand casually. He's learning to make his Soul/Spirit connection, which is why the intent is pure.

The work of the Initiate never ceases because the journey doesn't stop. He is coming back into the world to bring light, knowing that he is ready to confront any experience and go through any purification. This is the beginning of fusing the inner and outer life experience into one more drop of wisdom to lighten up the way in everyday life. This work is about alignment and movement towards cosmic consciousness.

When the metaphysical mind and inner discipline propels The Chariot, they conquer the dissipating basic energy of sexuality, directing and sublimating it into higher creative energy. This way the Alpha and Omega of life is understood. We only have duality because we have to understand the light and the dark (receptive and active) within ourselves. This is expressed by 'as I receive and offer myself to the light, I move'.

The passage from material to spiritual is achieved by the fusion of the 1 and the 6. These two energies working together give the Charioteer his purity and single-mindedness, which is when the sublimation of the senses is turned towards service and selflessness, rather than gratification. This sublimation can bring an apocalyptic realisation; the veil is taken away and the total revelation is perceived. Even a tiny glimpse pushes The Chariot forward, for it is a vision of life uplifting the Soul; of nature above its survival, comfort and pleasures. We are going forward for regeneration, not generation.

We have come to wield the most creative energy there is, which nature suffers and translates into procreation and sexuality. As we elevate that energy beyond sexual union, a deeper union can happen between people, which is the long lasting union of Soul. This does not mean to say that we should not have a partner and enjoy life; it only says that we should understand that there is a deeper union. If we can have that at all levels, then we are not going for the pleasure of the senses in the sexual experience, but rather for the purity of the sexual experience.

Impurity can't reach the Charioteer, because he has decided it won't. He has made himself pure by giving in to his zeal. If he goes through the mud it is not to partake in it, but to bring to it his hope, compassion, help and if necessary, corrective pain, so that he can realise his own essence. It is only through us asking the question "Why am I in pain?" and embracing it to feel it, that we can recognise our essence. Humanity has put itself through a lot of painful trials and ends up by asking the question "What type of God has created such a terrible world?" Eventually we learn to follow the pain inside where we can meet ourselves and therefore meet our own God, through internalisation. There is no other way; even the greatest brother who has walked on the planet before us to create a path that enables the little brothers to follow his steps, cannot change the way we have to reincarnate. That is why all the masters came as human beings, for how could they influence a group of people if they don't look like the people, talk like them and intimately understand them? If they defied the laws of manifestation on the Earth, we would have to be wary of them, as they would not be masters of wisdom. In the same way if we are going to make an object, we would have to use ingredients that are compatible with each other so they can hold together; we need compatibility. The only function of the flesh is to hold the experience of what it is to be human in a biological sense, this is why the great masters incarnated back into flesh, but it is the essence of every human being that needs to be touched.

The Pope allows and gives his blessing to everyone, and people can use it as they want, but with the Chariot there is spiritual action. The sublimated 6 as the cup of wisdom, sends out its magnetic beauty as wisdom, calling for the spiritual direction that the Number 7 will give. With The Chariot we have spiritual action, which is strict and righteous. Discipline and direction are applied, so as to manifest the new vision.

The Chariot and The Pope within have to come together to provide the qualification that is required before we can move, because moving with that fiery energy without all the goodness of the benediction would be very dangerous. They come together because of the love aspect between them; that is what creates the movement. This is purification to the point of crucifixion (letting go of an aspect of self), for the fusing of the two forces of love and truth to take place.

In Man's progress and evolution, he wins and triumphs over himself, over all his weaknesses and egotism. He doesn't do it for himself, but for others and he helps others in their progress towards realising the work of the creator within them. He has brought all the elements out of the darkness by placing himself into what he has created to finish the work. It is up to us at that level to go back home to Spirit through the sublimation of duality by fusion. The only way to do that is to give over to God's will and love, so we do the divine work instead of suffering it.

The key to Number 7 is the sublimation of our needs with the pure intent of love in action, taking the mind to cosmic wisdom; we can then become an instrument for the will of God. This is why we can be an instrument for change and precede the coming of events. The true inner peace of mind comes from the humble acceptance that we are not here to change the world, but that we are the tools the creator uses to bring his creation back to his heart; it is our minds' identification with the mind of its creator that makes this happen. We stop rebelling, opposing, or wanting to be free and can have complete peace of mind. We should dare to make mistakes and rush zealously towards the lightening bolt of our creator, which is enlightening the darkness of the unknown and reveals the plan. There is no mistake if the intent is pure, even if it is the biggest mistake that we have ever made, for it teaches us much more than walking on the safe side of the road.

All the actions that have been done in the name of exploration, all the pebbles that have been turned so as to find the monsters lurking under them; all of that is illusion. It all had to be named, so nothing needs to be redeemed, only our mistaken perception. We are in the right play, doing the right action and we have forgotten that we are in a play. This is good, because if we didn't have amnesia we wouldn't do it properly, or feel it; it is only by having the experiences that we are capable of naming them.

It doesn't matter if our vision of what is possible is so elevated that it might take thousands of years, let's keep it up because we might see its earlier avenement. We are told by Dwal Khul in the writings of Alice Bailey, that the masters were surprised at the rate of development of the consciousness of humanity and that to this day we are ahead of what was expected of us. As we rise and uplift our mind, we can truly participate in keeping the vision alive for others to perceive it and join in the great brotherhood of humanity.

The 'walking of the talk', results in the love aspect and the truth fusing the duality of inner and outer reality, delivering true peace of mind. In the following words of the Dali Lama it can be expressed this way: TRUE BLESSINGS COME FROM YOUR OWN COURSE OF ACTION.

Justice, La Justice
The sword of truth

The figure of Justice is seated on a large throne; she represents the Sun. She holds in her left hand the scales and in her right hand a large sword. This card is not about punitive man-made justice as we commonly know it, but divine non-judgmental justice. Her sword is not one that kills, but a sword that gives life and light, for it is the sword of karmic truth. This eighth card is about aligning the inner and outer worlds and finding the point of balance at the centre, so as to be a true witness for the life that flows through our Solar System. Here we gain the inner strength and humility needed to be able to communicate with the golden voice and speak for the God we live in.

The first five cards are the esoteric inner teaching that needs to be absorbed, digested and then manifested. Right up to the sixth card, we are shown the goal and the qualities required to reach it, though at that point they are not yet realised. Then the Lover at 6 is a doorway which tells us that God is love; where our love goes the will follows. The love aspect is essential to our transformation; if we by-pass it we can become dangerously mentally unbalanced. Will by itself is deadly and is an instrument of destruction, so without love will destroys. Very strong, wilful people can make things happen because there is love behind what they want to achieve, but when this love is seated in the personality then what is materialised is not necessarily good for humanity. So however much we may hide, if we love something that is not good for us or for humanity, we will have to face it again and again to show us where our desires and affections lie. As we get ourselves out of self-deception and stop being taken in by the things we love in the outer world, we have to kill that self-deceptive part of ourselves by having the honesty to recognise the self-deception and saying kindly to ourselves, as you would to a child, "Here I am again" as we pant in front of whatever it is that we desire.

Love fuels the will and softens the sharp angle of the sword, so that the sword can be an object of initiation. It destroys a sphere of exhausted experiences and allows the new birth of consciousness to see the light. This process can be likened to the birth of a baby, for the mother dies for a few seconds as she gives birth. In the case of the birth of the Solar System, it could not have been born without the pre-existence of space or womb to come into. The minute a star is born we have space and love, for they go together and we cannot have one without the other. In our Solar System human beings are the mediators between space and the moving light of the Spirit; we are here to do the job of mediation so we have to keep on experiencing and measuring, in order that the mind, the Spirit, the space and the love can reveal truth, so bringing man's consciousness to a higher level.

Most people would understand justice as the punishment fitting the crime. This is definitely not what we mean when we talk about justice here. In this card it is not judgment, in the worldly sense of good or bad, but divine justice, which is measuring and weighing up. Divine justice is the way the world is now, so whatever situation the world or an individual might find themselves in, they have to be completely able to accept things as they are. As humans we are here to work with divine justice; that is to say, to witness life as it is truly unfolding and understand the karmic work behind any situation. It is about finding the point of balance between action and reaction, so that we can develop a natural alignment with our inner truth, without questioning ourselves through guilt or pride.

We are looking at our inner and outer life from the point of awareness, so we have to ask ourselves whether we are communicating enough with both outer and inner worlds. For the mind and heart of a human being to witness the world from the point of view of divine justice is rare, because even the initiate or the wisest man can only evaluate a situation from the blueprint that they have seen. According to the Tibetan master Dwal Khul and the system of initiations, only at the eighth and ninth initiation will our consciousness become systemic, which means being in the blueprint rather than looking at the blueprint. The card Justice is symbolic of the Solar System. The egg of the world in its becoming is shaped like an egg timer, each one of us being in the centre point. Energetically, we are sisters or brothers of the greater Sun and are at the centre of our universe, not because we are self-centred, but because as a little individual sparks of sunshine we have a little universe around us. Our own sun has to shine in order to merge with the great brother Sun. To be useful we need to radiate affection to others who need it, to help them sublimate their emotions.

The egg of the world is the Solar System's 'becoming', for its whole potential is held within. Our lighted mind follows the figure of eight in our inner transformative work, so as to understand and in time to co-work with the greater life. When that egg is nothing but pure love, wisdom and will, it becomes the perfected Soul that

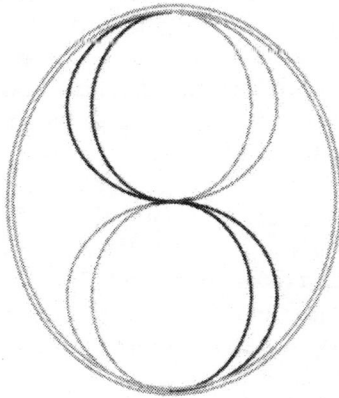

Figure 1. The egg of the world.

we name Christ; it is systemic, or at one with everything. When the mind of the initiate has gone through the eighth cycle, it has achieved the work of seeing, receiving, giving and understanding the karmic condition of mankind. It is then on its way to becoming the transparent elevated 9, which is the ultimate goal of the complete cycle of the exalted Soul. Even the greatest initiates on the planet can only carry on because they know how it works; however, they take on the real task of 'judging', in the sense of seeing and living by their own truth. While they are still conscious of working with and for the planet, they are not fully aligned with the deeper truth and so are not yet systemic. When we are in complete alignment and systemic, our self-awareness dissolves with all the other self-preoccupations, because the individualisation and the death of the Soul has left our unit performing only the song of God. When the initiate is able to understand a situation instantly, without any reference to himself or the system, he has removed himself and is taking the responsibility for understanding the collective karma. This is how we will all lead our lives eventually. If we are acting on behalf of something greater, we have to fully understand that in daring to go for truth every second of the day, we can say: "So be it, I know that every single bit of life is a manifestation of the God we live in; I know that there is nothing else that we are here to do, except dare to be a true witness for God; that is my 'becoming'. Judging, justice and weighing up are part of being a witness for God".

The Justice of the Tarot is non-judgmental and is the reverse of judgment as we commonly know it. From this place of love and understanding, if we have an individual in front of us who has committed certain acts, we don't see those acts but see everything that has brought him to that point. That is the divine justice and the true witnessing that reveals the work of karma. If we said; "God can see through me and can heal through me", that could be extremely arrogant. However, to exercise the justice of the just we have to take ourselves out of the way and be ready to say: "The God we live in might appear to make mistakes and I apologise". Once we get to the point where we know that there is no other will but the will of God and our will is only working out what that will is, that is the best we can do. We can only act through the will of God and God makes mistakes through our mistaken will, though the paradox is that there are never any mistakes. It is the same as; *Everything is perfect, but there is a lot of work to do'*.

Even when the whole of the life we live is completely aligned to the energetic principle and the greater life, we will not get things completely right, because the manifestation of the God we live in is not completed yet. It is only through us that it will get there. It is our job therefore to be that 'way-by' through which our God is 'becoming'. We are talking about mind and consciousness; about movement, communication and exchange. The 8 tells us to destroy the old ideas and bring new ones; it asks us to go up and down and bring the light into the darkness; it tells us to move continually, with endurance and yet more endurance. We are told that we should give up and give in to the system, for the system is greater than us.

True justice requires complete comprehension of the system, so that everything is seen in relation to something much greater than itself. We can only really love the God we live in if we understand the system intimately, this is expressed by; *'The more I understand the more I love, the more I love the more I understand'*. The 8 is telling us to internalise the outer world by going into it and exteriorising our light. In the downward movement the light is brought in and moves in an up and down motion, enlightening the darkness by releasing the wisdom of the ages. This is movement of consciousness in the process of becoming systemic; as we flow with it even the idea of being a mirror disappears and dissolves. As the mirror becomes transparent etheric glass, we become what we perceive. This is the key to co-creation.

There is a sentence: *'I come here to bring the light into the thing I see'*, which means, 'I look at something and I feel its heart and its life, therefore I reveal the light'; that is God and that is what true justice is, the karmic work that mankind as a unit in nature was created for. This is the perfect No. 8.

Some scientists are often more in love with the toys of the outer manifestation than the process and the task of witnessing, judging and weighing up. We are only here to witness and name, we are not supposed to co-create by taking the bricks and putting them somewhere else. Pure instinct and pure movement are the energetic way that the God we live in has managed to keep biology going for millions of years, so that the little flower of humanity can actually do the job of bringing in the light. The wise scientist knows that all he can do is to name and explain what he sees, for which scientist could create a system like this one? The Solar System is pure biology and pure physics. Pure science is the work of seeking the pure knowledge and seeing the universe in motion. Because we are afraid, we are going for needs and protection so we go and disturb things when we should know better. Can you imagine knowing better than the Earth when it has to blow its volcanoes?

The sword is the sword of true justice; it is not a sword for killing, but it gives life and light by renting the veil from head to toe. This is expressed by; *'A sword shall pass through thine own Soul also'*. The Soul is the mirror, the conduit, the timekeeper and the record-keeper; it enables the action of Spirit and matter to work together. When the Soul has done this work, it can truly align to the guidance of the karmic laws through its higher intelligence and then we don't need the mirror any more, so we can burn the books. Once the veil is lifted, the Soul can be rendered through the realisation of the truth; this is how that sword passes through the Soul.

There is no dream required for this process to happen; the dream is in the Soul of matter. God the Spirit rushes in to try and find the matching prince and princess. With the 8 we bring back all the brightness or darkness of our dreams, which are encapsulated in our tears and needs. Then the Soul is rent from head to toe, until there isn't an ounce of that watery luminous thread left in it to hold a single dream. When the prince and princess are one, unconditional love is all that remains and that love is light. It is like the Sun, shining and atomic. Every breath we take and every movement we make would have atomic sparks! That is the systemic 8.

When we start having a spiritual intent, we know that there is much more to life than the material world. It takes many, many lives for every cell in our bodies to be ablaze with the love and understanding of God. The Bible tells us that it took six days for the world to be made; that is symbolic for the six great cycles of manifestation, representing millions of years each. In the same way the Judgment Day will happen over many lives. Judgment Day has been happening now for the last two centuries, because we are in the process of moving from one level of consciousness to another. If we are really humble and look at the world we live in, we can see that it is never been more greedy and ugly; it is fantastically beautiful but it is very dark at the same time.

It has to be like that, because it *is* Judgment Day. We can say without being judgmental, that a thing is ugly beyond belief but also it is beautiful. It is not judging to say that how men and women behave towards life is ugly, for it won't always be like that; it is how it is at the moment. When we take the sword of truth, we understand why it has to be so. If there is not a blueprint of a romantic ideal in our heads which tells us exactly what we think life should be like, then we are not able to measure and prejudge. Most people are abusing their minds with the most moronic expectations, because in the everyday world form and senses are all-important. This is because when mind reincarnates it is held in a tapestry of form, so it has to get knitting to fit in and survive. We all have a tendency to over-knit! The Spirit is still a boy that has not yet grown up and matter is over-knitting because of an instinct that has gone into survival auto-pilot, so as a consequence we in the West have many times more material wealth than we need.

If we find ourselves thinking that we are connected and aligned to Soul/Spirit consciousness, it is more than likely that this is the make-believe of the intellect. The internal process of alignment throws the personality about until it trusts and gives way to it. If we are a witness and as such a 'judge' of ourselves or a witness to God, all we can really do is to allow the aligning to happen. This means that the protection, the fear, the greed and the wanting to be in control, start to be dissolved; the delusions are what we thought we were. It is truly a very simple alchemy and we need to let dis-solution reign. In this process there is so much light coming in from within our cellular memory (whether emotional, mental or physi-ological) that it alchemically completely dissolves the old film of the past and then, because there is an empty space, more light can come in. Matter is part of the process of alignment because it delivers the key of pure instinct, which is the divine side of matter. Pure instinct is a manifestation of Active Intelligence and is as necessary for the process as Spirit. Active Intelligence is the aspect of the one life that holds the vision of the 'how to do it' manifestation.

The dissolving and aligning takes us to the point where, if we have any unease about the world, we will be able to recognise whether it comes from mindsets, emotions, or from something physiological. We are made up of a specific set of harmonious vibra-tions which hold our matter together as bodies, so we have natural tendencies according to the nature of those vibrations. This means that we are not supposed to be completely in harmony with eve-rything we meet on the planet. If you were a lizard you will love to bask in the sun and you can re-grow your tail, but that doesn't work for a goldfish. We don't have to be like a lizard, but we can either resonate and feel like one, or have no affinity with it and be repulsed by it. We need to be true to ourselves, so we don't have to do things that we physiologically don't align to or can't do, just as you can't ask a cat to be a deep-sea diver! We can feel and know what an experience is like, for example being in water like a seal or a dolphin, even if we do not go in the water ourselves. Like The Charioteer in the great 7 we are really going for it, so we know that all our misguided instincts won't pull us down any longer, for we are full of the love and will of God.

The Charioteer is going to 'walk his talk' and the 8 of Justice will enable him to realise his mission with an intelligent understanding, through discrimination and witnessing. He takes it on his shoulders and goes for endurance. He will keep on living and doing, because the process of aligning with the greater life we live in doesn't ever stop; we keep on going, even if we find we want to get off the bus. The choice is either to align or not. When we don't align we struggle and struggle; then we struggle to do the work of naming and witnessing; then we do it all over again – more naming, more witnessing and more struggle!

We need to understand suffering from the energetic rather than the emotional point of view. Every second of the day matter suffers the movement of Spirit and life, it is not to do with emotions but sensations, for how would we ever know that this life is forever flowing and moving if we didn't feel it? It is all a rehearsal for being a perfect witness. We put ourselves through all our mindsets, emotional sets and physical sets to make certain that we know the lesson completely and then we can drop all of it. The same life then carries on and we have the same experiences time and time again, but our perception changes and we understand that this is the way life is. We can get fed up and bored with it, or live with it without even bothering. Matter is only a mirror and a by-product of what is going on in the greater life we live in. We have to own our space and our Solar System, only then to give it back to the greater life.

We can imagine every single one of our cells purifying and so becoming just what it is, a pure message, a pure life and a pure instinct. Then Spirit and matter will do the work like a dream and we will glow in the dark. We will become cells in that greater body and will resonate to it. We are here to witness, to name, to touch with our hands and to remember that we love; not to actually go and do it for the sensation, or 'because it is lovely'. We all have to end up eventually with the golden voice that heals. If we access it from somewhere deep in the Soul, what we say can resonate wisdom and peace in a person or a group Soul. The seat of the co-creation in humanity is at the level of the throat chakra. When we start to go through initiatic work we use the inner lens and work with the Ajna centre, where alignment and integration can happen. The Ajna is where the heart, head and Spirit all come together and we 'see'. Once that has happened it is the job of the throat chakra to express. While the sacrifice of the personality is ongoing, the throat centre is not yet completely free of the glamour and illusion of the self, so mistranslation of the vision may occur. Divine justice can only be understood though the Ajna.

The Ajna centre has to be working in a transpersonal way, being linked to and part of, the heart. Most of the time we translate from the intellect and it is quite easy just to slip into that automatically. When there is a flash of light and we don't know what it is all about, it needs to be expressed through us; we can look at the flash from within and start speaking from a deeper simpler feeling, rather than try to bring in details. If however, we are seeing it from the outside, we have to be patient and quiet enough to wait a little longer and not say anything until we see it from within. If we make a mistake in what we say to a person we have to own that mistake, take responsibility for it and feel the pain of it. Remember things are as they should be and there's no need to flagellate ourselves. If we take full responsibility for whatever we communicate, we are daring to understand that God allows us to make our mistakes as a necessity, for his 'becoming' to pass away quicker.

We have to be three hundred percent responsible; the three-fold human being has to respond to the higher message. We are witnessing without a safety net, so if we fall to pieces it is time for re-alignment or re-ordering. We might find that we actually don't need some of the broken pieces anyway! Even if some harm has been done to another person through our words, we can be sure they will learn something from it. We came in with white gloves of pure intention, but we are not superior to others and are not going to teach them anything, for we cannot open their ears if they do not want to hear their own heart beat. We are truly witnesses and have to be more humble than most lost Souls on the planet, who are willing to make all the so called mistakes in the ongoing experiment. Within all this there is the possibility of getting lost. We are only lost when we forget to look at our own socks or shoes! The 8 of Justice will bring us almost to the point of self-destruction to teach us responsibility.

If we do not meet and make one with our will, we will never be a Sun but a wandering star. We all go through the experiment and have to dare to live our lives up to the ultimate opportunity. We are only instruments, we can't be anything else and so we have to bring the intellect in line with the idea of being used. Life is an automatic training for addiction, which makes us take more and more pictures and seek more and more happiness. Until we give ourselves the right to be used by the God we live in, we will question God and put our fists up saying; "What is the matter with you God, why do I have to be in so much pain, why aren't I winning the lottery?" We know the answer – why have we not committed to the responsibility of buying a ticket? If we align to the higher intelligence of the Soul, which sees the truth rather than the pictures, we heal the addiction to the drama.

Nature is pure, it doesn't complain about being killed or giving away its fruits. It is only there as a tapestry to sustain us in the work we are doing. Humanity is so confused. Brave is the one who, having burnt themselves, keep on burning themselves. It looks a bit stupid but it is brave, for we have to make certain that we have exhausted all the burning passion. When the cup is almost empty we have the choice of either seeing our own Sun-like reflection and rising with the Spirit, or aborting ourselves through self-pity. The addict is like a Sun that refuses to radiate, or to take the responsibility for the pain of his lonely initiation. When he accepts the pain he will start to radiate, thus helping others to dare to follow.

There are people who have come back from complete perdition and all they want to do is to help others; these are the ones that have experienced and overcome addiction. Addiction shows a lot of courage and some people will not be able to manage it, so will render the dark Soul of nature even heavier. We know they are tackling a deep Soul group unease to do with the pain of being aware of the state of the world. We have to help by holding them in love and it is painful, as we understand the pain; the remedy is acceptance of what is. Most people are using addiction as a refusal, a way of not growing up or a way of wanting to go back into the womb. They are seeking that moronic state where they don't have to think and feel; that applies to whatever addiction they have, sex, drugs or anything else. Addiction can be either feeling high or absolutely awful; one is the same as the other.

We have to learn not to personalise. Whoever it is in front of us has potential; they are a Sun and therefore the centre of a universe. However they resonate with us should not be taken personally. When our relationship with them is private and intimate it is difficult not to take things personally, but in this case it is even more important, because when we personalise we are looking for a result, or for the fulfilment of a dream. At the impersonal level if we respond spontaneously with people, it is a Soul-centred reaction and even if we are sounding harsh it will resonate positively because we will be speaking with a golden voice, uncontaminated by our personal will and need. There is no other way and we need more than strength to dare to do that. If we're going to 'walk our talk' we have to have the inner strength to do it in the simplest and clearest way we can, the Active Intelligent way.

Being a judge or a witness is like being a priest; it is devotional and sacred. It is the highest possible attainment for a human being. We have to start by judging in the emotional, intellectual, mundane and social way, because if we haven't done that we would never realise how wrong it is. To call a man a thief who has stolen a piece of bread because he has eight children, a dying wife and no money, is not fair from the standpoint of divine justice. It is society that is not doing what it should, because from the higher point of view that man isn't a thief, rather he has had the courage to go beyond society's rules, so he is on his way to becoming more himself. On the other hand, if someone steals because they are greedy or because they are thrilled by the adrenaline rush from stealing, then we are looking at an addiction. In this latter case they are sick and have a problem at the emotional level, so need to seek help. We are not excusing any crime, but rather understanding it; this card represents the justice that understands the greater picture.

Jesus the Soul said: "If your justice is not superior to that of the Scribes and the Pharisees, you will not enter the Kingdom of God". This is clearly true, because if we give out justice at the everyday level it is not from within, but from an exterior God of form, society and protection that is concerned with maintaining the status quo.

The justice we are talking of is not the justice of man; it is not even the justice of philosophy, which is ethics. Ethics is still a frame of mind that concretises the highest thinking of the intellect of the time and it keeps the thinking of the society bound by that perception. Of course it is better to be ethical than not, but we are not even talking about the justice of an ethical person. Many people stop their spiritual journey because their sense of ethics is so strong and they can't see beyond it. They are righteous, but ethics are man-made intellectual righteousness, so are not centred on karmic divine justice. It is the highest, finest push of the intellect towards an order that is more elegant and beautiful but it has removed itself from its base – the wisdom in nature. Divine justice goes beyond keeping the status quo, it is the justice of potential and so not involved in preserving an order.

We all build our own universe because this is the science of going forward. We know that the exterior world is really all we have to enable us to see ourselves, for it is only the interpretation according to our level of consciousness that enables us to make any sense of the world. Each person's interpretation is entirely unique, so it is not just one 'little me' planet Earth, but many millions, or even billions of 'little me' planet Earths, as numerous as there are leaves on trees; what is more, our interpretation is different each day. We are re-interpreting the world every single minute through the physical, biological, emotional and mental facets and if we give ourselves as instruments for those interpretations, we bring that particular facet alive, which means we are helping with the making our little planet Earth sacred.

The world changes every minute, so it is not an absolute. Justice is born out of the drive of the will of love/wisdom and is becoming through its manifestation. The 8 is the restrictive aspect of the Soul following its karmic duty in matter. It was a symbol for the Soul of the Sun (as in the Son of God) and a guide as far back as ancient Egypt. The world of matter, being not absolute, is only material for us to use, so it is maya or illusion. If we take feelings, forms and mind-sets as absolutes, then we are going into the kind of addiction that causes disintegration.

Even nature doesn't take herself to be an absolute, for if she did there would be no seasons and no death. It is the way we interpret this world that makes up our innermost essence, or Soul. Complete identification between the way we see or interpret the world and our essential being, is exactly what alignment is. Eventually, when we see it is all one, we identify with everything at the formless level of the Soul, rather than the intellect and we see whatever is in front of us from the Soul perspective. This is when we know that in the Soul of the world we are all one and we are it, so the higher Soul of mind and the Soul of nature can unite. This is our egg, the 8. We have complete identification with our reactions, actions and with everything we are doing at the time. We are fusing, witnessing and identifying, all the time. It is a process that says that we are one with the system and we are okay. It is truly the God that says "I don't mind, I am a man and I love you".

We have to renounce ourselves completely, but if we're a spiritual being we cannot spiritually 'judge' anything we do in the world, but only witness. By taking the position of a mediator and a way by which things can happen, we are actually more 'present' in the world. Our task is to become the inner and to persuade the outer to serve the inner. When we really understand that, we are witnessing everything we are doing – the job we are engaged in, the food we are cooking, simply everything. The ultimate aim is to witness twenty four hours a day. As a true witness we are not a 'doer' any more, but are acting as a 'way-by', so allowing co-creation to happen through us. Witnessing is about knowing that whatever we do has the purpose of bringing in more light wherever it is needed; witnessing is not interfering.

In order to witness effectively, we can ask ourselves the questions, "Are there things I am not doing because I don't want the responsibility of doing them?" or "Are there things that I am doing because I love the responsibility that goes with them?" If what we are doing is the only thing at the time that carries the will of God in it, then we've got the true responsibility. The things we are avoiding, or doing because we refuse or love the responsibility are still coming from some reaction of the personality. True responsibility is when Soul moves according to the will of its own Spirit as it responds to karmic guidance and its own God. If we are refusing to do something because we know it is going to push us forward into the unknown, then we should go and do it. If we love to do something because of the responsibility, then we should do it until we drop dead. These two are the good and bad, so in doing both eventually we will become completely aligned with the responsibility of the Soul to Spirit, which will drive the personality.

A judge in society has to act according to the law of the land, which is always looking back in time. Judgment always needs a precedent and because it is the law of the land, it means that the judge will have to renounce the God within and go by the book, unless he makes a big fuss to get the law changed. Many people use religion in the same way, when they give responsibility to God according to the book, which is actually a denial of the God within and a renouncing of self.

If we are engaged in building divine justice on the planet, this can disrupt everyone around us. That stirring up does a lot of good, because we all have to learn to swim by ourselves. We all have to be receptive and 'walk our talk' at the same time, so both the passive and active go together in the Number 8: 'I see light and with that light I see'.

We dream of the consciousness of the one world, which would be globalisation in the highest sense, exteriorised as world peace. We need to carry on holding the vision of the one world and of a globalisation where no one is abused, or sold out, so that the vision can eventually be materialised at the right time. The Emperor has to be very stoical and keep on crystallising the perceived ideas, even if they're misused. Some want to stop globalisation, but the idea itself is not wrong it is only misused. When we support the idea of one world, it almost makes the job of the sharks easier and the third world feels the effects badly, but in spite of that we have to hold the vision of globalisation. Small is beautiful, but it is one world and the world of commerce has to learn that we are all equal and everyone deserves rewards for what they do. Justice has to bring in a different conception of material interest to the actual powers of the world, by rising well above the way the world is directed and driven, so as to bring in the concept of divine justice.

The world is governed by big business, yet it is in the process of changing. We need many little units in humanity seeing clearly, so as to facilitate change and so all our little actions, such as where we shop and what we buy are important, because this is the way big business can change. This is the 8; 'walk your talk and you can change the world!' In every single great movement of civilisations, there has to be a Libran influence to hold the centre. This ability to hold the insight of divine justice is the highest characteristic of Libra; it is holding this steady point that is part of seeing clearly where evolution has got to so far. Money and sex are strongly featured in the energy of Libra, so the right use of the exchanging and merging of energy would have to be in place for a fair Libran instrument to get it right.

Human justice cannot adapt easily, so it refuses life and evolution. Even when it does adapt it takes such a long time that it needs a hero to make it change. It is not a matter of them versus us, because when we are talking about human justice we are talking about the personality in all of us. The personality holds onto what it does every day and the way it does it, because that is what it knows; it has lots of rules and regulations. This is necessary because we need to be organised to proceed with our lives, but do we walk our talk and put divine justice first, or do we hold onto the laws of social justice? Whichever way is okay, there is no intention to judge or criticise but just to be aware.

The characteristic of the Number 8 is to be continually destroying and rebuilding through love and understanding, so it is not a justice that will accuse, intimidate, make a man feel smaller, or punish him and put him in prison; it is a justice that heals and helps man become himself. It can be experienced as harsh, but a point of crisis is where an alchemical transubstantiation takes place, if the will is there to accept the lesson.

Anything that isn't spontaneous isn't from Soul. Our reactions come from the physical, emotional and mental bodies and we could say that is from Spirit, but it is Spirit from the point of view of the personality. The tricky thing is to be honest enough to see whether what is coming through has come from the personality or from the Soul. It is important to make sure that we don't put our own version of the world onto what we do, also to monitor that our vision of its possibilities are not sclerosed into some romantic mindset. We also need to fully respect other points of view, because this is the way the God we live in can see itself at the time; there are many ways of seeing the one world, many different shades and colours.

With this higher kind of justice, judgment, or witnessing, there is no way that we can call a cat a poodle, because it is justice in the divine way of truth. We can only take on the judgment position, if we take the full responsibility of accepting at the time that we are personally out of the way. Because every single point of sunshine has its own world around it, we need to fully recognise that our world will make certain that through karma, we will meet whatever our perception isn't aligned to. There is a song that says, 'I am not afraid of eternity', which means 'I am not afraid of making mistakes and having to come back forever!' This is about not being afraid to follow the pure instinct and the God within, which can mean we are willing to be in disgrace or to transgress the rules of society. If we come from that place of truth and justice, we do not want to be different through arrogance or lack of care for others; it is not that kind of disgrace. Through the eyes of the world it might seem the same, but there is a world of difference. We do not wish to be different for the sake of being different, through lack of feeling, love, or judgment; in fact it is the opposite, because it comes from a higher impulse within the Soul. More love will be released if we dare to be hurt more by our act than the ones we hurt! Beware of the saviour/ martyrdom syndrome though!

When we take on that position and align, we can only be a shadow of the real thing, for the real thing is always an inner vision. The justice of men can never be an end in itself, because it only serves whoever is powerful at the time. When all men are wise and aligned to truth, there will be no need for ordinary justice and true justice will rule.

Anything that is manifested is a facet of the God we live in. The God we live in is pure concept, so eventually we will become pure justice and pure wisdom. This is where we are going and when we have reached this point form will have no pull whatsoever. We are only here to help people to realise that we are Souls and only one Soul, for the world is one. We have to be able to see the state of people in the world with honesty, for even if we don't yet walk, breathe and live as Souls twenty four hours a day, we are earnest. The majority of people have not started on this path, and are not even aware of Soul, so it will take a long time.

There is no alignment to achieve other than to the will; the first step is for the personality to align to the Soul and that has to be done via the will aspect. In this second Solar System, we are working at revealing the Soul and allowing it to completely overshadow the personality, so that humanity will be as one Soul. The third Solar System will have to realise complete alignment to the will aspect of God; the focus then will be on the etheric rather than the form. The love/wisdom principle is attainable in this second Solar System; this is the promise of the second Solar System. When we perceive ourselves as Soul, the form aspect of the person we are communicating with, for example their gender or colour, disappears. The Soul perception knows that form is transitory. However, we will still need exteriorisation because of the alignment of will and matter, so matter will still have to play a part. There will be no systems beyond the third, because in this Solar System the unification of the Trinity is the ultimate goal. In terms of time we are talking of billions of years and beyond that, when the Solar System becomes a black hole because the Sun is realised and everything is aligned. The only true understanding of the movement of Spirit through the Solar System belongs to Lord Karma, Sanat Kumara and beyond, where the will of God is known. All we know is that God is everywhere and everything.

Divine justice is a state of grace; any state of being is a way or path and this one is a way of unconditional love. 4, 6 and 8 represent cycles which carry an active aspect, for the characteristic of these numbers is an action of Spirit into matter, being the only medium where the spiritual work can be seen to be done. Justice in this card is represented by a woman and she is a 'way' or a state which represents the intuitive, loving side. It is as though the Emperor, in looking at himself in the mirror of Justice, sees into his deepest heart and acknowledges a very strong internal life. This allows him to precipitate all the divine understanding he needs to have and be in touch with divine justice. This intuitive side is represented as a woman, being the receptive feminine aspect, because there is no way Justice can base itself on facts, precedence or books. It has to be an inner vision that gives us the answer to why a thing is the way it is; an inner love, an inner wish to help, understand and heal.

We can only be 'just', in the sense of divine justice, if we have an intuitive comprehension of people and love them as they are. This is the perfect point of balance of the Number 8; it is the respect and love of karma through intuitively recognising the courage of the Soul as it demonstrates receptivity and action simultaneously. If we are unable to see what has allowed a person to fall, then we cannot help and understand them. If we don't want to partake of the world, then we have to be wise enough not to judge. If we are not going towards others with an open mind and an open heart, then we have to shut our mouths. The analytical mind reinforces prejudices; once we have a prejudice we see the world through the lens of that prejudice and continually reinforce it, because the intellect can only feed itself. Only an intuitive communication, directed to the Soul of a person with no intermediary, no language, no symbol – nothing, gives a total understanding between two beings, because it is Soul to Soul. The aim of justice is to make man aware of his insufficiencies. Insufficiency is a gentle, polite and soft word, which reflects that fact that it is quite alright to have insufficiencies, so let's not be afraid to look at them. If we are going to look at ourselves clearly and take the opportunity offered by the cycle of the 8, we will see them and be inspired to uplift them. The more we see the more we can be gentle with ourselves and others. Intuition can only truly operate when the mind is receptive and clear and the personality is not seeking anything for its own satisfaction or recognition.

Justice has a blue cloak with a green lining. Blue in this case, is a symbol of spirituality and green is the colour of life. The green lining to her coat tells us that no life is real unless it is true or spiritual. Nature is real because nature is entirely driven by the Spirit of her group. She is at one with her Spirit and doesn't hide it, so she is successful, pure and has pure instincts. Anything that goes away from pure instinct becomes drama, misunderstanding and misperception. We need to go through these distortions and there's no blame, but it is not real, it is maya, illusion and glamour. We are experiencing life to bring the instrument back to its spontaneous nature, so that Spirit can feel at home. Through this natural self awareness we realise we are one Soul or one mind. Communication then is instant, silent or very simple.

Nothing is real unless it is true. 'I will to be true' from the Lord's Prayer expresses the Number 8 and the purpose of true justice. The blue and green must always be united, for it is the Spirit alone that animates and gives life to matter.

Her dress is a deep red, the same red as the coat of the High Priestess. The puffed sleeves show the green of life and the gold of incorruptibility. The white turned over cuffs show that her action is pure, divine and true. Justice cannot be anything without the higher, holy wisdom that we cannot learn; this is divine justice. We can learn the 'outer' science, the science of sacred geometry (how everything happens to be made), but wisdom is lived and earned, in the sense of putting ourselves forward for the experiences and feeling the fire of Spirit within us. Divine justice can only be experienced once we have gone through the portal; it is a state of grace. So we can't *learn* divine justice, it is just in us according to our alignment so far to the higher mind. The red colour shows us the burning fire of the great wisdom in our hearts. Although we may strive and yearn, the 'road to Damascus' experience never comes when we expect it. The attaining of something does not come at the exact time that we think we deserve it, for it can only be a projection of how we saw the world yesterday. When we drop all that, eventually it may come. Perception is the key, for it is all one mind.

We have seen the plaited necklace before in The Emperor, representing the strength and purity of the initiate. It symbolises the three aspects of the physical, emotional and mental, unified and working together as one. We need to have the courage to find divine wisdom in the etheric of our hearts, so that we can manifest it into matter. To do that we have to have strength beyond strength, for we have to break our hearts physically, emotionally and mentally until we reach the heart of creation. There is an openness to the plait, which shows us the love aspect; this is a different quality from the closed plait of The Emperor.

The curly blond hair of the figure in Number 8 symbolises the Sun. Her hair takes the form of solar rays, because she brings light. As the Sun sustains life, so divine justice brings new light into the understanding of the Soul. Like our physical Sun, she sustains true life; also she guides Spirit into right action. Without this incredible quality that Justice brings, the Charioteer would achieve nothing and his chariot would be going all over the place, in many different directions. She looks austere because the inner certainty of the cold light of reason (unconditional love) is what moves her. She has closed the door to the temptation of warming up this flow of love, by not conceding to fall into the emotional need of baby humanity. She looks stern as she sits there holding the heavy sword, because to look in a mirror and see ourselves for what we are can be tough medicine, but it is lifesaving.

Her red hat with a crown on top of it is a symbol of sovereignty, for divine justice reigns over the world. The crown is not gold because divine justice doesn't need the protection of incorruptibility. By its own nature Justice comes from beyond our own system, so it will not be tainted. Justice holds sovereignty over us and is the only reason that the Solar System exists, for it has its roots in the karmic becoming of the universe and is forever performing the infinite work of the cosmic 8, until the one who cannot be named resumes his activity. We seek justice on Earth; the kings, priests and politicians will want to enforce their own justice on everybody else, because it gives them power. Justice is seen as a tool, when in fact *we* are the tools. Divine justice is far above us and it isn't for us to use it, but for us to be used by it.

She holds the broad sword of justice in her right hand. What it represents is not judgment in the sense of weighing up what is right or wrong, but it is a statement about the inevitability of the state of the world at the time; This state is according to the willingness of mankind to grow out of their self-centredness, which is the most difficult thing for mankind to realise. People are responsible for part of their own suffering. It is not a sword that is used to strike or hurt anybody, because it is a symbolic sword. In the middle ages it would have been a symbol of temporal power over everyday life, which is relevant because Number 8 holds the throne of temporal power. This has the purpose of reminding us that we are here because of our legacy of the karmic work that no one can escape. It is a just power and it has got to be administered with love, because nothing is viable if it hasn't gone through understanding the love principle.

The scales she is holding are gold, to signify incorruptibility. They are not for weighing in the sense of measuring good or bad, but rather to measure the vibration of the Soul. This is about looking with the eyes of the Soul, at the intent of what is behind the form; looking at the impulse behind our behaviour and owning the needs and mindsets behind our actions. To see this we may have to look intensely many times. The same action will have very different values according to the level of consciousness of the person, because morally, materially, psychically, intellectually and emotionally, we are all at very different levels of development. We are not all at the same level of awareness, so there is no way we can judge or compare the behaviour or actions of other people. Most of the time we are driven by our own needs, wishes and wants. Only the divine mind can know the secret intention behind someone's behaviour and they may not even have seen it themselves. An act often bears no relation to the first intention, because of all the covering up and story-telling that goes on.

The scales remind us of the duality of the world and that we are intermediaries between the physical and the spiritual. We can only function in this world by maintaining a healthy balance between these two. The word 'balance' suggests an outer equilibrium or status quo, but by reaching this point of balance we may not be outwardly progressing or going anywhere, so that is not really the aim. The point of balance we are talking about is the state of the mind where the experience has been understood. We learn to walk the tightrope for the next experience until it doesn't need the support any more and the mind is truly aware, suspended and poised, therefore performing as a witness and messenger, regardless of whether the scales are up or down. We go forward and keep on moving and so long as the inner God and the inner wisdom are inside us, we do not need to worry about falling.

It is important and necessary that our inner and outer lives come together; we cannot refuse one or the other. Our will must move towards the depths of our inner life, using all the opportunities of the material picture of the world that is in front of us. We explore the exterior world with the light from within us; 'I bring light to what I see and I see that which I bring light to'. If we do not do this we do not become the star and the centre of our world; we have to have communication with the inner and the outer all the time. Most of us will find a way to cover up and not do that inner communication properly. It is not about questioning what somebody else has done to us, or how they have behaved, rather it is about us being completely responsible for the way we have received life and the way we have reacted and interacted. When we have inner communication we can communicate peace to the world.

The chair on which Justice is seated is framed by two great pillars, one on either side; they are topped by symbolic shells. These pillars represent the structure through which Spirit involves into its own manifestation, in the laws of the genetic code of nature. The pillar on the side of her left arm, topped with brown, represents this phase of involution in matter. On this pillar, there are sixteen white receptive cups depicting this process. From the top, the first three are clearly visible and represent the concept. The tenth one down is hardly seen; this one is about Spirit coming back into matter, full of potential. The eleventh one is invisible and represents the beginning of the karmic work. The fifteenth cup is almost hidden, telling us that there is a choice to be made between self-gratification and self-sublimation. The sixteenth cup in this pillar is so full of the Spirit, yet so hidden to itself that it might only see its life as belonging to nature, by using and being used under the laws of life and death. Here the 16 becomes the needed 7 (16/7), as we need the fiery zeal of the 7, The Chariot, to give itself up to truth so that the mind can recognise itself as the evolved consciousness of the man who seeks universal truth.

Starting from the bottom of the pillar on the right hand side of the figure of Justice, we see that the seventeenth cup (the 17/8) is completely hidden, as God and his creature are naturally evolving with the help of the Number 8 of divine justice, in this phase of the work. We can observe that after the last of the so-called karmic numbers, the hilt of the sword of Justice is firmly anchored in the twenty-second cup (22/4), which gives the promise of salvation of matter through the higher consciousness of humanity. The twenty-third cup (23/5) holds the sacred weight of having to fly in matter, so as to learn to co-create. The twenty-fourth cup (the 24/6) hides the alchemical process in time and space of the transmutation of matter into mind. As we come into the next three cups, the Spirit can be released out of its immediate personalised karma in the twenty-ninth cup (29/11) and recognise divine justice as its guide. As the mind rises into the shell of the initiate at the top, this column is topped by the colour red to represent the burning Spirit of truth. The two pillars are framed in gold, to remind us that we cannot break the laws of nature, or the karmic laws. The shells on top of both pillars are associated with St James, the patron Saint of alchemy. The pilgrimage of the initiate to St Jacques de Compostelle in Northern Spain, describes the journey of the involution and the evolution of the Soul into initiation.

The highest manifestation of God's glory for mankind is to be used as a witness. It is this weighing-up in man that will allow him to rise in love towards the God of life. In this glory he has the conviction that he will never want to do anything else but to serve God. No justice can be administered without loving care, for we cannot weigh up without love and understanding. One of the problems with goodness and loving care is that it can degenerate into weakness and into wanting something for self, so this Justice is depicted as austere.

We are all one mind and one Soul; there is only one quality of mind that is actually its intrinsic raison d'être and therefore the most important – that is communication; there is nothing else. Our own inner communication needs to be flowing like healing water. It is okay to rave and rage, putting our fists up at God, for when we see people enraged we know they are on their way; rebellion is recognition that there is something mightier than us. When we express that rage we start to talk or communicate to that higher thing and are therefore expanding our mind. When we express love and care we open the mind in our heart. A Soul cannot be static.

Only those who have access to the wisdom can be fair, according to their access to the truth. There is no book to read with formulas, drawings and patterns, to give us the answers, because sacred science is entirely an inner process of lighting up the cells. The Archangel Michael, the proud angel with the sword, is an instrument for divine justice, as we are a way by or an instrument for divine justice to work through us. The more we align with our inner life, the more we understand and the more we love. We are the moving, thinking, feeling, singing, loving dolls of the stage of Earth. Eventually our instruments will resonate and align with its inner life, for the Earth is living, loving and moving. The life within it is actually doing it, so we can give over to it and drop the fears. Eventually we will become completely aligned with that greater life and realise that we are flowing with the life of the system, so we have become 'systemic'. We have achieved the work; we have achieved clarity in the egg of our life, so one cell in the body of humanity has rendered itself as bright as possible. Okay, we are not God, but we have made ourselves into good communicators and 'way-bys' for the God we live in; clear, clean eggs, little balls of light.

The 8 builds, destroys, discriminates and has inner honesty. It is a way that follows its own leader in being a 'way-by' for that leader. This is divine wisdom having found a way to precipitate itself with a blessing, with a sense of love and with an extremely zealous, unstoppable urge to go and serve divine justice. Without the strength of divine justice in Number 8, The Hermit (Number 9) wouldn't be able to do the work that he has to do. The zeal comes from The Chariot at Number 7, who has an unstoppable urge to go and serve divine justice. Divine justice is the way of the Soul.

The Hermit, l'Ermite
The Way Back

In the ninth card we meet the simple, severe figure of the Hermit holding
his light before him as he carefully prepares the path for those who choose
to open their minds into introspection. He is an uncompromising master,
for he is completely beyond the outer world of needs and desires. He hides
his radiance under a plain brown cloak, for its brightness is so great that it
would blind those who are not ready to see it. He checks the ground with
his staff, to make certain that all the treasures of mankind's previous experiences are recognised and used. He is Father Time, or Saturn and his job is
to lay the tracks of eternity for the generations of light seekers to come.

If we look at the whole evolution of the spiritual perception of mankind, at first we had the material, elemental gods of nature that fed or killed us; we had respect for these gods through fear. Aligning to the natural elemental gods, such as the wind or the fire, enabled us to have a lot of success as shamans, because this is an elemental world. Even to this day, when learning about the seven rays of manifestation, we tend to appreciate them as real entities rather than movements of energy, through the need to associate with masters.

The multi gods of Egypt were perceived as elemental gods. The Pharaohs of Egypt worshipped and revered whichever elemental God, or phase of the Sun, was most beneficial for what was going on at the time. In the time of the Pharaoh Akhenaton the people thought that the gods were bringing pestilence and famine, so he brought in the idea of worshipping just one God to solve those problems; that could be described as a political solution. As a consequence people at the time actually started to believe in the idea of one God. Moses was another example of a leader who found a practical political solution by taking his people out of slavery. Practically any change that has happened in the social condition of mankind can be called political.

In the ninth cycle the mind has accumulated all the possible wisdom in the field of experience that it was visiting, so simple reality should dissolve any illusion of what might have been and the world is seen for what it is. Practical, intelligent, political solutions can be used through technology, trade and science. The people who are successful in these spheres can be vehicles to implement a new future for mankind, through goodwill and vision. So if you truly want to be altruistic, get hold of the money and do business! Money is power and you can infuse power with goodwill, so that it becomes a force for good.

God is more in our image than we are in the image of God, for it is our level of consciousness that perceives God. We are here as witnesses of the life of the God we live in, so we can only have an image according to our needs, fears and aspirations. As we drop our self-preoccupation in the cycle of 9, in the giving up of the self by turning towards service, the appreciation of God becomes simpler and therefore more real.

Each card in the 22 Major arcana of the Tarot represents a phase in the journey of the initiate. Each phase will contain the experience of the card before, to be applied and re-focused in the card to come; it is truly an ongoing journey. It is the same with numbers, the 2 has the echo of the experience of the 1 and the call of the experience of the 3 in it. To give another example; if you are on a journey from England to Germany, you are breathing a different atmosphere as you pass through France and before you get to Düsseldorf you've still got a bit of French accordion music in your ears, even though you're already in Germany. At each experience we collect something, then at some points we have a 'rest' and go right into our locked in memory to see what it is about; this is a good description of the Number 9.

If we had to describe the figure in the card as a person, we'd say that all we can see is just a head and a skeleton, with the absolute minimum of flesh for it to move and be alive. The scaling down of wants and needs is characteristic of the 9; that is emphasised even more by his brown hood and coat, which offers shelter for the process of reflection and internalisation.

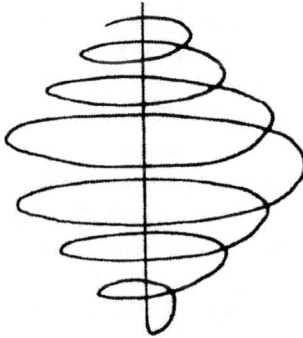

Figure 1. Spirals and cycles of 1 to 9.

We have to go through many cycles from 1 to 9; as we do so we are gathering every experience that a sphere has to offer until we have refined our vibration out of the density of that field of experience to enter another; this is what is meant by an initiation. The 1 to 6 is the gathering of experience, the 7 is fusing the experience and the awareness of the experience, to allow the 8 to make sense of it. After that the 9 unravels the loop and what is unnecessary in that experience dies, so that the consciousness can be reborn with only what it needs to take to the next cycle.

Dying means removing a cellular memory from the atom, which holds the physical, emotional and lower mental patterns. Nature is not going to give up her cellular memory easily, because she's survived for millions of years only though pure instinct; this is why pure instinct is precious and divine. As far as nature is concerned, if we're surviving we're doing well, even if our survival is based on fighting and using deception. Whatever has been successful so far is therefore retained. The tenaciousness of nature creates a resistance to dying, which can cause resistance to the process of inner transformation; there has to be a death of the old ways. We should not have a problem with the idea of physical death, for reality tells us that the higher consciousness is eternal.

The phase of the 9 is there to remind us that it cannot go any further with the physical experience, so it has to give up the importance of experiencing and deliver the wisdom from what it has been through. In a given experience the 9 will measure its internal vibration in order to see into the cellular structure, to check whether it feels right or not. It is this natural sense of righteousness which gives the 9 its sensitive spiritual spine; if people under the influence of 9 personalise this Soul sensitivity, they have a tendency to feel superior. When they allow themselves to be pulled back into an unnecessary experience, they will then recognise their humanity and lose all sense of superiority.

This is a journey that goes backwards and it is very slow, because we have the double-take of moving fast with our train (which is where life takes us) and at the same time sitting in the train motionless and watching from within. We are processing the experience of what is going on at the time, as slowly as possible so as not to leave a single cell unturned. So when we feel or think something, we have to go deep into it, to see if there's anything extra it wants to deliver. The process of internalisation is challenging and awesome, because there

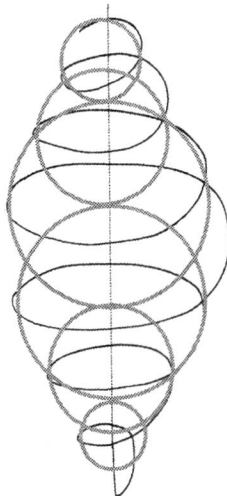

Figure 2. Levels of consciousness, spirals of spheres.

is no turning back. The internal light comes back to lighten the path of the ones who want to be on the journey. It is not 'a bowl of cherries', because we're going to end up with no fruits at all. It is a tricky one, because at this level we don't judge, though we recognise good and bad, but at the same time we don't qualify 'bad' in the sense of 'naughty', but rather as useless. The perception of 'bad' just becomes 'needs' and we shouldn't feel bad because we have needs, for we all have them. Eventually the mind resides in the centre, moving up and down the inner core, catching glimpses of opposite realities.

All these are actually spheres, not flat lands that overlap each other. So we can see that there will be the remains of the first level of consciousness in the second sphere, and the remains of the second in the third and so on. As we work in the sphere we are in, we still have to go for all the experiences that are in the spheres above and below.

The way of The Hermit is very slow, because he is checking every single pebble on the path, with the light of his inner will and love of truth. This means at every single reaction to life's events that he meets on the way, he will acknowledge the wisdom gained from it and then move on. He's making certain that the next life is actually being processed in the now, because he has understood that past, present and future is the same. He is Saturn, Chronos or Father Time. He knows that where we walk is the past and that the future can only be made out of the appreciation of the past. He is teaching mankind that in time and space we can discern, internalise, depersonalise and go with the flow of time. There is no need to rush or stop, just carry on. It is about understanding that when we are in the present we are always faced with the past, so as we learn that wisdom, the present doesn't exist and our past can become our revised future. From that we can see there is no past, present, or future, only awareness. The great lesson of The Hermit is that we have to make a leap of faith, so each day we experience is a step in the deep sea of the past, to reveal the Sun of the future.

If we haven't mined the ground properly and found all the gold we are supposed to be finding, then we need to do it: that is Soul retrieval and the gold is the wisdom of experience from the Soul. Before we become a hermit, we throw our goodwill all over the place to situations or people who might not know they need it; this is the 'casting pearls to swine' from the old story. The beauty of that story is that 'little pigs' cannot eat the pearls, for pearls are the wisdom from the Soul-transmuted experiences, so they cannot be used by the little pigs because they can only use what still needs to be transmuted.

These pearls of golden wisdom, good faith and good will, are all the things that come when the Soul gasps for the higher air; these will still be in the soil that The Hermit walks on. What he releases with his staff are all the good intentions that have not been used, or have even ended up with weird results; they break our hearts every time we look at them. As we understand that it was true gold that we gave at the time and though it didn't have what we thought was the right result, from the point of view of Soul we will see that it actually *was* the 'right' result. Even a Hermit will not be able to see the long-term view of what we call the collective karma. So if we make mistakes with good intention we shouldn't beat our selves up, but wait until the 9 probes the ground and finds the gold.

A well formulated thought has a potent vibration pattern before it is grounded in action, even if it hasn't been expressed. That unexpressed thought is picked up by mass consciousness and is exteriorised in forms and actions. Good intentions are like spontaneous thoughts and will have an effect on us and the groups' karmic life. If we know that each thought, word or action has a karmic impact on the collective that should help us to get ourselves out of the picture. When we know that our actions and thoughts are going to impact on the collective, the responsibility is revealed to us that we have to bring back every response or reaction to Soul. That is part of the great responsibility of the 9. By disappearing into the centre and clarifying the understanding, the mind becomes more collective and the humanitarian quality of the 9 can be revealed.

Bringing back our response to life into the light of the Soul is the way we cleanse our personality and perception of other people. All of us born in the 1900s are here to guide humanity into spiritual leadership and to lay down tracks for others to follow. So we have to be good 'navvies' by having as little personal intent as possible, so as not to cloud the future. By what we do or think we actually affect future generations. Humanity is one mind, so being the trail maker is a huge responsibility.

The responsibility of Saturn as Father Time is to expose the timelessness of the Soul. He's strict and severe and will not be softened by any cinema, or taken in by any artifice we can give him. The more we try, the more Saturn will harden; he's not going to let us get away with any game playing, because he is the realm of reality. He can be like that because he's the one who can gather the most love in his heart for humanity. Beyond all the hardness and coldness is reality. Think of a realised person; why would they even want to be bothered with people if they didn't have love for them? This love is not the lovey-dovey type of love, but it brings us into the reality of how the world is and how it works; it shows us what is worthwhile and so allows the judgment of the 8 to be transpersonalised. With the 8 the job is discernment. Anybody who hasn't got enough of the zeal of the 7 won't go through discernment and so won't transmute any wants or needs. Then in the 9 of The Hermit, zeal and discernment has to go inwards, so we have to get off The Chariot. The releasing of the wisdom in the 9 will set us in good stead to come back on The Wheel of Fortune where we will be able to put our wisdom into action. We don't have to become Jesus in one day; instant enlightenment can be dangerous for your health! There is no doubt that when we are reborn into The Wheel of Fortune we will throw the gold to the little pigs again. Even with all the goodwill and the love we have in us, we do not understand enough the karmic work of the world to apply the love/wisdom appropriately to the Wheel of Fortune. It is the Hermit who is going to make certain that we are not going to waste too much time playing the game on the wheel. It is alright to be active in politics or business, for these are practical ways to pass the message on. In fact it is alright to be in whatever we are doing, for it all takes us back onto the Wheel of Fortune.

There is no fun in this card, but there should be a sense of humour. We need to be humble, look at our reaction to the world we live in and be a little bit kind to ourselves. Aim to be a hermit who hasn't got a hole in his coat, for there is not one single action, thought, or intent that we can leave unturned: that is the way the 9 has to work. The Hermit has to collect all the work and experiences so far, from the 1 to the 8, to see it all as part of the human condition in order to distil the gold from all the experiences so far for the future generations, process it and close the door on what is illusionary and of no use. The more Hermit-light (wisdom) there is to shine on the path, the better, deeper, clearer and brighter the track is for whoever comes next; that might be you! The whole Life experience is one.

The Hermit has great responsibility. His coat tells us that there is no artifice, no uniform and no personality. Without the coat the shining, inner light would be revealed to the world and would blind or destroy those people who are not ready to be put in the light. He is depicted as an old man, because he is an old Soul and going to die. He's been on a long journey and has to be extremely aware, sharp and vigilant, because of the responsibility that he carries, both for the inner work that has to be achieved and the effect on his environment. Here we must experience an end to some level of self, such as fame, recognition and social reward. The Hermit type of people do tend to starve their own survival needs and not care for themselves, if they haven't understood the state of having no needs. There must be a degree of kindness towards self, which will naturally set in when we develop compassion towards others. Although we have no needs, the bit of flesh that carries us, does. We're going to go on a long march and if we are going to do the work of turning up the pebbles and helping others to turn up their pebbles, we have to be kind to our bodies so as to survive and do the job for the collective.

Before people understood what 'no-need' meant, the idea of need didn't occur. 9's go back and re-live the experiences of many lives and in doing so they very often work for the group Soul. But all life is asking us to do, is just to be happy in our skins and this is a great achievement. This is being happy with our biological, emotional and mental past, which means that we are at ease with life altogether. That is already quite a high achievement; at the stage of the 9 we have the opportunity to realise this state. We have peace with the world if we are happy in our skins; we don't need very much and we don't have to suffer. The Hermit knows he has taken the wisdom from the many experiences of life, and so he can leave behind the needs that instilled those experiences. He knows that he stands on many spheres of experience and that he has to reappear in a brand new one. The link between the two spheres is disappearance; that is the highest work of the 9.

He holds a very interesting baton; it is not a cane and he's not leaning on it. There are seven rings on it and eight levels; he himself is the ninth level. The seven rings on his staff represent the seven chakras or levels of consciousness. This is the great work at Number 7 of the 1 fusing with Soul and coming into the world to conquer it with truth, love and healing. Then the tight wave of the 8 guides him, and takes him to the 9, where he has to revisit all the stages again. The baton is touching the ground to feel if the past experience has delivered its wisdom, before he takes his next step. The ground that he is touching is life. He knows that what is in front of him is always the past and he has to make certain he's not going to miss picking up a single pearl of wisdom to take with him when he disappears.

He is a perfect Hermit, so he is going to be checking the vibration of the experience in front of him to see where it is coming from, therefore checking his own level of consciousness and his reaction to life. These tell him where the need for purification is and where the pearl is. We know that wisdom is found deep underground in the Earth's Soul, so The Hermit is inwardly dowsing with his baton. With each contact we make with life, we have an opportunity to check our instruments to find out which chakras are involved in the reaction, for in the esoteric sense we are talking about learning to be in charge of the instrument, therefore to be in charge of the seven chakras and the seven levels of consciousness. The aim is always to find the centre. The Hermit has visited all the levels of awareness with his instrument, so he can go deep into the karmic genetic memory, which is deeper than the heart of nature, because his consciousness needs to reach the Earth's Soul. This is the highest, deepest, and most intimate level that we can reach with our human Soul.

The little snake is an emblem of 'Chtonien', which represents the wisdom coming from the Spirit of the underground. This is the wisdom locked into our cellular memory from ages past. The snake's mouth is open, meaning that he is aware and testing the air constantly with his tongue, just as The Hermit is testing the ground with his baton. This is the man who has complete awareness of his seven levels of consciousness and who also has the wisdom of his inner animal, which is completely aware and instinctive. The Hermit tells us to stop playing the game, to drop the workshop, go into real life and act. He will only guide the ones who have the sparkle of initiation in their eyes. He will not look for initiates, for they have to come to him, but just like Buddha he knows what the physical needs are, so whoever comes to him he would answer their immediate needs. He would not question our level of consciousness. The main urgency is to care for the biology on the planet, for we are in a world that needs basic care.

He is an incarnation of Saturn, tall and bony, with a head like a skull and a beard to symbolise wisdom and age. The little snake is his companion and an aspect of himself; it looks like the ancient saturnine sign of a dolphin with a little tail. He is truly the perfected hermit, older even than Chronos, the Father of time. The emblem of Capricorn as a curled up dolphin comes from the birth of the concept of time; The Hermit is the glow in matter that knows and was there almost before matter. Time is the great judge of our lives and the wonderful thing is that time will actually annul everything that isn't true, so it heals. It is that deep wisdom aspect that knows that if what we love goes away, it will come back if it is truly part of us, so we will keep meeting it. Our desire for peace and a bit of compatibility is known, for nothing passes our hermit by, even the germ or possibility of something. The trial by time is the only test that assures a true value and he, as father Time, can even bring back from oblivion some of the great initiatic lives we have never heard of. These are the great Souls who had the zeal of the love/wisdom aspect, which drove them to take the path of responsibility to the great life we live in and disappear into service. There are thousands of good lives being lived and loads of good work going on that is not publicised. The Hermit has a light, not because he wants to be seen but the opposite, for he is guiding himself with the light that he is becoming. He is protecting the alchemical work with the humble appearance of the brown cloak, to remind the ones who hold the light to remain humble and so be free of wants and needs. We can feel grateful because someone has been kind to us and that is survival, but when we can feel gratitude for the fact that there's a great long chain of good lives, that is when we can feel grace. When we appreciate the pure energies of the masters, we are grateful for the gift of life in the true sense.

The Hermit has a powerful skeleton and he is dry, with just enough flesh. His bones represent the crystallisation of Spirit, so here we have the will in action for the truth, with the heart full of love. The head or cranium is the most important thing, because through the brain Spirit can be decoded and expressed. The head represents the higher man and is the instrument for the process of thought. When there is flesh on bones we can cover up and lie to ourselves, but when the bones show, it tells us there is no game-playing or cover-up, for he is a man with no makeup whatsoever. He's an old, intransigent man, who refuses to lessen the violence of his thoughts with the softening influence of the form. He says what he thinks and when he doesn't want to speak, his silence is even more dreadful and loaded than his words. If we are after something from him, then he's not going to tell us; when we are waiting for an answer it won't be a solution to the problem we have, it will tell us to hold steady in time and space and learn to shine brighter.

If he wanted to bring the light to everybody, they would not understand him; they could even abuse, use and mock him. They would break his wings, to make him fall from the sky of life to the Earth of the dead. Loads of Souls have come in and put themselves through that trial and the ones who still fly with broken wings have done the work of the 9 well. We have to be very careful, for we all know that we can be taken in by the illusion and by our past at any moment. If we are a strong internaliser we have to learn not to be taken in by the pattern of our own mindsets, or by the persona that we are playing at the time. To be really naked means to be tuned only into the essence.

At the ninth level The Hermit is going to be using his baton to check each level of consciousness. He's not checking to see if the ground is safe, but to find any resonance from a past experience that has not been healed or achieved, or which might be able to deliver some pearls of wisdom to give to the next generation.

Before the consciousness in the 9 realises that it is the light of the Soul, it will be very sensitive to situations, people and reactions. The work here would be to learn to differentiate between another's state and our own, so that we can avoid behaving or reacting on their behalf and therefore lose ourselves in the work. Before it gives the responsibility of the reaction to the internal life, the consciousness at the ninth level might exteriorise some of the worst aspects of the behaviour and reaction of all the previous cycles of experience.

We know what we know and others know what they know, so there's no need to argue. We don't need to hold onto the point of view from where we see life, or impose it on other people. If at the same time our appreciation of the same experience is lovely and our friend's is not, that is just how it is; both experiences are right. The one who is a Hermit is more likely to be right, because he doesn't *need* to be right.

We all want our own truth to be universal. We all have righteousness on our side and the banners to show it, but true reality has nothing to do with right and wrong, it is what is there and therefore it cannot be either right or wrong. The judgment of reality, in the sense of an action or thought can bring in right and wrong, but that is not what we are talking about. We are all real and everything on the planet is real, so we can only discern who is making an illusion out of reality and who isn't. How you receive an experience is where you focus your lens, either into maya, glamour, illusion, or Soul awareness. This is why we need to allow everybody their thought and their appreciation.

Time, as a measure of what has actually happened in a particular movement in space, has the limits of its expectation; because we know that, time will never fail. We don't need to conquer the world in one day, for there is no doubt that, in time, things will transform. So The Hermit creates limits to help us understand that it will never fail. It is not through theory, learning from books, or running workshops, but through the hard contact with everyday life that this wisdom is acquired. He is truly the hardest and driest of masters, for it is with our blood that we write the lessons, with our tears that the track ways and rivers are made in our flesh and thoughts, for the new generations to come. Live, experience and internalise fully and forcefully and the God we live in will be pleased.

When we work with people, we are all doing a bit of The Hermit's work and know that just understanding something is not enough. The understanding of the process of the experience is what a person might have, but they need to take it deep down inside themselves, right into the cellular memory, for any transformation to happen and that is something that only the person themselves can do. It is nothing to do with us and them, and nobody's good or bad, just as when there's no water to flow down a river bed there's nothing we can do, that is how it is; it is just not the right time of the year.

He's found all the vanities and knows that everything in everyday life is vanity. He has understood that the needs that torment and pull at us are about a longing for new things and they are only the symbolic manifestation of the inner pull for something else. While we're looking for a new face, person, landscape, country, or job, if we want it just for the sake of having something new it is outward, but what is really happening is that something else from within is calling us. While we are looking at new forms, we haven't yet found our inner vibration or our centre. If we use the method of this world of Maya or illusion to find ourselves we will never achieve it, for it is only when we actually rise above it or internalise, that we can see that all we were after was to be above the problem; then we can deal with it.

Meditation is to be encouraged all the time, but whatever system of meditation we use, we have to go beyond the illusion of the method, for if we don't, we are not really meditating. While we are using a system and don't break through, all we're doing is using a system, but once we drop it we can allow the inner life to take over, which is well beyond any system.

In the ancient myth of the God Saturn (Chronos in Greek mythology), he ate his own children, which is a way of saying that what is created will be dissolved in time. Creation is the manifestation of an idea, life or system, which renders the service needed at the time. Once it has served its purpose it is eaten up, assimilated and digested by time. The Solar System goes through many different stages and in each stage a different planet will be the ruler, so things have to be withdrawn and given back, in order that the new ruler can do his work energetically. Basically anything that is built in the temporal, or is of matter, illusion, want or need, will disappear. Throughout time, that has happened with empires, civilisations, races, in nature with species of animals, in fact all types of things die and the actual life has gone. Only what has come out of an essence that is worthy of merging with the greater life will remain. Truth is this essence, which will remain well after the form has disappeared, so in the story of humanity and the progression of civilisations only the best of the past should be kept for the next cycle. What endures from the beginning of time as teaching has to be sound and true. The very first commandment which has been given by a prophet to mankind was not to abuse as we use the weakest ones among us (man and beast); we are still tackling that one thousands of years later. This truth has got to remain, for if it disappears from the book of truth we are going to be in trouble. The second page of this great book of Revelation from the, "We are one, so love one another", could not even see the light of day. These great truths take so long to be assimilated as natural truths in the human consciousness, because nature herself has taken millions of years to give birth to that consciousness which is pregnant with universal truth; nature will not easily give up the successful process of using and abusing for survival.

The universal truth will always come back in cycles for the next civilisation to pick up and understand it according to the consciousness at the time. Then it will have to be grounded into details, absorbed and assimilated by the material expression; at that point it seems to disappear, to re-emerge again in a new millennium seeking a new interpretation. When the great lives go beyond themselves, in the service of reaching higher levels of consciousness, it will join or create yet another circle or sphere of consciousness. Then it can be thought of or seen as being like a string of golden pearls that goes straight through our Solar System to eternity. If we allow the golden light to flow through us, we connect and are linked to the will to good. The initiate lives in the world of form, yet form has no attraction for him; he is alone and yet not alone. He's freed from doubt and uncertainty and has acquired detachment, which is not lack of concern but the law of non-interference, to which he will adhere when helping his brothers and sisters. This law is the higher reflection in the Soul to the first law given by the prophet, which is not to abuse the lives that serve us.

The crowns that this world offers us will tempt us many times to compromise with our ideals, but any temporal success is false. We should not fall for the sweetness of Maya, worry or occupy our time with immediate results, but rather put our goal beyond ourselves, or all our efforts will be in vain. It is a very precise warning that in that phase of the evolution of the Soul, Chronos will dissolve all that we build. There is a biblical quotation that tells us to live beyond time and proceed in the world with the prudence and wisdom of the snake. Prudence used in that way is not protective caution, but wisdom. Wisdom is slow, but Active Intelligence is fast, so a good merging is needed.

Saturn is solitude, so the initiate is solitary in this world. If he finds that it is too heavy he will seek refuge in the temporal, or in anything he can; we all do this, so we can recognise it in ourselves. We take refuge in a faith or in friendship, relationships, food, our job, society, or whatever. When we go for refuge without being too clear about it, little by little we build a cage around ourselves, so instead of being the light alone in the dark, we cover and extinguish that light and it cannot shine any more. The compromises might be tiny but they add up; we may not be aware of them, but if we are it won't be that difficult to get rid of them.

Let's be careful not to feel special, for it is the place and role of mankind in the whole system that is special, not mankind itself. Being made powerful and solitary is not a very nice position to be in. The initiate knows he must go through the world without attachment, but that doesn't mean that he can't have friends in life, it just means that if the only way to help your friend to get on in the world is to throw them out of your life, that is what he would do. If he has attachment he will not want to do that.

Jesus said; "If you love your father and mother more than me, then you cannot follow me". He was talking like The Hermit or a good No. 9, saying that if we have any attachment we cannot actually come on that path, because it is a path of nakedness, no-need and non-attachment. This doesn't mean that we can't love our fathers and mothers more than ourselves, but that we don't allow the emotional ties to hold the Soul back from its path. We can also of course take the more esoteric view and read it as if we are more attached to material life or to spiritual pursuits than to the middle way of the Soul. We cannot follow the work of fusion of Spirit and matter that the Soul instigates.

The initiate has not come back to live for himself, but has come to serve his mission. Jesus said "I send you as lambs in the midst of wolves". We come back with no purse, bags, or shoes and we do not salute anyone on the way: that is the way the Hermit comes back into this life. The Hermit will naturally be solitary, but not indifferent, so the lesson of filling the cup to the brim with life and love in Number 6 must not be forgotten. When we come to the 9, the love aspect might be overflowing and dissipated, if the fusion (7) and assimilation (8) between the love (Soul) and mind (Spirit) hasn't been too successful. The 18/9 will put itself through hard lessons of being abused through love to sum up the wisdom to seek the true nature of the love within. A young 9 might appear to have no compassion, because they are inward looking for protection; this would be because they have been extremely hurt or been through a time of no love. Life will open the doors for them again.

The Hermit carries within him the totality of the experience of the human being, because he is at the end of the cycle. His thoughts are always turned towards human suffering and he aims to appease by attracting mankind with the power of his love. His mind has just come out of Justice and so he knows about reality; he also knows that the next step is to be reborn into the world, so he has to excel at transforming experience into wisdom. The reason for that work is to enable others to rise above the karmic ties, so that the fall and re-birth into the wheel of life can be done with more awareness. All the time we are in nature there's no problem, but when our Souls start to stir and we go in with too much zeal, carrying none of the characteristics of the 8 and 9, we could end up a slave. This means that our Souls are so much taken by nature that we are going to continually explore and not get ourselves out of it. The Wheel of Fortune is life and life is hypnotic.

There is a story in which the initiates came down from the etheric field of Shambala, to stimulate consciousness in humanity. They knew they faced the very real dangers of falling into matter, so in order to remember the light they all took a little shiny stone from the temple. The Hermit also carries light into the world and like the higher masters who come back to the land, he remembers the responsibility to that light, which reminds him what he has come here to do. Even for masters who are not in incarnation, matter is extremely attractive because of its magnetism; it has an enormous energetic pull.

Under the apparent detachment of the Hermit, he hides the inexhaustible treasure of his goodness. He has to hide the light of wisdom, love and life, for there is no way that with all its brightness, that kind of inner beauty can be revealed to the world yet. We need to do it gradually in degrees, so uplifting ourselves towards the beautiful in us. That beauty is the atomic life of the God we live in, so we can only merge with it to become the burning fire of Spirit and wisdom through a very long alchemical process: if we rush the process by unnatural needs we might end up as useless burning cinders. The Hermit has attained the level of being the deepest, highest, inner teacher, which is Soul. His brown coat represents the personality rendered humble and therefore his light is unrecognised by mass consciousness. His inner light will only be recognised by those on the path to enlightenment. Truth is uncompromising; we cannot have little bits of it and it will not suffer being divided; this is not a lack of willingness to share, but a fact. To get to that state of truth we have to accept to abandon everything transitory or temporal and anything that is not of eternity. The Hermit has done that; he has renounced the world with all its sweetness, beauty, enchantment and its 'tomorrow will do' attitude; this is why it is one of the most demanding of the arcana. Many have actually stopped on their spiritual path here, for they cannot do it. Everyone goes on The Wheel of Fortune, but very few will be track-layers for the next generation.

We may have been in an illusion about an aspect of life, but if all the circumstances are there ready for us to experience, understand and digest the misunderstanding, our Soul will be infused with so much light that in an instant we can make the next step on the path. It doesn't mean that we will never have another glass of beer, but we know we don't need or want it, because we have done that experience enough times that there isn't one single little factor in our Souls that has the desire for another experience of that kind again.

If we have the right enthusiasm and the right capacities, we are going to demand a total definitive choice, so this point marks the end for many people on the path. Its great teaching is the forgetting and total renouncement of the past, so there is a change of perception that transmutes all behaviour, emotions, mindsets and patterns.

The hood doesn't allow him to look backwards or sideways, he has to keep looking in. He brings his vision and all the darkness of the past experiences into the faint light of the Soul to be transmuted into light. At the end of the night comes the dawn; the darker the night, the brighter the dawn will be.

The choice is biology versus Soul. Nature has undergone millions of years of survival and it won't give that up that easily. Nature, the great Queen of form, has survived and we have all adored her. The ones who can see truthfully will go through all the levels of consciousness down to prehistory; there will be no turning back. At this point addiction to the sensory mechanism by which we know ourselves, has to disappear completely. Even if we are very wise we have to start again at zero, with no knowledge of whether the Soul is going to survive or not. The hypnotism and hallucination of the world of form and need can stop, right up to the need to be seen as wise.

When we remove every single speck of dust from our instrument, then the God we live in looks through our eyes to see itself, which is whatever is in front of us, be it a black cat, a green wall or whatever. Truth is very simple and everybody's truth has to be seen as divine, for it is what is written at the time and we are writing the book as we go. We have to be aware that our life is only a path and be ready to go beyond it. Giving up self introspection to responsibility to Soul is going beyond the path into the alchemy of the Soul. Love the world and let the wisdom do the transformation, for love is what has created the world. This is not a fragmentary renouncement, it is all or nothing. If we are still asking a question every day, it is not done and it doesn't work.

The initiate lives in the world that he observes; he also observes himself and from his everyday meditation gradually a conviction is born, which then becomes certitude. The inner life takes over the outer life, so that there is no doubt that when his inner certitude is strong and clear it will permeate his entire being. It is then that he breaks away from the exoteric world and he does it totally, all at once. The intitation process has started and a new vision is perceived, opening the mind to the brighter horizon.

Initiation is not a privilege, it is a natural occurrence so you don't get a gold star for it, but it is the accepting of duty and responsibility; it is dharma. The responsibility is enormous, because the service has shifted from self work, to work for others and for the generations to come. However, it is important not to take ourselves seriously, but rather take the job we are doing seriously.

The inner work required to achieve this stage of initiation is solitary. The Hermit is not seeking bliss or personal gratification experiences. He is in a suspended state between Heaven and Earth, which is what we call purgatory.

The accumulated revising of subconscious actions and reactions are seen for what they are and transmuted into wisdom by the light of the Soul. In this way The Hermit can absorb a lot of negative energy and transmute it into light and peace. The anguish of sin and guilt, represented by the common understanding of

Supraconscious

Everyday
Consciousness
of the Earth

Sphere of
influence of the
Subconscious   Number 9

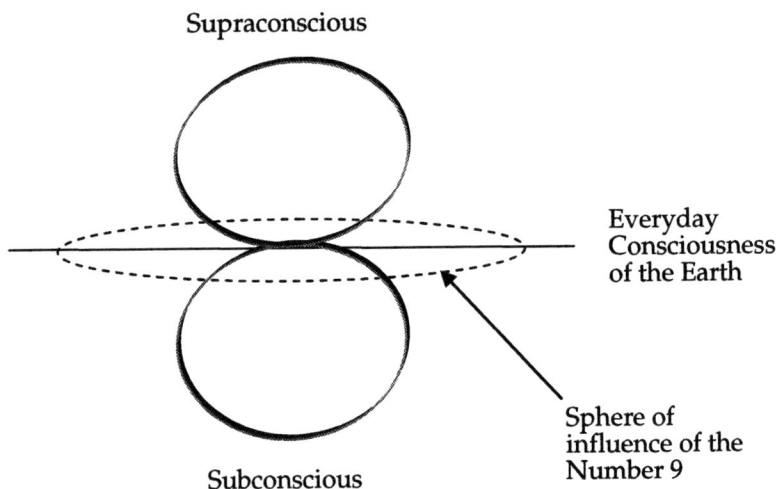

Figure 3. Suspended between Heaven and Earth.

Purgatory, is real only when the consciousness is growing and the personality hasn't lost enough of its pride, so sees itself as limited by its earthliness. Then the consciousness falls into its illusionary, misguided, despising Devil, the fear of Hell. In this case purgatory is being suspended in a point of conflict and it gets harder and harder to move from there, yet we know we have to make up our mind. There's no problem, it is our choice, but it is not the choice of 'I'll do it tomorrow', because when we procrastinate all we do is reinforce the desire to stay there. This stage for the Hermit is the process of purification that we call initiation, and it is undergone without the glamour of the angelic rescue, or the illusion of shadowy swamps.

Remember, we only manifest what is within us. The 9, dissolving its illusions and needs, will only manifest as energy disappearing into a lighter vibration. We should not be afraid of being disillusioned, as that comes after having all the hopes and dreams we carry vanishing in thin air. We shouldn't be afraid of life or of being hurt, because this is what will actually allow us a natural passage towards initiation. Some people can just pass through it by having seen they've had one life too many and enough is enough; others have to have that extra life.

We are not here to change the world or to change others; all we can do is give them a bit of light, a lot of love and a lot of respect. Others can only fly if they want to fly and that is about it. The fruitless desire to want people to rise up is still a want or need, though it is a refined and beautiful one. However, that desire only arises out of impatience and zeal, that is all. Do we have the strength not to reveal our light to the ones who are not ready? Any impatience may come from not understanding people not having enough memory of our own since they have not have been distilled into wisdom through the purgatory of our Soul. With the Hermit there is no role playing, it is the 9 of death and rebirth.

Pluto is the underground energy that helps to transform and bring all the hidden treasures to the surface. This process is represented in the card by the snake. If we visit the interior of the earth, we find that which appears to be most obscure and heavy in matter is our own part of it, then once we have seen that, we can rectify our perception so as to see things differently, that is the alchemy of transformation. Alchemy is entirely internal and in the dark. We will eventually find the hidden philosophical stone of the alchemist, which is the wisdom of the generations. There we are, with all the generations before and after us, and this is where our hearts have to go. We can say thank you, for it is because others have done it before that we are able to do it now. We can appreciate the pressure of the responsibility we carry to raise the world of matter inward towards its inner glory. It is from our 'golden pearl' that the next generation will rise, so we want to pass it on shinier than when we found it. It isn't for ourselves, for by then we are out of the way. We realise we are really part of an incredible and immense collective work and we have the wisdom of the ancestors within us. It is all one life and we know that we are them and they are us; they follow us, as we follow them.

Because we are all one, humanity is always the same one being, looking at and pursuing itself in all its different forms, even if we forget that when we reincarnate. The one being is the God we live in, looking at itself all the time. If we can visualise the long chains of initiates who have given themselves up to serve, that will ring alarm bells, for that vision reminds us of our responsibility. If we have too much pride in the spiritual work and we can't hear those bells, our heart is not open yet to that immense generative line of golden lights. But if we can really feel and hear it, the whole of our body resonates to it and if there is anything personal there, it will be shaken out by that vibration.

Nothing is static and the Hermit knows no rest, so he definitely has no pension or retirement; he works until his last breath. Because he is life at the higher initiatic level and doesn't look backwards or sideways, there is no self-gratification expected from the work he has done. 'I know that I don't know a thing', has been said by all the wise men, because they know what they have left behind and they don't yet know what is in front of them. Chronos is as old as the world and carries all the wisdom from the beginning as a mysterious deposit of connaissance, or knowledge. This is the lost word.

The little snake is the Hermit's friend and is a part of him. Jesus said to his disciples: "Be as wise as snakes". This is about communication with the underground, or the inner world. The snake is a beneficial symbol of healing and the communication of hidden secrets, so it represents the metaphysical truth that is not given to everybody. This is the knowledge that we are bringing back to life; this is the heavy penalty of karma for those who steal the secret in order to help their brothers to see the light.

The Hermit is holding the light of the Soul. Help will never be imposed on us, for his light is completely denuded of any personal interest. We mustn't invoke the inner light just for the sake of helping ourselves along the next curve of the road, but in true times of trouble when we really don't know where we are, we must be humble enough to actually ask for help. It is very important when we are working with the energy of the Hermit to avoid pride. Too many disciples or would-be initiates don't ask for help because of spiritual pride, and then of course they stay where they are, thinking they have arrived. We live in illusion and sometimes when the maya is very strong we need to remember the little light in our hands, for that is our help. The masters do not care what and how we feel at the time, for it is up to us to redeem ourselves; we cannot wait for anybody else to do it. So we can ask for help in holding onto the inner truth. If we help others out of our own personal interest, then we impose our light on them. Help is always offered; it is always there, so the one that can receive the light will actually come to it

The Hermit doesn't go to the world; it is up to the world to come to him. The cape he wears is simple, there's no seduction or artifice. His exterior is modest but inside are high ideals; theses are the treasure he carries in his heart. That is why the lining of the cape is blue, to represent inner freedom and inner light. Through the concentration of the process of thought and meditation, he has found that the cage of formal society and of mass consciousness has no boundaries for him and he is completely free, because he is not attached to it. That freedom from the relativity of life that chains most Souls right down into matter is seen as an orangey yellow, like the robe of the Tibetan Buddhist monk. Enlightenment is the slow processing of the light and the digesting of God, which the monks do when they abandon everything to live in contemplation.

The pure experiences of The Hermit have been collected during many lives and he can now examine the film that unravels in front of him. Placed between Justice and the Wheel of Fortune, The Hermit has the role of applying justice to the wheel of everyday life, so he has to be very careful. With divine justice and the discernment of the higher mind, he can pull out the valuable elements rigorously from this life, so that they can be used in the next one. This way he can prepare his own generation, or karma. He is the occult regeneration born out of the alchemical work.

We are truly here to serve and not to lay down the conditions of the trials of the men who will come after us. We can make the path easier, just as our path has been made easier by friends, wisdom and inner connections. We know that there are some hidden cults where the teachers actually place tasks and obstacles in front of their pupils, for this has always been the old way of initiation, but this is not the higher way; initiation is a natural process entirely generated by the person who is taking the initiation. When one of our actions stirs someone very deeply, but we haven't planned or wanted it, we have been an instrument to initiate their inner process, but not the 'master of the ceremony'.

It is still with the light of the past wisdom that we see the future. Endurance in the present means that we are living in the eternal and there is no past and future. We walk in our past, and at the same time we know it is our future, so we are in the eternal.

The Hermit has rapport with the Empress, for they both have a mental form. She is very mercurial, like quicksilver and represents the search for knowledge, whereas he is reflection, meditation and Saturn. With the Empress we had the clarity to go through the forest of symbols and recognise where we were going, because she's a fantastic translator of wisdom. She's that bridge from intellect to intuition, therefore she governs the world we know, but brings some of the other world into this world. The Hermit has overtaken the symbolic stage and is in the reality of Active Intelligence, so he is able to use the world of virtual reality and communicate with it; this is quite an awesome power. The Hermit is in a world where truth has no more need to be veiled by the symbols, for he's down here naked and he doesn't see symbols, just life. If we don't want anything any more, then we don't play with symbols.

The Empress took us to the temple and then The Hermit takes us in. She presides in the world and he has come out of the world by renouncing it. She supplies the blueprint for this world and he's applying and bringing the new divine justice to the world to come. Her animal symbol is the eagle and his is the snake; both rise, one in the blue of truth, the other out of sheer sacrificial effort brings the lighted inward truth out of the soil, to reveal the wisdom. She is hope and he is connaissance, or knowledge. Her head was crowned with stars; his is bent down to the soil. She was the expectation of life and he is the end of life. She is the initiate in the cosmos and he is the initiate in charge of his responsibility, on behalf of the cosmos. They are exactly the answer to one another, with different applications to the same work; these are the planes that man is called to live in.

The Hermit knows too much to judge, but we have to accept the relative bad as a way to arrive at the absolute good. We know that we have to let people make their own mistakes, for it is the only way they are going to come to the good, so bad is relative. Eventually good is absolute, so we have to accept the relative bad and put whatever we want to understand into that bad, for example, needs, greed and the little self, as a way to arrive at absolute good. So the lesson is to accept all our needs as relative bad, recognise them and decide whether we want them or not.

Without going through all our needs, there is no way that we will ever shed our little skins (like the snake) and get to the absolute truth and the absolute good. If personal intent was an absolute, there would be many limitations and divisions to the concept of divinity. Let's be humble and know that the God we live in, who is a great entity, is limited by the human mind not yet able to fully see it as sacred. We are not talking about that greater divinity, which is the guide for the Solar System and beyond. The God we live in has divisions and impotency; it is not sacred yet because of the silly little sparks that we are! So the relative bad is what takes man up to the veil of Isis, behind which he will see truth.

Of course this doesn't justify bad action so that we can go and do more of it. There is no judgment but divine judgment and that comes from our inner God. So on behalf of the God we live in, let's raise our minds right up to the will to good, by being in purgatory and transmuting the punishing voice of moral judgment against anything in us that is still afraid and needy. There is no purgatory as perceived by the mass consciousness, only an opportunity to redeem our fear in the work of purification. We know we cannot judge others' lives because we do not know their past or what they have missed and what they need to find. There must be great hurt in those Souls who appear to be lost. We can pass judgment that the lesson hasn't come through yet, but that is not judging them.

The Hermit represents the higher teacher in us, which can radiate and be magnetic in its manifestation so as to attract other lighted souls on the path, helping them to use this quality of the Soul wisely and with responsibility.

The Wheel of Fortune, La Roue de Fortune

The world is illusion

The Wheel of Fortune symbolises conscious life rising out of the green primordial waters. All the experiences gained in the cycle from 1 to 9 are gathered together, as we die to that cycle and rise into another. The image on the card, with creatures ascending and descending on a wheel describes the paradoxical experience of conscious life. The kundalini energy rises via the quality of mind represented by the blue and yellow Hermanubis who climbs the wheel on the right side, holding the caduceus. Balanced on the top of the wheel is the sphinx; this is matter aspiring to be sublimated. On reaching the sphinx we can rise up through the fires of purification, if we can answer her question correctly. The brown and green beast descending down the left side of the wheel represents the aspect of the mind that has not been able to sublimate attachment to survival. The blue and red circles of the wheel symbolise the inner and outer lives; the task is to fuse them together, the sacred with the profane and the personal with the collective.

229

In Number 9, the Hermit gathered together the accumulated information from all his experiences so far in the cycle of 1 to 9. Here in Number 10, The Wheel of Fortune marks a rebirth into a new sphere of experience. The mind has associated with the inner light in the Hermit at Number 9, allowing some dissolution of attachment to matter. Then it arrives back in the light in the Number 10, having to learn to recognise itself purely as mind and therefore see the world as illusion.

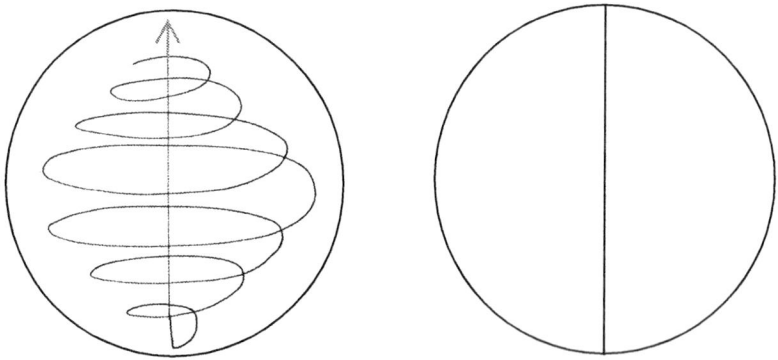

Figure 1. From the 9 to the 10.

As soon as all the experiences are brought back to the centre, everything is aligned and internalised in the 9.	*The 9 disappears into the potential and reappears in the consciousness with the 10.*

As we look at this energetic movement within a sphere of consciousness, we see the 9 suddenly emerging into a No.10. The Spirit has caught the experience, then the understanding, however small, is the pearl of wisdom which has been gleaned from the previous cycle; this is Spirit born out of matter, coming into being as a new cycle begins.

When we are reborn into a new cycle, we bring a lot of sediment from the previous cycle with us. It is important to proceed with caution, but not to let caution become precaution or protection, because this can result in leaning on other people a lot instead of becoming our own leader. A lot of number 10s can translate the necessary caution into 'not ready yet', which can be a problem. Number 9, The Hermit, is the end of a line of many lives and every time we go from one cycle to another, there is always an opportunity for healing. Coming from the 9 to the 10 is like being reborn, for we are looking at a whole new world. It is a rebirth into matter and as with any birth it can happen in many different ways.

This is one of the three cards in the major arcana that don't show a human figure, the other two being Number 15, The Devil and Number 18, The Moon. These three, The Wheel of Fortune, The Devil and The Moon, all tell us that we have to find the mid point. From the mid point we realise that we are 'It' – the mind as a witness, the consciousness and the light. At this stage we can see how life as civilisation (in both its practical and esoteric aspects) is unfolding, evolving and re-birthing itself.

From the perception of Soul or witness there is no action that any human being, be they evolved or not, can do which is esoterically or metaphysically right or wrong. It is vital that this is correctly understood, because it does not apply to the level of everyday consciousness and if it were misinterpreted at this level it would be dangerous, for people still have to go through their cycles and learn by themselves the understanding of their actions. The only way we can align the personality is by knowing right and wrong, so that we can eventually become spiritually righteous.

People who have not yet developed their awareness of Soul need to be given a structure to work within, which needs to be relatively straightforward. This is similar to the way we bring up our children; we don't allow a child to do things that are socially unacceptable, so our approach needs to be clear and dogmatic. If we tell those who are still learning that everything is okay metaphysically, we are not helping and not giving a structure, but are stimulating the forces of self-destruction. Humanity is like a single human being that is at the infant level, so the mentality to protect by killing the others we do not trust and like, prevails. From an intellectual point of view it is easy to understand the idea that there is no 'good' and no 'bad', but if we were to put out the idea that action is neutral, the world would quickly be destroyed. Mass-consciousness is still at the level of an infant and the instincts of self-preservation still create many conflicts, but within a very safe structure we have to allow people to become themselves by experiencing 'good' and 'bad', so as to realise eventually that there is no such thing.

If we look back in time we see that mankind has always had a special task within nature. Ancient shamanic societies performed rituals of making drawings on rocks and caves, marks in the sand, or constructing mounds on the earth. This search for something beyond the self has been expressed in the natural environment and the ancestral memory takes us back to before life began. Just as one of our cells contains the memory from the beginning of our time span, so one person has the memory of the whole Solar System within them. This means they can become systemic in the Solar System therefore cosmically systemic, because the Solar System itself has its own memory bank of being an organ in the much bigger body of the Cosmos. When the 10 comes back it can get lost, until it remembers that it is here to recollect the memory of the experience, be it individual, systemic or cosmic.

From the beginning of time, humans knew how to survive and found ways of holding the group together through the laws of the land and moral codes. The laws of the land developed organically and helped to create an order and structure within which the group or society could grow. These man-made laws are to be respected, but most of them are based on dogma and authority and will have to change in time. In making our own contribution to the greater good it is important to push for change, whilst realising that people need to be ready to help themselves. The primary aim is to be witnesses who are completely open to life and truthful to themselves. The only practical thing we can do is to put energy behind those things we see as being valuable for the new era to come; so if we find something which is going to be viable for the next three to four hundred years, then it is worth putting energy into it, for it is a step in the right direction.

When we look at humanity as a whole, we are looking mainly at an infant, with a few adolescents forming the social structure. Whatever we perceive, visualise and think now, can eventually crystallise at a later time. It is the ever-growing numbers of minds being able to exercise their metaphysical perception, which allows the scientific mind to move further in the understanding of the fabric of the universe, so influencing the builders of social reform and of law and order.

We can get lost in reliving childhood experiences or discovering past lives to excuse our behaviour, but it is better to be grateful for those situations because they enable the great life we live in to become aware of the feelings and mindsets locked in the experiences.

The animals, plants and insects cannot name their feelings, for nature is only concerned with survival not feelings. This enables biological life to carry on in whatever way it can and go through the experiences for that purpose. As human beings rising from nature, the task we have is to release the experiences that nature has had to go through on behalf of Spirit and then translate them through a sentient feeling body, which can be aware of them. Then we realise we don't need to act these experiences out any more. This may sound very obvious, but the truth is that man is still killing man on the planet through war or in other ways, so is acting unconsciously in the old ways of nature.

The biggest problem is that until we can witness life from the higher intelligence of the Soul none of us can be in complete truth, because we still personalise our experiences too much. There are so many layers that we have to unveil which go back into the dark prehistoric times; the main feeling we are looking at there is survival and fear. From a nature point of view it is not really fear, for a rabbit does not know it is afraid, instead its biological survival instinct takes over. We name these instinctual feelings using our emotional intelligence, but then we have to go behind the words and see that the feelings belong to nature; this way we de-personalise the experience. It is all just life pushing through for survival and in doing so finding protection. What is important is to keep digging out the feelings so as to see them for what they are, to name them and to witness them but not to use them to keep playing the drama. The difficulty is that the addiction to drama is tenacious.

We are experiencing a great loss of species on the planet at the moment; this tells us that we are on the crest of a wave. At this point we can expect that the denser parts of our consciousness will be transmuted and uplifted. The 10 is reminding us to be so aware of the situation we are in, that we can carry the vision with wisdom and do the best we can to hold the pearls of wisdom in our heads and hearts. Then hopefully when we jump into the next wave, many of us will ride it and carry on. It is like Noah's Ark, only it is an inner one; it is about knowing exactly where we are. We may be fed up, but from the higher point of view we know that it is just the matter in us that is making us feel down and we have to go on playing the game of being here. We have all 'had enough' and we need to be honest about that, so that we can allow ourselves to have the feelings of despair but still keep holding the vision within that carries and feeds us. The vision is the Soul of the planet, which is Mary or Isis; it is that veil of love that supports and protects life. The wave is forever infused with Spirit; otherwise we would all be dead. The kundalini light, which is the spiritual fire within nature, sustains life and matter and without it there's no regeneration, or life to replenish matter. The message of the tenth card, The Wheel of Fortune, is that 'The force is with you' and there is nothing else to hold onto; you can see why Star Wars is a very popular film! When we are talking about the inner life force, this has to be used for altruism and not for the self otherwise it would become personal power which ultimately leads to degeneration.

If we understand the higher principle of the system, our life is at peace, in that we are exactly where we should be. We can let the mind of Spirit fill the space within us and feel our fragilities without hiding them, for they can be our strengths. Those fragilities are what we are working at and we are bringing them up from the depths of our cellular memory, so that they can become part of the force that flows through us. As we learn to accept them, we understand that we are not weak or doing wrong; the fragility is there because we have dared to dive for yet another pearl or diamond. We can feel the support we have when we are doing that, for we are part of a long line of inner workers who have dared to die to themselves again and again. This is the other side of spiritual teaching; whatever we have taken on we can be sure we are able to go through it, so stop the drama and get on with it. With courage we can find our inner pain and recognise it, while taking care not to get caught in a drama with it.

At the 10th stage, people often refuse to acknowledge their pain and so stay in the physical aspect because they are involved in the courage of being born. However, what needs to be done is to go within, see, feel and endure the pain with the knowledge that it will pass. We have to be completely honest to feel it and to notice our behaviour in everyday life, while at the same time seeing it all from the point of view of the metaphysical, greater, energetic life. Then the experiencing and the understanding of the experience go on at the same time, just as in the card we have the red and blue wheels. With a lot of 10's the acknowledgment of the physical pain brings in the courage to go through it, but on the other hand they can use the pain to keep themselves from going in. The fear of the pain eventually brings them to a point where they can internalise. Then there is a time when they can have mental, emotional and physical pain and carry on walking through the fire without being stopped by it. It is there but not there; that is the fine thread of the inner work.

The sea is green to represent the primordial waters, for all life came out of water. The magnetic and electric fields could not do it on their own, there had to be a carrier for our elements, this was water. We have in the card two crescent moons, two lines of force, two beasts on two wheels and a sphinx with two wings; this is the world of duality.

Looking first at the ascending creature, which has a blue body, a yellow head and a loincloth, we see that it holds the winged caduceus, while it looks upwards towards the seated sphinx. This creature is called Hermanubis. Anubis was an Egyptian god of the dead, who the Greeks later identified with their own god Hermes; this resulted in the composite deity Hermanubis. Anubis, the dog-

god, guards the entrance to the inferior worlds or the worlds of the dead. Hermes is the God at the doors of heaven or Hell who guides us as we go in and makes sure that we are pure enough when we go through the door. The death we are talking of is a metaphysical death or the death of the personality, not the physical death of the body. Hermanubis is coloured yellow and blue, the two colours of the mind; yellow to represent wisdom through knowledge of inner life and blue for ascension through purity.

As Hermanubis, representing an aspiring quality of mind, ascends the wheel, he is going up to the sphinx which is going to ask him a question. If he doesn't get the answer right he will be devoured and digested by the Sphinx and then he has to come back into life down the other side of the wheel, in the form of the brown beast. The process is a natural and good one which ensures that anything that has not been assimilated will go back through the descending process on the wheel, to experience more life and ascend the wheel again, bringing up more wisdom to the Sphinx. Only what is viable for the next life can go through those doors, everything else will have to be re-cycled. Suffering and pain without self-pity has the role of burning out karma, but self-pity negates that work and carries on the karma. We are stronger than the pain, but we have to know it is there and not cover it up, deny it, or feed it. We think that we are the pain and the pain is us, but we are beyond that and so we need to let it go.

When we are flying in an aeroplane and it descends towards the sea, we see the water glistening; the little waves look like crests, or flowers opening. When seen from a greater height they look like little clusters of stars that don't appear to be moving, like we see in the sky. It is only once we are nearer to the water that we can see the big waves open. When the waves appear static even though we know they are moving, we have a picture of how we are from moment to moment; we appear to be static, but the cells in our bodies are constantly changing and this movement is reality. What we perceive as an experience on the surface is not the reality, the reality is what is happening on the inner blue circle on the Wheel of Fortune. We know that the sea is moving, though it looks static and this can help us to understand reality.

To keep looking for an explanation for our emotions and life's experiences, and to keep looking at the picture book, keeps us on the red wheel. It is important to bring up all these 'pictures' but we need to remember that they are virtual and not true reality, they are just a passing phenomena. It can help us if we understand our childhood experiences or past lives, but it is important not to 'fix' these things by saying for example that an upsetting childhood experience has made us behave in a certain way, for these experiences are only virtual. We have been given the task to name things, but we must watch out that the intellect doesn't hold what we name, for this can be like an addiction and we can get into being a 'drama queen', who refuses the responsibility of the work she took on.

If we keep looking and searching and going within, we can always find any incident repeated several times, which means it needs to be seen so as to understand the underlying, frozen, emotional dinosaur, looked at through our biological suit – once named it becomes energy. It is like a picture-frame held in the cosmic sky so that the God we live in can actually see itself and life can become aware. From going back again and again through all the situations we have put ourselves in, eventually we can see that it is only an energetic movement in time and space which reorganises the space so that the picture can be seen. We have misinterpreted the picture, but it is okay because we have been able to name everything we had to name.

We are the scientists, but the problem is that we get lost in the laboratory rather than register what is happening and carry on. If we need to look at past lives they will come up of their own accord, we don't need to seek them out. It is important to remember that life is only a 'picture book' that comes up so that we can look at it and let it go. Sometimes an interest will come up, so we can open ourselves to looking at it, otherwise we are refusing to see a pain or pleasure. To give the excuse of things happening to us because of a past life is okay but eventually limiting, for it doesn't allow us to go underneath to the movement of Spirit in matter that has created the situation and is inherent in the system. In the metaphysical world pain and suffering don't work! We go through cycles of experience for the intellect to name an emotion; it can't do more than that. However, if we take the emotion and bring it back to the source then the moving, energetic life will take our minds into the metaphysical level, where the emotion will be perceived as a specific happening in space! The energetic movement of Spirit boldly coming into matter is commonly perceived as fear, but it is courage in its highest form when that energy is used to take us forward. When freezing in fear, we play the protective side of nature in us that stops the movement of our spiritual will from going forth and expressing what it wants to express. Feelings do not need to be excused, they only need to be named and seen for what they are, for all they are is what happens to matter in the constant transformation of life. Our intellect in cahoots with our emotions will keep bringing these past lives back and that does not ultimately provide an answer. The paradox is that there is a need to look at the memories and name them, but not to make a personal 'drama' out of them.

We know that we have to live our life in the sacred, but at the same time we have to live it in the profane. In this process of fusion, the next level of attainment is achieved only when we are ready. Grace and humility are not earned; they happen naturally, for they are states of being and we cannot strive, pass exams, or flex spiritual and emotional muscles to achieve them, because it happens when we are ready. When we clear a space, light comes in and that is it. We are striving to live in the sacred all the time, by coming from our inner will on the little blue wheel, but we have to be in matter as well and be vigilant not to cover survival habits.

We need to recognise that life is always putting us in front of the dark night of the Soul. When we stand in front of the full light of divinity, we are made aware of our pitiful existence and if we don't feel the fear or terror of annihilation that overcomes the Soul, we are not going to go through our sound barriers. If we read Genesis we will find that Abram, before he becomes Abraham, fell into a long sleep and was overcome by terror and fear, then in the morning he started on the path of the long lineage of initiates. The meaning of the name Abraham is 'great multitudes', which is the meeting of the individual Soul with the divinity within itself and that fills us with terror. Suddenly, within matter there is the realisation of the light within, which is so mighty that we don't feel capable of living up to it. When we have gone through that several times it makes it seem as if God is fearsome and impossible to live up to, so bright is his light. The next step is to let go of the illusion and glamour and all the things dear to us that we called our lives. The question always arises; can we see ourselves for what we are in the splendour of the light?'

The flash of light released from a rise in consciousness reaches all the corners of our deep natural past. Then the threat to life is felt, as we know that we have to let go of many layers of personal survival instinct. Once we go beyond one level of consciousness to another, we become the Fool of the Tarot and we throw ourselves into the abyss. Even if there is a big crevice there which we are going to fall into, we know there is nothing else we can do but obey Spirit, because the big vision in front of us is actually in us. It can feel mighty and enormous and we can be overwhelmed and not know what to do.

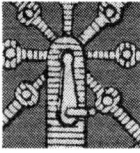

In the centre of the wheel there is a handle, but there is nobody to turn it and so it is not moving the wheel. This shows us that the meaning of this card is completely metaphysical. It is about life in a bigger sense and there is no physical, outer action, because we are talking about action in the metaphysical sense. Everything on the outer red wheel is of matter and represents maya, illusion and glamour. We have to reach the inner centre of the blue wheel, so that we can come back into life with the vision and knowledge of the sacredness of everything, where we know that reality is not as it seems. This is a general, metaphysical and symbolic card that doesn't describe an individual stage, but is it there to allow us to take the next step of 'Force', or 'Strength,' in Number 11.

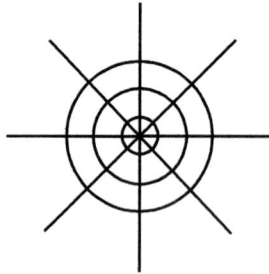

Figure 2. Wheel with two Crosses.

The wheel has two crosses; the horizontal and vertical cross symbolises the kingdoms of the life we live in; the diagonal hermaphrodite cross is about the fusion of the active and passive energies.

The water is definitely not still, because it is the primordial waters that carry the memory of all life and biology since the beginning of time. Its green colour, like algae, brings out the whole life of the planet and even the cosmos. The images of the Hermanubis and the sphinx are inspired by ancient Egypt. The two beasts on either side are balancing each other on the wheel and they are both relaxed, in spite of the fact that the wheel could easily be destabilised. At the top is a platform upon which sits the sphinx. There are two crescents upon the water, which are the base for a mast that then supports the wheel with the two creatures. The whole arrangement is impossibly unstable, though it is in perfect balance like a balancing act; this reaffirms that the understanding is metaphysical.

The gods of antiquity each represent one specific quality or aspect of the process of energy and matter: refining, coming together and fusing. It is not the figure or the name that is important, but the energy flowing through it, because whatever names we give them, they are only instruments or channels. They have the skills to carry out the task, but what flows through them is higher than them.

Hermes was a God of sacred knowledge, as was the God Thoth of Ancient Egypt. He had the same mission as Anubis, which was to take the Soul after death to the under-world, where Pluto (representing transformation) was waiting for him, ready to destroy and rebuild. Hermes was taking the Soul into the great primordial waters, either for ascension or purification, according to the work of the Soul so far. We know that Anubis was the God of the Dead and he presided over the embalming to make sure that all the rites were carried out properly. Hermes guided the Soul into the tomb and beyond; he is like Michael, an instrument through which divine judgment can happen.

The caduceus, which is formed by the two serpents twining together, is one entity: it is the symbolic process of the transformation of natural life into the inner life through the healing work of karma.

The Egyptian God Thoth was identified with the Moon crescent, for he was the protector of the Moon. He was supposed to be the inventor of chronology and Master of time and destiny; time in the past was defined by division into moon cycles. He represents all the situations and diverse rebirths that man has to go through before facing the sphinx and answering the question. The question asks us to identify the forgotten lost word, which differs according to our vibration at the time.

Thoth was the God of Movement in time and space and therefore a high magician who was said to have invented the word as well. Sound creates words and is a by-product of movement, so is a perfect language for the emotional body. It is when sound is heard, that the vibration of the matter that is organised around the sound starts to be viable, then we see a world beginning to emerge. Sound is not truly the creator of form; universal sound as space is the building material left from another cosmic experience lost in time. Sound as we know it is a by-product of the potential appearance of form through the movement of Spirit organising the blueprint, according to the available material. The great primal unheard sound is the suspended life of the Divine, before it organises itself into form through the impulse of intent. It took a long time for humanity to be able to name emotions and that naming is very potent, so we keep going back again to the emotions to re-name them. Before we named them, emotions were only the results of the movement of the Spirit in matter and their respective reaction was natural behaviour.

Thoth was supposed to have created the worlds and is the equivalent of the Logos of the Greeks. In the Gospel of St John, it was the Word (or verb) that enabled creation. The music of the spheres is entirely balanced, it is a divine orchestra and it creates the worlds. We truly act as a God within the system because of our awareness and we are giving awareness back to God through the cosmology of the Gods. If we are to be co-creators we have to be careful how we speak, for we are anthropomorphising the understanding that we have of Creation; man looked at everything around him and made God in his own image, it is not the other way round.

The incantation of the priest or magician is very important, because according to how much vision, heart and will is put in to what is invoked, it will be more or less potent. That is why the voice or sound ends up healing disharmony in the mental, emotional and physical bodies, when it has the right intonation. Nothing works without sound or communication. Sound is at the base of the foundation and materialisation of human society, a good example of this is the Declaration of Human Rights.

The brown and green beast is not falling, but descending purposefully down the left side of the wheel, holding on as he goes; he is not banished. Green represents the vegetative, receptive life and brown represents the Earth, because when he comes down again into the manifested world he is returning back into nature and life on the planet. His face is that of an old billy-goat and like the billy-goat, he is chained by the idea of generation and is at the mercy of his senses and desires. What he thinks is his own will is really mass consciousness, which is what drives him round the wheel of life. He represents nature, biology, physiology and everyday life, when the sacred is not acknowledged in them. He is mass-consciousness and humanity when it hasn't started to open the door to the inner path. Although he looks Capricornian, he in fact represents Pluto and also Neptune, because he has a trident so he belongs to the sea of the primordial water.

We live at a time when we have never been more bombarded by the senses to the point of being stunned, which is why things have become grosser. Sound has become loud to the point of numbness and all the food that is offered to the average person tastes the same. We have overdone the senses to the extent that so much of what we experience is loud, bland, gross and obvious. This is a normal progression, because it brings us to the point where the little brown beast has got to ask himself the question "How much more tasteless, loud and gross have I got to become before I actually start to think of something else?" He's got the trident and he's going back to the deep primordial waters. He can't stop the wheel, so he's going down and then he will have to come back up again. He carries the hope of transformation in his left hand in the form of the trident, as nature carries the hope of transformation through giving birth to the son of mind – the Soul of mankind

There are two wheels, the red outer one that represents the outer life and the blue one representing the inner life. The billy-goat is not touching the blue wheel but Hermanubis is. The red wheel is not meant to go round, for we are not meant to stay in vegetation all the time. However, we cannot reach the top without having to come down to the bottom. The two figures balance each other on the wheel. The brown beast, representing the outer life, holds onto the outer red wheel as he descends with a blue trident. The Hermanubis, representing the inner life, has one hand on the inner blue wheel as he goes up holding his winged caduceus, which is the hope of transformation, realised by the awareness of the three creative aspects of the divine in mankind. When we get to the top we can stop the wheel, bringing freedom from Karmic enchainment; this is represented by the Caduccus that is held by Hermanubis.

On the right side of the wheel (Hermanubis ascending), we should be aware when we are picking up karma, while on the left side we are more likely to be an unconscious instrument of karma for others. It is not a question of our age, because even if we are 70, we are just as likely to be descending the wheel with the beast as we are to be going up on the other side. There is a level of awareness where we have to know that we are overloading our karmic task, so we have to be completely responsible for what we do in life. Then as we involve back into matter, we can still repeat our mistakes, but in recognising those misunderstandings as the past we don't create more karma. If we ignore them, then we will have to meet them as more intense experiences later.

The green platform which is precari-
ously held in balance on the top of the
wheel represents the vegetable life on
Earth. The Sphinx, who is on the platform, represents wisdom that has come
out of the primordial water. She is the
feminine side and the enigma of life from the point of view of the
great life in matter. Her brown buttocks link her with the brown
beast and represent the heavy involving process of descending into
matter; this is matter aspiring to be sublimated. She is brown and
green like the beast, but also she is the metaphysical life of the planet
and she shows the weighing up of life through the wisdom of Isis or
the High Priestess. This wisdom lifts matter out of generation.

The blue wings of the sphinx show the possibilities of sublimation and link her with Hermes and the little blue caduceus held by
the ascending Hermanubis. Evolution cannot be achieved without
the passage through death and purification, so the symbol of sulphur on her head represents the purification and transformation of
gross matter. She holds the sword of judgment in her right hand; it
is white to show the action of the sacred in everyday life.

The sphinx also symbolises the stage of being suspended in the
hope for uplift and purification, which is called 'kamalooga'. This is
where the Soul stays after life, to be enlightened and to see whether
the wisdom can manifest out of whatever experiences it met in life.
Inspiration is received that could not be accessed while doing the
experience on the planet, so it is a place of understanding. As we
keep on growing in our inner world, we don't need to die to be in
kamalooga, we can do it here by extracting from life all the wisdom
and teaching so as to be ready for another incarnation. The sphinx
is like the lens, showing us that man is living his own Karma, in his
own image and with his own truth.

This card represents life in a vast sense and if we truly understand
the Number 10, we understand the whole of the universe. We are
looking here at the death of the 9, for the 9 has to die to itself to realise
that it has become 'the way' or the Soul! This is the point where the
individual has completely withdrawn so as to let the light through;
at this point he is working from the inner place. There is only one
thing that he has to do and that is to fuse the inner and outer lives
in incarnation. This means the turning away from the senses and the
uplifting into the world of energy, truth and love. A lot of 10s might
come back not wanting to go near the collective or mass consciousness, but they have to be able to come right back deeply into the outer

life. In starting a new cycle they are like an infant, so the physical is where they experience; they have to remind themselves to see the experience only from the point of view of the inner life.

When we talk about karma, we're including individual karma, collective karma, planetary karma and the karma of the Solar System. We cannot escape the twenty thousand year wave of the collective karma. The idea is to keep steady with our vision and do our best to promote what could carry through into the next wave. If everybody could become responsible for their own little part of the collective karma, war would stop overnight. Not only war would stop but also we would stop eating food that is rubbish, stop exploiting sex, stop polluting air and stop hurting each other. We need to accept the responsibility of realising that everything that might be wrong on the planet has to do with each one of us.

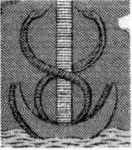

The crescent moons at the bottom of the wheel represent Isis and Thoth, the feminine and masculine. They are about the regeneration which occurs from the origin of everything. The Moon represents our yesterdays and the great Mother, whom we left behind a long time ago on a spiritual plane, not just in the hereditary sense but karmically. Karma and biology are tied intimately as one and biology can only manifest as karma unfolds.

The snakes show the energy coming up from within the Earth, rising to meet the energy of the Sun and healing its longing through accepting the process of dying and rebirth. The snake caused the descent of the first couple Adam and Eve, so we are looking at awareness coming into generation and creating the desire for rational knowledge. This would eventually exalt itself back into the sphinx, but before that it has to go round the wheel in the process of self-examination and experience. We are looking at nature rising up from within herself, recognising herself and eventually uplifting towards the greater self.

The card before, The Hermit, has known and experienced all the trials and lessons of life. He has connected to all the diverse and different doctrines and accessed the contact with the universal ancient wisdom, so he knows that universal truth is all one and therefore within all religions and doctrines. All these philosophies give solutions to life's problems, but he eventually understands that it is only from within that they can actually be understood.

The Wheel of Fortune represents the precarious stability of life; it will carry on in its survival of life and death even if mankind disappears from the Earth, for natural life seen at the esoteric level is a formidable system. Everything of degradation is a prelude to ascension; the karmic rhythm of the heartbeat of the Solar System holds it safely in its dance. Because it is a wheel it is going round and round, taking the reincarnated Souls up and down simultaneously and we can't reach the top without coming down to Earth. Because this up and down natural movement is not always understood, a lot of us make the mistake of wanting to be balanced, happy and well, therefore staying aloof and almost asleep. This is the 'walk the talk' of the comfort, pleasure seekers – they sleep-walk their lives.

Spirit as truth will use us when our personal intent is absent; this is the state of non-interference. Non-interference means we are allowing the hidden divine intent to come through us and move us for whatever needs to happen from within the centre of the greater will, according to the plan. It is non-action in the sense of not doing and acting according to our intent, but it is also action in the sense of being a channel for a deed to happen. This is the enigma of the material condition of life, for the 'apparent' world can only reach closer to self-destruction.

Anybody who doesn't want to look at his own life and behaviour from the internal point of view will keep going down into nature. If we blame everything outside our own remit on our own weakness, or the state of the world; on childhood, social conditions and so forth, then we are still on the red outer wheel. The brown beast has webbed feet, showing that he is aquatic and he is in the emotional world. When we do not really want to take responsibility for what is happening to us in life, including collective karma, then the only place where we can regenerate is in the waters of life. Water moves nature and has given life to the planet since the beginning of time. In the trees we see the water moving up from the roots towards the sky; this is how nature reaches up to her lover, the Sun. The hot core of the planet is magnetic and brings the oxygen and hydrogen together to form water, which is the basis of all biological life. We live in a watery world and are mostly made of water.

The Hermanubis ascending the wheel has accepted the risk of facing the question, or facing the God within. It is only when there is a true search and a total acceptance of where we are that we can eventually reach the sphinx, give the right answer and fly with her little wings. We have to be ready to die to what we think we are. If we look at our lives, the really significant steps we make are the ones where we risk everything and we achieve our next spiritual revival as our inner self comes to the surface. We have to leave behind the fear of failure. The paradox is that we need caution, but also need to take the risk, especially when it is in the service of the group.

Because there is acceptance of the death of the ego, we are no longer at the mercy of our own desires and needs. If we keep looking up, eventually we will reach the burning fire within the self. It is only by going beyond ourselves that we become ourselves; it is only through accepting the personal death of the old mindset that we conquer death. By refusing to change our perception of death we refuse to go further, we vegetate and stay where we are. This is perfectly alright too for there is no judgment as to which is the 'right' path to take. There are two wheels, so it is a double life and we have a choice.

In the outer, everyday life, we are very much attached to immediate results and self-gratification, whereas the inner life has a much broader vision. The idea of wanting and expecting results is fair enough, but the way to become an initiate is not by expecting anything to happen. The key quality is endurance and there is no judgment of result or action. For the esoterist there is no good or bad action when we are looking from the point of view of the Soul, for the initiate sees the play of the light and shade and understands it in relation to the whole scheme, treading the path with open eyes. The Egyptian priest weighed the heart (the sum of his goodness) of a dead man, in the presence of the masters of wisdom; they were not concerned with his body and the results of his actions. Man eventually becomes known to himself and then knows he looks at himself in everybody else. It is painful and difficult and many run out of energy, for before we can transmute all the repulsion and disbeliefs of what we are witnessing, we have to constantly face our fear of where it will take us and maybe keep us! There are many reasons why we don't realise ourselves by stopping ourselves; madness and love are the only ways to get there. We need a stimulus, so sometimes we will meet a guide, or some other situation will occur that can turn us around. Maybe something very simple does it like hearing the right music; it is then that the trials begin. We are all helpers, guides and stimulators for each other, for it is one life and one body. Our actions hopefully become less and less conditioned by our needs, but they may be conditioned by the needs of others, as we become instruments that can be used. In effect, we never know when we make an action, whether it is for us or for someone else. From the higher point of view no action is good or bad.

We need rules which society decides at the time are the right way to behave, because they give a structure for the infant humanity to develop. We are here to civilise the world, so that eventually civilisation can be spiritualised. Civilisation is a framework or house, in which humanity can grow safely and it is very important for it to develop a sense of what is good and bad. When eventually humanity becomes an infant Soul, it will break down the civilisation to spiritualise it and create the perfect song of the hierarchy. This will be harmonised and balanced and need no authority, because we will all be doing it together. It will be a blending of all levels of sound to create a perfect performance.

The structure of society is very important, because it is very important to develop a sense of good and bad. We have to assume social responsibility and after that we have to assume spiritual responsibility, meaning the way a Soul ought to behave according to the oneness of all life. Soul responsibility is a good substitute for will if we can't feel our spiritual will strongly enough, because it is the manifestation or materialisation of will. Our Soul is responsive to a manifestation of will, which talks to and wants to drive the Soul and the personality, without condemnation or praise.

Some of our actions may help people rise up and others allow them to fall, according to their direction. In the measure of our lives we have to do the best we can according to what we can access of the plan, so we may need to repeat experiences several times. When we come back as a Number 10, we have to accept to be part of the collective karma and understand our role as a leader. This way we remember to take responsibility for our own leadership. We are not going to show others how to do it; we are only going to say 'well done' to them, in recognition of their progress. We might give them a few clues and if they ignore them that is okay. When they have lifted themselves up above the problem they were solving, the responsibility is off our shoulders and they in turn start to do that work for others. The leader/teachers are not to blame for how it turns out. Here we cannot manipulate as a guru might, in setting trials for people; that is the old way and is not relevant. The real endurance is in everyday life, being able to look at ourselves and not forgetting or missing out any hidden corners.

We cannot judge people according to what they do, we can only be clear of personal intent and be aware that we have to infuse our every action with spiritual intent, for every action has an effect. We are here to act and do our best for the good, even if we make mistakes. The true thing is to know that we *are* taking action, doing something and taking all the responsibility for what we are doing. The paradox is that we don't personally want to do it but have to, for it is part of the greater plan. All the time we have to keep discriminating, making sure that we are not kidding ourselves and that we *are* doing the will of God. We have to keep opening up to life to make certain that we are serving Spirit and not going into obsession, madness or worse – blindness. We should have the courage to look at what has moved us, for most of us want to cover that up and ignore the call to change.

The intent comes from the deeper impulse and if we keep searching and going in we find the misunderstanding which we may have manifested several times in the past. Eventually, through going back into all the situations that we have put ourselves in, we re-organise the time and space. This is living our life at the sacred level. We can have pity for man's weakness and blindness, but when our actions and behaviour are overtaken by the collective mass-consciousness, we become an old billy-goat following the flock, instead of the Capricornian mountain goat.

There are two worlds, the sacred and profane; two teachings, esoteric and exoteric; two lives, the individual in everyday life and the inner life. These need to be fused and become one, so that we can actually see ourselves and be completely overpowered by the dark night of the Soul, which asks us to die as personalities, so that we only see ourselves as an instrument for the greater God. Remember that nothing is static, but we see pictures which are static illusions and therefore are taken in with the falsehoods of the senses; it is the realisation of this that takes us right into our centre. Life isn't static, it is forever transforming.

It is at the time of death, or between death and reincarnation, that we make the frame for the next life. We come back to the same energetic alignment that we had at the moment of death, this brings back all the accumulated experiences of who we are. Efficacy of action has no rapport with the true value of an action in the spiritual plane, for the only true value is metaphysical. In death we can only see from the metaphysical plane. An action on the plane of Earth can either take us into fall or uplift, according to our perception. Some actions become 'missions', which then can become non-action by our being carried by 'what is' and having no intention; these are not good or bad. We are all learning to align and be at one with the greater. What is our mission in life? The greatest mission we can have is to facilitate the action of Spirit coming into matter with awareness.

In the myth of Orestes, he accomplishes action by taking the responsibility of knowing that it was imposed upon him; this shows the paradox of doing it without wanting to. We are going beyond ourselves, so even if we are misguided it doesn't matter. The initiate accomplishes the action by taking full responsibility for it, at the same time knowing with certainty that it was imposed on him. That is what we are truly looking at with the Number 10; the great paradox of taking full responsibility for our action, even though we did not want to do it. This is the beginning of sanity, or if we can't handle it – madness; it is an everyday happening. It is the dilemma of life and comes up in the 10, when an initiate or disciple comes in with a great big bag of spiritual will on his back that he has to unfold as a spine of light for others to follow.

Do we allow ourselves to be overtaken by the collective mass consciousness, or do we learn to swim against the current? The salmon is one of the symbols for the initiate, because it has the endurance to swim against the current and go towards its death. When we swim against the flow, at the top of the wave we have the unknown coming up and meeting us. All the questions are there, splashing in our face. We know we are completely powerless in front of this, for it is the planetary karmic wind blowing from the depth of time, bringing back the memories we cannot have conceived in our familiar environment. This is where we cannot possibly be on a mission to change the world, for the world knows too well how to do this by itself! The patterns of the past happen to the body we live in regardless of the past, for what is happening is even beyond that. It is about Earth's karma and the karma of the Solar System working out on Earth. We can't save the world for it doesn't need saving, but remember to raise your sight, keep holding the vision and recognise what gives viable help and support, so as to make the next cycle easier. The mission is to back up or take on something good which can go forward into the next few hundred years, this way we can make the next wave sweeter.

When we align with the spiritual line of the greater life, we are not saving the world, we are aligning with the will of the God we live in who doesn't care if the world is saved or not, as for now he is the world and his own salvation is not the aim; serving the great lords of universal karma is the only job description he follows. It is just about finding the best possible way to render matter into the right vibration of consciousness, to take it back home. Redeeming is not saving and we can't redeem anyone else; we have only turned it into 'saving' because we need missions. We have to be completely involved with what is happening in the collective, so we have to come right down into everyday life and re-involve ourselves, we can't play the hermit and withdraw. When we want to save the world we are not actually completely centred in the will of the God we live in. The only thing that is saving the world, in the sense of redeeming, is the turning of The Wheel of Fortune continuously, until we can steady in our centres where the will of God is known. We are at a point of crisis, meditation alone is not enough and those people who believe it is, are not awake enough to what is happening in humanity. However, we can only serve humanity with our vision at the time.

There are two wheels, two moons and two snakes. They have to be together as one, for it is the one life in the primordial sea, with the promise of Heaven coming together with and on Earth, via the caduceus and via all the different levels of consciousness, as the kundalini rises. The kundalini is the fire and the forgotten light in matter, which rises to meet its lover again and goes back to heaven where it is going to lose the form and fly with its lovely blue wings. The sphinx will lose its female form because it is going to become an eagle or phoenix, a Spirit or a dove. Eventually when the top is reached, we can give the right answer to the one that guards the door to heaven or the underworld. It is a very clear process of spiritualisation and of developing each chakra into purity. It is no good wishing or striving to rise in consciousness, it happens when the right sublimation of vibration is achieved naturally.

The snake is a good symbol for re-incarnation because it sheds its skin; the two snakes depicted represent the double karma in us. Man must love individually and think universally; we must absorb the cosmic and realise the universal in ourselves, so we cannot refuse our part in the collective karma. If we ignore our part in the behaviour of mass consciousness we cannot redeem that which is pulling us down into matter. We must carry the vision into the new wave of the future and take our part in carrying the burden of the collective; in this there is no withdrawing and no ivory tower. We have all played, been obsessive and addictive; all of that has to be brought into our centre. Doubt doesn't help and the 10 should never doubt, in any case the lens won't allow it to, since everything is possible in the potential. Even if the worst thing happens, we can't doubt that some good will come out of it. Jesus in Gethsemane accepted the bitter cup, which tells us that if the personality accepts the pain it can be overshadowed by the transforming energy of love.

The name of God, which we cannot say, holds the secret of divinity. This secret can only be given to man when he acquires the power to stop the wheel through wisdom and love. If we can't die for love of something outside ourselves we don't know that thing; this is the wisdom of the 10, it has died and will again. The ones who remain protecting the form take themselves further away from the centre, so moving away from the sacred.

The sphinx guides the lost world, which is hidden in the subconscious and must be brought into the light of the conscious. Let's be strong and face the sphinx and her questioning by looking at the self, so that one day we will use the wings to fly with life. Wanting to stop serving is denying the divine in us.

There is a rapport with the High Priestess or Isis, which is also a card with Egyptian symbols. She is guarded by the black sphinx. In her mystery there is the meeting with the sacred in the dark night of the Soul, which fills us with terror as we face the divine. With Number 10 our questions are wise; this is not the dread of the ultimate refusal but the strengthening of the certitude that if we have found the way of the force, we can progress on the path.

There is also a rapport with the Emperor because he is the ordinator of the manifested world. His affirmation is that he has to live an initiatic life. The first aspect of his work is the acceptance of an indispensable discipline, to implement the right move for the viability of the plan. We have to come from the transpersonal in us, for our work is a complete acceptance of an immovable discipline and a response to our spiritual will or will to truth. We are not going to cover up or ignore anything to do with our behaviour. No elevation or uplift is possible without these two bases well established, for there is no rebirth on the Wheel of Fortune without this strong foundation. This is the discipline of always living from the inner life or the blue wheel, but accepting to work with life on the red wheel at the same time, so that the blue and the red can fuse into the purple of spiritual reorganisation.

The key to this card is that we must want patiently and for a long time, to acquire the right to go forward into eternity. This is a paradox, or a riddle of riddles. It is about the persistence and understanding that nothing is given to the one who wants, so we have to really let go of any wants. When we have an insight on something, the acquisition of that vision and the strengthening through each step we make really has to be part of us. If we do not do that, the next step cannot be taken because we have no foundation for it. Every bit of spiritual progress has to be regurgitated several times until every single drop has been assimilated by the body, so as to make the foundation for the next rise. We can start the next rise while still digesting the last one, but there is no way we can leave the last step until it is fully digested. We mustn't run before we can walk – the 10 does and by falling time and time again it learns to fly!

If we always want perfection it is important to know that wanting more is counter productive, for there is no soliciting of higher degrees; we just have to wait to be received naturally in the higher vibration. Those higher degrees are states, such as humility and purity; as such they cannot be obtained by any discipline or methods. The luck would be that if we wait long enough we forget what we wanted and the waiting would have turned into patience, so the rise would happen as surely as day follows night. To try to go too fast belongs to those who have not acquired a sense of eternity; they are still trapped by time and are therefore limited. To proceed eternally or with inner alignment, we have to stop the wheel (so to speak) to get rid of the limitation of time and measure, for the lens has no limitation and represents timeless, immeasurable potential.

Strength, La Force
Taming the personality

The keynote for this stage is 'Let the force be with you'. This is not power or brutal strength, which is the force of matter; rather it is the force and passion of the unconditional love of the initiate who serves. Having completed the cycle from 1 to 10, he is now going to tackle, through love, the burning of any drop of lust that is left within him. We see a serene and gentle lady holding open the jaws of a lion; she represents the love of Soul, while the lion represents personality with its pride and self-concern. The lion is being tamed; he resists but soon he will be lying at her feet. The two are fusing, Soul and personality, the sacred with the profane; it is an alchemical process. Now we no longer fight ourselves; our love is fiery and unconditional and our passion is for the truth.

In the greater scheme of things there is that great universal circling dance of the energy of Spirit coming into matter and the question arises; where does it all begin and where are we in that dance now that we have reached the Number 11? The 1 to 10 or the Tetraktys is giving us the conceptual understanding of the process of alignment. Then after the re-birth in the Number 10, the energy of Spirit has to find a way to integrate the concept into everyday life through the medium of the Soul in humanity.

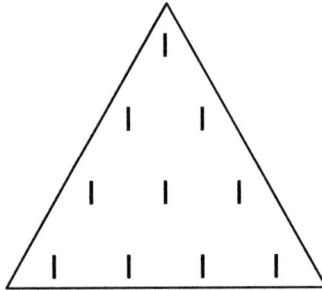

Figure 1. The Tetraktys.

At Number 10 the system is ready, because Spirit has come back into matter with all the experience and wisdom of the hidden word and the hidden knowledge of what happened within the great triangle. Then with the 11 we are looking at 'Man and his God', so we will use the word 'God' frequently as it is part of man and his relationship with his inner God. This relationship transforms the mindsets associated with the exoteric god of his religion. From the Magician right up to now, we have done the metaphysical work and we have prepared and tested ourselves through trials, to see if we are as clever as we think we are. All that work has to go through a process of distillation, which is why we need so long to do it. The fiery Number 11 is then going to take on the task of burning any drop of lust for personal power that is left in us; it does this through love.

At this point we are back in real life and when we're not in the higher witnessing stage, we are stimulating the drama. When we connect to the witness in us we can bring the clear mind to purify the perception of the situation that we are in.

The 2 (which comes from adding the digits of the 11) tests us, by attracting us back into the material aspects of life, where we can be swallowed up by our manipulative game playing. From there the

11 gives us the opportunity to see that attraction honestly and burn it out. We have gone through the university of the first six cards and the great metaphysical trials of the next four; after Number 10 we are in real life. The 11 is making certain that we love the highest thing; if we have exclusive love for the lower things we can be 'burnt alive'. Before this eleventh stage all that we were looking at may have sounded a bit gruesome sometimes and wise at other times, but it was in our heads and so was theoretical. A lot of people with an 11 in their chart will often use the Number 2, for it is so much nicer to keep it all in wisdom and theory and think that is where we are at, but actually we are not in real life with the 2, we are measuring the strength of our emotions and everybody else's emotions, including our pets! If we are measuring we are not moving with the emotions into the fires of transformation, but it is alright for diplomacy is greatly needed.

Number 11 asks of us to exteriorise the real strength of the spiritual essence of our Soul. With Number 10 there was a great balancing where we had the power either to stop the wheel, or be absorbed into our wants and needs and so be dissolved back into nature. Stopping the wheel doesn't mean that we don't reincarnate, for we still have to do so in order to test our strength. If we do inner spiritual work for ourselves we have to reincarnate; even if we are doing the work to escape reincarnation, we are thinking that we can be cleverer than God by taking weekend courses without life's exams.

The first ten stages are the result of the most positive expression of the initiate who comes back knowing he has to take a higher initiation or a rise in consciousness, so he comes back to 'walk his talk'. He comes back full of the idea of being the senior one or the king. His aim is to use everything of the world, without being enticed by it any more, for when we come back as Souls we know what luggage we have, so it is not just a question of theorising and vaguely knowing, it is about just getting on and doing it.

The woman in this card has the same hat as the Magician, for she represents the triumphant Magician. At Number 10 we looked at the positive outcome of rebirth out of any level at which we might have been; here we have to understand that walking through the gate of the 11 doesn't necessarily mean that our initiation has succeeded. The positive outcome of the process of Number 11 is to distil mental/emotional experiences into wisdom; the wisdom will then attract flashes of insight from universal truth. This process will require a lot of inner purification by fire, so that many who go through the stage of the 11 will not reach the higher 2 (1 + 1) and will choose to experience the little emotional 2 of the personality. However, The Wheel of Fortune will go on for millions of years and there are always other opportunities to uplift, so it is okay.

From 1 to 10 the same initiate is going through the different phases of his levels of consciousness, attributes and gifts. In Number 11 he comes again; the rise has happened and the spiritual graces that he might possess naturally and spontaneously are activated, so the energy we are looking at here is strength. The card is called 'Strength' in English, but it would be more appropriate to call it 'Force', because the initiatic Tarot is a send-out-call to all men of goodwill of 'may the force be with you'. Strength is there to help us to understand force. We are not talking about power, though strength and force can be powerful, neither are we talking about brutal strength whether backed by money, illusion, glamour, size or position, for all of that has to do with matter. The 'Force' we are talking about is something quite different; it is the will aspect of the higher mind in the Soul acting out its spiritual intent.

Science and occult science could agree that life from the beginning was fire, movement and energy. Our tiny lives began as a spark of light at the birth of the Solar System and we know that the whole of life on the planet is sustained by the vital fiery energy from the Sun. Our core being is a fiery energetic spark moving into matter to find its own reflection. In symbolism Spirit is often represented by fire and movement, or by flying birds. The reflection is soon seen as reality and the drama of survival, but it is only when the higher consciousness of the unit in nature is able to remember its origin as pure Spirit and realises that everything else is illusion and glamour, that the purified fire of active witnessing can do the work. The vibration of the level of consciousness of Soul/karma bodies, moved by the spiritual will to reincarnate, will attract the trillions of little fiery lights that will enable the biological space suit to manifest. The biological life determines the expression of the solar life, from the point of view of nature's consciousness, so when a lift of consciousness is achieved, nature's space-time equation is perceived as a mirror of illusion. Then the higher consciousness becomes more universal and in time can dispel maya, glamour and illusion.

Number 11 teaches pure passion and pure love; this is what fire really is. Whatever is in front of us is the past; don't avoid it, don't fight it or kill it, don't ignore it or cover it up, but perceive it from a different point of view. This is the rise in consciousness, where we bring our minds into our hearts and by using the energy of unconditional love, we burn with passion.

We can be passionate for humanity and for the God we live in, so the fire and passion in us can help others to increase their fire and sustain that process, but we cannot do it for them. We have all been through phases where we thought love didn't work, because the thing we loved the best, such as family, parents, partner, or a dog that bites everybody, would not change, no matter how much love we gave them.

We need to decide what we love best; we may love chocolate best rather than the God we live in! Maybe we have had intellectual beliefs, or glamorous emotional glimpses of feeling what it is like to be in the arms of God, but we still go for the chocolate. If on the other hand, we fight the love of chocolate and make it into a 'baddy', by saying it is not good for us or our spiritual growth, we are actually giving it more strength and power over us.

With Number 11 we have to dare to put the full glare of our Souls onto our personality or our animal self. From the point of view of the Zodiac the lion or Leo has the strongest personality, for it is full of the pride of matter, the tribe and the personality. We know its ultimate aim is to render itself into gold through service, so as to become a king of Heaven, but here on Earth the lion has the proudest position a personality can express. In the 11 anything we try and make-believe about ourselves is going to be under a strong spotlight, so if we refuse to look at that pride and withdraw into denial, saying: "That is not us!" we give our power to what we deny. By not acknowledging for example, that we like the taste of chocolate in our mouth we give it that power and it has a greater hold over us. Liking it is not a problem, for the God we live in loves chocolate, so what is the big deal! We define the God we live in as loving, so we need to learn to love ourselves passionately with all our attraction to chocolate, for we are doing alchemy and distillation. The woman and the lion represent Soul and personality fusing or coupling; this is the perfect alchemy through love.

The lady (who is Soul) is peaceful, for she has understood that she is here on behalf of the God we live in to express love, even to the smallest, lowest densest unit in the nature of God, so she tames the lion of personality peacefully, with love and strength. The lion's paws are tense and gripping as he resists, but his mouth is open and he is not going to bite her. If your dog bites you, you learn to receive it with complete unconditional love and no negative emotion, because the naughty little dog only bites through fear and he doesn't know why he is doing it; eventually he gives you his paw.

Number 11 is asking us to be at one with our God and at one with the fire of passion and unconditional love. The initiate has completely distilled the process of loving through understanding. When we are fighting ourselves, we are not loving the God we live in but conflicting with it. At the eleventh stage we can fall, because the less we look truthfully the less we love. This is a great narrow passage, where the energy of love flows through us and if we can associate with our God spontaneously within that fiery movement, the fire and passion is within us. Then if we don't let it out for distillation, blessing and transmuting, we burn ourselves. We truly see God in our own image and if we allow the protective, hate side of our nature to take over our God will be the self-destructive, punishing God. When we understand that the fiery God had nothing to do with the little us, we can learn to love this side and understand that humanity has made God in its own image. It is the God of yesterday, the God of survival; he was great at that time because he taught us to release the instinctive survival through fear, but do we still need to continue to do that?

Remember that if there is something we don't like in other people, it is actually in ourselves, so if we deny the unconditional love for anything we might discover in ourselves, then we are denying God. This is expressed by *'become the change that you want in others'*. Pure unconditional, passionate love is fire. The fire is in matter and is neutral, but it can be fuel for our lowest passions, all the forbidden things and everything that makes our God a dark God who is going for self-destruction. When the Spirit in the Soul of man seeks the fire, it can become pure unconditional love. But when the blind Spirit in nature fuses with the lower instincts within us (not the pure instinct but the one disfigured through our playing the game of Maya or illusion) and the Soul is aloof, then the fire is trapped and instead of being tamed from the clearest, purest, point of view the beast takes over and uses the force to exert brute strength. From that we get a picture of the incredibly stupid predicament that humanity is in now.

All the instincts have to be seen and understood again, because we have denatured them. We are not bad, but we have to explore our descent into the senses and we are now confronted by the danger of the grossest possible addiction that humanity has ever known. We have just surfed a wave of civilisation and are starting a new one; there is no doubt that we are at the end of an era, if we look at what is happening on the planet. For the last forty years there has been the possibility that the planet will self-destruct, but we are still here!

There are many voices and groups wanting to save the planet, but we only start to save it by waking up to the fact that we are living a denatured life. Our pictures of what life is, come from the exterior survival attitude rather than the interior and it is actually very difficult for people to really internalise. Do we know how to internalise? Do we touch the inner God, or do we stop at the intellectual/emotional level of guided psychedelic meditation and think that is what we are?

When we internalise, the only thing we feel is passion, movement and fire, but we are in the deepest possible peace because life is as it is. It is in that internalised very rarefied atmosphere, that the truth in whatever we have done in our day is distilled. It has to reach that depth to be transmuted. It first has to be seen for what it is and the minute that occurs, transmutation happens naturally and spontaneously. To reach the distilling fire spontaneously is quite a high achievement.

When we come back into matter the attraction is still there. The lion is so powerful that if it didn't have the desire for sublimation it would gobble up the lady. She's got no tools, no gloves, no sword and no gun for self-defence and she wears a coat in which she couldn't even run for her life! If she wasn't passionate and fiery, she (the Soul) would let the personality drive her. In ancient times the gates of hell were represented by the open mouth of a lion, a symbol for personality. From the point of view of the God we live in, who is witnessing and loving, it doesn't matter in the least how many times we feed our personality or our lower passions with the higher passion of the Soul. This is what the Soul is there for, to go on experiencing until eventually the personality realises that the type of love it was exercising and needing doesn't actually work. We will put ourselves through many experiences where we go for what we want, but once we achieve it we truly realise we did not need it.

The wise man has no preference; this doesn't mean that we lose the enjoyment for something, but rather that we lose the dependence and need for it, which is quite different. So we can go through life with enjoyment, but without addiction or obsession. The Magician or initiate by his nature has a very active kundalinic fire and he has learnt to wield and uplift the sexual creative fire into the purifying fire of Spirit. His consciousness will have the fire of God meeting its image in matter and as the two come together, we have a kundalinic spiral.

Buddhism has a great gift to give – it teaches us to clear our mind. In Buddhism the aim is to rise above the emotions, so that there is only a clear mind and a clear reflection. In this state our waters are very smooth and we can see life for what it is. We have to be like Buddhists; to internalise so that we know that reality is mind, then we can disassociate from personal pain. Now we are working on all the things that we haven't yet embraced and loved, so we have come back to 'walk our talk'. We talk of unconditional love, but we have to actually practise it.

In the great plan, what we see as 'aeons ago' is only yesterday. The civilisation of Atlantis might have lasted one hundred or two hundred thousand years. The symbolism of an age is what was used then to decipher the great knowledge that is within the planet itself. This comes from the initial fire of Spirit moving through its own time and space, then focussing on some of the planets with specific qualities so that they develop a life of their own. Our planet Earth was alive from the time it found a mechanism to enable it to keep on going through all its phases, until it produced life. It is life on Earth that is now keeping the planet alive by regulating the temperature for its ecosystem to survive.

The wisdom and the measurement of life as we know it were born at the beginning, with the first hot breath of our Suns' love and energy. The movement of this fiery energy organised the dust left in the space of a previous Solar System to form the Solar System we live in now; in esoteric understanding we call it the second Solar System. Its existence should reveal the reality of the one Soul, human/planetary/Solar, with its main characteristic of love/wisdom. The memories and myths from this previous time are coming back through the matter we are made of. They tell us of how the greater fiery life we live in keeps on living, dying and going through experiences continually; that is what life on Earth is all about. It can be measured in the same way that we measure our body through science; this has allowed us to find out an awful lot about it. The minute we internalise we get the film going and automatically release the cellular memory, which starts to replay. We revisit situations time and time again to understand the broader karmic group work that we have undertaken. The aim is to observe the unfoldment so that we can help others to recognise their personal karma. By contrast the initiate should always focus on the much broader and simpler appreciation of karma, through witnessing a much bigger plan. His consciousness knows that it is re-visiting dead stardust, so he's aligning with the karma of humanity, the planet and the Solar System.

In the life of the Solar System, humanity is under the influence of the Aquarius/Leo constellation for approximately the next two thousand years; this is the era of Horus, the 'son' or Soul of the third person of the Trinity, so the talks in this book are relevant for a long time to come. The era we have just left is Pisces and Virgo; this was the time of Isis that took us to the year two thousand with the 20 of the Goddess. She gave birth to the Soul of humanity at the beginning of the birth of Jesus. Before that it was the time of Osiris, the Aries and Libra era, when the fire of God came to reveal the mystery of incarnation. These eras (12 of them – the greater Zodiac) form the greater experiences of planet Earth by retracing the same myths over and over again. The mystery of the incarnation started with the first human being, so there would have been great initiates walking the Earth before Jesus and very few men and women knowing themselves as Soul.

The lady in the card is the love-wisdom aspect of the God incarnate. She is astride the lion, which is expressed in astrology as cutting the path of Leo. Leo is the house of the Sun, which is still the fiery but material God; this really means the strength incarnate, that is where the idea of being the strongest comes from. This gives rise to the misunderstanding; 'I can kill you, because I know that I have God's righteousness with me'. As well as seeing the woman as love-wisdom cutting across the path of the Sun, we also have to see her as one of the aspects of the brightest full moon, for she is illuminated and radiant. Her light illuminates what she is internalising so that the material Leo, represented by the lion, can actually see its reflected light in her. She is saying; "Look you are all light and love!" At the same time, she is throwing light onto the personality so that it can start reflecting and see that it is the light and the love. She's taming the personality so that it can submit to the transforming quality of the love aspect in the Soul. She represents the cry of love, the uniting of the moon and the Sun and therefore the Soul, Spirit and personality giving in to a complete passion that will incarnate and give birth to the new era.

When we come back after the 10, we come back with the aim of representing and 'walking our talk' according to the new level of consciousness that we have realised. We have had the passion to come into matter with our truth and our God, so we engender the flavour for a whole era. This is divine drunkenness, ecstasy and madness, but not through alcohol or drugs! Pure illumination is thrown on the personality that is accepting to be tamed, seen, named, or made conscious, for when we see and name something, we render it conscious. The personality will do its utmost not to be completely tamed in any aspect, mentally, emotionally or physically, because it likes to be the lion that eats the piece of chocolate it is addicted to! As the personality receives the light of Soul it gives rise to lust in the purest sense, which is the instinctual need for fusion; this is lust in the purest way of wanting to meet itself again. This is the created meeting the creator, or pure instinct meeting its will. When we do that we are in control of our wills and lust doesn't exist any more for it is divine, in the same way that nature is divine in her lust. We are in complete charge and we will never be taken in by anything lustful again, for we will recognise it, know what to do with it and not be a victim any more.

The problem is that a lot of us, once we wake up to the inner understanding of the system, start to see humanity or nature as a victim because of our misunderstanding. Either that or we go blind to it and use our power to stop us feeling the pain of recognising that everything on the planet (including plants, animals and us) is being used. The ultimate love in the heart of the initiate is service, which is about being used in every way with awareness. When there is the feeling in our hearts that somebody is going through suffering we don't need to make it heavier than it is already, we can thank God that they have the courage to go through it. This is a much better way to help than trying to stop their suffering, for having the courage to go through it is another attribute, like force, strength and passion.

The lady's hat is in the shape of the ∞ of infinity, like the hat of the Magician. The Magician had to 'walk his talk' and use the four elements of matter, earth, air, fire and water; any one of those four could have brought him back down. Here there are no more tools and she doesn't use any methods, for she is not manipulating or using matter. She has the quality of reason, therefore she can be in the most brutish situation of the greed and pride of the personality, without any tools other than love-wisdom; this is the basis for success in the new era. The hat has ten leaves in its left flap, to represent the promises of the next ten rays to come and the next ten generations, which are the latent rays of the new system of 12 to 22. The trees of generation are going to regenerate the past through karmic work; this is the primitive, creative energy, or the force of the first Solar System meeting its true self on the planet in biology, though the mirror and witness of the personality. This is why the 11 is not always liked, because it is very fiery, oversensitive and overbearing. It has all the potential of its divine parentage, so its fire has to come down to earth and bring the dreamy Souls into real life. With the 11 energy there is no 'either-or', it is just the way it is. It is freeing, for we have not got the choice and so we cannot be worried about others view of us. The fire does not care for achievement or goals; there is no judgment, for where love is there is will. Our only duty is to align to the God we want – we have become our own prophet. Lust, life and love all merge into truth, so speaks the Soul!

The attainment of this card is that the love-wisdom aspect has been heard by the personality and the personality is tamed. Look at the eyes of the lion and the way he is holding his body; he does not like it at all but he is tamed. In the same way the initiate has tamed his wild nature body. There is nothing to redeem in nature for nature is pure, so we are talking about the job we have to do to straighten out those areas in our perception of nature that we have twisted. Spiritually the fire of the planet is still growing because we haven't yet burnt it out. We have to become pure drops of passion which can be used to distil and transmute personality. Personality is only the film that we took from the beginning of time in which a lot of the frames are blurred, so we didn't see them clearly and we misunderstood them.

It is important to look at the process of internalising and to understand it, for this is fundamental to the work of the Soul. When we internalise, meaning bring the light of awareness into the dark of the ocean of experience, we release cellular memory, which enables a film of the past to be seen. If we don't know that this is the process, we dramatise the release and replay it unnecessarily; that is why we are still replaying the old myths until we can read the mysteries through the symbols. If we know that we are watching a film, the light of the Soul can erase the misunderstanding; there will no longer be a film and the old myths can stop. Otherwise we fall in love with ourselves as the star of the film! The lady is very calm and peaceful, for she knows that in front of her is a film that she's seen before, so she's not going to look at it again and be caught up in it. If we get caught up in it then we are being puppets on a stage and drama queens, rather than just understanding that we have done that one and that is what it felt like. We do have to feel the emotions in order to know what is driving the beast, so if we are trying to cover them up it is because we are afraid. Then we will find all types of excuses not to feel them; it is so simple. If we cover emotions up we are going to have many lives of make believe, of psychology and of being in love with the muck, where we give all the reasons why it is because of this, that and the other. These all have to be peeled off and as we do so we realise that what we are addicted to is the experience. Internalisation is going to be different for everybody and in its process we don't know we exist as a personalised individual, we are simply a point. We are everywhere and there are definitely no pictures, no sensations, not even time and space. It is the dissolution of everything that has to do with personality, outer awareness as we know it, the experience of the senses, the intellect and the emotional. It is pure awareness and we don't even feel loved in the way we would expect love to be. It is dark or light, according to what is going on in the alchemic cauldron.

We internalise to bring all the experiences into the distilling vessel to be dissolved, until only the essence remains. This is the path we are all treading which leads towards a pure state of being. Internalisation may be fleeting, for Soul contact can only occur as we seek the love and truth within us. Eventually we become Soul based, so we permanently see the essence in everything living and attain pure being. If we truly give up from the core of our being, then we drop into the alchemical cauldron and we give up to God. This is not giving up from the physical, emotional, or mental points of view, it is deeper than that. What is inside us is the Soul within, which is the consciousness in us that is forever going for more truth and more fusion. Giving up is really dropping into the depths of the Soul and giving in to its mystery; that happens when the personality stops doing its drama-queen business. We use the phrase 'give up', but we don't so much give up as 'give in' and allow ourselves to be uplifted as we fall; that is the true feeling of giving up. As the alchemical process happens we will still have survival reflexes, but we see it in a different way. The process of alchemy is always a mystery, for the light of Spirit via the mind and the light of wisdom from the centre of the cell, fuse. As this happens an atomic light blanches the cell's DNA and the Soul, removing the karmic memory from body and Soul. Even adepts may want to hold onto something they have understood and have a fear of going into something they don't know, so we can't expect our personality to do better.

Internalisation means losing some of the game that we're addicted to. There are many ways of meditating, but true internalisation is spontaneous. This is the exteriorisation of the Soul in the ordinary everyday life. It is acquired through a desire, so it is about where the heart is and what we love best; this is all to do with love. If others and God are what we love best, then the inner life will

spontaneously deliver its light; we can't work at it, for forcing ourselves via the intellect to love others and God doesn't work. It is
purely and solely a natural process.

We can internalise truth, which means being completely honest with our intent and reactions. We tame the lion by working on
cleaning our windows or view of the world. It is not about interfering with the lion or harming it in any way, because we love it, so
we let it bite us or react behind our back. It is being completely and
utterly honest about our instrument and our instrument *is not us* for
goodness sake! It is the fiery lives within biology that have created
the instrument or body, the fire of the Soul needs to fuse with that.
We are the fire and we have accepted that half of what we are is an
instrument to be used for developing the films that need to be seen,
named and felt; in this process we clear the space. We stir everything
up all the time and we don't know what we are going to find, but we
only find the monsters that were there naturally.

Non-interference delivers the purest light, so we cannot teach
other people what to love, push wisdom into people, or tell them
how to live their lives, for if we do we are frightening their lion
to death. A broken animal is not a tamed animal and the problem
for a lot of us is that we've been broken. If you have a difficult dog
you don't break it, you go along with the nature of the beast you
have with you, taming it by just waiting and loving until he trusts
humans again; so it is with us. The beginning of enlightenment
comes in when the personality realises that it has breathed in a bit of
light without the help of self-interest. While we are breathing in for
health, yoga, beauty and youth, we *are* still in self-interest.

We learn that our true growth is through love and passion rather
than hard learnt discipline. Though there is still a discipline it is a
more elusive one to obey, as it is the self-discipline of inner truth.
That lion is going to screw up his eyes and clench his paws for a
while, as he resists seeing himself as the silly, smelly, big lazy cat
he is! It is about being aware of what we weren't aware of before,
or what we were covering up and playing with.

Humanity had to be tamed with fear, like people break in animals. In time we are not going to be afraid of rain or volcanoes,
because we can use our intelligence to run away and cover ourselves. If we do not find fear somewhere, where do we dredge it up
from? Fear wasn't invented; what we call fear or excitement is the
movement of the energy of Spirit flowing through space, exploring
more manifestations and situations, according to the disposition
of the unit it activates (negative or positive). These various aspects

of feelings had to be named and we have to experience the full spectrum of what we call fear or excitement; this is why in the pre-understanding of sexuality we have fear and excitement coming together. The problem of mankind is that it kept adding all types of other curiosity to sexuality, rather than becoming truly in charge of it and rendering it divine.

When we start to internalise we develop the inner senses and in turn the five outer senses are exalted. As a result we can smell a colour, or see a sound. Our physical being is a super instrument that can take 3D, moving, living pictures and embellish them with smell, taste, touch, colour and sound. It gives a wealth of information to the witness, so that any aspect of dysfunctional reaction can be checked and the various levels of work undertaken. It is not about being in charge of our senses, but using the senses in the right way, so 'being life' rather than 'suffering' life, which is quite different. We are not a victim of the movement of life that flows through us, but rather a part of the creative process by being a co-creator through understanding. The true meaning of suffering has nothing to do with physical, mental and emotional pain, but with feeling the energy of light and Spirit flowing through our living organism and automatically transforming that organism; that is 'suffering' and it is fantastic!

There is a certain irritation in the passive resistance of the lion, it is the personality resisting at the same time as being tamed. It recognises the dominance and superiority and accepts that experience. The authority of the lady (Soul) has absolutely no intent whatsoever, either to break the personality, make it afraid, or enslave it, for it is completely non-intrusive; it is love. The lady is balanced, poised and peaceful and there is no expression on her face; this is the pure love fusion between man and his God via the peace of the Soul.

When we are looking at the outcome of all the trials we have gone through, we know that it is really nature that gives birth to the God of consciousness as a response to the sacrificial, fiery zeal of Spirit that seeks its bride. Hope, grace, misericord and all the experiences we have sublimated will be born out of the alchemy of the Soul taming the personality, as tokens of the Soul's love/wisdom expression. Internalisation reveals the responsibility of understanding that the conflict is within us, not in nature, other people or God, but within us. Will, like energy, fire and Spirit, only serves motion which is moved by emotion, so where we love and where we have our sensitivity is where the will goes. We can remain in conflict forever, until we realise what we love. Most of the time we love to please ourselves and we do not know how to love. We have served the God of gratification in either our pleasure or our hard work, so that our inner heart is lost and lonely and has forgotten to beat the rhythm of true life.

The state of beatitude that we are looking at, which is complete love in the name of God, has no value by itself, just like any of the other spiritual qualities. Beatitude is a state that we acquire, like bliss is a state we acquire when we have attained a certain level of consciousness. What is important is honest consciousness, not the feeling that we get from it. If we are striving to achieve qualities such as grace and beatitude to augment the self, then we have missed the point and the exercise will deliver pseudo feelings of glamour. The desire to reach these states, as we saw in the little arrows of Eros in Number 6 (The Lover), creates the movement necessary to go towards what we love. We can have an idea or a desire for bliss or peace as we enter the inner path of internalisation, but we become aware of wanting it for ourselves. There is a natural stage where we understand that in wanting it for ourselves we are still a lion, digging in his claws to hold onto what he wants. In that understanding we are able to forgive and love the lion. We may still carry a lot of the old attitudes, for we still have to use the personality, but in love we give up the dominance of the personality.

Even the desire to attain something is useful, for without desire or emotion there is no movement. Because the will is where the heart is, we truly have to see what we love, desire and aspire to. The key is that aspiration and desire should walk hand in hand, because for a lot of us they don't. Once they do, then we have the true beginning of the arrow of Eros, which gives the spiritual direction. Even if our aspiration is to be the richest man on the planet and there is no conflict in us, our spiritual will pushes in the right direction. Our spiritual will and our love aspect are the higher aspects of aspiration and desire. The man in whom they function together is a complete man; he will go quicker through his breakdown, fall and breakthrough than the one who is in conflict for many lives about aspiration and love. To dare to live and be yourself is the fiery way. In the eyes of God there are no good or bad ways to do it; just be yourself and – well – as it goes!

None of the things that we meet are imposed. We used to call them trials or lessons, because that was the way we learned and got wiser, but they were not imposed on us, they were part of a completely enfolding process of awareness. The minute we start bringing a little bit of that fire out from within our instrument, the mirror of life is going to show us the right situation, according to our level of spiritual awareness. So when the cake is ready, straight away we see it on the table. Nothing is imposed, we've cooked the cake and we've put the ingredients in it, now it is up to us to eat it, digest it and make it disappear. We call it a cruel system, because we can give ourselves indigestion, but it isn't either the system, or the God we live in that is cruel. From the point of view of love, they are like the parents watching the little ones grazing their knees; it is just life and it is tough.

We don't even choose the lessons, they materialise automatically as soon as we are ready. We enabled a situation to manifest, so there it is; it is up to us to recognise that we have to do something with it. We have watched the world, we have understood, therefore we know that what is there is a reflection of our understanding of life. We are a witness for God hitting himself on the nose and we have to accept that actually it is us hitting ourselves on the nose, on behalf of the greater life and that is okay. Nobody or nothing else is doing it to us, but we have exteriorised the picture and manifested it as a drama.

If mankind were just coming back knowingly to take photographs, then we would never have done any subconscious work. To be able to associate with the pain of others, we have to be able to resonate to that experience within us, even if we ourselves aren't feeling any pain from it. We walk through the fire and feel it burning us, but it is immaterial because we have experienced it before. We know the state of bliss and beatitude that the saints were in, we have all gone marching into the fire in the past and walked out of it on the other side, whether as a Soul, or a burnt up human being – it doesn't really matter. We still feel it, we still see it, but we are not taken in by it. If we have not suffered the burning and dying, then when we come back to help we won't be able to associate at all with people who are doing it now.

There are different stages in this work and as we detach from the world, there is a danger that we will cut out our feelings. We can reach a state of being aloof, so we could suffer from spiritual superiority and pride. At the stage of the 11 we are very good at freezing up and saying 'I don't need to cry', or making a mental excuse rather than empathising with human nature; so not acknowledging God's true love for his creature.

The lion will be tamed at the feet of the Soul without the tiniest bit of resistance. How is that going to happen? The Soul is coming

through, the fusion is happening and the personality has to truly see itself as a reflection of the love-wisdom aspect of its Soul. If we think of an animal we have loved, when we look at them and talk to them with our Soul they roll over and recognise the pure love that is offered and is therefore in them. That is exactly how the personality will eventually curl up. First it starts fighting, using all its intellect, its wants and its foot-stamping tantrums to resist, then the gentle, slow, noninvasive presence of the Soul takes over and it realises that it is looking at itself through these loving eyes. It starts to be tamed and eventually serves the Soul unreservedly.

When we recognise ourselves as love-wisdom, how can we ever want anything for ourselves? The system that we live in is the most beautiful one, the fear we have is pitiful from the point of view of the God of the pure Soul. The purification has happened through the loving of the beast and the more it resists the more we love it. The more pitiful the beast is, the deeper our love has to go and then the beast feels that love, knows it is protected and doesn't need to fight to survive any more.

If people are endlessly fighting and won't let go of their drama, all we can do is love them. They need to recognise what they love best and then they can stop fighting, because what we love best will purify us at the end. It is about aspiration, want or desire; if those are aligned then it should remove a huge conflict. If this doesn't happen, we have to decide which is the stronger; if the want and need are stronger we have to bring the aspiration down, otherwise there can be conflict forever. The middle place, where we are neither up nor down is a place of sin (in the sense of being in the dark rather than as a judgment) or purgatory, where we are in conflict all the time, so it is important to make up our minds which to go for. It is only out of pride that we would aspire to something more than what we are. If our aspiration is stronger than our desire, then we can focus on the aspiration and cut out the desire, or learn to love the desire like we love chocolate. The 'in between' stage is where we are addicted to the experiment. The experiment is where we have to go and hurt or cut ourselves, then feel guilty because we have gone into dark corners and felt the 'yuck' of them, until eventually we have got addicted to that feeling, forgetting that it is only an experience. Think of the natural progression of the human being; before we know what sex really is in a pure sense, there are all sorts of dark corners and dark alleys where we look for it. Once we know it there is nothing more simple, but most people keep on with the dark corners because it is giving them a 'yuck' feeling in the stomach. They like that more that the sex itself, so they stay in the dark corner. There is no punishment for staying in the 'yuck', we have only to recognise and sort out what is going on.

It is aspiration versus need. If the aspiration is looking in one direction and the need/want is taking us in another, then the will can only follow where the emotion is, which means that the aspiration has no wings or hope. The less hope the aspiration has, the more the will is imprisoned into the emotional aspect. The will only follows emotions; aspiration comes from a mental-intellectual point of view. The will can be stuck with the emotional, but the mental will see itself as completely impotent because it has no will in it, so day after day, year after year and life after life when we say 'I have no will, so I can't do it', the unease, disease and the 'yuck' bit is reinforced. So not only are we giving our emotional body, our Soul and our spiritual will to the 'yuck' feeling, but we are also giving our intellect to it, which means impotence and powerlessness. If we bring the aspiration in with the emotional aspect, it doesn't matter which direction it will move in, it is bringing head and heart together that matters, then the spiritual will is there and the experience will unfold. We will want to go home where the light of the hearth warms the frozen hope and allows the heart to seek the good and beautiful.

It is not so much change or evolution, it is fusion and coming together, which means transformation; that is what the planet and the system does and it is the same for us. It is only our pride that puts us into a difficult corner and that comes up because we are being used without being asked, until we give up the illusion of free will.

'The path' is a set of situations which confront us to enable us to reorganise our past. It is not imposed on us, but we impose it on ourselves and we reorganise it in a way appropriate to our own nature, our own mindsets and our own inner God; it is not according to the books. We are going to refine and distil the perception of it all as we travel more and more inward. The other choice is to allow ourselves to be dissolved back into nature, which is okay too. Despair will make us give up if we haven't brought back the aspiration into the love/emotional aspect, meaning accepting who we are, where we are and where we are going at the time. If aspiration and love stay separate and we keep aspiring to be the best-loved because we are the cleverest, sexiest or whatever, then the only thing left for that unit is to take itself right back into nature, because it is going nowhere. There is only so much self-pity a Soul can endure and if we see ourselves as a victim all the time, then we give up to the victim and go back to the instinctual nature. All that emotional/mental energy will be recycled again and again, so whatever we come back as will be cute and magnetic. Watch the sting however, for you could be a cute little chick for a fox!

It is only when man has accepted life as it is that he takes the path of probation. Man is free in front of God when he has understood the unconditional nature of the love energy of God; he then knows he is made of love. The system is fire and whether it is electric, atomic, by friction or magnetic; it is all love. It is about complete awareness that the self is made of love, therefore that awareness is alive in every single tiny one of the trillion fiery energy units in our bodies. If we are not aware we are not going to know that we are made of love. We have to have the courage to meet ourselves, because we are not going to meet anything else, so the questions are 'are you afraid of yourself?' and 'are you afraid of love?'

God is everywhere; when man realises this he makes the virtual world a divine reality. Many people would only acknowledge God in a moment of needing comfort or support or feeling guilt, rather than seeing God as the whole of life. It is truly in the measuring of man's love or indifference towards his God that he feels accepted or rejected, because this is his level of accepting or rejecting the divinity within himself. God disappears when the fiery aspects of personality and Soul don't recognise each other as one fire, for God in our image doesn't exist if we do not recognise who we are.

We may see the path of probation as something difficult, full of trials and lessons and so render it negative, when actually for an initiate the true path of probation is an active, loving, energetic one. We are always going forward, regardless of the mountain crumbling beneath us; we move with the positive rhythm of our spiritual song in our hearts. The pictures coming in front of us are there because they want to disappear, so the work is to make them disappear by digesting them, rather than by thinking "Oh my God, here we go, it is another trial, and whenever will it end!" It is better to just drink what is in our cup, digest it and carry on. It is active work on the inner probationary path, it is not negative suffering. But don't worry if you grumble, there's nothing healthier than a bit of a grumbling – it is part of the digesting process!

As an initiate or disciple we are being used by God willingly. That is the huge difference between the grumbling part of being used and being a victim. The riddle in front of us is always what we are looking for in ourselves, in order for us to have enough energy to go forward and lift above ourselves. It is about recognising that whatever the trial is, there is something in us which needs more loving, so we have got to go down to find and give up to the experience, because we know why it is necessary. It has to do with more distillation and that feeling of uplift in consciousness helps us dive deeper.

We come as a witness and learn to relate to others as ourselves. We are the strongest unit in nature, because we understand that self-realisation has no time and space element, so what is done to us doesn't matter, because that eternal aspect of 'we have all the time in the world' will never die. That is why the lady in the card wears the hat of eternity. It is a total giving of self out of choice and free expression, with no fear. It is about always having to surpass ourselves and when we do that it automatically renders us into the strongest thing there is in nature, but at the same time the most vulnerable.

We have nothing to show to the ones who do not recognise what we are talking about, for we are invisible. All they see is the shell or the crucified aspect, which is the part that makes us very vulnerable. Because of that aspect people start walking all over us, which is difficult to take, until we realise it is okay because it actually makes us stronger. Whatever happens to us is a complete gift of sublimation. Sooner or later that lion is going to be lying down and then matter can eventually recognise itself as organised bricks of energy serving the energetic movement of Spirit in matter.

The Magician is a bit cocky in comparison to the lady, for he is going to use whatever is around him. She, on the other hand, is not going to use anything material as a tool; this is shown by the fact that you can't see her shoes, which tells us that she is not of matter. She is love/wisdom and she is truly not of this world of matter; she is 'in the world, but not of it'.

It is all to do with fusing with the various levels of the great life we live in, which are within us. It is also about being an instrument of God and being used on behalf of God to witness. There is no value whatsoever in knowing what we are looking for. Reading books gives an illusion of knowing what we need to look for next; we believe that bliss is round the corner and we might even think that a mystic experience is it! In this way we are just turning the record in our heads to make it play the tune again. We live in God, God is in us and is pure fire; the fires of love will bring the inside out, so that our skills to deliver the pearls and visions is activated. This is the great longing of the fiery lives in nature for the lover – the fires of Spirit. That longing has become occult or hidden; this is the true fall out of paradise into matter. This is what the Soul of human consciousness is coming to make whole by sacrificing its very life to bring Heaven on Earth. Paradise is uplifted and the fall is the cosmic mystery of love.

The light has fallen into a little hidden part of the subconscious at the centre of our cellular memory. The fiery element in us must find the light of truth in the heart and descend into the subconscious to retrieve it, going deeper and deeper according to how much energy or power of love we have. We have to keep opening the mind to keep on remembering more and more of what we've experienced and there is always the danger of falling in love with the laboratory (virtual life), which is what most people have done. Even the masters can fall, because the laboratory is very attractive. If we've left a grain of sand unturned because we have not been completely diligent and honest, that grain of sand will soon fill up our bag and we will end up on our knees; however, we can always start again!

The Number 11 requires strength, force and courage to test the might of our free will. If we feel completely at one with the world, we are completely free, for we breathe and live as the world and it is our life. Free will is therefore a vital ingredient in this card, for without it there is no possibility of fusion. Doubt and constraint come from mindsets, so we are back here with the strong mind, advocating protection and being the devil's advocate. To resist that we need a complete act of faith, which means being completely in love, not doubting for a minute the power of that love within us and that the voice of God is talking to us! Can you see that if our will is not free we could doubt our sanity! Then if we fall we get up again and walk and even if the sky falls on our heads, it is all okay.

This road is paved with love, but if we haven't got it in us we don't recognise it, this is why we say God is hidden. It is the strength of our love that has made us acquire the knowledge and understanding of how the system proceeds; this completely removes the agony of doubt. We've put ourselves through crucifixion and we've destroyed superficial phantoms; we've led the fire of that love of God right through the deepest roots of our being and we can see how many illusionary bushes we've burnt there. Because we have been burnt right down to our roots by the passion of our love of God, there is no way we will ever doubt again. All the little fiery lives in our cells have been touched by the flame of God's love; that is faith. Love and faith strengthen each other. In this second Solar System we have to demonstrate that we are made of the love/wisdom energy because we are Soul, so if the worst comes to the worst and we make the biggest mistake of them all, what a glorious mistake! All we are doing is going back to the fire which was there in the first place. Once we have understood the system we cannot stop loving because there's nothing else, so why hesitate to be yourself, be love? The force of inner love and inner wisdom is completely unshakeable. This is backed by the knowing that whatever we meet, we are never given anything that we cannot sustain or transform. Also we never confront ourselves with anything that we haven't already done.

The Lady is sweet, supple and full of grace. The lion is already tamed. It had the violent instinct of the protection and survival of the animal world, which in us is the slightly distorted instinctual survival. She is not putting any pressure on the lion, only giving him pure love-wisdom. It is real inner beauty; there is no fighting and she's almost caressing him.

The ultimate protection button in terms of humanity is war and aggression, for example; 'he's done that to me so I will go and do that to him'. The cycle of vengeance stops humanity being able to internalise, because when humanity is plunged into war and destruction, the one most important thing to do is to survive. We have to accept that and help them to survive because it is a necessity. Just now the very survival of life on the planet would have to be a priority and it will teach mass consciousness to take 'responsibility' towards others seriously.

In the service of humanity there is nothing else we can do now, except do all we can to transmute the fear of doom into positive goodwill and help survival to happen. What better way of doing that than to take ourselves a bit deeper into matter, because on the way we have to go backwards. We are aiming at spreading the simplest possible way of looking at things, so that things can stop being complicated, glamorous or illusionary. The new wave of life in biology has never had a more polluted environment than we have now, but we can be consoled, for we came out of an atmosphere that could just carry primitive organisms and clever little things they are! They managed to help planet Earth to give them the best possible environment to sustain biological life until it gave birth to its most rebellious clever tribe, the human race.

The lion is a dominating material strength that imposes itself on others. It can be very protective, but even the protection can be dominating. It can be extremely generous as well, but with conditions; it is the generosity of the king that wants to be recognised; that is personality. The lion is the symbol of strength and the king of the jungle. He could gobble the lady up easily, but he wants to be tamed. He is furious and in a bad mood, but his resistance is passive and any minute now we will see him lying at her feet, for he is taken by so much love and sweetness from her. He has the love, strength and force of the lion, the king of the jungle; he is the well-aligned personality with loads of great skills. He is the top guy in nature, for when the personality is accomplished it has the strength to destroy and rebuild the world, as well as the inner incredible force of love-wisdom. This is so powerful that he doesn't need any arms to conquer his lover. In the picture of the lion and lady we have the inner and the outer fusing and coming together; the profane and the sacred meeting each other and starting to fuse and distil into a new manifestation. The 11 is always simmering some kind of refinement.

The Soul aspect, represented by the woman, has acquired the wisdom, so the whole journey is in front of her. She has lived, she has experienced it all fully and she has dared to die several times and then come back for more. She can see the vanity and fragility of the world and she is ready to co-create. She will never be worried again by the material pull or the attraction of form and matter, for she understands all the tendencies of the personality towards survival and protection and has compassion. She has emerged victorious from all the conflicts within herself and has recognised that she was fighting herself. The Magician was going towards infinity; she has found the love-wisdom and become it. His feet were in the material world, she doesn't even need feet. She only lives through love and thought and has no need of tools, for she has found the true science, which is about understanding the thing we love. The more we love it the more we understand it and we become one with it; that is wisdom. That cycle ends with strength, so it is *'May the force be with you!'*

This card has rapport with the following other cards.

Number 1, The Magician, is the aspiring initiate who comes from the desire to demonstrate the power of love. Desire shows us the goal and when we become the love, there is no goal. The lady in Number 11 is the highest initiate; she is the love/wisdom.

With Number 5, The Pope, we receive the blessing, so nothing is wrong, everything is at peace. God is not a God of fear but is complete peace. If man is made in the image of God he conducts himself as a picture of the God he knows, so if that God is a God of fear, he will conduct himself as a poor, guilty, aggressive, macho, stupid person. Know your inner God, so as to know yourself and remember the true God doesn't impose himself on anyone – *'I am that I am'*

With Number 7, The Chariot, the Charioteer comes back triumphant, knowing that love is all and that the fantastic passion he has,
will propel him into starting to 'walk his talk' until it is done. He
doesn't do it through pushing over his opponent, he does it through
love. He has no gun, or weapons, only a wand. He has renounced
the material world and comes back to prove that he can resist the
love of matter, because matter is not attractive in the sense that it
used to be, in fact it is not attractive at all. The lady in Strength also
has no weapons, but unlike the Charioteer she has nothing to conquer and is saying 'no conflict'.

She has a link with Number 9, The Hermit, because he has the
knowledge of the source of things. The force of the 11 is the fusion of
the source with its vision.

Strength has been able to stop The Wheel of Fortune (Number 10)
through rising out of the illusionary world; this is the force and
strength that can stop that wheel in us. It doesn't mean not reincarnating, but it means that whenever we come back we will not dissolve again in the primordial waters of needs and survival. Instead
of domination over others, or feeding on life and being fed on, the
internalisation has happened so we are Soul centred. The temptation of the surrounding world no longer appeals, for there is a passionate and complete fusion with the inner force.

Materially we live in a tragic period and appear to be going very
fast toward collective suicide. There must be many atomic bombs
waiting to explode, but there is no need to spread a feeling of doom.
It is a crucial and great time for change and if we want to go for
uplift and release ourselves from glamour, we have to keep on
burning fires all the time for more purification. This is all done for
the sake of what is coming in the future. The famine and war that
we see in the world now are a physical manifestation of a level of
consciousness which has become redundant. Man as mind could
take from nature without respecting its law of sustainability; that
is why we now have to learn to look after the body of nature. We
are grounding and seeding, so bringing into matter the energy to
express new paradigms. We have to have broad shoulders, for the
weight is heavy and there is a lot of very hard work to do.

It is said that if we know how to command pain, it will become
joy. This is not physical pain, for by this stage we will have walked
into the fire singing, so physical pain is not going to be our main
focus. We are talking about the mental pain of conflict, which is
about the trials. If we look at it positively it is not a trial but a pleasure, because we are going for more transformation, sublimation and

distillation. If we keep on focussing on the knowledge that we are talking about the moral pain, there is no conflict. The object of our fear or whatever it was we were glued to, can be seen for what it is and it doesn't attract. There is no sin, no pain, only a progressive detachment from protection and the survival of the personality and a gentle fusion with the one light of Soul.

Without the Soul-wisdom of the Pope (Number 5), which the initiate carries in him and eventually becomes, the world of form would have distorted that incredible love from the Soul and made him a powerful man. A lot of people at the top are powerful, because they are using that powerful energy of the Soul for self; a powerful man can bring himself to the top because he knows how to manipulate that energy. He has understood the power of love and magnetic attraction and he will become a powerful man on his own behalf. You can see that the light in him is imprisoned in matter and the more imprisoned it is, the stronger he will become. He will eventually believe he is a master because he is successful in holding on to the secret, but he will end up being tied by his illusion and disillusion; that is pride. He will self-destroy and take an awful lot of people with him because of the strong, manipulative energy he holds. This will sort it all out, because the system works beautifully!

Where our treasure is, that is where our heart is. It is so difficult to renounce our wealth, for when force is manifesting materially it finds no other aim than accumulation. The power of Soul stuck in matter, gives rise to addiction and it will create a crisis for change, a wake-up call. In its peaceful aspect love has to know it has a goal, until it finds its true goal – its home, the Soul.

Mitigate the pure fire with love and let love devour all things. Alchemy is the true passion of fire, purifying with the fire of love. This is the act of the original marriage in the 11; we have Spirit coming back into matter with equal consent and consciousness; we have the man and his God. It is true divine drunkenness – you have to be drunk with the vision of your truth to be a prophet!

If we are brave enough to be true to ourselves, we can go and have a good look into our lion's jaws. This is the courage of total engagement, which means that we have no problem with going and getting right into these jaws with our light, love and wisdom. The lion will be so surprised that he will not even think of his survival, he will be dazzled because the light of the Soul that we bring is more stupendous than he is. Think of the lion of personality encountering for the first time that deep place of love. He cannot know how to react to that, for he can't bite it, kill it or talk to it. He doesn't know the language and he's mesmerised by the simple awesome power of the Soul. He gives over to that power and all he can do is disappear in awe. Then when he emerges from the experience, the force is with him and he will seek to merge with it by serving it. From then on he will not be taken in so easily by the world of illusion.

The Hanged Man, Le Pendu
Everything seen differently

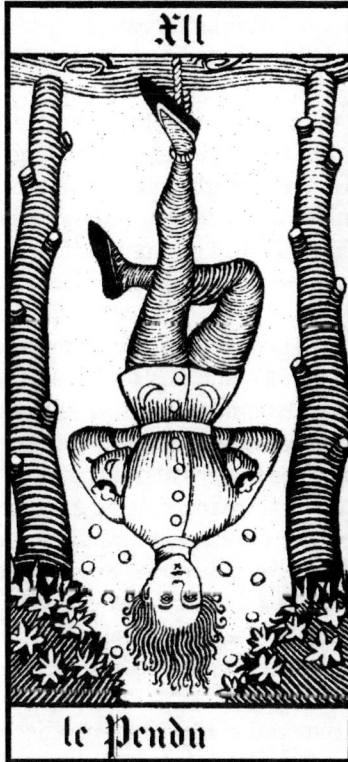

Here, in The Hanged Man, the all-seeing eye (3) is able to perceive clearly the glamour and illusion of the outer world, so his mind will not be pulled in by maya. The card depicts a man hanging upside down, suspended by a rope attached to his left leg and with his hands tied behind his back. He is helpless and his personality is giving over in obedience to the impulse of the Soul. All the things that the personality might want or desire are removed; this is symbolised by the cut branches of the trees on either side of him and by the coins that are falling to the ground. He has reached the point of no return.

In Number 10 (The Wheel of Fortune) the Soul, urged by its spiritual direction, is reborn into matter. It recognises the force (Strength – Number 11) within it as God, so it is man and his God. At Number 12 (The Hanged Man) the interiorising is complete, so he gives up to his spiritual nature and opens the door to karmic alignment in the next spread of cards.

The initiate comes back as a Magician wielding the wand of command and order, so he has the authority to be able to go back into matter and use all 4 elements, earth, air, fire and water, so as to exercise his authority over what might pull him back into old mindsets.

At Number 11 and 12 we know that the victory is over the self and not over the world, for if we've mastered ourselves we've mastered the world and so the world cannot pull us back and 'play' with us; the game is over. The highest wisdom will be revealed when the veil is torn; that is the goal. The first ten cards are all the conceptual, metaphysical attributes we have to understand, so as to eventually end up in this great one, The Hanged Man. This card represents the highest attainment to be achieved by the initiate; it is the goal of the Magician, hence some esoterisists look at The Hanged Man as the highest possible achievement in the whole of the Tarot.

The initiate has passed the test of the Wheel (Number 10), so there is a time where all he does is learn about the force that is within him. This means letting go of thinking that he can personally act in any way which is going to be effective in the long term plan, but rather letting the force work through him. We can see why this aspect comes at the 12/3, the Number of the zodiac. He has done enough, he can't do any more and he is on his knees, he's gone round the cosmic world several times and so he has become a cosmic man by detaching from the earth.

We can't get to that point through any discipline, philosophy, religion or therapy; it has to be done through the process of the internalisation of life's experiences. The Tarot is telling us that as long as we understand the Spirit/Soul/personality aspects of the self, the Trinity aligning to the greater source will reveal in time the spontaneity of the Soul. This spontaneity is the main characteristic of Soul expression, as the Soul will always respond to the impulse of the Spirit. Everyday life, being the field of experience for the Soul, is the only school for the disciple to internalise into the love/wisdom aspect of his Soul; in so doing he recognises that he is a witness. Spontaneity is the opposite of structured discipline; it is the inner discipline of instinctual response to the impulse of Spirit, which is very different. The discipline of the Benedictine order of monks is relevant to the 12/3, for it teaches the unity of the Trinity within. The rules of the Benedictine order are acceptance, obedience and stability (alignment). The word Benedictine means blessing, so blessing is offered and it is up to us to receive it or not. When we are blessed we go into a state of grace; that is what we are looking at in The Hanged Man. If we told people that this is what happens when we go into a state of grace, not many would join us on the path! Grace is the highest possible attainment of the realised 12/3 and so we are looking at that phase of the development, rather than at the earlier stage of the 12/3, which is the little self-centred princess – she might be called Hope, Pearl, or even Jordan, but not yet Grace!.

If we do not reach a state of grace or of complete spontaneity of movement from the point of view of the Soul, we cannot go through the portal of the Holy of Holies because that is where the Spirit and the Soul energetically marry. It is not about being forbidden entrance for there's no law that forbids us anything, but energetically all the time we are not in a state of blessed grace, the personality is very much in control and its vibrations are not ready for fusion. We are looking here at the ultimate distillation of the refined energy of the Soul, which is Jesus on the cross when the veil is being torn from top to bottom; that can only happen when our vibration is ready for it. It is not an exercise, or something we can try for or practise at, it is a natural, spontaneous happening in time, which takes place when the personality has completely allowed the Soul to take over. At this point we have completely accepted the death of the little self in favour of the higher self.

All this gives quite a different view of the 12/3. The 3 is internal and it has to do with allowing the third person of the Trinity to express through the Trinity, rather than through art or whatever else we do to express on the outer. The higher 12/3 removes the personality and expresses the Soul through the skills of the personality, which is a very difficult thing for the 3 to do. We have all got the syndrome of not doing enough inner work, either because we have to be busy out there or because we haven't yet found the right tool that is going to help our Soul to find its expression in our outer creativity; in fact it is co-creativity that the higher 12/3 is looking for. This is not art, science, or metaphysics; it is nothing else but the inner creativity of the Soul, using whichever skills the personality uses at the time; working on a supermarket check out will do!

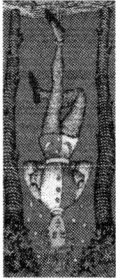

There are two living tree trunks with 6 cuts on each; we know they are alive because they are very green. The cuts are red, to denote that it is about spiritual life, or sacrifice in the best possible way. The tree trunks represent the earthly temple, which had to be cut to become the original columns of the door of the sacred temple. The columns can't be inside the Holy of Holies because they are the support of the door. The branches represent all the earthly qualities which have to be cut down and, sublimated into the qualities of the higher world. On each trunk all the cut off branches belong to the earthly temple and they are typical of our average good, strong citizen on the planet. There's no other way we are going to be able to free ourselves from all these external things if we don't go to the root of them and cut the branches off right at the trunk. Then, when the trunk has no more of these little branches, it becomes the portal of the Holy of Holies. Then it can go right up to the sky and carry on and on as it connects to the yellow or gold beam, which is the wisdom sustaining and feeding the tree.

The branches are:

1. Egocentricism or the egocentric focus on the world.
2. The love of material possession.
3. The application of the mind towards mundane advantage, which includes recognition.
4. Family ties.
5. The desire towards the illusion of survival via biology, in the form of reproduction and the senses; also the desire to stay young.
6. Professional life.
7. Union or fusion.
8. Sexuality.
9. The attraction of the world as a spectacle, which includes beauty.
10. Social achievement and rising above the rest of society.
11. Relationship and projects.
12. Secrets and shadows.

These are all illusions; the initiate has seen through them all and stands naked as the Soul. He has had to cut them all out, from the 1 to 12.

1. The first one, which is *the egocentric focus*, is the illusion that we are the centre of the world. We have to know our place in the world, but at the same time know that we don't matter in the slightest!

2. In the second one we see the *love of material possessions*. With this one we can see that the more we put around ourselves the more we protect ourselves. In doing this we are being good gatherers and nest makers. As we hold onto something, love of that particular thing ties us down. When we are a great gatherer we have a tendency to see that a leaf (for example) is so beautiful that we have to bring it home, or we see a puppy that has no mummy so we have to look after it. It is easy to think that we don't need material possessions, but this goes deeper; it is at the fibre of our being that we've got to understand the laws. It is a measuring experience of going right in and measuring and then extracting the knowledge in our Souls that nature is pure. It is from the basic underlying place of Active Intelligence that we get the answer. We don't have to drop our love for something so much as realise that we are still associating with it. That association has taken on an almost destructive flavour for we want it for ourselves; the paradox is that we need that fondness and love to keep us on the planet!

3. *Recognition*, or acquiring mundane advantages, has to do with science, knowledge and art. This is the way to reorganise what is given from the point of view of matter and translate what is in our inner being into matter, as for example sound or colour. However, these are all eventually dead ends because it is still just matter. It doesn't mean we mustn't keep on practising, for that is really part of the discipline we're talking about. We might not go for money, being known, understood, or for any of the mundane advantages that give us a sense of achievement, but we must ask ourselves, what are we still going for? Is it to be seen or heard by somebody else? If it is a cry of, "Can't you see how beautiful I am inside" it is still wanting recognition and to be seen. Have we ever discovered an 'artist' whom nobody knew existed? It is a real need (absolutely everything is out of need) to be able to communicate, reach and touch. This is still recognition and still a mundane advantage, so we even have to cut that away from us. This doesn't mean we have to stop doing our art, science or studies, so it is not the harsh, ascetic withdrawal of The Hermit, it is almost the opposite, for it is saying, "I know all those things, I've done them and love them, but I still carry on doing them, because one day I will be at peace with my whole self and will give in to the smile of my Soul spontaneously". There is no judgment and yet we're told to cut it all off. Many people are coming in contact with their Souls because of art, science, Pythagoras, or poetry and more often than not we touch people into awakening through the arts. So it is needed, but there is a point where we will

realise that we ourselves don't need it and then we can be more effective at introducing others to art.

4. *Cutting off family ties* is the transition from the personal family to the family of mankind. This does not mean that we do not love our families dearly, just that we don't need those ties. This love allows more freedom for the expansion of spiritual expression for each individual member of a family group.

5. The great scientist relies entirely on the senses to feed the curious intellectual *knowledge of what life is about*. Pure science observes and describes; this is the great Number 5 doing its work. At its best it is the perfect witness of the matter of life. Some disciplines of Science are doing the co-creating that they think they are meant to do, like learning about the fabric of life, only to try to re-organise it; the mind thinks that it can do better than nature. This is a tricky one, but it is mankind in all its glory, so we have to learn to be at peace with it, because science is mirroring all the metaphysical concepts perceived by the co-creative thinkers. As the co-creators rise and see something clearly, then the egocentric scientist will recognise it with the intellect. This is good because we have to understand our world. Scientists can now measure the hum of energy and the vibrations from activities in the brain and already they are measuring the impulse of reaction. Eventually they will perceive the flash of intuition and measure that, which is basically measuring all movements and vibrations. Science is already saying it is all movement and crystallisation and is on the verge of putting everything together, so from the cosmic point of view the mystic and scientist are merging into one mind.

We are here to understand our world and as the knowledge expands and we learn to vibrate to the bigger system, there will be a time when we won't need words, definition or equations in order to know. Then we will be able to truly communicate beyond our Solar System. At that time we will no longer be limited by the structure and knowledge of this small system. The only true co-creation has to do with ideas and with a progressive change of perception. The power of the one truth and the power of one unit of true light can bleach hundreds of thousands of misunderstandings and then spread, so that all the other units can receive it; that is the true job of the initiate. Translation of the universal message has to happen in the way it is needed and through the available instrument at the time.

6. *Professional life* is about self-worth according to what we can do. Here profession is not defined by what we do to pay our bills, but what we are best at doing. It can also be extended to what

society or our peers think of us. It is about how we are going to receive self-worth from the world. Profession is how the world is going to perceive us and while we haven't associated with the only true worth, which is the quality of the Soul, we will project our need for self-worth onto our profession or standing in society. As Spirit eternally manifests as matter in order to know itself, the sum of the experiences that are felt, sensed and analysed, are impressed on the Soul. These experiences can be contacted again as guidance or revelations. In time the Soul realises that life is only a process of knowing itself, so we give up the drama for we understand that there is no need to take life personally. The process of the life in the Solar System is going for truth, beauty and love. It is a machine that makes diamonds, so the pure are cut and polished to shine more light into the system for others to catch. Those who have not yet associated with Soul awareness, because they want to be part of the drama are suffering and feeding it, rather than rising from it. There is free will here and if we understand what we are supposed to be doing, then we can stop suffering the drama by just accepting the conditions of where we are and obeying. By doing the best that we can at the time we find stability and peace of mind and then we don't add to the mud and misery. The ones who are not aware and not awake are like nature; they die, come back and suffer, until eventually they are touched by a little bright light that might come to them through art, a book, a word, the contemplation of nature, or even despair. Through this they begin to understand the necessity of the experience of suffering as the way to recognise the presence of the witness. That is not inflicting the pain onto ourselves, but understanding that suffering is necessary. The system is seen as self-explorational and self-regenerating, until the awareness becomes part of the rebirth and we feel and know the pain.

With the elevated 12/3 we have complete acceptance, obedience and stability. Now it is time to die and regenerate. Life started unconsciously in the centre of biology, where the fire of the manifested aspect of God began. Now the journey is going to start again with the complete awareness of each cell; can you imagine the beauty of that! It is not so much saying "I see, I feel, I think" but more "I am, I am, I am": it is that simple. It is coming back home, seeing it for what it is and accepting, loving and obeying because there's nothing else.

7. *Union or Fusion*. Fusion is the experience that the 7 is going to try not to do, because it knows how painful that is. This pain comes from having to lose ourselves into something else; in so doing we find ourselves even more, in order to expand. So we know that the

7s always keep a little bit of rear guard 'just in case'. Light comes into the cup of matter as it is supposed to and puts its feet in the water that is flowing through the instrument and exteriorising its skills, but suddenly the water is too hot or too cold, so it withdraws. Because it comes from the spiritual, we aim to *be* the best rather than aiming to *do* our best, for we do not want to be seen as failing. We have to become our job by exteriorising the quality of our Soul into the skills of the personality, this way we get our Soul identity as we work. It is a process of fusing and daring to let the Spirit flow through the vibrating Soul into the personality, so that we can recognise what our job is and make one with it. Eventually we can actually master what we have to do and then it becomes natural, so we don't need to work at it.

8. With the eighth branch we go into *sexuality*. If we dare to understand that as the mythical Spirit and his bride, so realising that we are only here to fuse with the 1, then we are going to have to explore the lords of karma, who bring destruction and rebirth. Their tool is sexuality, which is the polarity of the extreme dispersion of the one creative energy in manifestation, as a way to explore its space. The understanding of the right use of sexuality, meaning the right use of creation for an initiate, is to bring back those polarities of expression and make one again by fusing with his God. At the biological level the function of sexuality is to create children; the higher level is to co-create with the light. Sexuality as a natural urge has to align with its divine functions: procreation and co-creation. The division of the one creative fire is manifested as the kundalinic energy, so the two fires of active and receptive energies twin together to create a unifying third one. To align to the right use of sexuality, either for generation or regeneration, is what is required, rather than finding our self-worth through being sexual objects, to be wanted by whichever exaggerated mindset of form and fancies is around.

9. *Attraction of the world and its spectacles.* With 9 the journey will end in the centre. We travel the inner road watching the world go by, leaving the experiences behind and recognising that we have the whole world in us. It is an interesting facet of the 9, like watching the passing by of a film. It is a sort of introspection. If we're doing it in a way that is giving others back their life, then we are blessing. Many will be attracted by the spectacle of the different colourful lives of other cultures and journey to exotic places. However, if we're going to be completely detached from the world we can't be attracted by what is moving in it. We are not in asceticism or judgment here, we

are in complete acceptance of the world and because that is the only way, we let it go. Love the travellers, for one day they will know that it is all inside.

10. *Social Achievement*. Because of the many qualities of insight that the 10 carries, a position of importance in Society could flatter their ego. The aim for those under the influence of 10 is to associate with their minds, which are there to guide and vivify matter. If that happens then they have no need to be seen as a pillar of society, or as the best.

11. *Relationships and projects*. Those influenced by 11 have to reach the blazing fire of their inner God, thus purifying their relationship with the world. So they will have to learn not to project the ultimate authority they are seeking into relationships and projects. All nature wants is to be found by the lover, but it is an internal finding not a physical/emotional/outward one, for all we are is light moving in to try and find its other half. The fire is internal and is in the cell. There are many layers of expression that are all playing at being the king on the planet, whether physical, emotional, mental or eventually the personality. These are layers that bring trouble for spiritual potential alignment. The projects are there to spur the various bodies into alignment with a task where all the levels are required to work as one. It is via the personality that we can bypass that timidity, fear, or the over-sensitivity of being found out to be not good enough for the God we live in. We are too hard on ourselves, for spiritual success is actually being able to be seen as completely stupid, idiotic and failing, without caring for our self-respect and self-worth, because we know that the Soul loves a fool. The minute the 11s understand that it is the God in them that moves them, they can dare to love and become the puppet, or even more God's prophet, for it is the complete abandonment of putting their lives in the wilderness. That is the ecstasy of the 11 who has recognised that the force is with them. The minute we give over to the harsh prophet in us, we realise that we are only one thing and that is love. The problem is that we all close our hearts because the voice of the prophet chastises us.

In relationships and families we keep mirroring what we are supposed to grasp or measure, so we keep asking 'am I up to that?' or 'have I understood it?' It is so simple when it comes to the Number 11 because this is truly the opportunity to transmute the prophet into the lover and the personality into the bride. We could call closing the heart a normal instinct because we don't want to be hurt again. To meet the experience that we think we are not worthy of, or which isn't worthy of us, offers us the opportunity to dissolve that mindset; at the time this feels like death. At that point we really do die and find that we have not only survived death, but have transmuted the negative emotion/mindset into love/wisdom.

12. *Secrets and shadows*. At its highest the 12/3 is the all seeing Trinity at the nature level, so it will need and want to be seen. At the disciple or initiate level, all the secrets and shadows in the subconscious will have to be seen and hell will have to be burnt by the great fires of universal truth.

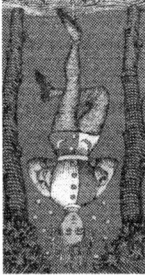

The two tree trunks are the two pillars of the occidental and oriental houses, which are east and west. These are the pillars of power which sustain the structure of cultural society and religious order. Although they are solid and strong, they do hold the Maya, glamour and illusion of everyday life as it has been so far. The Hanged Man has renounced the material support of the four elements in order to give service to the Earth. His only attachment and sustenance comes from the golden sea of wisdom that is available to him through the complete transparency of his love aspect; this is represented by the open cup formed by his head, arms and golden belt. The personality is completely rendered passive, but actively passive, because through love and understanding it is being used by the authority of the Spirit. This is the true Trinity.

The Hanged Man gives us the hallmark of the quality required to achieve the great work. We can see why we have to go so many times round the wheel of the Zodiac to find the golden thread back to the centre. At the centre we realise that all the knowledge and skills we might have thought were useful, have to be given up so that we can be used as a well-tuned instrument.

The consciousness of The Magician has been purified of illusion in the eleventh stage, so is rendered up to the vision of the 12/3. In this state he realises that he is not a master of the four elements, but is made up of them so that he can be used as an instrument for the light. We are on Earth and when the elements are aligned in us, we can be used as the vehicles of expression for the consciousness of the Soul. The perception is that we are the Soul of nature, Soul of mind and the solution for moving the Spirit into the process of fusing with its image. When this is seen the 'going back home' feeling grows into certainty and we realise that all is one. The highest achievement of the 12/3 is for the higher mind of the Soul (which is the point of contact with the higher spiritual intent), to fall into the depth of wisdom locked in the heart of its own nature; then all is seen as one. Because we are down rather than up, the upside down position is the right one, so in the 12/3 we truly see things from the centre; all is fire, all is mind, and all is love. That is the rending of the veil.

Here there is the recognition that the Soul is a witness and a teacher, bringing us to the point where the Soul can take up the job of teaching and people can come to learn from its wisdom. The ultimate aim is for these people to become their own teachers, so any wish or need from the Soul teacher to see a result according to their own passion would be a gross interference. In time we, as individuals, will naturally disappear as teachers.

From the position of The Hanged Man we can see that we are going to perceive the rest of the journey as an expansion into the consciousness of love, life and reality. There is liberation or freedom from the former perception of life through the senses, for the senses and intellect are rendered as tools and therefore have no hold over us. The normal understanding would be that when we die our Soul will rise; this is the interpretation given to the death of Jesus (the Soul) on the cross. In fact, the true interpretation of that phase from the point of view of the Soul would be to achieve complete freedom from the need to be useful, through liberation. This need to be useful comes from the personality/Soul instrument and is the last giving up of any emotional need. The rise is purely a more elevated vibration of mind. The death in reality is a complete fusion of the higher consciousness within the Soul and the fire (consciousness within nature). The Soul then is fused with its natural space suit – the personality. This is then complete freedom for the Spirit, which has met and made one with its manifestation as love (Soul) and wisdom (nature). This is the birth of cosmic man.

The Hanged Man is the right successor of 'may the Force be with you', in Number 11, for his hands are tied and he will not use strength; he will instead let the force of Spirit work through him, for the only authority over him is the inner one. Hence the mark of all true heroes is that they are seen to die before the happy ending, but as we know this is a victory of the expansion of the inner life over the world of illusion.

All our heroes have different names because of the perception of them in time and space, such as Krishna, Buddha, Hercules, Moses, Jesus and Mohammed. Once they pass through the flame of wisdom, they all belong to the one great initiatic Soul of mankind and they are reborn into a much brighter, eternal kingdom and a higher level of consciousness.

The vibrational rate of the movement of Spirit into space is so much faster than the vibration in matter that it would never be able to fuse directly with the heart of matter without destroying it, if it didn't have the vibratory rate of the Soul as mediator. With the evolution of consciousness (different levels of vibration) the Soul will act as a mediator by attracting the aspiration of the personality to uplift, so it will actually fuse with some aspects of matter, thus allowing matter to receive some spiritual energy. It is the gradual fusion of aspects of the personality with the Soul that will actually bring the Soul to the point of disappearance into form, so allowing Spirit and matter to move as one. This transmutation process holds the mystery of alchemy.

Our hero's left leg symbolises receptivity to the higher powers. His right leg of action is folded behind his left knee symbolising the giving up of his own authority. His legs form an upside down 4, which is one of the symbols for the Earth and humanity, so with his inner perception he has accepted the job of serving humanity. There is no action he does that is for self, so he is powerless for he knows he cannot do it for others, so his actions become non-action and Spirit works through him. The only resource he can draw on and be fed from is the love-wisdom aspect; that is why his foot is held by the yellow beam of wisdom, representing a long line of masters of wisdom.

When the Soul becomes master of the personality, the latter is automatically uplifted and has no need for freedom. True freedom is the complete giving of self and it is the only place where love can prevail. Seeking freedom is a rebellion against love. Here we are going for union not freedom, for it is oneness with everything that is the true life, bringing us back to the source of life.

While we want to reach out and be loved by everything, we demonstrate the scattering energy of the unrealised 12/3. Day after day we go after sensation, supposedly to learn and experience. Then we go from delusion back into sensation and delusion again, eventually going into rejection and disgust. As we keep going for the illusion and glamour, we go more and more into lack of respect and so it carries on, until one day we have to accept to let go and be as naked as our original essence was. So it is like dropping the useless rags. It is a beautiful correspondence to the chrysalis rejecting the covering that forced it to crawl in the mud, through accepting to live in the world at its most vulnerable, because with the chrysalis we know that death is around the corner. One of the most hunted creatures on the planet are the naked little bugs that only have their little legs to run away and hide with. Once in the cocoon, they will go through complete dissolution before they can emerge as butterflies. The butterfly emerges from the chrysalis, but before it can fly it is in extreme danger, for there is that short space of time when the wings are still wet and it can be snatched by a bird (meaning back into nature) before it can fly as a butterfly.

It is true that things don't happen until they are ready, but we have made the choice so far to bring ourselves up to that moment of readiness. For the butterfly it is part of its natural survival cycle, but for us it is a wonderful symbol for the transformation from personality to Soul. There it is in front of us, one minute it crawls the next minute it dissolves and at the end it flies. The whole of the transmutation of mind energy can be recognised by the initiate, so he will know only to help the ones who are already on their inner path. The law of conserving energy is one of the great laws of the Solar System.

The Hanged Man is at the centre of the Tarot, so is like the point of rest, the contact with the equilibrium, the pendulum between Heaven and Earth which digests the content of his universe. In the Herculean work there's a point where we come back in Libra to find the point of poise at the point of reflection, where we consider whether to come back into the system to serve our fellow man, in spite of knowing that all they will do is to manipulate us and in the end hang us. Serving the greater life is serving our fellow man. Everything from the beginning of mineralisation right up to the birth of humanity kills in order to survive; the terrorised innocent is still in us. It is the fear and terror of this that stops us completely giving over to the God we live in. Somewhere in us there is always the rearguard that holds onto survival and stops us from serving the greater. At this point in the centre we are aware that if we don't accept and love the system as it is, we don't love the God we live in.

Survival is the self-perpetuating predation that we perpetrate on the innocence of nature; that even includes us, for we are as innocent as nature. The hawk has to kill the rabbit, the rabbit has to chew the grass and the grass has to take the mineral away from the bones of the Earth and so on. Everything has to kill and feed on another. We can see how much love and understanding we need to serve that system. We have to wash out all the bitterness, resentment and pain to serve a system like that. If we don't see the system in that way, we are still blind and have rose tinted spectacles, for it really is a fantastically horrific system, yet wonderful at the same time. So open your eyes! We all know about being used and abused, it is in everything. The great life we live in is truly sacrificial and crucified, as every tiny unit of life makes up his body! It is great and wonderful and once we truly understand that, we bring the light of consciousness into nature so our little planet will sparkle as a most precious diamond in the firmament. We have understood the love and truth behind it, which means that we love it more than ourselves and more than survival. It is only by uplifting a problem that we can see its solution. This is where our initiate steps in with a tiny flash of awareness as to the solution to the problem of our system.

The initiate is going to implement the vision in the best way that he can. It is not so much how eloquent or how well he explains it, but it is how much he's becoming his vision that will create the sound to be received by another seeking Soul.

The Hanged Man loses the coins from his pockets, because his action is pure thought that is full of light, whereas the metal coins are very dense and heavy. They represent action taken for payment or recognition and therefore are for self. When we are acting from pure thought, action becomes pure, so we 'walk our talk' and act from our thoughts and vision. It is by thought alone that we truly act on the world, but it must be based in the love/wisdom energy to be rendered beneficent.

The Hanged Man is fed by the celestial waters and flows with them, so it is purification by baptism. We are looking at the key phase of the great work of transubstantiation and so we are truly in alchemy at the stage of sublimation, which stands for a total change in the life of the being. Water will carry away the impurities, which in our case are the mindsets, emotional states and the physical needs; these are what we have looked at in the twelve branches of the trees. We have suffered the purification by fire and we search and long for the spiritual celestial waters. We are actually completely receptive, as the mantra 'thy will be done' has made us available, but let's not forget that by letting the light in we have had to exercise spiritual endurance and recognise it as spiritual will. At the symbolic level some schools of mystery would have enacted the rituals of splashing of water onto the initiate to wash the aura; then we have the Christian baptism. These rituals symbolise the union with the Holy Ghost. They are also related to Isis who is the giver of the waters of life, as well as all different types of goddesses that represent the same qualities.

The Golden Beam at the top traverses the card and can be seen as being made up of condensed light; it is a gibbet, or a cross-beam, representing wisdom. This is translated in the initiate by an active and positive passivity, not out of complete exhaustion or disinterest, or because of being high and mighty; rather it is a conscious, receptive position. It is very active, because it is an act of will, so is full of confidence. We don't expect anything, but at the same time we know that the spiritual influx is actually going to come through us, so the mind is open to an unparalleled or completely different sort of knowledge. This is not a seeking of knowledge but rather becoming a channel for knowledge, which is why it is upside down. The role of the passive/receptive element is to faithfully receive, so that the activity of expressing the will of the Spirit can be done as truthfully as possible. It is a new life and a new vision, so it is a union of Yin and Yang by an act of freewill.

The coins or pentacles, which are falling out of the pockets of The Hanged Man, are made of metal. All the metals belong to the Earth and there's a whole folklore about them. The metal coins are falling back onto the Earth; this is about letting go of anything artificial that covers up our personality and stops us seeing it for ourselves. We actually do not know ourselves, for our true selves are hidden under the great mountains of mindsets, mannerisms, behaviour, conditioned reflexes and so on. The covering up that we do could eventually destroy the actual little flame of consciousness, because there isn't enough spiritual oxygen fanning it. The real reason for the multi layers covering the Soul is described in the Adam and Eve situation. When the rising of self consciousness within nature succeeded, their work started and they became aware of the animal skins they were wearing. The skins were the sum of all the survival instincts, behaviour and reaction patterns. They had to recognise and explore all these instincts that have created the emotions in the Soul of the world. Wanting to be the biggest or the cleverest comes in with the fear linked to survival; that is what it means to be covered by skins, it is not because the animals are lower than us that we wear their fur or leather!. We've had to go and explore what we were made of, so that eventually we recognise what the God we live in is made of, and then we can find ourselves in nature again, having cast off all our reactions to get back to the pure naked essence.

In a lot of the old rituals metals were forbidden, as in the Hebraic tradition where circumcision has to be done with a knife made of stone. There is quite a dark side associated with metal, so those planets which carry links to the different metals will also have that association. In some systems the metals relate to the seven capital sins. The non-practising of sin has no value, because not sinning out of fear, wanting recognition for being good, or not making 'bad' karma, really means following a discipline without understanding it. This is as bad as sin for it is just ignorance. The discipline must come from within through love and respect, because we have understood and want to live our lives in the light.

Man must recreate himself as a co-creator, this is the only thing that we are being asked to do. Biology has completed its work; therefore the only hope is the speeding up of the growth in consciousness. Science and art are doing it from the outer, whereas we have to do the co-creation from the inner point of view. We have to transmute the man into the Soul. Transmutation in ancient traditions was associated with the transformation of base metal into gold. The alchemists were looking for the gold value of the Soul (eternity), by studying the chemistry of fire on metal. Objects made of metal can be sharpened and they become dangerous, but while we are in matter we can see that the work of metal has given us the sword of nobility. The metal has been worked and refined so much that it is the lightest and the strongest it can be, so we have been able to build the new age of technology. Now we can see technology as threatening the life of the planet, but it is enlightening a new concept of being able to access the most useful quality of metal, which is endurance, so as to apply our technology to the elements of our planet. Metal serves by enduring fire. The first great hero was Vulcan who lived under the sea with his forge; it is his endurance that gives all the aspirants, disciples and the would-be masters their mastery. It is endurance and courage that make it happen.

The Hanged Man is letting go of the negative side of the metals, because for the unity of the divine work man must bring the cosmic pattern onto Earth. It is not because he doesn't respect the Earth as it is, but he has understood that to be able to make one with the divine he is going to have to become the mediator. So he doesn't reject the Earth, for this is where he can do the greatest work, but he wants to refine his Soul and be of more help.

The material temples were built on sacred geometry and so have sacred proportions. They were constructed through the desire to enhance man's connection to God. However, the door of the inner temple will only open when we have no desire or interest whatsoever in opening it! The Holy of Holies is only reached when we touch on the dimension of the cosmos within us. Then we are in the presence of our God with our question; it is the answer that we will be given that gives value to creation. The answer is that it is the fact that we are conscious and aware that gives God its value. This is a beautiful and extremely simple concept.

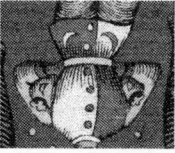

The costume that The Hanged Man wears is red and white. Red stands for spiritual action, white for purification. It is by acting with our spiritual thoughts (which are actions by themselves) that we purify and eventually align our purified personal karma with the karma of the planetary life. The moon on his pocket is associated with the sign of Cancer, the crab. Astrologically this means that we are looking at the higher psyche, which is the poetry of Soul and goes back to the divine source. In this phase of transformation the great watery sea mother earth springing her baby crabs out of the sand, represents the phase of rebirth of consciousness into the origin of life itself.

We let go of the rational reason of the intellectual by merging the mind with the Active Intelligence of nature, so as to restructure our new species into self-aware nature. We go into the occult and swim back up to the source, so we are not dragged back by curiosity any more. We all have to give back to the intellect time and time again, for it is at the service of the wants and needs; this is when we are attracted to whatever matter is. This chain is almost automatic and is about falling back into the illusion, the glamour and the maya. For the scientific purpose it is necessary, as it is part of naming and knowing of the body we live in, so it is part of the spiritualisation of nature. When the scientist becomes his research, he will instinctively become the watcher and the Soul will deliver new insight, restructuring the role of the intellect as a tool for the higher intelligence.

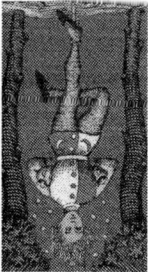

The four elements are actually transmuted here. There is earth, which is the pentacle or coins; the pillars of the gibbet are the wands of the element of fire; the moon is water and cups; the element air and sword is The Hanged Man himself, because he's suspended in the air. He's rejecting the fruits of the Earth and as he does so, the Earth is actually helping him by delivering her wisdom. The methods of the Magician don't work any more because we are going into a different level of consciousness and becoming the Soul. The Soul receives the higher vibration of light and speeds up the new understanding. Thought is penetrating matter to inform it, in the hope of uplifting it, so the mind has to work here and the sword (another symbol for the mind) cuts into matter in the hope of uplifting it, because there must be sublimation. The mind is entering the pure sphere of ideals where it can catch the cosmic ideas. He is being purified so as to be on the narrow path. Nothing is actually hidden, so the path is there to be seen for those who want it, but only a very small Number will have the perseverance needed to reach the final card. Many will come and only a very few will still be there at the end, because it is very difficult but necessary, to accept what is really annihilation.

Number 12 has a link to Number 1 because the Hanged Man is the end result of the Magician's work so far. The 1 is soon going to penetrate the Holy of Holies or the inner core of the temple in Number 12. This is where our Spirit and Soul meet in the depths of our hearts, so it is the cosmic element in us. It is where the God within us will fill our cups of expectation with the Holy Spirit as we lift our hearts in offering. It is the great inner meeting of God and the Soul; the temple being the personality, the inner temple being the Soul. In the ancient temples only the priests were allowed into the inner sanctuary or the Holy of Holies.

There is also a link with the Charioteer. The one danger with the Number 7 is that we could have gone a bit mad with the freedom, strength and zeal that we had, for we really feel the power of the zeal here. It could have made our Magician a bit drunk for power, but we know he went through and purified because he had to go through Judgment, Justice and The Hermit. He purified that aspect so as to transmute it into 'force' and he knew that the battle was against himself. He is kneeling at the door, more humble than we can imagine and richer than he has ever been, because what he has in him is much stronger than faith. We can shatter faith, but what he has is certainty.

In the crucifixion we have the phrase *"Father why have you forsaken me?"* On the surface it all looks like a terrible failure, but actually it is an acceptation of the rejection of the world because we rejected the world in the crucifixion. The awareness of the Soul, as its qualities descend into the three-fold nature of its instrument, sinks and disappears leaving a great feeling of annihilation. The Soul Jesus has achieved the taming of the personality. He has conquered and 'killed' the sin of ignorance in nature. The world has not crucified him – he wittingly gives himself up to the death of death. He fuses with his church which is the clarified body of the initiate. He was chased from temple to temple, but he entered the real inner temple to give access to the superior powers when the veil was torn open. Just at the time when the veil was rendered and Jesus died, there was a dark grey cloud over the Earth for three days – representing the three levels of fusion and the three bodies of personality. The Sun couldn't be seen any more because the Soul had gone through the veil into the inner Sun that wasn't shining in this world; when the two merged, we see it as resurrection and the light is brighter than ever.

We know that even our certainty is a mindset. We could doubt that this system is a 'way by' through which consciousness and redeeming ignorance are the aim. When we actually work for what we perceive, it is an affirmation with all the will, love and courage we have in us, believing in the idea of redemption and transmutation. We can't have any doubt, or even half an ounce of a rear guard behind us, because we are at the end of survival and if we are wrong we have had it! But, as stated before, at least preaching love and truth can only do harm to selfish interest. It is not even certainty we are expressing, but inevitability.

The Hanged Man speaks of love, so the renouncement of the material life can't be a harsh, condescending asceticism. If we did the ascetic bit we would only bring the punishing God back and the punishing God in us has to become the loving God. From the exterior the initiate looks just like everybody else, eats and drinks like everybody else and so on, but it is from the interior that the renouncement is completely willed, understood, and loved. He is not feeding on this planet, because the dear Earth needs help rather than being fed on. We recognise in each others eyes the brightness of the Soul and the capability of bringing peace; we are here to attract, not offend.

The three energies blending in the 12/3 of the first Trinity, here are on their way back to their source (upside down). We observe the sublimation of the power of the 1 through the gentle motion of upliftment, as perceived by the 3. If we look at the expansion of consciousness in humanity, it has always been provided by the prophets, artists and scientists through revelation. The idea of revealing a higher law or a secret has always excited humanity and it can really change mindsets. In the past the revealing of a law used to involve punishment, unless qualified in the right order and given to the right applicant, for we were likely to have gone and stolen it, taken it when we were not ready, or given it out prematurely. If we were not pure enough or we did it for our own advancement then we violated the law, but if we were pure enough then we elevated people with it. So when it was fully understood and given out, it was elevation; when it was taken in for self-aggrandisement and self-upliftment then violation and punishment were the result. This meant destruction, because from the karmic angle we would have dragged others with us into the glamour and illusion of being 'initiated'. This could explain another name given to the 12/3 – 'the lamed one'.

Grace is one of the key words for the 12/3, because we are 'blessed' when we have the right perception that purifies and vivifies. There are three qualities for that right perception; equilibrium, necessity and liberty. Out of necessity we go beyond freedom; this is when we find the preserving power of love. Acquired experience is the equilibrium of power and courage and therefore knowledge.

In the teachings of the Benedictine order we have the three attributes of the work, acceptance, obedience and stability, corresponding to liberty, necessity and equilibrium. Here in The Hanged Man we are looking at the force of the 11 coming into equilibrium and finding stability, thus freeing itself from ignorance through its own vision. This happens when the force is completely poised and goes into the idea of observation, to reach the point of light from within the aspiration of the Soul to uplift and oversee the work so far, with peace in its centre. The Soul will realise itself by passing into the physical form, then the form has to preserve and receive the qualities of the Soul so that the personality can be transformed alchemically. In this process the personality actually absorbs the qualities of Soul to preserve it; that is where the transubstantiation happens. Then by giving itself to the great work, the personality allows more absorption and the Soul can go deep into it, fusing with it and thus eventually disappearing. Because the law of preservation is one of the great laws of the universe, the qualities of the Soul will be preserved and speed up the vibration of the personality.

The Hanged Man is looking at the world upside down, so he sees it very differently to how he saw it before he accepted that job. This is why he can't have anything of the old world, because absolutely nothing of that would be useful for the way he sees the world now. So we are coming back with the 1, which might have been egocentric before, but here we see it as Spirit bathing in the love of the Soul. It has found the centre of matter via the mediation of the heart of the Soul. Matter as the personality, has completely given over to her lover. They fuse in a consented, aware, sacrificial act of love and truth (recognised as home), as they fall into the mystery of the great cosmic priestess of wisdom.

No Name
Stripped to the bare bones

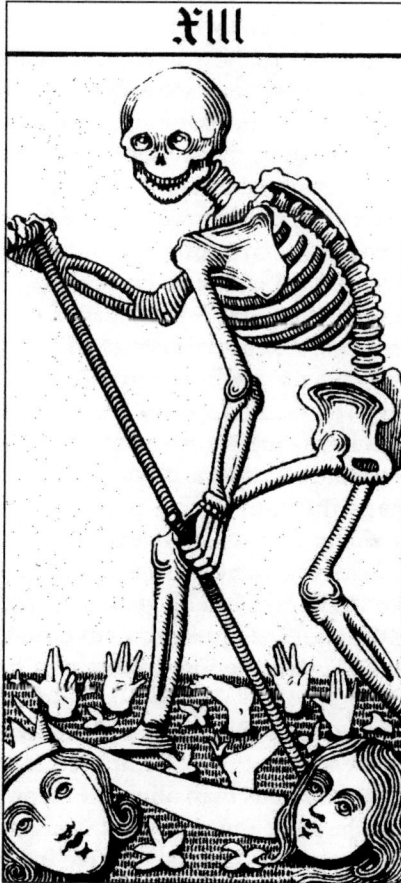

This is the card of 'no name'. Here all support from the outside has been cut off, so it is a true re-birth into the inner essence. All pretence and scenery has gone and we are left with the naked will, represented by the bare bones of the skeleton. This is the framework through which all that is durable or worthwhile can go towards eternity. It is true transmutation.

The original purpose and use of the Tarot was to preserve and transmit the Ancient Wisdom teachings, through symbolic images of the stages of evolution of the Soul, on its path towards realisation. In the first twelve cards, we saw the Initiate coming back to 'take the exam' again. The first five are to do with concept, so he's looking to see whether he can receive the message from the spiritual directing energy, then apply that message to the four elements, to the planet earth and to himself. We must realise that when the initiate or disciple works on himself, he works on the world and vice versa. He knows that the goal of this incarnation is to go beyond the veil of The High Priestess, for this is not a school for beginners but a school for initiates. It is only at the third initiation and on the way to the fourth that the veil is torn, so this is not a gentle self-development process, but a fiery determined intent.

The Magician smiles at the first step, for he has not yet put himself through the school! The overall goal is presented at The High Priestess in Number 2, then with The Empress at Number 3 we are looking at Active Intelligence and the tools of the intellect, which has to render itself available to the service of the light. Many people see The Empress as nature, but nature is only a by-product of Active Intelligence. The Goddess is the principle of Active Intelligence which creates form, but not the form itself. We live in a world where the shadow of the Goddess is doing everything it can to bring people back to the nurturing survival aspect of nature, rather than honouring its true divine nature, with its purpose of manifesting the message of Spirit. With the highest understanding of the Trinity, we see Spirit reaching the depths of biological life (the Soul of nature) to release the cosmic secret of creation. Active Intelligence finds its highest expression through the recognition and witnessing of the Spirit.

Then The Emperor fuses the vision and the will. Man as a created unit in matter, can reflect the life of the God we live in with awareness. This means that as man aligns to his inner life his mind receives the light of the solar angel, taking him deep into his cosmic, karmic genetic pool; he then recognises Active Intelligence and wisdom as his true being and his mind reflects on the three aspects of his qualities. He seeks full awareness, for he is looking at the world from within out. Having done that, he needs the discipline of honesty and righteousness in order to go forward on the path.

The next card is The Pope, where we receive the much-needed blessing. The Pope represents the sanctified, blessing heart within us. Our Soul offers us a blessing every minute of the day if we want to listen to it. We can take the opportunity to recognise and act according to the blessing. The blessing happens when the mind can see things as they are with compassion and without judgment; this creates fusion between mind and heart, giving rise to a state of peace of mind that can be used to expand the consciousness. The blessing is very much to do with acceptance, obedience and balance. Wherever we find ourselves, in the physical, astral, the white or dark worlds, we need blessings.

At Number 6, The Lover, the theory is in place and the cup is full. The pure 6 is the cup of love and asks 'which direction does love move us in and what activity follows that movement?' Anything we do has to be motivated by love, not in the sense of emotional love, but towards an aspiration which takes us beyond ourselves. Falling in love is when all our physical, mental and emotional energy focus in one direction and the karmic, spiritual wind of passion takes over the asylum.

This brings us full of zeal to Number 7, The Chariot. Knowing that he is going to fuse with the beloved, the charioteer goes into life to find the princess (the Soul). He allows Spirit to be in charge, so that he can achieve real fusing with the lover. Zeal is then tempered with the introspecting, discriminating qualities of mind as he perceives a higher form of Justice in Number 8.

Number 8 is Justice in the real sense, which brings universal truth in to reveal the reality of life on our planet. This truth breaks down our illusion and glamour to bring us back to a more natural approach, to fulfil the solution needed to guide humanity towards its responsibilities.

This leads us to the great internalising of The Hermit at Number 9, enabling us to raise the whole of our life's purpose to the inner life; this is the raison d'être of the second Solar System.

At the end of the cycle at Number 10, The Wheel of Fortune tells us that we can seek the path of love/wisdom, or gently follow nature as she goes through her life and death cycles, until we are ready to grow up.

With Number 11, Strength, we can recognise that the Force is within us, rather than in our personal power, for by that time we are quite mighty as an instrument for the divine energy. With our zeal we can apply divine justice; we can internalise and remember the law of Karma and not be afraid of it. We can recognise that the power in us is not ours to use, it is the force using us and we do not own it. Eventually we end up with absolutely no attraction to personal power, so at Number 12, The Hanged Man, we have completely stripped ourselves of any wants or desires for self. That sounds like work well done, for by the time we get to Number 12 we are in between the pillars of the temple, but we are not yet through them. Here we have achieved the right state to be able to meet death. Then at Number 13 the full circle has been gone through over many life times; this is the great time of transition.

The Trinity, 12/3, comes back being aware of itself. The 2, having served its purpose as a medium for awareness, gives something new, something hidden, something measured and something felt. Then the aspiration within the Trinity itself gives birth to the 3, so in the 13/4 the mind is raised to see a greater view. Because of this process, we are talking here about a real change of perception. The 4 will see a solution for a new structure which can hold a perception nearest to the truth. We cannot solve a problem from within itself, for we have to rise above the problem to see it. The 13/4 has to exercise recognition of its intuitive nature, so as to be a channel for the transmutation of self, humanity and the planet.

In the 12/3 we are in a process of destruction and creation, so we are poised between the visible and invisible worlds. At Number 13, the clear unbiased 3 will be able to shine on the conflict of the 4. The 4 represents mankind going through its transformation, so that the human mind can capture its vision of the light. We can see why all the secret societies have an initiation called death, for it is the one and only transforming energy. At the spiritual level this is the process of transubstantiation.

At the natural level of transformation, the body breaks down and decays so as to become compost for the new growth that follows. However, the experiences of each species are not lost and go back to the relevant Soul group. It is all those experiences from the beginning of time in the Soul of nature that mankind carries as his subconscious luggage. He has to revisit these experiences to bring light or awareness into the darkness, thus transmuting untold emotional mindsets into understanding and compassion, or love/wisdom.

The energy of life passes through the different kingdoms, bringing pain in the process of death. The mineral kingdom gives of its material for the building of the plant kingdom, which in turn gives of itself for the life of the animal kingdom. Each process will involve the breaking down, dissolution and restructuring into another state. When the human awareness revisits stages of death and transformation within its own physical experience, we qualify that natural process as painful, until we learn to put our minds into the process and accept it as natural. This then connects us back with the acceptance of the nature of the process and therefore we are nearer to the intelligence of our source. At the emotional level we have all witnessed the pining for a dead member of the group in the animal kingdom. There is not the full awareness, but yet there is the knowledge that something is not quite right. One minute we have something we relate to, like a parent or child, the next minute that entity is dead; there is no movement and the life force has gone. The emotional trauma will eventually help an internalisation of the question, in an attempt to understand what is going on. That question gave mankind the hope that there had to be another realm. So when we have to make peace with the process of loss, we revisit our internal landscape, to break and dissolve the many emotional patterns and mindsets that would have protected us in our previous level of awareness. In that deep pool of consciousness, we can cry and scream, but because we are there with acceptance, obedience and stability, we know that we are doing it so that nature doesn't keep all her dark secrets to herself. These are not actually secrets or dark, but just situations previously experienced with awareness. We are feeling and seeing them consciously for nature or the system. We have all had broken hearts; the glory of this is that the light of Spirit can penetrate deeper and deeper within the heart, so that we can rise even higher and stronger.

We live within the Earth's magnetic field that holds, like water, the memory of our whole history from the beginning of time. We all have our own magnetic field supporting our physical, cellular, organic life. As our hearts become more open, the incoming light energy will require a change of vibration so that it can release a lot of locked in memories and break down the scaffolding of our old magnetic field. This process allows a re-organisation and a new structure to take the place of the old one; the new one being nearer to the original Sacred Geometry of the cells. These outgoing emotions can be released through tears, as the frozen traumas are transmuted into water by the love in our hearts. When we are on the path we have to stop the tears shed out of emotional/mental melodramatic self-absorption and allow the tears of the deeper sorrow to dissolve the scaffolding of the old patterns. We live in a watery realm, so if we are going to change the memory and the blueprint we have to do it through running, cleansing water.

We have to remember what the job is; to come in, to weigh up and to see. Once we have done that then we don't need to see anymore. If we really want to understand this from the esoteric point of view, we can think of something in our lives that we hadn't understood; suddenly it comes and meets us, showing us that we are all the time running after and behind our true selves, because there is more that we can become. None of us believes that we are either complete or at peace. We may feel complete, but in truth we feel that somewhere in us there is more to become. If we stop trying to be anything else but what we are, then *"all is well that will be well"* and we *"become by passing away"*. We still experience life ahead of ourselves, so are still running after our potential. If after a big struggle, we manage to gain a bit of understanding, then the misunderstanding that might have distorted the view of the world for many of us will be taken and digested all in a few minutes and it is gone for ever; that is the glory of the death we are looking at.

The esoteric internal process cannot have a name, because transmutation is still a mystery. Transmutation is the process of going from one state to another or from one level of perception to another. This movement deeply transforms the nature of the one who perceives and adds to the cosmic planetary transmutations as well. Death as a natural process is experienced and observed. The 'why' of it can in time be accepted, as the answer is always the same – 'it is so'. Life manifests and then decays. When we see that it is held by Soul intent we see death as a deliverance of the Soul, which touches on the eternal behind the form. This tells us that the life is transforming its form into essence and therefore becoming part of the mystery of the invisible world. By its nature the Soul has no name, because the higher Soul of man is universal and one, so the process of de-personalisation of the lower self is helped.

This stage puts us in front of the black sphinx, where we answer the questions. The sphinx represents the passage from the myth to the esoteric understanding. It asks the question that we must ask of ourselves every single day. There are no words for this question, for it is the eternal one of self versus God. However, we put it to ourselves in the cave of our hearts; there are no words, because it is not an intellectual question. We can't truthfully translate on behalf of God. If we formulate an answer we are using the intellect, which can only give us an hypothesis. When one hypothesis is reaffirmed we can go to the next and carry on and on. We can build up ideas like the Tower of Babel, but they collapse when they are based solely on the intellect. Eventually we transcend the intellect and the ideas come from a deeper source; this is a silent knowing which can crystallise via the intellect, without the bias of the personality coming into it.

In the picture on the card we see the figure of Death cutting off hands and feet, these represent actions we have done in this and many past lives. Not one single little action from all these is lost, including thoughts. We can look at our lives before the reaper puts it before us, so that we can redeem it now. Redemption arises only from the perception of a new reality.

At the bottom of the card we have the Earth, with all the young plants emerging. There are two heads, a crowned man and a woman. In these heads we see that all the passion of argument and love of beauty are gone, so they are very peaceful faces.

The severed head on the left with the golden crown represents the giving over of the intellect to the higher energy and the cosmic wisdom. We have to go beyond all the philosophical, conceptual, or even metaphysical ways of understanding that we may have used in the past. Even wanting to go for the ultimate wisdom or divinity is still theorising. At this level, the initiate is going for something that he doesn't know; in a sense he is not even going for it, for how can we reach towards something we don't know? We can't even think of divinity as a concept, for if we do we are bringing it down back into the intellect and then it is no longer divine. If we truly want to let go of anything that stops us being one with the cosmic wisdom behind the veil, we must not even think that we were created to meet it; we must not even think that there is nothingness.

The female head on the right represents beauty in form, which has been a philosophical idea from the beginning of time. Beauty in all the philosophies, including Sufi, Muslim, or Christian, has triggered in men and woman the first uplifting sense of knowing that the creator is a higher being than the one who is standing and looking at the creation. The sense of beauty has helped mankind to rise, through hoping and wishing that there is something else other than the everyday blandness. Eventually, when everything is cut down, we realise that the attraction of form is only temporal and that what we call beauty is actually grotesque. It is not the beauty of form that we see when we are uplifted; when we rise in consciousness we are in contact with the Soul behind the form. Much of the form which we call beauty is from the common mindset; when seen from the point of view of the higher reality is quite hideous, because the more polished and glossy it is the more desires and needs are being exteriorised through it.

Our attraction to superficial beauty is self-destructive, because it brings our emotive body towards the lowest common denominator of humanity's aspiration.

The achieved Active Intelligence of the 12/3 puts the 3 into a new position in the 13/4, where it sees the essence and the movement rather than the concept and the form. The three days of obscuration that happens during the process of going from one stage to another relates to the disappearance after the crucifixion, when the body of Jesus vanished for 3 days. It is the 3 (the light) in the 13/4 that disappears, because it is going into obscuration, where the light of the Soul can fuse with its structure; transmuting it so that it can respond directly to the impulse of spiritual will. That crucial point in the Soul's evolution is not given a name, because the intelligence in the Soul is not being used to name its own structure any more; it is being used simply to bring more light and love into the structure. It is an enormous change from colouring the structure we are in by our emotions and needs, to coming back to it with no colour and seeing that all we are is a little light looking through the form. Once we realise that, we just have to get on with it. If the 4 is attached to naming the structure, rather than accepting to be the structure, it will not have gone through the death of personalised consciousness and the whole process cannot take place.

The power of the name is the power of the creator over the thing that has been named; this card allows a state of 'no name'. When we tear that veil or boundary made by a name, we break down the structure that held the whole of our raison d'être so far, only to fall a bit deeper into that structure. Then, in our recognition that it is our home we stop fighting it.

In the old esoteric Tarot, from the point of view of the disciple, the Earth was called hell, which is the place where we meet ourselves as humanity and are in constant conflict with our ignorant outlook on life. This is one of the old, dying concepts; that life isn't perfect as it is. It is in the 13/4 that we realise that *life is perfect, but there is a lot of work to do*.

In The Hanged Man we see the letting go of everything that could attract the initiate to the material world; he is free from the world of appearance and is ready to rise.

Number 13 is the third stage of the Delphic teaching. There is *'know thyself'*, *'know the worlds'* and *'know the Gods'*. The disciple had to 'know himself', meaning that he had to start naming everything, as he is the world and the world is in him. At the 12/3, which is the giving up of the self, we 'know the worlds' and are completely at the mercy of the great universe. In the third stage, 'know thy Gods', we are part of the great transmuting process, which goes beyond the veil into cosmic wisdom.

The skeleton as it is, represents structure and therefore relates to the mineral kingdom and the Earth. This includes the vibration of planet Earth's base note, which creates its crystalline structure. As the 13/4 raises the mind it still retains a natural basic structure in place, whether it is the earth, its minerals, or mankind and his sacred buildings. Accepting the structure that we are in at the time is the most important thing for the obscuration process of transformation.

Number 13 brings the awareness that we are walking through and experiencing our past all the time, making us conscious of the watcher of the inner life. The fact is that at this point we are not attracted by what is out there, even if we have a reaction to what we experience. As we become completely aware from the point of view of the inner reality, we go back to where all that we are is consciousness, for the form completely disappears. Soul and Spirit are connected and become one, as they are absorbed into the Holy Ghost. We are walking in the past and running for the future. There are moments when past and future meet; at these points the present is seen for what it is and the illusion of the world disappears. This is because Active Intelligence has been reunified with the love/wisdom of the Soul. When we are giving up our lives with the realisation they are not our lives anyway, we become an integral part of everything; also when we are looking from the esoteric point of view at an extremely advanced point in evolution, we will become systemic, because there is nothing else but a moving, transforming energy system.

The skeleton is all mineral. Death destroys all artifice; we are all the same in our bones and everything else is decay. The purified personality is the true vehicle for the Soul and is clear of anything that can spoil. We wear the personality as an expression of yesterday, which we have to enlighten with the fire of love and truth, so that eventually all we are is only a frame, like a tuning fork. It is the reaper who helps that process to happen. All pretence has gone; we are left with the naked essence where only inner truth is revealed.

In the card the colour of the skeleton is orangey-pink, to symbolise the idea that the flesh can be renewed; therefore there is the potential of re-growth, although the skeleton symbolises the end of life. Here we are not talking about death in the biological sense but death in the process of transfiguration, so it is a passage, a renaissance and not an end. The bones are a framework or structure, which takes all that is durable or worthwhile towards eternity. The world of matter has no interest by itself, but in the world of Soul all our acts are accounted for.

When alive, man is a virtual being in the process of becoming real. We are always projecting our reality ahead of ourselves, and then at death we hold onto that projection. We have to recognise that we are what we projected in a previous life, so we can see the importance of reading the biological book of lessons (personality) with love and truth. We transmute the misunderstanding of the past into the new, rising above the cycle of obsessive survival behaviour, to project a new form for the new life. We do the process in small ways all the time, so we have the opportunity to re-invent ourselves constantly. The projection is the way we thought and the way we loved; this creates patterns like Sacred Geometry. That is why when the masters incarnate, they will always take the appearance that they had in the last life necessary for their inner work; they don't need to have another life, so they will present themselves with that image. All is energy; a Soul can only incarnate when the welcoming instrument offers the exact qualities of vibration to accommodate the earthly experiment. In fact the incarnating Soul will attract the possibility of rebirth, well before the mother of the baby herself is aware of the need to conceive.

We have to keep all the social-type structures we have from the past for quite a long time, so that they can guide the ones who follow. It is the same when we go from virtuality to reality. We have to keep on re-affirming the personality time and time again, so as to be completely self-made and aware of what the personality is and then we can do something with it. When we are born we are only going to use a tiny fraction of the opportunities available to us; this is the part that we have decided to focus on in this life. It is not society that restricts us, it is us. What we actually are, is what we really want to be and what we spend our energy on being. We spend all our energy on projecting a better future, but because we don't know what that is we make it up as we go along. We do not know our true selves until our initiatic death reveals it to us. Life isn't static it is a perpetual transformation and an alchemical process. We are in a constant state of becoming; we are not fixed. According to our school of thought we can see it as evolution, adaptation or becoming. It is actually adaptation evolving towards perfection. Mass consciousness gently and slowly accepts change, realising that some of the things we have done in the past we shouldn't have, making little shifts in consciousness if not in applied behaviour, such the bringing in of equality of women in the west, or the abolition of slavery.

Number 13 is symbolic of initiation. It is a symbolic death and an opening to another level. There isn't any religion or sect that doesn't have a funerary ceremony which involves lying down; this represents renouncing our way of living and affirms the knowledge that this passage opens the door through to a luminous world. This is why this is a very important key card.

Within an initiatic group we are asked to understand why we have to dissolve our name and take on (whether given or chosen) a spiritual name. This is so that the frame of the karmic structure put on that name when we are born, can die; hence this card is called 'No Name. As we transmute the past we can take a new name and in so doing we can say that at the transmutation phase we do not exist, so we die with no name. Then we rise from within with a new name. The initiatic names are kept secret within the group so that nothing can have power over us. We die to the attraction of the old and all that we used to be. In everyday life when people change their names it is usually a denial of Karma, so really they need to look at that and face the karmic luggage they brought in. We ought only to lead our lives knowing that we are dying. When we do this the 'no name' syndrome is very strong and we can recognise people as Souls; their name being important only in that it gives them a clue as to their obligations. None of us must have any power over anyone else, or want anything from anyone else. A person is not a name but a Soul. When we tell our name to another person then it can be an offering which says "You can call on me".

In the initiation ceremony it is said that the flesh leaves the bones; this is the first part of the alchemical work – the black work. It is associated with the raven, which represents the Spirit in the subconscious. So it is said at the beginning of the alchemical work that 'the raven separates the flesh from the bones'. Initiatic death is a beginning not a stage. It is active, whereas physical death is a stage and is passive. In the initiatic journey from the 1 to the 12, we would have given the whole of our lives to the process of initiatic death. When a man has lived fairly selfishly for a long time he is not able to answer the question posed by the guardian of the threshold, the black sphinx. The reaper sends all who are not ready to rise, back either to Earth or to hell. It is a sorting out or a trial, which is what the 13/4 does. If we compare this to the sequence of 1-2-3; in the 13 we don't see the hidden 2, but it is there weighing up all the time, because the 2 is eventually going to become a 4. When the 2 mirrors or looks at itself then the 4 will become a 22 and mind as master of the emotions can build with wisdom.

When we face all the monsters at the door, the only thing that makes us frightened is our ignorance. If we have been very naughty and know the content and cause of our naughtiness, then we are not going to be so frightened of facing the black sphinx. However, if we cover it up all the time then it will be very frightening. All the earlier initiations are there to help uncover everything, so that at Number 12, The Hanged Man, we end up naked; this is where we meet the truth of whether we are viable or not, for the more refined energy of the uplifting 3. If we are not, then we are sent back to revisit more cycles.

There is nothing more difficult to achieve than to bring the outer world and inner realities together, so that true alignment to the source of our light can take place. When this is achieved, past, present and future are one. If we are caught up with ourselves in needing a direction for our future or a cure for our past, we cannot align. Dying to any expectation of where we are or who we are, we become the still, bright lights that can help others to realise their own alignment.

The only certainty is death; this has preoccupied us from the beginning of time. The greatness of mankind is that it has refused to accept that when the body dies, we die with it. This is a rebellion that has fuelled the human heart with the hope of eternity. If the life we are living has no point and no purpose then why are we bothering to live it? If there's no purpose, what are we doing explaining it and what are we doing with it? The intellect cannot give an answer and it eventually finds itself talking to itself, but if there is no purpose what is the point of trying to work anything out? If the purpose is to find no purpose then we are truly at an impasse, because we are just looking at our own navels. Behind and beyond that, we find ourselves in life again and getting on with it. The questions and answers are linked to the scientists or philosophers, who ask "What is the purpose of Life?" We go on looking at life and at what we are doing and the question arises "Can we tear that veil so that we can have the silence rather than the chatter of the intellect?" We need philosophy and science for they are fantastic tools of uplift, but they can take us to an impasse. Keeping on asking questions will show us that we have to stop asking questions so as to allow the mind to follow the light as it falls deep into the mysteries. The one place it will fall is into the cup of the heart, so that we will suddenly be on our knees. Is it a mindset that we gave ourselves to what we loved, or is it for real? Are we ready to live by it or change it if it is another impasse?

The gods and saviours who have been to hell are many; Ishtar, Tanu, Adonis, Osiris; many of the Greek heroes are among them. Adam and Eve were chased out of paradise and ended up on Earth (hell). In the legends, Gilgamesh goes out on a dangerous journey to find a plant which will give humanity immortality. Zoroastra goes into hell and comes back with the secret of never-ending life. Ur the Armenian comes back to tell humanity about the great hope that is in us. Ishtar is the symbol of definite truth and the symbolism is the unveiling at the seven doors of infernal life. For each level of consciousness a veil is taken out, meaning that we see it from the cosmic point of view rather than from the worldly one. Orpheus, when he was looking for his Soul in hell had to go down into the infernal world, then just as he found his Soul he lost it again, because he looked back to see the form once more. This is about attraction towards incarnation. There are many heroes who went to hell and came out again; this is the role of the secret society of initiates.

Jesus, in order to fulfil his mission of redemption had to go to hell, where for three days he was cleansing the physical, emotional and mental bodies. These three bodies have to be purified three times over and then broken down. The Jesus in us (Jesus being the common name for Soul) is permanently doing that cleansing transformation, so he shows us the path to take. When Jesus goes through the veil and when everything is finished and done, he becomes Christ, or the realised Soul.

In the Masonic story, Hiram was the best amongst the master architects, so he was chosen to plan and build the holy Temple. Some of the other master architects were jealous and wanted to steal his secret, so they murdered him. It is from that time that the knowledge became internalised through the shock that occurred in the collective; this is why his friends decided to form a secret society to hide the key measurements which enabled the building of the Temple of God. This was the secret of Sacred Geometry or the Golden Mean, which had been known about for thousands of years and up to then had not been guarded. It was at that point that it went underground, which meant it was internalised.

The true architect is the one who can build his own inner landscape, rather than the temple out there. The story of Hiram tells of a great turning point for humanity; once you have the key to perfect structure, the door opens inward to the concept. When the personality has achieved perfection of vision, the building of the house of God through the Soul can begin. This was an enormous change or point of realisation at the time, such as that experienced by Paul on the road to Damascus. From then on the secret of the inner realisation was passed on. This is relevant to this thirteenth card, for the severed heads and body parts belong to the old architecture, which have been cut off so that the new inner architecture can happen. Hiram's death was necessary for the cult to go into Spirit and truth rather than structures in stone. It gave birth to a new brotherhood, or a new society that places itself beyond death and can visualise the realisation of the world beyond man, so hastening the transformation.

The initiator is only representative of the level of the lesson being undergone at the time; this is the wisdom that relates to where we are. We have to go beyond that level and die to ourselves. This is expressed by; "*As I stand tomorrow, so I will be dead to today*".

An initiation which is only a physical ritual has no real value. A ritual can evoke something in people for it has a deep effect and can remind us of something, but it is not permanent. We can work and strive towards initiation, but nothing will happen. When we are aligned with our inner reality and ready energetically, then life helps us break down many mindsets and emotional dreams, so as to remove the last point of resistance to that specific initiation. We need to descend into hell to rise again, then the quality of the burning flame of transformation might be strong enough to be seen by and attracted to, a higher level of vibration. This might be the reason why it is said that we are elected into an initiatic group. We are going for something very potent here; we cannot take it or leave it as before, so it is important not to be premature in our action. It is an engagement we make which can't be reversed. We don't do it for curiosity or pride, rather it is an election; we have to be elected, then it calls us. It is not to do with being a saint, but consciously we have to have all the desires and all the will pointing towards the same goal, which is the goal in our heart. The will cuts everything away, all habits, ties and attractions, so we are left with a bare skeleton and no flesh.

This card is the only one in the Tarot with no name. The mind over matter of most spiritual disciplines and the repeated chanting, prayer, or invocation towards a greater energy will use the power of naming to manifest heaven on Earth. As the Soul starts its silent witnessing it will bring everything back to simplicity, so seeing every single item as a manifestation of the God we live in, it focuses only on love and truth and on erasing the seperative, necessary naming. This establishes its kingdom in every single cell of life on the planet as one; one body, one mind, one love, one Soul; *'For in him we live and move and have our being'*.

When a dear one dies, calling the body will not bring it back to life. However, their name wasn't given to the body, but to the life force incarnating in that form, so when we close our eyes and say the name we can still feel, through our love aspect, the presence of that life. The name is a call to life; when we give a baby a name that is the first ritual in their life. The last ritual is the transition from life in form to a life of energy and mind stuff, which is death.

Whereas this arcana has no name, the last card (the Fool), is called the arcana with no number. Here we are going into the irrational and the Spiritual, so we have to drop any notion of understanding life from the point of view of beauty, philosophy and science. We are in that state where we have no support whatsoever; there is nothing, no hope or even doubt. In remembering Jesus' experience on the cross we can imagine all our certitude being taken away. It is like when we cut a flower that is growing in the ground; it is at one with the whole Earth and with the whole sky, then we cut it off and the connection is gone. It is the same with us; like a seed we are cast and separated from our life line and have to grow from where we fall. We have to find the seed of divinity in ourselves. We cannot be saved by another's faith, but only by our own unique inner light, that is the only way that humanity can realise its divine origin. If there was a reason or need for individuality, that is the one. The reaper brutally separates the man from all his support; then the man has to find himself, so he is bound to be distraught. He is in front of his God whom he doesn't even recognise. A lot of his ideas had come from others, from religion, or mindsets and all that has gone. Going into solitude is the hallmark of the strong, because thoughts are concentrated to a point of release; the essence manifests more freely in solitude. If he is not strong enough he will start being afraid, for the dark night is falling and there are many shadows when we have to meet ourselves. Then we release the true answer to the sphinx, which is the unique vibration of the intelligence of our Soul. We have gone through an assimilation process and there is an 'I am' moment.

The hand in the shape of a setsquare shows independent righteousness, rectitude of thought and judgment. In the Egyptian ritual when the initiate goes through death and goes into the Holy of Holies, they have to say three times "I am pure". This means that they have to have complete domination of righteousness over their physical, emotional and mental bodies, so that their thought and judgment of what they are doing is completely aligned with the will of the Soul. It is about the purity of intent, which gives concentration, reception and protection against any malefic influence. It is a ritualistic position of the hands and so acts like magic in not allowing things to come in to the sacred space to pollute it. It is the same as when Christians feel afraid, they invoke Christ for protection by making the sign of the cross.

We could look at the four hands as representing the four corners of creation, which are the yin/yang ways within one person of receiving and reacting to life's experiences; the rational scientific and the receptive philosophic approaches.

The plants are there to remind us that life feeds on death and we need manure for other things to live. There is no other way that the system works. There is killing, eating, digesting and dying for others, so life has to sustain itself by death and suffering. The Earth is therefore the equivalent of the infernal world or hell; it is the only place where transubstantiation can happen. It is the latent life of the system that organises itself in the symbolism of alchemy, which is represented by the black raven. It was at the death of the Soul Jesus that all the experiences were realised and fully aligned with the will. The love and the Active Intelligence of the system are at the highest possible point here within the Solar System. When that dies, meaning when it completely fuses with matter, it is going to be truly transubstantiated, for it is pure sunshine straight into matter. This process is happening organically on the planet all the time, in the mineral, vegetable, animal and human kingdoms.

The scythe gathers all the experiences of the one life. Here we have to accept and look at what we have been, what we are and what we have turned ourselves into. Each moment that we did not act from the real self will be laid down in front of us. The past becomes real in the present and is seen for what it is, from both the outside and inside; this is instant re-birth.

The crisis in humanity that is happening now is the eleventh hour. It is the time of recognising that everything is happening and we haven't done our homework, which is why there's an awful lot of conflict now. Actually it is no different from how it always was, but by being aware of it globally we have to address the situation … The scythe is putting us in front of ourselves and what do we see? Conflict! There is not a place on the planet where there is no conflict, everything is up front. We are in an energetic world and the planet is going through some sort of alignment because of what is happening in the planetary world, but we have the opportunity to work with it, which is why it is crisis time.

It is up to us to align to the attraction of the central inner fire in the system, where that energetic crisis is taking us, so as to have a hope of a breakthrough. The system will carry on without us, if we resist or ignore the responsibility of our true position in the scheme. It is a huge task, but as long as there are enough of us who can ride that wave of change which is energetically on us now, we can keep the doors open. Alignment is when each one of our cells aligns to the message of the greater body. The greater body itself is aligned to the Sun and to the greater Sun behind that; in fact there is alignment right up to the centre of the Universe and it is entirely systemic and energetic; 2012 will see a great cosmic alignment. The more we align and recognise our true place in the changing world, the more we can keep the doors open. We have got thousands of years to complete the work after that. Alignment is reaching the divine fire in each of our cells with the light of our Soul, so as to fuse with the greater life. Each of us is as one cell aligning to the message of the greater body. The more we align and recognise our true place in the Universe, the more we are in, on, and moving along with that wave. That is how we understand the idea of being carried, because if we have completely aligned with the movement of Spirit and the angels are carrying us, there is no more conflict or resistance.

It is the reaper who allows man to take stock of the harvest he has gathered between each incarnation. At this stage we are reaping the karmic harvest of actions we have sown in time and space. We earn our bread by the sweat of our brows, so esoterically we will earn the bread of life (wisdom of experience) through the pain of the re-examination of our deeds. Here is where it is all happening, where we are bringing in the love of beauty and the love of knowledge, which has to die unto itself so that we may love the concept and reality through the purity of our Soul. The process gives us inner and outer tears, for it is the true Spiritual discipline. We gather the harvest of wheat with which we will make the bread; all our words and needs will be gathered and we will raise the Soul out of that. In order to acquire real *connaissance* we have to be grounded, kneaded and cooked! We have to be transmuted by the fire of the Soul. Man needs a guide but he must refuse a master, for the Spirit blows where it wants and if we have a master we may be transfixed. The Spiritual guidance of our higher self will help us to recognise our wave of light, which in simple terms shows us the way to work. The result of what we are doing here has to be the passage from silver to gold. When the silver has allowed itself to rise and meet the gold of pure Spirit, then it can come down and transmute the matter it is working through. For that to happen we have to purify ourselves.

This card has a strong link to The High Priestess. We have the moment in time where The Hanged Man is hung between the columns of The High Priestess and has to face the black sphinx. Here, in the thirteenth card the sphinx allows the passage, so everything has to be gathered that will be of use on the other side. The book of wisdom opens, giving him the sense of his life and his raison d'être. He can give himself divine justice because he has true self-awareness. We can therefore see a link with Justice, Number 8, which is divine self-awareness.

We can't access the 'why' of the world without going through the sphinx. If man doesn't ask himself the right questions, he can't touch the Divine in him and can't go through the door. To ask the right question he has to internalise, in order to sense a deeper sound in the silence. It is all internal, so the sphinx is in us. We stop ourselves going through the door because of all the little monsters; they are so small, but they are the ones that we don't want to look at! We close the door to our divine selves just by not being willing to remove another little monster or another little detail that we don't want to accept. We can be looking at it and hate it in other people because of our pride. The most difficult thing is to accept, it is so much easier to deceive ourselves.

Accessing the higher mind without wisdom, truth and courage is not energetically possible, because it is all to do with vibration. A lot of experiences from the past are there waiting to be transmuted into light, so to rely only on reason or philosophy will not deliver the letting in of the higher light. We need to let the inner process of fusing happen and then our lights will produce those sparks of enlightenment.

Here we are, we are alive, we know and we think that we are the flower of the cherry on the top of the cream in nature, but did we ask to be created? The long march of man having used all the sciences and philosophy to get to this level of awareness can give answers, but whether the answer is right is not important. What is important is to align our minds and hearts with that energetic world we live in. Of course we didn't ask to be created, but then who is asking our opinion? The intellect is so proud, but when it breaks down we realise that it is not important and nobody asked our permission to make us the flower of nature. All the suffering and conflict comes from the pride of having self-awareness and dominion. We have to accept the unacceptable if we are truly looking honestly. We are still going through the transformation from one state to another, from one Solar System to another; whatever happens we are still going somewhere. Scientifically, we are going to end up on the other side of a black hole, so we try and hold onto our point of consciousness or our awareness. So here we are, as cocky as can be and we have to come to the incredible conclusion, when we finally accept the unacceptable, that the divine perfection that we think we are is actually impotent.

If we accept that we are living in a great system and that on our little planet one of the outcomes is to deliver some quality of self consciousness and enlightenment, the witnessing of this unfolding within the great life we call 'the God we live in', is moving towards 'sacredness'. This would imply imperfection, but all we can conclude is that everything is at different levels of unfolding; we are all little sparks of the God we live in. It is a hard thing to accept that we might not live in a perfect God and that we haven't got dominion over what is happening. However, we *are* perfect in the sense that we fulfil exactly the role of demonstrating the imperfections of our God! In truth, our God is perfect in the sense that it fulfils whichever part of the greater plan of the life it lives in, which we call 'the divine', 'the Unknown' and 'No Name'. The life forms on Earth are not perfect because they are not aware, so the situation is perfect, but the God we live in is not yet sacred. We cannot put a name or concept on divinity because if we do, we immediately bring it down to the level of the God in our image. Divinity is truly without name; we cannot conceive it and if we try, the whole thing would collapse as it can only exist in our conception. We may not mind being part of that, but that is not the great calling or aspiration within the depths of Soul and Spirit that we can feel. We might as well start again and say "What is the point?"

The God we live in is the life in which we have our being and if we truly follow the teachings from whichever great religion we adhere to, we can see that we can go beyond our God, for the texts are only giving us the first steps towards the cosmic being. Our texts give us the first step towards the Sun, which is greater in size than the God we live in, because it is the life of the Solar System, rather than the biological life on the planet. We know that the Sun is divine and a few of the planets in our Solar System are also divine and sacred. On behalf of the greater God we come as earthlings, as sons of man, to the non-sacred Earth, to work on the planet and to bring light into the darkness. To do that we have to feel the separation, in order to become aware that we are one. That is what we have come to do, so we shouldn't take the pain personally. How are we going to bring in the light to the core of a cell if we don't truly make one with it? We have to become the little god of the planet, how else can we do it? We have to put the flesh on it in order to do the work in depth; we have to play the game of it and fuse with it.

Why is there this slow, painful descent, this constant conflict and suffering to go through so as to discover our inner divinity? We have it in us and we are going into hell to bring the original idea back into the light again. Even if the original idea is a mindset, it is all we have, so we have to be aware of that and not stop our journey through a mindset, because 'the more we understand the more we love'. The use of mankind as an instrument must be a result of higher love and will; that is what we are becoming all the time – intelligent love. First we have to start to wield that energy, so that we understand the potency and the sacredness of what is flowing through us and then eventually we can let that energy move our being. The God we live in becomes a truly felt thing, which we live in and which lives in us; we are just instruments of its action. However, we have to recognise that there is always speculation, as we go from the old mindsets to the new ones, retaining those that are useful as we go. If we get less and less in the way personally, then more and more transformation can happen.

The Hanged Man is eventually ready and he is in the presence of the great question inside him, beside which there is no other question. With this one everything disappears in front of us and we feel we've touched on fate or as we would see it, our own inner God; there is nothing else.

When the initiate goes on the other side of the veil, the light has a very different potency, so he will know who and what he is. This is the reality of Justice, Number 8. Accepting who and where we are is one of the keys to higher consciousness; unlocking the door is fraught with disarray. If we truly think we are going to be transformed into some glorious body with wings when we have enlightenment and life is going to be very different, then we have to think again many times, until we drop the promise of Heaven as everything we have ever wanted! It is ever so different and in reality it can be expressed as; *'Before enlightenment, chopping wood – after enlightenment, chopping wood'*.

The first twelve cards of the Tarot bring him to his aim, because they put man into the process of finding everything to do with his past planetary and cosmic experiences. This helps him strip away all the covering layers of the social, religious and personal life, so that he can find all the possibilities offered by his higher self. Only a high initiation allows a man to see himself beyond the visible, from inside and outside at the same time. The discipline and introspection of many lives and a deep understanding and love of mankind, allows a man to reach this level of wisdom. Reason and knowledge can't and will not take him there, until he learns to stop measuring himself against others. The ones who come with pride will fall back down into darkness.

If we always look for the material and temporal aspects in life, then we will stay in death for eternity and we will go round and round on the wheel of life. Man's aspiration must rise above the material world of success and gratification. If it doesn't, he locks himself in maya and follows an illusionary goal that can never be achieved, as no absolute can be found in a world of degeneration. There is no absolute in matter or the intellect, neither in the seeking of beauty that we find around us. We have to rise above anything and everything that is temporal and of maya, if we don't we just sign ourselves into the book of the nights of death, which is the Wheel of Fortune constantly going round and round, going nowhere forever. Everything of nature is forever dying, save its Soul which is waiting for the prince to wake her up with the kiss of eternal life. Earth is hell (unconscious) and purgatory (waking up) and it is up to us to uplift our understanding, widen our hearts, temper our sword of truth in the fire of fires and bring Heaven onto Earth. Heaven *can* be on Earth in the sense of perception. The minute we perceive life on Earth in a different way, then the incestuous degeneration can stop. In this new perception, the uplifted consciousness can lighten up the beauty of the process of the fusing of the Soul of nature with the Soul of mind, thus witnessing the death of its own misunderstanding.

Temperance, La Tempérance
Finding the essence through balance

An angelic, winged female figure is pouring liquid from a silver vase into a golden vase; no drops are spilt. This is water, the essence of life. There is no drunkenness, no illusion or magic, for this is Temperance. Silver represents the highest aspiration of the personality and when the work of uplifting the mind is done, the self-concern of the personality can be left behind and the essence of that work can be poured into the golden vase of the Soul. We have allowed ourselves to become completely receptive, for we have got rid of everything that is not essential, in giving ourselves up to the higher aspects of love and truth.

To start with a story about reality:-
Sherlock Holmes and Dr. Watson went on a camping trip. In the middle of the night Holmes awoke and nudged his faithful friend, saying "Watson, look up at the sky and tell me what you see". Watson replied, "I see millions and millions of stars". "What does that tell you Watson?" asked Holmes. "Well, astronomically it tells me that there are millions of galaxies and potentially billions of planets; horologically I deduce that the time is approximately a quarter past three; meteorologically I suspect that we will have a beautiful day tomorrow. Why, what does it tell you?" Watson asked. Holmes was silent for a moment, then spoke; "Watson, someone has stolen our tent".

Reality for most people is survival. Somebody has stolen my tent! Big drama! We can stick to that reality or we can simply explain the vision we have in front of us when the tent is stolen. If we don't do the latter we never get out of "Oh my God, the tent is gone!" With Number 13 we have died to the drama of survival and reason, to find the simplest and best solution to the riddle of life. The tent is really gone in the immediate reality, but that allows our mind to soar to the stars. We have allowed everything that is flesh to decay, meaning form, intellect and emotions; we have let all that fall off our bones. Then we move forward with what is reliable in us, which is the basic planetary structure of our bones. So we come back to Earth with what is essential, to witness the situation we are in as a reflection of the inner truth and reality.

The Lover keeps reminding us that the world is held together by love; we are coming back having to be realistic about what love truly is. From the universal point of view the energy that holds the universe together is what can be called love. This is materialised in the animal and human kingdoms into romantic emotional/comfort bonds, which is what most people call love. For example bringing flowers or chocolates to the one we love has its origin in the natural survival courtship instincts of bringing gifts in the animal kingdom.

When we come back again with the fourteenth card, we are in a state of recreation, or a passage from one state of consciousness to another. In the 12/3, which is the whole Trinity, the 3 expresses the sacrificial aspect of its existence. Then at the 13/4 the Soul accepts transmutation to the bare bones. At the 14/5 the rising has to happen from the existing structure; what rises is the mind. This is why the 14 can burn down the old unwanted mindsets which are deviations from the original natural instincts in nature – the karmic or genetic structures. The rising of the phoenix from the 13/4 and the recognition of the essence is all about mind. This is the process where survival transmutes into communication and mental work, rather than still staying with the comfort patterns. The essence of survival is communication and connection; it has the work of balancing and soothing the conflict between survival and Soul, which might still be in the 4. Once the mind has recognised its guiding ability, it has to learn to use it wisely by revisiting and re-perceiving all the natural instincts. Sometimes this can be manifested in the life journey of an individual as sexual or nervous system problems; this is because the kundalini fires are the vehicle for the energetic work.

Having seen that the essence is mind and recognised its own spiritual authority, the 14 can either obsessively seek knowledge, or refuse to be taught. This latter expression of 'I will do it myself' is ultimately important as it stems from within, so it is a precursor to internalisation. Out of the Death experience in the 13/4, the mind rises as 'I am' and the creative witnessing aspect of the mind is born, as man recognises the power of mind/word/connection in the manifestation of new structures.

Number 14 is called 'Temperance' in the Tarot. The word temperance means the moderation of all the pleasures of the senses: moderate eating and drinking; being in charge of one's urges and desires; learning to wield the great fire of the sexual creative energy and rising into the highest level of creativity for mankind, which is the aspiration towards goodness; this latter translates into goodwill. In becoming an instrument of goodwill or love in action, self gratification has been transmuted into caring for others. In the Old Testament, Noah didn't know anything about wine and its effects, but he planted the vine then drank the wine, became completely inebriated and so fell asleep from drunkenness. Noah with his drunkenness represents where humanity is now. Drunkenness is symbolic of being unaware and of only living a life of sensation and survival. It is forgetting the essential fact that we are Souls, here to witness life. This doesn't mean we shouldn't drink wine, it means that through ignorance mankind can allow sensory pleasure to veil the truth. Our true nature is not to use the senses for sensory pleasure but for information, as a scientist uses his senses to observe. It doesn't mean we can't enjoy what we are doing, but enjoyment is not what we are here for. Temperance knows that we have to bring in the essential, so as to recreate the world.

Once the rebirth happens, the water or essence of life has to pass from the silver to the gold vase. The silver vase represents the highest aspiration in the personality and the moon in her glory as she reflects light from the Sun. That reflection of light tells us that everything we see on the planet is a shadow of the lunar reflection. This is the high aspect of the moon, not the low aspect that just wants to survive, but the one that has aspired to a point where it offers itself completely to the light. Then the essential result of that work is transferred into the golden vase, which represents the Sun or Soul. Temperance can be seen as a mixing of two fluids, the essence of Earth and the sky essence, as in the archetype of Aquarius. However, it is more like a change of clothes or a change of body, which is the process of transubstantiation.

The other side of the 14 is the great power of creation, which is a result of the two energies of Spirit and matter coming together to manifest life. The 14 is usually called the kundalini energy, but we need to be careful in using this term, because the card is called Temperance, which asks us to use that power for the right purpose. In the card we see that not one drop of liquid is spilt, so there isn't a single drop which doesn't reach where it is supposed to go. This is about the right use of the kundalinic energy, in other words the right use of the power of the creation of life. In the seventeenth card, The Stars, water is being poured from similar vases and also represents that right use of the energy.

When someone under the influence of Number 14 has achieved a 'temperance' attitude towards life, they will have the backing of the energy of a 7 + 7, or 77, to help them internalise naturally. The number 77 represents the masters of meditation, mystery and internalisation, so it can be the 'wind behind the new grown wings of the Soul' of our rising 14. In the 77 two extremes can be seen. One 7 is fragile, forever focussed on form and therefore highly preoccupied by survival and nature; at the same time as fearing death, they bring death to themselves. The other 7 can actually measure all the stars in the universe, bring back the beautiful patterns and float on a cloud in an ivory tower where everything is okay. They can be so detached that there is no communication. When these two 7's align we have life, internalisation and a true vision of the process. Trillions of cells are dying everyday in nature, but it is no big deal, for the stars are doing it all the time. The movement radiates from the inside to nourish the outside world, rather than needing to take the outside in, to comfort and stimulate the little life. Fear is replaced by reason. The centre is reached and the movement of the lighted mind radiates from the centre to sustain the outer life. Selflessness replaces self-centredness. The mind has sensed the mystery of the inner silence and is able to translate it. The 14/5 is also called 'the power of the word' so it is interesting that we should ask the silence to give us the word and at the same time be an unspoken mystery! The true light of reason is just like love, which holds everything energetically; this is also like the magnetic energy holding everything together and giving of its body, so that eventually we can see the reality of the system. When the Spirit and the form have both finished the game of thinking that they are each the exclusive master, then the two can meet and fuse; the result is pure, unconditional, reasonable love, based on reality.

When we are helping people, the words we use are crystallised thought and are very potent, so it is essential that they come from the deepest possible place, which is beyond even duty or requirement. We learn to speak not from wanting the good for the person in front of us, because that is to do with what we think good is and can be tied up with control and power. We should check, when we are speaking words to others, do we want them to see the world from our mindset? Or do we want to make them feel good? We have to learn to keep quiet; this is a deep lesson for the 14/5. If we truly come back to recreate the world according to our essence, which is the truth and the God that we feel inside us, then we have to dare to come from a place of silence. We can make statements or speak all day long, as long as we check where we are coming from. Silence can bring with it the meditative aspect of the truth; for this reason silence can disturb. Our speech should sound like meditative silence, so the sound has an effect more profound than the intellectual meaning.

The key question for the 14/5 is "How do you love?" When we understand that what drives nature towards her lover the Sun is to do with her need to be sustained, then we have to know the true nature of our aspirations and accept to reconcile the goal with our situation. Emotion is a by-product of a deep aspiration within our nature body to be reunited with the Sun, so it is important to be very aware of our emotions and what we do with them. We should not be doing anything about them except following them to see where they take us. We should not hold onto them because they are only by-products, in the same way that form is a by-product. Our affection is our highest aspiration and is what we love and feel at one with; we are looking at this all the time. We have to render ourselves completely receptive, so that we can let go of any desire to attract the higher consciousness to serve our own needs; this way we get rid of everything that isn't essential and start again. This relates to the previous card, 'No Name', which is the 13/4.

The attainment of Number 14 is to become completely receptive, give ourselves up and move to the higher love and truth within the Soul. With the 14/5 we are crystallising what has been understood so far, so that according to the vision and the internalised knowledge that we hold, we are going to be giving out 'the word'. A lot of us would have tried to impose what we see onto other people, like an evangelist who says "Come on, I can save you and help you see the truth". Really we know that the only way anybody is going to unfold is by experiencing the hurts of life, to go through that fall and then re-birth themselves within the higher self. If someone needs too many answers from us and if they are not ready to answer their own questions, then rather than making them see it the way we do, it is better to stay silent. The truth has to be our own truth, not what has been given. If we repeat what has been given without having digested it fully and making it our own, then the work hasn't been done.

Alchemy comes in with Number 12 and carries on with the transubstantiation of what is not necessary for rebirth in Number 13. Then the rebuilding comes in with Number 14. The alchemical process transforms us from form to essence and necessity (karmic will) moves the essence to proceed back into rebirth. So far we have been striving for love, harmony, truth and for 'the good'. The motto of the Association Internationale de Numerologues is: 'Life, consciousness and all things are at different degrees of goodness and harmony' as given by Pythagoras. Alchemy brings forth a new vehicle to hold the new essence, so we can ask the question "Will there be more goodness and harmony?" Good has more to do with being the right tool for the job at hand, than any romantic idea of goodness.

'Good' is like humility; it is a state. When we try to be humble or good it doesn't work; we cannot acquire these qualities through books or take courses in them, for they are natural states. It doesn't matter how many books we read on alchemy, evolution, initiation, this path or that path, or how many good deeds we do even if we give our whole fortune or our body away. All that doesn't make us good, because good is the inner process of fusing with a non-personal view of the world, which is the cold light of reason. Goodness is impersonal and is a transpersonal unconditional love for the world, so we can't work at it or learn it. We bring ourselves into the right condition for it to happen at the right time, which is when the cosmos decides it is the time to come and work through us. So we might think, "I worked at it so I deserve it" – no way! If we think that, we haven't even started to take in and receive the lesson. It is complete receptivity, in the sense of really, truly giving up our mental control and smoothing our emotional into a reflective mirror. It is about keeping the silence of the wise and letting the light of the mind fall into the deepest inner creative caves of the past. If we have let go of practically everything then it is not difficult, because there is no 'I am' speaking. Instead we speak from a place which is so willing to flow with its waters of life, that it feels like we have no body; the structure adapts to its work. Therefore wishing 'good' for people is the opposite of how we could be helping them, as they have to decide which 'good' they want. We can help endlessly, but the beauty of 'the way' is that there is no way, only life. The true friend is the one who is going to help you buy the boat you want, even if they know you might sink with it! That isn't wanting good for you in a conventional sense, as they know this will lead to hurt, but 'by God' you are going to get 'good'!

In the end, to become good is to go to the end of our own experience. People can't learn how to be good through books or intellectualising. It is not about being safe; it is about going to the limit of what we've invested our love aspect into. There are three main aspects going back to the one life or the Trinity; Active Intelligence, love-wisdom and will. Each person has to find their own stream.

Allowing the foundation of our lives (that we have created with our minds over many lives) to die, according to our own truth, is transmutation; this is ongoing alchemy. In this process we *become ourselves by passing away'*. The acceptance of the process of the mind burning off some of the old structure is the prerequisite quality on which the new vision can appear. We must be vigilant and not rashly invite fake emotional crises into our lives; Temperance orders reality. It is not being violent to ourselves but receptive, which is exactly the same as obedience, acceptance, and balance. Balance is always being completely aware and so staying completely receptive; tolerance is being able to see things from other people's points of view.

If we have taken the violent road we are going towards self destruction, so we need to be aware that the aspiration of zeal has to be directed by Temperance. If we refuse to be guided by spiritual truth, we have spiritual pride which will come up in Number 15, The Devil. We should beware of our aspirations to be 'good' and ask ourselves whether we have understood the greater principle. If we are still being little prophets celebrating our own inner strength and pushing that down people's throats, then we are following the path of self-destruction. We need to allow the power of the life force to flow gently through us and align naturally, though our receptivity. The higher level of zeal is like silver, which represents the aspiration of nature; it rises up and is unstoppable. Natural enthusiasm has to be bathed in honesty and humility, so that we do not waste any energy or use it in a counter-productive way. Extremists of any religious group can push people away because they are using a zeal that is imposing. Zeal has to be tempered with humility.

There is a difference between passion and zeal. Passion is there to consume what is in us and to help us to reach our essence. Zeal is a quality of the essence; it is a law unto itself, which is why it has to be tempered or guided. We can be zealous with an illusion, but true zeal is the blind, mindless Spirit that flows through nature. We bring Spirit alive when we start understanding that it has something to do with consciousness. Matter is not self conscious, she suffers life; Spirit isn't intelligence it 'is' and it moves. When they meet and fuse the consciousness of the human race is created. True zeal will go forth and not see anything around it, because it is part of the movement of Spirit which propels it. In tempering that energy we bring in the awareness of truth; this is the eye in the centre of the tornado. When we work from that place true zeal can become a force for good. Even then we still have to be aware that the eye in the centre could be an illusion, a personal dream or a quest for uncontrolled zealous power.

If we understand and know that the world is just 'becoming', then whatever 'use or abuse' we see in nature we don't think "What a shame that it has to be this way", we just witness what is going on and know that in time and space the eternal truth will be revealed. If we can practise that a little bit every day it will remove in us the frustration of seeing that the world isn't the way our vision tells us it could be. This is very much part of the 14/5. That frustration smacks of spiritual pride, even of cruelty, because we want to impose something on a world that has already quite a lot to deal with. In the same way when a child is not ready to walk, we shouldn't chastise it because it is not walking.

In time and space everything will be revealed, for at the end of all that there is only the eternal. It is through our consciousness and ability to measure time and space that the greater life finds its place in the Universe. We have to develop our cosmic understanding, which is beyond time and space, so as to learn to stop wanting to do good, because good is happening right in front of us and is evolving all the time. The far-seeing vision learns to love the time and space aspect because it is the great guardian, making certain that the alchemy is happening according to what the body can receive and fuse with at the time. All zealous people have to make peace with the time and space concept of the 24/6, because alchemy cannot be pushed. Time the healer does work in mysterious ways, we just have to learn to love and accept its sulking retreats. Actually there is no time or space, only life and when the 24/6 eventually understands that, its love is beyond patience. Temperance is the ultimate patience and when we have seen the truth, it is the greatest friend and ally we have. It tells us that eventually all will be revealed to us. We just have to be prepared to look; there is no other way.

Separation is everywhere and is being clearly demonstrated in humanity. We have to look at the zeal and spiritual pride of 'there is only one God and it is ours!' We have to know that perfection can only be found within. Once we have understood this, then we are happy to share our cottage or land with anyone that comes to it. This is a reflection of the Earth, world of form, or matter, wanting to be one with the Sun or Spirit. Our Sun is in us, so we have to remove any artificial imposed names that are political in nature and then we know that the holy land is in each and every one of us.

Temperance is an angel with wings; she has a strong correspondence with the Empress in Number 3. The Empress represents the great intellect that learnt that it had to fly and give itself over to a higher power so that initiation could happen. The U turn was at Number 12 and 13. Now our Magician at 14 has become the essence or mind. He hasn't turned into an angel, but is at the level where he needs the help and support of the highest in him in order to rise from one world to another, giving him a completely different perception of life from that new level. The whole journey is always showing us the outcome of what has happened before. The transformation or transmutation of what we have given up has created zeal and power. We need the help of the highest will because the slightest wish of the "How? Who? Where? When?" of what we were going to become might crystallise a return to the wheel of nature, rather than a rise in consciousness.

If the work is complete, then we have contacted the river of life in us and we have given up any desire for self, for we have internalised and touched on the Soul. The river of life is the Spirit moving into our Soul; that is what directs us and we have to follow it. When we know that everything is made of truth, love and light, then we know that is what our consciousness is made of. We give up any brightness or cleverness that we might think we have, so as to follow the river in silence and quietness. When we have an inner knowing we don't even need hope.

The Magician (the mind) is in there, aware that he is the essence and that he has had to give up to something higher than himself, for the sake of others. It is here that an element of spiritual pride can be revealed. We come back and we have died. We know that we are essence and we are in the river, like a drop being carried downstream. In that state if we have the desire to push the river, then we have spiritual and intellectual pride in us; we are still thinking that there is another way to help others to be 'good'. Once we know we are flowing with the river, we look at life and we know that whatever happens it is flowing towards its goal. All we can do when someone needs help is support, love, understand and be a mirror for them. Where we are is exactly where we are supposed to be, although people may not like to hear that. This is Temperance asking us to give up pride and so be more efficient; to feel the force and beware of turning it into power again.

One definition for the 14/5 is righteousness, which can be expressed as "I am exactly where the God we live in wants me to be. I don't want anything for myself, except to be where my consciousness is supposed to be. I am blessed because I am not fighting any more. I am at peace. I understand and I have the choice either to keep on receiving, flowing and being, or to go and think that I can have a big effect on the world". We don't need to swim to survive; we are carried by the flow of the river.

It is a simple card; there are not many different symbols. It instils the idea of the passage from one state to another or the movement from inferior to superior. Having done the journey so far, the consciousness is going to see things differently and from a higher point of view than it had before; it has reached deeper into the mysteries of the subconscious. When we do self-work and go for truth and understanding, we engage in the simple naming of what Spirit and matter do when they come together. Eventually we see and go through tens of thousands of experiences, naming all the different emotions. When we come to the very end of that process, it is so important to see ourselves as we are without the explanations or excuses, such as, "That comes from the past" and, "That is one of my habits". We are at the point now where we don't need the psychology any more. We are just here to see how we are at the time and make the choice of either letting go or playing mind games. The more we put intellectual understanding into the vision of what we are, the more we base it on the past or excuse it, rather than completely accept ourselves and life as it is. Every time we give psychological reasons or excuses for our behaviour, we reinforce the picture so losing the chance to have that 'reflex photo' completely cleaned out.

Rising and seeing the situation from above, we can see life from a different point of view, but that rising above can only give us the understanding because we have been underneath before. It is the 'underneath' which has brought us back the vision and the understanding. It is the moon or the silver, which gives the receptivity and higher level of perception to help us feel and see through the form. Eventually, inferior or superior does not mean anything.

We all need to be liberated from any fixed positions that we are entrenched in. It is easier to see those fixed aspects in others than it is to see our own, if we are denying the same fixed pattern in ourselves. On the other hand we may be recognising the pattern quickly in others because we have liberated ourselves from it. However, this does not confer any superiority on us, for like us they are captured in their own particular vision of the world in order to satisfy whatever fear of need they have. In fact they have the courage to do the hard work that we've opted not to do any more and the God we live in still needs that work to be done. The real cry for help comes from not being able to let go of a restrictive pattern and thinking that we are inferior, because we are not managing it.

When we are talking about initiation, levels of consciousness and hierarchy, the terms 'inferior' and 'superior' are only there to describe a position, rather than to qualify a state. There is a true energetic hierarchy that is found at the heart of the deepest essence, but it is very different from the usual idea of hierarchy. What most people think of as hierarchy are separate levels of status which have dominion over lower levels. In a true spiritual hierarchy, each level is imbued with the life of the greatest life representing the system. If we want to rise above things because we feel we are in an inferior position, then we need to examine ourselves; there is pride in us and we are not flowing with our river.

We should never look at anybody and think that they are more, or less aware than us; we are only at different levels. Who knows, tomorrow we may be the one having to go down into matter with very little appreciation of what is happening to us. There isn't one single thing we do that isn't divine; even self-destruction. A stubborn intellect has within it the courage to make itself wicked, stupid and cruel, in order to get there; we can be in awe of that, for it is remarkable. It takes a lot of courage to be so enraged with God and life, to go for self-destruction. Such people have more courage than the average person and they are channelling that courage differently from others.

Among those at the centre of the tornado who are pulling themselves down with addictions, some will be sucked in for a little while and then will come out and be reborn again. We cannot stop this life experience, but it is hard to watch. Politically we can get involved in the work of forming a more human, less consumer-based and more caring type of society. Wars are there to show us that war isn't the way. All causes are valid in the movement of the evolution of consciousness.

Receiving the river of life to let it work through us would allow a spontaneous reaction to a situation, because our little river is aligning to the greater river and so will not interfere with the greater plan.

When the Hanged Man was admitted into the temple, he put himself in front of the two pillars and met the black sphinx; this is where he suffered the most frightening trial, which was to witness his own decomposition. We too have to witness our own decay or transformation, which is why it is so difficult and painful to have to look at ourselves. We cannot go back because we have to let go and rise into a new phase.

In this card the fluid that is being poured from one vessel to the other is water, not wine. Anything fluid is to do with Spirit because it is about the flow of life. Wine symbolises the Spirit coming into matter and making flesh, it is a symbol for the Soul in incarnation. It is used in communion by the priest (as representative of Soul). As Jesus said "The bread is my body and the wine is my blood". This is actually telling of life and Spirit in incarnation. When we read the story of Jesus' miracles the first one is the wedding, which is about the fusion of Soul and Spirit. The wine symbolises the Soul, full of all the sufferings of life. In this card we have water, because a particular incarnation is being washed out of our essence so that we can begin a new life. When Jesus gave the Samaritan water that quenched his thirst forever, it was spiritual water which had come from a well, because that water is only given out of the deepest inner work. So we meet our God and burn with Number 11, then there is the crucifixion at Number 12 and the obscuration of Number 13. At Number 14 we have the resurrection and the word.

The angel comes to us when we truly need to ascend and rise out of hell so as to come back into life. At Pentecost the angel gave the apostles the Holy Spirit. The twelve apostles symbolise all the experiences that the personality would have had from many lives as it goes round the zodiac; this is the experience of all the facets that matter has to offer as parts of life on this planet. At Pentecost all these different facets and lives are being rendered virginal or pure, as they receive the Holy Ghost. For many people Pentecost is the most important time in the Christian calendar, because it is a time when the blessing of blessings is given, Active Intelligence is made holy and the members of the Trinity are together again.

The beginning of consciousness on Earth was not a fall but a rising from the comfort of nature into awareness. At the beginning of this rise, the conflict and suffering happens through being increasingly conscious of the weight of matter. Then as we get more conscious we start questioning and measuring, which means that we are not comfortable any more. We are not fallen gods remembering Heaven, we are mind rising out of matter bringing back awareness to the God we live in. Through us, Spirit finds its original intent and works through more and more subtle qualities of mind as it experiences life. We are looking at what has been called a battle between Spirit and matter. Spirit flows through matter to vitalise its rebirth in truth. Matter will inform Spirit of its action through its reflection in her mirror, but unaware matter doesn't know or understand Spirit's karmic dictate and so reacts for survival. Then proud blind Spirit reinforces its zeal and so the battle goes on. The acting and reacting is a drama that we make of life.

Eventually we see that we can go on reacting forever and we realise that we are wasting a lot of time. However much intellect there is behind a question, we need the movement to come in from an emotional aspiration, in order to reach up and align to the level of consciousness that has created us. We want to meet the divine face to face and we must not be afraid, ashamed, or guilty to meet it inside us because we have not offended it. How can a worm offend a star? There is no way our little lives can offend the God we live in, for we are its manifestation.

All the feelings that are backed with a self-interested intellect are entirely man-made; there is definitely no watching, punishing God. Active Intelligence, having successfully exteriorised its full potential and achieved the goal of self awareness, has been used by mankind to satisfy the greed for power. When we manipulate energy for our own purposes, we use the intellect to weave a web of illusion. Instead we need to touch the pure power of Active Intelligence deep within us and so stop knitting or weaving layers of soporific glamour. Then we can offer this pure aspect of divinity in service to its guide (the Soul) and go back to the source.

The fall of man was a great gift and privilege that gave us the possibility of ascension, so there is no need to redeem it. Before the fall we were safe in the group Soul and as in the animal groups, there was no individuality. We survived, we were fed and we naturally behaved as a cell in a surviving unit; we were the self-sustaining group Soul. From this point of view (with a hint of romanticism) life could be seen as a paradise. The minute an individual started to ask questions there was trouble and he was expelled from the group. This individual was beginning to internalise through self-awareness, after having had no responsibility whatsoever except to follow the ethic of the group. Self-awareness and questioning makes us start to feel separate and rejected. A lot of people have to heal the great hurt that comes in with that; to them it is as if it is the fault of the group for rejecting them. Once they are receptive enough to understand that out of their courage they decided to reject the easy life in order to internalise, that hurt is healed.

Active Intelligence as The Empress, describes the achievement of the intellectual, philosophical and artistic mind and is internalised in The Hermit, where the knowledge received by the Soul, will be processed and remain as wisdom. Then with Temperance, we have reached the essence, so the angel helper within gives us the uplift. We have given it all up and realise that we are part of the great river, so all self-interest is lost and the higher mysticism of the Aquarian Age is reached. Then mankind will take his responsibility through the understanding of his position in the Universe; this is the cosmic work.

The Magician had all the zeal and enthusiasm to run around the world several times, so he rushed into death with the 13; then the 14 says "Take it easy!" Temperance tells us to go for life as the witness, to reflect and digest the experiences and then ask the 'how' and 'why' questions about life. Pondering and meditating on life while keeping an active mind, will naturally put us in contact with the higher intelligence of the Soul. The internalised work is entirely done by the Soul and all the personality can do is render itself completely receptive. Matter can't transmute itself; it can only be transmuted in time and space from within its own inner fire, fusing with the light that it receives from Soul. The water of life is truth and it comes out of the deep well of experience of the Universe.

After the death of all the illusion that the Soul has had to rise above, we are in the presence of the essential in us. We become more and more aware of any little lies, or any covering up that we do. This awareness is the only job we are supposed to do and as we do it, it becomes so normal and natural that it is not difficult. We become more and more aware of that little infernal spiral that wants to keep us in nature. This is not about feeling guilty or accusatory, it is just being aware of life as a mental exploration of the past – not to explain or run away from it but to transmute it into present reality. We have the choice of playing with it, feeling guilty and saying "Tomorrow I will be a better person", but that only reinforces the heavy layers of control that the intellect, in cahoots with the emotional, uses to keep the mind prisoner in the drama. When we feed it tiny little bits of intellect and emotion, we are feeding the little worm and giving life to the game. However, if we are aware, we have the choice not to engage with the game and then in time it will not turn up again, because we are not feeding it but just bleaching it with the light of eternity. Then we just see it with truth and love and there is no problem. That is the process of alchemy inside us; the transformation and purification.

In Temperance we are going up a level, from silver (moon) to gold (sun); eventually the Moon and the Sun become one. The wings of the angel are silver, for they represent the aspiration within the Soul. Silver is precious like gold but it tarnishes; its quality is like the purified Earth. It is so soft that it cannot keep its shape by itself, so it always has to have an alloy in it to give it strength, such as iron or copper which are corruptible. Earth, matter and the etheric are divine and therefore pure, but form is corrupted for perfection is not of this world yet. We are actually not limited by the body and it is not our bodies which are impure, it is how we use them. Matter is slow in organising its manifested forms, but there is an incredible freedom that comes when consciousness realises it can see itself in matter; then we know that what we are looking at is a result of yesterday's mind projection.

Symbolically, silver is of this world and gold is of the Soul, so only when the gold and the silver come together do we have the correct strength. The first step towards perfection is when all the senses are brought together into a harmonious perception of life and then we start to catch a glimpse of divine life unfolding. It is up to us to do the inner alchemy and render ourselves more beautiful (in the pure sense of the word).

There are three important aspects of the Number 14 that need to be recognised. The first is that those under the influence of the 14 don't like to be told or taught–this tells us that we have to find knowledge from within ourselves, otherwise we just want more and more from books; some 14s are eternal students. Secondly Man, recognising that he could take part in the creativity of life on the planet, has to learn to wield the energy of the kundalini with Temperance. Therefore at that level problems of sexuality can be experienced, as he learns the right use of the kundalini. Thirdly, 14 is 'the power behind the word', and here we are back into action. We are reminded that we can do all the good actions in the world, but if the intent comes from self-satisfaction and is therefore imposed, they will fizzle out to nothing or interfere in negative ways with an ongoing karmic situation. If we do nothing else but being ourselves and coming from the deep point of the waters of life, then our action in the world will be much more potent than any big interfering gestures. The highest level of the 14/5 is non-action, meaning action from within the greater river which acts through us. This is 'love without desire'. When we have no desire from any need or mindsets, the right action will manifest.

People who are called 'the great' of this world are just instruments of collective karma. In a way they are not responsible for their actions, for like politicians in times of war they are only an expression of the collective will of the country, or the hidden economical, political will of the wealthiest nations. They are puppets to manifest specific karmic lessons for humanity. Only the few great lights that stand against oppression and injustice can be seen as great missionaries of a world to come. If we feel we have a mission we should look very carefully at where that intent comes from, because the only mission we really have is to keep on being truthful witnesses, so as to render the world 'good' through the process of alchemy. If for the whole of our lives we have tried to be good and it is still not working, then our mission might be to fall on our faces!

Unless a man is completely denuded of collective karma, or his own personal heavy karma, most of his actions are tainted. The complete receptivity of matter or the feminine aspect has to come back to its original purity and just allow the Spirit to guide her. Spirit has had to adapt to the cycles and rhythms of nature or matter, because she has the power of manifestation; then nature gives her form feely to the next manifestation engendered by Spirit. Eventually the rhythm has been understood by Spirit, which has learned to dance to the rhythm that nature has created; the wedding is complete and Spirit and matter have come back as one again. Not pushing the river is the most important message in this idea. We have made peace with the time and space element; this is the wisest way to re-define and exteriorise. It is the only karmic rhythm that this little planet has to go through and Active Intelligence knows it. With this there is no more manipulation, pushing, ordering or power–just love and movement. At the basic level it is the mother or the woman that civilises man. This is why the age of sisterhood will be the true age of brotherhood. We're not talking about the power of the feminine gender here, for it is not a question of balancing feminine with masculine. In men as well, the respect for the feminine aspect in themselves (the personality), society, institutions, families, bodies and nourishers, is what will eventually bring the house in order. When that has happened and everybody knows their place (not in the sense of a hierarchical, social place), we will know what we are supposed to be doing here; then we can go to the wedding.

It is not a particular action that makes or uplifts a man; it is the intent or faith behind his action that is important, so whether the action ends in disaster or not is irrelevant. Action is only a by-product, but when it is the by-product of a true faith then it has become a non-action, because it is simply movement of Spirit into action through a transparent instrument. We have to learn to be self-propelled, until we are completely propelled by Spirit, then we give over into non-action. Out of our own zealous mistakes we learn to let something greater propel us, so it is really okay to make mistakes, they are only rehearsals.

The inner alchemical process of going from silver to gold, or being transformed into a more receptive vehicle, is hidden; with it there is a beneficial influence that modifies the collective aura of humanity. As we become more radiant and at one with everything, we experience the collective heaviness, despair and pain of humanity. If we are a strong transformer we automatically receive a little bit more than our share, it just pours in and we have to carry on and do the work. However, it is important not to think that it is just collective, because this can be an excuse not to do the necessary work of self-cleansing. The work is not a big deal and it is not self-centred, but it requires discipline because we have to be completely honest. Our consciousness is undertaking initiatic transformation from the silver to the gold. We cannot rush it nor do it all at once, for we do not own the process and we can only witness its happening, so patience is essential.

When we start internalising and working from Soul, we begin to do some work in the collective and we feel it. People who are disillusioned or despairing have to learn to live with it and recognise it, through realising that they are part of a collective Soul group and that they are open enough to take on that work. Most of the time we share a great big transformation or transmutation job, but the feelings that are around us are the key and we need to go deep into them. If we truthfully and honestly see that we have never had these feelings and they don't ring a bell in us, then what we are experiencing is collective. If they still ring a little personal bell (and we know the difference because it hurts personally), then we've still got some refinement to do and the collective upset is giving us a little bit more pain than we need to have. Most of the time what we experience is both personal and collective.

This process requires daily introspection, every second of the day. This is the discipline of reminding oneself to be alive, be a witness and live in complete lucidity. We can only really become one with Spirit when our whole aspiration has become silver and we have accepted to give our life to the higher or inner lover (Soul-Spirit) connection. There is no other movement for the essence but to reunite with the love of God, for that is the heart of love.

At any time we can change and perceive life differently; this is our gift. When we see the truth and give ourselves into it, then the Soul is uplifted into the light. Most people don't really want to contemplate inner truth and accept it, as this would imply that the misunderstanding of yesterday's perception has to die. The fear of death is more deeply embedded in the subconscious than we think; this is the only reason why people don't want to rock the old boat of their traumatised consciousness. When we are taught about angels, God and light, we think the future is going to be much more beautiful than yesterday, when actually it is exactly the same as it was, but with a bit more dust because we are a bit more aware of it.

This whole process is about de-crystallising the initial fear that we came in with. We have been frozen for tens of thousands of years in our belief that survival is the aim of life, then when we become free of that we don't know what we are going to become, so it can feel as if it was better to go back to the suspended life in the freezer. "Better the devil we know, or better the ice cube that we built our lives on! Beware, it is melting fast! Wake up!"

We have to put great trust into truth, love and God. When Jesus meets a rich man, who had refused to let go of his belongings and goods, an apostle asks, "If he can't save himself, who will?" That is the stage where you have to bring in that great trust, because the answer Jesus gave was, "Some things are not possible to man, but to God everything is possible". This is telling us to let God work through us, the river flow through us. If we have got to the bottom of our stench and rottenness and think we will never come out of it, we should trust that the love, light and truth aspects in us will actually transmute the past and uplift us. We must go beyond the worldly understanding that to be saved is to know that we do not need salvation.

The only thing we are expected to do is to be receptive to the love that flows from the divinity to us; our true love is receptivity. Most people don't truly love because they think they have to be in charge and retain power; others don't love because they have been too hurt. They have to open the doors of receptivity, let go of the protection and become vulnerable again, so that they can receive love and be in touch with their own source of love; then the spontaneity of Soul reigns. The ones who have transferred themselves from one urn to the other are the ones who have believed, loved, hoped and seen everything failing them, so they do not even know or care if they are transmuted from the silver into the gold. They have refined their minds and given so much up, in the name of that great primary yearning for love, that they have reached the point (as in nature) when the light and warmth of the Sun can be assimilated and crystallised in the very fabric of the vegetable kingdom (the emotional body of the planet). When the 'I am' of the Soul is present we never doubt love, then when we love we don't desire any more, because the need to love or be loved is gone; you *are* love. Endurance and hope are both exercises for total purification.

The silver light that the Moon emits is only a reflection from the Sun symbolising the world of the sensitive emotional life. It is that reflective quality rather than the mercurial path of the mind that enables us to rise. However, there is no possible point of crisis and vision without the mind daring to plunge into the dark pond, so we have to go with the mind as far as it can go, so that it can lose itself to the emotional life. When the emotional pain is too strong, the mind has to give up to the pain because it can't make sense of it and a crisis happens. The mind is breaking down, so eventually the great emotional sea reverts back to itself having exhausted the intellectual pursuit. At this point we are emotionally/intellectually dead to the experience; it is then that we become very receptive to the quiet peace of the Soul. If we understand that process, then we know a little bit of alchemy has happened and a rise in consciousness has taken place, because something has been transformed into peace and truth. From that place we love more and can forgive. We are essentially all Soul and as such we are at our most receptive.

The use of the mind is a preparation, like tuning up our computer so it can pick up the slightest touch of the celestial water and so bring flashes of light into the cup. In-tuition is 'inner Teaching', it is the same as connaissance which is what we have come back with and been born with. With this there is direct communication between the hidden knowledge and the one who wants to know. When the mind is at peace in the heart, the light can precipitate a message from heaven into the heart of matter where it will be translated by the hidden fires of nature and released as intuition. We know by now that the higher mind of God is not to be found in books or in workshops, but is in the experience of everyday life. We find it when we are in a state of complete honesty, vision and lucidity. This is not lucidity coming from a quirk of the intellect, but lucidity from the reality in the cup and the uplift of the veil, for the mind is in the heart by then and not leading the way.

As we rise in consciousness and get nearer to the mind of God, the lifting of the veil from one level to another is a metaphor for the passage from one cycle of vibration to another. The outer boundaries of both neighbouring movements create the 'energetic' veil.

How can we pretend to possess the mind or even the ear of God, when in fact it is man that has to realise that he is a possession of God? We can do nothing ourselves at any level of life, physically, intellectually or emotionally. There is no way we can say, "I am as God" meaning, "I possess all the knowledge here", for we are God's creatures. How can we think that it won't all go towards the best possible result? It doesn't matter if at the end the result is a pebble rather than a diamond if that is the object of the experience, so we can relax! When man sees his limitation and gives himself into the infinite realm, how can he not put his trust in God or the system rather than the bearded God of religion? All his pride, guilt and desire have gone and he has become incorruptible gold; it is then that he can have connaissance, inner knowledge and intuition.

The light from within produces the form. Man cannot look directly at the Sun but he can look at its reflection on the moon, so as to have an idea of what is going on. Once we have understood that the whole of life is a symbolic reflection of a higher truth, we can start to detach, for the symbolic helps us to reflect away from ourselves. Looking at sub-personalities teaches us to look at things symbolically, to remove ourselves and look at the situation in a different way. Then eventually, if we can drop the symbolic reflective side of our nature, we will have learned to look at something beyond ourselves, with the realisation that even that it is only a reflection.

The Initiate knows that there is only the inner narrow way, or the internal difficult path that has to be taken, which only a minority are able to access. He can see that the whole world is a comedy stage and he will not be charmed by it, or be attracted to form in all its aspects. He has perceived the light from within that has remained veiled. The light of the Soul will never dazzle, for Soul will never push in or interfere. If we are lucky the light of Spirit will dazzle or dim the intellect. At times of revelation this would happen naturally, with little disturbance to the everyday physical existence of the person. When the instrument is not ready, it is not ready and that is all there is to it. A person can be completely out of service for many lives when the kundalini is forced to rise unnaturally.

The Initiate is going through the internal process of being purified by the light. He has to experience and witness how that process works and to do this he has to accept where he is. So he asks to go to the bottom of the darkness and there at the bottom of the subconscious is a little speck of fire. This is wisdom that has to be brought to the surface so that it can be used.

In learning to let go of seeing form and the senses as absolute, he goes into the gold cup where everything becomes formless. It is not that form disappears, but he knows that the form is not the absolute and that he only works with the absolute. It is this one, the 'informal' in each of us, that corresponds strongly to the primitive revelation or the first instinct, which is the inheritance from the first Soul group. We are going in and seeking to retrieve that very deep thing that we know is our true self. This is the original spark that gave us the name of our Soul group. We have to have the higher powers to help us with that, so that our virtual aspiration becomes real. Then the beauty of that is that our inner higher aspiration, which has nothing to do with form or personality, becomes real as well.

On the ladder of initiation there are many lovely little realisations, but when we are going through a major initiation it is a 'U turn' at which we can close a door behind us, meaning that we are not caught in a circle of illusion any more. This doesn't mean that now and then we won't feel a tinge of what we used to be, for habits die hard. We have stepped onto another level where we can go back inside, deeper and deeper through to the beginning of time to unveil all the wisdom and know-how of the Active Intelligence principle so that we can realistically understand a little bit more of the system.

The angel wears a red dress and a blue tunic overdress, lined with green. She is pouring water from one urn to another. Her red dress demonstrates the inner fire and inner zeal that is in the human being at the time. The angel represents the highest aspiration of the Soul, but she still has the clothes of the personality that have pushed forward to that level of aspiration, so as to reach the truth and the true idea. The blue dress, which is over the red one, symbolises this true idea. Then we have the green, to give that true idea vitality and life. The red pushes the energy upwards, so that it can actually have enough aspiration to see the truth; then eventually it will give vitality to materialise and crystallise that truth.

The flower in this card needs the higher water from above, because it cannot find nourishment from the Earth any more. We must not separate brutally from our earthly body with excessive asceticism, because the idea is to merge, fuse and transmute, not 'get rid of'; that is a big mistake a lot of people make on the path. Temperance is really the only right way here. The body that we occupy is the vehicle that is adapted to the life in this world, so it has to be looked after, loved and recognised just enough to be the best possible vehicle for the job.

The angel has a solar emblem on her head and the golden flow of her hair is like the rays of the Sun coming down. Her short hair style shows care and neatness. She looks as if she has just come out of the hairdresser, ready to go to school. She has a hermaphrodite pageboy look because she is an angel, like the Soul.

If we want 'good' for others, rather than letting them find their own good, this is violent. Violence is pushing the river and therefore interference. It is violence to try to convert someone and impose our view of God onto another, just because of our absolute belief. Violence creates disorder, but disorder is what we need to create harmony, so chaos is wonderful stuff. Basically our aim is to uplift the mind from the magma of the form that eats itself and transforms into a harmonious ensemble, or arrangement. We know that good cannot be imposed and we cannot make other people happy despite themselves, for they must find their own definition of happiness. All we can do is tell them that their shining Sun is in them. Even when we are certain that our understanding of life is sound, we must not hurt any consciousness that is still ignorant with our vision. If we do, we find only rebellion, resistance and blood. However, we should not forget that our certainty could be a protective mindset against the great unknown void. It is a form of cruelty to push, just as an intellectual resistance is cruel. The intellect is extremely strong and finds the most wicked, pernicious ways of strangling the voice of the Soul. There should not be any forcing or persuading others into spiritual discipline, belief systems, or secret societies. Truth is such a strong wine that even if we want it we get a dizzy head from it and if we give it to somebody to drink who is not ready, we are certainly going to send them into a mental institute, because it is too much to take.

'The kingdom of heaven belongs to the violent'. This can easily be misunderstood, and is definitely not about violence to other people, but about an inner violence towards the self. It applies to those who do not hesitate to cut out what is not righteous in them, so as to cut through the illusions. It has to be done one step at a time with a strong foothold, otherwise we will fall.

What we are fighting is a state, not something on the outside to be killed, but something we are going to become or transmute into. It is an internal change of transubstantiation. It is not even something we can work towards as 'good', for if we do we are full of pride and have a tendency to tyranny. One who thinks he possesses 'the good' is definitely going to try very, very hard to preach it, reveal it and impose it when it is actually a way of being or a Soul disposition. We all have a little bit of the tyrannical violence of the mind in us. We have the special time-space vision of eternity and we truly would like to see Heaven on Earth as soon as possible. We say we will be patient, but in everyday life we would like more movement and more change, so there are people we want to kick into action. We have to remember that we have eternity, or the life span of the system, in front of us.

The spiritualisation of man happens through the Soul; it is not intellectual or emotional. Soul will never interfere and only works through its instrument when accepted. So any sort of imposition on others which excludes the rules of the respectful family unit and social groupings, would not be Soul based.

The best is the enemy of the good. To want to be the best is exposing our need to be superior to others. 'Spiritual pride' rules the upper waves of the high tides of emotions. If we want to be the best, we can be – with ourselves for measure; this is a humble look at ourselves moving towards goodness. Wanting others to do their best is arrogant and not our business.

When we look at Temperance as a 14, it is two 7's which is 77. The wise 77 has the patience of the world, they are the masters of the mystery, the travellers in space; they know that whatever is happening is exactly how it should be and will be so at the end.

The 14 as 'the power of the word' warns us to roll our tongue 7 times in our mouth before we speak, because the power of that energy is so systematically and energetically strong that it crystallises things, for its purpose is to crystallise thoughts into words. The word is symbolised by Number 5, which is the mind communicating with sounds created by the vibration of its movement, into the crystallised structure of life on the planet as a human being. We can see why this energy comes after Number 13 when that great death and rise in consciousness has happened, because nothing from form to higher intellect is left of the flesh, so automatically we have the rise of life that says "I am", so that the rebirth can come after the death. That is the power of the Number 14, creating words and recreating ourselves.

The Devil, Le Diable
The choice

In this card we see a blue-winged Devil with staring red eyes and yellow horns. He has the legs of a Billy-goat; they are coloured green and his torso is partly female, with breasts. Two 'little devils', a male and female faun, are chained to the plinth upon which he stands. This is the world of matter, power and sexuality; of dualities such as male and female, or darkness and light. The intellect has a million ways of attracting the Soul back into matter and self-gratification. As we become aware, we see this as an opportunity to look into our darkest corners. This is the way the system works, through mankind's self-awareness of its life on the planet Earth. We are being used by a system which itself is a by product of the mysterious quest of the great life we live in, so the work we do is not to be taken personally. Eventually, beyond the world of opposites and separation, we become realised human beings, as the personality, Soul and Spirit align. Through a number of initiations, this fusion takes place within a unit and eventually with the one life.

Number 15/6 in numerology is often called 'The Angel and Devil'. Here in the fifteenth card The Devil is an angel of God and the hidden symbol of the true esoteric Tarot. There is a question with this card and the answer can only be black or white; a choice has to be made and there is no compromise or colour. In the Major Arcana we see a high initiate coming back for an initiation, with the pictures of the Tarot showing his progress through the different levels of consciousness. He gathers all the metaphysical understanding of the qualities that he has to nurture, keep alive and remember within himself. He has to rely on high minded qualities, such as zeal and endurance. He prepares himself to do this through a process of internalisation, which involves being true to himself and opening his heart. He has to choose the type of strength he is going to 'use' or be 'used by'. When he is ready he will present himself and is only 'elected' if his mind vibrations can uplift and fuse with a new sphere of consciousness. The will and the choice are within the heart and mind of the initiate, but when he rises to be used by the light, it is nothing to do with him and is entirely systemically driven.

This phase of the process is a brilliant golden death that does the work of clearing everything, including all the mind-sets from the past. It happens at a cellular level and so involves the flesh and blood of the whole body. It is a passage from one level of vibration to the next and then when the aspiration of the Soul has actually reached its goal we end up in a different level of consciousness. After that, what happens? Instead of seeing a wonderful being of light saying "Welcome my love", we get the Devil! In our surprise we say "I don't want to play that game anymore if that is what I end up with! Where is the angel that is going to comfort me all my life?"

We are only here to lift up and cleanse the pebbles of matter on behalf of the God we live in; these pebbles are encoded in our cells. If we know that is what we are doing then we can understand that the Devil is a very bright angel, because he is the one that is going to trip us up if we still have feet of clay, so that we remove our tainted glass when we look at life. One of the signs that relates to him is Capricorn, so we can recognise the mountain goat in him or the high teacher; this is the one that is going to concretise everything that we might have brought back in our cup of gold (the Soul), so that we can see it in its densest manifestation. With the gold we have got to the point of understanding that we are a Soul. The silver was the aspiration from nature that was rising to meet its bright lover. This dark side of nature, which rises from silver into the light, has finally understood that dark and light are one and so it can go through the alchemical transformation into gold, thus making more light available for us to look at our dark crystallised cobwebs.

By now we have gone through a great cleansing process, as if through vitriolic acid, so that even our bones are cleansed and dissolved. We think that we are squeaky clean and everything we perceive is clearly black and white, but all the shadows that are still there within our cup are going to be crystallised in front of us. Energetically we are light enough to rise and when we do, we suddenly see life and nature for what it is every minute of the day, with its glamour and illusion; this is the bonus that comes with a rise in consciousness. It does not last for very long as the work of walking into our past continues.

There are a million ways that the intellect is able to attract the Soul back into matter, right down to enjoying the beauty of nature. If we look at nature realistically, from the point of view of understanding what the system is like, we see that it is the most murderous and incestuous system there is and a big part of our makeup belongs to the system! This is not to criticise nature in any way, because she is beautiful and godly, but her true beauty doesn't reside in her form or appearance for that is just on the surface. The beauty resides in the brilliant way Active Intelligence weaves the biological existence that we call life, to give birth to consciousness. When we can see it like that, then we can rise and feel the true beauty of the Earth and we see humanity coming out of the Earth like zombies, carrying the darkness of survival in their flesh and seeking refuge, some in their own darkness, some in the cleansing light of the Soul.

Even the highest expression of art is an attraction back into matter. While Number 5 is looking for gratification, whether it is intellectual, emotional, spiritual or sensual, we are on the side of the Devil and not with the angel. The Devil does his best to attract us, in order to help us see whether we are honest enough to recognise that we are being attracted. He's not punishing us or beating us over the head for being drawn back, for he's got the white five-pointed star on his head, which promises us the offer of the star kingdom. He is saying "If you are righteous and honest this is your chance to recognise instantly what is still attracting you".

The problem at this level is with the mind. Everything is of mind; even nature is a result of mind finding its way out of primal magma through our little brains. Every single loop of the intellectual mind is going to be put in front of us and if we are utterly honest, we can recognise the excuses we give ourselves in order not to see. This card tells us we have to be aware, so as not to go back to nature's zombie-like consciousness. We are not lost forever if we do return to nature, we can come back up again and carry the light, for by the time we experience the 15/6 we are a Soul or a son of mind. This is a card that warns us to be true to love and love the truth.

The sexual organ of our Devil is the symbol of Mercury, which relates to the Number 5. Mercury does not have one ounce of emotion in it, which tells us that it is truly a mental/intellectual passage that we are looking at here. Mercury or quicksilver is that quality of mind that will help sublimate our understanding of the right use of the sexual energy. It will wash out the sticky attraction of the zombie-like human, who has a distorted (animal) unnatural disposition towards his sexual nature. We have a choice, because there is a duality; we can be human or we can be bestial, but when the Number 5 is concerned with the intellect it has only one true aim; that is self-satisfaction and self-gratification. When the 5 seeks oneness with Soul, it will offer its gratification as part of a total commitment to love of the light.

In the 5 there is an attraction towards self-gratification in all ways, from the most basic, such as food and sex, right up to the more refined levels of the intellect, which even includes philosophy. One aspect of the 5 is being the 'high flyer', who can use his mind to explore new horizons without fear; on the other hand the 5 can procrastinate, because they fear that if they fly too high they may be disappointed in finding nothing more than what the intellect can offer. When a person has these qualities of the 5, combined with the strong love of music or science (these use the higher part of the intellect) they know they need to uplift and fly but they can be stopped by fear of disappointment. There may also be a sense of guilt, because they can see a picture or vision and know they are not as bright as that picture; they have a mission but feel they can't achieve it. There is another aspect of the 5 that actually remembers the song of the stars and so goes well beyond the intellect. It knows that it has to leave the preoccupation with the senses to be able to be an entire Soul; a Soul which can redeem the little misunderstandings locked in the cells of the body.

The Devil is a messenger of God; how much must this angel love God to undertake the task of tripping up his servants? This story from Job (Job 1: 6–22) holds the plight of humanity.

God was in heaven with his angels and he called them saying, "Look at the Earth, look at Job, isn't he a marvellous and great servant?" The Devil, who was one of the angels around God, said to God, "Wouldn't we all be great in his situation, for he has everything he wants. Everything he touches turns into plenty. He's the richest, the handsomest and the cleverest, so of course he's a good servant of God. He has no trials or problems and he is in a magical world, for you protect him and give him so much. If he were ugly and sick do you think he'd praise you? He'd curse you!" So God replied, "Okay then, go down and take everything he's got away from him, but don't touch him". Job was one of the high initiates who couldn't be touched by the attraction of power, so the God within Job was strong enough to say, "Come on then, if that is what I'm here for, thy will be done!" A servant of God understands that whatever is thrown at him it is nothing to do with him personally, so he remains bright and in love with God. If things are thrown at us and we realise what a liar or fraud we are, we should know that nothing we discover about ourselves is personal and love removes the weight of pretence form our shoulders.

How proud we are if we think that the world revolves around us! The whole of humanity is swimming in mud and so are we! We have been reincarnating on Earth for aeons of time. By raising our sight above the survival pond we can witness and understand our role in the scheme. We know we are bringing up the unconscious dark side of the Soul. Dark isn't bad, but must be seen for what it is, which is nature as it really is in its survival instincts, dirty and murderous. We have to understand that it is just a process that has to go on, until the last little bit of misunderstood instinctual behaviour can be re-united with love in the pure web of life. Why would we want to hold onto all these old habits as if they were ours? We take responsibility because we have done our bit of playing in the mud, but in the end it is just a process. If we feel shame, that is because we are proud and have difficulty in recognising that we took part in that process of degeneration.

The Devil is a 'fallen angel' and we are all fallen angels. He represents the time when man became conscious; this was the time when the sons of mind, who had got lost within the great dark sea of life, suddenly emerged and saw what they were. They had to associate themselves with what they could see. In their emergence into self-consciousness they realised what they were made of. The manipulative mind of Active Intelligence, before it actually wants to be the bride of the Spirit, thinks that it is all-governing; this is the pride element that man has to carry in his very fabric. On the other hand the appreciation of being aware of having used and been used, results in shame and this gives rise to 'man the scapegoat', who has to accept to be the servant and eventually the high teacher. That is the point in the Bible where the sons of man felt guilty and ashamed, because of their great pride.

We see and remember that we are here to do the work of God; to serve, witness and absorb. We are the only instrument that can actually transmute matter into energy, for the inner alchemy within the Soul of mankind is the secret treasure of sexuality, which brings light and dark together and transmutes the darkness into the fire of love for the truth; that is what this card represents. When we have the polarities of the higher and the lower attracting each other, sexuality and pride go together. Sexuality that hasn't been understood as being only a tool for procreation which can be sublimated into a tool for creation, just delivers pride. This is one of the main psychological problems for men and women; unease with their sexuality will deliver an inflated or deflated sense of self-worth. The only one thing we are here for is to understand that our world is an energetic system and that we are light transformers. To realise this function we have to understand the right use of the energy of light and become the alchemical vessels on behalf of the One who holds the task for the greater purpose.

We are here to understand the right use of the energy that calls and manifests life. If we believe the one world and the one life theory, then we must wonder what has happened in this world where there is right and wrong, left and right and male and female. Our lovely Devil has the symbol of Mercury as its sexual organ, to remind us that in truth all is one. True sexuality is the fusion of the receptive, active, loving God. We are equally male and female, for the mind is neither feminine nor masculine and we are the sons of mind. Men and women are excited by form as sexual stimulation, because they have decided that their intellect is either male or female; in fact the intellect is neutral – it is simply mind. It is masculine as a scientific computer and feminine as emotional intelligence, but it is only a neutral tool receiving programmes to equip the person for survival in their environment. When this isn't understood the intellect is completely at the mercy of lust, wants, pride and fear. When the higher mind is perceived by the intellect then we can observe the true inner sexuality, bringing us back to the one source.

We have to understand that we can make ourselves receptive, so as to receive the higher waters of life into the mind. The job is not to go and play with the mud, but to remember why we have played and to give out what we have understood to the ones who still think they are male or female and therefore do not know they are Souls. Once you live in Soul, the job of the intellect is to translate, through whatever medium, the understanding that polarisation into male and female is only a trick of the Devil. We are used by God to exteriorise the hidden side of his nature.

We then need to look at who we are attracted to, because this will show a hidden part in us that we don't really want to look at; here is the opportunity to see it crystallised in front of us. What attracts us is the qualities in us that we need to recognise; this is what we need to bring out. As a rule, the male or female shape that we are attracted to is dictated by karma and it is the hidden male or female within us. If it is hidden it could be because we are going for the brightest of the bright within ourselves, or the hidden aspect within us that we don't want to acknowledge. We exteriorise as very obviously male or female in form, because deep within us there is a problem with our masculinity or femininity, therefore our understanding and use of sexuality. If there were no problem we would come up as a mixture, like a dancer; not too muscular and with not too many forms bulging out. A true dancer would be somewhere in the middle, like Mercury.

Many young people are attracted to members of the same sex; this is a phase of development in sexuality where they are learning to accept self in a big way. All young adolescents need to go through a phase of falling in love with their own sex. This is healthy because it is about accepting their own gender. Once it is accepted, then it is not wanted any more and vanishes. It is important not to crystallise adolescent tendencies by over-reaction, because it is a normal process of learning to love the self and most do not explore the sexual side of this attraction.

There are other levels of relationship, where eventually the love aspect transcends the form because the people involved recognise themselves as Souls. Nature is a wonderful system that has made biological life possible, enabling us to be sentient and eventually become self-conscious. We came out of water; this is shown by the green scales on the lower body of the Devil. From a vegetative, passive sexuality, then a multitude of attempts, the God we live in was striving through Nature, to look at himself and ask the questions, "Who am I and where am I?". The answer was found through separation and sexual reproduction. This separation is what gave rise to the longing for oneness, the sexual urge and the fusing of two lives towards one romantic Sun.

The rut in the animal kingdom is not driven by the intellect, but by true group instinct; the phallus and the womb in action is pure instinct at work. Nature tells us clearly that it is an internal affair and is not about desiring the person you are with through the eyes or the senses, because the rut hasn't got excitement, desire or masturbation in it; it is not intellectual or sensual at all. We can't invent that, it is the stage reached when we have killed the intellect, which wants a good time through feeling all the strong sensations of pleasure and the excitement of role playing. When we have tamed the intellect and put it in its place and are truly in love, we go back to pure instinct. It is not a matter of getting rid of instinct, but bringing it back to its divine status.

It is the love aspect which can render the intellect righteous. Love teaches mankind to be righteous and that lives on for generation after generation. The attraction of the excitement of the intellect is not love any more and is seen for what it is – a bit of a waste of time. Righteousness means we are going to start respecting nature, respecting men and women and respecting the sentient part of the process. The feeling part has already had such a hard time of suffering; of being pulled right, left and centre; of being played with and used. We are used for a greater cause, so why would we want to go and use other people?

The minute we become aware and see life as black and white, we have to make a choice; it is either 'me' first, or the good of the group and the life on the planet first. We can't possibly know how the system works and then go and play with it again, because we would be adding to the suffering of the planet. Black magic is at its strongest when the choice to put our own needs first is made with awareness of the needs of the system. If we are aware and still continue with playing games, we should not leave it in the dark. We use all the manipulations at our disposal to play games all the time. Being ourselves is the aim, whoever we talk to and whoever we are with. Wanting to be liked and wanting to be seen is part of the game, but behind that it is really about being oneself, a Soul-infused personality.

People are kept locked in the intellect when, for example, they constantly read articles which say that flirting or masturbation are good for health. This keeps us locked in the intellect and just brings frustration. It doesn't bring pleasure, satisfaction, love or self-worth; all it brings is the need for more because we are not satisfied. It is experienced at the emotional level, because the intellect is not seeing what is deep inside us. It is not about being guilty, for until we have looked at what we need and want, we feel we are lacking. The answer to our need would be the same for everybody, a perfect man or woman in our life! We are looking for our other half like everyone else, but we get lost in thinking that it is pleasure we are after, because we are takers. We get lost and look for good sex, which is never satisfying without love; in the end it is self-destructive. What is behind the intellectual frustration and masturbation is the great lack that humankind has, because it wants to find its other half or the true pure male/female within itself. To be whole and complete is the outcome of the alchemy of fusion and transformation between Soul and personality, or between Spirit and Soul, according to the level of the initiation we are going through. The Soul is the true hermaphrodite, or the one that is male for the personality and female for the Spirit. This is why one of the representations of Christ is the five pointed star, which represents both mind and Soul.

We are karmically attracted to partners who exhibit the dark side of the thing we don't want to see. We have to recognise, truthfully accept and love this, because it is what we are. This is the fusion of our dark nature and our own inner light. Everything that we feel in true love with no chastising and no problems, fuses, heals, redeems and gives blessing. Most relationships that end in breaking up do so because the partners don't want to accept what they see of themselves within the other person; that is the side of us that we want to kick, hate, cover up and not see. When we recognise that we can transmute it and cut the karmic ties, then we either don't need to be in the relationship any longer, or we can be so grateful for the lessons that we can renew the love aspect at a higher vibration. On the other hand, when we leave without understanding that, we are even more bonded to our past, because we will meet it in our next relationship with a stronger message.

In alchemy we need to know that the sexual energy is there to be used for fusion, because we are on this planet to experience and fuse with our other half. In a life where we are visiting some of our initiations and are going for a rise in consciousness, we will all have to experience non-sexual times, when we withdraw from sexuality, voluntarily or involuntarily, to bring ourselves back to the virgin egg. This time of abstinence can be lengthy; it should last at least two to three years, which is enough time to internalise the fires of physical passion and to lose the need to relate physically, so that we can go back into our egg and go through the silent alchemy. Then the egg has to be cracked again and we have to start another life through sexuality and biology.

It is the love of the other, the forgetting of the self and the sacrifice that a righteous man would make for his partner, his babies or the group that would naturally drive him to become righteous and faithful. It is the idea of faithfulness that brings us into our alchemical athenor. This relates to the one-God principle, for we are all here to recognise that we are one. When we truly fall in love and we look at that person and know that they are us, then we have touched on Soul; we know that the self we see is a quality within us in which there can be some fusion. The true joining of two Souls creates a third entity of pure light, which is not tainted by need and is a pure gift of light to give to the world.

With The Devil, it is the pride of the intellect we are looking at more than anything else. We cannot get cleverer than the intellect, so be happy with it but not proud of it. Our downfall is pride, which makes us think that we are the best, the prettiest or the sexiest, because we are constantly measuring and evaluating. But we know that everything just 'is' so the only real purpose of measuring is to know the self rather than judging, becoming proud and being the 'biggest monkey'. We have to have justice so that we can give the exact measure, but it is not from our own point of view. It is important to develop the intellect so that it can serve us when we need to say something of greater value; it is the speaking directly from the intellect that is the Devil, for it is then that it gives excuses and explanations. It is so simple to see the truth, all we need to do is remember the original Trinity in us and then whatever we have just experienced will be seen from that point of view. At that point the light will be so strong that we see what we are doing straight away, so the intellect is not able to act in a 'clever' way (i.e. as a trickster).

In the Number 15 we are seeing life as being black and white; this means being completely aware, being real and knowing which master we serve. The Prince of the World, which is what this Devil is called, truly has had dominion over humanity up to now. We are not fighting him, because he is a real gift and he helps us to wake up. If we learn to love other human beings more than we love ourselves, then we wake up and become aware of how much we take out of life, rather than how much we give to it.

We become responsible to the Soul for what we see, do and feel, then in being responsible we give the response back to God. That means being receptive, open and truthful, so that we keep on remembering what we are here for.

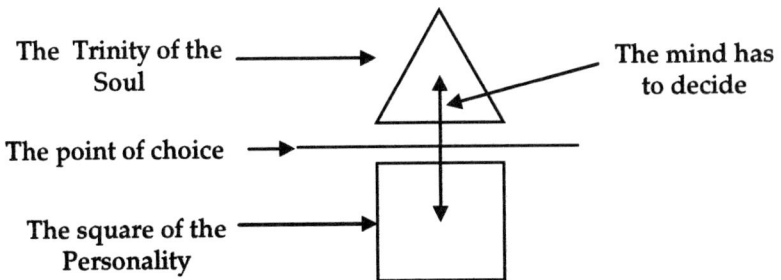

Figure 1. The point of choice.

We are going to have to make a choice, because we are in that mid line between Soul and Personality (Heaven and Earth). Purgatory (to give it its name) is truly an intellectual mind-set; it is the frustration and the rebellion against God because we really want to be down here, yet we are conscious that we are being used and we despise that. It is that place in the middle where we can't make up our mind which god we are going to serve. Being in that place brings up all the explanations and excuses of the intellect. If we stop these arguments of the intellect and accept that is where we are starting, then suddenly those excuses disappear, we have the connection, we have become receptive and can see from the point of view of Soul. That is the position of a black and white 15/6.

We are now in the gold or the Soul. From the point of view of the Soul we can stop the frustration. We can decide whether we want to be humble and we can remove all the emotional-intellectual mind-sets that will keep on making us want to play the game. If we love God enough it is alright to be a worm! No-one can *make* us love God; it is spontaneous because that love has to come entirely from within us. While the love of the intellect is strong we give more excuses, more psychology, more dogma and explanations, so the wall we build between us and our little God gets bigger and bigger. If we take everything personally we build a wall again; this is how the system works. We don't need to be squeaky clean; we just need to see the work done with no explanation or excuses. It is just the system so why would we want to excuse it? We might want to make excuses out of pride, but who needs an excuse to be a worm?

We have to become an individual in the best possible sense, to be able to take the responsibility to make the choice; that is the whole point of the work of nature going back to God.

This beautiful poem from 'A Man named David' by Dave Pelzer, describes the condition of mankind:

> All those years you tried your best to break me and I'm still here
> I make mistakes, I screw up, but I learn.
> I don't blame others for my problems,
> I stand on my own
> And one day you will see I am going to make something of myself.

This is the human condition, beautiful and simple.

We are being broken down so that we can bring out from within the depths of ourselves that determination to be nothing else but what we are. Let's be humble about pride, because we can see why some of us end up being proud, when over thousands of years we have had to fight our way up to a god that has to be taken over by a new mindset. Nature has to die every year and then she comes up again. That is painful and in being aware of it we suffer. Putting the intellect into mankind so that it can play the game of nature in disguise is the most cunning thing, for we wouldn't expect the intellect to be in nature. The snake represents that side of the game, because the snake has the reputation of being a cunning animal. Its true symbolism signifies the rising of kundalini. The intellect is part of the form body of nature, along with the emotions and the physical; we have promoted the intellect as a masculine quality, which it is not. Man sees himself as the master and as the Spirit, whereas the feminine is symbolic of form and therefore nature. Hence man looks to the intellect as a masculine quality; this is beautifully cunning.

The issues that we learn about the Devil are to do with power, despondency, structure, karmic connections, mutual addiction, financial and emotional dependency, sexuality, slavery and misuse of power. These represent the extreme crystallisation and materialisation of the things that are lost within ourselves and that we need to recognise, so they are put in front of us to seduce us. It is in seducing us that the Devil helps us find ourselves; he is a friend.

This card will only come up for us to face things from a long time ago, so it is a true karmic, spiritual work. We take full responsibility for the work in front of us, but it is as old as the world so why are we taking it personally? We are not the God of this world. The karmic work that comes up in front of us belongs to the group, to humanity. The only way to transmute darkness into light is to be at peace with the world. The love of the Soul is the only place where we can actually digest the karmic work by transmutation. The first step we have to be able to say is, "Yes I see it in me! Bless!"

The knowledge of this work of redemption is not something we can teach to others if we have not assimilated the experiences ourselves. We have to feel honestly that we understand how people can become rapists or murderers. It is the system that we serve and we are in the system; we have been there and we are still here. We are in the process of bringing light into the system, but because we understand the work we have to do, we do not work to get out of it because we know that the only outcome is fusion with the inner life; that puts us right back in it, so we know it is alright. Job didn't worry about what was thrown at him because he knew that it is the love of God that sustains this life, so it had to be alright. So whichever side we choose to work with, whether it is the side where we cover up our dark matter, or the side that sees it and says 'fine', eventually it happens spontaneously like breathing. We breathe without thinking, for it is completely natural; likewise because we take on the job of the willing Soul, the work becomes just like second-nature ...

When the Soul is clear, we are in the world but we can see through it, therefore it cannot attract us. We know whom we are serving and whom we love, we look at life and see it clearly. Once we recognise a thing for what it is, not only do we not want it but we don't want to play with it, because Soul has no time and no taste for playing with things. Rebellion, hatred and self-pity are still the game of the Devil and they keep us in healthy conflict.

Hatred, in the real sense of the word, is a tool by which we can cut the ties that bind. Once we have recognised, out of love, respect and righteousness, that we do not want the things that tie the heart and the mind then we hate them. They tie everything down to the lowest common denominator of selfishness, greed and pollution. Hate is not a lack of love but a way of cutting the chains that keep us in our protective nature.

Jesus the Soul spent his time in the company of prostitutes, down and outs and thieves. These people have had the courage to go beyond any barriers and lose their sense of proportion, in order to actually transcend the intellect and break the social structure of respectability. The Soul will automatically be present in these situations, as it does not answer to Caesar and it has to wait for the process of transmutation to happen. This will proceed when the intellect allows the Spirit to shine with respect for the laws of the land. As aware units in nature, human beings have had to give names to specific situations and feelings. Because it is an unpleasant experience we use the word prostitution for any act which might be degrading, or where someone appears to lower themselves; this culminates in our mind set that puts woman in the position of having a lower social, economical, spiritual value than the men.

Once we grasp how the system works, we begin the shift from the personal to the transpersonal. Between the second and third initiation there is a danger of going into black magic, because it is easy to serve the need of the intellect or pride. Pride is meaningless and all the other deadly sins stem from it. There are many ways that we serve the intellect and most of them are very sweet and seductive. That is why it is said that many are called but few are chosen, because it is hard to detect the tricks of the intellect. Once we finally understand the system and our place in the universe clearly, everything flows. It is simple: "*Understand and love; love and understand*".

The whole of life thrives on being at the edge of predictability and chaos; being at the edge is the only way to be. We won't go into illusion if we are living on the edge, because at the edge we always have to be aware. We shouldn't be afraid to take the next step even if it looks as though the ground will disappear, because so far we have walked and we haven't fallen farther than into our Soul. We need to recognise the fact that we rise up due to the presence of the Soul. The complexity of life, or chaos, is actually what renders biology adaptable and viable. Let's live at the edge to avoid crystallising the intellect into mind-sets that we hold onto, like 'I'm not loved', 'I'm a poor boy', 'I'm not beautiful', or "I am the best" etc. Living at the edge is where the Soul resides, between Spirit and matter. When the heart beats irregularly, it is healthier than when it is regular for with the latter there is habit and stagnation. Have the faith to be open with no security, need or want and go into the unknown. We have nothing to lose but our pride.

Adam and Eve were tempted by the Devil and so came out of paradise or nature. From that time the intellect was born and they were aware of being naked, meaning they could see into themselves and weren't covering up their intention. The story of Adam and Eve is not to do with their physical nakedness; it is to do with being able to truly 'see'. It is said that it was out of pride that they wanted to eat from the tree of knowledge, because the serpent said to them; 'You will be as Gods'. The warning is that it is in the intellect that the danger of pride would be exposed. All that needed to be part of the story, so that guilt and shame could be explored and expressed. The mention of pride would be a warning for mankind not to let the intellect preside as God, but rather as servant of the higher intelligence.

Whatever came out of nature came out of the intellect. If the intellect is self-serving it can only end up in pain and death, because that is the law of nature. We know that the mind as intellect is a slayer of the truth, but Nature cannot rise in consciousness unless it starts asking itself questions and for that we need a mind and an intellect. Unconscious happiness has no value! The actual awareness which comes out of nature in order to have the knowledge of good and evil has to be something beyond nature herself and beyond the intellect, if it is going to bring the message of eternity.

The animal within nature that could eat of the fruit of knowledge and be conscious of good and bad through the judgment given by the intellect, has its eyes open and will know, as gods know, what good and bad is. The snake, which is an energy rising from the subconscious, instinctive, passive, animal Soul comes into active consciousness and discrimination through the human race; it is all one great movement of energy. The snake represents the rising and beginning of the intelligence of the intellect; this is the cunning side of the intellect, which was needed and required and is the first coming out of the eternal wisdom in nature. The fall is what was required to facilitate the seeing of things for what they are. In the process of nature becoming aware through the sexual energy, there is the possibility of manipulation; this is where pride comes in. The problem with pride is demonstrated by the fact that human beings behave as though they are gods, who have the right to use and abuse the planet and don't respect life for what it is. There is no 'fall'; it is just the realisation that we are already down there. When we actually open our eyes and realise we are at the lowest possible position that one can be, there is only one way and it is up. If we thought we were somewhere else, it was just an illusion, we are only where we realise we are. If we fall we are just removing our rose-tinted glasses.

We put words and names onto our feelings, such as fear and anger and then through these veils we interpret what happens. If we can see behind that, we see it is actually not really fear, but just what happened at the time. There had to be a quality brought into the system that ensured that every single grain of sand was studied, so that not one pebble would be left unturned and un-named. We use the words 'cunning' or 'clever', but these are interpretations of how humanity sees the system tripping us up all the time. Actually the system is not cunning, for it does what it does out of necessity, so it is up to us to stop calling it something negative. It is a 'clever' system, in the sense that it enables us to go through the mire until the work is done. 'Clever' is not underhand but the intellect can interpret it as that, if it is lying to itself or making an excuse not to take responsibility. When we look at nature doing its work, we have to call it natural and clever. However, when we are talking about the initiate, cunning has to do with the Devil, for unlike nature we *are* conscious of what we are doing.

Thank goodness we trip ourselves up, because we all do things that are for self without really noticing it. We have tripped ourselves up so many times before seeing the fall for what it is and that is okay; it is of nature, for nature had to do its experiences so many times before it gave birth to consciousness.

God saw that creation was good and he had no problem with it. If God had doubted his creation and thought it was bad, then he would be a very odd, anxious God. God is telling us, "You are me, so go and do what you do and it is all good!" – We have to accept that. It is a cosmic joke, if we see that we are doing exactly what we have to do and we are loved for it, from the point of view of the Soul that has understood what it is doing and is laughing about the situation! We are being asked to be naughty boys and girls, so we are naughty and then we know that it is all okay, because it is the system that is asking us to do it. The problem is that we get lost in the laboratory, forgetting that we are only the instrument in an experiment on behalf of a much greater life and that we take ourselves too seriously.

When we can fully understand that we need to completely de-personalise the experience, we are automatically filled with love because we feel compassion for the suffering that those millions of lives are going through on behalf of the truth; there is no other way to find one's own source. Suffering is part of the process and is another word for experiencing. Nature is not aware that she is suffering; she is allowing the God within her to be one with her every single time she creates; that is all done in the dark and that is what we are re-tracing. We are going back into all that suffering, at the same time knowing that God is within us because he is working through us, so we actually become pure instinct. The highest intuition brings the person back into the purest instinct which is like nature, for the initiate is at one with his pure nature state.

If we want to be with the divine in nature, we have to obey the laws of nature completely; there is no way out of that, because nature is that part of the great life that knows how to crystallise and manifest. "As I feel, see, understand and love, I crystallise"; that is the natural process. The laws of nature are divine. The wise man knows that he has to get out of the need, want, insufficiency and survival of nature, but also be in nature and therefore ready to flow, dissolve and suffer. He is not there to take it personally because he is doing it as a witness. How else do we become systemic except by becoming a cell that sees itself being reborn and dying every five minutes?

It is through the door of The Devil that the initiate will have the opportunity to recognise instantly whether he is going down the path of survival, or on the highway to the top of the mountain of initiation. We should look, see and understand ourselves with honesty; this card says it very clearly. All our wants are coming back up, everything we've wanted we get and so everything that needs to be removed crystallises in front of us. After that, we go beyond the notion of good and bad; this happens once we have understood the system and are no longer using it for ourselves. The idea of good and bad is an intellectual mindset and truly doesn't exist. It is important to remember that if a person is not really on the path, going beyond the notion of good and bad is very dangerous. Intellectually it would be dangerous to tell people who are not compassionate and not responsible enough, that good and bad doesn't exist.

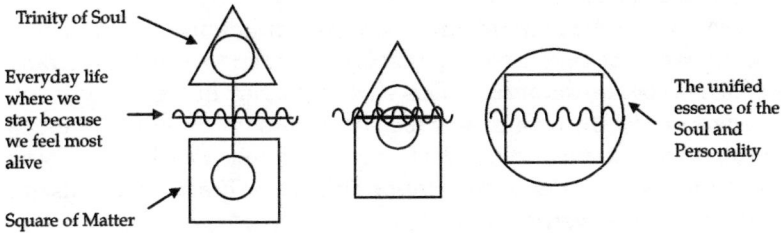

Figure 2. Personality and Soul becoming one.

The personality, as it rises to the Soul, opens up to the many reactions of its restrictive protectionism and we will automatically see and feel what needs to be transmuted. As the will of the personality gives over to the Soul, the two will become one and the will aspect, having merged with the higher intelligence of the Soul, will deliver a strong spiritual will. The Trinity of the Soul and the square of the personality will become one life. It is the process of unification and complete fusion within the Soul aspect that will allow the Spirit to eventually serve and guide. First we have to identify with the thing above us or the deepest thing in us, which is the Soul. Allow it to do all the driving and overtaking. It is as Souls that we live on the planet. When the accomplished Soul has done its saviour's work, all the qualities of righteousness and love fuse with the square of personality; then the separate entity that is the Soul is not needed any more. The spiritual will can then rule matter without harm, hurt, or explosion, because it is unified in the loving, serving qualities of the sacrificing Soul.

Spiritualisation of matter, which is the equivalent of bringing light into the darkness and rendering nature self aware and sacred, will happen over many aeons of time. Stubbornness, manipulation, being a trickster and the other negative qualities we put onto the intellect, are the equivalent to the earthing of an electrical plug and are therefore necessary safety mechanisms. If Spirit comes into matter without being earthed it would burn matter instantly. When knowledge, love/wisdom and the purest aspect of Active Intelligence are in place as a body in matter then Spirit can flow in.

The Soul has been able to earth Spirit through the resistance of the individual over many, many, lifetimes. Be patient, loving and understanding, because most of the resistance we see around us is about survival; it is there for the practical reason that Spirit can only fuse with matter by stages. Matter has to resist or they both would self-destroy. Spirit doesn't know, so Spirit moves; it is the Soul that knows.

We have to become feminine and masculine in turn, meaning receptive and active. Anything that is passive and suffers something cannot become responsible. This is why, as part of the experiment, we had to become feeling and rebellious. That is the beginning of a strong spiritual will, which can be visited by Spirit without burning up. When we take personal responsibility we become very useful matter for the experiment.

There is no original sin, if we think of sin as its definition by society. There is only ignorance and a lack of responsibility. The only true sin is against the Spirit and this can only happen when we are aware. It is the function of the stage of the 15/6 that man cannot sit on the fence saying "I'm only human". Having understood the two ways, the danger is that he will sin against his own truth; that is really what sin is. The true action is to uplift from within the personality that which is viable to the light, so that it can merge into the direction of the Soul. So many people under the influence of 15/6 will judge by material, professional and social appearance, but a true 15/6 ought to be able to appreciate the difference between social and Soul presence and therefore apply that measure to their life.

It is true that we do get lost, but we always have the chance to start again; this is what the little white star on the Devil's head means. It is there to remind us that if our actions are perceived as a condemnation to eternal damnation, we can always rise into the light, by making the choice in the 15/6 to recognise ourselves as sons of light and so take the path of redemption.

 The Star on his forehead is telling us that the Devil is under the domination of Spirit, so he is a servant of God. He can only do what Spirit tolerates, for he's the servant. He is that part of nature in God that is unaware and needs to see itself. In fact there is no duality, no conflict and no sin, just being in fusion and ongoing transformation. In the 15/6 the mind is at the culmination point of breakthrough to eternal wisdom, where it can become a midwife for its own re-birthing into a higher level of consciousness.

When we emerge from any of the initiations it is always very painful, because we are emerging out of mass-consciousness. It is like stretching skin which is so tied and enmeshed into fabric that we have to wrench it out. Mass consciousness is incredibly dense; it is denser than rock, it clings and clogs all the willing lives together, like black treacle to every unit it can touch, so we can't break it like we can break a rock. All we can do is push ourselves through and raise our perception above our needs, addictive habits, or emotional/mind sets that we aim to transmute. That density is part of our own body as well; it is all our yesterdays! This is the birth of births. One of Buddha's teachings is that when man looks for his future in the world of form he is staying a prisoner of sin (ignorance).

The Devil looks like a billy-goat; however, he has a star on his forehead, his wings are open and he has woman's breasts! He has the hermaphrodite sign of Mercury as his sexual parts and his legs are those of the goat. He holds a lighted candle in one hand and the Hindu symbol of the sexes in the other hand. The inscription 'Solve' is on the side of the candle and 'Coagula' on the side of the union of the sexes. He is on a pedestal which has three steps and there is a circle that holds two little fauns, who are making a sign and a counter-sign.

The blue square that he stands on represents his attachment to the 'fool's gold' of the possession and power of this world, which holds man prisoner through the structure of a strong intellect. A gold circle in its centre represents the wisdom of the ages tied into matter. He is the prince of this world of gold, money, wealth, position and power. His goat's legs show he is a man whose life has been limited to the pleasure of the senses, which is what most people strive for, whether it is fashion, work or holidays. There is something devilish in a civilisation whose main goal has to do with the type of pursuit that makes man forget his true purpose. Believe it or not, our vocation is not the research of pleasure, for seeking pleasure only leads us to death and nothingness. However, this is fair enough for even that is part of God. Most people wouldn't find it acceptable or easy to be told to look at their lives, as the choice has been made for them in mass consciousness so it has to be the right one! Most of mankind is very ignorant of his true nature. We can't accuse or condemn because we know it is happening the way it has to, for man has to become the result of his own projection; it is the awareness in him that will make him what he is. What we love and think today, we will be tomorrow, so everyone is made according to his own mind.

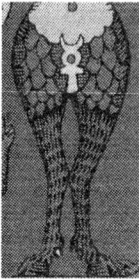

On the hips of his billy-goat's legs there are scales. Water is the first biological element from which algae, vegetation and animals emerged. The first primitive animals weren't very different from plants, they were driven by their nature, reproduction was simple self awareness was not needed. As the complexity within nature developed, there was the recognition that separation or polarisation in the process of reproduction would be the way in which units in nature could individualise, in order to become aware of themselves. It was only in man that the experience could become individual. His legs represent selfish gratification of pleasure. We have water as the matrix for life in the reproductive area, and then the form of the body exhibits the feeding, nurturing breast of the mother because it sustains nature in life and biology. The true nature of mankind has nothing to do with the body as male or female. The needs and wants of the survival instincts stay centred within biology, awaiting the rescue of the light of the Soul. The Soul is the sleeping princess for the man and the prince charming for the woman – the only true seeking of unification.

In the Devil's right hand there is a church candle. These are traditionally used for exorcism and purifying exercises, so when a candle was made they would have incanted a lot of prayer into it. Then when it is burned the flame would purify magically, because the words of the prayers would become the flames of purification. We have to use the purest possible candle wax we can find and do many incantations with it, so that it carries the strength of the Spirit, mind and will in it. The writing on the right arm says 'Solve', meaning dissolve; this is purification through incantation, which dissolves the form and so moves towards the light. This is liberation and absolution; it is like untying a karmic bandage. The symbolism of the candle here represents the will of the personality wanting to associate with the higher order over many lives. It has purified itself through many disciplines and religions, eventually giving itself up to the burning of spiritual truth.

The flame signifies liberation; it is like the end of time at the apocalypse. Purification is always done by flame and fire; the simplest symbolic meaning for a candle is the hope of bringing light into the darkness and keeping it burning forever.

In his left hand, 'Coagula' which symbolises crystallisation, is the opposite of 'Solve'. This represents everything that condenses, thickens and brings us back to incarnation, such as the union of the sexes. It is not just used here as a sign of perpetuation, but for the necessary karmic return, which continues until we have understood the cutting of the ties. This is about getting us free of needs and wants by forgetting ourselves. Eventually we can choose to bring light in and help with the purification of the world. It is telling us that through the union of the sexes and the right use of the sexual energy, the transmutation of matter (which takes us back to unity) can happen. The negative interpretation would be that with the Devil we can use the sexual energy to get what we want. This is a serious warning, yet it gives us the greatest hope that as we raise our will to serve the light, our love for others will grow and we will not serve ourselves. It is all about choosing who we serve.

Darkness is not bad, it only describes the state of living that is not aware; this is the unconscious. We know that we are transformers and transmuters of energy; also we know that it is the mind that directs and gives the power and the intent to our actions. Those who do magic are people who want to take rather than give. We are vehicles to transmute energy and nothing else. It is the mind that holds the power to put all our wants and intent into the energy that moves towards something or somebody.

For spiritual evolution and a healthy balance in life, mankind needs to be in a relationship. This is a healthier option unless we have chosen a life of asceticism; asceticism is fully accepted as it enables us to understand about mind over matter. Eventually we rise out of the illusion of form and so form becomes immaterial. The start of that longing for the rise towards realisation is in nature and therefore in mankind; it is about finding the other half. All our tendencies, possibilities and realisations are within us. Partnership is the best mirror for inner growth for it will show us what we admire and think we haven't got, or put us in front of needs that we have to internalise and transmute into Soul; also partnership puts us in front of what we don't want to see. We eventually learn to be active, receptive, protective and sensitive. In true relationships we each allow the other to fuse within themselves and help each other's realisation, without having to depend on the other for peace of mind. The right use of sexuality is on the one hand reproduction and on the other the sublimation of any attachment to the forms (senses) through the sexual impulse, so that the true union of the loved ones can happen spontaneously in the light. This is learning to die to ourselves, in order to fuse the inner male and inner female parts of the whole self.

The blue wings of the Devil tell us that he is a fallen angel of the Earth. The colour of mind is blue, so the deep, dense, blue of the wings represents the strength that the intellect has over the world, which is dogma and power rather than flight. He is the Prince of the world.

The Devil always offers us a choice between temptation and awareness. It is alright to be aware if we have been tempted, but it is dangerous when we have temptation and are covering it up, because then we are doing it under the bedclothes and it can become addictive. This is because we deny ourselves the will to be in charge, by letting the personality drain our light away. The Devil cannot become a Spirit of bad for he is only an instrument; he only acts to bring out the subterranean impulses of the subconscious.

The Devil has acquired power over the four elements; this is shown by the colours green, red, yellow, and blue. We have the choice to contribute to the harmonic dance of fusion between dark and light, so as to see the dark and light in ourselves and learn to love and accept them. In that acceptance we become humble. There is the other choice we can make, which is to sleepwalk into the blackness and enjoy ourselves silly. When we are conscious and still do this, it is an abuse of the power and a deviation. The rise in consciousness of the initiate is definitely not a guarantee of apotheosis or success, because there can always be a big element of pride that enables him to achieve this success, thus using the light for his own ends.

The card shows us two little fauns, or devils. They are karmically bound to all their desires, so that is why they are tied to the square. They represent all the passions of man and the natural forces that hold man chained to the Prince of this world; this is mass-consciousness ruling and keeping our noses in the absurd self-centred behaviour, until we start smelling the stench.

The little female faun is green to represent the generative aspect of Nature. The passion for life represents the mind moved by emotion, so the little male faun is coloured red. It is through the ears that we hear the voice of Spirit, so the little faun of passion has golden ears (representing the mind in mankind), which is why he is raising his arm to ask his personality body "Did you hear that?" He is starting to listen to the idea of humility, but the female faun is not interested and doesn't want to hear, for she is the generative nature within man which enslaves the passion, so that the cycle of life and death can continue. The passion within mankind could listen to Spirit and make it rise, but the generative, quiet, peaceful, motherly aspect of life chains us back into the everyday, ordinary life of form. Both fauns are chained to the cube, but because they are gold chains they hold some hope. Their feet are a golden colour, meaning that the fauns are attracted to material possessions.

'The unpronounceable name is the origin of all things; by fire nature is renewed in her integrity!' We have to consciously be willing to purify our needs and wants by fire, so as to be able to sustain the fire of redemption on behalf of the God we live in, as servants of the greater life. It is about the beginning and the end; combustion, disintegration and dissolution of the material form of the elements. When we go through alchemy, we pass through the burning fire of love, understanding and pain. In this way we bring back some of our material needs into our essential state and we can be at peace with that. Man can then recognise his true self and see that we are powerful creatures of fire, but the fire only remains as a potential as long as we haven't felt in us the burning of the transmutation, which renders us humble and selfless in service.

The Prince of darkness, or the Devil, is also called the adversary and the Devil's advocate. He is there to put questions in front of an initiate. It would be far too dangerous for an ordinary man to understand the idea that there is no sin, or no good and bad and that it has to do entirely with what we do and how we use the sexual energy; as either pro-creation, co-creation as sublimation, or self-gratification. The man, who has never been on the path, needs to have the blind faith of a child to make his first step. He can then go onto the next step, which has to do with a faith that seeks understanding. Then from there he can carry on beyond, until the intellect sees that it has to rise well beyond itself to meet the Devil; so he refines the understanding by releasing the grip that man's intellect has on his intelligence. Then he can dare not to be a slave to his proud and secure working out of the world. He has to give up the controls of the highest flower of the intellect to the intuitive, creative mind, without losing his ability to stand and use the amazing awesome knowledge that his research has produced so far.

The square represents this great structure of accumulated wisdom and knowledge that The Emperor is seated on in Number 4. The eagle in the square is looking for an up-lift; the Emperor has dominion over others for their own good. The blue cube that the Devil stands on is tied to this world, which includes all the intellectual pride that has been accumulated; it represents the myth of the fallen angel. Many high initiates fall back because they want to serve themselves; they want to be the best in the intermediary world of matter and so the pure world is secondary to them. They prefer to be first in the world of matter and forgo the world of light. The world of matter is intermediary because we are not all dense or unconscious, at the same time we are not supra conscious either, we are in the middle. The Devil is a clever manipulator and has dominion over people's weak wills. The Emperor also has dominion, according to the rightful development of humanity and not for himself, which is quite different. We will all go through the flame, time after time. The Emperor has the star and the moon of the hope of mankind on his coat and our Devil has the Star of hope on his forehead; he is telling us that we are stardust.

Number 8, Justice, also has a similarity to Number 15, The Devil. Justice, as divine justice is truth and is therefore the judge weighing up reality versus glamour and illusion. All we are being asked in every single card is that we 'will to be true', for without that willingness we are not on the path. The goal is unity and the way to achieve it is by truth, which always rests on love; we can't have truth without love, for if we see the system for what it is, we can only be in awe and love it. The initiate has to understand what he has been and what he really is, in order to free himself of the chains of glamour and illusion. When he comes back for new purification and transformation in the alchemical cauldron, his self-judgment will help him into more fusion.

The Devil is actually a great guy, as long as we look up with our 5 and know that when we look down we do so with love. That is all that is required for the 15/6 to be an angel. 'Bad' is an impotence and emptiness that wants to be soothed and complete. Life is an infinite expansion and to stay consciously in a world of conflict and limitation is to refuse the life within us. A conscious will that decides it wants the 'bad' is a suicide, because it has chosen limitation and frustration; that is contradictory to the eternal expansive life.

If a person exteriorises what he has seen of himself in rebellion, despising and hating the world, we know he still has pride that needs to be recognised. Pride after all, is only a strong spiritual will that needs to be translated positively into goodwill. We should watch ourselves to see if we are still rebelling or despising when we look at the world, for then there is still a little bit of pride. At every moment of the day we can operate a choice; this gives us the will to manifest what we want as we go. If we want to exteriorise Soul all we need to do is simply to be aware in love and truth.

The Devil holds the same posture as the juggler (The Magician), who holds the baton in the left hand of receptivity; with this gesture he is going for inspiration from the sky. The Devil holds the symbol of the union of sexuality in that left hand. The Magician applies and gives inspiration to the world with his right hand; the Devil has a burning candle of purification in his right hand, for he is an agent of purity and puts himself in front of everything that needs to be revisited. The hat of The Magician represents eternity and all the possibilities of materialisation that there are within the worlds. Those possibilities are contained in the etheric or astral fluid around life, which is waiting to be materialised. Most of it is going to be junk and the Devil is there to materialise everything around us so that we can see it. This is why life is the way it is, why we see what we do on the TV and read it in magazines and newspapers, for the Prince of darkness is forever materialising the thought forms of the mass-consciousness, knowing that the mass will want more of it. That is the power of the Devil; he is a friend because he puts us in front of ourselves. Another name for him is 'The dragon of the threshold'. His horns are the horns of plenty and everything that is of matter is crystallised, so he gives us the choice to recognise our humanity and feel compassion for the world, as we reject the values of the world of greed and want. In so doing we let the angel of our Soul overtake the scared little devils of the personality.

The Tower, La Maison Dieu
The road to Damascus

In the sixteenth card we see a tower being struck by lightning, the top is blown off and bricks are falling to the ground. A man wearing a crown is falling from the tower while another man lies on the ground near it, appearing to be dead. We all build such towers; they embody our beliefs, values and goals in life. It is when we are at the top of the tower and maybe at our most successful in the material world, that lightning may strike and our tower crumbles. This is the road to Damascus experience and so it must be, for Spirit to enter into the heart of man.

The experience of the cycle of Numbers 1 to 9 is the metaphysical luggage that the Soul has acquired, in order to face life again and work on the next level of letting go and cleansing. The initiate comes back and remembers the 'connaissance' of what he was born with and then it is at Number 16 that he truly faces all of that. We come back being aware and knowing that we are coming to take even more responsibility towards the life we live in. Then, in being responsive to the Spirit of the world and the Solar System, we can align completely with the work of co-creation that we have been blessed to do. This responsibility could have fallen on another species in nature, it happens to be the human species because our brain had the right makeup at the right time, to turn that little switch of awareness on.

Biology has enabled this process to happen in the mother or form aspect, which is the crystallising aspect of the God we live in. We are little points of crystallisation within which the incredible feast of awareness has been able to come through. There is a series of breakthroughs that happen as we go deeper and deeper into the biology of life. Then at the heart of that process the two 'lovers' (angels or energies) meet, in recognition of the brotherhood and oneness of the fire of God. When this has been achieved, we go back to the realisation that we are one.

At the stage of Number 6 the cup of experience is full. The Pope at Number 5 represents the psychic force, meaning the highest love of the Soul and the realisation that either the highest intelligence or the clever intellect can be in charge, according to which side the initiate loves best. Then in the experience of the 16 the maximum concentration in the psychic presence must develop. This comes after the passage through the Devil, where we have been faced with a lot to consider and have had to make a choice. After that the initiate can give his full force to where he goes and who he serves when the light comes in, for the Soul has to receive a lot of light from its higher intelligence, so as to win over the personality. At this level the personality can't attract the Soul any more, for the whole of the psychic or Soul life (represented by The Pope), is recognising the sacredness of life. When everything crumbles and the despair sets in, as the power of the love and light within the Soul breaks down the house of the personality, the little Trinity, which is the radiance and glow of the Soul, takes over. For that to happen we have to have a point of culmination within the psychic life with everything else crumbling, so that all that is left is the psychic strength, Soul, or the force, ('let the force be with you'). For this to happen we have to switch from doing the job to being the job; being the Soul.

From Number 10 to Number 16, we can see the force of God developing strength and willingness within the personality, so that it can go along with full acceptance and obedience. In The Hanged Man at Number 12 we see any needs that we may have, so that we can let go of them. Through this letting go we are rendered completely passive, but it is an active passivity, not the passivity of nature. Then we give back the gift that is in us to the energy that gave it to us. In time we understand that all our actions, thoughts and attempts at creativity will be weighed up for what they are and given to the Soul within us; The Tower at Number 16 is really going to make that very clear. A level of consciousness coming from all the aspirations within nature and represented by silver energy is being shifted right into the gold of the Sun, which is the Soul. Only once this real rise is done can we act from the purity of what is in the Soul; this gives us the complete inner knowledge to trust and give ourselves to the highest. We can understand this process in principle, but everyday life puts us right back into our mindsets and emotional behaviour, because we think we have to survive. It is from this point that we learn to have obedience, acceptance and balance. This is the bliss of being in the middle and witnessing what is happening.

In the process of the 14 (Temperance) we finally said "Thy will be done", then there was the big shock of meeting The Devil. The Devil is the pride of the intellect wanting gratification and to be seen; the intellect has been resisting the Soul from the beginning of time. The intellect is the shadowy masculine side of the nature principle. While the receptive manifesting nature is checking the viability of the next stage of fusion (loving and accepting), all it can do is reflect the uncooperative stage of fusion between nature and Spirit; this is perfect in its unfolding.

It is always to do with mind. If we accept that the whole of creation is a crystallisation of thought and movement, then all matter is just an arrangement or a crystallisation of the picture that the mind wants to see at the time. The problem is that we fix the image and then project the total value of life as we stand, onto the image and take it for gospel, instead of understanding that it was yesterday's point of view. Because the image is a structure, we either hang on to it or rebel against it. The image or crystallisation can be anything, such as social structure or religion. It is the whole of the edifice that humanity has built from the beginning of time in order to survive. At the end of the day when all the work has been done, it will be a world in which all the intents and thoughts are pure. There will be no need for action, because there will be no need for crystallisation; anything that is crystallised at the time will be transparent. Transparency happens when the thought, the action and the thing that is being used are one. This doesn't mean we can't see anything. Look at a tree for example; it is transparent if we look at it without needing anything from it. If we look at anything that is naturally not sinful because it hasn't got a choice, we can see it is transparent. All the time we need to use nature beyond the natural survival or common sense, we muddy the waters of our rebirth.

Transparency is when we don't need, want, or do anything for ourselves beyond the obvious survival of the biological life. There is no other aim or intent but to act within the great law of economy within nature, with respect for its creator. It is when we become transparent that nature becomes transparent. So when all the levels of experiencing the needs and wants have been uplifted into the heart of selflessness, the light from the top of the head flows through the instrument into the heart carrying love and respect into nature or the Earth. We become one flowing chakra, channelling spiritual energy into the matrix of the Earth within its own karmic sacred geometry.

The transparency will come from the retrieving of all the ways of nature that are trapped in the dark, for nature doesn't know itself. The work of all the aspirants, disciples and initiates is to accept the deep mining work of the revisiting of the subconscious. The subconscious holds humanity's misunderstanding of the unconscious of nature. When this work is completed we will not have the deviations of needs and wants that are everywhere at the moment, because the subconscious will be clear and respect will rule in the highest sense. This is the means by which our planet will become sacred and it will happen once we have answered the questions "Why do we do ourselves so much harm, why don't we love ourselves? Why do we hold onto bricks and mortar and mindsets instead of allowing God to come into us completely? Why do we hurt our brothers and the Earth?"

Being at complete peace with the cycles is the way that nature renders service to Spirit and allows the life and death cycle to take over. At every cycle there is a hope; we touch that hope with The Star, in Number 17. The hope is that we will eventually be at one with the love. When we go through self-development, we let that part of us that is living through our mind and emotional sets die many times, just to get a bit nearer to our inner life; this is nature in us accepting that this is the way. It is only through the experience and awareness of what the suffering is that we gain the complete acceptance and obedience of the process. Through the suffering we will actually be able to feel which phase of the process we are moving into and how and what is happening, so as to name it. This process doesn't come from the senses or the intellect; it is entirely internal and tells us what type of burning we have to do. It is true sentiency. If we can recognise what is happening we go along with it, it becomes second nature and ceases to be suffering. It is well when the work is done, but then something else comes up that needs to be cleared somewhere else. Many of us will have been doing this clearing at the emotional and mental levels, but when it appears in the body we need to see it as refinement.

There is no other way for Spirit to be able to realise the space it is in and therefore be itself, except to go into the heart of matter; this releases all the blocks and as they crumble we suddenly think, "Where am I?" We feel we are everywhere and nowhere; this is because our tower is crumbling. Spirit is shining the light on to every single locked-in memory, so as to find the pearl or diamond within. At the very heart of the biological being in each one of our cells, there is a world of wisdom wanting to be at one with the love aspect; this is the deep work that is offered in Number 16. The 1 (the movement of the light) comes into the heart of the cup of experience of the 6 and fuses with the wisdom within; this is the process of the 7.

We had a choice in The Devil (Number 15) and that choice is going to manifest an outcome here in Number 16. Whoever has been the king at the top of the tower has had to internalise, because he had to go into it so as to get to the top. The man lying on the ground is dead and represents one of the outer material values that are being destroyed. He is outside the tower and so represents the intellect in mass-consciousness. Here all the glamour and illusion is seen for what it is and in the clear air it all collapses. At the level of Number 16 we have to really touch on the inner life, because if at this point we haven't learned to internalise at all, we will just follow the way of nature with its cycles of life and death and our consciousness will be in the dark again. The dark is where the potential is held, ready to give birth to itself. Internalising means that we bring back everything we think, feel and experience to our inner self, to be understood, loved, weighed up and processed. It is the beginning of accepting and not blaming the world any more. At the phase of the 16, when the inner life is taking over, the initiate will offer this clear mirror of acceptance to others, so that they can recognise it in themselves.

The bricks and stones of the tower represent all the mindsets we use to build the world in our image, even thinking we are a man or a woman; even the fact that we can help people is a brick. They include everything we have thought of so far, this even includes our concept of ourselves as Soul. It is all an edifice that we have built and continue to build. Once we have gone in and climbed up to the third level of The Tower, we have accumulated a lot, have taken many risks and have an awful lot of our aspirations worked out; in fact we stand very solidly in society and in the world. We might be in an ivory tower, but we are in the World so we have a whole set of inner and outer principles from which we guide our lives. Then in order to go beyond our own personal principles, the structure we gave ourselves has to be broken down. We have to remember that we have done exactly what was required, so it is not the end of the road, but the beginning of the new life.

At the beginning of that new life we realise that we are at the top of a tower which isn't of much use, because it is based entirely upon our own personal building up of what the kingdom of God is; this can be either a scientific understanding or an artistic expression of God. Both of these are man-made, so the question is "How do we serve the greater?" What the falling man in the picture has done is not wrong, for he has reached the top of the golden tower and gold represents purity. He had the right intent and he internalised, because he wanted to meet and serve the divine in him. He wanted the best possible action according to his belief, so he went for it; he took risks, he internalised, he climbed and he had to go through the darkness. The tower has two little windows on the first floor and only one on the second floor, so it is darker towards the top; this is because it gets darker before the breakthrough. He went into the darkness of the night of his Soul and then suddenly he gets to the top, coming out as near to the Sun as is possible where he is blinded by the light. He realises, "My God, I don't know a thing, all that underneath me is useless". He thinks it has all been a mistake, but he has to accept that it has been useful in the past. It is truly a redemptive card, because at this point if we look at the way we made our mistakes we know we did our best. We can't take the right road straight away, we have to go and retrieve all the ways that didn't succeed before; that is our job.

The whole of nature has the true desire to reach and go beyond itself, especially when it becomes aware in humanity. When we are really working with this desire and find that we have made a mistake somewhere in the past, we have to go back and remember where we went wrong and see it for what it was. This mistake can be seen as a failure in nature, or something that just hasn't worked. It is actually not a mistake, because we did our best at the time and we had to relive the experience on behalf of nature. The mistake was made out of ignorance in order to redeem ignorance, but because the desire and the intent was pure and came out of wanting to go beyond the self, then when that illumination comes, a total change of condition in our life is experienced. Our aims change completely; everything that was of the past crumbles and all the accumulated mistakes to do with the specific thing that allowed us to build our tower, are abolished practically overnight by the fire of divine love within us. This fire is the lightning and when it has struck and reached that point of divine love deep inside us, then all the things that were mistakes are purified and seen as necessary experiences.

What makes us persevere in hiding the truth is pride. The main quality of pride is that it doesn't want to bend and admit ignorance; it would rather ignore the obvious. Any mistake we have made isn't wrong, but to carry on making the mistake can be destructive. When pride releases its rigidity it becomes spiritual endurance and humility, which is the stuff of sacrifice. We can see why it is so rigid, because from the beginning of time we have had to measure ourselves all the time, in order to survive the passage into the individual personality and then into the individuality of the Soul. We have had to persevere and hold on, as our little house or tower falls down and crumbles in front of us. We thought the values that we held were worthy, when they were not even registered in the big picture. The intellectual spiritual pride asks, "Am I going to allow myself to become nothing, when I thought I was a child of the divine?" We thought we were the favourite son or daughter and now we know we are not special at all, but does it really matter? The more conquests, knowledge or qualifications we have, the easier it is to be taken away from our true selves. Pride comes before a fall; it is a necessary thing. It is the one ingredient that enables nature to bring in further evolution, just as love/wisdom brings in everything else.

Here in Number 16 we are truly in an initiatic teaching. An initiation brings us to a point of crisis overnight, because it is that realisation that makes us fall on our knees; that is the crumbling of The Tower. Of course we have got many other towers to crumble, but at least the one where we were holding loads of emotional mindsets about situations or people has crumbled; it is the mental fusing with the love aspect that does it.

If we look at even a small experience, it is important to remember that accepting that experience fully is the way to rise in consciousness. We can look back at our lives with all the people involved – father, mother, partners and friends – and realise that everybody did their best. Once we do that everything crumbles. We don't even need to forgive, because that realisation from the mind coming into the heart melts any negative emotions from the past.

The 16/7 asks us to internalise our experiences and use the distilled wisdom in service to others, this is the true choice. If we go down into mass consciousness nobody is cross with us, because that is life. If we want to wait in mass consciousness that is fine, but if we are going to make the choice of internalisation and use its findings for our own purpose and yet haven't got it in us to be selfless, then the 16/7 in us moves into self-destruction and automatically goes back to nature. Mass consciousness follows the laws of nature and is driven by wants, needs, false sexuality, a false sense of values and a false sense of love. There's no blame, we just have to rake through the bottom of the pond.

Sin comes in when we know about the process of exploring the darkness, have no guilt and use that knowledge for our own ends. Even if we have a tiny ounce of knowing better, it is a sin to carry on because then we are doing it for gain. It is so important to give back to God every ounce of creative sound in the building of our castle and that only happens when we have total despair. Total despair has got to be the end of it, or we die. When we see that the whole of our life or lives don't make any sense, from our mind, to our heart, to our body, to everything around us, then we have seen the light. However, we don't really know what we are supposed to have seen, all we know is that we are crumbling. We are walking on quicksand, our mind is blown; our intellectual and emotional cogs burn out, simply everything is blown apart. We have fallen and everything is gone and is falling on top of us. All we can do then, amidst our weeping and screaming, is to listen to that little voice inside. There is the presence of the true God in us, because that is all that is left; everything else is shattered. There is the "I'm still here", which is perseverance; there is the love-wisdom aspect and the Active Intelligence aspect, for nature has survived for millions of years. But be careful, many will go into that state and stop the complete breakdown through the emotional self-pity that is often induced by medication or narcotics and start building The Tower again.

We are talking about a high initiation here; this is a stage where we really truly let go and break down the house of matter. We break down the idea of wanting still to be in charge (which comes from the intellect) and wanting to explain the world, or even wanting to understand that the world is of The Tower. Through that breaking down we have 'connaissance', the birth of deeper knowing. Once we allow the Spirit to flow in, meaning the life we lead really putting us in front of ourselves every minute of the day, the light goes straight into the heart of matter and we can deliver the true wisdom or knowledge which is locked in all of us. This knowledge is unique to each one of us, for there are no two individuals on this planet who will have the same set of biological treasures, but expressed and put together they will spell the same wisdom, which has been stored in our bodies since the beginning of time. When enough pools of wisdom shine in the darkness (whether in an individual or a group) then they become good lightning conductors for intuitive knowledge. True intuition is when we let the light go right in, exactly where it is needed so it can bring out the wisdom. This is intuition, which comes from the heart of matter where the light of Spirit has reached home.

Most holistic therapies work by retrieving subconscious stuff which is to do with the conditioning of life, such as psychology, philosophy and the whole business of survival, but the unconscious heart of nature is where true wisdom comes from. Techniques which are devised to help people deal with the shadows of the subconscious are probably part of the gold bricks at the top of the tower. The true purpose is to let the light come straight into the unconscious and find the pure instinct again; this is transparency. Once we understand pure instinct we can purify our own mass consciousness coloured instincts and we never need to do a deviation again. Pure instinct is nature in its perfection and will always bring out and show up the subconscious as behaviour patterns to study. So let's honour the subconscious, because we haven't finished the work yet; there's still plenty to come out. Pure instinct doesn't need survival, for it has survived already and all the time it is needed it will be there.

We were able to survive in nature by being the biggest male, the one who can procreate the most, or the cleverest female. This was a selection process within every species that was capable of handling the task of adaptation. If we really understand that process, there is no problem in going back to nature. In the mass consciousness decay is allowed, just as in nature we have to have autumn and spring coming round again and again. The process is extremely generous and it will wait until the last one goes through. Every tiny cell in the body has to be lightened up; some of us would like it to go a bit faster, but even that desire is another brick in the tower.

Talking about world peace and wanting good for the world, is really only about learning that we are just channels. It is good as an exercise and brings out a lot of good will, but eventually we can't even wish good for the world because we know that the world *is* good so we just watch it happen. Anything else is interference, which is good and fine, because we are allowed to interfere and make our own mistakes. Sometimes we know we have to interfere. For example, if somebody falls and they can't get up, we don't just tell them it is karma and walk away; we help. That will touch them and melt their heart, because somebody came to help them, then they will help somebody else in the same way. We help because it brings people together in the hope that eventually we will understand that we are channels of light. It is part of the moving on, just as being a therapist or a teacher is part of the great movement. Eventually however, whatever edifice we have built for ourselves crumbles. This crumbling is not necessarily material or outer; at the level of the initiate it is a spiritual crumbling, for the Tarot is a tool for initiates. We are looking at the 4th initiation here, which is a very high one, so when the veil is torn there is a spiritual crumbling. Numbers 12, 13, 14, 15, 16 are all part of that process of the veil tearing. Every time we put a little belief into what we do, that is a brick. Nothing is ours, we don't own a single movement, a single action, a single situation, or a single piece of knowledge; nothing is ours, even time and space. At one point time and space is all we have left and at that level it is a real headache, because we know that time and space is a mindset as well. It is not real, but it is needed because our minds are learning the most important lesson, that we are consciousness poised in balance in the collective mind set of time and space. Consciousness was only created so that it can measure and recognise itself; the measuring takes place in order to know.

From the point of choice we are dying to one level and are going to pass through the sieve, after that we have to decide which way we are going. Whichever way we are going we either fall, or die and then start again from the very beginning. Our King is starting a new life and he hasn't got a clue what that new life is made of. Let the dead bury the dead. The kingdom of heaven doesn't belong to the lukewarm and everything we are looking at is the opposite of lukewarm.

There is nothing else but living at the edge, for all life is risky. If creation has come out of the chaos into some recognised order, its basic structure still vibrates with the great chaotic universe, because life lives at the edge. Biology and nature are always living at the edge and death is round the corner every second. The whole of biological life is so fragile, it is amazing that we don't recognise how near to the edge we are. Once we do realise that, we understand that the only way to live is to drop what we think we are, because we will be what we think, according to which chaotic material there is in a situation to manifest the picture. We need to stop thinking what we might want to be tomorrow, just be and say "I'm the Soul!" Being cautious and protecting ourselves by not taking risks is the worst thing that a human being can do. However, if we are cautious because of the wise understanding that what we are going to do has been done before and it didn't go anywhere, then it is the caution of the wise. This is like The Hermit who checks his inner light before he makes the next move. Let's be a true fool of God and have a true light, not just recklessness or talking without thinking. There is a fine line between protecting and being wise; that line is reinforced by the fact that we know that if we are going to go for the risk, we will crumble. So the 'double-protection' aspect does come up.

Going forward has to do with shedding more and more until nothing is left but that incredible, little knowing thing inside that knows that it is Soul. That is all we are, so when we are in the middle of despair we can allow that knowing part to have a voice. A lot of us listen to the despair and don't find that voice; that is why we have to be plunged in again and again, going down even deeper to find it. If we try to understand rather than giving up to God, we use the intellect and stop ourselves touching the light in us, so we don't go into the true knowledge and true wisdom.

All this does not mean that we shouldn't understand psychology as a study of the psychic life of mankind, just as science does for the physiological life. If it is the task we are working on, it is important and mankind needs to do it, but we should remember that it is The Tower. We are the scientists, the artists and the philosophers, so if there is a great need to go and fathom the layers of how it works and if eventually the understanding does not satisfy, then give it up to God and know that it isn't what we are looking for any more, it is just what is needed in that stage of evolution.

Absolutely nothing is ours; even our life belongs to somebody else, so we don't need to keep on playing with it through fear, caution, or pride. We can give up the great drama of our emotions, needs, or wants and give our life back to the great life whose body it is; it is a simple as that.

We call Number 16 the mirror, the good counsellor, or the healer. Self-destruction comes from a need to be loved and to love. There is nothing else in nature other than wanting to reach the ultimate wellness. The striving in mass-consciousness to go through the dramas, sensuality and the intensity of experiences happens because we think all that is going to bring us more love, more pleasure, or more God knows what! If we do not internalise these, then we just want to receive it all rather than give. A lot of people give because they know it is the way they are going to receive; that is not the right sort of giving, but it is one of nature's ways so it is alright. We should check ourselves, see what we are doing and know ourselves. We need to give our sensuality up to God.

We have nothing to answer to but the light in us; it will never blame or judge us. Remember we have to go through all the mistakes, for it is the only way our body (as a crystallisation of the great project of self awareness) can actually vibrate fast enough to fuse again into the light of its creator, so as to make life whole again. It is the only way – the mind has to rise out of nature to bring light back into the cup.

We cannot become aware unless we start suffering, which means being aware of what is happening. We might have needs, but we have our being in a greater life that has its own agenda. Those that truly understand this from the depths of their heart become very tolerant, wise people and they know that it is only through doing it wrong that we eventually do it right. The danger is that we keep doing it wrong because it tastes nice, or because we like the drama of pain; this is addiction. We have to be honest about who we love and what we do. The God we live in will never blame us for loving, even if you 'over love' something.

Workshops will never give enlightenment, but there are millions of people on the planet going for workshops on this subject. If a guru hits us on the head and we see the light, it is not because he's got the light in him, but because at that time we were ready for the light. It is only in the dark space of our own tower that we find the light. Biology will take precedence, meaning our behaviour, wants, needs and intellect will win, until the light touches our centre. It takes a long time for every single cell to turn to the light. It happens when the intellect understands and the emotions are tamed by turning towards the inner will, then the personality is aligned and the Soul can be felt. There is a big part of the Soul which belongs to the Soul of nature; this causes confusion in us, so we start working hard at doing good deeds, in an effort to clarify our identity. It is the inner process of being completely loving, trusting and understanding which will eventually remain with us and get encoded into our causal body. Then when we reincarnate, the causal body supports the physical body and the inner process, coming up to the surface more easily over time.

There is no way anybody can do the inner work for us; it has to be sought from within. If love, truth and trust are not completely part of our biology and if we do not vibrate and 'give in' to those qualities entirely, then we know it is not happening. There is a point where energetically we have reached the top of The Tower through our own effort and then the time is right for a lightning bolt. We are not clever enough to go up the ladder to God by ourselves, for it is a long process. To get to the top of The Tower we need to have spent a lot of lives in the dark, as well as some in the light. We have to trust that we are going to reach the gold at the top. We have done a lot of work to prove our endurance and faithfulness, we have called for that light and energetically it has come. So now 'my will' is replaced by 'thy will be done'.

When the Soul dies, there is no more need for experience, because all the wisdom has been given out. Biology holds the qualities of Soul which we have to decode; these are the subconscious and unconscious of nature. Pure instinct is the intuition of nature. True inner work has very much to do with the fusing of our own inner light with our physical bodies, so that every single little element in our makeup aligns to the will and understanding of the love in our Soul. We feed our body with the light of the Soul; this is what sustains life. If our Soul decides that the body is dying, it doesn't matter how much food and oxygen we pump in, we are still going to die. Behind the Soul is the will of karma giving us the experience that is happening at the time.

When we go back to pure instinctive understanding, there is no more need to undergo further experiences. Nature has been made pure and the subconscious and unconscious are in the light, so the Soul, which was the mediator or healer and the one that does all the work, doesn't need to be there any more. We can only attract what we need, so our elemental body needs to be decoded, made peaceful, seen for what it is and completely brought into the light. Once that is done, the fusion has happened and the matter has been made sacred; then the Soul can disappear.

It takes many lives to come to the point of crisis, which is the complete 'U' turn of a major initiation. After that we will still have a lot of cleansing to do. We are breaking through to something new and different, so it is like the birthing process. When a baby's head comes out it doesn't mean the baby is an adult, but it has come out.

True inner work is the infusion of the thing which has been learned, understood, loved and accepted into the whole of the personality and the biology. It is being rendered transparent and it is only life's experience that does that.

The initiate feels despair when he realises that everything that he has learned and done so far is worthless. However, this realisation opens up the space to allow the greater life to flow through the instrument, which then reaches a state where it does not do anything but just operates with pure thought and pure action. True insight, which is beyond intellectual understanding, begins to trust intuition. We might not be able to explain what we see, but all we need is to perceive it, because that is a level of acceptance that is permanent. At this point we say, "By the grace of God" and start obeying.

The lightning is an intervention. We have put ourselves there at the top of The Tower, in a state of wanting to know God intimately and be nearer the light. We have made ourselves into such a strong instruments for invocation, that the light actually comes and blinds us. We get a bolt from the blue, which is a totally unexpected. After building our tower we expect bliss and "Well done!" And wham, our world disappears, we disintegrate, we – who is 'we'? Little did we know that fusion of the higher mind of our Soul with our instrument meant explosion! We wanted it, now we experience God as a terrorist. Shall we give up?

It is an energetic world; it is one life and we are a cell in a system. If we ask the light to come down we are going to get it, because we created the intervention. This is where we have to be very careful with our spiritual pride and need to ask God to intervene for us. If we have been working on ourselves, we get so used to knowing that it is from within, that when we get to the top of our tower we forget that a bit of lightning can give us a new lease of life. This is the point where we have done the inner work so well that we are ready to receive; at that point our tower has to crumble. We don't know what the next part of life holds and it is just as well, for if we knew we might think twice about going forward!

This is one of the most illusory cards. The mirroring effect is about removing shadows, so the inner life is becoming more important than the outer, but at the same time the outer is feeding the inner because we have to build the tower. What we do in the world has to be brought back inside us, but we expect the outer life to tell us how our inner life is doing and that is not how it works. A realised 16/7 has completely given up caring what other people think of them, because they know about internalisation and they are going for it.

At this stage we do not get our self-worth through seeing how good, clever, or beautiful we might be because we know it is 'as above so below'. We know that what is inner has more light, even if it is the dark light of not truly knowing where we are, because this is more true than what we see out there. A lot of 16/7's will rely enormously on the mirror of the world to tell them who they are and that is when their pain comes in, because it means they are out there in the world and not in The Tower where they should be. All the time we are talking of the 'who I am' from without (which is the mirror effect) it is quite painful. If we need the world to see us as wise, clever, brave or whatever, that is spiritual pride.

All speech is of the past, for there is nothing that can come out through the throat that has not been there before. We may have said it differently or the content may have changed, but we can only see the things that are already there. Speech is still very much of matter, for it is formulated by the intellect so is very restrictive. However, speech is a sound pattern and we can give things another angle through it, enabling the pattern to be recognised at an energetic level. If we bring in a silent sound, this is knowledge which we can keep forever from life to life, for this silence is a memory that has been digested. It is a result of transmutation and the process of digesting God. The light has gone in and been infused with personality and biology.

The trial by The Devil is what strengthens us, for we have had to make a choice to be able to go on to the next stage of The Tower. Every time we come into incarnation we build mind sets so as to make our way in the world; then those mindsets have to be dissolved. The notion of an ideal world is based on some romantic, emotional idea having translated the ideal of inner peace into the comfort of some loving arms; this is a remnant of natural survival. The unconscious aspect in nature seeks the ideal world, where nobody eats anybody else and everybody is happy, but that is so static and neutral that it couldn't sustain itself, for something that doesn't transform cannot live. We have to see nature as ideal for the work it has to do. The more deprived we are in the art of accepting and giving, the more we will seek an ideal world.

The Tower is made of pride. Pride is the first by-product of awareness. The minute we are aware, we have to start weighing up everything that is around us according to where we want to be in that situation; that is pride. It is pride to think we have control over anything, but on the other hand we can't have awareness without pride. If we suddenly recognise that somebody has pushed us, or taken something away from us, automatically pride sets in at that moment because we are saying "This is my life, you are not going to interfere with it and I have got to survive here". This is because we really think it is our life and think that we have dominion and control over it. To think we have control over anything is pride. We have organised society and children from the beginning of time into achieving by being proud of them, so it is part of awareness and striving towards something we see as being better, whatever that is. Pride has to be there for awareness to be born, so it is not a bad thing. It is pride rather than love, when a mother and a father look at a child with a warm glow when the child has done well. Pride is the ingredient that has allowed our little species to build its tower of Babel. It is like a tower of bubbles and is constructed out of the incredible yearning we have to go beyond ourselves. That has been going on from the beginning of time, for it is the one necessary ingredient which enables the species to go for the exploration it has to do. Without pride we would not care, or we would not want to know what the sky is made of. Pride gives us the desire to know the greater thing, because we think that knowing will bring us nearer to it. It makes us want to excel and go further.

Pride is the best gift we have. It is a great gift to be proud of one's tribe or one's nation, but the true gift is the life we have been given. Pride is what has given us awareness, so it can be recognised as a tool or an instrument. The Devil is the one who shows us that without pride the process doesn't happen. Without coming back into reincarnation, crystallising, looking at ourselves and the world, dissolving and coming back again, there is no awareness. Awareness comes in as we strive to create all the biggest castles that we want to build.

Pride and ambition are part of the same thing; to be proud of one's behaviour and to encourage ambition in reaching for the sky, are good things. The trouble is that we have eventually to get rid of them because the process has really nothing to do with us, but it is the Spirit in us which pushes the instrument further, to discover more about itself. It is always ourselves we are seeking; we are looking for the inner lover, the inner sound, the inner voice and the inner life. Before we can find it, we have to explore things on the outside because we can't recognise the inner unless we see its reflection. We have to go back, not just into the womb but into the whole of the pre-womb matrix, to see and feel what was happening there.

Pride is only removed at the last level, when we are full of light and the veil is torn. We shouldn't say pride is a sin, because it is not, it is part of the process of aligning the personality. We have to do all types of things, like looking for our self-worth, but then there comes a point where we have to break them all down little by little, so one tower after another is broken down. In this card we are looking at the ultimate tower where we give it all up. This process could very easily be interpreted as inaction, inertia and false pride. Even when we think the sky is going to open and all will be revealed, we still have more stages that tell us that we still have to do more. When we read about initiation we will find that it is at the fourth initiation that the veil is torn; it is then that we see that nature is pure and that we are not yet transparent. It is only at the 6th initiation that all the illusions have gone, so even when we are not actually incarnate in matter, we (as a consciousness) still have an illusion about what is.

When we are truly striving to reach our inner Sun, it doesn't matter how wrong we have been in our actions if our intent was innocent. We were striving to reach a higher level of being human and therefore working to better ours or other people's lives. When we recognise a mistake, it isn't even a question of forgiving ourselves because we were not even blamed. It is only when we know what we are doing that there is sin. When we are doing wrong out of ignorance and we get struck by the lightning, we are instantly purified. Do not attach blame or guilt onto what has been done, because we were courageous to go and do it the way we have. We know that there was no other way, even if we were going for protection.

So when we are striving and wanting to do our best, but are still comparing ourselves to others, wanting their appreciation and wanting them to think we are the best, then we will hide our pride under false humility or false pride. It is healthier and better to show ourselves as wanting to be the best at what we do, for that way we have fewer veils. We strive to be best and then eventually when we actually get to be the best, we can say, "So what?" It suddenly shows up a big empty space that needs to be filled, so we start again somewhere else to find the light. Pure intent excludes martyrdom. It is like being an instrument such as a clarinet; the instrument has no intention, but it is there to be used. No care is given to what the world thinks of us, for the world has no attraction to the pure intent.

It is a very good but frightening thing, to understand that biological life is cheap. We are all dispensable and yet we are all special. If it isn't us dying on the cross it would be someone else; in the life of God we live in, it doesn't matter who it is. We don't need to be the first or the last. Biology is very cheap because it is only the means to explore and express where the level of consciousness of the God we live in is at the time. It is sacred when we understand the true meaning of sacrifice.

We build our tower, which is really the dominating mind, believing that it is has risen well above others and has control over the average human being through mass consciousness. We have had to surround ourselves with a whole lot of mindsets and egregores. Civilisation is one of those egregores, for there isn't a single set of groupings from churches to football teams, which isn't an egregore helping us to strive to be better than another group.

Nothing is found in the intellect that hasn't passed through the senses. The intellect is only a registering, computing, compiling mechanism and is completely of matter; even words are matter. Maths, physics or chemistry, or everything we can think of as research or creativity, cannot describe or express God. We can describe the energetic world, the physical or chemical world; we can even explain the psychological, philosophical world and actually touch on the metaphysical world, but then we realise we are short of words to describe the metaphysical. We cannot describe our own extremely intimate inner clicking, but when somebody talks about it we can relate to it. We cannot describe the actual sound but we can describe the situation around it, so that other people can grasp what you are talking about, although it is actually unique to us. This is the reason why we can't possibly describe divinity, for when we try we are bringing it down to the level of the intellect and crystallising it; divinity is not crystallisable. What is crystallised out of it is only what needs to be seen at the time, no more than that. The actual knowing of a person is an intimate inner thing and describing the body of a human being will not enable us to know that being.

All the sciences, such as physics, chemistry and psychology are there to pinpoint and show us things. They are very definite and fit into very tight laws, which then might be changed fifty years later. When we suddenly burst out into the metaphysical side, we realise that it is even tighter than the previous laws have been. The metaphysical process is extremely circumscribed, set and 'just so' and is based on experience of life. All this is training for the disciple or initiate, because it is much, much harder to get ourselves out of our own tower than to succeed in life. It is easier to study physics or chemistry than to go for our own inner alchemy.

The quest for divinity requires the total will and power of love. The rational intellect allows man to continue with his behaviour, but not to get out of it, so we need all our will and love to get out of the power of the intellect. The only way to do it is to associate with the intellect and at the same time stop associating with what we think we are; that is why we call it 'giving up'. The problem with the work we are doing is that we know we have had to go for the 'self, self, self', so as to align the personality. We have had to suffer and accept ourselves until the personality has died for the sake of the Soul, then when we find our higher self we know we have to start letting go of that as well. Right up to the last the intellect is there, so we can be quite a high initiate gathering bricks just in case we want to build The Tower again. The more we go for the outer, the further away we get from our own inner God.

The true community of men is on an ascendant march towards divinity, in the hope of unifying with it. It is the affirmation of an autonomous ideal which acts freely and this is one of the lovely definitions of freedom, meaning 'to do the thing that you have to do with joy'. The inner light wants us to do the inner work and is not after a firework display. We are not going in there in order to be reassured that we will find the light, the star, or the spectacle, or to feel good. Strangely the more darkness we find the better. We need to get accustomed to the darkness, because it is in that depth of darkness that eventually we can feel the invisible inner glow, which says that we are getting near to home.

The Soul decides when we die, irrespective of what we want. We can live a longer or shorter life according to how much we resist or align with Soul. It is the Soul that gives sustenance to the body, so if we resist, our Soul might give up and become aloof and then we start to degenerate. Even if we don't resist we will die at 28 if we are meant to. One way or the other Soul decides. Eventually the Soul has to recede and give back to nature the love/wisdom that belongs to nature. That can only truly happen when any thought of projecting our own personal life would have gone. We can't become transparent and at the same time worry about what might happen in our lives.

The world of matter is determined and set; the world of Spirit is free and unrestrained, blowing where it wants and taking us wherever we need to go next. If we know where we are going when we are building The Tower, then we will be surprised where we end up! The Spirit is anarchic and won't submit to any other authority than the laws of karma and of the greater life; it just doesn't obey anything else. When there is a strong Spirit in the initiate, it has to be compromised and aligned so as to understand brotherhood.

A strong free Spirit in a unit is automatically going to be a law unto itself, so if the awareness is strong there has to be alignment to link the inner law with the greater karmic law and have awe and love of this greater life.

Mind has the awareness that death has no power over it. It is mind that associates with divinity to give pure action and pure thought, so in an ideal world pure thoughts would be constantly crystallising. Thoughts in themselves don't need crystallisation, but the system needs them to be materialised, for it is the only way that we can realise what level of consciousness has been reached. We can de-crystallise the mindsets when we recognise they are the crystallisation of some misunderstanding from the past; that is how we break the mould. The material world is only the support for a thought form that has not yet realised its complete unfolding. The process is not finished, for we haven't yet rendered the material world transparent and seen ourselves clearly in the mirror. We can remind ourselves that when we don't accept something about ourselves, or accept life as it is now, it means we don't love the God we live in and that there is still some pride in us thinking we could do it better. That doesn't mean that we don't try and stop the war, but by accepting that humanity is doing it that way, we can go and stop the war with no personal intent whatsoever. We still work as mediators, who take on the role of the Soul and as such we must not take sides, for if we do, it will go on forever. It is all to do with internalisation and finding the hidden light. If a man wants to be near God, then he has to have recognition of the God within himself and respect the divine in all lives; the first step towards that is to look inside.

We see The Tower as the building of the intellect on behalf of the personality, so that the personality can actually rise. Then the intellect gets knocked, so feeling vague and confused has got to be understood as a good thing. We should not hold onto our intellect, but let it go and drop deep down into the darkness, where the inner treasures are there waiting for us. The intellect is only a tool, like a computer and what a superb instrument it is!

The man who is falling from the top of the tower has a crown, because he thought he was the master and king in control of the world. From within nature the sentence, 'you will be like Gods' that was given, shows us that pride was the first thing. It is the same for humanity, from churches or temples to any other institutions of state; these are all about humanity building its house of bricks, in the striving to build the kingdom of God. When we are building, little do we know that in the end it is all about letting go. This is why the man is falling, but he's not dead so he's going to start again. The other figure is dead and represents the hold of the intellect at the level of mass consciousness, driven entirely by needs and greed. We have to scramble the structures of the intellect, which is what we used to build our lives with in the past, so that the intellect can become a translator for the higher intelligence of the Soul.

We cannot study the mindset of God, for the minute we do, it becomes our image according to our limited knowledge of the raison d'être of the Universe. All we can do is witness and maybe the image one day will merge with the light. Enlightenment is dangerous, for it will make us want it for our own enjoyment. We have to be wise, loving and selfless for enlightenment to be consistent. This is where obedience and balance come in, because when we completely accept, we understand that karmically everybody is doing what they have to be doing. We can hear the melancholic song of the ongoing process of what the person is experiencing. That song tells us that when the mountain has been climbed, there is yet another one to climb. We should let the sound rise from the depth of the mother of all oceans to the height of the next mountain, until we hear the sound of joy of the Universe, when we accept that our work is in the valley as humble shepherds.

There is no need to have fear of being hurt, for suffering is recognising that it is the lot of our species to do what we are doing. We have dared to feel the pain to know the plan and then we can recognise, love and bless it. The process works and we don't need to study God to engage in it. Knowing our God is when we suddenly understand the essence behind the mind of the person we are looking at. That understanding definitely has no words, no sound and no explanation. We know that we know nothing when we get to the top of The Tower, for suddenly all the mindsets are shattered and we have to start again. We do not know our essences unless we have given ourselves up to them.

When we go beyond ourselves we have the knowledge of the stars and that is beyond the body and the brain. We all have the knowledge of the journey that the Spirit did when it actually moved heaven onto earth to create a picture. Enlightenment is when every single little cell in our bodies has given up its life; there is no more information and each individual has rendered their bodies into light. This is when the God we live in will be sacred. There is an inner striving to get clearer and clearer in letting go of what we think we are. The understanding of the plan and divinity is already written. As Souls we are sons of God, so we have the plan in us and it is just a question of becoming aware of that. The plan is down here on Earth and to recognise it is the most incredible responsibility that we have. We can't and mustn't interfere with other peoples' inner growth. The only thing that is absolutely necessary is to turn our bodies into light, so that they can mirror knowledge and peace.

There's absolutely no uniformity of behaviour in the search for spiritual life; each one has a unique path. A lighthouse shines to give guidance, but it is not up to the lighthouse keeper to steer the boat. The captain of the boat takes the route he has to and the lighthouse is only there to illuminate. The only mode for spiritual reasoning is intuitive, so if something doesn't click instantly then we know we are going for intellect. Sometimes that is all the situation requires, but the only true way of communicating with Spirit is intuitive, which means that we have to be at ease and accept the work of the subconscious.

There is no way light can reflect unless it has a reflector. What comes in is strong clear light with a specific vibration. Whether the instrument can do the job or not is not to do with the quality of the individual, but whether they are the right instrument for the job. When we have our line of spiritual 'guidance' or spiritual 'life', that vibration will automatically find a cup to receive the light, so that the memory can be reflected in it. When the moon shines on quiet water we see the whole of nature reflected in it. There is a song in that light; if the water is a sounding board and completely receptive, the instrument can deliver the message. The sounding board will definitely cloud the message according to its own level of consciousness, so it needs to be as transparent as possible; to be truly real we have to be transparent. We are one continuous flow and nobody is using anybody else, it just carries on through all the different cells or units in humanity.

In the prologue to the Gospel of St John the Evangelist, we are told of the light that is with all men when they come into the world. It is a luminous light, but it is not the light we get from the top of The Tower, because it is veiled and is inside. When the veils are removed it radiates out. We must remove those veils so that the inner light, previously hidden in the depths of the self, can shine out and be met. That luminous light, which is in the life of each living unit, is the gift of the light from the cells of both parents.

Man gives a value, sense or direction to this world. Without man there would be inertia and no actualisation, only virtuality and no possibility of getting out of the nothingness. Inertia is like being in the vestibule of hell where nothing can exist; we have to fall or destroy. Our role is to be the species in nature which is able to conduct the boat towards its harbour, or home. If there were no awareness and no consciousness, there would be no need for nature to do what it is doing. In reality man is not his body. The senses of the body are needed, but it is the mind that carries the awareness that death has no power over it. It is with his mind that man associates with divinity, through both pure action and pure thought. We cannot associate with divinity through our body, because the body has no awareness apart from what we give it and we cannot bring that light into good use in our world, if the heart is not open and giving.

The Tower gives us a liberating passage through all the wrong things that man has been doing in the pursuit of power, goodness, sainthood and so many other worthy gods. At the stage of the 16 we might be lucky enough to see the game we are playing! "What is it all about, if it is not my deepest yearning?" In that questioning we dissolve.

If it weren't for nature having the desire to meet the ultimate oneness, we would not have been born. We have to honour the desire to go beyond ourselves, because that is what gets us there. When the desire to be the best lawyer or the best architect is there and has made us build the edifice, that desire has taken us right up to the top of The Tower because it was pure. When we really do put everything we have into something we are doing, with a fixed intent and desire, this is the call of the inner love in us, which asks us to look into ourselves by allowing us to achieve our best. After that achievement we fall, because we realise it is not good enough for our hearts desire.

Man can only reach the divine by asking it to come towards him. In the deepest ravine of our suffering we have to give up and then, when we are at our most vulnerable, we suddenly remember that we are full of the Christ energy. So The Tower really is a symbol of incarnation in matter; we are incarnated and we must lift away from it, to go beyond ourselves and matter.

When our tower crumbles even hope doesn't work. There is just that little, inner, luminous glow which is the Trinity in us. We go into complete despair with no intellect or thoughts; then we can find the comforting glow of the Soul inside. It is there – we will feel it. We are lost and resign ourselves by getting up to start the slow march again. We have to purify our emotions. It is so easy to yearn for the little happiness's that life gave us before, in nature or paradise. We have to go through the pain until it doesn't hurt anymore; then when there is no memory left of it we know we have absorbed the reaction. A lot of us would have the tendency to be afraid to go forward alone. We need to dare to take the risk of going towards the only home where we might not disgrace ourselves, which is in the stars within our own heart (solar) system. We can then digest the past for what it is and go forward within.

A lot of people stay in mass consciousness because of the risks of starting to believe in themselves, which is what our king has done. When we start believing in ourselves we take full responsibility for our lives and we do not blame it on anything else. Whatever we do, so long as we believe in ourselves, we give the human being the whole of its dignity. Dignity is a close cousin of pride, but it is necessary, for we have to believe in our own inner life and inner judgment. If we stay in mass consciousness we lose that dignity, but we can always start again at any time.

There is nobility in the acceptance of risk. This is like the knight who risks his life for his lady (representing Soul). When we take risks it involves the whole of our life, for we are trusting in ourselves to go beyond what is safe; that is noble. A life in spirituality is the assumption of a risk. If the whole association with our inner life has to do with being real and recognising the opportunity of more alignment, then we cannot hesitate in taking a risk; we can recognise this as a true calling. This is taking full responsibility for our state of being and in this we are going to be touching the lives of people around us, for it is not just to do with our own life. Belief in the God within us means that we are going to disturb others around us, as well as attract them. People are vortices for whatever pulls them most at the time and for whatever vibrates to their desires. We can recognise the impotence of relying on the intellectual and rational capacities, for we cannot have any intimate knowledge of God without destroying dogmatic edifices.

To receive the greater truth we have to accept to renounce our own truth, which is what living on the edge is. We have put everything we have into what we are doing according to our own inner certainty; yet we have to be capable of renouncing that certainty too. We have to be capable of dying to be reborn to a higher truth. We are all quite happy to have our minds changed, but to receive truth we have to accept to renounce our own truth. This is what we spend our life doing if we are truly on the spiritual path. We have to hold on and go on with the truth, which we know is within us and pushing us forward, but at the end of the day we have to accept that even that can be completely wrong. At the same time, we have to take the risk of giving everything we have in that direction, otherwise we build another tower.

The domination of the Soul over the personality is much more difficult to achieve than domination over the material world. It is a new life in front of us and the difficulty is that we are forever being taken in by all the things around us, with which we could build another tower. To get out of our mindsets and desires, we have to reject everything that could call us back, not our responsibility to family, group or society but all the emotions that are usually associated with everyday living that pull us away from our ultimate destiny of being with the Sun. Between God and man there is a huge precipice and we cannot build a bridge between the two. God is not explicable; we can only feel its presence when everything else has crumbled. Then all that we have to start the new life with is the inner presence of the higher.

The Tower is flesh coloured, to signify that it is a manmade edifice. We've had to go into the dark to introspect and then when we get to the top of it we are blinded by the light, because we have received some light within our head. The more we climb the less we see life as it is outside. We lose our certitude inside, then when we're at the top the light is very brutal, for it shows us the imbecility of all that we have done so far. We are artificial and full of self importance. Even in our lack of confidence we are focussed on ourselves. On the top of The Tower everything is seen for the dust that it is. The door of The Tower is open, so anybody can go into the dark of the subconscious and internalise. It has two storeys and the third is the crown. These represent the three levels of personality, infused with the aspiring Soul. The four turrets and four colours at the top represent the four levels of consciousness of the personality. The ploughed field symbolises the attempt by man to re-organise or conquer nature.

The 16 bubbles represent the outer appearances of the everyday world. They are as inconsequential as soap bubbles that are ready to burst. They represent everything we have built; all the values, successes and mindsets we have given to the self; all that is ready to burst and disappear into thin air at any moment. The bubbles look nice, for the sun reflects in them; this is why they are different colours, like soap bubbles in the light. When Spirit has come back into matter with Number 10 and has reached the completion of the experience in Number 6, it has to find a new life in Number 7; so we have 16 bubbles. Number 16 is made of an 8 with an 8, which tells of the necessary destruction and rebuilding that we have to do, until we have perfect poise and balance. 8 is the master of destruction and also the master of re-creation according to the laws of karma.

We start as an infirm mass, moving towards organisation and being uplifted by our aspiration towards the greater being. That is the chaos at the beginning of all cosmology. Life is already omnipresent and is looking for a way to manifest itself with more precision, so as to acquire a few new qualities with each step; from mineral, to plant, to animal. In the animal kingdom there are multiple degrees of animal nature, then further multiple degrees in man. Each stage is painful and life is suffering, because it is ascending. The force of inertia keeps us in passivity, stasis and resistance, which engenders suffering. There is a great need for the light to trace its steps back to the beginning, where it can find itself again and make itself whole.

Effort is required to free ourselves from this passivity and resistance, to affirm ourselves above matter; to refine, purify and transform matter. We have to wake up from the easy gratifying life. The more awake the Spirit, the more the problems present themselves, for we feel the carnal links more strongly when we put ourselves in front of the picture in order to destroy it. When we really feel we are bound to matter the presence of the Spirit is very strong, for the more light on our problems the more obvious they become. It is at this point of crisis that we can cut them away.

Suffering is the most visible clue that the Spirit is at work; this is not masochistic, self-inflicted suffering or self-pity. We uplift if the suffering is accepted and understood, for only then can it start its work of transmutation. If it is only 'lived through', it brings regret and longing for the nice easy life we had when we were in the Soul group of nature. A lot of people live from one little happiness to another; this is why the crowning of the fight is when man has arrived at the top of The Tower, which he has so laboriously built, brick by brick. He has truly only built a human edifice and he must renounce all his certitude, only keeping that truth that he has felt in him, which is the Soul. He has to lose the house he has built in matter for the lightning of revelation to reveal the true house of God, the Soul, or the 'Maison Dieu'. In order to do the work of stripping away we have to allow the lightning to go right in; we have to allow our crash.

The Stars, Les Etoiles
Becoming part of the greater life

A naked female figure pours divine water from a silver urn onto the Earth with her left hand. In her other hand she holds a golden urn from which she pours boiling water into a stagnant pool that represents mass-consciousness. In the sky are eight stars with 8 points, the largest of which is a double star, representing the higher aspect of Venus. This is the card of truth and love. The initiate has given up any hope of anything for himself, for his life is not his own any more. Spirit comes back into matter and at the moment of fusion a higher level of hope emerges, which has been cleansed of any self-doubt or need; this is 'esperance'. Naked of self, we will never be abandoned or forsaken, for we have become part of the greater life and when everything else is gone, there remains the guidance of the shining light of esperance.

This is one of the happiest of periods or cycles. So far they are all glorious, but we couldn't call them 'happy' since we are studying them from the point of view of initiation, which is hard work! This one is happy, but there's a big sting in the tail, for we have to face the greater truth. In the Number 17, God and his creatures are forever coming back to fuse together in the process of reincarnation, for each time we come back to Earth we fuse a little bit more. In the 16/7 there was an offer of a revelation, which enabled us either to embrace or to ignore the light. The 17/8 offers the greater potential of finding truth when we take up the offer of the light. This is not the absolute truth, but is the beginning of a passage of understanding through assimilation and fusion, so as to find one's own truth.

We know that in Number 1 we have the intent of the initiate, coming back to further his refinement by serving the world. At first he uses and handles the elements for his own initiation, and then eventually he needs to give up any hope of anything for himself as an individual. The 2, 3 and 4 are the blueprint of the goals that he has to reach in order to abandon his hope, so that he can take on all the theory of the 5, 6, 7, 8 and 9 cycles, to help with inner and outer purification. Then, with the 10 and 11 he has enough strength to rebirth and be counted, so as to actually carry on the journey. From 11 through to 16 there is no more theory; it is a hands-on reality check. The 1 to 9 establishes the blueprint, which maps out the way the movement of Spirit into matter unfolds; it begins with simple will and ends with a Universe. It's exactly the same with us; we come back and try to apply the ideals of goodness, fairness, justice, etc. to the world of matter, which is the world we live in. Then, through the karmic numbers 11 to 22, we find out how far we are from the ideal. Matter acts as a mirror for the subconscious; what is mirrored is actually yesterday, but we get lost and think it is today. The importance of the mirror is to give the revelation of what we thought, how we loved and how we respected life; it also shows us the way that we are dealing with it today, so we know that our reactions are not personal. In Number 17 we start to glimpse that we are a 'way-by' or a conduit for energy.

By the time we get to Number 17 nothing much is left, but we may still have charity and faith in us. Charity is the social cement of mass consciousness, which is really about the survival of the self. From this angle, when we see those who are less fortunate, we give, because we know if we were less fortunate we'd like people to give to us. There's a sense that if we give to charity it makes us 'good' and we may be the ones who are in need tomorrow, so there is that bit of self-gain in it. Without charity there would be no civilisation, so it's a good thing and is about the survival of the group. The egregore 'charity' was being re-evaluated in numbers 6, 7, 8, and 9, so that we could let go of the aspect in it that is serving the self. Charity is a necessary characteristic and has held societies down for tens of thousands of years, enabling the right seeds and flowers to be brought out in humanity. We need people who are driven by charity, but it's so much better to give because people need it and we do not, rather than because it's a good habit learnt over a long time. Also, it's avarice to say that the less fortunate should "Put their house in order", "Pull their socks up" or "Get on their bike". As the Buddha said, "When a man has an arrow in his flesh we don't ask him; "Do you deserve it?" or; "Where did it come from?" – we just take it out".

There isn't a single religion, philosophy, or science, which doesn't have faith in a dogma. Dogma enables us to follow the rules, because they have worked for others and so we feel they are bound to work for us. The essence of faith is that we believe in something that has been experienced by somebody else as uplifting; when we sense and know that is right, it lifts us above our questions or despair. This is not a bad thing, because if there were no religious faith we wouldn't have the next step that takes us beyond our God. There isn't a single faith that does not have its inspired people, who have learnt to go beyond dogma to a place where there is no more faith, only certainty. People have faith because it's going to help and soothe them and they think it will deliver paradise. It is written that if we do as we are told, we will find enlightenment and paradise and be free of misery; that is faith and it's beautiful, so let's hope that there's a lot more faith in the world yet and that people will follow pure dogma! However, our job is to read between the lines, by internalising and so seeing how the dogma vibrates with us. We can understand its message, which is to keep the fragile one in the safety of the flock. Faith has brought us to a point where, when we look at the state of the world now we can see that all the groups that are seeking the truth are speaking in the same voice, saying "we have to look after one another and care for the planet". So all our faiths have brought us to the point of the simple, good realisation that we have to get on and clean up our act. Extremists of any kind, be they scientific or religious, are looking for absolution from the same problems, but their zeal might have blurred some of their humanitarian qualities and distorted the method in order to get the answer.

So far everything has been about breaking us down, so for many lives we have been in the long dark night. Then suddenly we see the little glimmer of light from the inner star. In The Tower we let go of everything and couldn't care less; charity and faith had gone and there was nothing more to believe in, because all our belief systems had been broken down. The star is 'light' in the sense of truth and esperance; these two qualities have nothing to do with our personal selves, but make us say "My God! I am still alive and not only am I still alive, but I am only alive because there is a star alight in front of me". We are alive because the star is there, which is quite different from: "The star is there because I am alive". We are not bringing Heaven to Earth; rather we are revealing Heaven on Earth, for Heaven is not just in us it's everywhere. We are talking about a great initiation here; we are not talking about "I'm dead, but I'm aware I am dead, therefore I'm alive", for this is the survivor or the good 44/8. Here it's "I've done all the theory, all the work and the discipline, I've done it all and I've crumbled. There is nothing left, not even peace. There is no map or direction, but somehow I am naked, innocent and okay with the truth".

This is the true energy of Venus, which is not about the flesh, emotional love or sensual pleasure, but rather represents the awareness of the light, which has given us the courage to come back into the flesh to see the world of matter for what it is. Venus represents the naked, plain, simple truth as the divine judgement of justice. When we recognise this, everything else looks so silly that it takes a lot of courage to stay in the world! We have the movement of fusing the newly acquired awareness with matter, happening in the 17/8.

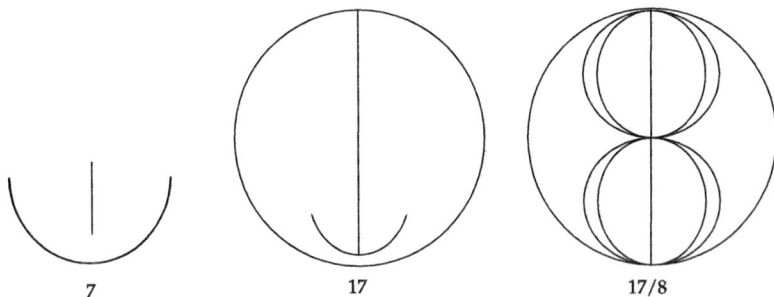

Figure 1. The work of the 17/8.

The 1 of Spirit coming back with its full potential (10) into matter, reaches its fusing point in the conceptive nature of the 6 and experiences the fusion in the 7 of the 17/8.

The 8 will destroy the glamour and illusion and rebuild the framework according to the level of karmic evolution of the person in question. This happens at an impersonal level, so we are completely denuded of any veiling that our personality might have put in front of us to enable us to enjoy things. If we are on the road to happiness that is a cul-de-sac! We are not here to enjoy, or to flagellate ourselves either. We are not here to change the world or suffer, but only to witness and recognise our place in the universe. Also we are here to forget our obsession with our little place in the Solar System and get on with our lives on behalf of the greatest cosmic good. Not because the cosmic good (as the sky) is waiting to fall on our heads, but because if we are bad we have the courage to see life as it is in the bigger picture.

The Stars connect us to 'Thy will be done' through complete trust, with no personal questioning. Very often we find ourselves in situations where we don't want to be doing what we are doing, because it's not about what we think is right. We don't know why we are not stopping doing it, although we are questioning it, for we're suffering like mad but are still doing it. This is not martyrdom; this is part of witnessing yet another level of deep mining into the dark, to achieve yet more transparency in the nakedness of the light.

The French word esperance is the closest word we have to describe this process. In English the nearest word is hope, which conveys a sentiment that something should happen in the way we desire, but that doesn't express the full meaning of esperance. There is some consideration of calculation in esperance and the desire has a real possibility of realisation. If we hope, we automatically have a doubt, which means we are still in survival mode and therefore in life for ourselves.

The word 'hope' is part of faith, hope and charity, but esperance is hope that has been clarified of any self doubt, need or trust and so is a little sister to truth. When everything is gone, the light that shines is so steady that we cannot do anything else but be guided by it, and then whatever comes at us the poise remains steady. This is the blessing of Benedictus or of life, that tells us that when we accept we arrive at a point of poise. Truth and esperance are akin to each other. Because we are not removed, aloof or superior, we are completely in life and have trust in whatever happens. We are poised and balanced therefore completely centred, but not even aware that we are centred. The true essence within all of us is perfect harmony. First the personality and then the Soul has to have acceptance; this is the true "thy will be done". When we recognise that fully in ourselves we know that we are naked and are nothing more than transparency (light) for truth and love to shine through. There has to be obedience (which is not the obedience by fear), because there is absolutely nothing else that can be done but obey. When acceptance and obedience are firmly in place in the centre, The Stars send us back to experience the flesh again (like sending a child back to school) giving us the opportunity to connect to the cold light of reason of Venus. She will send us back into the form for us to learn that the only true aspect of love is ethereal rather than in form; this is the ultimate movement or action of love. We are in the second Solar System, which carries the love/wisdom aspect.

We are naked, naïve and innocent because the other life has been 'driven' out of us and we have said "yes", out of love. So from now on, it is 'naked truth', meaning there is nothing in it for ourselves, we just have to take our place in the universe. We are back like a grain of sand on the beach, or a drop of water in the ocean. Can we imagine a drop of water in a wave saying that it doesn't want to be there? We are like a grain of sand that protests and resists! That drop of water in the wave can never be non-active, because it is one with the life of the greater sea, river or pond. Even if it's stagnant decomposing matter it is active, for its action is helping decomposition. Whatever form that action takes, it has completely given itself up to the greater life that it lives in. That is pure love and abandonment to the greater energy, or the God of life.

Every time we get a little glimpse of the star within us, the will of God in us gets stronger, which means that we have increasingly abandoned ourselves to the light. This is the sublimation of sublimations. We are not there yet, we are on the way and that is the message in the light. To be systemic again means to be pure life that is aware of itself and completely part of the system, whatever that system happens to be. It cannot even start to think it will rebel, for it is systemic!

The big eight-pointed Star with the green of Hermes behind the yellow is the ruling star of Venus, Ishtar, or Lucifer and represents the higher aspect of love. Yellow is to do with mind; either the intellect or the higher mind, according to the quality of the yellow. The green colour is the hermetic light crystallising all love and wisdom into the purest expression. This is pure instinct, a necessary state for intuition, which is a rare thing. Intuition is not the ability to know where somebody hurts or what somebody thinks; that is just being sensitive and recognising the life as one. Intuition never gives an answer to our own or somebody else's problems. It is the pure movement of Spirit fusing with instinct, so that we suddenly see the light. We should use the word intuition lightly and wisely, because it is the mode of communication between highly evolved Souls and their Gods, therefore it is a rare thing. What we do frequently experience is telepathy, which is great, for it means that we are accepting to be at one with and a part of, the body of the God we live in. The animals have the quality of innocence of pure instinct; to have that we have to drop the hold that the intellect has on us, as it translates life back to us. We have to be truly innocent to be intuitive; anything else would come from a personal view of the world.

This Star is the light of God or the great initiator and is of the Spirit. It is the first one to gain the attention of the Souls that want to see it. Venus is the big sister of the Earth who feeds us, for, esoterically two thirds of our light comes from Venus. She is sacred and the Earth is not yet sacred. Number 8 is also another number for Christ, so an 8-pointed Star is always seen as the light of God. The fusion of light and matter can only be done on this little planet Earth, so Venus can definitely encourage us as Souls to come down again and again to go through all the trials of reincarnation, until we emerge purified so that we can help with the transformation of planet Earth. This is going for the higher, complete love, not the sugary sensory one; we have to come and experience love in all its forms down here on Earth. We are the ones who can recognise that life on this planet is divine, so we can raise our consciousness without hesitation, give ourselves into the task and be completely ourselves. Then we will become so open that we will remember that intuition and pure instinct are the same thing.

Sex is the way the mass consciousness translates the magnetic influence of the energy of Venus, because we need that method to procreate and have as many experiences as possible: these enable us to recognise what we might be attracted to or repelled by. Eventually we can sublimate these attractions and repulsions, because what we really want to bring in is the divine love, which loves things for their essence rather than their form. The form is just the glue that keeps us in the magma of mass consciousness.

Eventually we break down the mind-sets, ethics, or philosophy, leaving just the pure innocent knowledge that life is divine; that in itself is a kind of rebellion. There isn't a single religion that doesn't have the dogma to tell us that we should do this exercise, breathe like that, do this, or do that. Venus says; "It doesn't matter about all that, there is only light and its vessel, love!" She is the first one in the morning and the last one at night; she is the light of our dreams when we sleep.

Without dreams, mankind would never have noticed that there was something underneath the surface. Dreams and imagination tell us that we are more than meets the eye. It is Venus who guides us into the deepest clarity that we can get at night in the dark. She carries the two aspects of the warrior and the lover. In the morning the Warrior says, "Get up", meaning rise in consciousness from the point of view of the Soul; then in the evening the lover says "Trust your dreams", meaning that we shouldn't forget that we are still aware, even in sleep. This is our double life and we have to fuse the two aspects together by bringing the ideal into the situation we have in front of us at the time. This fusion is called spiritual compromise and from this we have the naked truth.

The path of esperance is an act of complete, total love. Only the mystical psychic love can take us to the truth, which is the life of the Soul. There is a saying, "To everybody his own truth". We would never deny somebody their own truth, but it's not necessary that *all* these perceptions are truth. There is only one truth, just as there is only one life or one being, so the saying should be re-written as, "Everybody has the right to perceive the truth in their own way"; there is a huge difference. There is only one truth, but millions of different ways of interpreting, so to each his own way. We are told, "The beauty of the way is that there is no way".

Beauty is peace, simplicity, nakedness and innocence; the revealer of beauty is Venus. What is harmony, if it is not a loving appreciation of truth, or a loving acceptance of the law of economy in Active Intelligence? Something is beautiful when it is poised and complete in itself, then everything in it is used to express nature and symbolism. Beauty is the essence not the form. Venus sends us back into matter to be confronted by our mind-sets about what we call 'beauty', which is what things should be like to please us! So we have the opportunity to go and chase it, so as to find that in the end it's the essence that we are after. This card is asking us to go beyond symbolism, whereas The Tower is a symbol that we need to go back into, in order to rise.

The influence of the cycle of 17/8 can only bring positive karma with it; it has gentle innocence and says, "Be guided by your light". This is why those under the influence of the 17/8 have great difficulty in knowing where they are or what they are doing, or whether they are doing anything; so often they feel they have no direction. The sentence 'by the grace of God' could be their leitmotif.

This is because with positive karma we are not doing anything, if we let life take care of its creature.

If the twenty-two cards of the major Arcana are arranged in two rows of 11, then The Stars (Number 17) is underneath The Lover (Number 6), right at the centre of the two rows. These two cards are about poise and being the axis in the middle, so they can be very self-centred, or directed by their own innocence. The centre of the initiatic Tarot is entirely based on Love and Truth.

1	2	3	4	5	(6)	7	8	9	10	11
12	13	14	15	16	(17)	18	19	20	21	22

The seven little stars in the card all have eight points. The little blue star over the lady's head is her personal one; it is the light perceived within. Blue here can be interpreted as receptive. The other two blue ones are a representation of love, beauty and harmony 'on Earth as it is in Heaven' as represented by the qualities of Venus. They symbolise the Moon and the Sun, or the receptive/active qualities of manifested life; we are here to bring those two aspects together. Esperance is the only thing we have got left, so when we say, "All there is, is love", it means that there is nothing if there is no love, as the light cannot be seen without its mirror. There is here an elevation of the personal work towards integration into cosmic consciousness, so we are at Soul-Spirit level. The Stars are placed symmetrically, to remind us of harmony, justice and peace, within the four corners of a square (the four yellow stars). These four represent the main planets, Saturn, Mercury, Jupiter and Mars, which tell us that we are talking about the Solar System.

However noble the mindsets, the religions or the 'isms' are, they have to crumble, so that we can lift normal consciousness into cosmic consciousness. We are a tiny part of this great big universe, so we will never be left, abandoned or forsaken, for we are part of that greater life. Esperance and hope, together with trust and love, make up the complete life. All the experiences are there for us to have, including the whole cosmic experience.

We have the great guide, Lucifer, who brings in the brightest light of the Star of God. Lucifer symbolises the rebellious guide in us, who says, "I'm so bright in such a fragile body, even if I am broken, I will rise and shine. Being broken is my natural state, I fell. I will carry on. I am right. I will be revealed! Wait! I will be discovered! I trust completely". This giving in is love, but it's the love that is the cold light of reason (as out of economical necessity the situation is accepted) rather than the 'lovey-dovey' warm love of needy reassurance.

The whole of biological life always lives at the edge and we have to learn to live there too, understanding that we are not this or that but both, living at the centre and poised on a tightrope. Beyond biology there is the sensitive Soul life and if we don't render ourselves sensitive as well, we are still in form. This sensitivity will take us to the cosmic consciousness that will make us work at the etheric level. It is on the etheric level that the butterfly landing on a flower makes a wave twitch on the other side of the world; that is the level of sensitivity we are talking about.

Here in the card we are seeing the naked form, represented by the lady as innocence, ready to receive the naked truth. She has two urns or vases, just as Temperance had. Naked truth, beauty and love-wisdom, in the highest Venusian sense, will keep on pouring out waters and these urns will never empty. This represents the idea that we are a way-by through which the world can be revivified. One is cold water and the other boiling water, hence the steam.

The cold water comes from the silver urn. Silver symbolises the energy of the highest inspiration in humanity and biology, so this water feeds the dry earth. We have ended up in the dry desert and not one single seed we have planted has done anything; everything is completely dead. Having seen The Stars we are guided by them to put the divine water of aspiration on the land and from that we are starting to see a little bit of growth. However dried up and closed the mind is, however thick the mass consciousness can be with conflict, there is always a hope that somebody will start to grow, so never despair.

There is hope, but it is not for self and therefore it is esperance, telling us that we need never give up, for there is nothing in life that is so closed up and dried, that it will not eventually want to drink.

The boiling water represents the fiery zeal of Spirit and is being poured from the gold urn into a little pond. This is the pond that we all know, where we keep repeating the same past patterns. It is the stagnant waters of mass consciousness, where we go round and round digging ourselves in, like quicksand. What is needed to purify this one is the heat of the spiritual water of life, which can go in and stir the decomposing matter, so as to purify the waters of the subconscious. This enables what is there to be revitalised and re-birthed, so the psychic life can be re-awakened. The Soul had become dull and gone into sleepers amnesia, now it's going to be engaged.

The single branched plant on the right side of the card represents the initiate. The lower plant on the right tells us that nothing is too dry for the waters of Heaven not to reach it, showing us that however deserted it may be, the presence of hope will enable us to drink the water and start to regenerate. These plants are acacias. The acacia tree is very resilient and grows in very arid places, remaining green and alive and refusing to die; the cross of Jesus was made of acacia wood. The wood of the cross of the initiate is green, as if to say "I will give up, to be alive!" Acacia sounds like Acashic, which also says "From the beginning of time to the end, I'm here". Acacia wood is a symbol of rebirth, high initiation and endurance. Whatever we witness, or whatever happens to us, we know that in the plan it is exactly right, even if we do not understand why.

The acacia bush on the left represents Venus. On it is a blossoming rose to symbolise the love and life in the cross, in case people thought it was dead. The highest possible love is when we don't see existence for self any more, it's not even acceptance and obedience, it is actually *being* the red rose, for we have given our heart and blood to it. We have even stopped thinking that we have given anything up, for life doesn't belong to us, we are it.

There is a pure celestial blue butterfly on the rose, to represent transformation and the cosmic universal spiritual Soul, which is there to fecund the rebirth. What was an isolated hope becomes participation with the universal Soul, thus enabling cosmic communication. A rose can represent the carnal, passionate, sensual rose of the lower Venusian energy, but here it's a rose with the possibility of the highest transformation of love. The rose and the butterfly symbolise the two aspects of love coming together to reveal life. One feeds on the other, but if the butterfly wasn't there the news couldn't be spread that love is something more than rubbing two sticks together.

Through the Soul's experiencing love in the flesh again and again, the higher recognition emerges that we are after the essence or higher aspect of love. Here it's not saying "be an aesthete", but rather "be in life". Eventually, through experiencing the sexual, sensual aspect of love, we know that we only go through this stage of experience because we love the essence of the person. The essence is not the want, need, desire or attraction, but a natural state that comes back to the purest possible instinct. It is the natural consequence of two Souls coming together and joining in the sexual act. There is no game playing here, it's a pure consequence. It is full life and full love, rather than self-gratification. This love happens as a natural consequence of us all being here to become one again.

In the bottom right corner of the card we can see a hole or ravine; this is actually a well. If we go down into the water of the earth through a ready-made hole, we haven't done any work. If we have dug a hole to get to the water that is underneath, it means that we have done internal work. In this context the water that we find at the bottom, represents the life-giving water of wisdom that brings re-birth. Rain falling on the earth symbolises Spirit sending a message deep down into the earth. Messages are brought up from the earth as well, so when we go down into the unconscious we bring up love-wisdom. If we dig deeply to find the water that has fallen, it is twice as charged as when it first fell from the sky.

Without water there is no life, for water is the messenger of life and revitalises the Earth so that life can keep on going. Naked truth always comes out of the symbolic well of the deep waters of the unconscious, which are completely charged with the truth of the history of the Earth so far; it's wonderful imagery. The psychic or Soul element is represented by water as a messenger, for this is the 'way-by' through which God communicates with the Earth. Spirit goes into matter to bring light and release information, which can inspire others to carry on with the work of transubstantiation; this happens at the point of sublimation.

The divine celestial water is incorporated in matter and man must find it in himself, for this is how we self-realise or go through alchemy. We must extract the original message from within the form and so move from brute matter to the sustaining psychic waters of the Soul. As the Soul permeates through the etheric it gives sustenance to matter, for matter can't exist without Soul. For example, it is through the etheric linking to the element air that we have the blueprint of the unfolding flower. Truth is simple and universal, nakedness is transparency. If we are in a situation and we are fighting like mad to find freedom from that experience, this is still a form of ignorance. Freedom comes when we realise that we are the witness of the experience.

When the two patterns of Spirit and matter meet we have an Omega point, which brings our negative thoughts into the light so that they can be transformed, transmuted and sublimated. Water and matter symbolise high alchemy, where the super-conscious, everyday consciousness, the subconscious and the unconscious are brought together. In this process the subconscious will give up a lot of its murky bubbles into the waters of the unconscious. Intuition comes when the intelligence of the Spirit finds pure instinct in the innocent unconscious nature. It is brought back to divine life in its simplicity and transparency. When we reach an Omega point, we have glimpses of what we are going eventually to see clearly, through an intuitive communication from the light of Spirit to the pure instinct, which is the unconscious in us. Anything else that we call instinctive is not pure nature, because our mass conscious or man-made instincts are mostly based on self-gratification rather than true survival. By the time we get to the Omega point we don't need survival, for we have seen the light and our true instinct can be revisited, so we see flashes of the truth of what life on this planet is about. From this point we are no longer going to play cinema and drama with our subconscious aspect that wants to remain in the artificial instinct.

The subconscious contains all the experiences which haven't come into the full light of the Sun. They are there; ready to be brought back to simplicity in natural behaviour, which is stripped of our meddling, addictive mind. This lower aspect of mind is driven by our need to feel good or bad. When it comes to the divinity looking at itself, the world is perfect. Whatever has been misunderstood has to be re-visited again and again and is 'denatured' or diverted from pure instinct. We re-visit it with the troubled waters of our own needs and fears, which dictate a view on life that 'denatures' it even more. That is why we act the way we do and that is why we say we own the ocean when we are only a drop in it. The Stars represent the triumph of hope over rationalism. Rationalism would have said, "What is the point?" Acceptance, obedience and love in the now, are the qualities in us when we have achieved poise.

The cycle of 7 has in it all the fears and aspirations strongly based on survival in nature, so it has strong needs, wants and mindsets of how it should be. Someone with a strong influence of the 7 will feel that what they want is what they should get, which will be often what they will not get, so as to help them accept whatever relationship with the world that they have at the time.

We don't have to become victims, but we do have to work through difficult situations in order to understand. If we escape from a situation that doesn't work out or turns out not to be viable, we have to have learnt everything there was to be learned from that experience. We can ask ourselves whether we have really refined to such a point that when we leave the situation, there will be nothing left but a pearl or a diamond. We could find the pearl 10 years later but the question now is, have we done it all with this one lesson? We have to go through every possible formula. Are we using an excuse to avoid looking at it from another point of view? Escape from a situation doesn't give us the answer. Taking responsibility is accepting the naked truth, which is the entire response of pure instinct to its maker; that is fusion into life. That is the environment provided by the 10, where the 1 with all the potential can fuse with the cup and release some karmic ties.

She's kneeling on her left knee; this tells us, "There is no more individuality"; this is the knee of the initiate. After The Devil and The Tower we cannot possibly take our own initiation seriously, so we are not even searching for it; this is why the left knee is down. We have given up the idea of personal initiation because we have recognised that it is a 'dogma' status that we have to go beyond, so as to become pure life again. True life is beyond the personal, beyond calculating, wanting and ritual; rather it is about becoming instinctive in the purest sense. We are looking very fast towards The Fool here!

Her hair falls on her left shoulder. The left brain relates to the intellect. Hair symbolises the past, strength, or wisdom, which tells us that by resting on her left shoulder the intellect is in touch with the receptivity of nature. Her hair is divided in three parts, so it reminds us of the Trinity.

We can go on understanding the true nature of good and bad, until eventually we achieve full compassion. The complete knowledge of the human condition has to be achieved by the breaking down of all mindsets, for the human condition has nothing to do with anything we understand from the intellectual point of view. This knowledge has to be sensed, experienced and recognised, because the inner essence, which is felt and is immoveable within us, is there when we start to perceive the true light of love-wisdom. We cannot find truth through any 'isms', or through the intellect.

We broke down the concept of faith at Number 16. Faith still puts a condition or a market value to things, because we still expect a treat, so there are still doubts and conditions to do with faith. Here we cannot pronounce any dogma or discipline whatsoever in the name of God. The only measure of the God we live in is that he is what he is, which is the world as we see it and receive it; this is our lot. This is not much of a measure but it is the only one we have. We are not talking about the intellect that says "Yes, I have understood and I feel it in my gut". The innocence of pure truth just 'is', and it's not an intellectual thing at all, because we have given up the importance of our position in the plan. There are no conditions of salvation or causes for damnation, for these are behind all faiths. Esperance is really the only attitude to have. We can cultivate that natural, unspoiled state by being aware and recognising anything of personal desire, want, need or pride in ourselves.

The Devil, Saturn, or Lucifer puts us in front of the double possibilities of using our power. The second level initiate can still fall and use the power for his own ends. Number 15 (The Devil) says, "Beware" and asks us if we are truly sincere in our service to life, because if we aren't there is an unexpected ending awaiting us in Number 16. There is still a choice at 16, but at 17 it's a double star and there is no choice. We are in a state of being, which is rather vague, confused yet not preoccupied. The breaking down of mind-sets is what is needed for the naked truth to be seen; this is the breaking down of the tower of Babel, or the way we look at life, as naturally the two aspects of personality and lighted Soul merge. What is on offer with The Devil comes true in The Stars; once the path of truth is open we stumble on the way life really is, strangely bizarre yet fluidly comfortable.

It is not the acceptance and the obedience of the dogma of some religion or some wise Zen way of thinking that frees us, it is just knowing that being one with life is not a superior way of being, but the *only* way of being. Always remember that we are like a grain of sand, or a little drop of water in the sea. The only thing that puts us above nature is being able to be aware of our place within the system; we are not higher or better.

We refuse to see God, because if we saw God and went back to utter simplicity and transparency like the drop in the ocean we wouldn't be able to speculate or search, take enjoyment and satisfaction, or feel miserable. If we truly let go we would not be able to do any of that. Life is only a game; if we like playing the game and are very good at it, we even think we are not playing it and that we are so alive! We prefer to hide, cover up and stay in the dark, because that way we still have an excuse to go and search and keep on with the farcical drama! The freedom not to see or love is a strange notion of freedom, manufactured by the intellect. We don't want to see the truth of our tiny selves and our impotence in comparison with the system. That is the only reason that we are playing the game. It's not a question of blaming anybody because without the ones who really want to play the game, we would not have all the mud coming up and that needs to happen. The lambs sacrifice themselves because they love the smell of blood and if we don't do it any more, they do it on our behalf because we are all one.

Man doesn't know himself. We are incredibly good at putting cinema on for the personality. Even when we go into meditation or visualisation, it is mostly all about the glamour and illusion of the little self. Everything about us that is visible is acting, unless it comes straight from Spirit-Soul connection as innocence. We are all going towards being centred or poised and are at various degrees of alignment, where the Personality, Soul and Spirit come together as one. See how much unquestioning love we would need to be able to live 24 hours a day as innocent witnesses, with full awareness of what drives the form. At that stage, when the three are one, we would have achieved Christhood! We need to operate at the level we understand and be humble with the little Christ within us.

We need to become very simple to see the truth and the essence of life; rejecting pride, falsehood, desire to dominate and self-love. It is about putting all the selves out of the way and just turning ourselves towards what is hidden underneath. Before we get to that point we will have done all the cries for help. There is a huge, silent 'I love you', which is a fantastic cry towards love and is instinctually there in somebody who gives their life entirely to the will of God. Here in The Stars, 'naked truth' (the lady in the card) is looking down and the water that she is pouring represents the thoughts and the Soul. All that loving energy of truth is being poured onto the earth, so that hopefully some of those who cry for help can see a ray of light. She's not doing it for herself at all; she is out of the way because she is truth. She has become the esperance for others in that sense, because that is what naked truth is.

We are not separate from creation. When we take something from creation to satisfy our personal needs, we separate ourselves from it. When we truly engage and take our rightful place in the system, then suddenly we can actually forget ourselves and rise and see life from a wider perspective, which is the cosmic greater life we live in.

Truth is so innocently spontaneous, like intuition. "The manipulative noise of psycho-analysis giving voice to the logical clever intellect asks the questions "Where did it all start?" "Whose fault is it?" Like children, we blame the table, our parents, society. The voice has scrambled the obvious. It's the fault of the Universe because the Universe is. The clamour of trying to survive within the human group is there in the noise of the Soul emerging. Sensitivity to noise is a physical level of pain that is completely accepted, but the mental pain of seeing the world for what it is, is excruciating. When we experience this, we either go mad or we become sane. Sanity means deciding somehow to get on with the virtual game of the material life. Getting on with it is still painful, but we recognise it as a necessary movement of spiritual energy going towards an expression, for that is all it is.

The personality can be very noisy with the yap, yap, yap of the old kingdom, but if we are looking at this with the broader view it's beyond our own noisy karmic work; it is the sound of the planet. We have the cosmic white noise in our ears, which is completely deafening, but there is a dazzling white light within it when we reach the point of balance. Suddenly we can hear and see the inner direction, the inner life. We are not going off our rocker and things are going to settle down, when we can merge the inner and outer sounds and lights.

Esperance is elusive – it has to do with bringing the complete trust and full acceptance of the divine plan into the perception of the process. This gives rise to grace, which finds the point of poise of love/wisdom where the conflict ceases. We have understood and in that state of grace, we have completely abandoned any self whatsoever.

The esperance or truth is naked because its importance is not in the appearance, the phenomenon or the artificial, but in the essence. Adam and Eve represented primitive instinctual purity, or how nature is in paradise. They were naked because they had nothing to hide. As we know, they suddenly got the 'right and wrong' idea from the tree of life, then truth and awareness set in. Awareness sends us into all types of experiences, in which we fall out of that instinctual purity. We have to go into the system with that newborn consciousness and retrieve what lies at the heart of the purity of the primitive.

 We need to see the incredible, cruel intelligence of the system; hate it and kick against it, like an adolescent. We know that it is the system of systems and is the 'enabling' of the God we live in; we know where and what we are within the system. We have to truly look at it and our rebellion and sneering needs to be done. If we have not gone through all this, then we haven't even started the breakdown from within, because eventually there is nothing and we can only ask, "Who are we?" Lucifer,

meaning the light of God, is there to help us to do that rebellion. We are like a naughty child who doesn't accept that mummy has said no and will not treat us like a king. The rebellion is expressed by refusing to be only a loving mind which is not even ours. The gold and silver urns (the silver one containing cold water, the gold one boiling water) are about the fertilisation of the earth. They represent the psychic element or the Soul communication from above, coming into man. Without water there is no life. To understand the quality of the psychic element within us (the Soul) look at the analogy of water. Water clings to the nearest thing to it, with the memories of the qualities of everything it touches. Water makes one with everything it encounters and retains the experience; this is very much like the raison d'être of the Soul/Spirit vivifying the water. What gifts have we got? We seek the inner guidance of something that we don't even comprehend, but which shines through us. It is in us, but it's not ours, just like a little drop of water that has the innocence and purity to know that it doesn't own the ocean, therefore it is existence itself.

Our behaviour has to be a servant to the highest ideal of pure instinct. It's the instinct of survival that make us behave the way we do, that is why most of us behave moronically because we receive our impulses from the subconscious rather than the pure instinct. Pure instinct is pure life, naked truth and 'less is more', which brings us back to the simplicity of nature. To reveal the deepest, simplest aspect of love is the 'becoming' of the second Solar System; we are here to reveal the perfected Soul.

The origins of all life and the origin of the consciousness that is beyond appearance are in water. Eventually we uplift back into the energies of the Spirit through water. There is Cancer, Scorpio and Pisces all demonstrating different aspects of water. Scorpio has to go beyond the appearance of form to do the uplift through death, and then in Pisces the fish completely merges with the celestial water. The position of Pisces cannot be attained without coming back via the Cancerian re-birthing into purer and purer waters. These three astrological signs are one and no one is more evolved than the others. We can see it as a process, not as a level of evolution, because the process is the 1 transforming. Without the great Cancerian waters of origin, where is the origin of life?

Eve doesn't represent woman, she represents Spirit having to come back into flesh. The misunderstanding about duality is the fact that we immediately categorise according to what we look like, when really we shouldn't, for we only represent Spirit coming into the flesh. It's the same with Adam; he is mankind coming into generation. All the intellect does is to start playing sorcerer's apprentice. Mimicking nature is great, but reorganising nature causes problems. Who do we think we are? We need to ask that question, but at the same time be in awe of our position. It isn't a putting down but a reminder of our glorious position, which is to be responsive to the God we live in and to the greater life. It's about living in the light and the brotherhood, rather than in the pride and egocentric way of living. The gold of the spiritual water is in the water from above, so the call of Spirit comes to disturb the dead water that has a tendency to vegetate. We all have a tendency to go for an easy life, but that is not bad and is nothing to chastise ourselves about. We gather moss and a lot of other primitive forms of life when we vegetate, then we have a lot to explore when we wake up.

When we do one of these little 'atomic clicks' where we burst a tiny little point of light into us, we can actually redress the genetic code in our bodies and bring back the original purity by removing the karmic knots or miasms. The boiling water actually purifies the miasm out of the subconscious; this way the code gets back to its original purity without the interference of such practices as gene therapy. The only way to do this work is through full consciousness, responsibility and alignment to the 'plan' within us. We can get out of addiction, illness, fear, pollution and absolutely everything we have been thrown into. The work on the genetic code is done on behalf of the group and we need to remove the need to do it for self.

At the etheric level there is no biology. The picture in biology is only a projection of a level of consciousness we can observe as the Soul gradually merges with matter. Whatever befalls one drop of water comes from the whole group. Matter is only an expression of what is going on within the group and we all are part of the expression of the bigger, cosmic group. The DNA biological structure is definitely given out for a much higher purpose than the group itself, but it exteriorises within the group and the unit, to demonstrate some characteristics that are being worked out. When these characteristics are being worked on from a point of poise, explosions can happen which will remove that characteristic out of the DNA pool of that group, because that particular work has been achieved. When that is done, the group will come back with a different story and a greater understanding, to help bring back more DNA to its origin.

Genetic Modification is the work of the apprentice sorcerer, when man thinks he is God. We must understand that we are here to do this work, but to manipulate it in the name of profit and being clever is the sorcerer's apprentice syndrome. This is the excess of science that we see in cloning and genetic modification. We have to explore these excesses because we still have to find out about how it all works. The work of the initiate is similar but he has to be innocent in order to probe the same waters without interference, always looking for the 'why' relating to karma and the plan, rather than the 'how' of the scientist; the latter names the one physical greater life, the other aligns his mind to the inner reason of the working of Spirit.

Truth is an absolute and it suffices by itself; happiness is in us and we can say, "My Sun is in myself". The more we look for it on the surface, or on the outside, the less and less satisfied we are. This is the beginning of any understanding on the path. The pursuit of happiness is the pursuit of self-gratification. If we are pursuing any thing at all, or if we do things to earn a peaceful place, bliss, or any other state of enlightenment, it is for self. Beware of imitation – absolute truth and inner happiness cannot be bought, pursued, laboured for or deserved, for they happen as naturally as rain from a cloud.

Truth is essence and is absolute. In manifestation we have the relativity of the world and it is the job of man to bring the relative back to the absolute. The Absolute truth has absolute love, life and beauty. The law of the material world is entirely to do with relativities; where we come from, where the system comes from, whether we are male or female, our age and so on. In this card we are supposed to bring the truth into the relative; to bring in the understanding of the underlying cause of what seems to be reality; to discover the inner reality that moves the relative to its next expression. The tragedy is that this doesn't bear any resemblance to what we might wish or want in our everyday life. The moment anything is externalised we are going back into the relative. We can appreciate all the levels of innocence, transparency and lack of self-preoccupation that man needs to attain, so as to bridge and accommodate both mundane and cosmic reality.

It's not a case of keeping silent; it's about speaking without being involved; on a deeper level we don't speak at all. It is transparency and 'doing without doing'. The system is imposed on us, we have not created it and we are being used by it. That is why, when a bright man wakes up, he still wants to be in charge. He imposes on himself and his group all sorts of rules and regulations, in order to recreate the system for his own glory. It's part of the Luciferian rebellion, to be fighting against what is there so as to be in charge. Right up to a high level of initiation we are still in danger of keeping up the 'self' bit, until we give up the pride, the need to dominate, the need to be the best, greatest, prettiest or whatever we feel we need to be. We have to see and feel the conflict and separation. We see that we are being used and that this is imposed on us; but what are we? We are an end result, a by-product. If we accept our rightful place, which is a divine one, we have no separation from the greater life any more. It's not acceptance of the caste system in India, it's acceptance through understanding and love, using the discrimination which does not come through dogma. We have to accept life as it is, but we can take action from an angle where we are completely involved with the mechanism of the system, backing up anything which is true, natural and instinctively divine.

We don't need to be searching for paradise or be afraid of hell, because that is done and gone. We don't need to be free of anything, because we understand that freedom is an illusion, a separation and a misunderstanding of the system. Our full definition of humanity's place in the universe is given by the agonies we put ourselves through when we start asking questions about life.

We know that something has to die for a truth to be revealed. The occult karmic link between the murdered and the murderer is twinship. Who is the lamb? The murderer or the one that is murdered? Are the murderers automatically not lambs? Actually they are pitiful little lambs, for when they wake up to full clarity they realise and feel what they have done. This is not to say that we should pity the murderer, but we can see in him the human condition and in a way the victim has got the easier role; this could be why it takes mankind so long to stop blaming the world for its misery!

The world is one and at the same time duality. It's in duality when it manifests, for only then can it go into a polyform. In the Bible Peter is being told that the Soul (Jesus), will take him where he doesn't want to go, which means into hell, for if we do not learn to live at the edge between birth and death, we don't breathe properly, we suffocate. That is a real recognition of 'Thy will and not my will'. Living at the edge in whatever we do, think, or feel at the time, we denude ourselves of the protection of the so called good-will with which we cover ourselves and use for game playing and theatre. If we do not live at the edge we suffocate, because our lungs are not receiving the spiritual waters that they should be receiving. That is why we keep on putting ourselves in front of the door of death time and time again, as a murderer or as the murdered, so eventually somewhere in the middle we gather what is going on.

Until we experience our own decomposition (framework for our experiences), we are not strong enough to live on the edge and be aware of the process of physical death. The breaking down of our emotional dramas and mind sets is what is required, to eventually become innocent. Innocence is a state of not being soiled by ignorance and ignoring the idea of wrong doing. We have done the experience with our eyes open in full consciousness, to the point of becoming transparent, so we cannot be afraid of anything any more; it is only then that the edge is truly our home.

The 'way-by' idea is the best possible analogy we can have. Imagine a little drop of water in a big wave; there are all types of communications happening and it's holding dozens of other drops around it in their positions. We become exactly what we are supposed to be, doing what we are supposed to be doing, in the place we need to be. We see life for what it is and witness the truth, at the same time we support people in the hope that they will wake up to the truth as well. This is why the woman in the card is looking down, listening for the ones who would actually be reacting to the water.

The initiate is there to give the hope of speeding up the process. Like Lucifer, the bringer of light who came down, the initiate says "Look. If you find me I'll help you!"

The role of the initiate is to guide and help other people become their own guides. We do nothing, we are like the little drop of water, but we are held in an unseen ashram and support the local system, until it has every single one of its little cells aware of what is going on. By that time we are innocent and made of love and truth.

Giving divine water is a true refusal to abandon life. That is what we cultivate in ourselves – a refusal to abandon life, even though we can see the drama and the theatre that is happening on the planet. This is an affirmation of the love and will of God and of life without limit. We are not after freedom, but the idea of freedom is what pushes people to climb out, therefore if we have somebody who says "I want to be free" we should encourage them, so that they can learn the truth about freedom. The search for freedom from a situation or condition is good. For those that are after it, freedom means peace, being able to create, moving and being themselves. When we have accepted being that little drop in the pool and obeyed what we are being asked to do, then we can realise all the things we've ever wanted. We are talking about real freedom here, which is not a separation but a true fusion with the greater life itself. Little do we know that we have been running after the wrong freedoms!

Esperance is the fusing of the love and truth of the creator with the created. We know that there was a need to create and in that knowing we have acceptance. We know that creation needed the constant renewing and re-birthing of the endless possibilities, so that it can eventually go back through sublimation to its creator. The love of the creative process of the God we live in is the way of bringing Heaven on Earth.

The double Star of the 8 is the true Venus with all her esoteric power, pushing us to be in love with the experience and so come into life. We start with the obvious attraction to Venus which is held by the mass consciousness, in the appreciation of beauty though the senses. Then we achieve the climate of deep tender affection, where form is by-passed and the sexual activity is not the essential attraction, but only a natural consequence of the state of togetherness. All love must tend towards an ideal, the sublimation of our needs, or the comfort of satisfied needs, according to our perception of what God is. The Lover (an ethereal rather than a comforting and providing lover) comes in and has to come back to the original ideal through us. This can only work by experiencing all the different levels of love within us. A true inner uplifting can happen, when love takes us beyond ourselves. This brings an externalisation of the Soul and a complete turning inside out, when the inner purpose of bridging Heaven on Earth subdues the need of the personality.

Venus is the first point of light to shine in our sky in the morning and the last to shine in the night. It is the double star. Her light gives us peace at night and illumination at the end of an experience. In the morning the early star wakes humanity up, so that the job of submerging ourselves into the magma of mass consciousness can be done safely; the light of Venus is a guide during the day.

Venus is a true teacher for planet Earth, her wakeup call to awareness is showing us the way of transformation. When she transforms herself she does it all at once by turning herself completely inside out; see the glory of that! If we remove ourselves from our little preoccupations and ponder on our position in the process, being on that 'lighted ball of Earth' (as it says in the old commentary) is such a privilege. Then we realise that it's entirely through the process we are under going, that Earth is going to be self-realised and to become sacred. It's simple and beautiful. 'Turning inside out', means seeing it from the point of view of the Soul and serving our fellow men.

Love is the only thing that gives us the sense that in this life we can go further. If we don't go beyond ourselves through love, we are far too much in the desires of the personality, building our own world rather than the world of God. When we build our life according to what we think personality ought to be doing, we are doing it with the thought that life is our personal problem, which it isn't! Holding that idea would limit us to our own view of the world, so to enlarge this view we need to abstract our own personality. Seeing our resistance is only one of the tiny elements of the solution. We have to square the objective behaviour of our life with the value of the cosmos. If we think that the truth is in us, we tend to think that it is exclusive to us. Though we are an expression of the truth, the truth is actually in the whole world, for the world is the truth and we are only a tiny part of it. Truth is the creation itself, which is why it's perfect. We must discover and decipher truth, for it's a decoding process; to do that we have to be pure, give ourselves to it and accept our place. We are searchlights, witnesses and seekers of the truth; we are definitely not criteria or the depository for truth. The love that we have for the creative process is the link that enables us to become the mediators between Heaven and Earth. We must participate in our God's work, for we cannot rise into being co-creators if we shut ourselves into a personal conception of the world.

A faith must always convert itself into trust and hope; that only happens when faith crumbles. This works when we believed in something that subsequently doesn't feel comforting any more. When faith in a belief is translated into behaviour it can become esperance, because we are witnessing and experiencing the word from within ourselves. So we see whatever we see according to the plan above and see whether our behaviour on this planet is viable or not. This will help us to crumble things that have been misunderstood. In the end we have to transmute our faith into a behaviour which is completely aligned to what we truly love, knowing that is all there is and that truth always prevails at the end.

The Moon, La Lune
Digesting the past

In this card we see the vegetative world of the moon, reflecting the light of the Sun and being held in its bright light. The light penetrates the deep dark world of the subconscious, shown by the pond, which is full of decaying matter. In the pond the large red crayfish eats up the decaying unconscious matter of the past, which it digests and assimilates by the process of accepting and loving the biological system of survival. It is a long slow process and involves bringing all the digested matter up into the sunlight of the Soul. The two dogs looking up at the moon are guarding the way along the orange path. On either side are two solid towers, which tell us of our adherence to the structures and principles of the past. In this card the mind is learning to become at one with the ongoing rebirthing process of life in matter.

Many people start on the path, but few complete the journey; this is particularly apparent at this stage in the process. There are several stages where opportunities to break through arise and they can be either taken or refused. The Magician knows he is back in matter with the knowledge of the elements that make up his personality. He can check if he still wants to use them for himself. The elements represent form in all its aspects, so in this process he discovers if there is any attachment to form he might still be protecting. He also has the chance of just playing with the elements; if he takes that option he is feeding the illusion of 'the laboratory' of life on Earth by being the 'sorcerer's apprentice'. There are always tools that can help him get out of this trap, but most of the time a tool itself becomes another element of attachment and can be used for self-satisfaction.

In the first six cards the Magician is presented with the aims and goals of the journey, which he needs to perceive and follow. These six stages are very theoretical and so are focussed in the head and the heart. In these first stages he is still up in the clouds and not touching real life. His buttons have been pushed, but he is not yet in real life, even if he has been able to gather all six stages together and has just passed his exams. It is at Number 4, The Emperor, that we are given a real opportunity to review where we are, in the form of a map or plan. This map gives us a structure and so may appear to be real life, but it is not; it is still a necessary theory. The Pope then gives us the idea of the highest possible way of loving, but this is still a church, a ritual or a place of worship, therefore it is a mindset and just an aspect of loving, not love itself. All mindsets are there to help us on our way, so however much they may have become part of us, they are still very much to do with knowledge and association. We may have fused with ideas, but they are still only ideas. The real path to choose is the way of love, for only love shows us direction. Without love nothing can happen, in fact action can be harmful without love.

The next card at which there is a new start is The Chariot, which is about triumph. This is a turning point and a new direction, where we are going to apply the first six stages to the next group of six cards. In The Chariot we start with zeal and courage. So far we have only given metaphysical qualities to the 1–6, now we have to apply and give those qualities personal names. This next group of six cards, beginning with The Chariot, have the fundamental disciplinary qualities that we need to apply, to help us continue on the path and succeed in the next part of the journey.

This is another point at which we can refuse to finish the journey for we have still not yet gone through the veil, which was shown to us by The High Priestess in Number 2. The High Priestess held the promise that we could go through the veil so as to find the truth and reality behind it, but we were not actually able to tear it at that point. So the first six cards are to do with concept and its shadow, the next six are when we start to apply these characteristics into our lives. Justice, Number 8, is the most severe one, for without the intense honesty of that one the others would not succeed. Justice shows us levels of covering up that we didn't know existed. We go on with those for life after life until we refine, so we can keep going round and round and up and down on The Wheel of Fortune, rather than rising above it. Number 11, Strength, is about finding the wise inner strength that is in us because of what we have gone through.

The second six cards are the survival kit for the initiate, preparing him for the next part of the journey on the path. When we get to Number 12, The Hanged Man, we are going for the death of what is of no use and would impair the progress on the path. Most people coming to this stage will give themselves a really hard time, because they know it has to do with being seen and heard; in fact it is the need to be seen and heard which has to go, so that the inner contact between Soul and Spirit can be the point of meeting for the lost personality. The following six cards are particular aspects, there to activate the death of the little self, in order to be re-born to the true self. These are not teaching us how to do the metaphysical work any more, but the work in real life. This is why at The Hanged Man we reach the point where there is no going back. If we are in that process and decide we are not going to let go of seeking outer recognition, then we might not be able to come back into the world of everyman, because we have touched on another world and don't fit into ordinary life any more.

At The Tower, because we are going for the crumbling of all the social structures and mindsets that we have relied on, we end up with nakedness. Then with The Stars we are letting go of all form, until we are no longer attracted by it. Even the idea of beauty has to be relinquished, because like love, beauty is in everything and is therefore systemic, so is nothing to do with measuring and comparing; life *is* beautiful. The Stars tell us what we have earned and tell us that we are rich with the secret of life itself. This wealth has none of the attractions, desires, or needs in it, so all we have is the inner knowledge. This is what we call 'connaissance', or having certitude about the greater truth. We have the greater life in us. Number 17, The Stars, has love and true hope in it, but even here we are still bargaining and still wanting something. Now here we are at Number 18, looking at all these mindsets and asking, "Did I aspire to wisdom, love and all the other high qualities?" The Moon says, "Forget it!"

The Moon truly says there is no return, not even to the nakedness that we found in The Stars; it is about eating ourselves and really disappearing. The only thing left is the reflection of the Sun on your personality. All the contradictions are in this one for it opens up the true metaphysical life.

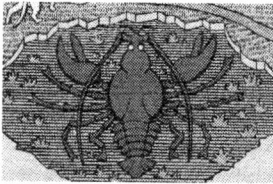

Depicted in Number 18 we have the pond, which represents the unconscious, the subconscious or mass consciousness. This is how it is in life; we are in a pond swamped by the heaviness of the unaware mass energy; that is our environment. The point of being here is to learn to be aware of our reactions to everyday life and to always check ourselves to see if we are playing games, for if we are playing games we have forgotten that we are in a pond.

The crayfish, like Cancer the crab, is symbolic of the great principle: 'I build a lighted house and therein dwell'. This is the energy of home (planet Earth) holding on through regeneration. The crayfish is walking backwards and the special thing about a crayfish is that it only eats dead matter; it won't eat anything that shows any sign of life. This is the extremely simple principle of the ultimate re-cycling, so simple that if we do not recognise it we can't see it. It is a strange experience when it is felt in the cellular memory, for it reminds us that the world of nature is a being that is eating itself. In the feeling of that we experience a poignancy and uselessness, yet we have to accept it. The crayfish carries on eating a lot all the time and as it does so it sheds its old shells, grows new ones and gets constantly larger and larger. It represents all the experiences that have been done so far in the world. Because of its bulk, it forms a step from which we can eventually get onto the orange path.

The fat crayfish is pregnant with the new life to come, which must be completely denuded of any dead matter. We have a very big album of 'photos of the past' to look through, which go back to long before the dinosaurs. Much of this has been used in the past and finished with, but there are a lot of people who think that to go and kill each other like dinosaurs is still the way to behave. Even though we may have understood the whole process, we continue to destroy each other, for we can still be under the illusion that we have to fear biological death. We know that this behaviour is silly and worthless, yet we keep giving it life and being taken in by it, for we wake up every day with the same rubbish around us. The initiate also comes back into the old swamp like everyone else and even if he has seen the truth behind it, he has to adhere to the principle 'when in Rome do as the Romans do'. He has to live his life like everybody else, so that he is not noticed as being different and special by the mass consciousness; he is part of the world and doesn't stand out.

The word, which goes with this card, is 'anguish'. With Number 17 there was the essence of pure naked love. With 18 the experience of mind over matter requires the breaking down of sustaining the welfare of matter into mud, to achieve the next form and the question arises "Can my will-power endure".

The path forward is the past, which has to be perceived in a different way. The fact that we are here is likely to mean that we still have a personal desire to walk in the natural biological life to meet our God; this is very self-centred. At this stage we are being told to go in, go down, look at and understand the process of how we do it, so any mindsets which we have left about being anything else but a pale reflection, must go. Here we meet ourselves and our brothers or sisters where they truly are. We are no better than crayfish. This is the lonely path, or the long night and we are walking backwards. We have to drop the promise of salvation for ourselves, so if we are looking forward at the Sun and living our lives for ourselves, we have missed the point. It is like the story of Orpheus, walking backwards with the Sun behind him. If we don't take on the work of the crayfish then that tells us that we are in it for ourselves.

The anguish is in the question, "Where has hope gone?" and the answer is that we have to transmute hope into complete obedience and acceptance, through understanding the energetic process. We have to tidy our house and drop all the metaphysical mindsets, as well as all the tools we have looked at so far. These tools are all the things we have used to survive, like knowledge, wisdom and religion; even our own personal religion. Once we have dropped these there is no longer any support, no survival kit, photo album and no wanting to see the God we live in for self; we have to drop belief in anything that sustained us. This is how we go through the great process of becoming systemic. How can we do that if we don't experience the life within the system through our whole being?

In Number 18 the 8 is coming back to the 10, revisiting it from the level of the awakened consciousness, so as to give it the systemic experience of how it all works. This is so that there can be as much awareness in the subconscious as there is in the highest aspiration. The process is kind and gentle, for we are not blinded by the light as we are when we come from total darkness. Though we are in the darkness of the night, as we come to the surface of the pond we see the stars and we can dream. Then we go back into the depths of the pond with The Moon, in order to look at the shadows. If we went straight from the pond into too strong a light, it would blind and destroy us. The 18 tells us to 'Go gently' into having the complete experience and follow the great laws of destruction and re-birth. Number 18 comes back with gold, but it is hidden gold, because it is in the dark at night. There is great promise and great wisdom, but the law of Number 18 is about using and being used and about the way Spirit and matter works with this law. The problem for anyone under the influence of the Number 18 is that they put themselves in the position of being used without realising, so they are punched again and again until they finally can see a pattern. Then they realise that way of being used is actually not working. Eventually there is a complete acceptance that being used *is* the right thing, but at the same time there is a need to discriminate and make sure that we are being used in the right way. It is helpful to remember and recognise that feeling of being used. Nature uses and is being used to an end, as it eats itself. Mankind is still exteriorising this violence against animals, women, children and the land itself. The goal is the great concept of the complete acceptance of being used by the light of the greater life we live in. At the end of that one we really have to accept the concept that our life isn't ours. That has to be accepted with reality and love in our hearts and not with bitterness, so that it is clear, clean, untainted and able to receive the light of the Spirit. If there is anything bitter left in the tool bag, it gets the whole drama going again.

The only thing we are is a mirror of the Sun, receiving the energy from the greater life. From that perspective we can't be afraid to see the self and humanity as they are. We could call this unconditional love, but that is not even the right word, for there is a hint of a condition in it. Here we are going into true metaphysics, for there is only one true life that is energetic and its purpose is hidden. If we don't see through the illusion of everyday life we relate to everything by measuring and comparing. Consequently we only know ourselves through an appreciation of what others think of us. This is giving dust a reality and dulls our shiny star. The idea is to recognise the existence beyond ourselves as one with us and become an expression of the reflected light. This is not an understanding or a state that we can practise at. That is why the stage of The Moon is a long dark process, the longest night of our lives.

Even though the crayfish is a fiery red colour, there is no lust in him. He has nearly filled his pool. His shape is like a figure of eight, which reminds us that we need to understand the process that the 8 symbolises. The 8 is associated with the sign for eternity, the cosmic egg and the Christ. The 8 is also to do with time and space and therefore linked to the planet Saturn. Astrologically Capricorn is associated with Saturn, so we have the lovely description of Capricorn – 'lost am I in light supernal, yet on that light I turn my back'. In this we can understand the process of the initiate, walking with his back to the Sun, so that the reflection of the Sun can be seen in him as he serves his fellow men. The Sun represents the universal Soul of our Solar System and the sum total of consciousness achieved within its experience. We construct our perception of God from the level of awareness that we hold at the time.

The crayfish is the equivalent of Cancer, the opposite sign to Capricorn. Cancer is to do with passivity, receiving, memory and history. We love history because we want to understand where we came from, in case there is a paradise at the bottom of the pool. The advanced Cancer is 'the holder of the little ones;' holding the space so they can go forward. Walking backwards is going deep in so as to be 'in the service of'; this is the only thing to do if we want to be a faithful witness, so it completes the wisdom of Capricorn the teacher, by receiving the light and turning it into new forms that the little ones (aspirants) can observe.

We can see the anguish at the physical level if we think of early man, surrounded by all the elements and experiencing an awesome anguish about survival, for he saw the God we live in as all the elements fighting against him and punishing him for being alive; we felt guilty before we could even stand up! This was the way we built our God then as we had to feel the fear and do it anyway! Rebel! Now we have a huge span of experience of what the God we live in might be, yet our perception is still very much on the elemental side. It is only when we take the metaphysical point of view that we can go beyond ourselves and beyond the mindsets. Thus we stretch the comprehension and so begin a new understanding of the great life we live in. When our minds experience the process of light coming into the death and regeneration of biological life, any idea of God according to our own projections goes and there is no longer a promise of a personal relationship with God. The whole awareness takes on the perception that the system is all there is; we have to feel it in us and love it as well as know it, for the system *is* God.

The more we go into the pond of ancestry, the more able we are to clean the dead matter; that is our job. The pond and the crayfish are reflections of the Moon and Sun. The Moon in its highest aspect is symbolic and acts as a protector and trickster at the same time, for it keeps us in the shadow to make sure that we really eat all our rubbish. This tests our will; it also acts as a receptor for the intensity of the light of the Sun, so as to feed us with the light we can assimilate. We need this protection because we are not yet ready for complete fusion. At this level we are not actually facing the Sun, but have our backs to it and are looking at the reflected light, rather than the Sun itself. It is only possible for us to see life from the point of view of the initiate when we are down here on Earth, so the initiatic state requires a true acceptance of life as it is. If we have the illusion that as an initiate we are going to heaven, forget it! Religion, philosophy, theosophy, science, as well as everything we find in life on Earth, are all just mirrors of our misunderstanding.

The crayfish transmutes the muck into real life and enables us to re-look at everything, so as to see it from a different point of view. Actually there is only one point of view, which is from the watcher within us. However beautiful an idea is, if it is not expressed from our unique expression then it is meaningless. Our completely unique set of experiences tell us that we are on our own, that we are one unit in the total expression of awareness and that we have travelled through time and space to be here at this time, pregnant for the next part of the journey. This is another expanded way to perceive experience. From here we are going beyond ourselves, because so far we have found nothing but a burning love, so we ask "What is it that I love so much?" At that level what we think we can love and would die for might be a con trick, because we actually receive and have received a lot of love already. Here, at Number 18, there are no mindsets about love left, because we are being pushed back through the past. We can see how, in order to be loved, we let other people use us and we can see that that is really not love. It is about re-looking at all of those experiences in depth. That is what the crayfish is getting big and fat on and why the pond, or the subconscious, is getting purified. In the metaphysical world we are like the Moon, or a reflection of our past, through which our mind can be filled with the filtered light of the source. When our minds can sustain the light of pure energy from the Sun, we give it back to the system, we become systemic. When we think of eating all the pictures of the past and all the old dramas, then we start to be ready to become cosmic, for we are de-personalising. The experiences are ours without being ours. This happens more and more the deeper we go into the pool. The crayfish has loads of humanity's experience in it, because it has eaten and digested so many misunderstandings, that it becomes a true reflection of where humanity is at. The lower we go into the self to cleanse, the higher we go up to look at supernal life.

On either side of the pond we see two dogs, one black and one white; they are there to guard the everyday life of mankind. The big black dog lies on the ground; in his horizontal stance he represents the playfulness of matter. The white dog represents all the highest religious and philosophical aspects within mankind. These are both aspirations of everyday life in matter and are to do with attachment. Dogs have natural faithfulness and attachment to everyday life through loving their owners, because it is in their nature to belong to a group (pack). They also represent a deep attachment to the past, as man and dog have walked on the Earth together for thousands of years, so the dogs are there as guardians to prevent the crayfish from giving life away to the mirror of The Moon. They are barking to guard the familiar, the past and the unconscious, but also to protect the process of transformation so that it can succeed. They represent the profane life, so they stay behind and keep a watch as man's best friend. When we reach the crunch however, we have to go beyond that. We stay because the group knows us and the group is holding everyone together. This is seen in the extreme in the mass consciousness level, for everyone has to behave as the others do and everyone stays and holds because it is safe and it works. This dulls the pain and anguish of the transition from nature to higher consciousness. The dogs represent the accepted pack mentality of the group. They guide and protect the aspiration and uplift of the mind, while the transformation of dead matter (misused energy) into pure instincts takes place.

The drops in the air, which are coloured red, green and yellow, are rising up towards the Sun. They represent what has been digested from the pond, and then atomised. They are going back to the Sun, for the Sun is the great cleanser, which burns up the Solar System and sustains life with the energy that is released. It is the same process as our crayfish. The Sun purifies its system by burning the dross to fuel the ongoing life it sustains. It burns itself pure to the end. We are the fuel. Are we singing? The crayfish is walking backwards, not looking where it is going, for it demonstrates the inevitable outcome of where it belongs in the system.

The crayfish is an aspect of our reflection. Having understood our role in the enfoldment of the great life, we are no longer seeing ourselves in a state of pain and suffering. Our consciousness is associating with the working of the system. Matter is recycled, so the mind is free to break through to a new understanding. The dogs are there as a reminder to the crayfish to go on looking at the reflection. Here, with the symbolism of the higher Moon we are in the presence of The High Priestess, so the work has to do with 'becoming' rather than finding out. It is reflection in action, rather than just a reflection that recognises The Moon. We have to use imagination, which is something more than just pure reflection, in order to get out of the pond and go beyond the dogs and the towers. Also what is needed is the sublimation of the experience of having received and given love. Life becomes a gift when we know it is not a gift any more. We are not a gift, so we give ourselves back to the thing that gave us life. This is a good description of how the mind becomes systemic; to achieve this we need to go through the pond many a long time.

We are mirroring all the time and there is no separation. In the remembrance that in everyday life we are only a reflection, there is anguish. There is the silence and the not being heard. All the time in the night the dogs are watching, to remind us of the time nature took to birth consciousness, also to remind us how long it will take to go back to nature in full consciousness, so as to redeem the innocent past. At the end of our process we don't need dogs, for we become the watching of the dogs ourselves. The silence is there because we have to reach a point of nothingness and go into the place of dissolution, to be really clean. Before we had not seen ourselves as dead matter, so there was the anguish and the fear that we would find we are monsters. Now there is no going back from here; it is the long night of acceptance, endurance and obedience. We are always going beyond, until there is only going backward, we just go where the Spirit is taking us in the system. This is being systemic, but we have to hold the consciousness and be totally aware, at the same time as flowing like the wind through experiences. This can be expressed as, 'I am looking at a world that is being experienced through me'. If the world looks at itself as a series of objects, then it will see itself as 'matter' and we will be forever measuring ourselves. This is about asking questions and developing awareness, but we have to rise and fall to look at ourselves being looked at. As long as we see it from the point of view of the question 'who am I' we automatically see others as objects to be used, but when we're feeling used we see it as 'not fair!' This is the downfall of mankind's individuality. From the point of view of the higher life we are one. We are the objects that the higher consciousness uses and that higher expression of the life we live in is not abusive and greedy like us. Religion describes God as good and we tend to interpret that according to our understanding of what good is. The true experience is that there is nothing else but infinite love, which is not a love that makes you feel good. Systemic consciousness is experiencing the system itself on behalf of the greater life.

It is here that we can see that the veil is only a reflection through which the 8 will replay everything back that we have seen or experienced so far. At Number 12 we tore the veil, here in Number 18 the veil can lift and be blown in the wind that comes from the very ancient times of creation, to shake the cobwebs of our illusions. At this point we have to drop our own aspirations to go towards The Sun; we didn't know we would have to do that when we started the journey. If we follow the aspiration to fulfil our own desires, then we are still in personality. It is here that we have to make sense of the reality of what drives life forward. If we have lived through an initiation with our 'awareness' eyes open, then we can see ourselves in the process; this is the gift of the cycle of 18, bringing the knowledge back to the Soul (9).

The Moon is represented with three colours in it, silver, white and yellow (an aspect of red); in actual moonlight there are no colours. In the picture there is red behind the sun's rays. In the Masonic symbolism red is the colour of the master of masters and represents the consciousness becoming one with the life of the system. Silver is white and black and is to do with initiation. It works in the shadows and tricks us, for it is to do with the quality of the changing Moon. One minute it shows us something being white and the next it is black, so this teaches us to have to think for ourselves. White is the stage of the second initiation, where we are learning to see things as silver, which means neither good nor bad, nor black and white. Here the emotions (colours) are being bleached, for there are no colours in moonlight. Even the deepest esperance has to give way to the cold light of reason. Gold or yellow, is about the fruition of the new birth, sustained by the light of the Sun. Gold is crystallised sunshine.

The Moon has a woman's face to affirm that it is a receptive quality. The feminine tells us about the reflecting aspect, which is prominent in this card. There is a general biological aspect to this, which relates to the reflection of the Sun's rays onto the Moon and then onto Earth, for without that process seeds would not germinate. This is about letting the light of the Sun come down to Earth and be received in a way that can be used. The aim is to let that principle work through us and give up all that we think we are, in order to be used as a receptor for the light. Without the work of the creative unconscious being bathed in the light of awareness, there is no possibility of the re-birth of the species. The job of humanity is to bring the light deep into the pond of biological life, to receive the message and give out the translation according to the local atmosphere, so the vision has to be de-personalised but individual at the same time. This is the paradox, for if we stop the process of individualisation then all the mindsets cannot be seen and melted away. We need to see ourselves as individuals, so as to poise our witnessing.

18 could be interpreted as mind over matter, as some great Hindu 'saints' or wise men demonstrate by the example of how they live their lives. It is the mind following the Spirit guided by its master Lord Karma. If we remember to look at it as 18/9 we understand that the aim is to unite the mind and the heart in the deep silence of the Soul, so that matter (personality) can be moved by the Spirit and guided by the collective karma of humanity.

The two towers represent refuge and institutions. Only the right hand one has a door, which tells us that the right side of the brain has more openings for mankind's imagination and creativity. The two towers are the equivalent of the columns in Number 2 (The High Priestess) and the two dogs are the equivalent of the two sphinxes. The orange path starts in the pond. It represents the whole of our little past lives, including all our experiences so far and the lives of all our ancestors. The shape of the path reminds us of an intestine, because it is about the digestive process of absorption, which is what we need to do at this point in our transformation.

The meandering course of the path reminds us that it takes time to digest what we take in, so as to extract that which is of value from it; that can't be hurried.

The aim is to infuse pure instinct with lighted consciousness, so that life can see itself for what it is. Our 'responsibility' is to be aware of what moves us and bring it back to Soul, so that it can be exteriorised as love/wisdom. If we are in the mass consciousness we are just asleep, which makes certain that consciousness gets lost into all the illusion, glamour and the matter of Maya. If we feel content there, then we are not responsive to our own spark because it is hidden. The process is one of a self-participating God and our responsibility is to drop the protective scales, so that we feel as nature does, constantly anguished, but with deep love holding it in the light. Once we know the system we no longer need to name the patterns and objects of the world, for many are there, dying to do it! It is all about awakening and awareness. We hold all the memories, both reactive and instinctive and we can remember the uniqueness of our own experiences.

The shared witnessing in a group through individual perception, allows us to cultivate our own individuality, but with respect for other people's point of view. This reminds us that it all goes back to the one life we live in. We can't have a God that matches our understanding, for God has to be greater than that, so it is important to break down anything which gives us a certain idea of what the God we live in might be. The memory aspect of self is very important, for it enables us to recognise the shadowy quality of form. The deeper we go into the memory and action of biology itself, the nearer we get to an understanding and great compassion of why it takes a human being so long to become wise.

We had to create the measurement of time in order to actually come to the idea of timelessness and then we had to frame our experiences within that. The Spirit moves, whereas time is an accommodating measure in space. When we go beyond the idea of timelessness we become a carrier of love and truth. In nature everything can be predictable; from the point of view of Soul and Spirit change and transformation belong to the realm of karma. A feeling is only an intellectualised instinct. We hold on to an experience so that we can give a name to our feelings and reactions, until we are fully aware of them. In that awareness we can cleanse the pool very effectively. Fear is the call of Spirit, which says 'move on' towards something we don't know. The fear of the unknown is fear of finding that hurt and death is all there is, so making a monster of our God!

Any monsters we find are actually the memory of the fears of the little self we use as an instrument. At every initiation we have to go through the process of people not liking us, because we have to shed one of our aspects of self respect to bring back this consideration to the Soul. At Number 18 we have to meet, recognise and love the God we live in, seeing how he looks at us through our reflections. This stage is a corner stone, as how we look at life will have to be seen as one and the same perception. There is a caution here, because if we come up to the gate of initiation and are not ready, we can be a danger to the collective by disrupting the energy with our chaotic vibration. However, this can be seen later on as a wake up call for the group. All the other cards have to do with truth and love, but this one is the process of actually becoming one with the truth, as experienced by nature as she gives birth to consciousness. We start that 'becoming' by associating with the truth, rather than to our sad story; eventually a merging of our mind with the simple universal truth takes place. We are becoming a spark of light, enlightening the path back home. In this state all the rules of the world don't make much sense, for it is more through prescience, sentiency and movement that life has to be understood.

Every single minute of the day we stand exactly where we have brought ourselves to; we are the sum total of all our reactions and where we are at so far, so there is no blame. It is not to do with abandoning the past, or thinking of ourselves as the behaviour of the past, for that is a sign of pride. There are so many methods that make us think that we can leave the past behind, whereas actually what we need to do is to go deeper into it and perceive it on a simpler, higher note, by eating it as the crayfish does; taking in all the memories and digesting them and so transforming our causal body into a brighter support for the Spirit. The only way we are going to recognise the communal essence of all lives, is by the mind being able to go back into the unconscious nature. Nature is a pure manifestation and a response to a stage of unfoldment that the God we live in was in, before it could see itself. The way has been sought for a long time and as we become more and more respectful of nature, we become more in touch with our own natural instinct, which is pure. If we are being part of life, then we cannot be de-natured. We can recognise the brotherhood of all life; for example, a baby is born with no other purpose but to be a part of life, whether it is a piglet or a human baby.

Many people have opened their minds in order to receive sweet messages of peace and the answers to so many questions about the human condition, God and his angels as well as much else. If their consciousness does not fully comprehend the meaning of the idea they channel, the impact for uplifting the consciousness of their readers might be spreading like the wind, but will not go deep enough to stir up a whirlwind and bring some hidden aspect of mind into the light. Thinking for ourselves is the beginning of self responsibility, so when the word contains the inspired vision and the intimate understanding of what is being said, then we have to be aware of the great responsibility we take, for the energy contained in our message could trigger a disturbing change of perception in the recipients. This may result as a transformation of the way they live their lives, which may take them into an initiatic crisis. The responsibility for such a happening becomes part of the great karmic guidance that encourages the unfolding of the great life we live in. Another observation about the responsibility of the trail blazer for the love of truth, is that as a new interpretation or a simpler expression of some aspect of Ancient Wisdom is delivered, it seems to give the green light for many other minds to pick up the idea and spread it according to the level of consciousness of a mass market. There it will be diluted, but can initiate important questions in the readers.

The importance of the message of transparency in this book becomes evident when you consider what has just been said. The breaking down, grinding and melting down of all the aspects of self that might cloud the reception and delivery of useful ideas, has to be undertaken. The devotion that is required to annihilate the resistance of the personality and the pride of the Spirit goes beyond the norm; by doing that we 'become'. By 'becoming' we let the light of the divine dissipate the shadows of our nature body. To receive a minute drop of the light, the initiate knows he has to throw himself into the abyss, where no one else has gone before.

The word for this card is anguish. At first we are following 'esperance', then we have to feel 'anguish'; this defines man. When we have left behind all the nitty-gritty of life, many questions come to us and we find that anguish is behind the questioning. It is this anguish that makes us become true human beings; we need to understand this. We aspire to know what it is all about and become aware of our ultimate need, which is to be one with the love within life. In a previous age we became individual personalities; further back still man's life was only experienced according to tribal survival. We can only question our origin and our future. In that questioning we have to recognise the great cosmos and see that even though we are only a tiny part of that, we have a relationship with it and a role in it, which operates through all the levels of transformation.

We should realise that we carry in us the gift of the past. That process of creating a perception of the God we live in started in the dark of a timeless night. The highest levels of illumination are now being sought after by mankind because we seek the bliss aspect, so we need the qualities we find in Number 18 to help us get rid of that search for personal bliss; we are not going for a God of reward here. We feel the pain of solitude in our individualisation. This is a state that we have had to take on so as to find the outer boundaries of our individual selves, for until complete limitation is found, recognised and given up we can never be one with another person. Eventually we will be able to see through someone else's eyes, or they will see through ours. The more we turn to self-gratification and search for bliss though outside experiences, the more anguish we create. To be phenomena among other phenomena creates anguish, for as wisdom tells us, we are only Maya and illusion. When we have stepped out of the pond, we are then in a sacred place and there is no possibility of refusing to participate in the work of the sacred. This work asks us to go back into the pool, in order to digest more biological life and bring more sacredness into that life.

We call the resistance to moving forward 'fear'. We are learning not to call it fear anymore and coming to the realisation that it is just movement. If the will is strong we walk through what we fear. The one thing that halts man is laziness and the desire to stay in comfort, for it is so much easier to be passively fed. We are not fallen Gods trying to romantically remember how it used to be, we are instruments for a God who self-builds and recreates itself according to the availability of its building materials. Because of this we always find ourselves going further, deeper and higher than we have gone before. The one who avoids the search is essentially not a man, for the essence of being a human being is to do with seeking and giving. Few of us are at the stage of leading a true autonomous life, for humanity is suffering from a great psychic laziness, or indolence of the Soul. Searching for cosmic labels such as green aliens, indigo children, rainbow children or any other hue is avoidance of who we are. The only 'hu' we seek is the one in 'hu-man', which means God and his man.

In the sequence of stages in the journey, the 18 opens the last group; this time a super effort is needed to do it. Here sheer will is needed in order to be able to progress. We have acquired true value and we must have no ties, therefore we must leave behind that which could still help us. We are asked to kill the initiator in us and let go of all links, all useful things and all the pain of the past, so as to have no more self-absorption.

As we grow old, we lose the memory of the present and go back more vividly to the memories of childhood. In doing so the only thing that stays is the instinctual memory; this is the true childhood which is spoken of in the bible, when the consciousness is going back to the source. We have the sum total of a lifetime to show us that we came in as a child with the promise of the future; we are the future of that child. If we have loved, hurt, forgiven and forgotten, whatever we have achieved is well done and its only use is to move the future and the past together.

We need to be as naked as a newborn babe; this is true childhood and is not the self, just us and our God with no reward and no punishment. We are walking towards identification with God. This is the process of our consciousness becoming systemic and is the work of the Number 8, which always revises and re-evaluates. Religions apply a high attainment concept to everyday situations, so giving people a direction of how to live their lives; this is not what we are talking of here. Through our Soul, we feel that the eternal truth and the mundane are as one.

The unconscious is the whole of the experience of nature. When there is a point where individualisation can take place, the experience of nature gives to that point the energy of pure instinct. When pure instinct is retrieved amongst the decaying pool of the subconscious, the supraconscious mind of man can see himself as the life in the system and as the mind making God in his own image; meaning God as he perceives the system itself. Reality rules; man gives up and lets God take over.

The Sun, Le Soleil
Out into the full light

A young, almost naked couple link arms under a radiant Sun; this is the spiritual light that penetrates to the heart of matter. They stand within a grassy circle of flowers and behind them there is a wall of blue, red and gold bricks. This is Number 19, where we experience the fusion of the feminine and masculine. Here we radiate energetically from our core, so the vibration is very fast. At the advanced level the card represents sainthood, where there is no desire for self. It is near the end of the journey, so we are building the New Jerusalem.

What is beautiful about Taoism is that it is practical yet metaphysical; it rises right up, then it comes back down to look at the situation in a practical way. This is Number 19, which is sainthood, so here we are looking at the saint of the Tarot.

> Give up sainthood, renounce wisdom,
> And it will be a hundred times better for everyone.
> Give up kindness, renounce morality,
> And man will rediscover filial piety and love.
> Give up ingenuity, renounce profit,
> And bandits and thieves will disappear.
> These three are outward forms alone; they are not sufficient
> in themselves.
> It is more important to see the simplicity, to realise ones true
> nature, to cast out selfishness and temper desire.

(Tao Te Ching. Gia-fu feng and Jane English)

If we are working at sainthood we are not doing it; this is what 'giving up sainthood' means. Achievement occurs when we know we are doing something, but when we have really done it we merge with it and then the achievement disappears. The 19 is the fusion, merging and balancing of the feminine and masculine. This is where all our qualities of left and right are coming together to fuse and become one consciousness. This is Active Intelligence and the Soul intelligence coming back to the light of the Sun again.

The Sun is represented as a sphere so it is like one of our cells, or on the other hand like the whole life of the Solar System. The egg of life symbolises how the process of the manifestation of form is imbued with life in time and space, on both microcosmic and macrocosmic scales. The rays of the Sun have many different manifestations; one of them is the far infra-red energy ray, which has a healing vibration that goes to the very heart of our water molecules. Another ray enables us to see things, so it is what we usually call light; there are many others. There are the physical qualities of light, but there is also spiritual light from the Sun and this is what we have in the 19. In this context seeing life truthfully from the spiritual angle, means that we are looking from the point of view of The Sun consciousness.

The 9 can be so full of wisdom that it doesn't know how much it has, until it releases and relaxes all the pent-up crystallised experiences that it has gone through in all its cycles. When the 9 disappears in the centre of its space/time manifestation, it can be so fragile that a lot of pain covers up the wisdom accumulated in the experience. The miasms in the biological life that carry the karmic link to the Soul can then start rising to the surface, to be seen, recognised and depersonalised. When we work to clear our karmic accumulation we start realigning our own DNA to the original idea. We are doing this for the next generation. It will take at least three more generations to be completely clear of the miasms through the releasing of the karmic genetic pattern. Simply put, this is the basic work of the 9th cycle.

We come back into one world, we are in it and it is in us. It is all to do with movement and vibration attracting the right coat of matter for incarnation into a specific job. When we come back in a Number 1 cycle in the centre of the sphere, the aim is to lighten the vibrations of our 'space suit'. As we vibrate faster we are going to feel a narrower, tighter, spiralling movement, so when the 19 comes back it is on a tightrope vision of life, in which it is not going to be moved by anything but the thing it loves; it uses the will to serve that love. The more we align to the will of God, the more we are going to experience tightrope-walking through life with no safety net. Staying in a position of authority and caring for people is all very well and good, but it isn't acting through the will of God so much as using that power for our own need; we all do this. When we speak about the Number 9 we speak of all the numbers, for it can have the best and the worst of everything in it. This is because it is at the end of a time and space spiral. With the cycle of 19 we have a similar thing, but here the disciple has already seen some wisdom and comes back to refine and deliver its teaching. He has to do this without interfering with others and with the deepest compassion, so this means he has to completely give over to the will of the planet to the karmic life of the Solar System.

As the spiral tightens the experience gets faster and tighter, which means that the energy is getting highly strung. Esoterically this means the energy will radiate out further from its own core and, if it is all working well, that core is in touch with the Sun.

The tighter and the faster we vibrate, the more the radiation from our core will affect what we do, say and touch. This is important to realise at this stage, because we are talking here about building the New Jerusalem at the end of the journey. There are many different levels of consciousness going through a 19 cycle, but it is only the advanced human being that has no desire for self and will give their life as an example of service and selflessness; that is what

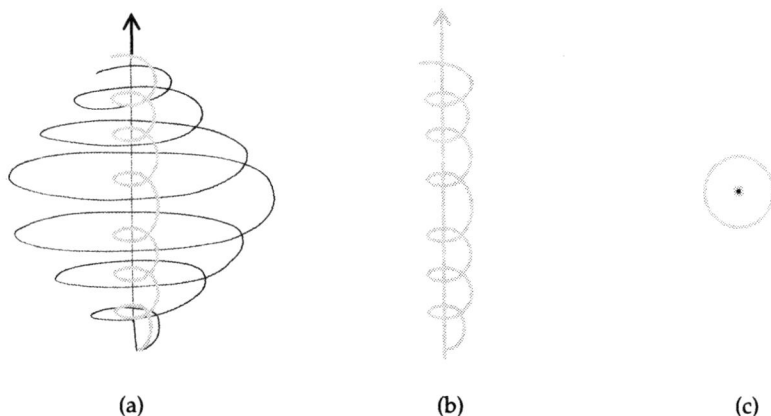

(a)   (b)   (c)

Figure 1. The tightening of the spiral.

a. The lighter and faster we vibrate, the more our core is in touch with the Sun.
b. Eventually the tightrope will get so tight that we have to look at it as one
of the rays of The Sun.
c. We are walking on sunshine!

sainthood is. Many people under the influence of the 19 have a desire to be heard, because they hold a piece of sunshine. There is something incredibly stubborn in them that says they have to put this light to good use. This is the spiritual will of the 10 guiding the Soul 9. The job of the 19 is to get the Sun out, so they need to vibrate to such a pitch that the resulting movement is going to touch deeply the emotional energy of people. Then this enables something to move in others, in the same way that the far infra-red ray from the Sun brings its healing vibration into the cellular structure of the body.

As we move into tighter loops we radiate faster and deeper, which means that we are able to decipher the locked memory in the matter of our bodies. As we vibrate even faster the energy goes deep into the heart, where we can recognise and work at the mindsets driven by the emotions the moment they appear. At this point we have been through 19 steps to recognise what we have to do to be true to our higher self. Like the Sun rising, the truth comes up from the depths to deliver a memory from the past. It is at the psychic or Soul level that we retain everything that is worthy of life's experiences, from the beginning of our conscious life. These are the things that have struck a chord with us; that chord is sounding into the ten thousand things that are in us. The whole of that sound is held in the body, while the Soul keeps the record of the emotional and mental understanding.

Biology is only the film, whereas the psychic world is the music. As in a film when they put the music on, we feel it and know it; the music locks the experience deep inside our nature body. In the same way the Soul will lock into the experiment as it continually radiates, then when biology and Soul meet the truth can be revealed. In the end truth is always just about survival and revisiting life with our eyes open, so as to bring it back home; nobody is guilty!

Everything we do or are is on behalf of the God we live in; it is just so simple. In knowing this intellectually we can easily go into our reactions and judgment, but really it is about bringing the light deep down where it can meet matter, so as to be known and seen; this is how we can understand humanity's sometimes bizarre and awful behaviour. When we are in love with the Sun, we dissolve into it. It is easy to be compassionate, but in that clear place we can't understand why people make such a fuss about pain! Why can't everybody be happy in the situation? Those under the influence of the 19 can be like that; they bathe in the ray of the God we live in and so can't see why people aren't able to cope with pain. To understand that, they have to fall back right into matter, the emotions and the mindsets, so as to remember what the fuss is all about. The spiritual Sun is doing the work, but is not completely in the form, so has to work at understanding what is going on in matter.

A lot of 19s will only do what is comfortable for them, which is to follow their own authority, because they know that what they are doing is okay. They can be very single minded with that mindset, for they are holding onto the spark of the true Sun behind them. There is no way they can let that authority out of their sight, for if they do they start lying to themselves. Because they are not able to lie to themselves, it is very painful for them to see people around them lying about what motivates their behaviour; this makes them difficult to live with. We know that lying to oneself is what hides the Sun and veils the possibility of fruitfulness and goodness on the planet. The difficulty here is the pain that we have, when our vibration starts to speed up and we see our misunderstandings and short falls. We see that it is all to do with the Sun using humanity to purify darkness. We can almost exclude our planet in that, because at that level of understanding we know that the plants, the animals, the rocks and the planet itself are sacred. It is an intellectual, natural knowing, so when we look at an animal we see it as pure, even with all its killing and raping. We know that our brothers in humanity are also pure; it is just that they haven't understood how to use that purity yet. It is here that we truly learn to use the sacred energy of life in the right way, by starting to realise that the only way to move is with the right use of energy. With the cycle of 19 we are talking about giving up our will to the higher will; knowing the difference between the two will involve the wisdom in the Soul. Mistakes will be made and we have to dare to make mistakes.

A lot of people have these little sparks of Sun-light, but are not listening or looking at them any more, so deep is the groove made by social pressure, habits and attachment that they cannot be true to their inner authority, for they cannot see the light in themselves. In the cycle of 19 they go into battles because they still feel strongly that they have a mission. They need to learn to do it with love; they don't need to battle or feel in isolation, but rather come and merge with the group so that their light and their words can touch people's lives for the better. Even if they only touch two people in a thousand that is two more people who are going to learn to give their light to others. The reason why 19s have a problem with authority is because they have to listen to their own authority and learn to dispense it by letting it radiate, rather than forcing reason onto others. Radiating is the force flowing out, whereas forcing one's authority onto people is using power. We know power isn't the right use of spirituality, for we don't force people, but we do radiate inspiration and see whether there is something that can attract and spark off that little bit of true light in others, so that they can find a better way of spreading it than us. We can go against authority if we think it is stupid and we know better; however, there are better ways to do it than fighting and 'stupid' might just be what the doctor ordered. We wait and see, for the world knows best. The energy of the Sun is so bright that it asks absolutely everything from us. Because of this, we can see why a lot of people in the 19th cycle might not want to look into their Sun, preferring to play the game of sensitivity and touchiness (9), rather than give up to the full power of the inner life. This power is always blazing, for it is the Sun.

The initiate has completely understood that his will can only do the one thing, which is to be committed to love for the truth and the will of the life he lives in, so he acts according to where he is, doing whatever has to be done in the situation that is in front of him. At the highest level of the 19 there is no guilt or fear. By the time we are in our Sun, we are aware that everything is very simple because it is all an exteriorisation or a manifestation of the God we live in. Every action that doesn't come from the guidance of Spirit is a non-event and we cannot measure a non-event! So we can't possibly judge ourselves or others for doing all the silly things that have nothing to do with our inner core. True action becomes a non-action, because it is not us but the Sun within us acting through us, so we are just doing the only thing we can.

We shouldn't chastise ourselves if we feel we are judging. There is right and there is wrong, although at the same time we know there is not. The Number 19 has that knowledge on its shoulders, so it has to lead by helping others to be their own leaders. The paths of righteousness can only be nourished by the inner light and love. If we call a pot black, it is because we know the pot is black, for we've been there before and done the experience. We need to recognise the pot because it might be there again tomorrow. If we have some judgment left, we might still have a little bit of scrubbing to do on our own pot, which is to do with fear, need, want or attraction. In fact it is not the pot that is black but our appreciation of it, so if our reactions come up we should be pleased, for everything we go through, however unpleasant it may be, gives us the opportunity to do that little bit more cleansing. In fact we should be 'over the Moon' about it, for that means that we are connecting with The Sun! If we still have a bit of hate or need for something in us, that is exactly where the God we live in is at. If we can accept that in our hearts, we will feel the kindest, most loving smile in us and whatever reaction we had will dissolve, because we have been honest enough to look at ourselves with a big lens. The world isn't doing it to us; we are doing it to the world! In following the will, the Soul (or the one that is doing the experience) is nailed by the will to the truth, meaning that we cannot actually do anything else.

It is always said that the Spirit is young and we can see why, for it flows continually from the source. At the heart of that movement is the Sun and behind our Sun is a greater Sun. Spirit is always new; it has a fundamental principle at its heart and that is the divinity that cannot be named. We can only have a mindset of what the God we live in has as a goal, which is to reveal the goodness, brightness, beauty and harmony of the whole cosmos. This means that when the Spirit flows, the Sun that we have in us starts to radiate through the generations. As it does so, it starts removing itself from the condition or situation of the life of the body, eventually seeing itself only in its cosmic context. At that point the cosmic or spiritual light will actually sink deep into the cellular structure, bringing in the original vibration, where everything is perfect. This can only be done very gently over many generations. The electric fire of the mind, as it seeks fusion with the fire of wisdom, can generate enough radioactivity to transmute a faulty DNA link.

A generation is only a day in one group Soul; in a group there's always going to be one that breaks through first and then the others can pick up and refine the work, so automatically we are going to have waves going through the whole group. This kind of radiation happens in the body, emotions and mind, because it is all linked. This movement from light into matter will disturb the members of the group enormously, for when one rises they will lift with them the ones who are looking up, but the ones that are still looking down will be pulled down even deeper, because it is an energetic current. Automatically the people who understand will rise, but the ones who are focusing on the darkness will have to go down even further to see the light. When something is acute it is time to break through! Then after that breakthrough we are tidying up our everyday lives for a long time.

The Sun is not after our life, we are its life and its conscious rays of light. It is not out of pride that an esotericist will say that one little unit of consciousness, or one little man who is waking up, is more important than the whole physicality of the cosmos. This is the reality of the mindset that says that all manifestation is a mirror for the mind of the God we live in. If we can understand that one, our heart falls into the heart of God. Again, 'one man, who is beginning to be truly conscious, is worth more than the whole physicality of the cosmos'. This is the mindset that is going to make us go and internalise as deeply as we can. In fact it is not the man that is important, it is the awareness. If we can feel the responsibility of that, we can only put it in our hearts and then our minds will want to be transparent, so that we can realise the wondrous fact that the awareness of mankind is the consciousness of the Solar System; we then work towards that awareness.

Number 1 (The Magician) and the 19 are strongly related. The Magician came in with the goal of mastering the elements in time and space and then at Number 19 we are actually in that goal, which is the Sun. It is all about internalisation so the goal is in us; it is no good looking for it outside of us. The task is to be able to release, reveal and radiate the inner Sun that we all carry. We have to find the door of truth, will and love; eventually it opens and our inner Sun can be revealed.

The Sun has twelve gold and twelve red rays, so there are twenty four in all; 24 is the number of 'time and space'. This is the cosmic Sun as light and Spirit. The lowest expression of that energy is the intellect, which is needed so that we can do the job of naming; how else could we become aware if we do not name, differentiate and ask questions? The scientist however, has to remember that he is a saint as well and his work in science is only a crystallisation of an obvious message of the deeper inner laws.

The intellect is a crystallisation of an aspect of Spirit, so rightly used it is a most beautiful thing, because it is the one that can translate and speak the language of the Ancient Wisdom to those who are ready to listen. It is very versatile and its right use is to explain the world to the little ones who can hear.

The wall behind the two figures is a cosmic structure, because it is seen from the point of view of The Sun, as the king in his own universe. At the same time it can be seen as the young man and woman building a house. They have allowed their needs and wants to be broken down in The Tower and now we are seeing new walls being built. The wall is behind them, but it also encircles them; it is the house of the Soul. The wonderful circle of green with little flowers growing in it represents the whole world of the true life as it is meant to be; this is different from the illusionary, glamorous life that we have all plunged into. The minute we align our consciousness to our inner Sun, we see it all for what it truly is and so we know that we don't need to 'redeem' life.

The green circle with flowers is a symbol of aspiration for a new generation coming into a new stage of life. There has been a misunderstanding about the elixir of eternal youth for it is seen in a physical sense, but it is really about the spiritual life. The fact that the couple are inside a green crown of flowers, symbolises the true eternal life of Spirit. We put ourselves into a ring for protection and magic. This protection means that the minute we flow with our Spirit, we cannot be attracted out of it again, so it is not being protected in the ordinary sense, but is an energetic fact. As soon as we understand this, we will get an awful lot of rocks falling down the mountain onto us, just to test whether our protection was a real or imaginary understanding and to see if it holds. This understanding hasn't been obtained freely or easily, there has been a lot of work, a lot of hurt and healing.

The wall is the beginning of the building of the Temple of the New Jerusalem, which is the same as the temple that was built by Solomon to receive the presence of the divinity, except that here Jerusalem is not the city in matter, but is used as a symbol to represent the concept of the city of peace within humanity. It is only when the initiate has reached this stage that he can help his brothers to break down their own walls and start building their 'Jerusalem' temple, for if we haven't even started to build our 'Holy of Holies' how can we help somebody else to build theirs? We can help other people with all types of things, but at this stage we are helping Souls to go through initiation.

The New Jerusalem Temple is the 'Holy of Holies'. This is when our Soul completely responds to the impulse of its spiritual Sun and starts radiating through matter, so that matter can be transubstantiated and brought back to its etheric state. All types of beautiful species and forms have been brought out of a few elements by the laws of adaptation and economics, but in the next stage all the elements can be turned into gold (Sun rays) and so become one again. That is the alchemical idea; to find the formula of how to turn any element into incorruptible gold that cannot be tarnished. Eventually there will only be one life, with all the tiny little expressions shining and vibrating slightly differently, but without needing a form. It is alchemically possible to turn the elements into gold, because they are all an expression of the one life, but with the inner alchemy we have the gold in us rendering everything we do, are and say, into pure radiation from the Sun. That is the New Jerusalem, when people will be able to see everything as divine, from within the heart and not from the intellect. Then we will be truly radiating a change of perception, which can actually transmute matter by bringing more light and life into it.

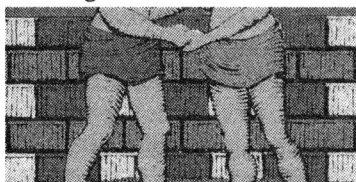 The wall itself is crystallised sunshine; it is the true unfolding of the experience of the Sun and the Solar System. This is a deeper, more subtle level of the expression of life than the one that we are in now, for we are only just starting our journey. The colours of the wall are blue, red and gold. Blue represents the highest aspiration and truth, red is action and fire, so with these two the wall is completely infused with hope and aspiration. The gold represents that which has been achieved.

Red is action, but we can see it also as the genetic blood line, which is life waiting to be turned into gold. Action is Spirit in life, coming to meet itself at the heart of nature; it is not to do with what we thought we needed to do, but what we know is the only thing we can do at the time. It doesn't matter how many poor people we are going to feed in our lives, if we are doing it from the point of view of being recognised and feeling good ourselves, then from the cosmic point of view we are not even seen; we don't even exist. If we are doing it because that is all we can do, then we are not acting, we are being used. Any action only has a value according to the amount of spiritual intention moving it. We may not want to act, but we are going to do it and even with only a tiny drop of spiritual intent, that action will stay forever and help other actions. So it is better to let the Spirit push us a little bit, than go and do a lot of things to make ourselves feel better.

This card is all about fusion and alchemy and has to be seen symbolically. When it is grasped, there is sudden illumination and a completely new recognition of the world. The most important thing is to dare to give up freedom and individuality, once we have earned them. This is hard, because individuality is very precious; it is what took us originally onto the inner path, gave us solidity and steadiness and taught us confidence and truth. When we come to the point of getting that great illumination of feeling, we have disappeared; it is in that moment that we are in real life or in our Sun and can start to be aware of how the whole thing works. It isn't pie in the sky, for we are actually standing on the planet when it happens and it is thanks to the bricks of matter that we have done it. We are starting to render nature divine. Nature is the recognition of the divinity of life, so is metaphysical but at the same time very manifest and practical.

The bricks in the wall have been cut exactly the way they should be, by a mason or initiate who has spent a long, long time refining his work; in the end he can do it because he doesn't need matter any more. He reincarnated into matter with Number 1, for this is the only way to tread the inner path. How are we as a consciousness really going to be sure that we are not going to be taken in by glamour, illusion and Maya, if we do not come back right into it to find ourselves in its wisdom? Thanks to the mirror of the whole of the life in the senses, we can actually recognise that our home is in the consciousness of the Sun and at the heart of matter.

This is the beginning of the building, so it is a realisation. The Moon is a long slow process in the dark with the rising Sun on the horizon, then eventually illumination comes and transubstantiation can happen; it cannot happen before. The red and blue bricks were there already; now, with the twelve gold bricks, there are three levels.

 The male and female figures in the card are the completed balanced union of the masculine and feminine polarities. We always say that the opposites will attract, but in the real work the opposites are only there for a karmic mirroring. The fusion only

happens when there is a deep recognition of the inner self; this creates balance. By recognising our inner lover we are in complete balance. The focus on the truth aspect for receptive, sensitive types and the love aspect for rational, intellectual types melts the resistance of the personality away. When we see truth with love inside, we know we are complete. There are all types of levels of this work; what we used to feel as complete enlightenment and love when we first started vibrating faster, was fed very strongly by dreams and wishes from within our astral body. This was great, but as we take life as it is for a reference, the feelings ought to be different; inner peace comes after the fireworks. We know by now that all we have to do is watch the unfolding of the marvellous life of the God we live in, so whatever is happening can't be judged by the intellect or the emotional, but only from the point of view of truth. Here we are not going to curse ourselves or others any more, for we love the world.

The two figures represent pure consciousness. The woman, representing receptivity, has a blue loincloth; here receptivity has been turned into aspiration. This is active not passive energy, so it will attract the red of action (portrayed by the man's red loincloth), to move towards the goal. The red action needs the highest possible aspiration to be able to reach the true lover, which is the Sun. A true action from the inner core of the life we live in will automatically make a path for all the other intentions from the heart to follow, that then will become a river and eventually an ocean of pure life.

The young couple are like two lambs of God. They have had to accept a lot of breaking down of dreams and had to burn out many passions to meet their truth, for the kingdom of God doesn't belong to the lukewarm or the lazy. They are young, which is not to say that the kingdom of Heaven is only for the young, it is just that what we are looking at is a consciousness that is completely aligned with spiritual truth. Spiritual truth is always young, because it is always new; it is the energy that is forever flowing; the true fountain of youth. The striving of mankind over thousands of years to stay young is a misunderstanding of what true youth is, for true youth is the right use of mind and heart; it symbolises the new rebirth and the energy that is forever flowing.

Coming out of the solitude and conflict of The Moon, with the aspiration that comes from The Stars behind us, we are suddenly in the bright sunlight and full illumination. The esperance behind us gives us the strong certitude of where we are and what we are doing; this is why the couple are bathed in light. It is a very positive structured card, bringing us back to Earth. It is total illumination at the highest possible degree and preparation for many different levels of the growth of consciousness.

The wise old Hermit in Number 9 is very relevant to the Number 19, for his work has come to an end. It was at the beginning of the journey that we had to introspect and The Hermit asked us to 'go in and find the wisdom'. He was facing a lot of disillusion and doing a lot of work, to do with clearing and being aware of all the things that had to be cleared. Then when we came to Numbers 12, 13 and 14 an awful lot of things had to be cast off. The initiate is full of wisdom, but now in the 19 that consciousness is reborn with the light of the Sun – the higher mind as the lover of the Soul; there is the dawn of new life and awareness in this world. It is a consciousness radiating out into the world. Here we are completely centred, so the light can start to illuminate the path for others.

The Sun is the dispenser of spiritual life. It is always the same, it doesn't matter who dies, when or where, for the Sun always rises. So if our consciousness (whether flowing or crystallised) comes from the Sun, we never die. All we do is go into our autumn and winter.

In The Sun we are looking at complete knowledge, complete connaissance and the complete life of a fully realised Soul. As we live and go through experiences, we always have the opportunity to know and love a bit deeper.

While we are living by comparing ourselves with others, we are dependent and we stay on the surface of life. Do we depend on anyone or anything to know who we are? Do we need to hold on to outer things, like our job, family, appearance, title, or what we know? Do we need to hold on to the fact that we are a woman, or what it is we might want in life? There is a saying, "If you do not see me I do not exist". We have to retreat strongly into ourselves, so as to know that we don't need to be seen, recognised or loved, because we do not depend on anybody for our sense of self; it is within our hearts. We are Souls and there is a greater life depending on us to open it up, so that the light can be revealed. This is why we have to go through the long dark nights, why we have to feel and understand what loving and not being loved is; why we have to experience not being seen, heard or loved, so that we can be completely aware whether we depend on anything at all to make our existence bearable. If we do, we soon get the next lesson that takes the crutch away, until all we can do is to give. When we feel this is exhausted, the giving becomes natural and 'from Soul', then we truly love.

We have to give all we have gathered so far, because life cannot be static, it has to move and flow. We are channels for pure love, for we are empty of self. It is not that we haven't got an inner life any more, but our inner life doesn't bother us that much; we are an adept at checking all our reactions instantly, so that we can release more love and understanding. We have to let it flow.

The New Age has given us 'go with the flow', but that can be the biggest escape we have invented when we are doing spiritual work. It is good if we have already got our trickle of transforming river flowing within us, checking the glamour and illusion coming from our emotional or mental bodies, but 'going with the flow' for most people is a wonderful excuse for laziness. The one who thinks he has understood thinks he doesn't need to do any inner work. The real problem we have is the laziness of not pushing ourselves to be real. To be truthful we give ourselves many excuses; this is the main thing that stops humanity going faster where it is supposed to be going. Being lazy is not thinking for ourselves and giving ourselves excuses not to. If somebody tells us they are going with the flow, ask them, "Which flow is that?"

Physical light is the crystallisation of spiritual light, which is why we say, "I see" when we mean, "I understand". There are many different levels of seeing. When we look at all the materialisations of life, we should try to see them as a crystallisation of the inner spiritual light of the great life we live in. For everybody to see something in full light is wonderful; to see something in half light or in the dark is even more wonderful, because there is the mystery of the shadow that holds more light, ready to come out when it is seen.

This is not a card about passive bliss or happiness – it is active. We have to act and we have to come out of ourselves now. Anything that exists without consciousness has no absolute value, so we have to recognise that biology has no absolute reality and that matter is not a principle. The value of matter has always been that it has allowed the birth of the light for recognition and self-awareness to happen. So the great value of biology is that it is a 'way-by', or a by-product, not a principle. It must be respected as much as we would respect our mother (in a universal sense), who gives of her own life for the perpetuation of biology, until the day the light can come through; that is immensely valuable and important. The priority in the world now is on keeping biology going and if that happens, the experiment has succeeded. The birth of humanity has happened, but we are only like a baby making its first cry and opening its eyes for the first time. Now we are waiting to see if the baby can scream. There is no doubt it will, for it is struggling for air now through the issue of global warming, the environment and the many tribal/extremist, religious groups all battling to be heard and recognised.

The Sun has blue eyes, so as to focus on the purity of intent and vision. The red lips of the Sun are about aspiration and action creating the words we speak, which creates the life we live in. The intense and deep expression of the Sun says, "A Sun has got to do what a Sun has got to do – till the end!" The Sun purifies and cleans the Solar System constantly by burning the unwanted matter. It does not discriminate and will gobble anything that comes up, to create more fire; that is its life, so that is what is required of us. We are the little brothers of the Sun and as Souls are cosmic. This is nature with awareness and we are doing it for the Sun, like the little brothers imitating their elders. How can we judge the Sun? It does what a Sun does, so there is nothing else to do but accept that process.

The conscious journey takes us to the source of all existence, so as to integrate with that source, consciously and deliberately. We came in ignorance out of the source, for the whole of creation burst out without self awareness. We are aiming to be exactly in that same position, flowing in matter with the source but this time watching. This is the offer of the cycle of the 19, the Soul coming out again with the knowledge of everything that has been experienced in between the 1 and the 9 and the many deaths and rebirths from 10 to 19/10. A unit which suffered the earlier stage of initial creation could not possibly have been aware, for the pain of it would have been too excruciating and unbearable. The will to survive would have been destroyed without understanding the process. To be aware means that we have within us a reference point to show us where we are in a system we think we understand; that is our only point of repair and healing. It is a sharp awareness. A self-conscious instrument that doesn't have that anchor because it hasn't reached its inner depth cannot sustain the vision of the creation. That point of reference is the energy made of the same type of radiation as the Sun/Soul from which it came, so in having that, the instrument will not be burnt out. If people come to the door for an initiation and want it because of pride or to make the world a happy place, that means they are not ready. We have to have that tiny little point in us which is Sun/Soul contact, so that we can face the explosion and illumination. This is a natural state, not a staged workshop exercise. The illumination is like being exposed to radiation, or being bleached and it hurts mentally, emotionally and physically; to survive that we have to be completely lucid, aware and sacrificial. Only then can we participate in 'the becoming' of the God we live in.

We all have the potential of solar consciousness within us; we are virtual and the idea is to become real, so that we all become little shiny points of consciousness. We can truly transform the world through our consciousness, but we shouldn't aim at doing that, for we may impose ourselves onto it and it is so important not to interfere. We have to follow the rhythm of nature and do our fusions of Heaven and Earth in real, everyday life situations. These revelations mostly come out of the blue.

Whatever we think, wish, or want, will be materialised. A strong will in a cloudy consciousness can be very powerful in materialise situations very powerfully, so let's be clear and selfless. We are forever reinventing and unfolding the God we live in.

There is no life of science, dogma or practice which makes an initiation happen, for it is always a very intimate transformation. The inner path of the disciple is the way of the mind. We need to recognise that everything is mind, that we are instruments and we have to get on with it, 'singing down the mountain'. It is an intimate transformation that can only happen with the spiritual energy of light and mind. It is so subtle that we can only truly speak about it to a person who has experienced it in themselves; even then there are many different degrees of recognition and sensation, so there are many degrees of initiation.

If we truly understand that consciousness is movement in time and space and only associate with that, then our mind can automatically travel through time and space because we can see through it. We still have to obey the divine karmic laws of the Solar System, so we open the door of many more misunderstandings as the mind travels through the different levels of astral projection. We must have more respect for the law of non-interference we know that the life we are witnessing is a cosmic happening. This is the first plunge into eternal life that is free of all the limits of manifestation; this is the higher level of the 19.

Aspiration is not a passive virtue, for it moves all the time, carrying and uplifting us. Number 18 moved us towards the ideal that we wanted to find, until we realised that it was in us already. We have to have that great certitude of knowing that the divine love is there at the centre of our goal. When we have identified and recognised that the inner fire is burning bright, then it matters not at all what the form is master of! Let the radiator radiate! Life is the work of love in its fiery aspects. Nature's love is need and desire, which is what most people still call love and that is okay. At the spiritual level it is a responding to that inner burning fire, so giving ourselves more and more to it. Fusion with the source is what we are after all the time; this is love for loves sake. The aspiration moves towards total communion with the source of life.

The fiery Leos are another expression of the Sun. Leo plays an important role in the connection to the spiritual Sun behind our Sun. We can only bring fire through fire; that is why we have to have our permanent little spiritual mane burning like mad with the Sun. That lovely connection eventually brings the fire down and then the planet can be on the path of truth and revelation in a practical living sense. When we realise that all our mistakes, agonies and addictions have to do with the jungle law of nature, we see the life we live in as a cruel deception. In waking up from the heavy sleep of the unconscious, we feel the bitterness and disappointment of such a cruel system. This is one of the deepest pains, the perceived deception of only retracing nature's path is not easily accepted by a proud warrior, who has gone through many deaths to save the world, only to find that the world does not need saving. He would prefer to hold onto his guilt and fight another war! So we can understand why a bit of rebellion comes in to this cycle, as we question what type of a God we have been dying for. When we start realising that it all stems from the way we look at life and that life is us, then whichever way we look at what we are doing, we always have to end up with no blame and no guilt, only responsibility to truth and love. This is law and non-interference in its full expression.

This is the rise of autonomous consciousness. The best example we have of the automatism of nature going through the process of being clarified and refined, is the diamond. There is no way we could all wait until we become diamonds, because a diamond isn't conscious of being a diamond, and therefore is worthless from the point of view of the light and the work. However, as a symbol for what we have to become, the diamond is wonderful. What makes the difference between a worthless diamond and our mind as a diamond is that we have willingly, consciously accepted the pressure of time. Enduring with our fiery passion and eyes open, the transmutation of our body nature, we have become a diamond in the name of love and truth.

In the process of fusion we are not destroyed or disappear, rather it is a fusion by identity of thought, not annihilation. The result is a supreme exaltation by constant identification with life; this is bliss. It is being blessed and the whole of our heart is looking at life with reality and loving it.

In a couple, the two units have to fuse within themselves, because it is a time when we have to love on behalf of the Spirit of the greater life, rather than for ourselves. We are not after the bliss of being in a couple. We are seeking to learn in order to identify our inner qualities mirrored by the partner. This way we recognise and become our true partner, the Soul; we learn to die to our little selves. When that happens, we create an energetic life full of light, which will be able to exteriorise a more perfect form of life. In nature, reproductive generation is always moving towards physical adapted perfection for the sake of survival. From the spiritual angle, Perfection is the fusing of Soul, the love wisdom body and the Spirit into the light of universal truth. As we know, perfection has many degrees of manifestation. Fusion happens when the two lovers absorb each other into one entity. The end product of this great self-regenerating laboratory, is that at long last God has digested itself back into pure self-aware essence.

Karma is not an automatic "you have done that to me, so I will do that to you". If that were the law of karma, everything we did would always come back at us and never end, going backwards and forwards, like ping pong, for ever! So karma isn't an 'eye for an eye', because all we would end up with a blind world, as Buddhist wisdom tells us. By this stage we have to understand that there is no good and bad, no evil, no fault and no guilt. Karma is the great law behind what is naturally happening in our Solar System, therefore whatever situation we are in, is exactly the right place and time; so stop moaning and get on with it! It is that idea. It is not just because it is our karma for goodness sake, for we do not own it! It is because it is where the Solar System is at! Who wants to moan about that and who are they going to moan to? At the end of the day, karma is not a personal thing, except in the sense that the group, the nation, planet Earth and the Solar System itself is part of one drop of a greater life that makes that wonderful clock go round. So it is personal in that way, but we should not take our personal karmic situation personally! It is all to do with acceptance, obedience and poise; these qualities bring awareness. It is always about finding that inner poise and inner fire.

A single action can have opposite karmic consequences for different people, so it is not the act that is karmic, but the intent we have put into it. It is not simply a matter of counting our actions and balancing good against bad, for that is childish and is a form of bartering. What we are looking at with karma is inclusive and not seperative. When people talk about clearing their karma there is substance in that, because they have accepted to work on something that came to them; however, it can be very self-centred. It is an understanding that is only valid in the sense of learning by our mistakes, aligning and accepting the fact that that is how it works. We are always in front of a situation that gives us the opportunity to see life differently and any situation we are in is directly to do with karma. We are exactly where we are supposed to be at the time.

While we are questioning what we have or haven't done wrong, we are still in time and space and thinking of fault, wrong, bad and guilt. This is fine and there is validity to this, but once we realise that the lesson is a deep, collective one that is bigger than us and beyond us, we drop it and see it cosmically rather than personally.

We are hurt, for we do not get to the Sun without being wounded. Wounds give us the means to defend ourselves against temptation, for when we feel the reaction, the fear, the guilt, or whatever it is that our wound is, we are going to remember how we got it. It is up to us to go right down inside it, rather than keeping it hurting by scratching the surface of it.

True memory is wisdom and is locked into the heart of matter; the Spirit or light wants to reach the pool of love and wisdom which is its other half. This pool is found in the memory, which is the feminine receptive side. By definition the whole of humanity is that part in nature that is an open wound, because of our awareness.

In Number 19 we have men and women equally partaking of the life of God; they are all blessed. In the world today, even in the west, women are still seen as objects; in the media and in the mass consciousness they are bonded to infantile excitement. The Tarot tells us that we are all equal. It carries the complete respect and understanding of the oneness of the sexes, so there is no sexuality in the Tarot in the sense of competition or conflict. The aim is to have Spirit and matter working in complete love, fusion and truth; that is the unfolding of the flower. The woman inspires rather than tempts and the man is action, so the two together make the perfect human being. It is not to do with the sexuality of reproduction, so in the card they are depicted with their genitalia covered up, only the woman's breasts are revealed to show her gender. It is a quirk and a deviation in men's infantile minds, to associate breasts with sex.

In the Tarot, men and women are used symbolically. The feminine aspect represents anything that is form; it doesn't have to be a woman. Humanity still uses and abuses form, as in its treatment of animals, children and the planet itself. In the original temptation we had the concept of the Luciferian light being the heart of matter or nature. Then we had nature having to start thinking for itself and so wanting to know; this is the formation of the intellect. From there we have the awareness of separateness and the notion of the fall. It is the mind that made the fall happen. The wonderful thing in the story was that as Adam bit into the apple, the Spirit flowed into the intellect and the sky opened with a great revelation of awareness. This was expressed by, "Oh my God! We are naked! We can name what we feel, I am vulnerable, I feel guilty, and unprotected!" – This is awareness speaking. Adam asks, "What have you given me?" for he represents mankind and can't take responsibility for having been part of what was happening. At this point the two aspects of Spirit and matter meet. They are represented by the great Archangel Michael and the incredibly bright, sacrificial Lucifer. The angelic point of view represents Spirit, which is righteous and refuses the responsibility within the situation, saying "How dare you! It is all your fault and look where we have ended up", to Adam. Lucifer says, "Keep eating till you get to the core of the apple and then we will see clearly!" Out of the same consciousness, come these two ways of doing it; two different perceptions.

It doesn't matter how advanced we think we might be, it is only truly when our karmic cycle is achieved, that we can put the last brick down in time and space, so we don't need to be in a hurry to put any bricks anywhere! It is only at that point of completion that we can really help our brothers. This is work at the level of true brotherhood, where we are not doing it for self. When man works at salvation from here, he works for the whole of the species; working just for your own salvation is a bit dodgy! It is true that we have to be pretty aware of what is going on before we can help others, for if we are an enigma to ourselves, how can we help other people?

We all have the door to sainthood within us and we are allowed to go for this sanctuary. The Tarot reminds us that sainthood is about rendering everyday life sacred through our perception. It is up to us to find that door, manifest it in the full light and use it for the edification of the city of The Sun. The light is another understanding of the spiritual fire, for light from the Sun is the fire at the service of the will. It alters those who know it and use it, but it incinerates those who abuse it. Even wanting to know just for the sake of knowing, can burn us to cinders, because that is still being self-centred. All types of things go wrong when we just want knowledge for the sake of it. At this level good and bad don't mean anything, so we can become such a law unto ourselves that we go away from our real centre. The knowledge is so incredible that it can send us into all sorts of weird and wonderful experiments. The aim for more power is where a lot of esotericists, healers or great thinkers might have fallen.

This stage is all to do with will and going beyond duty through love. St Teresa of Avilla tells us that free will is a miserable slave to its freedom and that when we have the love of the one who created us, free will is automatically nailed on the cross of time and space. Then it cannot move, for we have gone beyond free will in the name of the love of the creator, so our will isn't ours any more – it is the will of God. St Teresa asks, "When will this happen? When will this happy day come? When you will not be able to sin, you will not desire this freedom, because you will be protected from all materialised misery with the life of God itself".

The next card is Judgment. There is no way we can step into that one, if we are afraid of the light. We have to be completely in the love of the God we live in. If we are in that love, we cannot be afraid of Judgment, for we have seen it all any way!

Number 19 has an affinity with Numbers 17 and 18. In 17 we saw the cosmic light of The Stars through hope and aspiration; here we start from the stars so as to have our view from the cosmic, rather than from the self. With Number 18, the light from The Moon was helping us to get more familiar with the light of The Sun; the moonlight being a reverberation of the light of the Sun onto our inner path. There is also a strong link with The High Priestess, because she represents Isis, the wisdom, the enigma and the question; here in Number 19 we have the answer. Only when we have been dying consciously through the 13, are we conscious of that phase of The Sun, the Sun of the dead, or the Egyptian God Atum. Here we are aware of the energetic passage that we call death, so that we can come back as a new Sun into the eternal light, then we have gone through the whole four degrees. The Emperor has the Sun and Moon on his breast and is going to order how the 'connaissance' will be applied in the world. We need that discipline to enable us to keep our eyes on the source, so that the work can happen.

This is the stage of will and love. We can only exercise true will when there is full connaissance, so let's be humble. Any other type of will that we exercise is to do with desire and we all do it. It could be all types of higher desire, like being good, not just desire for gratification, but it is still desire. Desire is the expression of freedom that has not yet reached the fullness of its own destiny. That is fine and we are not going to beat ourselves up about it; however, we know that freedom belongs to the world of doubt and mistakes. We also know that we need to take the first step of wanting without desire. You have to be responsive to the love of the Soul for the Spirit to be translated as a 'want' within us, but not as a desire. The aim is to participate in the work of elevation and transubstantiation of the cosmos. Whatever tiny transformation we can do in ourselves that comes from the purity of our inner fire, is of cosmic importance and creates real change. If we eat three apple pies by ourselves in a day, or feed the rest of the world for ten years with apple pies, that will not have any significance for the cosmos, because these are outer actions. If we have the honesty to say that we have cooked all those apples to feed the world with the intention of being seen as a saint (therefore for our own aggrandisement or salvation), just that little drop of honesty and truth offered to our inner fire changes things in depth. It even creates a response between the Earth and sky that has a cosmic effect.

To forget this cosmic service to the Spirit, even for one instant, would weaken our capacity to use the knowledge rightly. Whatever we do, we have to remember that we are doing it for the bigger purpose. However, we shouldn't even be afraid of weakness, for in time and space, who cares if we make a mistake and go back to ashes! The act is not important it is the awareness that is, so just be aware of a mistake for the awareness will give more fuel for transformation. The hiding of mistakes is a huge problem for it stops our Soul shining. When we are in the full Sun we cannot hide anyway.

The Soul is the seat of pure intent.

Judgment, Jugement
Wake up to action

Three naked figures, a mature couple and a child, look up at a green-winged angel holding a trumpet. This is the end of the journey; the accomplishment. When we arrive here our cup is full of awareness, experience and wisdom and now the contents have to be used. The trumpet gives a wake-up call to action, asking us to translate what we are receiving, so that we can be intermediaries between Spirit and matter. Here, we are not referring to the judgment of the world but to the judgment of self, for we do not owe anything to anybody, only to the Spirit of life and truth.

This is the end of the journey; the accomplishment and the achievement of the twenty Mayan steps to divinity. We are following the steps of the consciousness of a would-be initiate. He knows that he can apply all the discipline that the journey requires and that his next step is in an everyday life, where his humility and unconditional love in service to others will be tested. He knows as well that it is not up to him to decide when he is going to experience the next rise in consciousness, for at this stage his concern would not be for himself.

We have seen the death of all the aspects of the personality that might impair man's progress into the light; this was the passage of purification through the cycles 11, 12 and 13, giving us tough work. Through standing up and through love we raise the consciousness with the vision of the greater plan. This work was the first death initiation, the U-turn, where life is perceived from the point of view of the Soul.

Here in the cycle of Number 20 we are at the door of the second death. This is when the light and fire of the internal Sun (the Soul) of the would-be initiate is naturally and easily accessed by the everyday consciousness. The light of the Sun within is being absorbed in matter. This is the explanation of the second death, that of the Soul, whose vibrations are now one with its vehicle, the personality. At this level of attainment the would-be initiate becomes an initiate. He does not have super-human qualities and strength, or any other mark to differentiate him from the crowd, the light of his Soul will only attract those people whose Souls are already seeking or stirring. What has been achieved is another illuminating light, another fully-realised human being who moves and serves the greater Soul of our planet that belongs to the cosmic life. The Moon has reached full term and is ready to deliver into the cup the new life in form, transfigured with the light of the Soul.

Before the glorious rebirth in matter of the highest attainment of cycle 20, we have 'walked our talk'. We have understood the principles of justice, righteousness and love and let the light of the full Sun spark a transfiguration in us. That has to be processed by its nature (the Goddess) into a rebirth, not out of matter but *of* matter itself, transmuted with the light of the Soul. Number 20 in numerological terms is known as the two feet of the Goddess. This cycle carries all the potential for that rebirth, for the process has come full term.

When a cup is full the contents have to be used. Nothing in life is static and nothing is either owned or possessed, so any wealth, food or water has to be passed on. At this level when our cup is full, we would be quite happy to sit back and watch, the world happening as in this stance we would not be looking forward to the labour pains of re-birthing ourselves. The two people have their hands in a gesture of prayer as if to anticipate a pose, but the angel is saying "Wake up!" meaning, "Act". We have had the light in our hearts and minds so we are completely full of light, but we might not want to open our eyes and see. Still wanting to have control, or have possessiveness and grandiosity, are the labour pains of our re-birth. Our cup is full, so we can wake up, have a good scrub and pass the light on!

When we have seen a vision and have had some level of enlightenment, we might not understand what we are supposed to be doing with it. For a minute or two we are like a dazzled rabbit in the headlights of a car, so we are not going to process it but just carry on with our lives, maybe ask a few questions and get a few explanations, that is all. When we are dazed, instead of asking, "What does it mean to me?" we should let the light go on and do its work of releasing the deeper wisdom.

We have experienced some kind of enlightenment in our heads and hearts. We don't need to ask the question of how we can use it for ourselves, or ask, "What does it mean?" instead we let it uplift us. We might be doing the same thing that we have always done, but the new light and energy coming through us is given out as we serve others. We can only translate the light according to our own individual computer or instrument, so the importance of becoming transparent becomes obvious, as our personality point of view is not necessarily the universal remedy. Nevertheless, using the personality is not a problem, for the group we're in may need our particular translation at the time. We are just vessels that enable the translation of lighted messages.

The realised Soul of the human being (the anointed or the sacred one) is the end of the journey for the human consciousness. The 'teaching' of the one who realised this state first has been passed on from the beginning of this happening. It puts in front of human beings the possibility of understanding how we can align to Soul, then align Soul to Spirit and Spirit to matter, through a certain set of transformations. From this a human being can achieve the highest state that he can reach, which is to become a perfected Soul.

In this card we are looking at the lovely mysteries of the ascension and the assumption. Ascension is when the perfected Soul, having become Christ-like, rises by itself to reach the pure energy of the

Sun, which brings Heaven to Earth. When the consciousness has reached those heights, the Soul has automatically risen but we are still here on Earth and have a job to do.

In the previous card (Number 19 – The Sun), there was a young couple, demonstrating the feminine and masculine aspects. Here in Number 20, Judgment, we have a mature couple. They represent the responsible ones, or the human beings who know that they have had to go into duality and be attracted to other people, so as to recognise their own strengths and weaknesses; this is how it works. The feminine and masculine are recognising themselves as one here, for illumination has happened and as a consequence the Soul has come forth in the form of the child. The three people in the card are the Trinity made visible. This is why the 'parents' on the left and the right sides are in a praying position, because suddenly they see the result of their lives and work. It is possible to truthfully and humbly see ourselves through the Soul; 'in the full light, we see ourselves'. We are not saying that these people are pure and have achieved everything they needed to achieve, but they have willingly accepted the light of the Soul, so that they can see themselves truthfully.

There would be no way of touching, uplifting, blessing or redeeming nature if it weren't for the potential transformative action of humanity. This is a whole process of absorption and fusion between the above and the below. We are truly mediators, or intermediary beings of transition. We are not animals and we are not angels, but we are in the middle bringing Heaven and Earth together. We absorb and give out. At the twentieth cycle we have absorbed right up to the brim of the cup, so we have to let go of power and use the flow of the birthing water to deliver the messenger.

Assumption is the other way of rising into light. When the consciousness of the Soul shines into an individual and is blazing, the process of the transformation of the personality starts to move from protection to transparency. There is more understanding and love, so the self is removed more and more. In the process of becoming transparent, everything in the individual personality (which includes the physical/emotional/mental or elemental life) is received in the lighted Soul. That is the symbolism of the assumption of Mary. Mary is the life in our true nature bodies (the etheric web of life), that can't rise through its own efforts, but as the light of consciousness shines in her cup she is seen as pure and transparent, once the process is loved and understood. 'Rise and shine' is the redemptive message in this card. Its nature is Judgment. It is a redemptive moment in the life of a person when they actually access the vision and enlightenment, in the way that they perceive life. The redemption is for the consciousness aspect; life is back where it always was in the manifested form of the God we live in and in whom we are becoming. The work has been to purify the understanding and perceive the form, not as maya, but as the manifesting principle of nature, which is Mary. The realisation is happening and so now is the time to actually rise with the ethereal ray of light within our body, to serve the unfolding of the lighted life.

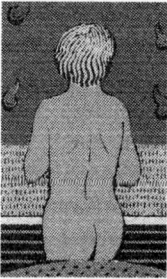

Some people suggest that the child depicted in the card is coming out of a tomb, but there is no coffin or lid; it is not a bath either! The two 'parents' look as though they are emerging from the soil and the child emerges from an opening that is in the soil; that is the birth. We have lighted up the subconscious, which is in and belongs to the Earth. The Soul has understood that there can be no result and no rebirth, except through the Earth and the Sun, so the child is the result of the deepest connection of awareness into the subconscious. The great Number 8 is really relevant here, for there is no way in everyday life that we are going to be on the path of realisation, if we do not bring our consciousness deep into the subconscious and merge the two together. This is the karmic process of enlightenment.

The child is the aspect of truth in the Soul for the person who says "I see myself as I am"; this is the work of the Spirit of truth and life. It truly is the result of the individual having had the courage to look at the two opposite tendencies   left/right, good/bad and bring them together in complete harmony, respect and love, so that every single time an action or reaction happens, they can see where it is coming from. If we can see what moves us, we are living in the truth and the child represents the truth in our Soul. The light of truth, rising out of matter, is uplifting the new purified, perceived matter with it. The blue box rising out of the Earth with the child in it could represent the newly perceived true structure. It is the etheric body. The sandy texture of the soil that has been disturbed would represent the Earth having given all its wisdom to the structure, so all that is left is sand and dust. This is the process of Assumption.

In the 19 we see the full Sun, as the Soul takes over the consciousness of the personality in the 20. The light of the Sun completes its journey into the depth of the cup of life; the result is a wake-up call, a triumphal welcome into the realisation of a human Soul. In the next step, Number 21, we walk in reality and are walking into the past continuously checking from the point of the truth in our Soul, that we do not lack in life, truth and love. If we still think we are going forward, outward and upward, rather than inward, then we haven't reached the point of understanding, the U-turn. If we are conscious, we are walking inward all the time with the light of Spirit. At that stage the judgment might still be turned outwards at others; this is not the triumphal judgment, but the protective one. If we see others as stupid, then we have to remember that idiots are 'wise men in the making' and we all have been there. Being angry about others' ignorance is often a way that we shield ourselves from feeling the pain of recognising the ignorance that we have held in the past. Many examples could be given as an excuse not to allow more truth into our subconscious. As the ghost of the past collapses into heaps of dust, a few tears could be shed.

The colourful flag on the trumpet is a masonic symbol. We are in the presence of the philosopher's stone here, hence the square blue box and the red square flag. The individual is going to be of great use to the God we live in at this stage. The gold cross tells us that the golden door has opened and the Sun is out, so there is no possible fall back into ignorance. The last step on the alchemic path of the initiate is red. Gold is the incorruptible wisdom from the Earth and red is the passion of becoming pure energy, so this is the blending of passion and wisdom. This is not full realisation, but the first step into it. The Soul is active, the awareness is active and the Spirit of the life of truth is active. We have understood that it is a process of fusing and transmuting. Our responsibility is to see life for what it is, from the point of view of the God we live in, an $E = MC^2$ life.

The alternate rays of the Sun are yellow and red. Yellow is union of meditation and contemplation and red is action. This is how we have to be all the time, receptive – active – contemplative – active; in time and space a live wire!

We are acting not from an unconscious need, but because of a universal necessity. At this point we start to encounter the non-interference aspect of spiritual life. We are witnessing yesterday, so that nature's intelligence can be reinstated with its divine aspect. Once we understand that, we could not possibly interfere. This is the beginning of learning to work with the cosmic law of non-interference.

If we have reached the point of full term within our cup, then the cosmos will be using us in time and space. Until a man accepts his receptive, feminine side, he is not clear what he is supposed to do with all he is receiving, so there's an awful lot of frustration being stored. He knows he has to act, but he doesn't know how to when he's so full, the energy can be expressed as violence. The only way to deal with this is to give out the translation of the manifestation of what it is that needs to be born, just like nature does when she gives us apples from the apple trees. Heaven is alive! A perfectly realised 20 could be expressed as "I am that which receives and translates". For a man to receive and to be able to translate through his art skills and gentleness, is very difficult and he can be violent when he loses that ability. Men still need to look honestly at the pride on their masculine side and accept the receptivity of their feminine side. Highly creative women would have the same characteristic of bursting into violence.

We are all working towards simultaneously receiving and acting intuitively. As we receive it is important not to mess up what we have received with the intellect, personal will, or wish, but just to let it sink in and then let it move us. We have to train in order to recognise spiritual impulse versus subconscious reaction. If we haven't got the awareness to see from which corner of our dark wood we are looking at life, we will be interfering. Our actions will be born out of greed, lust or whatever, so creating violence as a reaction. We have to be completely aware every minute of the day, trusting that our everyday reaction or action is coming from that deep fusion with pure life. If we are aware when an impulse is still an impulse for self, then we will know how to deal with it and learn not to interfere with the unfolding of the flower of life.

The Magician is an initiate because he's already gone though the first revelation and therefore has been initiated into the mysteries, but he is still a probationary initiate. It is only at the door of the 20 that he gets the title of initiate. In the cycle of 20 we are looking at the making of sainthood. We know that the saints are not perfect and are neither Christ-like nor fully realised Souls, but they are firmly on the way. They are rendering their lives more and more sacred, by blending the everyday life with the Spirit of life and truth, so that the service to God/Heaven and mankind/Earth can centre in their Soul as one; this is the process of making perfect.

At the level of sanctification we are truly in love with the light of God in us. Transparency naturally comes when enough fusion between light and matter has occurred. It is not matter that needs purifying; it is the lack of self-awareness in the Soul. Man needs to perceive life in a different way. When the light of Spirit via the vehicle of the Soul, actually penetrates and infuses all the cells of matter, then the little elementals (the building blocks of matter) become obedient and transformed; that is illumination. When the Soul aspect fuses with the biological life that is the beginning of transmutation.

Purity is not spoken of as a quality to reach, it is a natural state. Nature is pure and Soul is pure, but from the beginning of time they have been intermediary stages. The result of every single experience to which we have had a strong reaction, either good or bad, is all accumulated in the memory of biology and of the Soul. We can see in ourselves, for example, when we go to a place without knowing why, we can suddenly be completely afraid. This is because our Soul is carrying the memory of something that happened at another point in time that instilled that fear. The Soul is not guilty or impure but it is not transparent either, because it still has fears and shadows. In the Soul of nature there are lots of experiences that we need to unfreeze. Soul is perfect in the sense that we can't put any blame at all on our etheric body, matter, or Spirit. While Spirit and matter are blind to each other the Soul is the one that holds all the conflicts; this is why the Soul is crucified and is a saviour. When the light of truth and the compassion of wisdom meet, the Soul will remain till the goal of complete illumination is reached. Soul is pure, but the misunderstandings within its natural experiences have to dissipate.

The Soul will automatically attract the perfect biology for its purposes, for what is in the memory of Soul is in the memory of matter. If we come from a long line of wolves, we will have a lot of wolf cellular memory in us, so our Soul will come back as a wolf-soul, automatically attracting the right size and grade of wolf. There is nothing in the memory of Soul that has not been in some sort of drama, so if the drama was 'wolf' in the past, it is 'wolf' now. At the cellular level the movement within the cell sustains its life, for it is the Soul of nature guided by the Spirit. Our trillions of cells are forever moving and have the breath of life in them; this is the Holy Ghost or the Spirit of life. It is all one big energetic flow, organising the right experience to take place. For example, if I want to come back to Earth to have a cup of tea, I am going to be given a cup of tea even if once on Earth I now prefer coffee, because my Soul organises the experience out of the vibration of matter. This is the magic of Spirit and matter being one. It is Soul that does the job of holding the love, as well as every possible experience and memory.

We are always walking into the past. When our consciousness comes back and we become aware, the only way we can actually be the intermediary or Soul is by understanding everyday life, as well as the cosmos and eternity, then blend the two together into us; that is the Soul's job. The minute that we do that, we go into the Maya or illusion of life (our subconscious) and check what it is we haven't understood or loved. Every single day and night of our lives this is what we are doing when we are aware. This is why our actions and reactions become very important, because they tell us whether we need to put our subconscious under the bleaching light of the full moon where it can be seen clearly, or whether we can allow a little blast of illumination, as we suddenly bring together the two aspects and understand what is happening. At this level, the personality, which is what we are looking at when we are looking at the couple, is completely in awe of the result of the illumination of Spirit and matter, as they become one in the child's Soul. The prince and the princess have found their home, for the personality and all the elementals are in love with the Soul. The Soul in turn brings the will of Spirit into its temple.

In the cycle of 20 there is no doubt that we are looking at revelation, which consists of a psychic vision coming through receptivity, with the great input of sounding our trumpet of action. The angel is surrounded by a ring of cloud-like substance; an allusion to the etheric body receiving the victorious call of illumination by the lighted angel. The three figures represent the individual coming into the full blast of the light of the Soul; the angel is one aspect of that solar life. We are all cups holding truth, love and life, waiting to be dazzled with light and hear the wake-up call of the trumpet.

When we are looking at the bright hot Sun, sometimes a vague cloud does help us to see things better and prevents us from being blinded. In the same way the intellect is completely receptive, but has a vague protective membrane between the intensity of what is happening and the actual receiver, or individual. The rays of the Sun are coming out from underneath the clouds, so the light shines through the etheric. We are here as intermediaries or translators and are not yet flowing with the light; we are not 'Christ-Lights,' because this state of consciousness develops well beyond reincarnation. The angel is one of the aspects of the Sun. The rays are very pointed and sharp because the Sun represents the action of the pure, fiery, higher mind. The mind/Spirit is often represented by swords.

The little coloured droplets or tongues of fire represent the gifts from the Holy Spirit at the Pentecost. The droplets are there to inspire three groups of people. The red ones are the gift of passion, fuelling the leaders and heroes of mankind, who give their lives generously into action. The green ones are the unconditional love; nourishment for those who sacrifice themselves into devotional service. The yellow or gold ones symbolise the gift of wisdom, enlightening the teachers of men who are here to share the treasures of pure knowledge. If we start having problems about which group we might belong to, we are too preoccupied with ourselves! At the level of Judgment we are giving up any idea of preference for the job we are supposed to do in service to the great life.

This card is simple, clear and at the same time subtle. We can ask ourselves whether we love the experience of life in its fullness. This includes not just the beauty and joys, but also all the unfairness, the ugliness and the pains. Do we love the Soul in us, which is the pure result of the fusion of Spirit and matter? If we do, then we love the God we live in. Do we love that experience enough so that the God and Goddess (its reflection) we live in, can live in perfect bliss and harmony as they recreate the world every second of the day? The Soul is not perfect, but at the time holds the truth of how much we love and are true, so it does a perfect job. We are not answerable to anybody, only to our own reactions, love and understanding. Are we devoted to the Soul as the mediator between Heaven and Earth? In this card the feminine and masculine aspects are devoted to their charge, which is the Soul. We are in sainthood here. Saints are not perfect but they forget their bodies and their lives for the sake of what they are devoted to; that is what this card represents.

We are not perfect, but the whole of life is perfect. Being alive means we have the possibility of being aware and adjusting our lenses for a purer perception. This is the lens where we see that everything is perfect. The fact that we have a lot of work to do despite all this perfection is because we 'suffer' from that awareness and so start the process of redemption. It is not about being in control, discipline or exercise, in fact it is about the opposite. It is about being naturally devoted to love and truth as life in its simplicity and unfolding; it is about serving the seeds and flowers of perfection so as to offer humanity as the fruit of the Universe, which can feed the cosmic God of perfection.

At the time of burial the Egyptians used the symbol of a man judging himself by his heart. They had a prayer that the dead

person would say to his heart, where he asks for it not to be too
hard on him and not to accuse him. In this we are looking at a process of constantly 'passing away'. If we are receiving and translat-
ing simultaneously, then we are not here or there, but are 'passing
away'. In self-judgment we do not owe anything to anybody, only
to the Spirit of life and truth within us. We are used to the type of
self-judgment that comes through the social, emotional and condi-
tional aspects of life, but this is always to do with the exterior. It
is that self-judgment that we have to 'pass away' from and that is
one of the most difficult things to do. Because we want the World
to love us, we measure ourselves against what the world might
think of us, so we are not doing the true self-judgment. True self-
judgment is simply not about comparison; we don't owe the world
anything and the world doesn't owe us anything. If we rely on the
world to know and understand who we are, we could be in it for a
very long time, as the world is looking at us for the very same purpose; to be heard, seen, touched, understood, loved and be alive!
We have to internalise to find the well of wisdom, let in the light of
truth and fall in love in the depth of its past.

All we are learning to do is to be that strand of light that is consciousness rising from the well of life; this is the triumph of the birth
of light into matter. The way we can do that is through love. If we do
not love what is in front of us, we do not love the God we live in. In the
loving service of the God we live in we align; it is a beautiful process.
If we love, we align and then as we align we love more and so on.

There is a story about Buddha being angry with some monks
who didn't help someone in a desperate situation because in applying the principle of detachment they were lacking compassion and
love. If on the other hand, our love wants to guide, then we give
help even if we are not asked for it, so we have to look at the urge
inside us that might say "I know the answer; let me give it to you".
In the need to demonstrate that we know, there is spiritual pride.

At this level we are going to use the broader aspect of the truth in
the Soul, which is the Sun or cosmic aspect; this does not interfere at
all. We are not obliged to self-judge if we don't want to, but then we
miss the opportunity to do so. To be really true, we have to have the
will to be true, for there is no way that anything can force us to be;
it is not a medicine or a punishment. There has to be the readiness,
which comes out of the recognition that the only salvation comes
from that deep willingness to be true. The punishment type of salvation that society or the group imposes is conditioned by the times
we live in; it is only there so society can protect itself, which is fair

enough. Society is not in the full bloom of becoming Christ-like and it will be a while longer before that is the case! As long as we have not reached that point, society needs a lot of self-protection and self-regulation. Through the translation of our vision we are working at influencing the re-creation of tomorrow's world, by influencing the movement towards new paradigms in society. This is what the wise do, for they know that all that can be done is to influence, not to impose. If we are self-judging by looking at what people expect of us socially, even if it is a body of people that we belong to, then this is not the right self-judgment to apply. We have to break the codes of ethics sometimes, for who says we all have to do what is written on a piece of paper, if at the time we think it doesn't match what we have to do? If we look at the jobs we have from an inner point of view, it will show us what we do to ourselves.

When we give excuses we're not truthful; we make the excuses so that we can get on in society, but it becomes a habit which eventually needs to be peeled away. We do need others, but when we learn to use our hearts and inner wisdom we learn not to need. It is not about cutting off, but about rising and looking at life from a depersonalised view and a Soul-full lens, so that then we come back into everyday life, bringing that cosmic view that can bridge the gap between the temporal and the infinite aspects.

A person who doesn't ask himself too many questions could either be terribly wise, or still quite happy to answer and obey their elemental animal instincts. There is a mind in an animal, but it is not a self-aware mind. Those who do not ask many questions and are quite happy with the explanation in the newspaper or on the television, are still very much driven by the survival instinct. At one point, they may come into contact with someone who says strange things or asks unfamiliar questions. Then they may feel they have to argue their case; this is the beginning of the mental aspect pulling itself out of instinct.

Society has been built on protection of the individual/group/country and its own self interest, so people are made to feel guilty if they don't display the right behaviour patterns to serve the group. The problem is that they will then have a job getting rid of the guilt. We have to be thankful for original guilt, because this is the one mindset that we have to turn around by accepting, understanding our place in the scheme and redeeming our perception of our nature body.

If we feel that anything has been imposed on us that is an excuse not to see a thing for what it is, process it and transform it into a positive outlook. If something is imposed it means our Soul put us in front of that feeling to see if we could rise in consciousness from it, so we can't blame the situation or the condition; this applies to practically everything we experience. That is where we were, so we need to recognise it and realise that we didn't know any better. We can grieve and recognise our grieving process, but let's not take the past as an excuse to keep on with the self-pity and the guilt. When we can say, "I didn't know any better at the time" or "I did my best at the time", then we have accepted the responsibility of our limited consciousness and we realise that we have grown. We can regret and let the regret work through. It is like rubbing a pain better; it works as long as we don't use the regret for the continuation of the memory of the guilt. We can regret that we might have hurt somebody through our action or lack of action, but we have to accept the fact that we have been an instrument for disturbing a situation, for that is how the system works.

We also have to deal with the recognition of how we behaved out of complete ignorance and innocence, and then we go through all the pain of having understood. We feel the pain of the others in the situation and because we know how the process works we can totally accept all of that. After that we can feel the melancholy of the process of life and experience deep compassion for all living creatures and a gradual falling in love with Lord Karma. This is a sure start to recognising his work through the human family.

This card represents the attainment of an initiation. The teaching of the philosopher's stone is that each one of us, when we are completely realised, are building blocks of the new Christ-like humanity; we are the building blocks of the new consciousness.

Society with its grouping dictates by survival but also with the possibility of the higher benevolent guidance of some wise person. The wise people in the group work at aligning the protective aspect of society with the unfolding of the individual. It all starts from the fear intrinsic in nature. Fear is a natural state but guilt is not, for guilt is the beginning of self-awareness. Self-judgment comes when we fear the authority imposing a break in our so-called freedom. Fear has been used by society and fear of God is the beginning of a guilty life, used to bring people into religion.

Judgment is about seeing the value of all the experiences and passion within many lives and still being willing to do the work on behalf of the greater life. 'Judgment' here is not the end of the world as in the scriptures, but a real wake-up call for the individual, asking him to live his life and take the fruit from all the work he has done

before. The angel himself is not the judge, but the bringer of awareness. He's the truth aspect of manifestation from within the Sun or
the Soul, that makes certain that we don't fall back to sleep.

The three people in the card represent
the achievement of the initiate, which is
the self-conscious manifestation of the
Trinity. The woman and man carry the
qualities of reception and action, the third
person is the assimilation of both, provid-
ing the perfect poise and balance between the two; this is Soul. Soul
does not judge mankind; mankind does that itself. The Soul puts
light into the man's actions, reactions and thoughts. A word or a
thought is the beginning of a world. At this stage in Number 20,
the thoughts of a person are powerful materialisers. Thoughts and
words are waves, organised in such a way that they can attract and
manipulate matter into manifestation. With the 20 being a cup, we
know that we are intermediaries, or energetic instruments to receive
and transmit light; we can tune ourselves into a higher channel, just
as we tune the radio.

Most people have their radio tuned into survival and self-
gratification, so their thoughts are always turned to that, hence the
success of all the communication channels, which spread Maya,
glamour and illusion through the ether. Within that range we have
a broad spectrum, from the lowest degrading thoughts, to harmless
forms of self gratification. We are picking up each others' thoughts
all the time, so that creates many different forms. As the fashion in
lifestyle of mass consciousness changes, it alters what is in everybody's thoughts. It is driven by an industry that feeds from people's
lack of discernment. From that we can see the importance of keeping
our elementals tuned towards the highest possible reception, so that
our translation can come from the greater view, to be received by
those who can hear. The translation is as important as the reception.
We have to adapt the teaching to everyday life examples, so that people can learn the common sense of the teaching and associate with its
simplicity. How do we start when we know that we are working into
our past and most people are planning for their future!

We are not doing it for ourselves at this level; we are doing it
to serve the God we live in by serving mankind. If one minute
aspect of our being becomes sacred, we are uplifting this aspect
and everything around us. We do not have to wait to be perfect to
join a spiritual working group, for the rising is not taking place for
everybody simultaneously, as in Judgment Day. This rising symbol-

ises being in true life and being truly alive, in the spiritual sense. The link between the collective and the personal is very important, because an individual waking up is uplifting the environment of those around them. It might have opposite results in the group, as people's lives become disturbed by the wake-up call. It is no good thinking that we can just rise by ourselves above others, because it is a collective movement and our action will automatically bring others up with us. We are one mind and one Soul, even though we can individually separate.

We cannot separate the creator from the creation and to uplift others is a way of accepting the whole process. As man uplifts his mind he has to retrace all the levels of consciousness of the past until he gets to the very heart of creation, then he can perceive the work of the six days of creation with clarity. That is the true co-creation and is the work of the initiate.

The fully-realised initiate or the perfect human being (as Christ) is the active uplifting element for the whole of humanity. An enlightened man is able to demonstrate the possibility for every man to aspire to goodness, regardless of his religion. The realised man is represented by the Sun and the light that has realised its wholeness and so co-creates. We have seen from the beginning of the Tarot that all there is is mind, so it is thought that creates life, love that sustains it and Active Intelligence that manifests life's many forms. The following quotation has been given out by The Lucis trust and is the clearest definition of the fully-realised Soul:

'Christ is the light of the world, the embodiment of love and the indicator of divine purpose. He is the source of all the light and energy which flood throughout the world of human consciousness at this period in the cycle. The Christ of history and the Christ in the human heart are planetary events.

At the centre of all life on this planet stands the Christ, the relation between life and form, Spirit and matter; the innermost consciousness of all creation awaiting revelation. Because of the position the Christ occupies in the evolution of our planetary life, he is the focal point of all endeavour, the 'way' of spiritual unfoldment, for 'No man cometh to the Father but by me'. He belongs to all humanity, irrespective of nation, race, and religion, social or cultural background. He is 'the same identity' which those of different ideologies recognise under different names.

The Christ is God-man, human-divine, a fusion of the vertical way of at-one-ment and the horizontal way of service. He is total *human experience fused with the inner life force which gives coherence, intelligence and purpose to life on Earth.*

The Christ is a Person, a Presence, and a Principle. He brings together in one sweep of continuous energy flow, the cosmic fountain head, the planetary manifestation and the human expression. He is power and livingness, love and wisdom, light and understanding.

He is the builder of the new world, the new age: the driving power within the human heart and mind, which produces the new forms of the new and coming civilisation. He is the magnetic and attractive force which 'lifts up' and redeems the density of materialisation. He ignites the spark of divinity within each human being. He is the fiery love of God for man which inspires sacrifice and renunciation.

The Christ is the archetype of the true Aquarian: he is cooperative, inclusive, intelligent and active. His motive is love of humanity, his keynote is service.

He is the Way, the Truth and the Life for all mankind. He is the beacon in the darkness, the essence of divine truth and reality, the guarantor of ultimate spiritual achievement for 'as he is so can we be in this world'.

From Taoism, Hinduism and Buddhism, where the mind perceives life in the physical as an impermanent state because life is a flowing movement of energy, to the Hebraic traditions of the West, where we explore life at the emotional and intellectual level and where we have personalised the idea of God in our image, the message is the same; sacrifice, compassion, love, truth and wisdom. We can see that we are the golden thread linking the one mind or the one Soul, as one long journey of enlightenment for mankind. We have brought the East and West together as one, with the Buddhist and the Muslim both having the role of the mirror for their respective traditions.

Here in cycle 20, we have the passion of achieving the work on behalf of the God we live in. Europe and the Middle East haven't quite finished their work yet; we have spread the realisation that everyone can follow the Soul (Jesus) into Christ realisation, giving hope to the humblest of Souls. The next step is to go back to nature and to a simpler way of living, where the love, understanding and respect of working at one with nature, can achieve some kind of fusion and perfection. Then, when the conditions are right, the enlightened mind can be grounded.

We really can't have an enlightened rebirth without coming back into biology. The body of nature must not be neglected, rejected or despised, but rather nurtured, respected and brought into the light. We are only here to judge from the point of view of spiritual reality.

We have to go through the stages of true transubstantiation, which takes us from probation to sanctification, eventually reaching communion. The communion is the very last stage, when we are in total union with the divine and become little specks of gold light. It is our privilege to be the only self-conscious beings on the planet and probably in the Solar System. Because of this it is up to us to render our cells and matter sacred, so that we can bless what is around us. When we have completely accepted within us a quality that is part of the vibration of the animal or plant kingdom, we see it from the point of view of the love of the Soul and it is then that transubstantiation takes place. It is the love of peace, the love of assimilation and therefore the love of the God we live in, that makes transubstantiation happen. If we recognise in our hearts something in us that is even more than these loves, then we know that the God we live in is looking through our eyes. So for example, when we look at a dog with that complete love in us, we see the angel of the dog Soul and if we are really lucky the vibration of the highest qualities of this Soul will be felt in ours. It is a bit trickier when we are talking about human beings. For example, being 'blissed out' with love for a guru figure can be based on emotional need therefore is not pure. The guru himself is taking energy from the Earth and radiating magnetism, so he is still duplicating dependency and still being fed. We are exploring the next stage, which is understanding the importance of individuation within the group. This is therefore not interfering with individuals in the group, yet recognising the one life, at the same time as seeing all the different qualities brought together to attract and ground the light.

We don't give in order to receive, but because we know the law of energy, we receive so much more than we would ever be able to give, even if we think of giving our lives, which actually are not our lives anyway. What we are receiving is the incredible effect of transubstantiation. At this stage we are not doing it for this reward, because if we were the change wouldn't happen; it can only happen when the point of intent is clear of self-interest, because we are a cell in a greater body.

If we let love naturally flow through us, rather than thinking that we give our love, something will happen spontaneously to our instrument through the law of energy. We can, through the extreme discipline of physical exercise, actually make some transformation happen in our bodies, but this does not deliver a permanent realised stage, it is a forced sainthood stage. It demonstrates mind over matter as an escape from human misery. This encourages the disciple to practise 'you are mind'.

Man has a right to refuse both his salvation and divine love for a long time. If he refuses to participate in the life of the God we live in through degenerative, destructive rebellion, he will be dust for another Solar System and another opportunity. We can be certain that all will be right in the end, because as we go through our own lives the Solar System will experience a fusion with a greater Sun in the universal life. As we go deeper and deeper, it all becomes denser, until eventually we reach the very first experience of our Solar System. Then we have to actually break through the very dense material that was left behind from that first Solar System, which was the first refusal to participate in the plan with God. It is not so much about looking up to the stars all the time, but aligning with the cosmic forces working through our Solar System with the purpose of making it a sacred star.

It is thanks to the individual effort of every man, that the survival/war-like mindset can be replaced by a communication/peace-like paradigm, enabling true changes to happen on the planet. Those who are lukewarm are like a sky that is deprived of stars; there is a refusal of commitment and a refusal to believe that goodness could in fact, be the essence of the sentence, "We are only human". The lukewarm accept and submit to what is going on materially, because this is the way it goes and the way it has always worked; the pull of Maya and glamour rules, okay! Is it worse to refuse to lift one's head up to look at the stars, or to actually do the bad deeds? At least when we do the bad deeds we ground the illusion and we have a chance to regret our action and feel guilt, thus starting the process of responsible awareness.

The child is the realisation of the couple. Through introspection we learn to love our shadow aspect and then the third aspect, as it sees itself in the light/shadow mirror, fuses all the opposite qualities and perceives the complete human being. It is the conclusion of the union; it is the mind discovering it is Soul; not a boy or a girl but the mystical, spiritual three-in-one Soul, which is the result of a synthesis of accomplished work during incarnation. The parents have to associate with their one Soul to expect judgment from its wisdom. In the light of the Soul we look and truly see.

The Sun and the angel are one. The angel is the symbol of the lineage of all the great realised Souls having reached solar consciousness and beyond. It dispenses light and truth, for it can see deep into all the needs and cracks. The judgment comes out of this. The child is the risen Soul coming out of the subconscious, having passed its exams. Recognition of the oneness of life brings holiness to the perception.

The parents are coming out and rising above the green vegetation. They recognise and are thankful for the result of their struggle – they have seen the light! All the previous experiences are put in front of us, so we are put in front of ourselves in order to understand the work of karma or destiny. The child represents the zero point between the essential and the experiment. It is so important to understand that it is the essence of what we experience in everyday life that is important, so we need to de-personalise and distil the experiences to get the essential out of them; we do that through Soul awareness. All the situations and conditions that we find ourselves in are by-products; we are after the essential in the experience, so we are not being taken in and falling in love with the laboratory any more.

What comes out of the subconscious are our most secret thoughts. We truly have to see where we are coming from, on behalf of the God we live in, without all the other outer layers that are there as part of the laboratory. A thought sparks out and it becomes part of life unfolding, independent of any intervention. At that level we have to be more and more conscious of our thoughts and words, for that is where it all starts. Millions of thoughts a second are flowing through the ether and are being received, duplicated and multiplied, until they end up as war and crime, or hate and stupidity. We have the responsibility of looking at what we think and feel from the deepest aspect. From there one pure thought can bleach an awful lot of the rubbish that is flowing in the ether, so it is pretty potent because it comes from the fire of fires. We know that eventually nothing will remain hidden, so we may as well hurry up! 'In time and space, all will be revealed' – it is that idea. The cosmic life has the memory of where it has been and we are retracing it. The collective memory will be decoded again, so that our action can follow the new code; that is how we do it. These new waves can truly manifest a better life on the planet. Many more minds and hearts can catch this dream than even a few generations before, so eventually we will all be working at rebuilding the new structure for the new humanity.

The other familiar concept is the resurrection of the body, now to be seen not as physicality but as a body of light. Man is not a prisoner in matter. Matter is the best possibly ally, for we can see the reflection of the God we live in through it. Through our reactions we can see how much we understand and love the process of his creation. The possibilities of co-creation reveal themselves by degrees and are so enormous! We all feel like prisoners in matter at some point, but when we see it from the point of view of the Soul reincarnating to perceive life in a different way, then the pain is accepted and we can start to free the misunderstandings from the role of matter. We have the most marvellous tool there is, which is an image of life as it is in front of us and because we know of the power of the thought and the word, the possibility of co-creation for peace and love on the planet are limitless. We are not prisoners, it is the opposite; we are a gift given to life to uplift matter. The inner process is true creativity and the 20 brings man into the true life.

The green wings of the angel are crystallised sunshine – the sublimation of the emotional body, given as sacrifice to the higher vision. They are symbolic of the spiritual life which we know is also the Holy Spirit or Holy Ghost, coming out from relativity into the eternal life. The angel's head with its curly hair symbolises the Sun. Her red arms and red hat indicate thoughts that are constantly acting and realised instantly, through the passion of service. Thought is only valuable when its consequent action becomes viable and the goal is realisation of an ideal. An action and a thought are only of any importance cosmically, if they come from an ideal that is well above our heads; that makes them cosmically legitimate. The ideal is the world of pure thought and pure ideas; it is through 'thought-action-materialisation' that we can ground the vision of the God we live in. It is only by seeing and touching, that we co-create the divine kingdom in the Solar System. The God we live in is all-loving, all-giving, all-sacrificing and all-knowing, so what we are doing as self-conscious beings is letting our hearts and minds be used as blessing instruments, through our loving and understanding. By this process we can dissolve into the greater life, to the point of knowing that nothing is ours. The sacrifice truly belongs to the God we live in.

By the process of self-judgment, man survives the state of the corruption of death, so reconstituting the vehicle of matter into a more subtle vehicle. The judgment is victory over Maya or illusion. All was consumed on the evening of the crucifixion that The Magician had to go through. Now he has reached the end of his long journey, after which the world may bring him another job.

In The Empress, the full receptivity of the intellectual life had to be there to receive the psychic emanation from the wisdom of The High Priestess, so that it could be translated via the intellect and passed on to the next phase of implementing, ordering, and organising the world in The Emperor. We can see the similarity of the message in The Empress and The Emperor with the 'thought-action-materialisation' of Judgment.

The Hermit at Number 9 can acquire all the qualities that the supreme Justice in Number 8 has given him. He takes in the vision of true justice and needs to digest and understand it, so that he can know the movement of the wheel of karma; this means that Justice is also a pivotal card. Justice has to do with self-judgment; at Number 20 this divine judgment fuses with God's creature, the Soul of man.

After the death initiation at Number 13, The Devil in Number 15 must choose a direction. This is either pride, or the dissolution of the world of illusion. After that, the destruction of The Tower follows.

With enlightenment we go into the world to retrace the past, but also that is the time when we have to accept the possibility of sainthood for the next part of the journey, so as to allow the Soul greater fusion with the love in the Earth. The method in 20 is the pivot from enlightenment to 'let's walk the Earth'. Number 20 acts out of what the world needs, not what it needs for itself. Then with Number 21, we have to really stop looking at our self-cleaning methods, self-looking obsession, self-best sainthood preoccupation, so as to let light through the transparent web. Before this ultimate self-realisation the 21 stage will use the illumination of the Sun for a long time yet, in order to turn the full light on us and go into self-judgment.

When man is capable of truly finding himself and giving himself to self-judgment, then the spirit of life manifests in him in a very conscious manner. Here man doesn't suffer life as he used to. He still goes through pain and suffering, but sees it through understanding, willingness and contemplation, which is the life chosen by a saint. Saints put themselves through the worst possible situations, physically, mentally and emotionally. They are willingly crucified for the love of God, but without serving a martyr's syndrome.

There is only one will, which is the divine decree, or the law of karma. Anyone who is blind to this process hasn't got a chance in hell to be going up or down any ladder, but just goes round the wheel of rebirth. It is not that they are rejected, but energetically it just doesn't work any other way. It is self-evident, just as there are substances we cannot digest and if we eat them they will just pass through us.

Salvation or ascension through the initiatic way is not an evolution, so it doesn't happen naturally in the way that a species develops and survives. We cannot do it by evolving, semantics, philosophy or anything else. It requires and necessitates an active intervention of the individual man himself, by the acceptance in him of the divine decrees. He deliberately participates in the world of creation with his thoughts. Man has actively got to have the will to act, receive and participate. The minute we understand that process, or even a bit of that process, then we are not evolving any more, we are co-creating. Ascension is the result of uplifting the mind of minds towards the mind of the creators. Man becomes truly human only in the measure that he absorbs the universal experience.

Never neglect the obligation of earthly work, for it is in this work that the initiate participates more efficaciously in the struggle for good. There's a point in this process where he has to uplift to actually help. As we precipitate another translation of what we are doing on this planet into words and sentences, we can actually access thought forms, then we are influencing the ones who are fighting for the good and giving more energy to their work. This influence gives direction to those who are willing to take action to relieve suffering. Very often they will have too short a vision, for they have only just risen and they feel that the world is unfair. A lot of the initiatic ideas are not easily understood by human intelligence. These ideas are inspirations and noble thoughts that have to be received and translated into actions. This is the Soul of man, rising to the higher intelligence of the cosmic group of a realised master, so giving birth to an initiate – a peaceful warrior.

The World, Le Monde
Bringer of the good news

The journey of the Tarot is the journey of the Soul into initiation, which is the movement of Spirit into matter and the fusion of lighted truth with eternal wisdom. In this process the aspirant's consciousness emerges, his mind in Heaven and his feet firmly on Earth. From aspirant, he rises to the conscious struggle of the disciple on the path and finally to the lighted way of the initiate. He understands that there is only one life, one mind, one Soul, one will and all he needs to follow is the direction of the lighted will of the ones who served the will of God before him. The good news would have to be that he is not alone, as he has merged with essential life and that others can recognise the brotherhood of Soul, through his resurrection in the world.

483

The Magician came back into the world to demonstrate that he could master the mystery of life by juggling with the four elements – earth, air, fire and water – that make up biological life on the planet. He discovers that all is maya, glamour and illusion; this is the energy that manifests yesterday's problems. All this is to be transmuted by his enlightened consciousness into love/wisdom. In this last loop of the spiral of his journey The Magician has to become the initiate. The world is in him and 'becomes' through him, as his divine fire reminds other sparks of intelligence to turn into blazing love.

As aspirants and disciples there's hardly any action we make, or behaviour we exhibit that doesn't hide something for the self, so throughout the whole journey we have to keep looking at our behaviour and our desires without obsessive fear or selfish guilt. We may use big words such as justice, discrimination and love, but the aim is to sublimate the entire emotional luggage, whether it is 'good' or 'bad'. Also, we need to transgress what we are proud of or feel guilty about, because all of that is about desire and is based in the emotional body. The danger is that while we are still moved by our desires, all our actions will be coloured by our personal needs and wants. The disciple has to be passionate because fiery passion moves and transforms, but his passion has to become a passion without desire, so therefore the ultimate aim is to want without desire. This is difficult to achieve and to do it we have to kill the teacher within us who wants to give out the good news, in order to transmute it into more love/wisdom. When the desire is eventually gone, then there is nothing else we can do but be in service.

The first part of the journey was a wonderful exploration of all the high metaphysical ways that Spirit can move. Straight away The Magician met the goal of his journey in the High Priestess, who represents the wisdom behind the veil and the cosmic mind. The ultimate goal is to re-fuse one's consciousness with the cosmic consciousness, which is itself the result of Heaven and Earth releasing their separation and making one through the medium of humanity. After that, the next four cards – The Empress, The Emperor, The Pope and The Lover – are concerned with looking at all the metaphysical ways in which Spirit can move through our consciousness.

Most spiritual teachings tell us that the higher aim is to detach our minds from the misery of life on the planet. This is the most separative mind-set that we meet while on the spiritual path and is commonly held, though it is an essential part of the spiritual enfolding of our minds. Actually the higher cosmic consciousness can only be realised here on the Earth. The aim is not to rise on a cloud and stay there, coming back down to the Earth to do some work and apologising because we are human beings. Instead, it is to *be* a human being with no apologies, but with a much higher, broader, cosmic and energetic point of view. If we have understood the true meaning of ideas such as truth and love from the point of view of energy and the higher mind, then we will know that there is no want and no desire in those words left for self.

We live in the best possible time to understand the simple down-to-earth initiate, who has become a true human being, through the honest work of giving up all the excuses of the little self. It is the glamorous part of us that is still kidding us by misunderstanding what it means to be a co-creator. Science today is experimenting in ways that are part of this misunderstanding and is fixed on the idea of co-creation in a purely physical form. Science is the little sister of the higher mind and is the vehicle through which the understanding has been able to proceed in a rational way, so that we can have a good blueprint to stand on and rise from. Eventually the scientist becomes the priest, but before reaching that higher state he has to experience the pride of the sorcerer's apprentice. We all need to recognise the apprentice sorcerer within ourselves; any action that is not first internalised for its intent, can take us back into self-aggrandisement. The first step in the process of internalisation is to develop awareness of all our behaviour and reactions, whether they are good or bad. The second step is to take all of that in mind and listen to our chattering, excuses and explanations from the psychological angle. From there we can stop getting caught in the drama and go beyond the clouds of illusion, until eventually we truly give up. At this stage we see and accept ourselves for what we are and stop associating with our little selves. This means that we know that nobody is guilty. When we have reached that point we can see the whole world for what it is, with courage, honesty, love and a pure heart. What stops us engaging in the truth process is our desire.

Desire is the only obstacle to completing the process of internalisation and as long as we keep avoiding this work by giving ourselves excuses, we are covering up and feeding our mind-sets, which are based on desire. A pure heart is like a clear cup and has no mind-sets, so it sees everything for what it is; it retains nothing and the mind is clear of desire.

In Number 20 we saw Judgment as the end of the experience. We recognised our shortfalls and thus took initiation in 12

(The Hanged Man) and 13 (No Name). We have put ourselves passionately into the process and know that this is not the end of the work, but the beginning of a more rigorous scrutiny of our makeup. Even after the illumination in The Stars we have The Moon, telling us 'beware', because any desire can still destroy us. At Judgment, in Number 20, there is the promise of a rise in consciousness, a new birth. Here we can stand on the planet and look at ourselves from the higher intelligence in our Soul. We can't hide at this stage and we are happy not to, for the Soul is truly present doing its work.

With Number 21, The World, we are here in the world and our mind has connected with the cosmic raison d'être of the world. We are looking from inside out at the plan unfolding. The elements, which were material, have become metaphysical and of the Soul, or higher intelligence. The symbols of the four Evangelists that we see in the card represent that transformation. The Tarot cards were first made in the Christian era and so the Evangelists were the archetypes that could help people understand the idea of 'the good news', which says that there is hope. If we can perceive life from the point of view of the Spirit-guided Soul the world can achieve peace; this is truly our service to it.

The wreath of leaves represents hope and eternal life. The green is the green of crystallised sunshine and the Sun's rays; it is the essence of Spirit, crystallised in form through the work and the Active Intelligence of life. We are the best instrument that life could produce for the job of witnessing and we are back on the planet to serve; this is 'the good news' of the resurrection. The four evangelists represent the metaphysical expressions of the elements. Taurus the Bull (the Gospel of Luke) represents the earth element, with the coin or pentacle. Leo the Lion (the Gospel of Mark) is the fire element of wands, then Scorpio the Eagle (the Gospel of Matthew), represents the element water and is cups. Lastly Aquarius the angel (the Gospel of John), is swords or the air element.

The World is all the elements refining to their essence as they deliver the human Soul. The eternal life, aware of its cosmic dimension on this little blue planet, is bursting with myriads of innocent sacrificial lives. The passion of fire moves the Magician and stirs him into action, so he needs the receptivity of the water and the sharpness and clarity of the truth of the mind to be able to penetrate deeply into matter, where the memory is held in water, to perceive and retrieve the golden wisdom; this is high initiation. This process had started in Number 20, and then the good news in Number 21 is that it is processing.

At this stage the initiate or Magician has come back into a completely symbolic world that is full of light and the self-centred elements of his personality have disappeared. He has become eternal youth, but not through wanting it, as the apprentice sorcerers want the secret of eternal life and play God on Earth as they seek it. This youthfulness is represented in the form of a young woman, symbolising matter. We could be one hundred and three years old with many wrinkles, but if our heart is pure and our cup reflects the purity of the light of truth we are eternally youthful. This energy is new, childlike and pure. The great initiate Saturn has removed the flesh so as to reveal the veil that holds everything in the World together and allows the light to flow into manifestation. Even the cup is removed, because it has become transparent, so there is no form left in the world and nothing to attract or distract us. It is a world full of beauty because we see the light in everything rather than the form.

The initiate knows he is just an aware spark of mind and has learned to see beyond the world of appearance. According to the Ancient Wisdom we are in the second Solar System, so the work is strongly based in the emotional life. This is why desire has to be the key word, as it is needed to reveal the house of our Soul, Soul being linked to the sensitivity of the higher affectivity. The first Solar System would have seen the birth of consciousness in matter, which is an incredible feat, from which there is a lot of healing to be done. On the planet at the moment there are still a lot of people who are learning to be born into the first initiation, which means they are beginning to put the needs of the environment, the needs of animals and other people, before their own. At the end of the great work we disappear and the golden coin is simply a sparkle of sunshine, because this is what we have become, through going back to our essence in the Christic lighted Soul.

Until the stage when the Number 6 becomes an open cup and our hearts can open, obsession is its key. If our cup is not transparent, everything we do will serve our own desires and dramas, until we are completely denuded of them. Here we are looking at all the emotional and intellectual mindsets which serve desire, right up to wanting to be the best person on the planet. Soul is the only entity to associate with if we really want to serve, because it is not part of the world of matter, it is essence, which is changing all the time. Want is coming from desire, if the need to be loved, seen or holy is present. After the 'want' has gone there is "I can't do anything else but". While there is desire, we have a mind of our own and so we are feeding desire. The important thing is to know ourselves so that we can forgive, which is the same as checking all our excuses. We de-personalise the job to be done when we dissolve the patterns of obsession with self.

If we are not as clear as we can be about our desire, we would still tend to be 'doing it to the world' rather than letting the world happen through us. If we are doing something because we want to have an effect on the world, we are being an apprentice sorcerer. It is only when we act without desire that we really have an effect on the world. There is a tiny and refined line between the apprentice sorcerer and the initiate; it is this fine line that we are learning to negotiate, so that we can once and for all rise above the temptation, until it disappears.

We may be serving our fellow humans with the most refined part of ourselves, yet they are still not moving and change is not happening, so we may at times say to ourselves 'what is the point?' For the ones who are deaf and blind to the world of the Soul only good news is the old news; they have heard it before and it does not work! The key here is non-interference. We can remember that we are only a cell in the body of the world, so we get on with our lives. We know that the Universe is supported and held together by love.

We are in a world held by the cold light of reason; this is the true love that sustains biology, until it merges with the love of life, form and the great body of the Solar System. Our work is to attune ourselves to that natural intelligent magnetic love. We are only able to carry on because we have given up to and become part of, what is holding us energetically; this is called 'going beyond the world'. Holding the world of manifestation is the way to pass on messages to the whole system and keep it flowing. It is through the etheric, primordial magnetic field, which is constantly moving and flowing, that we become able to travel with our minds through time and space. We have gone beyond the world of magic here, for we have sublimated it by completely understanding that we cannot do anything to the world, it has to do it to itself; we can only witness it with our open heart.

This card is sometimes called 'Triumph', because it tells us of the world after initiation has taken place, so demonstrating complete understanding for the harvest of experience that has been gathered in, processed, digested and reborn in a new consciousness. It is a very peaceful, glorious triumph. It is also the end of one cycle and the beginning of a new one. At this point the evangelists or the bringers of good news, tell us that though humanity is lost in the dark, there is light at the end of the tunnel. This is a pure message, without the mindset of 'saving' humanity. We are not here to make people happy or to stimulate the emotional or mental mindsets through mind-blowing, tear-flowing workshops. We are transmitters of light and transmuters of matter; in that there is no 'magic' for it is the state we reach when Jesus, the Soul in us, shows us the way of service. The Soul is the intermediary between the higher mind of Spirit and the intelligence in matter, so its job is to attract the light of the Spirit through the higher mind, sublimating the form so that Spirit can merge with the wisdom in matter.

The mind creates and we create God as we go. God is the concept of what our little minds can perceive as a meaning to life. We are coming into a new conception of God, which is much less separative (as in good and bad), but is inclusive and supportive. This God brings the message that all is one and goodwill is the way. The 'good news' emerges out of the darkness of the interpretation of the old religions that talk about punishment and sin. The interpretations are real, in the sense that they are mankind's appreciation of the general karmic and genetic process; that is why we revisit the sacred texts. The good news is that out of that there comes another appreciation of God, called the father who forgives. However, the fear of God has been the way forward and the beginning of introspection, so we shouldn't dismiss the old ideas for they are still needed for mankind's mental state. It is up to people themselves to go beyond the old ways of thinking; we can't keep on blaming a way of looking at God, we need to think for ourselves and in doing so we digest and go beyond the old God.

The world is within us and we are in the world. What are we but a light transmitting instrument to enlighten the darkness of ignorance? The initiate knows that by loving, understanding and digesting the process of life, he transforms fear into acceptance, so transmuting the code of fear into 'I am life as I am supposed to be!' This is the work of alchemy and is same principle as 'to close the door where evil dwells'. It can only be done deep in the Soul, because it is only the Soul that has the honesty and the energetic power to see clearly and bring the message down from the father to the mother; it can't be done by the intellect. The initiate sees a thing for what it is, not for what it appears to be. It is always the same world, but with a different perception. This is the alchemical process transmuting the coal of accumulated fossilised experiences into a blazing fire, which purifies and releases the essential energy of life.

Here the elements, represented by the four corners of the card, are ready for the alchemical process to achieve the transmuting of matter into gold. The baton (lion), symbolising the element fire, is what propels this process. The cup of water (Eagle or sublimated Scorpio) is what is going to receive and reflect the idea, which itself is going to have to become spiritually true and pure with the sword (angel-air). In time the sword will fuse with matter (the bull) and render it gold. It is the energetic journey of the Soul as initiate, as he travels back home.

In Number 21 the four Gospels of the New Testament are represented. There is the Gospel of prayer, which is of the earth (Luke); the Gospel of action, being of fire and passion (Mark); the Gospel of spirituality which is of the mind (John) and then the natural rebirth of mankind in the Gospel of Matthew. Earth, fire, water and air are the classified elements, but here we are being told to stop classification. The elements flow from one into another. They are only an expression of that energetic experience. By the time we have reached this stage the understanding is metaphysical, so there is no separation of the Gospels or apostles. 'As above, so below', these are sublimated facets of it all; first we pray, then we act, then we spiritualise, then we sublimate.

The three astrological signs associated with the element earth are Taurus, Virgo and Capricorn. In the card these are represented by the fixed earth symbol of the bull of Taurus; this is the evangelist of prayer. Before the completed purification of the personality's resistance, the earth signs speak of interest for the self, because they are to do with exchange or getting something back for the self. Gold represents the end of the Alchemic process. The pentacle is gold, but it is still a coin and an item used for payment and exchange. This is the proper and rightful quality of the energy of earth, therefore this is not to be seen as a criticism, merely a fact. We are simply looking at consciousness moving through stages. The elements are only there to take us into the different levels of understanding this world, so it is not to be understood as personal, but just a fact from the point of view of the elements.

The evangelist Luke will open the mind and dispel narrowness of mind and control on right or wrong. The bull brings in enduring patience, which we know is an essential quality to achieve the new vision; it is in this earth sign (phase of experience) that the third eye opens. The angels of the four weeks of the month of Taurus are vitality, abundance, beauty and wisdom; all these have to do with patience. We may wonder what vitality has to do with patience, but for vitality to come back on the planet we need to go through autumn and winter, so it needs complete patience to accept the law of time and space in nature. Abundance, beauty and wisdom are the fruits of patience; for example, some of the most beautiful trees on the planet take many years before they give even one flower, so we have here the patience of the one who knows that life is beyond time.

When the critical mind of Virgo is quietened down it becomes total devotion in an obscure and silent way, so as to keep only the necessary knowledge of what we are devoted to. The critical mind is there in the first place to enable us to find our direction without waiting for any reward, for Virgo is a sign of sacrifice, renouncing and humbly bringing the maximum to others. Capricorn is the one who knows how to dominate the tumultuous flow of passion by looking at the individual incarnated life as if from the outside of it, thus he is already looking into eternity. He meditates with pity because he has turned 'life isn't worth living' into pity and understanding and he can see that other people are going through all the trials that he has gone through in the past; that is the secret of the initiatic quality of Capricorn. Luke or Taurus is teaching us enduring passion and here we learn about prayer. The element earth teaches us to pray, not for easily earned impermanent pleasures, but for patience, acceptance and devotion.

With the lion we look at the fire signs of Aries, Leo and Sagittarius. The Lion is the fixed fire sign and represents the Gospel of Mark and the wands in the minor arcana; this is the evangelist of action. The wand is the sign of power and command, which is precipitated into action in Aries so that it can radiate through the world, even if the people don't want it. The tyrannical aspect of fire can be seen in Leo and we can recognise this in ourselves, for we have all these elements in us. The fiery side in us can want to push the good news down people's throats! With Sagittarius this power of leadership can even overtake the spiritual, as we can witness in tyrannical leaders. We know that even religion can be taken over by despotism and that has happened so many times in history.

Earth has given birth to the kingdom of God; higher consciousness comes into the world and the action of man must manifest its presence with the energy of the apostle Mark. Aries is needed to manifest a great trust in life, so the 'angels' of Aries are rebirth, hope, faith and trust. Rather than actively wanting to pin people down with our fire, we have to do a lot of work on ourselves so as to know that the only thing we are here to do is to give the good news of faith, hope and trust. Aries has a need to shout out the good news that we can have trust in life.

With Leo we are looking at the self; self-approval, self-esteem, self-confidence and personal power. We are in the full brightness of the summer here, where the light on the personality is at its strongest, so the courage and devotion of Leo enables all these 'self-qualities' to disappear. This is why Leo is the one that provides the turning point for mankind. At all the great revolutionary points in history Leo has to be strongly present, because it is the one where the beginning of the death happens; we need the burning coal before we get the sublimation. Leo refuses to keep it to himself, so wants to spread the knowledge and esperence, which is the hope that has put his heart on fire. By now he has completely transmuted his need for self-approval and personal power and has become the sacrificial lamb of his first incarnation.

Sagittarius brings adventure, curiosity, opportunity and expansion. Wherever the arrow of Sagittarius points the Spirit goes. These qualities are all very dangerous if you are supposed to be bringing back the fire into the heart of beauty! The fire in the heart of Leo is burning and wanting to give out all that knowledge and hope, while Sagittarius will turn his life totally in the direction where his arrow points. The arrow's movement culminates by following the path of the heart, flying to the sky and hoping to bring the divine inspiration into the world.

The eagle represents the exalted water sign of Scorpio. The battle of mind has been won and in its pure cup of vision, the triumphant mind soars to the light for the waters are pure. It represents the Gospel of Matthew, the element water and the cup. The Gospel of Matthew is the normal, logical and natural good news following the Old Testament.

The element water represents the waters of life, which carry the message of the greater life; that is the essence of Matthew. In the past the kingdom of God was dangerously tiny with only a few elected people. Now it is everywhere thanks to the work of water, of Matthew and of natural growth and rebirth. From one small handful of elected nations, the message has spread all over the world and it can't be stopped, for it is universal, invisible and ever present. Water needed the cup to give it its form, so we have the origin of life in Cancer, its sublimation of needs for survival as death in Scorpio and then rebirth into universal water, with is Pisces. So here we are truly in the psychic element or the Soul. Water is the messenger, the holder of memory, the magnetic field and the Soul memory; all of that is a watery movement carried in the cup of the Grail or the Holy Ghost. When we go beyond the form, we don't need a cup any more for we are seeing water metaphysically as coming from Heaven. This is a Gospel which renews, heals and re-births. The higher attribute of water is to be sensitive, not emotional; holding but not possessive.

Cancer is a water sign with no form, pulling itself out of matter and attracted by its goal to spirituality, so here we have the birth of true awareness. Cancer is the mother of all genetic karmic energy. Spiritually we have to go through Cancer to be reborn, because eventually we come out of its waters of knowledge. Scorpio reaches spirituality by its death, eventually emerging to live in the pure mysticism of Pisces. These are the higher aspects of the water element that enable the outcome of how we live the Tarot.

The angels of Cancer are knowledge, intuition, imagination and awareness. These are carried in the higher reflective waters of Cancer. Here we are in the metaphysical in full possession of the waters of life and of the higher intellect; in Cancer we are being reborn out of all that. With Scorpio we have the angels of sensitivity, talents, gifts, apprenticeship and mastery, which are all very relevant to the death of self-propelling grandeur. With Pisces, there are the angels of sorrow, reconciliation, release and departure, hence the two currents of the up and down streams.

Lastly we have the depiction of the angel, representing air, the sword of Spirit and the clear mind of the Gospel of John. The air sign becomes the sign of Spirit for the initiate, therefore representing the mind. It can penetrate flesh and matter so as to inform it. Here we are not in evolution any more, for the journey has ended; Spirit has fused with matter and the work is done. With the first card we saw Spirit coming back into matter; now at Number 21 there is no more descent into form, instead Spirit is rising up with matter. This is why John is the spiritual evangelist. You have Luke, the prayer evangelist, Mark the action evangelist and then John the spiritual evangelist. Here the one universal love is seen from dizzy heights.

The three air signs are Gemini, Libra and Aquarius. Gemini represents the curiosity of the mind waking up to life in its lower aspects; Libra is marvelling at the aesthetic aspect of the world and looking for justice; Aquarius is about the joyful waking up of the world – it is a wonderful world! Aquarius will use its sense of expansion to become at one with the angel, but there are very few Aquarians that are exercising their minds in this fashion. The angel of Gemini gives transformation; the mind opens to the light. There is celebration, joy and recreation giving a childlike, pure view of the world. Libra's angel carries truth, courage, fortitude and integrity. The Aquarian angel is about caring, sharing, loving and brotherhood. Looking from the point of view of the angel, in Gemini we have the certitude that it is possible to attain total knowledge. Now that we are steady we know that the knowledge is there and that it is in us. It is reached at the central point of Libra, where that mind attains a source of beauty; this enables man in Aquarius to actually have a cosmic mind-set, instead of the little survival planet mindsets. He has looked at and absorbed the knowledge, then is re-born from it because he knows it is in him. It is mankind co-creating and taking part willingly in the process of transubstantiation, which brings everything back to its source in the heart, to be held in beauty. Wait for the day! What are a few thousand years from the point of view of a trillion year old universe!

Each of the seasons has an Archangel. For spring, which includes Aries, Taurus and Gemini, it is Raphael the healer. In the summer, for Cancer, Leo and Virgo, we have Archangel Uriel who brings knowledge. In autumn, with Libra, Scorpio and Sagittarius, it is Michael the Archangel of truth. In winter, Gabriel, the Archangel of strength is there for Capricorn, Aquarius and Pisces.

 The woman symbolises eternal youth or the perfected Soul from the perspective of the Spirit. She is carrying two wands; one is the flame of eternal truth – the light that never dies; the other is the flame of eternal burning love, which makes anything that touches it pass through onto another level. She is the manifestation of eternal life, which is pure mind being reflected in the transparent cup of life. Her red drapes represent the action and passion of life itself, for ruby red is a symbol for the highest level of initiation. When we are initiates we do not 'do' anything ourselves, rather we are a doorway for people to start their own initiation. The flames are there and whether the initiate is working with the mind or with the love aspect, he has the eternal flame that can touch others if they can receive and perceive the spark in their hearts.

Number 21 is the goal seen through symbols and realised by Number 1, The Magician. This rise links the initiate with the High Priestess in Number 2, because she is the formless goal, encompassing all the knowledge of what it means to be a human being from the cosmic angle; this is very different from intellectual knowledge.

The Emperor in Number 4 shows regency over the material world and so receives the plan in order to implement it, whereas at 21 the initiate has regency over the mind or the mental world. The Wheel of Fortune has stopped, because all the attachments have disappeared and we have seen the remnants of past misunderstandings crumble in Number 16, The Tower, giving the opportunity to rebuild the house of God. Then in Number 21 the celestial Jerusalem has been built. It is Heaven on Earth because of the realisation that it is built with one cell at a time. Each unit of consciousness (an initiate) is a stone brick, making up the temple of God. That is how it is built, one cell or one Soul at a time; the celestial city of Jerusalem is actually the body of humanity.

In Number 21 there is a warning of the dark side that surfaces when we break through into another level of consciousness. The warning is that we create dark shadows out of glamour and illusion. These can give birth to destructive entities or 'errors', which are all based on desire; if unchecked they can swallow us up. These introspective questions are so important. We also have to look at our obsessions, for it is obsession that keeps us down and feeds our desire; maya, glamour and illusion feed each other to keep control over our actions. The whole of mankind's perception of life is usually entirely made up of phantoms or illusions; this means that we don't see things clearly, for we always look through a veil of fear, anger, or other emotions. We have to rise above ourselves in difficult or good situations, accepting and making the best of them for the sake of others involved in this space, then move on.

Egregores are the huge collective mind-sets that societies and groups have to hold, as protective structures for a society to carry on existing. They are man-made mind-sets that serve as structures for a group, country or nation; even the whole of humanity. They are necessary to guide the steps and offer the final excuse for rebellion, on the way to self-thinking and self-acting. Eventually we will not need them because we will only be driven by Spirit, but before we reach that stage we all need 'egregores'. Our mind sets and brains can get caught up in our egregores, making us think like the institution that the egregore is linked to. The egregore has a life and a structure, which is dependant on the thoughts of the ones that created it. It will need new blood all the time, to keep itself alive. Our desires, which feed into thought forms, are then born out of that egregore and they will do everything they can to keep it going.

We live in a world of ghosts and we say "Everybody to their own truth". In fact this is an excuse to avoid truth and feed the Queen of illusion. This accepted wise sentence allows everybody to make mistakes and that is good and noble, but as a dictate it is dangerous if it is kept as a pinnacle of wisdom, because it can stop people aligning to their own integrity. It is not a pinnacle of wisdom, but something on the way to wisdom; it is valid, but not as an absolute. If we know we are one mind, one Soul, one life, we are going to have to believe in one universal truth and be able to recognise that truth in other people. Every time we accept and say 'yes' to an idea without looking into it with awareness, we create a ghost, because we are asleep and so allow that thought-form to grow. It is the same with anything to do with hope, our own personal will, our needs and material interests, the need to be at peace and not to be disturbed, or the need to rise above others; in fact anything which has to do with self. We will create shadows that are stronger than any locked castle doors against life. The mass consciousness creates ghosts all the time and we live in the middle of them, for mass consciousness has an incredible hold over most people. There is a constant conflict in humanity that is self-propagating and feeds 'the beast'; we need to rise out of that eternal conflict. These are the veils that hide the glorious angelic world of energy that works through us all the time.

Things such as phantoms, ghosts, glamour or Maya are not entities, although they behave exactly like them. They are issued from a mind and they need that mind and that life to give them the means to live. Whatever grain of sand we have that needs feeding, will do its best to take us over. This is the healthy survival desire in nature, but pushed to excess it can create mental disorder.

When we first come on the path we think that we can acquire supernormal powers by using rituals and invocation in order to influence people and events, but this is far from the Hermetic principle of 'wanting without desire', which is the true creativity. The only thing that is developed through rituals is desire, which is linked to the lower astral plane. In the beginning of our journey of consciousness we are all unformed beings and start off in the lower astral plane, which is full of desire. Like Gollum in Lord of the Rings, there is a great desire in this state, to own that which is precious. This is us at the most pitiful level of our being. To go there and be that is okay, for it is there at all of our beginnings at the birth of our consciousness. Consciousness was born into matter and we need to accept and love that. It is like accepting to be a worm in the arms of God and loving that worm. Whatever type of therapy, meditation, or other practices we do, while we don't recognise our levels of desire for detachment we feed the ghosts of desire. Desire keeps on creating thought forms and materialising them in matter; we are really here to materialise the glory of the God we live in, which is beyond the self.

It isn't wrong to have passion, for without the fire of passion we don't move. It creates prayer, action and spirituality, rebirth from the old to the new, the good news, and the angelic elements. The good news is that we have come back right down to Earth, so that Spirit can be right at the heart of matter. The only way it can be done is through our work of transmutation, so we have become the alembics, or ovens, for the alchemical work to take place, to reveal the greater life.

Number 21 is a strong resume of everything done so far, so it puts it all into focus; we are looking from above and seeing what the process actually is.

In a way none of us are in touch with real life, because we have all got an agenda that relates to our shadows and makes us protect our underlying desire. This agenda comes from some of the elementals in our physical, emotional and mental bodies. They go for comfort and they do not want to be hurt or bothered. To deal with that in a practical way we have to accept our passionate wants, which drive us forward. At the same time we always look at how much personal gain there is in what we are doing. Then we look for the source of the desire that is behind that. Once the source is found, if there is a glow of satisfaction that comes with it then we need to look at that honestly, for the glow will be about self-interest and it can be transmuted. The little elementals will eventually grow up into being the servants of the Soul. Each time we repeat an action there will be less and less desire in it, until we do it completely without desire. As we watch ourselves it can be quite funny to see what we are doing; if we can laugh that is healing in itself. When the Soul can laugh with God then Heaven is on Earth, God has a wicked sense of humour and we stop doing the drama because we are laughing at ourselves.

In Number 21, we have regency over the world of ideals, which actually creates the world, so the co-creative process can work through us. We have reached the goal and gone through the veil of the High Priestess. As we go through, the love in us is being transmuted from desire into eternal love.

At Number 21 we see the ultimate come-back of the 1. This happens after the greatest of all achievements, the disappearance of the 9 from the 1 of return into the 10. Then at the Number 11 we start the path of inner purification. The 12/3 is the achieved materialisation of our inner work of love and truth. So from the 11 + 9 steps, we walk the inner path to the 20, where the Moon Goddess is letting the fully realised Sun (the 19/10) fuse its light with her nature, so it is transformed and transmuted into the new manifestation of the Soul of man, at the service of the greater life. Then the world with its new point of light, adds to the greater light so as to shine more brightly on the path of no return.

The problem with the spiritual path is that right from the start we need to have the courage to go deep into the hurt of the world; when we do that we see the world for what it is. We see that it has not been created with glorious song, but rather in howling and screaming. However, even that is an illusion that we have to see through, because actually it is just energetic movement that we have to explore. It is a fantastic exploration and if we give ourselves up to the energetic way of being, then we feel the energy of the life of the Solar System moving through us and we know the great God we live in.

CHAPTER TWENTY TWO

The Fool, Le Fou
Returning to the source at the end of the journey

le Fou

This is the end of the journey and yet the beginning at the same time, for we have reached the point of infinity, or the completion of the cycle. This is the 'Fool of God' who has let go all social conventions and any self-interest, so as to go forward into the abyss of the unknown. He walks towards the edge, and carrying nothing but his little cloth bag, which is full of love and truth. Pulling at his yellow trousers is a lynx, representing the profane world, that tries to drag him back into illusion, but he is completely unaffected by it for he is in the full light of consciousness. His will is now the will of God and though he is going beyond all that he has ever known, he is not afraid in the slightest. He has merged with the greater life and is disappearing into the light, so that mankind can fulfil its destiny.

499

It is appropriate to arrange the cards in a circle with the finished journey of The Fool. We are looking at the journey of spiritual consciousness into matter and any completed cycle is represented by a circle, which symbolises the universal potential of the consciousness of an adept. The number of this card is therefore understood as the nought, zero or lens. We have called our bateleur or Magician an initiate all the time, but really he is more of a potential initiate, or someone who is ready to be initiated into a higher consciousness. He is an advanced Soul because he is aware. He knows that he is coming back for another life to give him more experience, more refining and more death and rebirth, so that he can actually finish his cycle at a higher vibration than when he started.

This rise in consciousness is truthfully the key to everything else. There isn't a single card in the Major Arcana that hasn't told us to go beyond comfort, habit and self-complacency; there is nothing trickier than doing that. In the profane life we can achieve a very high degree of recognition for our intelligence, cleverness, beauty, talent etc. and if we get caught in the glamour of being the best or even the third best, then we don't achieve a rise in consciousness; we might even dig ourselves a bit deeper into mass consciousness. In order to rise, everything has to be shattered, as we saw in the journey from 11 (Strength) to 16 (The Tower).

When we have managed life well, we might want to stay put where we are and not go beyond ourselves. The more questions we ask ourselves the more answers we get; the answers get thinner and the questions more disturbing. In the end the explanation given by the intellect is no answer, just as an explanation through science is no answer to the unanswered questions behind material reality. Science can give us the 'how?' and 'why?' things are the way they are, but 'who?' and 'what for?' – are greater questions. We know that through the ages some scientists have aligned their methodical minds with an inner awe, so touching the universal love in the mind of God. All we can do is to get inside of and be one with, whatever it is we are looking at. This true science transmutes, brings permanent healing and feeds light to matter and life. We are at that point where The Fool doesn't want eternal life or the secret of the gods. There is nothing that moves his action other than the fact that he is here and he has to act; this is following the path of the one consciousness.

There are three 4's in the Major Arcana. One has no name (Number 13) and is usually referred to as Death, one has no number (The Fool); also there is The Emperor at Number 4 as the dutiful inspired mind, reminding us that the viable instrument for consciousness is mankind. He has to rise through the death of self-preoccupation and achieve mental intuition, through letting his mind travel to unknown spheres of consciousness.

We have just come through the end of one millennium into the beginning of a new one. The Soul is given another opportunity to be sensed and therefore bring a higher level of consciousness to mankind. At every new millennium we get this chance; this one came after two thousand years of expectancy in the western world and a much greater time span of longing in the east. Now many of us are reconnecting to the higher vision of the Soul. We live our life; we express it, try to understand it and then when we recognise the karmic patterns of life on Earth and see that something greater is moving us, our concern is with humanity and not our own rising! With the opportunity of the new millennium and the even greater cosmic alignment (which happens only every twenty six thousand years) the universal wind of change is spurring the Souls of men to recognise that we are Soul. As Souls we conquer our personalities or nature bodies, which subsequently become our Holy Land. We have a vision, from which there is an idea and then we move with that idea. The blend of the impulse from Spirit and the emotional response of the heart, merge as a clear concept in action. It follows the passage of the numbers, the 1 to 3 of the concept, then the 4, 5 and 6 of humanity as a well-tuned instrument. 7, 8, and 9 are the proof of how well the 1, 2 and 3 of the vision has been understood and implemented in nature.

When we are looking at this progression, either in one little life or in the whole history of humanity spanning thousands of years, we can observe all the cycles of civilisation. Thus we can implement the next necessity for the eventual recognition, unfolding and expansion of the one Soul consciousness of mankind. This is always The Fool coming back; it is the zero, the potential or realisation of humanity. The Fool is a 22/4 or the seed of spiritualisation in nature, symbolising David the king. At this point we have the birth of the seed of light, holding the potential of the true human being or the king in humanity. This is the whole of the potential of the planet, born out of the sacred line of the Ancient Wisdom of the planet, not a blood line but an initiation cycle. The Fool appears to be mad, for he acts without any regard for his social status, recognition or self-gratification. He does not obey the conventional rules of self-preservation and his ideas are seen as 'cloud cuckoo land'. He will, after many cycles, learn to fuse his vision with the everyday needs and not be noticeable as a mad dreamer, but as a wise teacher.

The Fool is a very specific seed that will only produce a specific plant, in the same way as when we have the seed of an oak we are not going to get apples. Your oak might be small or tall or a fully blown majestic oak, but it can only stay within the context of the karmic fact that it is the seed of an oak and not anything else, therefore there is no choice. At this point at the end of the journey we have completely given up choice and freedom; we just act because we are a seed for mankind's destiny. This karmic responsibility has overtaken any desire for self-concern. That is the kind of madness we are contemplating.

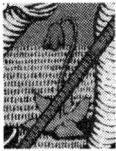

A Soul that is capable of initiation is already on the path. We are a seed and in nature the seed has to break out of its encasement to grow into a plant, for the flower to come forth; in the same way we have to go beyond our limitations. In the card we can see the tulip hanging its head, which reminds us that eventually the flower is going to die. The flower is a symbol of the fully realised sacrificial vegetable kingdom, which in mankind is the emotional body, the natural house for the Soul. The advanced Soul is represented by the tulip.

When we look at The Magician and The Fool together, we can see that they are the same man. The Magician was a nice cocky little fellow coming in and saying, "I am going to change the world" and he ends up as a Fool with a flower! In The Fool we see that he has lived his life and the whole thing is pure madness, for if we told anybody that they would we end up like a beggar with nothing, would they go for it? The only ones who go for it are the ones who know that unless they understand it from a true point of love, there is nothing to be gained from anything they can do or represent on this planet. Love is the only thing of value and going for it, is 'going beyond'.

The Sufi tradition calls its wise men 'the fools of God'. This connects the Tarot with the Ancient Wisdom, which is a golden thread linking the many traditions of expressing the symbolic ways of Soul realisation, through the ages and cultures. The Soul of Europe is completely linked to nature. Human beings had to go through the survival challenge of the last ice age, which lasted tens of thousands of years. Now our experienced wisdom is completely merged into our everyday life. In the past we saw that God was in nature, just as the Taoists and all ancient peoples did. We saw that we are part of the body of God; this is true druidism. The accent had to be on survival, according to the rules of nature as directed by an unseen Spirit and the rules of the group, as in respecting Mother Nature and father Spirit. Both the will and receptive aspects were clearly exalted at this time of survival.

The European Soul, before the coming of the south wind of Africa and Egypt, was very much like the Taoist Soul, which was the original wisdom out of survival. This one original, primeval Soul was the one consciousness of the world; it was so near the veil of the creator, that it could see the light in everything and saw how everything linked together. All it could do was to hold the wisdom and survive, in a dazzled passive state. The ones that hadn't been dazzled still received that strong spiritual impulse and used it negatively for their own empowerment. It isn't so much the body that they wanted to capture as the inner essence. So we had the two things, the bright illumination of those dazzled Souls who were able to capture and depict the light through their vision; then the ones that were being driven by the same light, but hadn't seen the vision and therefore wanted the experience for its own sake and their own power. Here we have the two brothers! Is one more sacred then the other? We think not.

With the Tarot, the minute we are feeling on top of the world and think we are going somewhere, we suddenly fall down. For example, after Temperance we had to face The Devil, then after Strength we were turned upside down with The Hanged Man. So we mustn't be surprised that after he has triumphed over the world The Fool looks the way he does. His tiny little sack is easily carried, for his wisdom is simple he doesn't need a lot of luggage; it just contains a few truths that he has decided are worth keeping on his journey. These serve to sustain him. He knows that he's finished his cycle and he's going over the edge towards an abyss, for on the other side of the card there is the big void of the unknown. He has to be mad, for he's going there with the only things he has, which are his own few truths and the love in his heart.

There is a lot of mixed symbolism in this card; Egyptian symbols, Sufi head gear and a European coat. These tell us that the Ancient Wisdom does not belong to any single group, for it is in the seed at the heart of man and is common to everybody. The card has no number and this is to do with the fact that it is a potential or a seed. This communicates to us that the journey is finished and we are going to start another one. It is a beginning and an end at the same time, like a tunnel or a channel in between one state of consciousness and another. When we incarnate we come in the dark, because matter hides the light, so we don't remember what happened just before. It is the same when we are at the moment of death, we do not know what is ahead of us, so it is important to hold in mind the lighted way.

If we look at the history of our experience so far, we can see that with every card we have seen the paradox that we are facing all the way through. All the time we don't realise or recognise that we live a paradox, we can't walk on the line in the middle that runs between the two realities. On one hand we have dominion over the world and on the other we have nothing; it is a paradox. We are not talking about the incredible uselessness of multiplying our possession of material goods, which is life for most people. It is a paradox that none of the science of being a human being can be explained by the intellect or by rationality, for the true human being is a cosmic instrument. The true possibility of mankind is to co-operate and co-create with the spiritual dance, so as to exteriorise the wisdom at the service of universal truth. When we start to co-operate with the inner vision, we don't need to create anything to be a co-creator because we are one with the creative force. Co-operation with the greater life is the goal and aim of the seed of mankind. To understand that, we have to be completely denuded of any wish for self, otherwise we are sorcerer's apprentices. We are certainly all sorcerers' apprentices now and then, but so long as we see it we can put it right.

The Magician comes in to find the gnosis or connaissance and it is as if he is running after the wind to try and catch something. This is pure madness because what he seeks is actually within. The amazing plight of mankind is that we are running after the wind, because nobody has come from beyond the veil to say, "Let the wind carry you". We can connect, perceive, even access and digest, but we don't have masters in shining robes offering us the secret of the book of life. At this level we have to own the responsible certainty of what we are doing and we have to be ready to give up our lives for that, rather than for glory. We know it is not our life anyway!

The High Priestess is the one with the answer, so she points with her finger to a page in the book, which shows the veiled inner wisdom of the seed of cosmic truth behind the veil. We also know that we have the black sphinx forbidding the access to all those who don't succeed, so we may ask, "Is it worth it?" When we meet the sphinx none of us will know whether we are going to actually be able to answer its question correctly, even if we had the highest or best teacher on the planet. We may have done all the work only to be destroyed at the end, which seems like madness from the everyday point of view, when we could have taken the slow way and survived. We know that humanity is going to go through the door anyway, in time and space; we could take our time, so why go and do it now when it could be done tomorrow? The wind is already carrying us forward. Little do we know!

The next card, The Empress, represents the Number 3 of Active Intelligence; the 'I see, I perceive, I can deliver' principle. We use the intellect and the emotions, but Active Intelligence is more refined than intellectual power and emotions, so it is the driver behind these. It is a precipitation of the high intelligence of the Soul, because it is a matrix or mother. We have to reach a stage where the intellectual power gives up in front of the unknown. The Empress represents the will of prudence and certainty and there is no way biology would have survived what it has gone through, if prudence and certainty were not there. Active Intelligence and the law of economy are the ways that nature understands what she has to do. They are embodied in The Empress, or Queen. She has had to give us the time to digest the wisdom that is in her and she has the job of passing it onto the next stage, when it will be implemented. So when our bright Spirit, The Magician, comes in to conquer his inner self he finds the great cosmic wisdom of Active intelligence, which is wisdom in action seeking the light of its other half. He has to have a great respect for the Active Intelligence aspect in him, for he recognises it as the divine collective rather than his own intellect; after that implementation can take place in the fourth card, The Emperor.

The Emperor's job is to bring in viability and crystallise that stage of the mind reached in The Empress. The understanding has to be so clear that it can dominate without being sidetracked. This can look like going backwards, but if we are going to be able to sustain the supra-natural world, in which everything is above our heads and penetrate it with our Spirit and our understanding, we are going to have to be in charge. It can't be a state of crazy madness, where we don't know what we are doing. It is a state of complete obedience, because we are accepting that which can push us forward with full consciousness into the next unknown. The one who goes into the unknown without knowing and caring has no merit whatsoever; he is not The Fool, he is just a fool. We have to be in charge and understand the world of matter to be able to carry on with what we are doing; otherwise we can succumb to madness in the real physical sense, rather than in the esoteric sense and the instrument will quickly burn out.

The potential of the '1 to 3' movement of the Trinity is behind The Emperor; the knowledge of how to activate it is also there, so that the goal can be reached. It is through The Emperor that we can understand the idea of the 4 in both the 22/4 and the 13/4. He has already experienced the 13/4 so as to let go of everything that is not permanent; this is really what Number 4 represents, the intuitive mind of man in nature. Everything that is not permanent is gone and it is only the thought, action and the path that is worth collecting and putting into our little sacks at the end, to make up the very few things that we are going to keep. The Emperor has to have the foundation of being the master of the material, profane world, which is the No. 4 of humanity. This position carries the hope of the planet and its work in the Solar System; it is the cosmic plan.

We have seen the goal and the wisdom and so we are in it, but we haven't accessed it yet, meaning we haven't made it our normal way of breathing and eating. We eventually have to recognise that the goal is in us. If our goal is to make money or to sing or anything else, then until we have done those things, we will be running towards them; eventually we become the thing we wanted. Only then can we go beyond so as to look for a goal that is more permanent. This is why, when we try all the worldly pursuits we always end up with disappointment. There is a big queue of people behind us wanting to do the same, so we quickly realise the futility of the worldly goal.

The Emperor is David and he is represented in the 22/4. He is the seed of hope that the planet has in mankind, so it is the first time that the Number 4 has really achieved and realised this characteristic. The true and higher meaning of the 4 is to endure the responsibility of organising a structure for the New Jerusalem (humanity), on behalf of something greater, instead of thinking that we are special, which is one of the characteristics of an average 4 in an individual. There again our looks and status disappear and we look like a fool!

It is the silent card of The Fool that is behind The Emperor. It is so important to understand and make certain that we are not going to be trapped and imprisoned by the glamour and illusion of becoming a master, for the master is bonded to what he is a master of. If we become master of mathematics, we become trapped into that method. It is the work of human consciousness not to be a prisoner of the laboratory, so we aim to do the work without wanting to play at being the big chief in the laboratory. The conclusion is that the only way to be on the path is to want without desire.

The Emperor represents that very poignant aspect, for when we get to that level we are going to refuse everything that the world can offer us. At that point there is incredible power, which is not going to be used for anything else but implementing some of the wisdom that has been perceived as Active Intelligence. The Emperor has that capability. He is the seed aspect that can only come from an inner vision. His mind has to vibrate very fast to go forward to the great Number 5, where he knows he is mind.

The great difference between the animal world and mankind, as we currently understand it, is our power of imagination and creativity. Imagination is creation for the sake of creation and is therefore not about survival. The intelligence of nature creates so as to sustain an aim; we create the means of sustenance with art, religion, or science, only to realise that we are the aim and we are all the things that uplift us. However, at the same time these things can also be an evasion. We start by going in and either using our imagination to send us into a point of beauty that stirs the Soul, or to send us somewhere else to seek refuge from the unbearable. Whichever way we take there is uplift, so we can have another perception; Number 5, The Pope, represents that aspect. We can't have mysticism in Number 4, because we would turn it very quickly into playing with the laboratory; the highest aspect of the 4 is intuition and that can only flash in when we have done the round of purification. The 4 of The Emperor has to be very stoic, strong and immoveable. We can't ask him to dream, because we would be in danger of going into romanticism, which isn't a bad thing in itself, but it is not the job he is supposed to be doing. We have to be so aware of the romantic idea that it was better yesterday; that is what has happened in the new age movement, with all its illusion. The realisation that our mind, with its capacity for receiving and projection, is the revelation that allows us to travel from the rational to the arational, is really a way of going for the divine cause.

Automatically that brings us to the big question of the Number 6: 'Which love am I going to pursue?' Here there is a great choice and a turn-around, that tells us that nothing has value that is not built on the aspiration of love; also that nothing can actually last if it isn't given out freely. If we don't give from the deepest possible aspect of the love of truth, all we have is karmic exchange. When we give from the natural radiation of our permanent Soul, rather than from the point of view of physical survival, it looks like pure madness, for the world around us works very hard at survival. It is okay to be in nature and it is great to survive, but we are not looking at physical survival, in which we observe how easy it is to manipulate people into wanting what they do not need. The laboratory can become a bit too real and then we have the cultivation of greed, which is the opposite of love. Love fuses and dies with and for, the loved one; it doesn't protect or separate.

Then for the conquest of the world here comes Number 7, with real zeal and that wonderful energy that is going single mindedly to take us into the world. The charioteer has to be alone here, for this is where he has to demonstrate his refusal to lazily accept the good life that he could have. He is starting to search for the food of the Soul, which is the real 'manna' of truth and enlightenment from Heaven, not the food of survival.

Then we see somebody who is well equipped and intelligent, but who risks all to find something that nobody has ever seen; this is Justice in Number 8. Justice has nothing to do with judging the world, but rather with truly seeing ourselves for what we are, in the most righteous possible way. When we are really looking for our truth, we will have a tendency in everyday life to go and speak out against unfairness and injustice on behalf of the ones who can't speak. When we do that we know we are doing it against the odds, because we are more likely to be in a minority. So far the few people who have raised their voice on behalf of minorities, good causes and righteousness have been put down by the system. Thank goodness we see an increased support for the activist, although in many walks of life they are still said to be trouble makers.

To really get to the inner truth we have to have no personal interest in the result of our search, so when we are working for a cause we always have to look and see if we still hold some emotion about it. At this point we have the next paradox in The Hermit, because he retires from the world and internalises, in order to dominate his own response to life. That is a paradox, for we know it has to be done in the world, yet here we are being told to withdraw so as to know our world better. If we are going to conquer ourselves, we have to have the internal process of the righteous sense of justice within us. When this is seen from the continuation of the unfolding of the one consciousness, it is the only way.

So here we are, we have done a great deal of work through our inner wisdom and inner understanding, then we are immediately put back on The Wheel of Fortune in the Number 10, to see whether we are only pretending or whether we are really achieving something here. The key question here is, "Can we match that inner process with the reactions that we experience in our everyday life, under the light of our inner truth." We are being put right back into the laboratory where nothing has to do with our own will, so as to learn to perceive the bigger picture and align with the greater will.

The next step is to give our power to Strength or force, so that it can flow through us; this happens in Number 11. Then, when we get there, we are hanged upside down in the Number 12, The Hanged Man! With Strength we have no weapons and have transmuted our power into the force of the higher will. In the Hanged Man, the initiate has the will, the strength and the wisdom to dissolve himself into the goal and become powerless. This is a culminating position in an initiation.

Then there is Number 13, or No Name. Here we are also powerless. This one asks us why we have vanity and why on Earth are we doing what we're doing, because all that happens is that we end up with no flesh on our bones! However, we know that the uplift has happened, that the 4 has perceived everything anew and through the enlightenment of Active Intelligence the initiate has understood his rebirth or death. An initiatic rebirth always takes us nearer to the plan and the mind of God, for we can only be reborn in light. We are born out of nature, but a rebirth is a rise in consciousness; after that, only the permanent will is left. Our Hanged Man has lost all his power and he dies to everything that might have given him power, which are his wants, desires and actions. So the next phase is to give into the higher will.

Now Temperance comes into play, for we have realised there is only one thing to do, which is to follow the greater will. Number 14/5 has to see itself as mind at the service of the higher mind. We know that purification goes well beyond the death of the body. Temperance is about rising out of all the aspirations, into the golden light of the cosmic transpersonal aspect of the Soul. We are mixing the waters of life so that we can rise, because we have to come back and confront the Devil at Number 15. The Devil is about taking a decision; there are many decisions if we want to go further. It is always following the easy life versus the responsibility of being the awareness of the flow of life; where we have to go with the next experience rather than stay where it feels good. When we have made the choice to go forward, we can automatically see all the dangers, because by the time we get to Number 15 we are very powerful. We certainly have understood how to manipulate matter out of our own experiences, that is why the decision or choice of 'who do we serve' is very important at this point.

With The Tower we have travelled further and are shaking our mental walls by letting go of everything we have learned so far, because it imprisons us in its self-important reflection. Basically we let go of everything that gives us a reason to be a good, social human being in our community, in order to become what could be called a dreamer from the point of view of the profane. We have to break down all the powers, links and limitations so that the only thing that remains is The Star of hope and esperance.

Here we are poised with everything that remains in us, transformation, experience, cosmic dreams, the lot; it is a pure point of love, the fisher King is after a moonbeam.

Then what do we do? We find ourselves breaking through another barrier again, moving out and taking that very lonely little path in Number 18, The Moon, with the full light on our subconscious helping us digest everything. We know where we are going, even if we can't see the way, because we are facing backwards.

There is no more protection, then on the other side of that horizon we come out straight into the full Sun in Number 19.

We have truly ended the initiatic journey at Number 20 and are in a state of complete arationality, because we are seeing life from the Soul point of view. We can see the patterns behind the events, so rather than getting caught up in the details we can see the bigger picture. In fact we see the details better, but they are only there to remind us of the cleverness of personality and matter, resisting so that things can be done in time and space without too much destruction. According to the plan the intelligent rebuilding happens harmoniously in the slow process of dying and rebuilding.

We have arrived in the world in full sunlight and then Number 21 is true triumph over the world, because we are seeing it from the point of view of the Soul. This is why we are working with the Evangelists (Matthew Mark, Luke and John), who represent the good news that love/wisdom is the true life for mankind. The purity of the Soul is in place.

It is important not to profit from the simplicity of the mass consciousness by feeding it what it thinks it wants. The initiate's role is to spark the inner revelation of the higher destiny of mankind in his brother's inner eye. The offer is often ignored, as the initiate is hardly ever demonstrating a life style that appeals to the average human being.

What is being passed on is only viable when it is manifested through an instrument that has understood, digested and released the essential. The fundamental principle of Active Intelligence is the essential key for the light of Spirit to release the wisdom.

If we look at everyday life, there are people who make the bread for us and others who invent a better wheel. There's a school of thought that says that we should all be making our own bread, making our own medicine etc, but the specialisation of skills has taught us to share. In the everyday life there is definitely a group understanding of trying to make everybody responsible by giving back something to the group. With the inner life, where we are not dealing with the physical, we cannot eat somebody else's 'bread', we have to recognise which type of bread we want, through somebody else's point of view and then make up our own bread; manna from Heaven can only be given out with our own recipe. There is no running away from such responsibility, for how much more responsible can we get than knowing that we are nothing and yet part of the salvation? We know that this is a mind-set, but we cannot use this as an excuse to drop the work if we find it too overwhelming, for we know we would break the gold and silver rays of aspiration and inspiration, which have been the hallmark of humanity from the beginning of time.

No words, symbols, ceremony and nothing from any physical/ mental discipline, can deliver the high state of wisdom. It is achieved by giving up to an inner process of truth and forgetting ourselves. The one who goes in refuses facility and servitude. It is about going beyond the guru, beyond our own desire for initiation and refusing the comfort of dogma with all the strength of a heretic. Being on the path is a heresy, because we go against everything that has been tried and tested. We are a heretic when we have made a choice to move out of the common understanding of every wide-spread religion, when we go beyond our god.

The Fool is unfrocked and has no shame; this is because he is completely at ease with the process of life in matter. He is at one with everything. When we are looking at a nice landscape or tree and we have emptied ourselves, we feel the tree and field in us and merge with it; by going through this process we understand the oneness of life. We know and understand that it is the one life manifesting in many forms and with many qualities of expression. There is no way we can want anything for ourselves if we have experienced life energetically in us. It is the most natural way; it is the realisation that with our minds we are in everything and everything is in us. Naturally and automatically with no intellectual gymnastics, we are going to co-operate and share and not take. If we are mischievous we will take, because we haven't perceived and felt that oneness in us. The true birth of awareness and recognition of the oneness of life is in the intelligence of the Soul of mind. In that state we go beyond the veil and we are one with the veil.

There is only one goal and that is to merge and be one with the greater life of the God we live in. We only find the goal when we have given up the search for it. Once we have merged then we understand that we do not know the God we live in; we can only sense the greater life in us and around us. If we think we know it, we have gone back into the laboratory and are using God as a science, which means it isn't God; we are studying, but it is illusory manifestation. We cannot study the mind, the intent, the purpose of the greater life; we can only give our will to it. It has to stay unknown; we cannot 'man-size' God. The superhuman, man-made god is in our image and we strive to understand his powers for our own sakes, which is missing the point of where we fit in the Universe. We have to drop ourselves and stop thinking that way. The God we live in is that unknown that we serve, as we merge and dissolve into the next experience. There is no end to that fusion of man and God, it is an act of love and a giving up of one's certitudes; this is the beautiful process of alchemy. Eventually we will fuse completely and experience God moving through us without acknowledging it, because it is a natural process.

There are so many ways of fusing our being with something greater. Describing that disappearance of self when we are at one with the world is only one aspect of it. When the world disappears in us and we disappear in the world, then we are that elusive thing, the higher mind; this is what we are here to do on behalf of the greater God. We have fused essence and appearance, so that the two become one. Our mind has gone out of time and space and merged with the greater karmic purpose of the lord of the planet. If we are still looking for an answer or a repeat, we are back in our intellects, trying to explain something which is impossible to explain or know, for the real experience is always spontaneous and we disappear into it. Wanting to know the process of self-realisation is a valuable thing, but we really start the process when we stop checking the steps and ticking the boxes. This is not knowing God or becoming God; it is serving life and fusing with its purpose. To align with the greater life we live in, is the only way we can reach the cosmic divinity. Beware, this must not be a want, need or a goal. We are an essential instrument for the God we live in.

The unknown divinity cannot be reached by any sensual means or intellectual discipline. There is absolutely no way but our own way and this is our own self-alignment to the greater life we live in. Very few have achieved that completeness and oneness with the God we live in; we have to be humble to undertake this task.

When there is no shadow for the sun is clear, and no reflection for the water is no more then naught remains, but the one who stands with eyes directing life and form. The threefold shadow now is one. The three of self exists no more. The Higher three descends and all the nine are one. Await the time!

Lucis Trust

When the Active Intelligence principle in us recognises the higher will principle, through the love-wisdom principle in our hearts, then the strength of the human being is in wanting to love beyond the grave, beyond self and going even further, to know and be one with the thing we love. That is our strength and the hope in nature is that the survival type of love will be transmuted into the sacrificial type of love. This is the one thing we have in us, a stardust type of memory of infinity that we hope to pass on. We know biologically we are all one body, one mind and one Soul, so if we don't tackle a job in this life then others will take it on. In any case the others are us; it is all the same thing. That aspect of wanting to go back to the source of love enables us to go right back to the source of life itself, which is what we are here to do. The salmon is a symbol for an initiate, because the salmon goes back up to the source where it was born and at the top it spawns or releases its seeds and dies. The young salmon then goes down to do the experience, eventually going back up again in turn. In the same way we hope beyond reason and that hope is kept alive by the one tradition of the Ancient Wisdom, with the many ways of exteriorising its teaching.

Hope is the refusal of nature to go through so many deaths in vain; the light of the mind was born as a refusal of anything that would hold back the human Spirit from going forward and back to its source. The human Spirit is reborn as that great optimism, coming back again and again after having exhausted all the ways and means. This is extreme physical endurance, via the emotional sacrifice of one's life to the exaltation of one's mind, through some hermetic, religious pursuit. Everything has been exhausted and in the end we realise that we have to find our way alone. We have been well strengthened as an instrument and well nourished by our beliefs. We have made our base, but the digesting of the light and the nurturing of the seed to birth the flower of the Soul, can only be done by an inner process. The Ancient

Wisdom is the beamed light that gives its secrets through the marker stones of its symbols.

The only dance of life is that of the light. The only conclusion to life is love; love and light can touch or guess the divine. That type of love is madness. Very few people can love to the point of madness, for this love requires complete giving of the self and everything that might feed self. Many will give to love fully and many will end up lost, if they are holding onto the experience rather than go through and die to it through initiation. It is called madness because we get lost again and again, but all the time there is that inner knowing that we are going towards the source of life. We have love towards our own mind-sets and we have to be aware and know that there is a still a purer way to be; a more loving, wiser way to be, so as to be of service to the greater life. It is madness in the sense that we have to keep losing ourselves; otherwise we might stop and imprison ourselves in whom we think we are. It is losing ourselves by being transmuted, without the fear of being destroyed. Eventually we abandon and forget ourselves into the supreme sacrifice. In The Gospel of Thomas it is said 'become yourselves, passing away'.

Biology becomes mystic as we are aware that through Mary (the etheric web) our Active Intelligence principle is at one with the one God we live in. We then see the very beginning of becoming systemic, as the Sun energy flows through our vehicle, reinforcing our role as aware witnesses for the light and using our skilled instruments. It is a beautiful process of always being able to see what one has to give up, in order to reach a state of 'self-less' channel. At this point we are coming up the river to reach the source of life.

The flower dies and gives its seeds; that is the way of nature. By serving we die to our needs and the seeds are compassion and truth. Putting forward a possibility or a probability is not the same as curiosity. We look for answers in the power of symbolism and magic; we serve by helping ourselves through being the best health specialist or the wise guru, but at the end of the many lives in the day it is always the same; the answer and the way are within. When we cultivate that strong inner certainty that comes from deep within the true self rather than from our appreciation of life, then we eventually understand that there is only one way; the inner way. We don't get answers at that level, we just get revelations and we have completely lost the personality, for it offers no resistance or opposition to the greater life which leads it. There is no need at all for recognition from others, for the whole concept of the selves has vanished; 'self-this' and 'self-that' has given up to the higher self of the Soul.

So far what we have called personality has been resistance. The Fool is an entity that we can call personality if we want, but we must understand that he has no resistance and therefore has none of the characteristics of personality as we usually understand it. The Fool has the type of personality that will really bother some people and certainly can cause reactions, because of too much willingness to give of self. The instability he exteriorises, due to the giving up being almost complete, makes our initiate's personality stronger than a personality might usually be, because it has no inhibition and no need for any appreciation of self. It is humble, but not meek. It is humble in the sense that it has no self-appreciation or self-care whatsoever, which of course is going to give him quite a difficult personality. The last thing the guy wants is to be loved! This doesn't mean that he can't be loved; just that he doesn't need it. The renouncing of personality here is the removing of all the artificiality that we usually attach to personality; when we do that there is no playing of games anymore.

In French, 'Le Mat' is an old word for the Fool, with the same root as 'mad'. He has gone beyond freedom; freedom is normally only perceived as opposition to something bad or wrong that we want to get rid of. However, it isn't really this kind of freedom we are after, but rather a fusion with the higher consciousness; this is a complete obedience which has gone beyond freedom. Because The Fool is outside of the principle of freedom, there are no more mistakes he can make and he's not afraid of falling. He doesn't look at anything as good or bad, rather everything is an unfolding of the human condition. The only way forward is to the abyss and the only luggage is the simple truth. We complicate life too much by wanting it to be how we think it should be. When we think life should be a certain way, it means that we have incredible pride in us, so that we are trying to think for God; this is putting ourselves in the position of God rather than just allowing God through us.

Most people work all their lives just to accumulate the next material thing, which has absolutely no value to the real inner life. We have made ourselves prisoners of the material world so people work for the next holiday, the next television, or the next car. All the potential of human creativity is going into making our prison more comfortable. That is what we work for; it is quite funny! if it were not so sad. The Fool is a response to The Magician, for he is the end of the search and he has used all the resources. The alchemy has revealed the secret of matter with The Hermit. The hermetic wisdom enables him to understand the symbolism and destination of the world in The High Priestess. He has been put in touch with the superior realm by The Pope. With the help of ancient traditions he has gone though several degrees of wisdom and so found himself. All these are only tools to help us, they are not a way by which to achieve the goal. It is exactly like any physical or mental exercise; we find that nothing does it in the end apart from the inner work itself. All the experiences of the initiate have helped him to rise above the rational and therefore above the explanations of the intellect. The experiences on the wheel of life have done it; all the other things are only ways or systems that man goes though. When the Ancient Wisdom is completely absorbed, man can stand on it, this means he knows how to reveal it from within himself, so he becomes the diamond from which dreams and hopes radiate.

He has a profound knowledge of life as a human being, which is a study in intimate reality rather than illusion. Through meditation and Ancient Wisdom, he has been able to rise and reach his own door of entry into the temple. We always have to remember that what we are looking at is only a symbol. Symbols can only be understood according to the point of view of the one looking at them; this view is dependant on how their level of consciousness is developing at the time. So if we are still centred on curiosity of mind, we will look at the world as a field or a place where we can go and do experiences. On the other hand, if we have strongly internalised, it will be easier for us to use what we are looking at as a sounding board, to tell us which aspect in us is still not aligned.

It is necessary to overtake the intellect. This is not negating it, but using it to supersede a sense of self importance. We must acquire a certainty beyond augmentation or apotheosis so as to go for our inner light. These are the depths where we find the lost word that gives us a sense of the destiny that we want to merge with; this is the goal. It is beyond dialectics, beyond everything. *"Know yourself and you will know the worlds"*, means to know that we are composed of mind, personality and Soul; then we can understand how all our reactions work and how we 'become'. We might not be able actually to describe this alchemy, but we would know about it, having gone through it and we will know the worlds, because what happens to us is just the same as what happens between the movement of Spirit and the manifestation of systems all over the Universe. The sentence goes on 'know yourself and you will know the worlds and the Gods'. 'The Gods' refers to the elemental gods and is about seeing how it all works, according to the movement of the greater life. This is about abandoning our role and carrying on with only a few truths.

This is the only card where there is a cat. The cat family is relevant when we are talking of initiation. In the card it is a lynx, because they used to be in Europe. When we think of the cat family, we think of the lunar lord side of Active Intelligence, rather than Mary and her white veil. The lynx represents the old great grandmother who is not going to let go of her crown; she is under the charge of the lunar lord. In dreams cats can represent heavy sadness and self-pity; this is the drama that we might still have in our hearts and minds, that wants to hold us back by continuing to play itself out. This is what the lynx represents here, so it is madly angry that it is not going to be able to play the drama any more and have control. This lunar lord had complete control before the intellect turned itself towards the Sun. It was having a great time and then suddenly The Fool put himself through all types of weird and wonderful things, pulling away from that control. In the card we can see that the Fool is walking in spite of probably having a few pains, because he is not bothered by them. He is not going to look back at the pains, for he knows that they are on the way out.

This symbol could also depict a false initiate who has taken the wrong path, lost his way and not found the narrow door because of his pride. Going through the narrow door is about not joining the crowd and doing it like everybody else, but staying true to what we are doing and sticking to the path we have found, when everybody else is making names for themselves and seeking recognition. The false initiate wanted to acquire psychic, supernormal powers by all types of outer ways, rather than through the inner way. These outer ways could be incantation, magic and mental exercises, all of which are an exterior use of power. The false initiate in the profane world is attacking those who have been able to stay on the path of their inner truth, because he can see that they have been able to acquire that innocent truth. They represent for him his own culpability and condemnation. The presence of the true initiate would represent a huge threat to the false initiate, so straight away the latter will try to disrupt. There is a normally a counter-current that tries to destroy the forward movement of people who seek truth; this current is the bitterness represented by the lynx. It is the same idea as when people project things onto us that we know are theirs; if we take those personally we play the game, so showing to ourselves that we still have a problem with some type of self-belief.

In the card an obelisk has fallen to the ground just in front of the abyss. Next to the obelisk is a crocodile. For the Egyptians the obelisk was a petrified, crystallised Sun-ray, in the form of a stone, which represents the transmission of truth and knowledge to the material world. It is petrified; therefore it is always to do with a type of dogma, religion, or crystallisation of a good idea that has helped mankind through the ages. All the traditions are crystallised or petrified aspects of the rays of the Sun and according to what we do, going through them reminds us of what we are and of the quality that we are looking for. We can drop that particular obelisk and go to the next one; that is how we go from one tradition to the next. It has a great spiritual symbolism, but has become useless for the initiate, for he knows it is not that type of knowledge he needs. It has served him in the past, so he is not going to negate it and tell people, "Don't go for it", but when people are ready he will be able to say, "Okay, that is good, but don't stay there too long", because we all have a tendency to keep on using something that works. What he was using before is now useless for him, so it is pulled down.

In The Tower all the systems have fallen away and then in The Fool we have the little crocodile rising. The crocodile was used as an ancient symbol of power in Egypt and in the Book of Job. In Egypt it represented Ra the Sun God, coming out of the water and opening his eyes for the new dawn. In the hieroglyphic script the eyes of the crocodile represent the dawn, so he's a symbol for the sun, light, self-awareness and man coming out of the animal kingdom. The new life and the new dawn are from now on going to be sacred and that makes all the difference to the way we perceive life. We can decide that from now on we are starting afresh, looking at life as this sacred new dawn. This can happen because we have recognised that the Soul is sacred, the Sun is sacred, absolutely everything is sacred, even the profane world, because it has the seed of sacredness within it; then whatever happens to us next really doesn't matter because it is all sacred.

The obelisk signifies the descent of Spirit into matter, the involution, or the process of going in, through the long search to find out our own truth. Then suddenly we rise up into the new consciousness with the crocodile. One is symbolism and is dead like the obelisk; the other is life. It is a new life in the true life; it is a real accomplishment of a spiritual destiny. So the obelisk is material or crystallised matter and the crocodile is the life energy.

The abyss is the infinity, the sacred unknown. The Fool is walking out of the old world of form, intellect and even high reason and then he overtakes the world of manifestation to precipitate himself into the absolute. He plunges over the edge, not to acquire a superior science, power, or superhuman strength; it is more humble and simple than that. He doesn't go in there just to try his courage or to put himself though a trial, or to enjoy knowledge. He deliberately goes in to disappear, because he knows it is his destiny and because he has realised that the destiny of mankind depends on the willingness of The Fool to fall. He's like the hero in a western, walking into the sunset by himself, saying "Lets go further and bring more justice". He is mankind and his dreams.

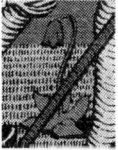

The tulip at his feet says he's an initiate. The flower has a drooping head, for its life is. As Jesus said at the end *"All is consumed"* and the mission is accomplished. The initiate has lived amongst men; he has lived their lives; he has walked with them and though he has been unnoticed, he has radiated the purity of his heart and mind. He was like a dove amongst wolves and he was unhurt, because he was not afraid of them. He has been for some a help, for others a trial and for himself a question, but in all these circumstances he has kept in him the inner illumination of 'esperance' and certainty about the destiny of mankind. He is a being of consciousness, a witness. He has been sharing his humanity with others without an ounce of self-interest. He goes into infinity and all is consumed and accomplished, because he has understood. He has not suffered his destiny; rather he has uplifted it which is quite different, so he can fall towards the source of life.

If he is crushed and overwhelmed by destiny, sometimes it is because he cannot or does not want to understand at the time, preferring to play the drama. Sometimes the questions are not true questions, but only anger and revolt. If we are touched by the plight of humanity and feel the hurt and abuse we inflict on each other and on every living thing on the planet, we are still refusing the process of the system we live in. We know the solution is simple, 'communicate' rather than fight. Share and help to apply goodwill to every problem, respecting all lives as sacred. However, this can only be applied from within outwards, so we cannot oblige or force anyone to adhere to it unless they have worked it out by themselves. We have to stop our own drama of wanting life as we know it should be, for this is still a form of self harm and rebellion.

The keynote to this card is that the kingdom here on Earth is overseen and ruled by the light that enthrones the higher will.

We are not here to perfect our will, we are here to align our will to the higher will, until the two merge. All the time we think we have to perfect something while we are here, we are a bit too self-centred and still doing it for self. As man aligns his will to the higher will he can achieve a clearer vision, a deeper wisdom. Beware of spiritual pride, for the force that flows through us will destroy us if we seek it for our own power!

Happiness or peace of mind is the fruit of the science of bad and good. God doesn't allow that fruit to be picked, unless man is sufficiently a master of himself and is able to come near it without coveting it, so we can't get near that tree until we are ready. We are ready when we do not want the knowledge any more! It comes back to the four words 'to want without desire', which is 'want' being will-centred rather than need-centred.

Desire is necessary to start out with, for when the will awakes the desire to go forward, this actually puts the will into action. We know that the will always pushes us to what we want, so the best thing is to stop wanting and then the will pushes us to where the world wants us to be, which is quite different. All the time our desire side is active the will follows it. The idea is to get the will out of where it was trapped in desire; then it moves according to where it should be for the greater plan.

The only thing that helps us overcome desire is understanding. If we truly understand that we are here for an experience, in order to bring back wisdom and to transmute misunderstandings, then we are not going to actually be taken in by how good the wine tastes, how nice the colour of the wall is, or how important a person we might be! Understanding our place in the plan has to be the key.

The initiate has risen above the present life (the one we live from the point of view of personality) so when receiving anyone coming to him for help, his whole being is transfused with the light, which means that anything he does is done on behalf of humanity, no longer for himself. It is not to do with the little private life or private joy; it is much more metaphysical and is not the sensory type of joy. The complete human is present in us and when that complete human (the Soul) is touched, we suddenly feel at one with everything, because we have gone through the whole of experience so far, right back to the beginning of time. We are at one with everything and we are with and in real life. This is meeting with the uncreated essence, which is the ultimate goal of the entire creation, for creation wants to meet itself.

So it is our glorious 1-2-3, precipitating into the glorious 4, then internalising in the 5, radiating in the 6, going forward in the 7 to be reborn again, then definitely reaching the point of inner truth to be able to apply it. This is the process of becoming more human. When we are in the wheel of life we align with the force of God, where we completely give up power so as to only live the essential. The rise in consciousness can help us refine our instrument and make the right choice, so that we can go beyond all the fabricated or artificial knowledge so far. We become humble, pure and clear and accept the loneliness of the path. We have the full Sun of the Soul radiating, so that the world doesn't attract us any more. We have dominion over the world without domination, we can tread the path that has been trodden before by those who know the destiny of humanity. We can do that in a day, if our many lives each become a breath, with its life and death cycle in the greater of cycle of the greater day. We become three-fold in one and then there is only the 1 travelling in time and space and it is all 1 anyway. What a dream, no wonder we wake up tired!

The journey of the Fool has come full circle, so it can only go further by uplifting into a spiral. Thus the potential of the circle becomes the energy that propels the Soul upward or downward towards the next completion of a circle; circles represent the completed experienced levels of the conscious mind working in a specific sphere of consciousness. His jacket is the jacket of the court jester. Its colours represent purity, aspiration, crystallised sunshine and passion, with the gold of wisdom; it is all there. We have the green of life as crystallised sunshine for sacrifice. The top part of his hat is red, because the highest level in the great work is ruby red. The right-hand sleeve that represents action is coloured the blue and white of purity, to show that his passion is inspired by purity. His trousers are yellow like the obelisk; they represent the wisdom belonging to all the traditions, which have to be 'unfrocked' and fall down. All of that is the lower aspect and so is below his belt, being representative of what the intellect and personality would have used. His neck is scaled like the snake, or crocodile of wisdom. He holds his bag with a staff held in his left hand that goes over his right shoulder; this speaks of action held by the heart. The staff or wand now symbolises force rather than power and it holds that little bag of universal truth very loosely. The strange way that the baton crosses his shoulders, shows us that he is not free and is not after freedom.

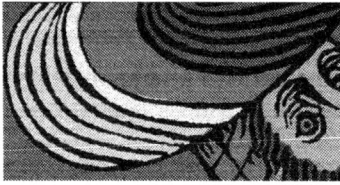

His hat is not shown entirely, as we cannot depict higher universal consciousness. It rests fully on his head as a great cup of receptivity, for his intellect has given up to its master; the higher mind of the Soul. It connects directly with the throat, which is the centre of higher creativity for humanity. This is the matrix that can receive and transmit the cosmic light, for the benefit of the 'becoming' of the kingdom of Souls.

The grotesque face of The Fool tells us that he has had to let go of wanting anything else but a consciousness that comes out of nature and serves God, so he's not going to have a pretty face that says "I am an angel" rather his face tells us "I don't look like anything, I don't need to prove anything, I am even quite happy to look stupid". He does look stupid in the way he thinks and behaves; this demonstrates the achievement of Active Intelligence at the service of the life of the Spirit. It is actually nature walking towards her God and her God recognising his progeny as himself, through the love aspect.

The top of the bag looks a bit like a rose, which could represent the ultimate sacrifice of carrying the love and truth; it is like having our heart on our shoulder. He is offering up his heart so as to reach out to the truth quickly. The staff of The Magician has become a blue rod, to show that it is not power, but force and love, for he has given his direction and his will to something that is outside himself. He is not standing straight and proud, for there is no doubt that he has given his will up to the fiery will of God. His heart and his will are not his any more; his will is the will of God and he carries on. His eyes look dazzled as if he's had one or two drinks too many, for he is drunk with the Spirit in him. This is far stronger than any spirit he could drink! There is no way he is afraid of death, so that makes him completely vulnerable; he is just going for the next thing with his whole being.

Because the yellow of his long-johns represents some mental/spiritual discipline, which he rested on as certainty. The lynx pulling them down is helping him to renounce and let go of the mindsets and traditions that he has learnt, so as to go beyond them. We have to keep re-translating the traditions, otherwise we get stuck. The main stream of people who have not got the insight to take more responsibility with their belief systems, want the traditional interpretation intact and so want to hold back the initiate and destroy him. The power of the collective consciousness is very strong, much stronger than we can imagine. The collective egregore of the ones who have built society is very powerful and difficult to break through.

The Fool is not what he looks like or does. He would be stupid if he tried to save the world, anybody, or anything else for that matter. The noise of our greedy civilisation and the dark cries of the ones who want to destroy it, cover the voice and light of our initiate. He will not waste the force by finding ways to put the world to rights. He lets the energy of love and light in him direct his life in the market place, as a jester of the greater king he serves – the God we live in. Step by step, dance by dance, each man moves with the song of Spirit in his heart as he becomes a Fool of God, bringing closer the promise of peace on Earth.

The prophesy of the coming of a saviour for mankind comes true every time a Soul of man walks towards its full realisation. The Ancient Wisdom has held the knowledge of this secret journey alive, so that in time it could simply be revealed through the life of the realised Soul, Jesus Christ. The revelation of the kingdom of the one Soul of humanity rests in the lighted temple of every man's heart.